THE UNIVERSITY OF

coins
photos
archaeology

General view of the Roman town of *Venta Icenorum* from the west

The site of the Caistor cemetery is indicated by marginal arrows; the Markshall cemetery lies about 300 yards north of the north-west corner of the town wall (photograph by J. K. St. Joseph, Cambridge University Collection, copyright reserved)

Reports of the Research Committee
of the
Society of Antiquaries of London
No. XXX

The Anglo-Saxon Cemeteries of Caistor-by-Norwich and Markshall, Norfolk

By

J. N. L. Myres, C.B.E., LL.D., D.Litt., D.Lit., F.B.A., P.S.A.

and

Barbara Green, B.Sc., F.S.A., A.M.A.

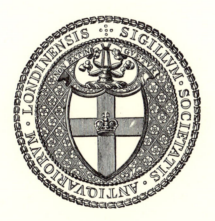

Published by
The Society of Antiquaries of London
Distributed by
Thames and Hudson Ltd.
1973

OXFORD
PRINTED AT THE UNIVERSITY PRESS
FOR THE SOCIETY OF ANTIQUARIES
BURLINGTON HOUSE, LONDON

CONTENTS

III. THE CAISTOR-BY-NORWICH CEMETERY—INHUMATIONS

IV. THE MARKSHALL CEMETERY

V. APPENDICES

LIST OF TEXT-FIGURES

LIST OF FIGURES

(pp. 263–333)

LIST OF PLATES

LIST OF MAPS

BIBLIOGRAPHY

The following abbreviations are used:

F.R.M.	F. R. Mann
N.C.M.	Norwich Castle Museum
Antiq.	*Antiquity*
Ant. J.	*Antiquaries Journal*
Arch.	*Archaeologia*
Arch. Cant.	*Archaeologia Cantiana*
Arch. J.	*Archaeological Journal*
J.B.A.A.	*Journal of the British Archaeological Association*
J.R.S.	*Journal of Roman Studies*
L.R.B.C.	*Late Roman Bronze Coinage* (Carson, Hill, and Kent, 1960)
Med. Arch.	*Medieval Archaeology*
Norf. Arch.	*Norfolk Archaeology*
P.C.A.S.	*Proceedings of the Cambridge Antiquarian Society*
P.S.A.L.	*Proceedings of the Society of Antiquaries of London*
P.S.A.S.	*Proceedings of the Society of Antiquaries of Scotland*
P.S.I.A.	*Proceedings of the Suffolk Institute of Archaeology*
R.I.C.	*Roman Imperial Coinage* (Mattingly and Sydenham, 1923–)
V.C.H.	*Victoria County History*

Note: In the case of *Norf. Arch.* and *P.S.I.A.*, a volume is made up of several parts issued over several years, which may give rise to inconsistencies in dates of publication.

The principal references to Caistor-by-Norwich are to be found in Clarke and Myres 1939–40.

ABERG, N. 1926. *The Anglo-Saxons in England during the Early Centuries after the Invasion.*

AKERMAN, J. Y. 1853. 'An account of excavations in an Anglo-Saxon burial ground at Harnham Hill, near Salisbury', *Arch.* xxxv (1853) 259–78.

—— 1855. *Remains of Pagan Saxondom.*

ALBRECTSEN, E. 1968. *Fynske Jernaldergrave*, iii.

—— 1971. —— iv.

ARBMAN, H. 1940. *Birka. Untersuchungen und Studien I: Die Graber.*

ARNTZ, H., and ZEISS, H. 1939. *Die einheimischen Runendenkmäler des Festlandes.*

ATKINSON, D. 1931. 'Caistor excavations', *Norf. Arch.* xxiv (1931) 93–139.

—— 1932. 'Three Caistor pottery kilns', *J.R.S.* xxii (1932) 33–46.

—— 1937. 'Roman pottery from Caistor-next-Norwich', *Norf. Arch.* xxvi. 2 (1937) 197–230.

AUSTIN, R. G. 1934–5. 'Roman board games', *Greece and Rome*, iv (1934–5) 24–34, 76–82.

AUSTIN, W. 1928. 'A Saxon cemetery at Luton, Beds.', *Ant. J.* viii (1928) 177–92.

BALDWIN BROWN, G. 1915. *The Arts in Early England*, iv.

BECK, H. C. 1927. 'Classification and Nomenclature of Beads and Pendants', *Arch.* lxxvii (1927) 1–76.

BEHMER, E. 1939. *Das zweischneidige Schwert der germanischen Völkerwanderungszeit.*

BELL, R. C. 1960. *Board and Table Games from Many Civilizations.*

BIDDER, H. F., and MORRIS, J. 1959. 'The Anglo-Saxon cemetery at Mitcham', *Surrey Arch. Coll.* lvi (1959) 51–131.

BIDDLE, M. 1970. 'Excavations at Winchester, 1969: eighth interim report', *Ant. J.* l (1970) 277–326.

—— et al. (Lambrick, H. T. and Myres, J. N. L.) 1968. 'The early history of Abingdon, Berkshire, and its Abbey', *Med. Arch.* xii (1968) 26–69.

BØE, J. 1931. *Jernalderens Keramikk i Norge.*

BOELES, P. C. J. A. 1951. *Friesland tot de elfde eeuw. Zijn voor- en vroege- geschiednis.*

Boon, G. C. 1957. *Roman Silchester: the Archaeology of a Romano-British Town.*

Boube-Picot, C. 1964. 'Une phalère de harnais à décor de trompettes', *Bulletin d'Archéologie Marocaine*, v (1964) 183–94.

Breuer, J., and Roosens, H. 1957. 'La Cimetière franc de Haillot', *Archaeologia Belgica*, xxxiv (1957) 171–376.

British Museum. 1923. *A Guide to the Anglo-Saxon and Foreign Teutonic Antiquities.*

—— 1951. *Guide to Antiquities of Roman Britain.*

Brogan, O. 1953. *Roman Gaul.*

Brown, B. J. W. *et al.* (Knocker, G. M., Smedley, N., and West, S. E.) 1955. 'Excavations at Grimstone End, Pakenham', *P.S.I.A.* xxvi. 3 (1955) 189–207.

Bruce-Mitford, R. L. S. 1968. *The Sutton Hoo Ship-Burial: a Handbook* (2nd. edn. 1972).

Bushe-Fox, J. P. 1926. *First Report on the Excavation of the Roman Fort at Richborough, Kent.*

—— 1928. *Second Report on . . . Richborough, Kent.*

—— 1932. *Third Report on . . . Richborough, Kent.*

—— 1949. *Fourth Report on . . . Richborough, Kent.*

Callender, M. H. 1965. *Roman Amphorae, with Index of Stamps.*

Carson, R. A. G., Hill, P. V., and Kent, J. P. C. 1960. *Late Roman Bronze Coinage: A.D. 324–498.*

Chadwick, S. E. 1958. 'The Anglo-Saxon cemetery at Finglesham, Kent: a reconsideration', *Med. Arch.* ii (1958) 1–71.

Clarke, G. 1970. 'Lankhills School', in Biddle 1970, 292–8.

Clarke, R. R. 1950. 'Roman Norfolk since Haverfield: a survey of discovery from 1901', *Norf. Arch.* xxx. 2 (1950) 140–55.

—— 1957. 'Archaeological discoveries in Norfolk, 1949–54', *Norf. Arch.* xxxi (1957) 395–416.

—— 1960. *East Anglia.*

—— and Myres, J. N. L. 1939–40. 'Norfolk in the Dark Ages, 400–800 A.D.', *Norf. Arch.* xxvii. 1 (1939) 163–214 and xxvii. 2 (1940) 215–49.

Collingwood, R. G., and Myres, J. N. L. 1937. *Roman Britain and the English Settlements* (2nd edn.).

—— and Richmond, I. A. 1969. *The Archaeology of Roman Britain* (revised edn.).

Conway, M. 1917–18. 'Burgundian buckles and Coptic influences', *P.S.A.L.* 2nd ser. xxx (1917–18) 63–89.

Cook, J. M. 1958. 'An Anglo-Saxon cemetery at Broadway Hill, Broadway, Worcestershire', *Ant. J.* xxxviii (1958) 58–84.

Cumont, G. 1908. 'Vase de type saxon', *Ann. Soc. Arch. de Bruxelles*, xxii (1908) 301–11.

Cunliffe, B. W. (ed.) 1968. *Fifth Report on the Excavations of the Roman Fort at Richborough, Kent.*

Curle, A. O., and Cree, J. E. 1915–16. 'Account of excavations on Traprain Law in the parish of Prestonkirk, county of Haddington, in 1915', *P.S.A.S.* l (1915–16) 64–144.

Curle, J. 1911. *A Roman Frontier Post and its People: the Fort of Newstead in the Parish of Melrose.*

Dannheimer, H. 1962. *Die germanischen Funde der späten Kaiserzeit und des frühen Mittelalters in Mittelfranken.*

Davidson, H. R. E. 1962. *The Sword in Anglo-Saxon England: its Archaeology and Literature.*

—— and Webster, L. 1967. 'The Anglo-Saxon burial at Coombe (Woodnesborough), Kent', *Med. Arch.* xi (1967) 1–41.

Dickins, B. 1932. 'A system of transliteration for Old English runic inscriptions', *Leeds Studies in English*, i (1932) 15.

Dolley, R. H. M. (ed.) 1961. *Anglo-Saxon Coins: Studies Presented to F. M. Stenton on the Occasion of his 80th Birthday.*

Dunning, G. C. 1956, in Knocker, G. M., 'Excavations at Framlingham Castle, 1954', *P.S.I.A.* xxvii. 2 (1956) 78–9.

Ekwall, E. 1960. *The Concise Oxford Dictionary of English Place-Names* (4th edn.).

van Es, W. A. 1967. *Wijster, a Native Village beyond the Imperial Frontier, 150–425 A.D.* (Palaeohistoria xi).

Evison, V. I. 1956. 'An Anglo-Saxon cemetery at Holborough, Kent', *Arch. Cant.* lxx (1956) 84–141.

—— 1965. *The Fifth-century Invasions South of the Thames.*

—— 1968. 'Quoit brooch style buckles', *Ant. J.* xlviii (1968) 231–49.

Faussett, B. 1856. *Inventorium Sepulchrale.*

Fowler, E. 1968. 'Hanging bowls' in Coles, J. M., and Simpson, D. D. A. (eds.), *Studies in Ancient Europe*, 287–310.

Fox, C. F. 1923. *The Archaeology of the Cambridge Region.*

Frere, S. S. 1966. 'The end of towns in Roman Britain', in Wacher 1966, 87–100.

—— 1967. *Britannia: a History of Roman Britain.*

—— 1971. 'The Forum and Baths at Caistor by Norwich', *Britannia* ii (1971) 1–26.

FRERE, S. S., and CLARKE, R. 1945. 'The Romano-British village at Needham, Norfolk', *Norf. Arch.* xxviii. 4 (1945) 187–216.

FRISCH, T. G., and TOLL, N. P. 1949. *The Excavations at Dura-Europos*. Final Report IV, pt. IV, fasc. i, *The Bronze Objects*.

GELLING, P., and DAVIDSON, H. E. 1969. *The Chariot of the Sun and other Rites and Symbols of the Northern Bronze Age*.

GENRICH, A. 1954. *Formenkreise und Stammesgruppen in Schleswig-Holstein nach geschlossenen Funden des 3 bis 6 Jahrhunderts*.

—— 1964. 'Über einige Funde der Völkerwanderungszeit aus Brandgräbern des gemischtbelegten Friedhofes bei Liebenau, Landkreis Nienburg/Weser', *Nachrichten aus Niedersachsens Urgeschichte*, xxxiii (1964) 24–51.

GORDON, E. V. 1927. *An Introduction to Old Norse*.

GREEN, C. 1963. *Sutton Hoo: the Excavation of a Royal Ship-burial*.

GROHNE, E. 1953. *Mahndorf: Frühgeschichte des bremischen Raums*.

HAARNAGEL, W. 1957. 'Vorläufer Bericht über das Ergebnis der Wurtengrabung auf der Feddersen Wierde bei Bremerhaven in Jahre 1956', *Germania*, xxxv (1957) 275–317.

HARDEN, D. B. (ed.) 1956. *Dark Age Britain: Studies presented to E. T. Leeds*.

HARTLEY, B. R. 1960. *Notes on the Roman Pottery Industry in the Nene Valley* (Peterborough Museum Society, Occasional Papers, No. 2).

HAWKES, C. F. C. 1949. 'Caistor-by-Norwich: the Roman town of *Venta Icenorum*', *Arch. J.* cvi (1949) 62–5.

HAWKES, S. C., and DUNNING, G. C. 1961. 'Soldiers and settlers in Britain, fourth to fifth century', *Med. Arch.* v (1961) 1–70.

—— —— 1962–3. 'Krieger und Siedler in Britannien während des 4 und 5 Jahrhunderts', *Bericht der Römisch-Germanischen Kommission*, xliii/xliv (1962–3) 155–231.

HOLLINGWORTH, E. J., and O'REILLY, M. M. 1925. *The Anglo-Saxon Cemetery at Girton College, Cambridge*.

HOUSMAN, H. 1895. 'Exploration of an Anglo-Saxon cemetery in the parish of Castleacre, Norfolk', *Norf. Arch.* xii (1895) 100–4.

HULL, M. R. 1958. *Roman Colchester*.

—— 1963. *The Roman Potters' Kilns of Colchester*.

HUMPHREYS, J. *et al.* (Ryland, J. W.; Barnard, E. A. B.; Wellstood, F. C.; Barnett, T. G.) 1923. 'An Anglo-Saxon cemetery at Bidford-on-Avon, Warwickshire', *Arch.* lxxiii (1923) 89–116.

HURST, J. G. 1959. 'Middle Saxon pottery' in G. C. Dunning *et al.* 'Anglo-Saxon pottery: a symposium', *Med. Arch.* iii (1959) 13–31.

—— and WEST, S. E. 1957. 'Saxo-Norman pottery in East Anglia: part II. Thetford ware, with an account of Middle Saxon Ipswich ware', *P.C.A.S.* l (1957) 29–60.

HUTCHINSON, P. 1966. 'The Anglo-Saxon cemetery at Little Eriswell, Suffolk', *P.C.A.S.* lix (1966) 1–32.

HYSLOP, M. 1963. 'Two Anglo-Saxon cemeteries at Chamberlains Barn, Leighton Buzzard, Bedfordshire', *Arch. J.* cxx (1963) 161–200.

JANKUHN, H. 1952. 'The continental home of the English', *Antiq.* xxvi (1952) 14–24.

JESSUP, R. F. 1946. 'An Anglo-Saxon cemetery at Westbere, Kent', *Ant. J.* xxvi (1946) 11–21.

JONES, M. U. *et al.* (Evison, V. I., and Myres, J. N. L.) 1968. 'Crop-Mark Sites at Mucking, Essex, *Ant. J.* xlviii (1968) 210–30.

KENDRICK, T. D. 1937. 'Ivory mounts from a casket', *Ant. J.* xvii (1937) 448.

KENT, E. A. 1929. 'The Roman fortified town at Caistor-next-Norwich', *Norf. Arch.* xxiii (1929) 269–84.

KENT, J. P. C. 1961. 'From Roman Britain to Saxon England', in Dolley 1961, 1–22.

KENYON, K. M. 1948. *Excavations at the Jewry Wall Site, Leicester*.

LANTIER, R. 1937. 'Le Trésor d'argenterie de Chalon-sur-Saône', *Gazette des Beaux-Arts*, xvii (1937) 185–6.

LAYARD, N. 1907. 'Anglo-Saxon cemetery, Hadleigh Road, Ipswich', *P.S.I.A.* xiii. 1 (1907) 1–19.

LEEDS, E. T. 1913. *The Archaeology of the Anglo-Saxon Settlements*.

—— 1923. 'A Saxon village near Sutton Courtenay, Berkshire', *Arch.* lxxiii (1923) 147–92.

—— 1924. 'An Anglo-Saxon cremation-burial of the seventh century in Asthall Barrow, Oxfordshire', *Ant. J.* iv (1924) 113–26.

—— 1927. 'A Saxon village at Sutton Courtenay, Berkshire (second report)', *Arch.* lxxvi (1927) 59–80.

—— 1936. *Early Anglo Saxon Art and Archaeology*.

—— 1945. 'The distribution of the Angles and Saxons archaeologically considered', *Arch.* xci (1945) 1–106.

LEEDS, E. T. 1949. *A Corpus of Early Anglo-Saxon Great Square-Headed Brooches.*

—— and ATKINSON, R. J. C. 1944. 'An Anglo-Saxon cemetery at Nassington, Northants.', *Ant. J.* xxiv (1944) 100–28.

—— and HARDEN, D. B. 1936. *The Anglo-Saxon Cemetery at Abingdon, Berkshire.*

—— and SHORTT, H. de S. 1953. *An Anglo-Saxon Cemetery at Petersfinger, near Salisbury, Wilts.*

LEICESTER MUSEUM (n.d.). *Anglo-Saxon Leicestershire and Rutland.*

LETHBRIDGE, T. C. 1927. 'An Anglo-Saxon hut on the Car Dyke, at Waterbeach', *Ant. J.* vii (1927) 141–6.

—— 1931. *Recent Excavations in Anglo-Saxon Cemeteries in Cambridgeshire and Suffolk.*

—— 1936. *A Cemetery at Shudy Camps, Cambridgeshire.*

—— 1951. *A Cemetery at Lackford, Suffolk.*

LINDENSCHMIT, L. (ed.). 1858/1870/1881. *Alterthümer unserer heidnischen Vorzeit*, i/ii/iii.

DE LOË, Baron. 1939. *Belgique ancienne IV: La Période franque.*

LONDON MUSEUM. 1930. *London in Roman Times.*

LOWTHER, A. W. G. 1931. 'The Saxon cemetery at Guildown, Guildford, Surrey', *Surrey Arch. Coll.* xxxix (1931) 1–50.

MACKEPRANG, M. B. 1943. *Kulturbeziehungen im nordischen Raum des 3–5 Jahrhunderts.*

MARQUARDT, H. 1961. *Bibliographie der Runeninschriften nach Fundorten*, i.

MEANEY, A. 1964. *A Gazetteer of Early Anglo-Saxon Burial Sites.*

MORTIMER, J. R. 1905. *Forty Years' Researches in British and Saxon Burial Mounds of East Yorkshire.*

MURRAY, H. J. R. 1952. *A History of Board-games other than Chess.*

MYRES, J. N. L. 1937a. 'Three styles of decoration on Anglo-Saxon pottery', *Ant. J.* xvii (1937) 424–37.

—— 1937b. 'Some Anglo-Saxon potters', *Antiq.* xi (1937) 389–99.

—— 1942. 'Cremation and inhumation in the Anglo-Saxon cemeteries', *Antiq.* xvi (1942) 330–41.

—— 1954. 'Two Saxon urns from Ickwell Bury, Beds., and the Saxon penetration of the Eastern Midlands', *Ant. J.* xxxiv (1954) 201–8.

—— 1956. 'Romano-Saxon pottery' in Harden 1956, 16–39.

—— 1969. *Anglo-Saxon Pottery and the Settlement of England.*

NASH-WILLIAMS, V. E. 1932. *The Roman Legionary Fortress at Caerleon, in Monmouthshire: Report on the Excavations Carried out in the Prysg Field, 1927–9: part II —the Finds (pottery excepted).*

NENQUIN, J. A. 1953. *La Nécropole de Furfooz.*

NERMAN, B. 1935. *Die Völkerwanderungszeit Gotlands.*

NEVILLE, The Hon. R. C. 1852. *Saxon Obsequies illustrated by Ornaments and Weapons.*

NORFOLK AND NORWICH ARCHAEOLOGICAL SOCIETY. 1853. *A Catalogue of the Antiquities in the Norfolk and Norwich Museum.*

NORLING-CHRISTENSEN, H. 1956. 'Haraldstedgravpladsen og Ældre Germansk Jærnalder i Danmark', *Aarbøger for Nordisk Oldkyndighed og Historie*, 1956, 14–143.

NORWICH CASTLE MUSEUM. 1909. *Catalogue of Antiquities found principally in East Anglia.*

ORDNANCE SURVEY. 1966. *Britain in the Dark Ages* (2nd edn.).

OSWALD, F. 1931. *Index of Potters' Stamps on Terra Sigillata.*

—— 1936. *Index of Figure-Types on Terra Sigillata.*

—— and PRYCE, T. D. 1920. *An Introduction to the Study of Terra Sigillata.*

OWLES, E., and SMEDLEY, N. 1965. 'Archaeology in Suffolk, 1965', *P.S.I.A.* xxx. 2 (1965) 188–97.

OZANNE, A. 1962–3. 'The Peak dwellers', *Med. Arch.* vi/vii (1962–3) 15–52.

PAGE, R. I. 1964. 'Anglo-Saxon runes and magic', *J.B.A.A.* 3rd ser. xxvii (1964) 14–31.

—— 1968. 'The Old English rune *eoh, íh*, "yew-tree"', *Medium Ævum*, xxxvii (1968) 125–36.

PAULY-WISSOWA, 1894– , *Realencyclopädie der classischen Altertumswissenschaft.*

PLETTKE, A. 1920. *Ursprung und Ausbreitung der Angeln und Sachsen.*

POKORNY, J. 1959. *Indogermanisches etymologisches Wörterbuch.*

RICHARDSON, K. M. 1944. 'Report on excavations at Verulamium: insula XVII, 1938', *Arch.* xc (1944) 81–126.

RICHMOND, I. A., and CRAWFORD, O. G. S. 1949. 'The British section of the Ravenna Cosmography', *Arch.* xciii (1949) 1–50.

RODWELL, W. 1970. 'Some Romano-Saxon pottery from Essex', *Ant. J.* l (1970) 262–76.

ROES, A. 1963. *Bone and Antler Objects from the Frisian Terp Mounds.*

ROLLESTON, G. 1869. 'Researches and excavations carried on in an ancient cemetery at Frilford, near Abingdon, Berks., in the years 1867–1868', *Arch.* xlii (1869) 415–85.

ST. JOSEPH, J. K. 1966. 'The contribution of aerial photography' in Wacher 1966, 21–30.

SCHACH-DÖRGES, H. 1970. 'Die Bodenfunde . . . zwischen unterer Elbe und Oder', *Offa-Bücher* xxiii (1970).

SCHMIDT, B. 1961. *Die späte Völkerwanderungszeit in Mitteldeutschland.*

SCHOPPA, H. 1953. 'Ein fränkisches Holzkästchen aus Weilbach', *Germania*, xxxi (1953) 44–50.

SELLYE, I. 1969. 'Recueil de bronzes ajourés de Pannonie faits par les maîtres celtiques, à l'époque de l'Empire Romain, *Collection Latomus*, 103 (1969) 518–41 (J. Bibauw (ed.), *Hommages à Marcel Renard*, iii).

SHEPPARD, T. 1909. *Some Anglo-Saxon Vases in the Hull Museum.*

—— 1913. *An Anglo-Saxon Cemetery at Hornsea.*

—— 1940. *Saxon Relics from Barton, Lincs., and from Elloughton, E. Yorks.*

SMEDLEY, N., and OWLES, E. J. 1963. 'Some Suffolk kilns, IV. Kilns in Cox Lane, Ipswich, 1961', *P.S.I.A.* xxix. 3 (1964) 304–35.

—— —— 1967. 'A sherd of Ipswich ware with face-mask decoration', *P.S.I.A.* xxxi. 1 (1967) 84–7.

SMITH, C. R. 1852. 'Anglo-Saxon remains found in Suffolk and Leicestershire', *Collectanea Antiqua*, ii (1852) 155–68.

SMITH, R. A. 1907–9. *P.S.A.L.* 2nd ser. xxii (1907–9) 63–86.

—— 1935. 'A Celtic bronze from Suffolk', *British Museum Quarterly*, x (1935) 27–8.

STANFIELD, J. A., and SIMPSON, G. 1958. *Central Gaulish Potters.*

TESTER, P. J. 1968. 'An Anglo-Saxon cemetery at Orpington', *Arch. Cant.* lxxxiii (1968) 125–50.

—— 1969. 'Excavations at Fordcroft, Orpington', *Arch. Cant.* lxxxiv (1969) 39–78.

THOMAS, G. W. 1887. 'On excavations in an Anglo-Saxon cemetery at Sleaford, in Lincolnshire', *Arch.* l (1887) 383–406.

THOMPSON, F. H. 1958. 'A Romano-British pottery kiln at North Hykeham, Lincolnshire: with an appendix on the typology, dating and distribution of "Rustic" ware in Great Britain', *Ant. J.* xxxviii (1958) 15–51.

TISCHLER, F. 1937. *Fuhlsbüttel: ein Beitrag zur Sachsenfrage.*

—— 1954a. *Das Gräberfeld Hamburg–Fuhlsbüttel.*

—— 1954b. 'Der Stand der Sachsenforschung archäologisch gesehen', *Bericht der Römisch-Germanischen Kommission*, xxxv (1954) 21–215.

—— 1955. *Das Gräberfeld Oberjersdal Kreis Hadersleben.*

VOGT, E. 1960. 'Interpretation und museale Auswertung alamannischer Grabfunde', *Zeitschrifte für Schweizerische Archäologie und Kunstgeschichte*, xx (1960) 70–90.

WACHER, J. S. (ed.) 1966. *The Civitas Capitals of Roman Britain.*

WADE-MARTINS, P. 1969. 'Excavations at North Elmham, 1967–8: an interim report', *Norf. Arch.* xxxiv. 4 (1969) 352–97.

WALLER, K. 1938. *Der Galgenberg bei Cuxhaven.*

—— 1957. *Das Gräberfeld von Altenwalde Kreis Land Hadeln.*

—— 1959. *Die Gräberfelder von Hemmoor, Quelkhorn, Gudendorf und Duhnen-Wehrberg in Niedersachsen.*

—— 1961. *Der Urnenfriedhof in Wehden.*

WATERER, J. W. 1968. 'Irish book-satchels or budgets', *Med. Arch.* xii (1968) 70–82.

WATERMAN, D. M. 1959. 'Late Saxon, Viking and Early Medieval finds from York', *Arch.* xcvii (1959) 59–106.

WEBSTER, G., and MYRES, J. N. L. 1951. 'An Anglo-Saxon urnfield at South Elkington, Louth, Lincolnshire', *Arch. J.* cviii (1951) 25–64.

WEGEWITZ, W. 1944. *Der . . . Urnenfriedhof von Tostedt-Wüstenhöfen.*

WELLS, C. 1960. 'A study of cremation', *Antiq.* xxxiv (1960) 29–37.

WERNER, J. 1962. 'Das Frauengrab von Fécamp (Seine-Maritime): Ein reiches Laetengrab der Zeit um 400 n. Chr. aus Fécamp', *Archaeologia Belgica*, lxi (1962) 145–54.

WEST, S. E. 1963. 'Excavations at Cox Lane (1958) and at the town defences, Shire Hall Yard, Ipswich (1959)', *P.S.I.A.* xxix. 3 (1963) 233–303.

—— 1969. 'The Anglo-Saxon village of West Stow: an interim report of the excavations 1965–8', *Med. Arch.* xiii (1969) 1–20.

WHEELER, R. E. M., and WHEELER, T. V. 1932. *Report on the Excavation of the Prehistoric, Roman and Post-Roman Site in Lydney Park, Gloucestershire.*

WHITWELL, J. R. 1918. 'Bronze Patera found at Wickham Market, Suffolk', *P.S.I.A.* xvi (1918) 179–80.

WOODWARD, H. B. 1881. *The Geology of the Country around Norwich.*

WRENN, C. L. 1959. 'Saxons and Celts in South-west Britain', *Transactions of the Honourable Society of Cymmrodorion* (1959) 40 f.

—— 1962. 'Magic in an Anglo-Saxon cemetery' in Davis, N. and Wrenn, C. L. (eds.), *English and Medieval studies . . . presented to J. R. R. Tolkien,* 306–20.

—— 1965. 'Some earliest Anglo-Saxon cult symbols' in Bessinger, J. B. and Creed, R. P. (eds.), *Franciplegius. Medieval and linguistic studies in honor of F. P. Magoun,* 42–50.

ZIMMER-LINNFELD, K. *et al.* (Gummel, H.; Waller, K.) 1960. *Westerwanna,* i.

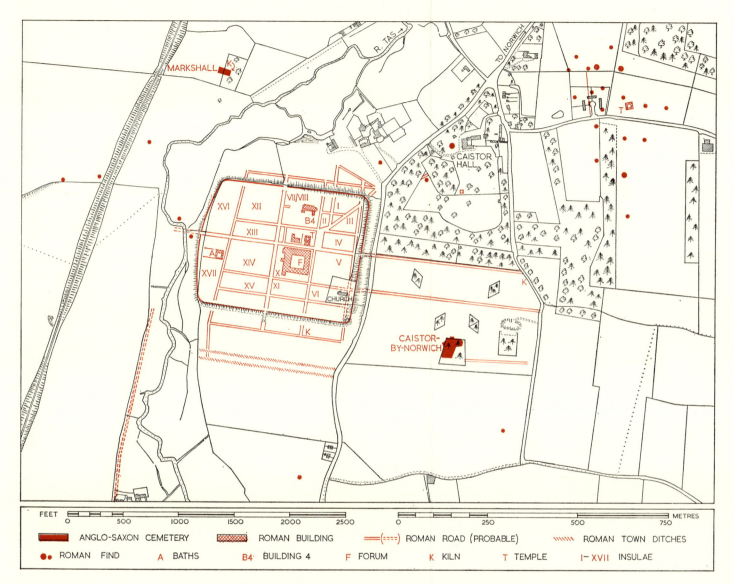

FEET · 0 · 500 · 1000 · 1500 · 2000 · 2500 · 0 · 250 · 500 · 750 · METRES

ANGLO-SAXON CEMETERY	ROMAN BUILDING	═══(====) ROMAN ROAD (PROBABLE)	ROMAN TOWN DITCHES
●● ROMAN FIND	A BATHS · B4 BUILDING 4 · F FORUM	K KILN · T TEMPLE	I – XVII INSULAE

MAP 1. Plan of *Venta Icenorum* showing the location of the Anglo-Saxon cemeteries

I

THE ANGLO-SAXON CEMETERIES OF CAISTOR-BY-NORWICH AND MARKSHALL: DISCOVERY AND BACKGROUND

GENERAL INTRODUCTION

By J. N. L. Myres

THE Anglo-Saxon cemeteries of Caistor-by-Norwich and Markshall both lie in the present civil parish of Caistor St. Edmund,[1] the one to the south-east and the other to the north of the Roman walled town of *Venta Icenorum* (map 1). While both are situated in close and obvious relationship to it, and so must be treated together, their history in recent times has been quite different. The material here published from Markshall comes either from a few chance discoveries of earlier times or from the recent attempt to re-examine this destroyed site: no information is available from which a plan of the cemetery can be constructed; the urns, though including several of exceptional interest, are mostly represented only by fragments, and there are very few reliably associated grave goods. Caistor, on the other hand, though to a great extent disturbed and in part destroyed in earlier days, has been the subject of recent excavation in which several hundred urns were recovered in controlled conditions and a great deal of information was recorded both on their contents and on their relationship to one another in the ground. This introduction will thus be concerned mainly with the conditions in which the excavation of Caistor took place, and with the circumstances which have so long delayed its publication. It is only against the background which this information gives that the importance of both cemeteries, especially as type-sites for the study of Anglo-Saxon cremation pottery, can be properly assessed.

The Caistor cemetery occupies the north-eastern point of a tongue of comparatively high ground on the east side of the Tas valley about 300 yards due east of the south-east corner of *Venta Icenorum*. Although no more than 100 feet above sea level the site is conspicuous from all sides except the south-east, and itself commands extensive views up and down the valley of the Tas. It is included within the bounds of Caistor Park, which has been laid down to grass for at least sixty years but was previously ploughed.

The first recorded mention of the site occurs, appropriately enough, in the Minutes of the Society of Antiquaries for 23 May 1754.[2] It takes the form of a note by Henry Baker and runs as follows:

My Friend [Mr. W. Arderon of Norwich] . . . informs me that on the Declivity of a Hill about three Furlongs nearly South of Caistor Camp he discover'd (two years agoe) three urns, about 14 Inches below

---

[1] Grid References: Caistor-by-Norwich, TG 23500325; Markshall, TG 22850395. [2] Soc. Ant. Mins. vii, 128.

the surface, placed in a Bed of Sand: but the Place was so overgrown with the Roots of Trees, he was unable to get any one of them up whole which was a great Disappointment to him. Two of them were large enough to hold each a couple of wine Gallons but the third was small, not holding more than about a wine Quart. The matter or clay they were made of was quite different from Those of Elmham, being paler and much coarser . . .

London May 23rd 1754.   Hen: Baker

This notice was observed by J. M. Kemble and was copied by him into Vol. II of his MS. notebooks now in the Department of Medieval and Later Antiquities of the British Museum. It would appear that at the time of Mr. Arderon's activities the site of the cemetery was overgrown in much the same way that it is now, for the description would very well fit its present condition. But in 1814, when it is next recorded, urns were being disturbed by plough- ing, and it would seem that the undergrowth had then been cleared. It is certain that the present plantation of Scots pines and larches which covers the greater part of the cemetery dates only from shortly after the conversion of the Park from ploughland back to grass.

It is evident that these successive changes of use caused much damage to the cemetery, for, in addition to the destruction of many urns, several more or less complete ones found their way during the nineteenth century into the Norwich Castle Museum,[1] and one each into the British Museum (fig. 17)[2] and the Wisbech Museum (fig. 58). In recent times a small collection mainly due to the activities of rabbiters and estate workers also accumu- lated in the possession of the Revd. J. W. Corbould-Warren at Caistor Hall.[3] During the excavations some areas of the cemetery were found to have been more or less completely dug out in consequence of these fossickings and these are indicated on the site-plan here published (map 2).

The plantation, which was enclosed within a wooden fence, seems never to have been satisfactorily maintained and soon became infested with rabbits and covered with an under- growth of elder bushes and stinging nettles. The roots of the close-set trees and bushes, and the activities of rabbits and rabbiters in the loose sandy soil, already deeply disturbed by ploughing and planting, had by 1930 produced conditions on the site about as unpropitious for archaeological investigation as could be imagined.

The excavation of the cemetery was carried out between 1932 and 1937 by the late Surgeon-Commander F. R. Mann[4] of Longwood House in the nearby village of Tasburgh. The digging was done by him personally with a little local assistance and he also undertook the whole work of recording, surveying, cleaning, preserving, and repairing the urns which he found, and their contents.

The circumstances in which the work was undertaken were thus described by F. R. M.:

In 1931 Professor Donald Atkinson, who was then engaged in the excavation of *Venta Icenorum*, paid a visit to the site of the cemetery. He was appalled by the signs of destruction he saw on the surface and not unnaturally concluded that unless the cemetery was explored at once there would be nothing left to explore. He therefore obtained permission from the Rev. J. W. Corbould-Warren [the owner and occupier of Caistor Hall and the Park in which the site lay] to excavate the cemetery, but, as his duties

---

[1] Two were illustrated in the printed catalogue of 1853 (Norfolk & Norwich Arch. Soc. 1853) and are here pub- lished as R 17 (fig. 19) and R 18 (fig. 43). Others, known only from sketches in the papers of various antiquaries, are here shown on pls. XVI–XVIII.

[2] B.M. 1870. 12–6.1.

[3] These form the bulk of the R series.

[4] Hereinafter referred to as F. R. M.

prevented him from staying longer in Norfolk, he deputed me to do the digging and provided me with money to hire labour. I was fortunate enough to procure the services of Mr. A. J. Dicks, the foreman of the labourers employed on the *Venta Icenorum* excavations. He has assisted me throughout my exploration of the cemetery and I owe a great deal to his enthusiasm and skill as a digger.

We began digging on the 28th January 1932. The nettles by then had died down and it was possible to get a good view of the surface of the ground. We did not find this encouraging. The ground all round had all the appearance of having been thoroughly upheaved and churned up by the activities of rabbits and rabbiters. Fragments of Anglo-Saxon and Roman pottery were strewn about everywhere and there were also large numbers of big flints and fragments of roofing and bonding tiles lying about on the surface. Many of the flints had been faced, which makes it probable that they, as well as the tiles, had once formed part of some building. At one spot there was a large, freshly dug hole. Near it lay the fragments of a newly broken-up urn with its former contents of burnt bones lying around it. We subsequently learnt that this urn, together with another whole one,[1] had . . . been dug out by a rabbiter. I bagged up the fragments of the broken-up urn and later repaired it. At this time, of course, our ideas about the lie and extent of the cemetery were very vague. . . . It seemed then obvious that we should make the hole dug by the rabbiter our starting place. This we did after having picked out a line from it over ground that looked comparatively little disturbed, and where a fairly straight course could be steered among the trees. The line . . . happened to run due north to the north fence of the plantation, and we started digging, one at each end of the trench, working towards each other. We soon began to find urns, all of which lay over to the west part of the trench. Years afterwards I found that, had we started our first trench a yard further to the east, we should not have found a single urn, as they had all been previously dug out.

This account of the first systematic excavations in the cemetery, which probably resulted in the recovery of urns A 1–10, indicates graphically enough the conditions which prevailed throughout, and the difficulties constantly encountered: the soft sandy soil, encumbered with the roots of fir trees and nettles, and everywhere disturbed by rabbit burrows and the grubbings of rabbiters; the impossibility of laying a regular grid of trenches among the numerous tree trunks, and the consequent difficulty of accurate plotting of the urns found; the complications presented by the presence of demolished Roman structures, and previously dug-out areas, the nature and exact limits of which were often impossible to ascertain.

Some further quotations from F. R. M.'s account may illustrate the ways in which these difficulties were overcome.

The urns, with a few exceptions, are found with their bases resting on a layer of sand which lies immediately beneath the loam in undisturbed ground. . . . The depth . . . beneath the surface seems to depend mainly on the thickness of the layer of loam above them.

The excavator began by digging

a hole large enough . . . to work in . . . to the sand layer . . . standing on the sand layer, he would then remove the soil . . . layer by layer until he reached a level about a foot above the sand on which he stands. This foot of soil he would then carefully examine with his trowel to find out whether it contained an urn. . . . The next step was to probe with the trowel the soil all round the sides of the trench which lay just above the sandy layer . . . urns lying a foot or more beyond the edge of the trench could be

---

[1] The whole urn was probably R 12, described in a letter from the Revd. J. W. Corbould-Warren as having been 'discovered by Cmdr. Mann at the very beginning of his excavations'.

located in this way. This method increased the effective width of . . . a three foot trench to a five foot one . . . most useful for digging in the narrow spaces between trees. When an urn was located we . . . cut the side of the trench down to its level. . . . For . . . recording the position of the urns . . . we marked . . . trees growing in suitable positions. . . . The position of any urn . . . could . . . be put down by taking measurements from it to two . . . marked trees. We also had marks on the fence for the same purpose.

Unfortunately for the accuracy of his general plan F. R. M. apparently assumed that the north and west fences of the plantation joined at a right angle while in fact the angle is about 104°. In consequence, while the position of urns measured from either fence or from near-by trees is fairly accurate in the northern part of the cemetery, the position of those in the central, southern, and eastern areas is increasingly inaccurate as the distance from the corner of the fence increases. In the plan here published (map 2) the angle of the fence is correctly shown, and the position of the doubtful urns has been adjusted accordingly. Inevitably, however, this has involved a degree of uncertainty in the mutual relationship of some groups of urns, and some of the blank areas shown in the eastern side of the plan were probably more evenly filled with urns than can now be indicated.

F. R. M.'s method of handling and recording the urns is best given in his own words.

Each urn was given a number and a serial letter and marked down on the plan. If it happened to be a whole or nearly whole urn, after marking it in pencil, I took it home to empty at leisure. But if it were in fragments, as was generally the case, the sherds were collected and put in a bag. The burnt bones were . . . carefully examined. If they had any associated object it was put in a tin and placed in the bag with the sherds. The bag was then marked with the number of the urn contained in it and the depth at which the urn had been found was written on it. If there had been anything unusual about its surroundings in the ground . . . a note . . . was also written on the bag. This system of using a bag as a notebook I found saved endless bother when details concerning the urn came to be written up . . .

It is indeed largely due to the care with which F. R. M. wrote up his notes recorded in the field on the urn-bags that the amount of detailed information about each urn contained in the Inventory (pp. 122–208) has been preserved. Moreover in every case in which he found it possible to reconstruct a shattered urn F. R. M. reconstructed it. This meant that, as the work proceeded, an increasing number of bags could be discarded, and, as this was done, the records on each were transferred to a separate foolscap sheet accompanied by a note of the dimensions of the urn and a quarter-scale sketch of it. The restored urn was also marked with its serial number in white paint. Eventually he added a sheet for every bag containing fragmentary or unrestorable urns. The Inventory here published is based directly on these foolscap sheets, which have been checked individually against the relevant urns or the contents of the relevant bags. F. R. M.'s descriptions have been amplified and rewritten in conformity with a standard terminology worked out for the purpose, but they are based directly on his material. Indeed this invaluable record and sketch of each individual urn has very greatly facilitated the comparative study and classification of the material contained in this report.

Something should be said about the serial letters and numbers used by F. R. M. for identifying urns. He left no record to explain his system of numbering. Urns were recorded under every letter (except I and J) from A to K (though very few under some letters and only one each under C and H), followed by long series under M, N, P, X, and Y. The intervening letters were not used by F. R. M.[1] and no reason can be given for their omission. It is quite certain that no groups bearing these letters have been lost, because there is a complete coherence between the written records and the numbered urns corresponding to them. Moreover it will be seen from the plan that no urns bearing the missing letters are recorded on it. But while, on the whole, urns recorded under the same letter come from the same part of the cemetery, and sometimes form contiguous groups, this is not always so, nor are the groups so formed, especially the larger ones, arranged on any apparent system.

The explanation is probably that F. R. M. began by starting a new lettered series for every separate period of digging, perhaps even for each new trench. His method was to alternate work in the field with the writing up and repair of the material excavated, and, since this process of alternate spells of field-work and home-work went on for some five years, it was obviously convenient to have a simple method of distinguishing the batches of material produced by successive periods of excavation. That some series are long and some short is due partly to fortuitous circumstances such as good or bad weather, varying availability of labour, or the different density of urns in different areas, which determined the length or productivity of his spells of field-work. This would also account for the apparent lack of system in the distribution of the various series on the plan. Sometimes a long trench running about among the trees of the plantation would produce comparatively few urns scattered over a considerable distance; at other times work might be concentrated on the complete clearance of a compact but productive area. Later on the system of using a separate letter for each individual trench was abandoned and, if two trenches and their offshoots were being worked simultaneously in different parts of the cemetery, it seems that F. R. M. would record the urns found under the same letter. It will be noticed that the longer series M, N, P, X, and Y belong to the latest letters in the alphabet to be used: it is probable that by the time F. R. M. reached M he had a clearer picture of the size of the task he had undertaken, and resolved that future spells of excavation should be on a more intensive scale, so as to complete the clearance of the cemetery in a reasonable time.

By 1938 F. R. M. had finished most of the digging that he considered likely to be worth the time spent on it. He had cleared all the most productive areas inside the plantation so far as the trees allowed. He found that on the slopes outside the plantation fence to the west and north the denudation by ploughing of the loam overlying the natural sand on which the urns rested had proceeded so far that most of them had been completely removed or were represented only by their bases remaining a few inches below the plough-soil; in some parts similar conditions prevailed inside the west fence, while on the sloping ground outside nothing was left at all. To the east and south where the loam is thicker and the urns lie deeper there may still remain some undiscovered burials, but on this side considerable areas seem to have been completely dug away, presumably in the nineteenth century, and re-excavation of this part was not found to be profitable.

[1] The R series in the present inventory has been formed from the group of urns formerly kept by the Revd. J. W. Corbould-Warren at Caistor Hall and from those already in the Museum. Most of these had been brought in to him by rabbiters before the excavations began, and those of which the findspots are unknown do not appear on the plan. The W series has been formed from the considerable quantities of pottery fragments to which F. R. M. gave no individual letters, because they were derived from surface finds, grave-diggers' dumps, or urns too fragmentary for individual record.

By the time F. R. M. stopped systematic digging the total of lettered and numbered crema-tions was 376 and in addition about 60 inhumations in 39 graves had been found. But this does not give a complete picture of the number of interments in the excavated areas, for, in addition to large quantities of surface finds and other pottery fragments from destroyed urns (of which 94 of the best are now incorporated in the W series), F. R. M. marked on his plan without a number the position of about a hundred urns of which only the base re-mained *in situ*, all the rest of the vessel and its contents having been dispersed by ploughing or rabbits. Moreover there were what he called 'grave-diggers' dumps', collections disturbed by the diggers of the later inhumation graves. In addition a number of the bags containing broken urns to which serial numbers had been given in the field were found on later examina-tion to contain parts of two or more urns, either because later cremations had disturbed earlier ones on the same spot or because small grave-diggers' dumps or fortuitous collec-tions of sherds had been mistaken during excavation for the remains of a single urn. Allowing for all these factors there must have been at least 700 burials and perhaps as many as 1,000 in the excavated areas. The original area of the cemetery was certainly much greater than this, but the numbered series alone formed by far the largest run of Anglo-Saxon cremations excavated with proper records up to that time from a single English cemetery.

It is worth noting at this point the conclusions to which F. R. M. came during the excava-tions as to the historical development of this great burial place. They are important as the views formed by an acute observer who saw every phase of the work but whose judgement was entirely unaffected by any preconceived notions about the dating of Anglo-Saxon pottery. At the time of my first visit to Caistor in the spring of 1935 he explained his ideas about the growth of the cemetery to me at some length, and it was of immediate interest to me to note the degree to which his views, based entirely on his observation of conditions in the cemetery, cohered with the conclusions on the relative dating of the different sorts of pottery to which I was being led from typological studies of those found in other places. Later F. R. M. put his conclusions on paper and the following extracts contain the essentials of his account. After explaining how in the early stages of the excavation trenching was carried out first in the northern and later in the central and southern areas he continues:

Numbers of urns were found in both the northern trenches and in the exploratory trenches further south, and we noticed that there was a considerable difference between the urns coming from the two areas. . . . Nearly all the urns from the northern part were decorated with grooved or incised lines and sometimes bosses. Very few were stamped but, if they were, only one stamp was made use of. . . . On the other hand, the urns from . . . further south were generally decorated in a much more elaborate style. In some cases three or more stamps were made use of. . . . These urns rarely had grooved lines, their decoration being generally carried out with incised lines. . . . Also we found in the southern trenches that the urns were less deeply buried and that there was less space between them. Taking all these facts into consideration it then seemed not unlikely that there might be two parts of the cemetery—a north part yielding an Anglian type of urn and a south part yielding urns with elaborate decoration. At the time I remember that I thought this difference in decoration could be explained by supposing that the urns from the south part were of later date than those of the north part.

F. R. M. goes on to explain how his ideas on the historical sequence were developed first by the discovery in the north part of intrusive urns, such as the E 7 group, or D 7 with its elaborate surround of tiles and flints (pl. XV*a*), similar to those found further south; and secondly by unexpectedly finding near the west fence several inhumations, one of which, Grave 3, 'had obviously . . . been dug in a pre-existing urnfield'. He continues:

It was now evident that the cemetery was a mixed burial one, and that the digging of some of the graves at any rate had caused the destruction of previously buried urns. Also the conditions under which the urn D 7 had been found made it seem likely that some of the urns were intrusive as well. It seemed to me therefore that a theory which best fitted in with these new facts was to suppose that a pure cremation cemetery was first established on the site, and that, later on . . . a mixed-burial people arrived on the scene and made use of the previously existing cemetery for cremation burials and inhumations.

I have observed nothing during more recent excavations to contradict this theoretical history of the cemetery but a great deal to support it: and I still think it best explains the facts.

It is clear from this that F. R. M. had a firm grasp of the essential points which his excavations had revealed: the distinction between the types of pottery which he rightly calls Anglian and early, and the more elaborately stamped wares that succeeded them; and the fact that the inhumations belonged to the later (in fact they are the latest) burials on the site. The distinction he was at first inclined to draw between an earlier northern and a later southern section of the cemetery was subsequently modified. At one time he believed that a relatively blank strip between the two parts marked a path perhaps separating burial areas used by two different communities, but he later came to the conclusion that the blank strip was simply a dug-out area resulting from the activities of earlier excavators or rabbiters. It is not in fact possible to press very far this distinction between north and south. If the early Anglian pots are plotted on the plan they are found to occur in the central and southern parts as well as in the north; and there are other examples besides D 7 of elaborately stamped urns in the north, by no means all of which are demonstrably intrusive. Such urns are in fact particularly common among the P series, which comes from the north-eastern section of the cemetery. On the other hand, the N series, which comes mainly from the south, contains a high proportion of the early Anglian unstamped urns.

It may perhaps also be doubted whether the evidence for the use of the site by two distinct and successive communities is as strong as F. R. M. believed. It was natural for him to interpret the not infrequent cases of the intrusive burial of one urn upon another as implying a lack of continuity in the use of the site or at least a significant lack of interest in the later period about pre-existing burials. But while such phenomena might well arise from a break in the occupation, they do not prove that such a break occurred. Not all intrusive urns are in fact of the elaborately decorated kind and, while an intrusive urn in the nature of the case can be presumed later in date than the burial it disturbs, there are no means of knowing how much later it may be, and no reason to suppose that such occurrences took place only in the final period of the cemetery's use. The plan certainly suggests that at no time was there systematic alignment of the burials,[1] and if, as seems probable, their positions were not marked by any permanent surface indication, the chance that an earlier burial would be disturbed by a later was present throughout the whole period of the cemetery's use, though naturally such collisions would occur more frequently as time went on and the available space became more thickly filled with urns.

[1] The apparent north–south alignment of such groups as A 1, 2, 4, 6, N 5–7 and N 88–91 is more likely due to the position of F. R. M.'s trenches among the surrounding trees than to any significant original arrangement in the cemetery.

On the whole the evidence, though not conclusive, is more strongly in favour of continuous use for well over two hundred years by a single community, which may of course have been reinforced from time to time by newcomers of somewhat different cultural antecedents, and was certainly subject to changing methods and fashions in the production and decoration of its funeral pottery. It was not until near the end of its effective use that the major change in burial custom from cremation to inhumation is in evidence in the cemetery at all, and the fact that the inhumations at Caistor are comparatively few, and all so late, may well indicate that the conversion from paganism to Christianity was imminent, if indeed it had not already occurred, when they took place. If this is so, the evidence from Caistor suggests strongly the use of the cemetery throughout the pagan period by one community with a homogeneous but continuously developing culture. It is in marked contrast to those mixed burial grounds which cremating and inhuming communities or families seem to have used indiscriminately throughout pagan times.

An aspect of the chronology of the Caistor cemetery on which F. R. M. never felt that he had the technical competence to form a decided opinion was the date of its beginning. His excavations showed that the site had been occupied in Roman times by various flimsy and rather indeterminate structures whose nature is discussed elsewhere (pp. 19 ff.). He thought that he had evidence for a general clearance of these and a levelling-off and tidying-up of the whole area, presumably by the first Anglo-Saxon settlers, prior to its use as a pagan cemetery. But he found no certain indication of the date of this change of use which could throw light on the connected questions of the beginning of the cemetery and the end of Roman life in *Venta Icenorum*. Moreover, while, as has been noted above, F. R. M. was quick to record any evidence he encountered which bore on the relative dates of different types of urns, his knowledge of the background material, both in this country and on the Continent, was insufficient to tempt him into proposing any absolute dating for the ones which he believed to be the earliest.

These questions will be discussed in greater detail in the later sections of this report. But it may be convenient just to mention here the principal local factors that are relevant to the solution of the historical problems involved. There is, first of all, the evidence from Professor Donald Atkinson's excavations that some houses in the Roman town were occupied until at least the end of the fourth century, when he believed that one of them, the so-called Building 4, was violently destroyed.[1] Secondly there is the evidence of certain small objects from his excavations which suggest the presence at *Venta* of persons in possession of the type of military equipment used by barbarian troops in Roman service at the end of the fourth and early in the fifth century.[2] Thirdly there is the fact that a few cremation burials of normal Germanic type but contained in Romano-British coarse pots were found both in the Anglo-Saxon cemetery and on the berm outside the south wall of the Roman town.[3] Fourthly it will be

---

[1] The excavations as a whole still await detailed publication. But some publicity was given to Atkinson's interpretation of the evidence for the end of Building 4: see *J.R.S.* xxi (1931), 232. In view of its relevance to our cemetery, we have attempted (pp. 33–40) a critical reappraisal of this evidence, and are grateful to Professor Sheppard Frere for permission to include in this a full description of the coins found in the building, kindly revised by Mr. R. A. G. Carson from the list made by the excavator at the time.

[2] See pp. 41–2. The significance of those pieces was not appreciated at the time of Atkinson's excavations. With them may perhaps be considered the unstratified sherd of 'Romano-Saxon' pottery illustrated in Myres 1956, 20 and pl. IV A. Three further pieces of this kind are here illustrated (fig. 64).

[3] Those from the cemetery were included by F. R. M. in his numbered series, and will be found on fig. 33, together with that subsequently found outside the south wall of *Venta*. For an assessment of their date and significance, see pp. 74–6.

suggested that a significant number of the Anglo-Saxon cremation urns themselves are of types likely to be datable in the fourth and early fifth centuries, if not earlier.[1] It will thus be seen that the excavation of the Caistor cemetery, taken in conjunction with that of *Venta Icenorum*, throws exceptionally interesting light on the process of transition from Roman Britain to Saxon England. There are in fact very few excavated sites in this country where the evidence for cultural overlap is so significantly present and so closely datable from both sides.

In this as in so many other ways the importance of F. R. M.'s work at Caistor can hardly be overestimated. To have excavated, recorded, and repaired, almost single-handed, the longest series of urns hitherto recovered from an Anglo-Saxon cemetery in this country is in itself a personal achievement difficult to parallel in the annals of British archaeology. But he also made interesting experiments on the technical questions presented by the manufacture and decoration of pottery of this type, the results of which are summarized below (p. 257). It was indeed obvious long before his work on the cemetery was finished that it deserved early and detailed publication and that Caistor with its great numbers and wide variety of urns was exceptionally well suited to become a type-site for the study of Anglo-Saxon pottery.

From 1935 onwards F. R. M. had been generously supplying me with information about his discoveries including a long series of photographs of the urns he had repaired. In 1938 we agreed to collaborate in the production of a joint communication which could be offered to the Society of Antiquaries as a first step towards the publication of his work. To this end he sent me the bulk of his records early in 1939, and it was arranged that we should together address a meeting of the Society in the winter of 1939–40. I was working on this material when war broke out in September 1939, and a sudden end was put to such activities. The proposed paper was thus neither completed nor delivered. For nearly seven years I was in no position to give much thought to Anglo-Saxon pottery, and F. R. M.'s records of Caistor fortunately remained undisturbed in the cupboard where I had placed them on the outbreak of war.

In the spring of 1944, before it was possible to resume work on them, I learnt with profound regret that F. R. M. had recently died. Moreover the Revd. J. W. Corbould-Warren, the owner of the site and of everything excavated from it, in whose outbuildings at Caistor Hall a great number of the repaired urns had been stored, died also in April of that year. Apart from the authorities of Norwich Castle Museum, who were of course aware of the importance of the material and had made arrangements to take into safe keeping what was in store at the Hall, I was the sole remaining repository of detailed information about the site and the plans for its publication, and I still had in my possession most of the essential records.

When the war was over Mrs. Mann kindly agreed to present to the Norwich Museum all the material and records remaining at her house at Tasburgh. I accordingly arranged with Mr. R. Rainbird Clarke, who in 1946 became responsible for the archaeological collections at Norwich Castle Museum, that we should jointly undertake its publication. He undertook the general description and history of the site, its Roman remains, and the small objects, while I was to describe and discuss the pottery. In April 1948 we read a joint communication

[1] See pp. 43–8.

on the cemetery before a meeting of the Society of Antiquaries on the lines of that which I had planned to read with F. R. M. eight years before. Subsequently the Society undertook to publish the cemetery in detail in its series of Research Reports, and assisted financially in the necessary drawing of all the pottery. The material collected from Caistor Hall and Tasburgh, much of it by then inevitably in some confusion, was sorted and arranged by Mr. Clarke with the help of F. R. M.'s notes and memoranda, and, as time allowed, I visited Norwich at intervals over the next ten years, and gradually worked through all the pottery, checking it against F. R. M.'s notes and drawings, and redescribing it to form the Inventory here published. In 1956 I was invited, at the suggestion of Sir Llewellyn Woodward, to spend three months as a member of the Institute for Advanced Study at Princeton, New Jersey, and I used the leisure provided by my stay there to classify and arrange the drawings of the pottery, and to draft preliminary notes on the different groups in the light of comparative material at home and abroad. I am deeply indebted to the Trustees and the Director of the Institute for providing me with the welcome opportunity of this continuous period of study without which it would have been impossible to make solid progress with my part of the work.

In the following years both Mr. Rainbird Clarke and I devoted what time was possible from busy official careers to the preparation of further parts of the report. He had completed a revision of F. R. M.'s site plan and a draft account, here published in revised form, of the evidence for the Roman structures on the site of the cemetery before it was used for Anglo-Saxon burials, when his untimely death in the spring of 1963 again deferred hopes of early publication. Fortunately his assistant, Miss Barbara Green, who was already conversant with the Caistor work and had played a major part in preparing and mounting the line drawings for publication, was shortly afterwards appointed Keeper of the Department of Archaeology in the Castle Museum, Norwich, and was thus in a position to undertake the unfinished parts of his work on the report. After I left the Bodleian Library at the end of 1965 I was myself able to spend more time on it than had hitherto been possible.

Meanwhile, however, we had agreed that the remains salvaged from the closely related cemetery at Markshall ought to be published along with the Caistor material. A detailed examination of the boxes of potsherds rescued from that site revealed a far larger number of pieces worthy of publication than had been anticipated. All these had to be sorted, and in some cases repaired, before being drawn and described. The evaluation of their significance in its turn necessitated some revision of what had already been written about Caistor. Inevitably this involved further delays, and I had in fact to rewrite most of what I had written some ten years earlier at Princeton. In all the later stages, and particularly for his work in assembling, drawing, and mounting the Markshall pottery, and for revising some of the Caistor drawings that had been made many years before,[1] we are greatly indebted to the cheerful co-operation, technical skill, and timely criticism of Mr. William Milligan. The typing of the report has been most competently performed by Miss Norma Watt, whose skill in combining in one fair copy emendations and corrections derived from several more or less illegible manuscripts has evoked our constant admiration and gratitude.

Many others have contributed over the years, and we would like to acknowledge our

[1] A few discrepancies between the drawings and the Inventory descriptions are due to further work on the objects since the blocks were made.

thanks to them all. We are especially grateful to the present Director of the City of Norwich Museums, Mr. F. W. Cheetham, and to his predecessors, Mr. R. Rainbird Clarke and Miss G. V. Barnard, and their staffs, for their co-operation and tolerance during the whole period of this report's preparation; particularly in the final stages to Mr. T. H. McK. Clough, who prepared the maps, plans, and bibliography and helped in many other ways, Mr. P. Lambley, who identified the wood, and Mr. B. McWilliams, who identified the animal bones. For specialist help and contributions to the report on the subjects indicated we are indebted to Mr. M. Allen, Mr. A. P. Baggs, Miss H. Bamford, Mr. D. R. Howlett, Dr. G. P. Larwood, and Mrs. A. Parker, for drawings; to Mr. R. A. G. Carson, for the report on Roman coins; to Dr. D. B. Harden, for that on glass; to Mr. J. G. Hurst, for that on Middle Saxon pottery; to Mrs. H. E. Davidson, Miss V. I. Evison, and Mrs. S. C. Hawkes, for help with the Roman military equipment; to Miss V. I. Evison and Mrs. E. Okasha, in connection with the drawing on R 9/10; to Dr. Calvin Wells, for his reports on the human remains; to Dr. R. I. Page, for that on the runic inscription from N 59; to Mrs. B. Chambers and Miss E. Crowfoot, for that on textiles; and to Mr. S. E. Ellis, for advice on the whetstone. Mr. Hallam Ashley supplied most of the photographs for half-tone illustrations, apart from those of continental pottery which we owe to Dr. A. Genrich and Dr. K. F. Raddatz. Mr. C. Green gave us valuable help with the gazetteer of Anglo-Saxon cemeteries, as did Professor S. S. Frere and Mrs. K. Hartley with some of the Roman material, and Mr. Eric Higgs and colleagues with the animal bones. We are grateful to Dr. K. R. Fennell, the late Group-Captain G. M. Knocker, Mr. S. E. West, and Mr. John Bartlett, for permission to quote unpublished information. Mr. F. H. Thompson has helped us in many ways, especially with the production of the volume and with the Roman material.

IN MEMORIAM

It will be seen that the work involved in the excavation and publication of these two cemeteries has covered a period of forty years, including of course the six war years, when no progress could be made. Inevitably, after such a length of time, most of those closely concerned in its earlier stages are no longer alive. These include, as has already been noted, Professor Donald Atkinson and the Revd. J. W. Corbould-Warren, from whose collaboration, as excavator and landlord, the pre-war exploration of the whole Caistor complex of Roman town and Anglo-Saxon cemetery originated. They include also to our great sorrow two who played a major part in the detailed work which it has been left to us to see finally into print, F. R. M. and R. Rainbird Clarke. This book is as much theirs as ours, and we dedicate it to their memory.

J. N. L. M.

B. G.

HISTORICAL SUMMARY

By J. N. L. Myres

IT may be convenient to begin this report with a brief summary of the main points of interest for the early history of this country on which the evidence here presented from the Caistor and Markshall cemeteries may be thought to throw light. These historical problems largely concern the nature of the overlap between Roman Britain and Anglo-Saxon England, but there is also something to be learnt about the continental origins of the Germanic settlers in this part of the country, the early development of their arts and crafts, and the nature and duration of the pagan phase of their culture before they were converted to Christianity in the course of the seventh century.

On the overlap between Roman Britain and Anglo-Saxon England these cemeteries have an obvious interest because of their immediate juxtaposition with a Roman walled town. But they are not the only cemeteries in such a situation. Other examples, as at York and Cambridge, at once spring to mind. What makes the situation here especially significant is partly that *Venta Icenorum* was the administrative centre of an important Romano-British tribe, and partly that the sites of both the town and the Caistor cemetery are devoid of modern buildings and so present a unique opportunity for studying the relationship between them. Much remains to be done before this relationship is fully intelligible. In particular we need to know more precisely the dating of the successive phases in the defences of *Venta*. But already some facts of great historical interest have become clear. One is that the Caistor cemetery occupied a site originally within the rectangular street plan of the early Roman town (map 1). It had also contained, until perhaps the beginning of the third century, the same loose development of flimsy huts and workshops as prevailed in much of the central area of *Venta* even later than that period. It would moreover appear that this shanty-town occupation on the cemetery site ended at approximately the earliest date at which the present defences enclosing a much smaller central urban nucleus could have been laid out.

These two events could well have been connected. In other words, one consequence of the major change in the status of *Venta* implied by its conversion from a very large but mainly undefended area of rectangular *insulae*, that were never fully built up, into an impressively defended nucleus of some 35 acres, was to release for eventual use as a barbarian cemetery an area no longer required for civic purposes. It has been suggested that the only building to survive for a while in this area may have been a small recently built shrine or temple, but this too was in ruins, and perhaps deliberately demolished, by the end of the third century (pp. 29–30). Its existence, even its ruins or its memory, might have determined the subsequent allocation of this site for barbarian burials.

When did such burials begin? And what was the function of the folk whose dead were buried there? These questions admit at present of no certain answers. The first cannot be settled with precision until it is possible to date more exactly than at present the successive phases in the development of proto-Anglian and proto-Saxon pottery. What is already clear is that a number of the earlier cremation urns in the cemetery echo ceramic fashions preva-lent on the Continent in the fourth century, and that the decoration of a few even suggests that their makers were conversant with styles that were largely obsolete at that time but had been popular in the second and third centuries. What inferences should be drawn from these unexpected facts remain obscure. But it is clear that, surprising as these facts may be, the topographical evidence makes it quite possible for the site to have been cleared for use as a barbarian cemetery as early as the later part of the third century. That it was so used on an increasing scale from at least the middle of the fourth century can be taken as certain.

There is thus an overlap of perhaps a hundred years here between the first Anglo-Saxon arrivals, which may have been on a very small scale, and the end of Romanized life in *Venta Icenorum*. What was the function of these newcomers, and what were their relations with the Romano-British authorities of the town and its dependent canton? Certainty again eludes us, but it is difficult to believe that their settlement in such close proximity was not deliberate, and that they were not employed in some way that was supposed to improve the security and prosperity of the town and its environs. Whether the visible defences were laid out in the third or the fourth century they are dramatic evidence of the need for improved security in the later Roman period, and their rectangular design with gates centrally set in each side and apparent disregard for the earlier street-grid suggests at least a para-military purpose in their construction.

Whatever end the new barbarian settlers were designed to serve there is no evidence for more than a minimum of social contact between them and their employers. Their burial customs in particular, with a rigid adherence to cremation just at the time when inhumation was becoming general in the Roman world, and their all but universal use of their own hand-made Germanic pottery as containers for the cremated bones in preference to the com-mercial products of local Romano-British kilns, mark them as folk living their own lives rigidly distinct from the Icenian tribesmen of *Venta* and its neighbourhood. The occasional use of a Roman jar and the even rarer occurrence of vessels hybrid between the two cultures are so uncommon in the cemetery as to emphasize rather than bridge the gulf between them. We do not know where they lived, but the total absence of Germanic domestic rubbish within the walls of *Venta* itself makes it quite certain that in life as in death they remained essentially outsiders.[1]

It is true that in the later part of the fourth century there is evidence from within the town of the presence of troops equipped with the standard Roman military belt-fittings charac-teristic of that time. Such equipment was certainly issued to barbarian mercenaries in Roman service, but its use was not confined to them. It must remain at present an open question whether the pieces from *Venta* are evidence for a body of local militia, or for Germanic irregulars, and in the latter case whether the wearers are likely to be identical with, or dis-tinct from, the folk who cremated their dead in the Caistor and Markshall cemeteries.

It is certain that as Romanized life declined and finally ceased within the walled town at some ill-defined date after the collapse of Roman rule the population using the cemeteries

[1] It will be noted that the urn here illustrated on pl. XVIII from a drawing by Miss Anna Gurney is described as one of 'a great number . . . found in 1814 in the Roman Encampment', but in view of the absence of corroborative evidence for any subsequent discoveries of this kind from the walled town itself, it is probably best to take Miss Gurney's statement as a general reference to the area at Caistor in which such antiquities were known to have been found.

greatly increased and came to replace the old native order. Before long competing groups of Anglo-Saxon chieftains and their followers superseded in a spread of village communities the tattered relics of a tribal economy administered *more Romano* from *Venta Icenorum*. The cemeteries throw no light on the stages in this complex process which by the middle of the sixth century had produced the kingdom of the East Angles ruled by the *Wuffingas*. But they do illuminate very sharply the continental connections and tribal origins of the new Anglo-Saxon population.

This, it is clear, was far from uniform. The most distinctive element among the earliest users of the Caistor cemetery was an unusually pure-blooded body of Angles whose culture so closely mirrors that of fourth-century Schleswig and Fünen as to imply a fairly direct transference in considerable numbers from continental Anglia. There were also smaller groups whose pottery may suggest an even more northerly origin. And certainly from the end of the fourth century, perhaps earlier, there was a considerable body whose direct antecedents were among the less coherent Saxon peoples of the lower Elbe valley, and the coastlands extending to the Weser and the Ems. It is not possible to analyse with such confidence the earliest users of the Markshall cemetery owing to the confused and fragmentary condition of its surviving contents. But what remains suggests a different emphasis: very little sign of the pure Anglian component that is so marked a feature of the earliest Caistor burials, but a much stronger strain of direct Saxon origin, especially from the mid-fifth century onwards, including one or two pieces that imply a direct personal link with potters working for cemeteries around the estuary of the Weser (p. 237 and pls. X, XI). It is therefore quite possible, though far from proved, that, while the dominant element of the Caistor folk was Angle in origin, the Markshall cemetery was developed, certainly from the middle of the fifth century, for use by a more distinctively Saxon body of newcomers.

However that may be, there is little sign that these differences of tribal origin inhibited a rapid intermingling of the various groups. There is no indication at Caistor that any part of the cemetery was reserved for exclusive use by any one tribal element. Although the excavator at first concluded that the early Anglian burials were concentrated in the northern area, the plan shows that they occur elsewhere also. If any valid distinction can be made between different parts of the cemetery, it is more likely to be due to a difference of date than of race. Even so, there are plenty of intrusive or late burials to be found in parts where most of the interments appear early, whether these are predominantly of Angle or of Saxon character. Before very long in any case these original distinctions became blurred, and by the sixth century were rapidly converging to produce a mixed Anglo-Saxon culture showing only minor local differences from the outcome of similar developments in other parts of East and Middle Anglia. In this part of England, it is true, Anglian fashions in brooches and other metalwork came to supersede those of Saxon antecedents, except in the southern and western parts of Middle Anglia. This Anglian dominance no doubt reflected the fact that noble families of Angle stock were prominent in building up the new political arrangements that soon led to the creation of kingdoms in East Anglia, Lindsey, and Mercia, and of smaller principalities in and around the Fens. It was their Anglian cultural background that determined fashions in jewellery and other luxury goods. But in the humbler craft of pot-making, whose development is so well illustrated in the great cremation cemeteries, Saxon influences continued to play a full part in the evolution of this mixed Anglo-Saxon culture.

At Caistor and Markshall cremation remained, as apparently at a number of other Norfolk cemeteries, the almost universal rite until near the end of the pagan period. There is no sign here of that gradual 'flight from cremation' that has been noted in Middle Anglia and the southern midlands, still less of any sudden intrusion of extraneous inhuming elements into the earlier cremating population. This can only mean that for nearly two centuries after the breakdown of Roman rule the folk who used these cemeteries followed their ancestral traditions of Germanic paganism and developed their own social arrangements entirely uninfluenced by any surviving Romano-British ways of life and thought.

The cemeteries do not supply much evidence for the character of this pagan culture. The decoration of a few pots may suggest a devotion to Thor and Tiw especially among the gods of the northern pantheon, and there is a hint that at least one tale from the Götterdämmerung cycle, known to us only from literary sources of much later date, may already have been familiar at Caistor around the turn of the sixth and seventh centuries (pp. 62, 118, text-fig. 5 and pl. VI*a*). There is evidence for some knowledge of the Runic *futhorc*, perhaps as early as the fifth century, but not for its use in any literary context (p. 114). Of economic growth or of contacts with neighbouring Anglo-Saxon communities there is little indication. Several more or less professional potters were at work at Caistor by the middle of the sixth century, but little trace of their wares has been found in other cemeteries, even at such comparable Norfolk sites as Castle Acre and North Elmham. The most striking exception is an urn, probably from the most prolific Caistor workshop, which has turned up unexpectedly as far away as Thurmaston, Leics. Nor did many products of potters based elsewhere in East Anglia find their way to Caistor: no certain pieces, for example, from the workshop of the very productive Illington/Lackford potter have been noted here.

The end of these cemeteries can with fair certainty be linked directly with the spread of Christianity in East Anglia during the seventh century. The first influence of the new faith can perhaps be seen in the group of inhumation burials which mark the first breach in the pagan tradition of cremation and belong to the final period of the Caistor cemetery's use. Those buried in what at Caistor was this novel fashion were not necessarily themselves Christian, for there were stringent prohibitions against Christian interments among the 'heathen burials' of pagan cemeteries. But they could well be witness to the spread of new ideas and to the beginnings of that religious syncretism which led King Rædwald of East Anglia in the second or third decade of the seventh century to add a Christian altar to the equipment of his pagan temple.[1] If we are right in suggesting that the animal-stamps used by potters at Caistor and Markshall could have been used to ornament the bindings or booksatchels of seventh-century Christian service-books (p. 61), our cemeteries provide a final proof of that overlap between the old and the new faiths with which this summary of their historic interest may fitly end.

[1] Bede, *Hist. Eccles.* ii, 15.

THE ROMAN OCCUPATION OF THE SITE

By the late R. R. Clarke

This section is substantially that written by R. R. Clarke in 1962 and is based largely on the accounts and interpretations of Professor Donald Atkinson and F. R. M. Subsequent work on comparable sites elsewhere suggests that some of the conclusions may require modification, but until further excavations are carried out in the Roman town a reassessment of the site is impossible. In particular, more precise dating should be obtainable for the successive phases of the defences. We have therefore thought it best to leave this section very much as it was written apart from a few minor emendations and a more extensive revision of the final part.

J. N. L. M.
B. G.

AS indicated in the General Introduction the Anglo-Saxon cemetery at Caistor occupies the brow of a low hill overlooking the walls of the Roman town known as *Venta Icenorum* in the Antonine Itineraries. The centre of the cemetery lies about 1,100 ft. (335 m.) south-east of the site of the Roman east gate and is thus extra-mural (map 1). Various structures and refuse pits of Roman date were disturbed by the urns and graves of the Anglo-Saxon cemetery and prove that this area on the eastern outskirts of the town was inhabited in the Roman period. It is clearly important to define and date the close of the Roman occupation of the site when evaluating the evidence for the earliest use of the cemetery. Similarly the function of the first Anglo-Saxon inhabitants of Caistor can only be determined in the light of our knowledge of the last phase of Romanized culture in the town as a whole. A brief account must therefore be given of the principal features in the history of the town as revealed by the excavations directed by Professor Donald Atkinson between 1929 and 1935, before describing the less satisfactory Roman material found in F. R. M.'s investigation of the cemetery site.

No large Iron Age centre of population or fortification has yet been detected in the immediate vicinity of the Roman town, and consequently it is uncertain if the selection of the site of the latter was influenced by the existence of an earlier administrative centre. The main topographical reason for the choice of this site for the Roman cantonal capital was an abundant water supply and the presence of an extensive area of relatively level ground on the gravel terrace lying on the east side of the River Tas. This terrain closely resembles that chosen in Claudian times for the similar but smaller settlement at Coddenham in Suffolk. The foundation of the town of *Venta Icenorum*, a name to be interpreted as 'the market-place of the Iceni',[1] was an important factor in the pacification which followed the harsh repression of Boudicca's revolt of A.D. 60–1. Some pottery of Claudian date has been found on the north-east outskirts of the town (TG 241036)[2] but is inadequate to prove anything more than very small-scale occupation.[3] Pottery and coins in much greater quantity suggest that a grid of gravelled streets dividing the area from the Tas to the higher ground to the east into rectangular *insulae* was laid down about A.D. 70 and certainly not more than a few years earlier.

---

[1] Richmond and Crawford 1949, 48.
[2] Clarke 1957, 404.

[3] Clarke 1950, 147, records Samian ware of Claudian type from excavations inside the walled area of the town.

The first occupants dwelt in small huts while the town was being developed and nothing more substantial was erected until the early second century. The sites for the principal public buildings were left vacant until about A.D. 125, when the Hadrianic zeal for public works led to the construction of the *forum* and *basilica*,[1] and baths, the first masonry structures in the town. While this massive construction was in progress or contemplation, at least four pottery kilns were in production in Insula VII/VIII[2] between A.D. 110 and 140.[3] Wattle and daub timber-framed houses were in use in Insula IX during the early second century and were not replaced by masonry structures until the following century. Later in the second century a fire occurred in the baths and *forum* and this was followed by repairs. Another development, probably also of the second century, was the laying out of a temple precinct over half a mile north-east of the town centre.[4]

Either in the third century, or perhaps later, and probably as part of a general scheme for putting the province in a state of defence, a central area of the town, comprising about 35 acres, was fortified with a formidable wall with a rampart behind and a broad ditch in front. Bastions, alternately rectangular and circular, are possibly a later addition to this defensive scheme. These fortifications truncated earlier streets on the north, east, and south and cut a street leading to the north-east, possibly to the temple precinct.[5] Henceforth, access to the extra-mural areas of settlement from the town centre was restricted to the four gates provided in the centre of each of the four walls.

After the fire the *forum* remained in ruins for the first two generations of the third century, but there was considerable building activity elsewhere in the town. Soon after 200, two temples of Romano-Celtic type were built in Insula IX, and between about 225 and 250 the public baths were rebuilt. Capital investment was not confined to public edifices, for in the early years of the third century houses in Insula IX were reconstructed as a shop and house respectively, with a timber framework enclosing wattle and daub on flint and tile sleeper walls. These buildings lasted till about the end of the century. Over the disused kilns in Insula VII/VIII another substantial house, with sleeper walls of masonry (Building 4), was built and a large house in the grounds of Caistor Hall, partly excavated in 1846,[6] is probably of similar date. About 270, or soon after, resources were available for rebuilding the *forum* on a simpler plan and this important structure continued in use until the late fourth century. About 300 the shop in Insula IX was superseded by a furnace for manufacturing glass. This juxtaposition of public buildings, houses, shops, and workshops was a normal feature of the life of this market town.

The final phase of Romanized culture in this town is difficult to evaluate. On the evidence of coins and pottery, occupation in the areas excavated in the walled sector of the town continued steadily until about 360, but lasted in diminished form until at least the end of the

[1] But now Professor Frere (1970a), reinterpreting Professor Atkinson's records, suggests that this building may date from A.D. 150–60 or later.

[2] The numeration of the *insulae* follows Kent 1929.

[3] Three were excavated in 1930 (Atkinson 1932) and one in 1958, on the berm between the north town wall and the edge of the ditch, by M. Brely (N.C.M. records).

[4] Clarke 1957, 404–5.

[5] An air photograph by Dr. J. K. St. Joseph (1966, pl. III) clearly shows two parallel ditches, one *c.* 140 yards (*c.* 130 m.) and one *c.* 158 yards (*c.* 145 m.) south of the southern line of visible defences, which on analogy with earthwork defences elsewhere may belong to the second century. Recent work on the walled town suggests that the defences excavated by Professor Atkinson, which enclosed a more restricted area, may have been constructed in the period 240–75; the bastions being added in the fourth century. We are indebted to Professor S. S. Frere for information on this point.

[6] *Arch. J.* iv (1847), 72–3.

fourth century. The temple precinct to the north-east was still in use in the fourth century and the Romano-Celtic temple partly excavated in 1957[1] may even date from this time. Atkinson suggested that among the buildings excavated there was no indication of destruction by fire save in one house, Building 4,[2] at the west of which he identified a layer of burnt material containing thirty-six human skulls and other bones not formally buried. This gruesome assemblage has been ascribed to enemy action[3] but it is not certain that this is the only interpretation.

The house contained over 100 coins of which more than a third date from *c.* 390 or later, the latest being a solidus of Honorius of *c.* A.D. 404.[4] On the evidence of these coins and associated pottery, this house must have been occupied as late as the opening years of the fifth century, and probably later.[5]

THE CEMETERY SITE IN THE ROMAN PERIOD (map 2)

Interpretation of the Roman occupation of the site as revealed by F. R. M.'s excavations is especially difficult owing to the almost total absence of adequate records. There is no detailed plan of any structure, no measured record of any section, and no photograph of any Roman feature. Most of the Roman pottery found has not been preserved and, of the fragmentary material which now survives, the precise location has usually not been recorded.[6] F. R. M. was consciously digging an Anglo-Saxon cemetery and, regarding the Roman material as a complicating factor in this investigation, he underestimated the vital importance of studying the inter-relationship of these successive phases, particularly from the chronological viewpoint. It must, however, be remembered that conditions in the cemetery would have tested the skill of the most experienced excavator. F. R. M. had no training to equip him for the difficulties encountered in this part of his task. The following account must therefore lack much of the precision to be expected in the report of a present-day investigation of such a site: it has been based on F. R. M.'s notes and a study of the surviving material. The measurements given are only approximate and have been taken from revised versions of F. R. M.'s field plans.[7] The structures will be described in the alphabetical order which he gave them, but this has no significance either geographically or chronologically. The refuse pits and their contents will then be described in numerical order and, finally, an attempt will be made to assess the evidence for the Roman occupation of the site as a whole.

Soil Conditions

The disturbances of the cemetery site since Anglo-Saxon times have been noted in the General Introduction (p. 2). Medieval marling and ploughing, the burrowing of rabbits and the diggings of rabbiters, and finally the growth of the plantation have conspired to

[1] *J.R.S.* xlvii (1958), 142.
[2] But see p. 33.
[3] *J.R.S.* xxi (1931), 232–3, whence Collingwood and Myres 1937, 302; Hawkes 1949, 65; Clarke 1960, 130, 132; Hawkes and Dunning 1961, 25–6; Frere 1966, 91, and Frere 1967, 376–7.
[4] The coins have been checked by Mr. R. A. G. Carson of the Department of Coins and Medals, British Museum. His list is given on pp. 34–40.

[5] The problems presented by Building 4 are further considered on pp. 33–4.
[6] Because of this R. R. Clarke's notes on dates and parallels have not been revised.
[7] Map 2 was redrawn from F. R. M.'s several plans of the cemetery. The measurements given on pp. 19–24 were taken by R. R. Clarke from his own amended version of one or more of these plans. There are certain discrepancies between the two.

effect the maximum confusion in interpreting stratigraphy. It is clear, however, that where definite floor levels in structures of Roman date can be recognized, they lie about two feet below the modern surface. The top 2 ft. (60 cm.), composed of about 9 in. (23 cm.) of leaf mould inside the plantation and of turf outside its limits overlying about 1 ft. 3 in. (37 cm.) of 'loam', must therefore have accumulated since the Roman occupation ended. The accumulation may even have been greater than 2 ft. (60 cm.), for ploughing, especially on the western side, and soil erosion have probably been responsible for some diminution. F. R. M. suggested that 1 ft. 6 in. (45 cm.) might have been removed by ploughing but this is perhaps an overestimate. Unless some of the Roman floors were themselves sunk below contemporary ground level, as the account of Structure M suggests in that instance, humus must have accumulated after the cessation of occupation in the Roman dwellings at a rate sufficient for a layer of loamy soil at least 1 ft. (30 cm.) thick and probably nearer 2 ft. (60 cm.) thick to form before the Anglo-Saxon cremation urns were inserted.[1] Their bases normally rest on the top surface of the dingy yellow sand or less frequently on the bright yellow pebbly gravel which underlies the loam throughout the cemetery area except at the north-west corner where the loam is absent.

Structure A

The remains of this structure, one of the larger found on the site, consisted of a layer of gravel, 3–4 in. (8–10 cm.) thick, lying 2 ft. 1 in. (63 cm.) below the modern surface and spread over the natural sand. The limits of this floor were not clearly defined owing to tree roots and modern digging, but it was at least 14 ft. (4·25 m.) long. The northern half of a clay hearth survived with its long axis oriented east–west for a distance of 2 ft. 6 in. (75 cm.). The adjacent gravel was reddened by heat. At the south-east corner of this dwelling was an oven (Structure I, p. 21). Eight feet (2·4 m.) south-east of this was an area of fired daub classified as Structure J (p. 21), but it is uncertain if this represents a separate hut or is a dump of building material from Structure A, which was presumably a timber-framed building, though no post-holes were noticed. It is likewise uncertain if Pit 9 (p. 24), which lay close to the east side of Structure A, was dug by its occupants. 'Plenty of Roman sherds and objects' lay on the gravel floor, but cannot now be identified and the only surviving associated find from this floor is a denarius of Septimius Severus (minted 197/8). Holes for the insertion of several Anglo-Saxon cremation urns (A 3–A 7, A 10, A 11) were dug later so that their bases rested on the surface of the gravel floor.

Structure B

F. R. M. noted that 'conditions were very complicated and hard to disentangle at this spot, but I think there is little doubt that a building of some sort had existed here'. On his field plan he marked the edge of an apparent clay floor at least 7 ft. (2·1 m.) wide from east to west, but gives no further details apart from noting at a depth of 2 ft. (60 cm.) a layer of black earth just over 1 ft. (30 cm.) thick containing numerous sherds, fragments of charcoal, fired daub, and lumps of burnt clay flooring. In excavating a few feet north of Structure B,

---

[1] Professor Frere has suggested that this may have formed from the debris of timber-framed daub buildings and *terre pisée* walls.

F. R. M. recorded daub, and to the south-west flints, tiles, and sherds. None of this pottery is now identifiable, but a hint as to the date of this wattle and daub dwelling may be derived from the contents of Pit 6 (p. 23), probably dug about the beginning of the third century. Pit 6 contained carbonized wood, daub, and fragments of clay flooring and may represent part of the process of clearing up the site of a burnt wattle and daub timber-framed house prior to constructing a new house with sleeper walls of tiles and flints. Of this only the building debris found west of the pit now survives; the remainder must presumably have been robbed in Anglo-Saxon or later times for the building materials or to facilitate agriculture. This scanty evidence points to a second-century date for the wattle and daub house, a conclusion consonant with the dating for the houses of similar construction excavated in Insula IX. Urns X 8, X 9, and X 10 had been inserted on part of the site of this building.

Structure C

The remains of this dwelling consisted of several square feet of an unburnt clay floor approximately 6 ft. by 3 ft. (1·8 m. by 0·9 m.) lying 1 ft. 2 in. (35 cm.) beneath the modern surface. At the north end of the floor were the remains of a horseshoe-shaped clay hearth of which the northern edge had been destroyed by those who dug Grave 27. No post-holes were noted and there is no record of Roman pottery or other objects associated with it except for a fragment of *opus signinum*, the surface of which is slightly curved and bears the remains of a red wash. The relationship of this fragment to the structure is unknown. Urn M 42 lay in fragments on this clay floor.

Structure D

This comprised a clay floor of irregular outline at least 12 ft. (3·7 m.) from north to south by about 6 ft. (1·8 m.) wide, with a soak-away or urinal at the north end and a refuse pit (Pit 8, p. 23) to the south. A hearth, Structure N (p. 22), was about 6 ft. (1·8 m.) away to the east and was probably connected, as the intervening space was filled with black soil containing carbonized wood and large numbers of twisted iron nails suggesting that the building might have been deliberately dismantled. To the west of the floor, which lay at a depth of 2 ft. (60 cm.) and was 5–6 in. (13–15 cm.) thick, was a considerable spread of fired daub, of which a few fragments were incised for keying on plaster, together with Roman sherds. The floor was much broken, but its brick-red colour and the white and shattered condition of its contained flints left no doubt that this house or its materials had been burnt. The soak-away on the northern edge of the floor was semi-circular in plan and rested on the sand. It was constructed of two courses of fragments of gritstone rotary querns with the gaps plugged with clay.

The remains of cremation urn P 54 lay on the east side of the floor and a Roman jar containing a cremation (P 43, p. 74) was on the west side. Near the centre of the floor, in a hole which had been dug through to the sand, was cremation urn P 42, and in another hole on the western side, P 44, while P 36 and P 41 were east of the floor in the area of black soil. Just west of the soak-away was a broken Roman jar (P 45) in grey ware of mid-second-century date.

If Pit 8 may be associated with this dwelling, its contents suggest occupation from about 140 to 225. The latter provides an approximate date for the burning of the house, though this is only inference.

Structure E

This was a clay oven, oval in plan, with its long axis east and west. Originally it had been about 3 ft. (90 cm.) long and 2 ft. (60 cm.) wide but the higher east end has been destroyed. The clay walls were 1 ft. 1 in. (33 cm.) high and were unfired, but the floor of the oven at a depth of 2 ft. 2 in. (66 cm.) was burnt red. The interior of the oven was filled with fragments of burnt clay mixed with Roman sherds, animal bones, and oyster shells. At the bottom was a mortarium, intact except for a hole in the bottom, but this cannot now be traced.

Structure F

This was a clay hearth, oval in plan and measuring about 3 ft. (90 cm.) from south-west to north-east by 2 ft. (60 cm.) wide. No futher details recorded.

Structure G

This was a clay hearth, oval in plan and measuring about 4 ft. (12·2 m.) from south-west to north-east (both ends were damaged) by 3 ft. (90 cm.) wide. No further details recorded.

Structure H

This was a semi-circular clay hearth approximately 2 ft. (60 cm.) in diameter, which had been cut into on the east side by Grave 36. No further details recorded.

Structure I

This oven or hearth has already been noted in connection with Structure A (p. 19), at the south-east corner of which it lay, though it is uncertain if it was inside or outside that dwelling. F. R. M. recorded this as 'a large mass of burnt clay resting on a spread of more burnt clay that may have been a floor', but on his plan he shows an oval area about 1 ft. 6 in. (45 cm.) east–west and about 1 ft. (30 cm.) wide.

Structure J

This was an area about 2 ft. 6 in. (75 cm.) in diameter with a concentration of fired daub bearing wattle impressions. It is uncertain if this is the remains of a structure or merely a dump of material from the adjacent dwelling.

Structure K

This was a roughly circular hut represented by a mass of fired daub with some unburnt clay, a few fragments of carbonized wood, and iron nails lying about 1 ft. (30 cm.) below the modern surface. The daub was spread over a wide area, but there was a concentration about 1 ft. (30 cm.) thick in the centre, diminishing to 3 in. (7 cm.) at the perimeter, which suggests that the hut was 9–10 ft. (2·7–3 m.) in diameter. Beneath the daub were Roman sherds and iron fragments (not now identifiable) and fragments of glass vessels. These survive and have been identified by Dr. D. B. Harden as portions of five glass bottles of early second-century date.

Structure L

As this structure lay on the margin of the excavated area of the cemetery its limits were not ascertained, but a gravel floor about 1 ft. (30 cm.) thick and stretching at least 17 ft. (5 m.) from north-west to south-east by at least 8 ft. (2·4 m.) wide was identified. Overlying the gravel was a layer of black earth about 4 in. (10 cm.) thick which contained quantities of Roman sherds and fragments of iron, but this material cannot now be identified. It would seem probable that this floor was part of a rectangular hut of timber.

Structure M

This consisted of a fan-shaped area with a radius of 22–3 ft. (6·7–7 m.). From about 1 ft. (30 cm.) below the surface to a sandy clay at a depth of 2 ft. 8 in. (80 cm.) on the west and 2 ft. (60 cm.) deep on the east there was a loam infill in which large flints, tiles, wall plaster, and daub were scattered 'like plums in a pudding'. There was a hearth in the northern part of the area, but its relationship to the infill is not recorded. Inside this fan-shaped area were several cremation urns (N 9, N 15, N 16, N 17, N 19, N 21) found resting on the sandy clay and apparently undisturbed. From this circumstance F. R. M. deduced that the infill took place prior to the insertion of the urns and attributed the filling of this hollow with building material to the Romans. It may be suggested that the building debris is the remains of a rectangular Roman building on the site, possibly a temple, which was demolished and spread before the cemetery came into use. Unfortunately there is nothing to suggest any precise date for the structure. A socketed iron gouge (fig. 63, 1 and p. 26) is recorded to have been found by the side of the hearth and an amphora sherd, probably not later than about A.D. 150, came from an unrecorded spot in the loam.

Structure N

This was an oval hearth about 2 ft. 6 in. (75 cm.) long, but no details were recorded by F. R. M. From its location it is almost certain that it formed part of dwelling D (p. 20).

Structure O

A floor or hearth about 4 ft. (1·2 m.) square is marked on F. R. M.'s field plan but he left no notes on it and its function and exact position must remain uncertain. Its proximity to Structure A suggests that it may have formed part of that dwelling and for that reason it is not shown as map 2.

Pit 1

This refuse pit was about 6 ft. (1·8 m.) long from east to west by 2 ft. 6 in. (75 cm.) from north to south and was 4 ft. 2 in. (1·3 m.) deep. The black soil of its infill had later been disturbed by the insertion of cremation urn N 54 (found complete),[1] and that in its turn by an inhumation burial, Grave 32. The original contents of the pit had included many sherds of coarse Roman wares, and one sherd of Samian ware, but these cannot now be identified. A fragment of Roman window glass and a bronze brooch in the form of a fly, inlaid with

---

[1] This urn has inadvertently been omitted from map 2.

light blue enamel (fig. 63, 2 and p. 26), remain from the contents of this pit, which may have been filled in during the late second century. F. R. M. also recorded a leg bone of horse from this pit.

Pits 2–5

F. R. M. left no records of these Roman refuse pits or of their contents. From his field plan their approximate dimensions may be recorded as follows:

Pit 2—oval in plan, 8 ft. (2·4 m.) north–south by 4 ft. (1·2 m.) east–west.

Pit 3—not completely excavated, about 9 ft. (2·7 m.) east–west by at least 4 ft. (1·2 m.) north–south.

Pit 4—circular, about 2 ft. 6 in. (75 cm.) in diameter.

Pit 5—circular, about 3 ft. (90 cm.) in diameter.

Pit 6

The association of this roughly circular pit, 5–6 ft. (1·5–1·8 m.) in diameter and 8 ft. 8 in. (2·6 m.) deep, with Structure B has already been noted (p. 19). The infilling of the pit was dry loam and contained fragments of daub with wattle impressions, burnt clay flooring, charcoal, animal bones, and Roman sherds. Lying over the northern part of the pit was Grave 12, in which the two skeletons had sagged owing to the settlement of the contents of the pit. The only object from the infill which can now be recognized is over half a beaker ('Hunt-cup') of Castor ware with barbotine decoration (fig. 63, 8 and p. 28). Beakers of this type were current in the earlier third century[1] and the presence of this example suggests that Pit 6 may have been dug and filled after A.D. 200.

Pit 7

This was a circular pit about 2 ft. 6 in. (75 cm.) in diameter but F. R. M. left no record of its contents.

Pit 8

This pit, described by F. R. M. as 'more of a spread than a pit', lay only 2 ft. (60 cm.) south of Structure D and was probably used by the occupants of that dwelling (p. 20). It was oval in plan with a length from north to south of about 8 ft. (2·4 m.) and a width of about 3 ft. 6 in. (1·1 m.), and was apparently shallow. Fortunately a number of Roman sherds have been preserved from this pit, but there is nothing to show if this broken pottery was a gradual accumulation or was tipped there together. Roman sherds in some quantity and daub were also found beyond the south side of the pit. In addition to sherds, the pit contained a fragment of a glass bottle, probably of second-century date, and a lead plummet with a bronze loop for suspension (fig. 63, 4 and p. 27). The surviving pottery ranges in date from about A.D. 140 to 225 and includes the following fragments to which a more precise date may be assigned.

Samian Ware. There are two fragments of form 33 and one of form 36, all Antonine, and a base of form 80 stamped SENILIS FE, attributable to Senilis of Lezoux (also Antonine).[2]

---

[1] Collingwood and Richmond 1969, 262.   [2] Oswald 1931, 292.

Castor Ware. One sherd of white paste with green-brown slip decorated with incised line and line of raised dots,[1] late second–early third century.

Rusticated Ware. Two sherds with vertical linear rustication—probably early second century; and one sherd with oblique lines of rustication, a type characteristic of East Anglia,[2] A.D. 200–30.

Buff Ware. Rim of flagon,[3] probably mid-second century.

Mortaria. One example in buff paste and large flinty grits,[4] about A.D. 140–60. One example in coarse grey paste,[5] about A.D. 180–220.

Pit 9

This was a small circular pit about 2 ft. (60 cm.) in diameter, 6 ft. (1·8 m.) east of Structure A with which it was probably associated. There is no record of its contents.

Pit 10

This was a shallow pit, 2 ft. (60 cm.) deep and about 6 ft. (1·8 m.) in diameter, lying some 20 ft. (6 m.) west of Structure K, but any association can only be guesswork. The black soil infill of this pit had been much disturbed by the later insertions of urns D 1, D 2, D 3, D 4, D 5, and D 11. F. R. M. recorded that the pit was 'full of Roman pottery' but none of this can now be identified, and the only two objects assignable to this pit are a small broken and worn bronze coin of Theodora (337–41) found at a depth of 1 ft. 6 in. (45 cm.) and a circular bronze mount with openwork decoration, probably from a belt (fig. 63, 3 and p. 27; pl. XIX*d*). This is of considerable interest from three points of view. It forms part of the small group of objects from *Venta Icenorum* which are likely to be military equipment;[6] it is an addition to the relatively few examples of openwork mounts in trumpet style from British localities; and this particular example is distinctive from its combination of motifs derived from abstract and naturalistic art.

In the absence of the pottery from this pit it is impossible to date the period of its infill. The coin of Theodora shows that either the pit was still open or further disturbance occurred in the second half of the fourth century or later. This might have been due to the deposition of one or more of the Anglo-Saxon urns. D 2 and D 11 are both early types, not later than the fifth century.

Pit 11

This was a small oval pit about 4 ft. (1·2 m.) from east to west by about 2 ft. (60 cm.). No record of its contents has been preserved.

OTHER ROMAN MATERIAL FROM THE AREA OF THE CEMETERY

In addition to those relatively few objects which can still be identified as coming from the structures or pits, other Roman material from the area of the cemetery is preserved but with-

[1] Cf. Richardson 1944, 118, fig. 16, 6.
[2] Cf. Thompson 1958, pl. IX*a*, *b*; Atkinson 1937, 219–20, types S 42, S 43.
[3] Cf. Hull 1958, 283, type 160.
[4] Cf. Atkinson 1937, 213, type R 21.
[5] Cf. Atkinson 1937, 214, type R 33.

[6] Dr. G. Webster has identified the following bronze objects from the 1929–35 excavations as probably of military origin: hinge from the back of a cuirass, a cuirass hook, and a lunate pendant from a belt or strap. These may have been lost by military engineers laying out the town streets.

out, in most cases, any record of exact provenance. Despite this handicap this material must be considered in assessing the date and intensity of the Roman occupation of the cemetery site. In addition there are six Roman jars from the site numbered by F. R. M. as part of the burial urn series. Four of these contained cremations, but it is very doubtful if the other two were used for this purpose. All six—N 6, N 72, P 43, P 45, P 48, and P 74—are discussed on pp. 74–6 (figs. 33 and 58).

Samian Ware

Apart from the fragments already noted in the account of Pit 8, and disregarding undatable pieces, over twenty fragments, which may be dated with reasonable accuracy, are still preserved. F. R. M. noted that 'great quantities of fragments of this were found on the site'.

Form 18. Two fragments—not closely datable.

Form 18/31. One fragment Hadrianic and another Antonine.

Form 31. Four fragments Antonine including a base stamped PA(......) F—possibly Paternus of Lezoux (Oswald 1931, 231).

Form 27. One fragment Hadrianic.

Form 33. Base stamped PISTILLI (Pistillus of Lezoux, Antonine) (Oswald 1931, 241). This was found with Anglo-Saxon urn P 34, probably a child's cremation, and was perhaps used as a toy.

Form 80. Three fragments—Antonine.

Ludowici Form SMB. One fragment Rheinzabern ware—Antonine.

Form 46. Two fragments much worn (cf. Oswald and Pryce 1920, pl. LV, 24) about A.D. 190–200.

Form 37. Fragments of six bowls, five being of Antonine date and one Trajanic.

There are several fragments of a bowl in the style of LAXTVCISSA of Lezoux (c. A.D. 150–80—Stanfield and Simpson 1958, 188 and pl. 98, no. 10, where a reconstruction drawing of this Caistor bowl by Dr. F. Oswald is given). The decorative elements include his ovolo, leaves, acanthus tips, and characteristic demi-acanthus as well as his doe (Oswald 1936, no. 1815) and goat (Oswald 1936, no. 1842). The demi-acanthus is used as a basal border, while the acanthus tips alternate with seven-beaded rosettes to form a median zone.

There is one fragment of a bowl in the style of IOENALIS of Lezoux (c. A.D. 100–20—Stanfield and Simpson 1958, 40). It bears his ovolo, warrior, Hercules, and Nemean Lion (near Oswald 1936, no. 796).

The Samian ware from the cemetery site is thus all of second-century date, apart from the two fragments of Form 18, but the bulk of the surviving fragments were made in the period A.D. 140–80.

Roman Coins

Eight Roman coins are known from the site of the cemetery but only one of them, a very worn perforated radiate, probably of Valerian I, found in urn Y 40 (pp. 44, 204) was certainly utilized by the Anglo-Saxons. It is true that two coins were found in Grave 17 and one in Grave 29, but there is no reason to think that this is other than an accidental association resulting from the digging of graves through a deposit littered with Roman debris. The following seven coins may therefore be losses by the Romanized inhabitants of the site between the second and fourth centuries, though in at least two cases (5 and 7) the possibility of later intrusion cannot be ruled out.

1. Trajan, sestertius, originally identified as *R.I.C.* ii, no. 519, A.D. 103–11, but legends now almost completely illegible.
   From Grave 17.

2. Lucius Verus, sestertius, *R.I.C.* iii, A.D. 165–9, legends largely illegible.
   From near Grave 13.

3. Commodus, sestertius, originally identified as *R.I.C.* iii, no. 608, A.D. 172, but legends almost completely illegible or missing.
   From Grave 17.

4. Julia Domna, denarius; coin now missing but originally identified as minted A.D. 193–211.
   From north of Y 22, Trench Y.

5. Septimius Severus, denarius; obv. L.SEPT.SEV.PERT.AVG. IMP.X; rev. VICT.AVGG.COS. II P.P; *R.I.C.* iv, pt. I, no. 120(c), A.D. 197–8.
   From Structure A; 9 in. (23 cm.) east of A 5. F. R. M. suggested possible association with the group of urns A 4–6: of these A 4 is a small plain biconical pot of early type.

6. Constantine II as Caesar, Æ 3, rev. GLORIA EXERCITVS (one standard), m.m. TRS, Trier, *R.I.C.* vii, no. 586, A.D. 335–7.
   From Grave 29.

7. Theodora, Æ 3, rev. PIETAS ROMANA, m.m. TRP laurel leaf, Trier, *L.R.B.C.* i, no. 129, A.D. 337–41.
   From Pit 10. See p. 24 for possible association with intrusive urns D 1, 2, 3, 4, 5, 11.

Miscellaneous Roman Material

A few other objects of Roman date remain to be recorded. With the exception of a sawn tine of stag's antler found below Grave 16, the exact locality of the following material was not noted by F. R. M.: clay counter, bone pin, strip of sheet bronze, iron stylus, two iron locks (now missing), and the bronze terminal of an iron key (fig. 63, 5 and p. 28).

Illustrated Roman Material (fig. 63)

1. Socketed iron gouge, with oval spoon; cf. gouge from 1890 hoard from Silchester[1] and one from Newstead,[2] but longer than the latter. L. 11·3 in. (28·7 cm.).
   From Structure M (p. 22).

2. Bronze brooch in the form of a fly, inlaid with light blue enamel. Fly brooches are a variety of enamelled trumpet-headed brooches (Collingwood type Sii). An example

---

[1] Boon 1957, fig, 35. 6.   [2] Curle 1911, pl. LIX, 13.

identical in form with that from Caistor, and apparently from Lincoln, is now in the British Museum[1] and somewhat similar specimens come from Lime Street, London,[2] and Brough under Stainmore.[3] Brooches of this type can be dated to the middle part of the second century.

From Pit 1.

3. Circular bronze mount with central triskele of peltas in developed 'trumpet' style springing from an outer ring which is divided into six segments and decorated with three scallop shells (pl. XIX*d*). On the back were three studs, each set beneath a scallop shell; diameter 1·25 in. (3·2 cm.).

Openwork mounts with trumpet patterns of Celtic inspiration were made in Pannonia[4] and possibly also in the Rhineland or northern Gaul from the second century onwards.[5] They are commonly found in the forts of the German Limes[6] and along the Danube but are relatively uncommon in Britain. Examples from this country have been recorded from military sites at Richborough[7] (unstratified), Caerleon[8] in a second-century deposit, Newstead[9] probably Antonine, and from Traprain, Scotland,[10] and from Icklingham, Suffolk. The Icklingham specimen with its triskele of peltas in trumpet style was regarded as Iron Age by R. A. Smith[11] but has been correctly assigned to the Roman period by Brailsford;[12] it compares very closely with one from Volubilis, Morocco.[13] None of the British examples provides a very close parallel to the Caistor mount and the best analogy comes from the opposite end of the empire at Dura-Europos on the Euphrates,[14] though this lacks the scallop shells of the Caistor specimen. The Dura-Europos mount probably formed part of the equipment of a Roman occupation force which included elements from the Rhineland or adjacent areas and must have reached that city and been lost between A.D. 165 and 256 when the city was destroyed.

Scallop shells are employed to decorate the handle of a silver patera of Gaulish make in a hoard of first-century A.D. silver objects from Chalon-sur-Saône, France,[15] but the shells are treated in a less naturalistic manner than those on the Caistor mount which, on the basis of the parallels to its general form already cited, should be assigned to the late second or, at the latest, to the early third century.

4. Hemispherical bronze steelyard weight or plummet, with a single bronze loop and one link of bronze chain. The weight is 394 gm., well above that of the standard Roman pound; in addition, quite a lot of metal has been lost. The chain is similar to one attached to a weight found at Richborough[16] but the shape of the Caistor weight is different from those found at Richborough. The shape of the Caistor object does seem more suitable for a weight, rather than a plummet. Diameter 2 in. (5·1 cm.).

From Pit 8.

[1] British Museum 1951, 23, fig. 11, no. 23.
[2] London Museum 1930, 99, fig. 29, no. 32.
[3] Collingwood and Richmond 1969, 297–8 and fig. 104, 67.
[4] Sellye 1969.
[5] Brogan 1953, 152–3.
[6] Lindenschmidt 1858, 10, pl. vi; 1870, 8, pl. v; 1881, 7, pl. v.
[7] Bushe-Fox 1932, 81–2; pl. XII, fig. 1, no. 38.
[8] Nash-Williams 1932, 39–40, fig. 33, no. 30.
[9] Curle 1911, 304 with pl. LXXVI, fig. 2.
[10] Curle and Cree 1915–16, 111, fig. 28, no. 1.
[11] Smith 1935, 27–8, pl. XIII*c*.
[12] British Museum 1951, 28, fig. 14, 5.
[13] Boube-Picot 1964, 188 and pls. IV. 1, V.
[14] Frisch and Toll 1949, 8 and pl. I, no. 1.
[15] Lantier 1937, 185–6 and fig. 7.
[16] Bushe-Fox 1932, 83 and pl. XIV. 47.

5. Iron key with bronze handle. Existing length 3·5 in. (9 cm.). This is similar to a key, all in bronze, of late first-century date from Richborough[1] but iron keys with terminals of this type generally date from about A.D. 150. A somewhat similar specimen came from the *forum* site at Caistor (B 205).

6. Handle of globular amphora, reddish with a buff core, stamped L.I.T.[2] This is an example of Callender's type 878 which is south Spanish in origin and dated to A.D. 150–98?
   Labelled 'REF. PIT' but number of pit not known.

7. Mortarium, pink clay with cream surface stamped REGAL. Mrs. K. Hartley has examined this example and kindly reports that mortaria by REGALIS have been found at the Colchester kilns (at least six specimens)[3] and the fabric and rim-forms suggest *c*. A.D. 170–200 as a probable date. Four other examples are known from Atkinson's excavations at Caistor-by-Norwich, two from Grimstone End, Pakenham, Suffolk, and one each from Brundall, Norfolk, Great Chesterford, Essex, and South Shields, co. Durham.
   From Trench Y.

8. 'Hunt-cup'—Castor ware beaker with cornice rim and barbotine decoration of a hunting scene. There is a single row of animals of which a hare and a single hound survive. Four rows of rouletting below the animals. The form is very similar to one illustrated by Hartley.[4] This group belongs to the earlier third century and barely reaches its last quarter.[5] Height 6 in. (15·2 cm.).
   From Pit 6.

DISCUSSION

In the absence of detailed records and our ignorance of the full range of the archaeological material recovered by F. R. M., it is clearly unwise to be dogmatic about the interpretation of what he discovered of the Roman occupation of the site. Yet the attempt must be made, for Roman debris forms the basal layer of the cemetery and the existence of the Roman town provides its *raison d'être*. The excavations showed that over almost the whole area subsequently used as a cemetery there was evidence for Roman occupation in the form of refuse pits, buildings, and ancillary structures, together with a general scatter of building debris and sherds.

In his draft report F. R. M. interpreted this group of buildings as a 'village' and its inhabitants as 'villagers'. Though he gave no reasons for this view, he was perhaps swayed by the apparent isolation of this inhabited hilltop from the walled town 1,100 ft. (335 m.) away. Many more air photographs of the site are now available than when he wrote and these seem to show that the street-grid—the rectangular grid of streets laid out when the town was established—extended at least as far east as this site.[6] Three parallel streets can be seen stretching eastwards and a length of the southernmost one is visible running east from the east side of the cemetery plantation which it must have passed through just south of the southern limit of the excavated area (map 1). The reason for the apparent gap in these streets

[1] Bushe-Fox 1949, 19, 125, pl. XXXIV, no. 86.
[2] Cf. Callender 1965, fig. 9. 15.
[3] Hull 1958, 248 ff.
[4] Hartley 1960, 24 and 25, fig. 4. 1.

[5] Collingwood and Richmond 1969, 262.
[6] The plan here published does not agree with that in Collingwood and Richmond 1969, fig. 34; it is based on a reinterpretation of the air photographs.

and the absence of Roman occupational debris on the surface in the area west of the cemetery is again supplied by Dr. St. Joseph's air photographs, which show clear indications of subsequent disturbance on a large scale. These are represented on the ground by a deep depression at the foot of the hill on which the cemetery was sited, which may have been a loam, sand, and gravel pit of medieval date. The field to the south still bears the name 'Clay Pit Field'. The cemetery area in the early Roman period thus lay within the confines of a rectangular *insula* and formed an integral part of the town, which from this and much other evidence was clearly at one stage very much more extensive than the subsequent walled area of a mere 35 acres.

On the basis of the evidence revealed by Professor Atkinson's excavations in Insula IX, we should expect that the earliest development on the cemetery site would consist of unsubstantial huts with clay hearths, a persistence of the native idiom in architecture. It may well be that the cemetery sequence began in this manner and that the isolated hearths (Structures C, G, and F) and oven (Structure E) are the only recognizable remains of former circular hutments. Structure K seems more definitely to have been a circular hut with walls of daub. There is nothing surviving to show that these huts, if such they were, were Flavian. The only datable material surviving is from Structure K and this was early second century, but whether this corresponds to the beginning or end of the occupation of the hut we have no means of knowing.

We are on more certain ground in assigning the apparently rectangular huts (Structures A, B, D, and L) to the second century, if the evidence of stray finds and the contents of adjacent refuse pits may be accepted. The floors were gravel or clay and their walls were timber-framed and filled with wattle and daub, a technique shown in Insula IX[1] to be characteristic of the town in the early second century. These buildings are probably part of the Hadrianic development of the town which culminated in the construction of the *forum*. Two of these buildings (Structures B and D) were burnt down, by accident or design, about A.D. 200 or soon after, and with this the main occupation of the site ends. There is no decisive evidence for the activities of its occupants during the second century but, in default of evidence to the contrary, it may be surmised that they were workmen employed in industrial activities, such as pottery-making, elsewhere in the town, or were engaged in farming outside the limits of the built-up area.

The surviving pottery and coins indicate little occupation after about A.D. 225 at latest, but the mass of building debris from near Structure B and from Structure M probably indicates a new development early in the third century. It will be recalled that large quantities of mortared flints, roofing tiles, daub, and plaster were found and it is improbable that this material was carted to the hilltop merely to dispose of it. It would appear more probable that a new structure, possibly a temple, was built soon after A.D. 200, a date which would be consonant with the use of similar materials for this purpose in the central area of the town and a purpose which would be consistent with an absence of the occupation debris such as that which had existed in the previous century. It may be objected that no footings were discovered to support this attribution but F. R. M.'s technique of excavation was not likely to have identified robber trenches made either in the eventual clearance of the site or by the Anglo-Saxons in grubbing out flints and tiles for funerary purposes. The fact must be faced

[1] Atkinson 1931, 130–1.

that among the surviving material there is virtually nothing to prove domestic use during the later third and early fourth centuries, and if the area was occupied at all it seems to have been for a purpose which did not result in the accumulation of broken crockery. If such a building existed we have no means of dating its abandonment, though it may well have been superfluous for the needs of a declining, or perhaps increasingly Christianized, population, served by at least three other temples, before the middle of the fourth century. The latest evidence for Roman culture on the cemetery site to which a precise date may be assigned consists of the two coins of Constantine II and Theodora. But two isolated coins do not constitute proof of occupation, especially as they could well have been introduced in the cemetery period. By 300 therefore, if not earlier, the hilltop may have been crowned by the ruins of a hypothetical temple with grass and bushes covering the unsubstantial debris of the collapsed hutments of the second century. If there had been a temple there it might have seemed an appropriate spot for reuse as a cemetery for pagan barbarian mercenaries and their families at any time after this date, but there is no evidence from the site itself to show how soon the first cremation fires were lit. F. R. M. thought that there were 'faint indications' to support the view[1] that the first Anglo-Saxons spread what remained of the buildings and levelled up the hummocky ground before its use for a cemetery began. The grubbing out of the ruins of Structures B and M, and the accumulation of loamy material burying the Roman floors, and no doubt derived largely from the flimsy walls and roofs of the earlier shanties, suggests that such a tidying-up operation must have preceded this new phase in its history.

[1] Clarke and Myres 1939–40, 217.

VENTA ICENORUM—THE FINAL PHASE

By J. N. L. Myres and Barbara Green

AS at other Roman towns in Britain it is impossible to date closely either the breakdown of civic control at Caistor or the final abandonment of the site. The extent of the fourth-century occupation is also uncertain. Insula IX, a central site given over to glass-making in the early fourth century, was perhaps abandoned, but coins of the House of Theodosius and Arcadius were found in the topsoil. Effective occupation in the late fourth century is, at present, attested only from the site of the *forum* in Insula X and from Building 4 in Insula VII/VIII; but further excavation might well enlarge the area. A number of coins from these two sites, apparently minted during the last decade of the fourth century and the first decade of the fifth, indicate that a community[1] was still in existence at that time. It has been convincingly argued[2] that many coins minted in the late fourth and early fifth centuries remained in circulation in Roman Britain for a further three or four decades, later coinage being only rarely brought into the country. Such coins cannot therefore be used to date closely the deposits in which they are found.

The suggested reorganization of the town defences in the third century[3] implies a community still sufficiently large and viable to warrant such an expense. The enclosure of some 35 acres must indicate that this area was thought worth defending. Until the whole system is securely dated uncertainty must remain. But the existence of external bastions does indicate that the defences were probably improved in the later part of the fourth century. Further evidence for the existence of an adequate defensive system at that time comes from the *forum* and Building 4. Five pieces of military equipment of the type associated with barbarian troops of this period have been found on these two sites, while a sixth was included in a nineteenth-century collection.[4] All are late fourth- or early fifth-century types[5] and indicate the presence of a military force stationed in or near the town at this time. A bone sword guard was picked up after ploughing in 1969 in the area of the Baths. This too can perhaps be associated with the users of the metal objects. By this time also, if the dating here suggested for the earliest barbarian burials in the Anglo-Saxon cemetery is correct, Germanic folk were already cremating their dead only some 400 yards outside the east gate of *Venta*.

It may be significant in this context to note that a number of pieces of so-called 'Romano-Saxon' pottery have been recorded from the Roman town. One such, unstratified, has already been published;[6] three others are here illustrated on fig. 70. Pottery of this kind has

---

[1] A detailed account of the coins from Building 4 is given on pp. 34–40. An analysis of the coins from the *forum* was made using identifications given in Professor Atkinson's coin list: thirty-eight Theodosian coins were recorded in addition to five of Arcadius and four of Honorius—nearly all came from topsoil, and were in very poor condition.

[2] Kent 1961.

[3] See footnote 5, p. 17.

[4] Hawkes and Dunning (1961) describe three of these

pieces. The other three were recognized subsequently in the N.C.M. collections. All are described and illustrated below, pp. 41–2 and fig. 64. In spring 1972 part of a bronze strap-end was recovered from the ploughsoil in the area of Insula V or the *forum* (N.C.M. 271.972).

[5] Ibid. and information from Mrs. S. C. Hawkes on unpublished items.

[6] Myres 1956, pl. IV A, where this piece is described as 'lost'; it has since been found.

been held to indicate the impact of Germanic decorative taste on ceramic fashions in the later days of Roman Britain. It certainly displays motifs that were popular beyond the Roman frontiers at this time; where datable, it occurs mostly in late fourth-century contexts, and its distribution lies mainly in those eastern parts of Britain where barbarian influence was likely to be felt at the earliest date.[1] The presence of this hybrid pottery is another piece of evidence for the cultural conditions prevailing at *Venta* in its final phase.

Caistor is in fact one of the few Roman towns in Britain where Romano-Saxon pottery, late Roman military equipment, and early Germanic cremation cemeteries have all been recorded in close association. The relationship between the soldiery to whom the military equipment found in the town belonged and the folk whose cremated remains were buried outside the walls is difficult to determine. It is most natural to suppose that these finds represent two aspects of the same phenomenon, a body of Germanic mercenaries who in life defended the walls in their final form and in death were buried, in accordance with continuing Roman practice, outside. If, as is suggested by the presence of beads in some of the earliest urns, they had their families with them, they too would have been settled somewhere close at hand. It may be objected that barbarian irregulars in Roman or sub-Roman employment would be unlikely to cremate their dead with such persistence as the earliest users of the cemetery appear to have done. It is true that most cemeteries of Germanic troops that have been recognized in Roman frontier areas on the Continent consist of inhumations, and the well-known Dorchester burials are a similar instance in this country.[2] But it has to be remembered that most of the continental *laeti* in northern Gaul came of Frankish stock or from related German tribes beyond the Rhine who had long been familiar with Roman ways, while the Angles and Saxons who first settled at Caistor came from regions much further afield in north Germany and southern Scandinavia on which Roman civilization had made little cultural impact. And, while it is true that no objects of Roman uniform equipment have been recognized in our cremation urns, such instances have been recorded occasionally in north German cremation cemeteries, indicating no doubt that individual Saxons who had served in Roman irregular units did sometimes return home to die and be cremated in accordance with their own ancestral customs. At Caistor and elsewhere in eastern England such folk had fewer opportunities to return home to the Continent: they had come to stay, and they continued to cremate their dead in their new homeland, unaffected by Romano-British habits, for which, in any case, they probably had some contempt.

It is of course possible that the scraps of Roman military equipment from *Venta* itself may have been dropped not by barbarian mercenaries but, in part at least, by members of a local militia, operating perhaps as early as the defensive reforms of Count Theodosius in 369, and paid in coin or kind by the cantonal authorities. The external bastions added to town defences in the second half of the fourth century were perhaps intended to take catapults, and these existed on the walls of *Venta*. Trained crews would have been needed to operate this system and it is surely not unreasonable to envisage small detachments of uniformed men being stationed in towns to work the catapults. A high proportion of the belt fittings listed by Hawkes and Dunning come either from Roman towns or from Saxon shore forts, which were also provided with catapults. This is not to suggest that the military belt fittings were the

[1] For the distribution and date of this type of pottery in Essex see Rodwell 1970.

[2] The burials recently found at Lankhills, Winchester, (Clarke, G. 1970) and Gloucester, 1972, are others.

accoutrements distinctive only of such 'Roman artillerymen'. They were undoubtedly used by barbarians in Roman service and such mercenaries could have been employed inside the walls of Caistor. They might then form a barbarian group distinct from those who were being buried contemporaneously outside the walls. As noted above there is no record of any such belt fittings having been found in cremation burials in this country though they are so found in Germany. In Britain those recorded from burials have been from inhumations either in a late Roman context, as at Dorchester or Richborough, or in an Anglo-Saxon context suggesting the reuse of single items as pieces of jewellery. There seems no real reason why there should not be these two grades of employment for the Germanic barbarians, as they can be envisaged as serving different purposes in the defence scheme for Britain, and their terms of employment could have been different. When the Roman military command withdrew, the 'regular' barbarians may have remained in Britain and joined their irregular compatriots, keeping their uniform equipment much as many modern retired soldiers still do. Other members of the family could have worn some of the more attractive or useful pieces, and treasured them sometimes for a good many years. If there were two such groups they would eventually have amalgamated. Whatever the explanation it seems certain that some proportion of those settlers were established before the breakdown of centralized Roman rule in the first decade of the fifth century, and that they were reinforced by further mercenary bands introduced by sub-Roman authority in the following generation.

At the time of Professor Atkinson's excavations some publicity was given to his discovery of the skeletal remains of probably thirty-five men, women, and children at the western end of Building 4 in the heart of the Roman town. Professor Atkinson suggested that this provided evidence for a violent end to Romanized life in this part of *Venta*, and that a massacre in Building 4 had been accompanied or followed by the burning of the house over the victims. He dated the disaster on the evidence of associated coins as probably late in the first decade of the fifth century. Recent reconsideration of the evidence has raised doubts on the case for such a dramatic and violent end to the cantonal capital. The floor on which the human bones, coins, and other objects lay was only 15 to 18 inches below the surface of the ploughed field[1] and there is reason to think that it formed the bottom of the hypocaust of a small bath suite. The layer of ash, hitherto interpreted as coming from the burning of the house, could thus have resulted from the firing of the bath-house furnace. There is no mention in Sir Arthur Keith's report of any fire damage to the bones and this makes it unlikely that they were present at the time of the fire.[2] The fragmentary nature of the skeletal material and the high proportion of surviving fragments of skull bones compared with the number of bones from other parts of the bodies also suggest that the deposit contains at least some intruded material.

The fragments of skull bones represent about thirty-five individuals, but the fragments of limb bones cannot be attributed to more than six individuals. Soil action does not seem to have been responsible for the destruction of the missing bones, as a complete skeleton of a full-term child is recorded from the gravel bed under Room 8.[3] Sir Arthur Keith reports '. . . the population represented is predominantly of young men 20–35 years of age but old

[1] Professor Frere has examined Professor Atkinson's records and has provided many of the following details.

[2] The bones seem to have been destroyed during the

1939–45 war, but Sir Arthur Keith's report survives among the excavation records.

[3] Plan of building in Atkinson 1932, 33.

men and women at various ages were also present and at least two children of about 8 years of age.' There was some evidence that these people were done violently to death. Keith states '. . . on the occipital and frontal fragments of quite a number of the skulls, one could detect evidence of blows made by blunt rather than with sharp weapons and the blows were apparently made when the skulls were fresh before or just after death. I did not see signs of such blows on the bones from skulls of women or of children.'

It is now impossible to be certain of the date or the circumstances which led to the mass disposal of the bodies or portions of the bodies of these people. It is possible to think of them in terms of the disposal of casualties incurred or of criminals executed elsewhere, rather than as evidence for a massacre on the spot. Whatever the explanation may be, this large dump of human remains in the hypocaust of a perhaps already derelict bath suite remains a dramatic illustration of the circumstances in which, after more than three centuries, Roman town life at *Venta Icenorum* came finally to its close.

THE ROMAN COINS FROM BUILDING 4
(1930 EXCAVATIONS)

By R. A. G. Carson

THE numbers and information about the findspot are taken from Professor Atkinson's coin log now in the possession of Professor S. S. Frere. Nearly all these coins were in very poor condition, the only exception being No. 447, solidus of Honorius *c.* A.D. 404, which could be described as 'very fine'.[1]

No.		Details	Mint-mark	Findspot
321	Æ 3	Constantius II Gloria Exercitus (2 standards) *LRBC* 370 A.D. 330–5	⚼ SCONST	W. end
324	Æ 3	Urbs Roma (imitation) Cf. *LRBC* 224 *c.* A.D. 335	PLG	,,
325	Æ 4	Constans (imitation) Two Victories Cf. *LRBC* 449 A.D. 341–6	P̣	,,
329	Æ 3	Constantine II (imitation) Gloria Exercitus (2 standards) *c.* A.D. 335	m.m.?	,,

[1] As indicated above, it has been thought desirable to publish in detail the coins from Building 4 that were used by Professor Atkinson to suggest the probable date of the supposed massacre. We are greatly indebted to Mr. R. A. G. Carson for his report on them. It could be argued that these coins suggest rather that some occupation continued in *Venta* through the early decades of the fifth century than that it came to a sudden end soon after A.D. 400.

No.		Details	Mint-mark	Findspot
445	Æ 4	Magnus Maximus Spes Romanorum *LRBC* 156　A.D. 387–8	TRS	Rooms 3–4
446	Æ 4	Uncertain emperor (double struck obv.) Salus Reipublicae Cf. *LRBC* 1105　*c.* A.D. 390	m.m.?	,,
447	Solidus	Honorius Victoria Auggg Cohen 44　*c.* A.D. 404	R|V COMOB	N. corridor trench, top-soil
450	Ant.	Gallienus (sole reign) ? Provid Aug Cf. *RIC* 266　A.D. 259–68		Rooms 3–4
451	Æ 3	Constans Fel Temp Reparatio　Phoenix on globe Cf. *LRBC* 34　A.D. 346–50	m.m.?	,,
452	Æ 3	Valentinian I or Valens Securitas Reipublicae Cf. *LRBC* 527　A.D. 364–75	m.m.?	,,
453	Æ 3	Valens Securitas Reipublicae *LRBC* 528　A.D. 367–75	S(CON)	,,
454	Æ 3	Valentinian I Securitas Reipublicae *LRBC* 525　A.D. 367–75	PCON	,,
461	Æ 3	Constans Two Victories *LRBC* 148　A.D. 341–6	D TRP	,,　Beside skull
462	Æ	Uncertain Late fourth century		,,　　　,,
466	Æ 4	Victor Spes Romanorum *LRBC* 561　A.D. 387–8	SCON	Rooms 3–4
467	Æ 3	Constans Gloria Exercitus (1 standard) *LRBC* 400　A.D. 335–7	⚹ SCONST	,,
468	Æ 4	Arcadius Victor-ia Auggg *LRBC* 164　A.D. 388–92	? TR	,,
469	Æ 4	Arcadius Salus Reipublicae Cf. *LRBC* 1105　*c.* A.D. 390	m.m.?	,,
470	Æ 4	Theodosius I Victoria Auggg *LRBC* 565/568　A.D. 392–4	(S)CON	,,

No.		Details	Mint-mark	Findspot
471	Æ 4	Imitation Fel Temp Reparatio Falling horseman Prototype *LRBC* 2295 *c.* A.D. 355		Rooms 3–4
472	Æ 4	Theodosius I Victoria Auggg *LRBC* 565/568 A.D. 388–92	SCON	,,
473	Æ 4	Theodosian Victoria Auggg Cf. *LRBC* 562 ff. *c.* A.D. 390	SCON	,,
474	Æ 4	Arcadius Victoria Auggg Cf. *LRBC* 389 *c.* A.D. 390	m.m.?	,,
475	Æ 4	Arcadius Victoria Auggg *LRBC* 566 ff. *c.* A.D. 390	///CON	,,
476	Æ 4	? Theodosius I Salus Reipublicae *LRBC* 1106 ff. *c.* A.D. 390	AQP	,,
477	Æ 3	Imitation Fel Temp Reparatio Falling horseman Prototype *LRBC* 2295 *c.* A.D. 355		,,
478	Æ 4	Theodosian Victoria Auggg Cf. *LRBC* 389 *c.* A.D. 390	m.m.?	,,
479	Æ 4	Theodosian Victoria Auggg Cf. *LRBC* 562 ff. *c.* A.D. 390	PCON	,,
480	Æ 4	Theodosian Victoria Auggg Cf. *LRBC* 389 *c.* A.D. 390	m.m.?	,,
481	Æ 4	Constans Two Victories *LRBC* 138 A.D. 341–6	$\frac{M}{TRS}$	,,
483	Æ 3	Imitation Fel Temp Reparatio Falling horseman Prototype *LRBC* 2295 *c.* A.D. 355		,,
484	Æ 3	Constantine II Gloria Exercitus (2 standards) *LRBC* 63 A.D. 330–5	TR·S	,,
485	Æ 4	Theodosian Salus Reipublicae Cf. *LRBC* 1105 *c.* A.D. 390	m.m.?	,,
486	Æ 4	Arcadius Victoria Auggg Cf. *LRBC* 389 *c.* A.D. 390	m.m.?	,,

No.		Details	Mint-mark	Findspot
487	Æ 4	Honorius Salus Reipublicae Cf. *LRBC* 1105 *c.* A.D. 390	m.m.?	Rooms 3–4
490	Æ 4	Theodosian Salus Reipublicae Cf. *LRBC* 1105 *c.* A.D. 390	m.m.?	,,
491	Æ 4	Theodosian Victoria Auggg Cf. *LRBC* 389 *c.* A.D. 390	m.m.?	,,
492	Æ 4	Theodosian Victoria Auggg Cf. *LRBC* 389 *c.* A.D. 390	m.m.?	,,
493	Æ 4	Honorius Salus Reipublicae Cf. *LRBC* 1105 *c.* A.D. 390	m.m.?	,,
494	Æ 4	Imitation Constantius II Fel Temp Reparatio Falling horseman Prototype *LRBC* 2295 *c.* A.D. 355		,,
495	Æ 4	Theodosius I Victoria Auggg *LRBC* 391/394 A.D. 388–95	LVGP	,,
496	Æ 4	Arcadius Victoria Auggg Cf. *LRBC* 389 *c.* A.D. 390	m.m.?	,,
497	Æ 4	Theodosian Victoria Auggg Cf. *LRBC* 389 *c.* A.D. 390	m.m.?	,,
498	Æ 4	Theodosian Victoria Auggg Cf. *LRBC* 389 *c.* A.D. 390	m.m.?	,,
499	Æ 4	Imitation Fel Temp Reparatio Falling horseman Prototype *LRBC* 2295 *c.* A.D. 355		,,
500	Æ 3	Uncertain. Diademed Fourth century		
501	Æ 4	Theodosius I Salus Reipublicae Cf. *LRBC* 1105 *c.* A.D. 390	m.m.?	,,
502	Æ 4	Uncertain. Possibly fourth century		,,
503	Æ 4	Theodosian Vot (XV) mult XX Cf. *LRBC* 552 *c.* A.D. 380		

No.		Details	Mint-mark	Findspot
504	Æ 3	Gratian Gloria Romanorum *LRBC* 1424 A.D. 367–75	F|R|A ASISCP	Rooms 3–4
505	Æ 3	Valens Securitas Reipublicae *LRBC* 303 A.D. 367–75	OF|I LVGPA	,,
506	Æ 4	Imitation Tetricus I Pax Aug Prototype *RIC* 100 *c.* A.D. 275		,,
507	Æ 4	Theodosius I Salus Reipublicae Cf. *LRBC* 1105 *c.* A.D. 390	m.m.?	,,
508	Æ 4	Honorius Salus Reipublicae *LRBC* 1111/1113 A.D. 394–402	AQS	,,
519	Æ 4	Arcadius Victoria Auggg Cf. *LRBC* 389 *c.* A.D. 390	m.m.?	,,
520	Æ 4	Theodosian Salus Reipublicae Cf. *LRBC* 1105 *c.* A.D. 390	m.m.?	,,
521	Æ 4	Theodosian Victoria Auggg Cf. *LRBC* 389 *c.* A.D. 390	m.m.?	,,
522	Æ 4	Theodosian Salus Reipublicae *LRBC* 804/811 A.D. 394–402	RQ	,,
523	Æ 4	Valentinian II Salus Reipublicae *LRBC* 796 A.D. 388–92	R·P	,,
524	Ant.	Victorinus Invictus *RIC* 114 A.D. 268–70		,,
525	Æ 4	Theodosian Salus Reipublicae Cf. *LRBC* 1105 *c.* A.D. 390	m.m.?	,,
526	Æ 4	Theodosian Victoria Auggg Cf. *LRBC* 389 *c.* A.D. 390	m.m.?	,,
527	Æ 4	Theodosian Victoria Auggg Cf. *LRBC* 389 A.D. 390	m.m.?	,,
528–30	Æ 4	Theodosian Reverses uncertain Late fourth century		,,

No.		Details	Mint-mark	Findspot
531	Æ 4	Imitation Urbs Roma Cf. *LRBC* 224 *c.* A.D. 340		Rooms 3–4
532	Æ 4	Theodosian Victoria Auggg Cf. *LRBC* 389 *c.* A.D. 390	m.m.?	,,
533	Æ 4	Arcadius Victoria Auggg Cf. *LRBC* 389 *c.* A.D. 390	m.m.?	,,
534–47	Æ 4	Theodosian Reverses uncertain: Victoria or Salus *c.* A.D. 390		,,
548	Æ 4	Constantinian Gloria Exercitus (1 standard) Cf. *LRBC* 1028 A.D. 335–41	m.m.?	,,
549	Æ 4	Theodosian Reverse uncertain Late fourth century		,,
554	Æ 4	Theodosian Reverse uncertain Late fourth century NOTE: in MS. list this is identified as Severus Alexander Æ		W. wall below floor level
556		Imitation Tetricus I Reverse uncertain *c.* A.D. 275		Rooms 3–4
557	Æ 4	Arcadius Victoria Auggg Cf. *LRBC* 389 *c.* A.D. 390	m.m.?	,,
558	Æ 4	Constantinian Gloria Exercitus (1 standard) *LRBC* 92 ff. A.D. 335–7	·TRP·	,,
560	Æ 3	Constantinopolis *LRBC* 52 A.D. 330–5	TRS	In burnt layer immediately under cement floor
561	Æ 4	Helena Pax Publica *LRBC* 128 A.D. 337–41	TRS ⚹	,,
566	Æ 4	Honorius Victoria Auggg Cf. *LRBC* 389 *c.* A.D. 395	m.m.?	Rooms 3–4
567	Æ 4	Theodosian Salus Reipublicae Cf. *LRBC* 1105 *c.* A.D. 390	m.m.?	,,

No.		Details	Mint-mark	Findspot
569	Æ 4	Valentinian II Victoria Auggg *LRBC* 389 A.D. 388–92	? LVGP	Rooms 3–4
571	Æ 4	Constantinian Two Victories Cf. *LRBC* 630 A.D. 341–6	m.m.?	In burnt layer immediately under cement floor
572	Æ 4	Constans Gloria Exercitus (1 standard) *LRBC* 131 A.D. 337–41	TRS ◡	,,
573	Æ	Urbs Roma Wolf and twins *LRBC* 376 A.D. 330–5	Ω (PCONST)	,,
574	Æ 4	Imitation Constantinopolis *LRBC* 221 A.D. 330–5	Ω PLG	,,
575	Æ 4	Constantius II Gloria Exercitus (1 standard) *LRBC* 242 A.D. 337–41	☧ PLG	,,
576	Æ 3	Constantine II Gloria Exercitus (2 standards) *LRBC* 49 A.D. 330–5	TRS	,,
579	Æ 3	Constantius II Fel Temp Reparatio Falling horseman *LRBC* 253 A.D. 353–4	CPLG	Room 5 on upper floor, SE corner
580	Æ 4	Theodosian Victoria Auggg Cf. *LRBC* 389 *c.* A.D. 390	m.m.?	Room 5 above upper floor
591	Æ 4	Imitation Urbs Roma Cf. *LRBC* 376 *c.* A.D. 335	Ω PCONST	Rooms 3–4, NW corner on lower floor

(568 and 604 on original list not found)

LATE ROMAN MILITARY EQUIPMENT[1] (fig. 64)

By Barbara Green

Nos. 3, 4, and 5, described in Hawkes and Dunning (1961), are also now in N.C.M.

1. Iron *francisca* with rectangular butt and oval perforation. L. 5·1 in. (12·9 cm.). Mrs. Hawkes comments that it is close to the most evolved of the group from Furfooz[2] which date from the second half of the fourth century. It is less curved than the fifth-century series from Haillot,[3] but not too unlike that from grave 7[4] which is dated mid-fifth, and distinctly less elegant than one from the late fifth-century grave 8.[5] Thus, on the typology of the form, the Caistor example could be dated to the end of the fourth or beginning of the fifth century. Two similar examples were found in the topsoil at Richborough.[6]

Small find F 77 from Building 4, Cross-wall 2.

2. Part of a bronze *strap-tag* with a central flat oval plate decorated with two large engraved concentric circles in the centre and four 'bull's-eyes' surrounding it; there is a long moulded terminal ending in a faceted knob; only the lower parts of two openwork wings survive, flanking a central bar which is decorated with a single 'bull's-eye'; on one side only, between the wing and the central plate, there is a small pointed projection. Surviving L. 2 in. (5·1 cm.).

It is uncertain if this tag was attached to the strap with one or more rivets[7] or if it was hinged to a plate.[8] A rather ornate example with openwork wings was found in a grave at Champdolent, St. Germain-les-Corbeil,[9] in association with other belt fittings including a buckle plate of Hawkes and Dunning Type IIa. This and other examples differ from the Caistor tag in having simple knob terminals. Two examples from Richborough[10] are long

like the Caistor piece, but they are much simpler in design, with solid wings and a plain, elongated, pear-shaped plate ending in a knob. Mrs. Hawkes considers that most if not all the Richborough examples form part of an insular series and would place the Caistor example with these. The date of these pieces is second half fourth or early fifth century.

This piece is part of the Fitch Collection presented to N.C.M. in 1894 (Accession no. 76.94 (715)). Found 1859 or before, spot not recorded but presumably from within the walls of the Roman town.[11]

3. Part of loop of Type IIA *bronze buckle*[12] in the form of a stylized dolphin with no crest, incised triple collar, broken eye circlet; tail forked; single hinge loop complete. It is likely that there was a horizontal bar connecting the snouts of the two dolphins unless the buckle was originally more curved than it is now, although there is no evidence that this was the case.

Small Find B 80 from Building 4.

4. Openwork bronze Type IIA *buckle plate*[13] with four pairs of opposed arches with rounded heads, each partly divided off by projections from the pillars. The four hinge loops are grooved; one had been broken and replaced by a patch which was itself grooved. 1·8 × 1·7 in. (4·6 × 4·4 cm.).

Small Find B 119 from Building 4.

5. Bronze *tubular object*, open on one side, with seven pairs of ribs running round the tube. L. 1·9 in. (4·8 cm.). Mrs. Hawkes considers that this is likely to form part of a buckle-plate such as was found at Misèry (Somme)[14] and Vermand (Aisne);[15] these date from the second half of the fourth century.

---

[1] We are indebted to Mrs. S. C. Hawkes for comments on nos. 1, 2, 5, and 7.

[2] Nenquin 1953, fig. 18, no. 16.

[3] Breuer and Roosens 1957.

[4] Ibid., fig. 8, no. 7.

[5] Ibid., fig. 9, no. 7.

[6] Bushe-Fox 1949, 154 and pl. LXI, 341, 342; Hawkes and Dunning 1962–3, Abb. 7, 4 and 5.

[7] Cf. Bushe-Fox 1928, pl. XXI, 47.

[8] Cf. Bushe-Fox 1949, pl. XXXVII, 119; Clarke, G. 1970, fig. 4. 94.

[9] Hawkes and Dunning 1962–3, Tafel 6

[10] Bushe-Fox 1928, pl. XXI, 46, 49.

[11] Norwich Castle Museum 1909, 43, no. 388; other refs. given there.

[12] Hawkes and Dunning 1961, 51 and fig. 17 c.

[13] Ibid. 51 and fig. 17 g.

[14] Evison 1965, fig. 2, 2 and 3. [15] Ibid., fig. 26 b.

Early fifth-century examples are also known from, for instance, Vieuxville and Lüttich. [1]

Small Find B 158 from site of *forum*, 1931.

6. Bronze *disc-attachment* (Type VI)[2] with decorated disc and suspension loop to which is attached a cast bronze ring. The disc has a frilled border with small triangles and concentric circles surrounding central rivet which links disc with suspension loop. Diameter of disc 0·8 in. (2·0 cm.).

Small Find B 180 from site of the *forum*, unstratified.

7. Antler *sword guard*[3] of pointed oval shape, decorated with two rather shallow grooves. There is an approximately central rectangular hole, which on one face is extended into tapering grooves indicating that this is a lower guard which fitted over a blade with sloping shoulders. The groove and tang hole are slightly iron-stained. The antler is probably from a red deer. Max. L. 2·95 in. (7·5 cm.), thickness 0·6 in. (1·5 cm.). Max. length of groove on underside 1·9 in. (4·85 cm.); tang hole 0·45 in. (1·15 cm.)×0·35 in. (0·85 cm.).

This guard belongs to Behmer's Group A Type I,[4] which are of organic material; their absolute chronology, he considers, is very difficult. The Caistor guard is most nearly paralleled by one from Nydam,[5] which dates from about A.D. 400. A similar guard, grooved to take a sword with sloping shoulders, but rather longer in proportion to its width than the Caistor guard, was found in a Frisian terp.[6] Roes states that this was a Nordic type of which many examples were found in Danish bog deposits, where they date from the second half of the fourth century. The guard of the Cumberland sword, although of wood, is not dissimilar[7] and it is likely that it was originally plain, the decoration being a seventh-century addition.[8]

So few datable examples of these short straight guards survive, doubtless because they were of bone, antler, or wood,[9] that it is not possible to state that the Caistor guard, a stray find, is certainly of late Roman or early post-Roman date. However, the evidence does suggest that a late fourth- or fifth-century date is not unreasonable and that it could well have been the property of a barbarian warrior.

N.C.M. 35.970. Stray find from surface in area of Baths.

[1] Breuer and Roosens 1957, annexe VII, 343 ff., fig. 33, nos. 3, 5, and 8.
[2] Hawkes and Dunning 1961, 65 and fig. 24 b.
[3] We are indebted to Mrs. H. E. Davidson for comments on this piece.
[4] Behmer 1939.
[5] Behmer 1939, Tafel II, 1.
[6] Roes 1963, 75 and pl. LVIII, 5.
[7] Behmer 1939, Tafel II. 3; Davidson 1962, pl. X. 63.
[8] Davidson 1962, 58.
[9] The use of the word 'horn' to describe some is incorrect.

II

THE CAISTOR-BY-NORWICH CEMETERY— CREMATIONS

GENERAL NOTE ON THE POTTERY

By J. N. L. Myres

THE pottery from the cemetery is notable not only for its quantity and for the quality of some individual pieces but for the variety of styles which are represented and for the chronological range which it covers. It includes both some of the earliest and some of the latest types found in pagan cemeteries in the country, and a continuous series of the intervening forms. It provides a good deal of evidence for the dating of different types not only from the objects contained in the urns but also from the considerable number of cases in which one urn or a group of urns was found to be intrusive upon, and so later than, another.[1] It illustrates the variety of continental sources from which the Anglo-Saxon settlers were derived, and, owing to its close proximity to the most important Roman administrative centre in East Anglia, it throws unique light on the circumstances in which the transition from Roman Britain to Anglo-Saxon England may have taken place in these parts.[2] It is the purpose of this note to draw attention to the more significant evidence which this great collection of pottery can provide on all these matters.

First there is the question of the date at which the cemetery came into use for Germanic burials. Discussion of this must begin with the earliest pieces of purely Germanic pottery recorded from the cemetery. One is undoubtedly P 15 (pl. IIa and fig. 12), a beautifully made biconical bowl decorated with a zone of three-line chevrons demarcated above and below by groups of horizontal lines on the upper part, a line of nicks on the carination, and shallow three-line swags below. This is both in form and decoration a purely continental piece, difficult to match in Britain, but with plenty of antecedents and parallels in the second- and third-century pottery of north Germany, from the Oberjersdal culture of Schleswig[3] and that of East Holstein[4] in the north and east as far west as the mouth of the Weser.[5] It also occurs further north, especially in Fünen, where bowls of this kind, mostly carrying handles, are common in graves of the period A.D. 175–250. Thus a close parallel to P 15 is to be found

---

[1] A summary of the more significant of these stratigraphical relationships is on pp. 72–3.

[2] I have discussed in general terms the importance of the Caistor cemetery for early Anglo-Saxon history in Myres 1969, 5–6.

[3] Tischler 1955, especially the pot from Gr. 19, Tafel 7.

[4] Genrich 1954, 28. Of the thirty pottery types from East Holstein on Abb. 1 at least five show this type of ornament with enclosed chevron zones.

[5] See the piece from second-century levels at Feddersen Wierde: Haarnagel 1957, 307, Abb. 9. 2.

in two bowls with handles from Ringe, Fünen, one of which is conveniently dated by an associated third-century brooch.[1] Others with the same form and type of decoration, some without handles, come from Oregård, Fravde, Ørbæk, Nybølle, Møllegårdsmark, Alenbækhuse, and elsewhere.[2] P 15 is without handles, and perhaps should not be placed before the middle of the third century; it is typologically closer to this group than it is, for example, to a less carefully decorated but somewhat similar bowl from Hammoor which was found with an early fifth-century brooch.[3] Vessels of this kind do not appear to occur as late as this in the stratified levels at Feddersen Wierde near Bremerhaven,[4] and, whatever the circumstances may have been which brought it to Britain, it is difficult to believe that P 15, which is in remarkably fresh condition, can have been still in use at Caistor as late as the closing years of the fourth century.

P 15 may not have been the only urn of its kind at Caistor. Among the pieces of broken-up pots in the W series there are several, such as W 38 (fig. 10), W 55 (fig. 15), W 56 (fig. 14), which, if not so distinctive, come from vessels in the same tradition and can be readily matched among the third- and early fourth-century pottery from the cemeteries of Fünen.[5] Indeed the familiar practice of decorating pots with one or more broad bands of chevrons demarcated above and below by horizontal lines (see figs. 12–15) seems to derive from the fashion prevalent in the Anglian areas on the Continent at this early date, for it is not at all characteristic of the fourth- and fifth-century wares in those parts. Thus an elaborate scheme of this kind on W 57 (fig. 14) looks just like a developed version of that on a late third-century piece from Møllegårdsmark,[6] though it is of course impossible to say what period of years may separate their dates.

A variety of this style in which the triangular spaces left on each side of the chevron lines are filled with diagonal hatching set at right angles in alternate spaces to produce a basketry effect is also a decorative trick taken over by the earliest Caistor potters from third-century fashions. Hatched triangles are a very popular motif at this time not only in what became the Anglian homelands of Schleswig and Fünen but also in the proto-Saxon cultures of Oberjersdal and Fuhlsbüttel farther south.[7] The Caistor examples, Y 40, N 11, and W 9 (fig. 12) or N 102 (fig. 10) can be closely matched at Næsby and Fravde in Fünen by pieces datable before A.D. 325.[8] It may not be without significance in that connection that Y 40 contained a much-worn Roman coin of the mid-third century (probably of Valerian), a very rare instance of such an association in the Caistor cemetery, but one that is occasionally found in the cremation burials of Denmark at this period.[9]

Certainly deriving from this hatched triangle style, and providing a direct link between it and the Anglian corrugated technique which came in before the middle of the fourth cen-

[1] Mackeprang 1943, 42 and Tafel 12.

[2] Albrectsen 1968, Tavle 78b, 8od. 1, 83a–f, 84h, 89b, 91a, e, 94d, etc.

[3] Genrich 1954, Tafel 15 E.

[4] Dr. P. Schmid tells me that P 15 would not be in place much later than the third century at Feddersen Wierde.

[5] Compare these, and N 88 (fig. 14), with Albrectsen 1968, Tavle 95a, b from Alenbækhuse.

[6] Albrectsen 1968, Tavle 99b.

[7] Tischler 1955, Grab 13, and Tischler 1954a, Grs. 1, 32, 82, 85, 155, 166, 178, 183, 185, 208, 217. See also

Wegewitz 1944, 22, Urne 30; and an urn with a fine array of third-century grave-goods from Krummensee-Pötterberg, Kr. Eutin, no. 105 (Genrich 1954, Tafel 19 C).

[8] Albrectsen 1968, Næsby, Tavle 79c, d; Fravde, Tavle 96d, e. The somewhat similar trick of alternating blocks of horizontal and vertical lines, as on N 7 (fig. 3), N 44 (fig. 5), N 94 (fig. 6), also occurs on third-century handled cups from Næsby and Fravde (Albrectsen 1968, Tavle 79f, 80d), but it continues later in the fourth-century corrugated wares (Tavle 120d, 121h from Hiallese.)

[9] Albrectsen 1968, 352–4.

tury, is the decoration on Y 23 (fig. 11), which can be exactly matched on urns of the same size and shape from Oregård in Fünen[1] and from Süderbrarup in Schleswig.[2] That the irregularly massed groups of diagonal, vertical, and horizontal grooves that are seen on these pots indicate a breakdown of the earlier fashion for hatched triangles is neatly illustrated by N 102[3] (fig. 10) where the process can be seen actually occurring, one side of the pot carrying hatched triangles like Y 40, and the other a confused arrangement like Y 23.

This early dating suggested by the continental parallels for Y 40 is strengthened by its association with Y 41 (fig. 11) which was apparently buried at the same time. Y 41 is a remarkable piece with a tall conical neck ornamented with a vigorous but irregular design in broad grooves and large dots. The only parallel to this at Caistor is the fragmentary urn X 9 (b) (fig. 11) which could be from the same workshop. The decoration of Y 41, though carried out in grooves rather than applied strips, is reminiscent of that arising on the handle attachments of some urns of the proto-Saxon Fuhlsbüttel culture,[4] as developed later, for example, in the extravagant fashion displayed by one of the pots from Altenwalde.[5] If Y 41 can be rightly thought of in these terms, it too seems to be echoing third-century continental fashions, even though true handles of this kind hardly ever occur on the English pottery.

But these, though typologically among the earliest, are by no means the only Caistor urns which must have been made well before the breakdown of Roman rule in Britain. On figs. 1–3 are a number of large powerfully built urns with wide mouths, well-made rims and base angles, and simple linear or grooved ornament, which are closely related to Plettke's types A3–5.[6] These types were dated by Plettke from the late third to the mid-fourth century, and though these dates, as Tischler has shown,[7] are perhaps fifty years too high, and the types less distinguishable chronologically from one another than Plettke supposed, the whole complex which they represent is one which in north Germany runs across the central and later years of the fourth century. A comparison of these great urns from Caistor with examples from Westerwanna that are dated by association with fourth-century brooches and the like, leaves little doubt that a number of our pieces belong to a time at least a generation before the end of the Roman occupation.[8] Not much later are likely to be urns like P 14 (fig. 2) whose more rounded profile and narrower neck suggest a closer relationship to Plettke's type A6 which may have lasted into the early years of the fifth century. It is worth noting that several of these early urns contained a wide range of grave goods (E 5, E 14, N 52) and that two of them, X 35 (fig. 1) and N 52, were buried with some care in cists of flints or broken Roman tiles. One of these, N 52, was accompanied in such a cist by an early Anglian urn with corrugated decoration, N 53 (fig. 5), which can thus be taken as contemporary with it.

This may therefore be the point at which the date and significance of the substantial and distinctive group of these corrugated urns at Caistor (pls. IV, V, and figs. 4–8) should be

[1] Albrectsen 1968, Tavle 77c. 1.

[2] Genrich 1954, 29, Abb. 2. 25.

[3] It is significant that N 102 contained part of a comb (c) probably belonging to a Rhenish type that can be dated with some certainty to the decades around 400: see p. 93.

[4] Tischler 1954a, Tafel 42, 423.

[5] Waller 1957, Tafel 7, 46.

[6] Plettke 1920, 42–5 and Tafel 28 and 29.

[7] Tischler 1954b, 66–7.

[8] Compare, e.g., E 5 (fig. 1) with Westerwanna 388 (two

fourth-century brooches) and 454 (tutulus brooch); N 52 (fig. 1) with Westerwanna 11 (fourth-century brooch); P 23 (fig. 1) and N 50 (fig. 2) with Westerwanna 861 (early type of equal-armed brooch); E 14 (fig. 2) with Westerwanna 848 (fourth-century brooch); N 39 (fig. 3) with Westerwanna 443 (fourth-century brooch). P 53 (fig. 2) is almost exactly the same size and shape as Westerwanna 1347 (fourth-century brooch), and has the same type of line-and-dot decoration. References are all to Zimmer-Linnfeld et al. 1960.

considered. The association of N 52 with N 53, itself a corrugated bowl of the simple early kind, is one of the few direct pieces of dating evidence for the style, for neither on the Continent nor in England do they normally contain much in the way of associated grave goods.[1] The style is of course characteristic of the Anglian *Kulturkreis* on the Continent, and occurs little, if at all, in its pure form outside the Anglian homeland in Schleswig and Fünen, except for outliers in Norway and in England. Of the latter by far the largest groups are those at Caistor and at Sancton in east Yorkshire; elsewhere examples, though not unknown, are less numerous and mostly derivative in character. The Caistor series is thus of prime importance for the earliest Anglian settlement in Britain.

The principal forms of these corrugated urns at Caistor are wide-mouthed bowls, vessels with tall conical necks, and large shouldered jars. There is also one example, M 50 (fig. 6), of a big globular urn with narrow neck and short upright rim decorated in this style. It provides a link with the undecorated globular urns of this form which are also typically Anglian and occur frequently in continental and English cemeteries.[2] The Caistor group is on figs. 24 (M 14, N 89) and 25 (the whole):[3] it includes many close parallels with pots from cemeteries in Fünen that are dated in the years 325 to 400.[4] M 19 (fig. 25) is certainly early as it underlay M 18, a stamped urn of the sixth century.

Corrugated urns of all types occur both without and with shoulder bosses. Unbossed examples are on figs. 4–6, and bossed ones on figs. 7–8. Related types of both kinds, in which massed lines are used but in a sharper form without producing the true corrugated effect, are on fig. 9. There is no doubt that the Anglian folk using these corrugated wares and their derivatives must have come direct to Caistor from Schleswig and Fünen at a very early stage in the history of the settlement. In Fünen, where the Stiftsmuseum at Odense is full of corrugated pottery from such sites as Alenbækhuse, Broholm, Nybølle, and Lundehøj that could well have been found at Caistor, the style is dated mainly in the second half of the fourth century and is believed to end about 400.[5] At Signekær Skov a little corrugated bowl, not far removed in type from N 53 (fig. 5), was found with two brooches of that date.[6]

In Schleswig,[7] where perhaps a higher proportion of the corrugated pottery has shoulder bosses, the style may have lasted longer. A shoulder-boss bowl from Hamburg/Alt Rahlstedt,

---

[1] It is curious that at Caistor several corrugated urns contain iron manicure sets, M 8, N 96 (fig. 4), M 51, N 12 (fig. 7), M 52 (fig. 8), X 23 (fig. 9); unfortunately these are of little help for dating purposes: see p. 110.

[2] As was first pointed out in Jankuhn 1952.

[3] It will be seen that these, like the corrugated urns, often contain manicure sets of iron: A 9, M 43, N 18, N 63 (all on fig. 25).

[4] Compare, e.g., M 43 (fig. 25) with Albrectsen 1968, Tavle 109b and c, and 123d. 2 from Hjadstrup and Fravde; N 61 (fig. 25) with Tavle 115d from Alenbækhuse; N 63 (fig. 25) with Tavle 117h from Korup; and P 42 (fig. 25) with Tavle 114a from Alenbækhuse. The type persists into the fifth century in Schleswig: see examples from Borgstedt and Süderbrarup in Genrich 1954, Tafeln 6E, 26A.

[5] N 95 (fig. 4) is a perfect example of Albrectsen's Type 24 (Albrectsen 1968, 248) from Alenbækhuse; N 14 (fig. 4) is very close to his Type 17 from the same site, both dated

325–400. Compare also N 2 (fig. 6) with Albrectsen 1968, Tavle 125g from Ringe, and Tavle 112d and 113a from Alenbækhuse; the shouldered forms N 3, N 21 (fig. 6) with Tavle 116c from Signekær Skov; M 21 (fig. 4) with Tavle 127d from Møllegårdsmark; and the tall conical neck and horizontal grooving of P 3 (fig. 9) with Tavle 125a 2 from Rosilde.

[6] Norling-Christensen 1956, fig. 15. The vessel from Oregård Gr. 45, there illustrated fig. 33, is very close in shape and decoration to N 14, N 95, N 96 (all fig. 4).

[7] Close parallels from Caistor can be quoted to a number of the standard Angle forms from Schleswig illustrated in Genrich 1954, Abb. 2. Thus his bowl types 6 and 7 from Borgstedt correspond to our E 9, M 54, N 22, etc.; his shoulder-boss types with tall conical neck 27 from Borgstedt to our K 5, and 13 from Bordesholm to our M 55; his shouldered jar type 12 from Süder-Schmedeby to our N 12, etc.

very similar in form and corrugated decoration to E 9, M 54, N 22, and Y 34 (all fig. 8), was found with a cruciform brooch of the first half of the fifth century.[1] It would seem likely that the more elaborately bossed types, such as B 2 (pl. VIIIa and fig. 8), which in addition to shoulder bosses has horizontal and vertical strips laid over the corrugation on the tall neck, may belong to the years after the middle of the fifth century when the taste for elaborate plastic decoration on pottery was widespread in the Germanic world and culminated in the Saxon areas further south in the extravagances of the *Buckelurnen*. B 2 is, however, alone at Caistor as an Anglian example of this exuberant manner: it is almost certainly an import, for it is very closely related in style to two larger urns of the same general form from Hammoor and Sørup in Angeln, and probably comes from the same workshop (pls. VIIIb, IXa).[2]

Most of the Caistor corrugated pottery is of simpler forms and a good deal of it is without bosses and likely to be early in the series. Much of it should thus date on these continental parallels between 350 and 400, continuing, especially with the shoulder-boss types, through the fifth century. What little internal evidence there is from Caistor itself is consistent with, if it does not positively prove, this dating. That the series as a whole falls early in the history of the cemetery is clear not only from such associations as that of N 53 with N 52 but from the fact that several corrugated urns were disturbed by later burials. Y 11(d) is a corrugated fragment perhaps from an urn broken up by the burial of the late Y 9 group. X 2 underlay X 1, a stamped urn probably of the sixth century, and must be earlier than the burial of the latter. M 54 was apparently disturbed by M 55, another corrugated shoulder-boss urn of a more elaborate kind, but it is just possible that the damage to both urns was due to M 54 being the later burial: they are in any case close in date. More interesting perhaps is the fact that X 24 (fig. 17), an elaborate Saxon *Buckelurne* of early type perhaps dating about 450, rested on the shoulder of X 23 (fig. 9), a large shoulder-boss urn with tall conical neck, and somewhat decadent-looking corrugation. If X 24 is a subsequent burial it would argue an earlier fifth-century date for X 23, but it seems more likely that this is a matter of two urns being buried together, in which case their association is good evidence for an overlap at Caistor between the later phases of Anglian corrugation and the earlier types of Saxon *Buckelurnen* in the central years of the fifth century.

It is, however, quite clear that there were folk of Saxon antecedents established at Caistor at least as early as the earliest Angle users of the corrugated wares. The presence of some large urns related to Plettke's Types A 3–6 has already been noted as evidence for Saxon interments in the cemetery before 400, and another small group is even more significant of such an origin. These are urns of, or related to, Plettke's Type A 7(a),[3] the 'Cuxhaven/Galgenberg Typ' of Tischler,[4] whose continental focus is in the coastlands between the Elbe and the Weser in the later part of the fourth and the early years of the fifth century. They are marked by a rounded contour with upright or concave necks and well-moulded rims. Their decoration includes raised and slashed collars and strong linear designs often in the line-and-groove technique with a preference for chevron and, above all, curvilinear patterns. What the

---

[1] Genrich 1954, Tafel 12D. Very little of the corrugated pottery from Fünen has bosses.

[2] Albrectsen's Type 17 (Albrectsen 1968, 248) from Alenbækhuse is the prototype of B 2: it already has horizontal and vertical strips laid over the corrugation, but has not yet developed shoulder bosses.

[3] Plettke 1920, 46 and Tafel 32.

[4] Tischler 1954b, 48 and Abb. 8. I have discussed the style further in Myres 1969, 42–4.

Germans term *stehende Bogen*, standing arches, are the hallmark of this style. There is a certain amount of stamped ornament sparingly used, but a much greater fondness for finger-tip rosettes and similar motifs executed in dots and dimples.

Of this distinctive style in its purest continental form Caistor has the best example recorded in Britain. This is R 12 (pl. IIIa and fig. 16), whose form and decoration with its slashed collar, three-line *stehende Bogen*, and neat finger-tip rosettes, could well be taken as a model for the type. It is matched in this country most closely by another Norfolk piece, that from Brundall,[1] unfortunately incomplete, but continental parallels could be quoted from most of the cemeteries in the Elbe/Weser region and further west in Friesland. Almost its double is a fourth-century urn from Midlaren in Drenthe, now in the museum at Assen.[2] Vessels of this kind are most unlikely to have reached Caistor (R 12 must surely be an import) after 400 and may well be earlier.

The fashion which they started is well illustrated by the other urns on fig. 16, several of which have useful associations for dating. It will be noticed that most of them (E 13, N 92, Y 8, possibly Markshall IX, as well as R 12) were accompanied by combs, or bits of combs, and this is an association that occurs in other cemeteries besides Caistor with vessels of this type.[3] E 13 (pl. IIIb), which had the finest comb of the group, is certainly an early piece: both in form and decoration it is very like Westerwanna 45, which is dated by a fifth-century equal-armed brooch.[4] The rather slipshod decoration of Y 8 suggests that it may belong to a time when memories of the more stylish treatment of the design displayed by R 12 were fading.

The *stehende Bogen* style is important as providing one of the main sources for the ornament found on the elaborate *Buckelurnen* of the second half of the fifth century, and it no doubt continued in parallel with these more exuberant fashions and may even have outlasted them.[5] Markshall IX (fig. 16) provides an interesting example of the transition between its early phase and that of the *Buckelurnen*, for here the grooved *stehende Bogen* and the multiple raised collars are so strongly moulded as to give almost the plastic effect of bosses, and the vessel is, like many early *Buckelurnen*, mounted on a well-made footring. Its apparent association with the full-round knob of a Group I cruciform brooch is unfortunately dubious and cannot be used to support the date here suggested for the urn (see p. 235).

The fully developed *Buckelurne* style is represented at Caistor by the examples on fig. 17. Of these C 1 is a fine urn of my Group I,[6] simply decorated with grooved horizontal and vertical bosses and mounted on a well-moulded footstand. It is a simplified statement of the design displayed on one of the urns from the Galgenberg near Cuxhaven that was found with a pair of late Roman bronze tweezers.[7] A close but rather more elaborate English parallel to C 1 is that from Luton, Beds.[8] Y 38 is another, more unusual, example of my Group I with vertical and circular bosses, some rather indefinite line-and-dot ornament, and a footstand originally perforated with several 'open windows', as if intended at first for use as a strainer. Some interest attaches to the association of M 48(a) and (b), both of which have footstands, though M 48(a) is decorated only with a couple of grooves on the neck

[1] Clarke and Myres 1939–40, 189 and 191, fig. 1. 1.

[2] Van Es 1967, 164, fig. 81.

[3] e.g. Lackford 50. 125 (Lethbridge 1951, fig. 5), or Sancton 150.

[4] Zimmer-Linnfeld *et al.* 1960, Tafel 8.

[5] An example from Castle Acre, Norfolk, now at New-castle upon Tyne, is dated to the early part of the sixth century by a Group II cruciform brooch.

[6] I have given a provisional classification of the English *Buckelurnen* in Myres 1969, 45–7.

[7] Waller 1938, Tafel 34. 6.

[8] Austin 1928, 177 and pl. XXXVII, 1.

above a line of shoulder bosses,[1] while the smaller urn M 48(b) has an elaborate design of bosses and stamps covering its lower as well as its upper half, which is a broken-down version of that on the well-known urn from Newark-on-Trent.[2] Both M 48 urns were overlaid by M 49(a),[3] a stylish biconical vessel with two zones of chevron lines, which can itself hardly be later than the fifth century. It is evident that there was only a brief interval in time between these two burials, and it is interesting to know that such a wide variety of different ceramic styles was in virtually simultaneous use at Caistor at this date.

Of the *Buckelurnen* without feet M 28, X 24, and the British Museum urn 1870.12–6.1 are examples of my early Group II. The British Museum urn with its tall conical neck and double row of bosses seems to show the influence of the more elaborate Anglian shoulder-boss urns of the type of Hammoor KS 12084.24 (pl. IX*a*), though its own linear decoration is not corrugated. Its truncated appearance is due to the fact that the upper part of its neck and rim has been planed off along one of its upper neck-lines, having evidently suffered damage in ancient times: it may therefore have had some period of use before burial. M 28, whose remains were found in confusion with those of two other urns (see Inventory) and which may have contained a pair of late Roman bronze tweezers, is a fine example of a not uncommon type displaying alternate vertical and horizontal bosses each covered with groups of *stehende Bogen* lines; its closest English parallels, both rather simpler, are from Lackford, Suffolk,[4] and Wallingford, Berks.[5] No very close parallel to X 24 appears to be on record; apart from the three different sizes of bosses on its shoulder, of which the larger are covered with *stehende Bogen* lines and accompanied by irregular line-and-dot patterns, the row of solid lugs immediately below the rim, which could have served to sustain a cord securing a handle or lid, is most unusual. As already noted, the association of this urn with X 23 serves to show that there was an overlap in time between the early *Buckelurnen* and the later Anglian corrugated wares at Caistor around the central years of the fifth century. A 8, which was carefully buried under a layer of flints and Roman tile, also belongs to the group whose bosses, in this case feathered, are covered by *stehende Bogen* lines; it also contained a broken comb, and the curiously hesitant use of stamped ornament (a single impression of one stamp which puts it in my Group IV) seems to place A 8 before the period when this method of decoration became really popular.

It may be significant that the closest parallels to so many of the Caistor *Buckelurnen* are to be found at places far away from the East Anglian coast. The links of C 1 with Luton, of M 48(a) with Frilford and M 28 with Wallingford (both in Berkshire), and of M 48(b) with Newark-on-Trent remind us that the second half of the fifth century was an age of the greatest confusion during which the remaining restraints imposed by the sub-Roman regimes that had succeeded to imperial rule were broken, and the surviving relics of Romano-British civilization were destroyed by waves of uncontrolled invaders. I have suggested elsewhere[6] how the distribution of Group I *Buckelurnen* can be used to indicate the rapid spread of

[1] It is not unlike the urn from Frilford, Berks., Ashmolean Museum 1886–1401, figured in Rolleston 1869, 469 and pl. 23. 2.

[2] Myres 1937*a*, 429, fig. 1 (*a*), formerly at Hull, now at Newark.

[3] Also possibly by M 49(b) (fig. 18), but the relationship is not certain; see Inventory. M 49(b) is itself an early type

of bowl related in style to the two-handled bowl M 42 (fig. 18); its unusual bosses apparently derive from the applied flat handles found on continental prototypes.

[4] Cambridge Museum of Arch. and Eth. 50.100, not illustrated in Lethbridge 1951.

[5] Ashmolean Museum, Accession No. 1939–446.

[6] Myres 1954. See also Myres 1969, 100–5.

one group of these newcomers from East Anglia to the Upper Thames: the Caistor *Buckel-urnen* as a whole indicate ways in which this line of thought may be given even wider applications.

In addition to these groups of pottery which indicate the settlement of folk of both Anglian and Saxon antecedents in the earliest days of the cemetery's use, one other group deserves mention for its suggestion of a distinctive origin. This is the group of undecorated vessels, most of which are on figs. 28–30, with the special features of a markedly hollow neck above a sharply carinated shoulder. These features characterize pots of several forms, bowls such as Y 17, tall jars such as Y 12, wide-mouthed urns like M 53, and biconical types like X 5. They merge of course into more normal kinds of shouldered and biconical shapes, but the more distinctive examples are something of a Norfolk speciality,[1] and of those on record from the whole country about a third are from Caistor itself. That their users may have arrived as a coherent social group is suggested by the fact that two of them, M 53 and Y 17, contained elaborate combs of a kind very rare in Britain,[2] and that a number of them, Y 12, Y 17, Y 26 and some related forms such as Y 30, Y 46, Y 47(c) and the decorated pieces Y 16, Y 24, Y 28, Y 40, are concentrated in the Y area of the cemetery.[3]

This sharp-shouldered, hollow-necked type of pottery has basic northern associations on the Continent, particularly in Norway and Denmark,[4] but it early affected ceramic fashions both in the Anglian areas and in East Holstein. It is only in rare cases in this country, such as Caistor, that it occurs in a pure form in sufficient strength, both quantitatively and qualitatively, to justify the suspicion that a distinct social group of northern origin may be present. If so, they are likely to have been early arrivals. An undecorated urn from Hammoor, strikingly similar to X 5, is dated by an early fifth-century brooch,[5] and the influence of this form on such early Anglian corrugated vessels as N 14 (fig. 4) and others with tall conical necks like N 95 suggests that they are close in date. The same can be said of the early bowl with linear decoration K 7 (fig. 3), which contained bronze tweezers of late Roman type, or of the sharply shouldered bowl N 34 (fig. 3) with its combination of continuous diagonal corrugation and triangular groups of dots, a sure sign of influence from fashions of the Roman Iron Age. Anglian corrugated urns like N 2 with markedly hollow necks, or strongly emphasized shoulders like N 3, N 4, N 21 (all fig. 6) owe much to the same influence.[6] That the type persisted in a modified form into the sixth century is shown by the association of N 45 (fig. 29) with a Group III cruciform brooch.

Before leaving the pottery to which a fifth-century date can be properly assigned several other less distinctive groups can be mentioned. One is that consisting of biconical or sub-

[1] Other Norfolk examples are Markshall XVIII (fig. 69) and Illington 168a.

[2] See p. 92. There may have been others with Y 8, an early Saxon urn, and with E 1.

[3] The influence of this form can be seen also on some later stamped and/or bossed pots, e.g. Y 1, Y 7(a), Y 45 (all fig. 36), Y 2(c) (fig. 45), Y 44 (fig. 56), to take examples only from the Y series.

[4] See, e.g., Bøe 1931, figs. 151–74 for some exaggerated Norwegian examples.

[5] Genrich 1954, Tafel 15C. Another close parallel to X 5 is from Næsby, Fünen: Albrectsen 1968, Tavle 134e, not certainly dated.

[6] N 2, 3, and 4 were in contact as an associated group, apparently surrounding N 1, an urn with simple linear and stamped decoration (fig. 41), which could well be dated soon after 500. The association of the others with N 1 is not, however, certain (see Inventory), but it is worth noting that, though decorated in what might seem a rather later fashion, N 1 is, in shape, of the hollow-necked biconical form here under discussion. The group might represent a family burial of about 500, for which some older urns in the same tradition were employed (see pl. XIVa).

biconical vessels decorated simply with one or more groups of horizontal lines or grooves above the carination. Of these the sharply biconical forms M 11 and W 34 (fig. 15) are among the earliest, being related on the one hand to a type of biconical bowl very common among the *Schalenurnen* of East Holstein around the turn of the fourth and fifth centuries, and on the other to some of the Anglian pottery of Fünen of even earlier date.[1] It will be noted that M 11 contains an iron manicure set like those already noted as characteristic of the earlier Anglian pottery at Caistor. M 11 is a larger version of a little bowl from Peterborough,[2] itself very like one from Liebenau near Hanover, that was found with one of the earliest types of equal-armed brooch datable about 400.[3] That M 11 is early is shown by the fact that it underlay not only M 6, but probably also M 10, a corrugated shoulder-boss urn itself likely to be earlier than 500.

K 2 (fig. 15) is also likely to be early. It belongs to a group of English urns most of which, like K 2 itself, come from cemeteries in the immediate neighbourhood of Roman walled towns or significantly set on important roads linking them.[4] The continental parallels suggest that they date mainly from the first half of the fifth century,[5] a period in which sub-Roman regimes based on these towns may have been employing barbarian forces in an effort to maintain their independence. While K 2 has a more upright rim and a less hollow neck than many of the others, its decoration and proportions place it with some probability in this group.

A close parallel to R 2 (fig. 15), which has a flat slashed collar included in the group of horizontal lines, is an urn from Lackford with a flat feathered collar in this position: it was regarded as early by Lethbridge on account of the bronze tweezers of late Roman type found with it in very fresh condition.[6]

The only vessel in the Caistor collection with true handles, as distinct from the lugs common on cook-pot types (fig. 32) and an occasional miniature such as N 71 C (fig. 32), is M 42 (fig. 18). This remarkable bowl originally had two rounded and pierced handles set vertically on the maximum diameter, though both had been broken before it was buried. It is decorated otherwise with rather slapdash groups of vertical or diagonal lines and of dots, some of which are set in triangular groups. No close English parallels are on record and it is not easy to find comparable two-handled forms on the Continent that are much later than the third century. In Norway, however, two two-handled bowls, apparently of the early fifth century, are on record from Kirkesole, Håland, and Høiland, Rogaland, but in these the decoration is quite different and is executed in a much neater and less careless manner.[7] A closer parallel to the decoration of M 42 is one of the two-handled urns from Mahndorf, near Bremen,[8] also apparently of the early fifth century, but in form this is more of a wide-mouthed jar than a bowl. The decoration of M 42, though carelessly executed, includes

[1] Compare, e.g., M 11 with a third-century pot from Hesselager: Albrectsen 1968, Tavle 88g.

[2] Myres 1969, fig. 14, 2102.

[3] Genrich 1964, Brandgrab II/28.

[4] e.g. Great Chesterford 128, with fifth-century glass; Leicester, Court A, Churchgate, just outside the Roman walls; Thurmaston 36, on the Fosse Way north of Leicester; Castle Acre 31. Similar urns from Flixborough Warren, Scunthorpe, Lincs., and Lackford, Suffolk, are from sites less obviously related to the Roman administrative pattern.

[5] They occur, e.g., in the latest levels at Feddersen Wierde, nr. Bremerhaven, abandoned about 450, and at Wijster as Van Es's Type VIII B of the same date. The urn from Liebenau II/58, which is not unlike that from Leicester, had somewhat later associations: Genrich 1964.

[6] Lethbridge 1951, 16 and fig. 5, 49. 580.

[7] Bøe 1931, 155 and figs. 240, 241. These are somewhat exceptional as a Norwegian type.

[8] Grohne 1953, 84, Abb. 21d.

triangular groups of dots, a motif characteristic of the transition from fourth- to fifth-century pottery, as is also the chevron-and-dot pattern of the Mahndorf piece.[1] It is difficult to believe that either can have been made later than the second quarter of the fifth century. M 42, however, contained the badly burnt foot of a cruciform brooch of either late Group I or Group II, and is therefore unlikely to have been buried much before 500. That it was something of an antique by this time is suggested not only by its rather battered appearance but by the fact that it had already lost both its handles.

It has already been noted that M 49(b) (fig. 18) is similar in form to M 42; it also carried triangular groups of dots. Although it has no true handles, the solid curved bosses set horizontally on its shoulder are vestigial handles of the kind often found on continental pottery of proto-Saxon type.[2] It is no doubt of much the same date as M 42 and could well come from the same workshop; if it overlay the two M 48 *Buckelurnen*, which is not certain, it too, like M 42, may have had a long life before burial.

Line-and-dot decoration of this general character, a familiar feature of the pottery of Fünen, occurs on a number of other early Caistor pieces. It is found on more normal types of shoulder-boss urns such as E 2, E 4 (fig. 18), M 37 (fig. 19), P 19 (fig. 20), on the very large bossed biconical urn N 9 (fig. 19), or emphasizing chevron patterns as on P 25, Y 19, W 16 (fig. 11), N 32, M 44(a), W 38 (fig. 10). There is little internal evidence for the date of these except that M 44(a) was buried with, or possibly after, M 44(b), an early biconical urn with simple line-and-groove ornament. It is also probable that a stamped urn by the sixth-century Potter IV (M 15) was intrusively buried on several urns, one of which had line-and-dot decoration. Line-and-dot is also used for the broad biconical schemes on N 17 and N 42 (fig. 13), of which the latter includes *stehende Bogen* lines, thus linking it to the pre-*Buckelurne* Saxon phase. Its design is in fact a simplified version of that on one of the Galgen-berg urns, which includes finger-tip rosettes and restrained use of a rosette stamp.[3] N 17 has an interesting design featuring large freehand swastikas as well as the triangular groups of dots already noted as an early sign in connection with M 42 and M 49(b); it formed the centre of a group burial which included not only the remains of a plain urn but also N 16, a small urn also with line-and-dot decoration, probably from the same workshop, containing a child cremation. This group could well represent a simultaneous family burial of man, woman, and child, at a date probably before 450 (pl. XIV*b*).

Linked to these elaborate line-and-dot designs are urns such as N 10 (fig. 13), Y 30, and W 1 (fig. 55), of which certainly the two last, and perhaps all three, come from the same workshop (Potter VII). These have decoration of a coarser kind, carried out rather with grooves and finger-tipping than the neater line-and-dot. N 10, which had a large collection of grave goods including part of a comb, probably of Rhineland type datable around 400,[4] has two zones of continuous chevron grooves with a finger-tip in each triangular space, a motif especially popular in the first half of the fifth century, though apparently not later.[5]

---

[1] And of the somewhat similar Westerwanna 1128 (Zimmer-Linnfeld *et al.* 1960). A possible prototype for M 42 might be seen in the two-handled jar from Røgnehoj, Fünen, dated by a brooch of about 300: Albrectsen 1968, Tavle 106b.

[2] As, e.g., on some of the *Zweihenkeltöpfe* and *Dreiknubbentöpfe* of the Fuhlsbüttel culture: Tischler 1937, Abb. 10, 14, 18, 19.

[3] Waller 1938, Tafel 29. 2, not directly datable, but probably of the early fifth century.

[4] See pp. 95–6.

[5] The chevron-and-dot motif appears in the later fourth century on Group F of the Romano-Saxon pottery (Myres 1956, 30, fig. 5), on contemporary Germanic pottery of several kinds, including pieces associated with *Krieger-*

A bungled version of the same motif seems to have been attempted also on Y 30. These are not likely to be much later than the middle of the fifth century.[1]

Vessels with the basic biconical design of one or more wide zones of linear chevrons were common at Caistor, and most of them are not closely datable. It has been suggested above (p. 44) that such designs derive from third-century continental types, but this kind of decoration certainly had a long life and came to be used on vessels of shapes very different from the biconical forms to which it is primarily appropriate. There is no reason to suppose that urns like Y 3, or Y 2(a) and Z 4 (fig. 14), of which the last two may be from the same workshop, are earlier than the sixth century. The fact that Z 4 had been broken up by the diggers of the late Grave 7 is consistent with this view. The same may well be true of N 79 and W 55 (fig. 15) and X 22 (fig. 12). Even so stylish a piece as M 49(a) (fig. 14) with its sharply biconical form and neatly drawn double zone of chevrons is a secondary burial, as has been noted, intruded above M 48(a) and (b), both fifth-century *Buckelurnen*. On the other hand X 28 (fig. 12) not only has *stehende Bogen* grooves in what would normally be the chevron zone, but also has its sharp carination marked by a raised cabled band,[2] both indications of fifth-century date. It also contained an iron manicure set, as do so many early pieces at Caistor. A 12 (fig. 10), however, though of comparatively early biconical form, has a very broken-down arrangement of its chevron zone, which lacks a lower line, and its comparatively late date is confirmed by its association with a cruciform brooch of Group III/IV which takes it well into the central years of the sixth century. Among the latest examples typologically of this form at Caistor is probably E 12 (fig. 45) where the chevron zone has broken down into a meaningless jumble of vertical, horizontal, and diagonal lines. It formed part of the E 7 group, the evidence for whose very late date is analysed below (pp. 59–61).

Before going on to consider further the development of all these forms in the pottery of the sixth century something should be said at this point about the use in the cemetery of Roman coarse pottery as containers for Anglo-Saxon cremations, and on the related question of the influence, if any, which may have been exerted by local Romano-British fashions on the ceramic traditions of the first barbarian settlers. Both these phenomena may have a bearing on the date and circumstances in which the cemetery came into use. Four cases of ordinary Roman coarse pots used for cremations, N 6, P 43, P 48, Y 4, are on fig. 33, as is another, containing a cremation, probably but not certainly of Anglo-Saxon date, that was found away from the cemetery on the berm outside the south wall of the Roman town. Although these pots may not fall late in the Roman period (see pp. 74–6), there need be little doubt that the burials they contain are Anglo-Saxon. One of them, P 43, had part of a bone comb among the burnt bones. Moreover there is no reason to suppose that there was a Romano-British cemetery on this site before the Anglo-Saxons occupied it for this purpose: had there been, many more such burials, disturbed or undisturbed, would have come to

---

grab burials of Dorchester type, such as the pot from Liebenau Gr. 57/1, on some early fifth-century metal-work such as the Mucking buckle (Evison 1968), and on a few of the earliest *Buckelurnen*, such as those from Sandy, Beds. (B.M. 1937.11–11.8), St. John's, Cambridge, Lackford 50.54, Markshall LXX (all Group I); Kempston, Beds., Souldern, Oxon. (Group II); Osney, Oxon., Abingdon CX,

Berks. (Group IV). It does not seem to occur on the elaborately stamped examples (Group V).

[1] For the decoration of N 10 cf. Westerwanna 501 though the form of the latter is somewhat earlier.

[2] An unusual feature, paralleled, however, by a plain urn from Little Wilbraham (Neville 1852, pl. 32).

light during the excavations. In fact, the earlier Roman use of the site was not for funerary purposes at all but apparently for minor domestic or workshop occupation (see pp. 28–9). None the less, such evidence as exists suggests, as one might expect, that the use of Roman pots to hold Anglo-Saxon cremations was a feature of the early days of the cemetery's existence. Thus Y 4 underlay, and was certainly buried before, Y 5 (fig. 26), itself an early globular urn of Angle type with some irregular line-and-dot ornament. The questions posed by the presence of the Roman pots are further considered below (pp. 74–6).

It is perhaps surprising that the cemetery has produced so few examples of pots suggesting the surviving influence of Romano-British ceramic traditions on the newcomers. Two possible cases are M 46 and Y 15 (fig. 33). Y 15, with its well-moulded foot and rim and smooth red fabric, suggests a businesslike adaptation of Roman technical skill to the manufacture of hand-made pottery. M 46, whose rim and smooth buff/brown fabric are a good deal more stylish than seems appropriate to its rather hump-shouldered profile, is very much the type of pot that might have been made by someone familiar with late Roman coarse pottery, who had been caught up into the social and economic life of the invaders. That it belongs to an early phase of the cemetery is shown by the fact that it underlay M 47, which is dated to the early sixth century by a Group II cruciform brooch.

By far the most remarkable instance of the fusion of Roman and Saxon ceramic traditions is provided by Y 36 (pl. I*a* and fig. 33), a large biconical bowl decorated with a single row of stamps between groups of close-set lines above a trellis of criss-cross lines. It is exceptionally well made in a hard, thin, light grey ware indistinguishable from a Romano-British commercial fabric. Detached pieces from undecorated areas would not be out of place in a collection of Romano-British coarse potsherds. Its regularity suggests that some kind of mechanical aid was used to turn it, though it was evidently not wheel-made in the usual sense. The stamped decoration also markedly recalls Romano-British fashions in that the stamps (two are used) are set so close together that they often touch or even overlap, as is often the case on Roman stamped wares of the fourth century but hardly ever on Anglo-Saxon stamped pottery. The criss-cross trellised lines are also, of course, a characteristic feature of Romano-British jars and bowls, but one that occurs only rarely on Anglo-Saxon pottery.

Germanic parallels to the form and decoration of Y 36 are not easy to find, but those that have been noted supply from that side also evidence for its extremely early date. Most striking are two vessels from Møllegårdsmark, Fünen (pl. I*b, c*), which are almost exactly similar in size, shape, and decoration, except that they have cabled collars where Y 36 has a line of stamps. These urns are dated by Albrectsen A.D. 175–325 and thus fall well within the period which the Romanizing features of Y 36 might suggest.

It thus seems clear that Y 36 was made by someone familiar both with third-century barbarian taste and with the living tradition of later Roman pot-making, and so presumably within the time when commercial pottery was still being used by the British citizens of *Venta Icenorum*. The first half of the fourth century would seem to be the latest period when these conditions can have existed at Caistor, and Y 36 could well have been made even earlier than this. Whatever its exact date it remains a remarkable monument to someone's conscious or unconscious effort to reconcile *Romanitas* with *Barbaries*, while such compromise was still possible and the skills of the former had not yet finally succumbed before the onslaught of the latter.

Y 36 can thus serve as a reminder that stamped ornament, though most popular on the later pottery of the pagan period, can sometimes be found on very early pieces where its employment may provide a link with late Romano-British fashions. Caistor has also produced a small group of large stamped bowls whose antecedents are more specifically Germanic. These derive from one of the elements comprised in Plettke's somewhat composite Type C, a fourth/fifth-century group which originated in south and east Germany but, perhaps owing partly to the movement of the Suebi and related peoples, became popular in the lower Elbe valley and Holstein.[1] The earlier examples of these large bowls are mostly decorated with raised slashed collars and massed diagonal lines on the shoulder interspersed with dots and finger-tip rosettes, but stamped ornament finds its way onto them during the fifth century.

M 1 (fig. 34) is a very fine example, difficult to parallel in this country, of an early stage in the development of the type. Its features can be matched individually or in combination by a number of pieces from Westerwanna, a few of which are dated by association with late fourth- or fifth-century brooches.[2] Most of these have no stamped ornament, while on M 1 this occurs (two stamps) in a very restrained and inconspicuous manner, supporting a design still basically composed of groups of diagonal lines, dots, and finger-tip rosettes. One of the Westerwanna urns displays stamps more freely than M 1 in such a design, having both a collar of dots and stamps and a stamp in the centre of each rosette.[3] M 1, which could well be an import from the Elbe–Weser area, is hardly likely, in view of these analogies, to be later than 450.

But the type soon came to attract the attention of potters who favoured a less restrained use of stamps. N 54 and P 44 (both fig. 56) and N 56 (fig. 34), which could all be from the same workshop, show some of the different lines which this development could take. While all three retain the raised and decorated collar typical of the earlier phase, they have dropped finger-tip rosettes. N 56 uses stamps to emphasize the groups of diagonal and chevron lines on the shoulder, N 54 (pl. II*b*) combines them with the *stehende Bogen* motif already noted as characteristic of the earlier 'Cuxhaven–Galgenberg Typ', and P 44 introduces groups of shoulder bosses and vertical lines into the stamped chevron zone, as a hint of Anglian influence from further north. P 36(a) (fig. 35) is an urn, still of the wide-mouthed but now more shouldered form, in which such influence is dominant: it has in fact become a straightforward example of the bossed panel style with grouped bosses separating vertical panels of lines and stamps. N 54 and P 44 are by Potter VIII.

All these developments can of course be traced further in the great variety of stamped designs which characterize the pottery of the sixth century. Thus the stamped chevron style, well illustrated by such a straightforward example as N 41(a) (fig. 40), grows out of the beginnings suggested by N 56, and the stamped *stehende Bogen* style of R 18 and M 27 (both fig. 43) arises from a design like that of N 54. There is no need to follow in detail the ways in

[1] Plettke 1920, 48–9 and Tafel 40.
[2] e.g. Westerwanna 207 with a large group of objects, none closely datable; 646; 682 and 879, both very similar to M 1 in size, shape, and decoration; 755, rather earlier in form, with a fourth-century brooch (not illustrated); 920; 1190, rather later in form, with an equal-armed brooch; 1202; 1351, with simpler decoration and parts of

two fourth-century brooches; 1554 (Zimmer-Linnfeld *et al.* 1960).
[3] Ibid. 1547. A similar collar of mixed dots and stamps occurs on the small pedestal pot from Reading Gr. 13 (Hawkes and Dunning, 1961, 44, fig. 14(b)) that was buried, perhaps about 450, with an early fifth-century zoomorphic buckle: see Myres 1969, 91, for a fuller discussion.

which these and other patterns derived from the horizontal linear style (e.g. M 4, P 46, Y 9 on fig. 43), or the biconical style (e.g. N 93, R 3 on fig. 42), of earlier days are combined on the unbossed stamped pottery of the Caistor cemetery during the sixth century. Examples can be found on figs. 40–3, and among the stamped fragments from broken-up urns on figs. 45 and 46.

Direct evidence for the date of many of these pieces is less satisfactory than one would like, partly because the placing of datable objects with the ashes became less popular as time passed, and partly because close continental parallels are now much scarcer, itself an indication that English pottery styles were developing on their own independently of conditions in the lands from which the invaders had come.[1] But there is a good deal of internal evidence to show that this type of stamped pottery at Caistor falls late in the history of the cemetery. Thus X 3 (fig. 38), which displays an elaborate stamped chevron design, overlay, and was buried later than, X 4 (fig. 9), an early wide-mouthed urn with simple linear decoration and highly burnished finish. So too M 6 (fig. 54) with a simple stamped design by Potter VI seems to have been one of several urns that overlay M 11 (fig. 15), the early biconical urn with horizontal linear decoration discussed above (p. 51). A similar case is that of X 1 (fig. 40), with rather elaborate stamped biconical decoration, which partly overlay (pl. XIIc), and must be later than, X 2 (fig. 5), a typical early Anglian corrugated urn of the wide-mouthed variety.

All but the earliest phases in the development of panel-style decoration are also likely to have taken place after 500, and the cemetery has a good range of the successive stages with some useful indications of their dates. At Caistor the beginnings of this style are to be found in the corrugated shoulder-boss urns of Anglian character shown on figs. 7–9, many of which, as has been suggested (p. 46–7), may be earlier than 500. As the fashion for corrugation went out the panels between the shoulder bosses on this type of pottery were left partly or wholly empty, as with Y 18 (fig. 18) or Y 11(b) (fig. 20). Both of these were included in group burials whose date cannot be before the early part of the sixth century. The Y 9 group (pl. XVb), to which Y 11(b) belonged, probably disturbed an earlier corrugated urn (Y 11(d)); it included not only another early piece (Y 12)but also two stamped urns (Y 9 and Y 11(a)) that look to be later than 550. The whole group was surrounded with a ring of flints and tile, suggesting a contemporary burial but, in view of the confused and fragmentary state of some of the pots (the group of sherds originally bagged up as Y 11 was found to comprise parts of at least four urns), it is possible that subsequent disturbance introduced Y 9 and Y 11(a) into an early sixth-century group comprising at least Y 10, Y 11(b), and Y 12: but this is far from certain.[2] The group containing Y 18 looks more homogeneous. It included Y 19

[1] Although it is often assumed by scholars that the north German cemeteries went out of use by about 500, perhaps as a consequence of the main movement to Britain, they do contain a few pieces that would be dated well into the sixth century in this country, and some of these have a very English look. Thus Westerwanna 1116 (Zimmer-Linnfeld et al. 1960), Galgenberg, Tafel 26, 4 (Waller 1938), and Wehden, Tafeln 18.537 and 19.256 (Waller 1961) are examples of the fully developed stamped chevron style, represented here by, for example, N 41(a) (fig. 40). Wehden, Tafel 34.749 echoes almost exactly the stamped *stehende Bogen* style of M 27; and the stamped biconical scheme of Wehden, Tafel 36.558 is very similar to that of R 3 (fig. 42), though the pots are of different shapes. Pots of this kind could be used as evidence for a cultural backwash from Britain to the Continent in the early sixth century of which there are other indications in both the literary and archaeological sources.

[2] The range of types comprised in the Y 9 group could be readily explained if it represented a family burial plot used for successive burials over a considerable period of time. In that case it was most probably marked in some permanent way on the surface, but the area was so restricted that later burials almost inevitably broke up the earlier ones in it.

(fig. 11), with line-and-dot chevrons and the distorted remains of a cruciform brooch certainly earlier than Group IV, an undecorated shouldered bowl (Y 20, fig. 29), and part of another undecorated urn with conical neck (Y 21, not illustrated), all of which are consistent with a date early in the sixth century.

The next stage in the typology of the bossed panel style occurs with the intrusion of stamped ornament into the neck-lines or the panels or both. This is well illustrated at Caistor by M 47 (fig. 34), a shoulder-boss bowl with conical neck, almost empty panels, and a single row of stamps among the neck-lines. It is conveniently dated by a Group II cruciform brooch to the early part of the sixth century, and, as noted above, was buried above and later than M 46 (fig. 33), one of the few vessels of specifically sub-Roman character from the cemetery. Stamped ornament soon comes to play a more dominant part in bossed panel designs than is shown in its tentative use on urns like M 47, or H 1 and N 100 (fig. 35). Elaborate designs involving the use not merely of one stamp, as Y 7(a) (fig. 36), or two (W 23 (fig. 37)), but three (Y 45) or even five (X 7), both on fig. 36, fill the panels and the gaps in the neck-lines above them.

Pre-eminent among the practitioners of this fashion at Caistor is Potter I of whose work at least ten examples are preserved (figs. 47 and 48), though mostly in a sadly fragmentary state. This potter occasionally retains early features such as the raised slashed collars of M 16(a) and W 81, and sometimes leaves the panels empty, as on X 39, suggesting links with the preceding phases of the style. But most of the urns are distinguished by an exuberant variety of stamps—six on X 12, and nine on M 16 (a)—and by an elaborate treatment of the panels, which are filled either with horizontal and/or vertical zones of stamps and lines (M 16(a), P 22, W 77) or with groups of stamps separated by diagonal lines arranged as a St. Andrew's cross (X 12). The work of this potter is given a *terminus post quem* in the sixth century by two of the best-preserved urns which are intrusive: the burial of M 16(a) broke up M 16(b) (fig. 23), a shouldered urn with simple linear decoration, not necessarily earlier than about 500; and X 12 disturbed X 13 (fig. 21), an urn with line-and-grove decoration including an irregular chevron zone and two stamps; if it also disturbed X 13(d) (fig. 45), as is possible, a date at least as late as 550 is likely, for this was an urn with a developed pattern of biconical ornament involving the use of at least four stamps. Potter I was evidently in production around the central years of the sixth century, and may have started earlier.[1]

Another Caistor potter, who used the shoulder-boss panel style with stamps, is Potter IV, six examples of whose work are on fig. 53. This was a less versatile practitioner, with a more limited range of stamps—never more than three on a pot, as on the largest, P 26—and a standard scheme of grouped solid bosses, and horizontal zones of stamps and lines in the panels. This potter also retains a raised collar, but this is sometimes stamped (M 15, P 21, P 26) rather than slashed (P 41, Y 39). In one case, P 34, the collar and bosses are omitted, but are both replaced by a line of stamps, horizontal for the collar and vertical for the bosses, thus maintaining the characteristic design. There is no direct evidence for the date of Potter IV, who seems to have specialized in child cremations (P 34, P 41, Y 39), but the use of solid instead of hollow bosses, and the substitution, on P 34, of stamps for features of a design otherwise rendered by bosses suggest that bossed decoration was now going out of fashion.

[1] Urn 62 from Thurmaston, Leics., is closely related to the style of Potter I. Although it carries stamps not known to have been used by Potter I, its general design is so similar that it most probably came from the same workshop.

Potter IV may thus be taken to mark the transition to the stage when panel style designs dispensed with raised collars and bosses altogether.

This transitional stage may perhaps also be indicated in another way by X 7 (fig. 36), an urn with an extremely florid display of stamped ornament in five horizontal zones above large pendent triangles also filled with stamps: five are used. But the pendent triangles are made to hang, as it were, from diminutive shoulder bosses set in the lowest horizontal zone, which are almost lost in the profusion of stamps. An earlier version of the same type of design can be seen in Y 45 (fig. 36) where the bosses are both larger and more numerous, and the pendent triangles are narrow and do not extend below them.

These two urns are somewhat exceptional at Caistor in the use on shoulder-boss pots of stamped pendent triangles in the panels. The device is far more characteristic of Middle Anglian fashions, and indeed of the midlands generally, than it is of East Anglia in this phase.[1] At Caistor the panels more often contain either horizontal lines of stamps, as noted in the work of Potter IV, or chevron patterns, as on Y 7(a) (fig. 36) and W 23 (fig. 37); sometimes broad linear zones derived from the biconical style enclose both panels and bosses as on N 46 and Y 1 (both fig. 36).

Bosses and raised collars are dropped altogether in the final stage of the panel style, leaving stamped triangles or swags hanging free from the neck-lines. In adopting this style the Caistor potters show themselves strongly influenced by what, once again, was a fashion based in Middle Anglia but now spreading both east into Norfolk and west across the southern midlands to the upper Thames.[2] This is the style illustrated by W 75 (fig. 37), M 18, Y 6, Y 11(a), W 90, and W 94 (all fig. 39), and W 7, W 39, and Y 7(b) (fig. 41). It is securely dated at Lackford to the later part of the sixth century by florid square-headed brooches found with two examples of the type. One of these was made by the so-called Illington/Lackford potter, by far the most prolific practitioner in pottery of this kind.[3] At Illington in west Norfolk a Group II/III cruciform brooch was found in another pot with stamped pendent triangles from this workshop,[4] which is consistent with a date soon after 550. No such definite associations help to date the Caistor group, but two of them were intrusive upon earlier burials: thus M 18 (fig. 39) overlay M 19 (fig. 25), a plain globular urn of Anglian type which could be as late as 500; and N 81(a) (fig. 46) had crushed N 81, a shouldered jar with linear chevrons and perhaps a zone of unfinished stamped ornament above, which is unlikely to be earlier than about 525. It is perhaps significant of the local differences between east and west Norfolk at this time that no certain examples of pots from the Illington/Lackford workshop have been noted at Caistor, though the decoration of an urn like W 39 (fig. 41) may have been influenced by its distinctive style.[5] At Illington, on the other hand, nearly a quarter of all the stamped pottery from the cemetery appears to have been supplied from this source.[6]

That such direct contacts with west Suffolk were occurring towards the end of the pagan

[1] It occurs with some frequency in the west Suffolk, Cambridge, and Northamptonshire cemeteries, and as far west as Baginton in the valley of the Warwickshire Avon.

[2] Myres 1969, 118, and Map 9 show the wide distribution of the type, which is contemporary with, and may perhaps be taken as the main ceramic hallmark of, the age of the second Bretwalda, Ceawlin of Wessex (550–93).

[3] Lethbridge 1951, fig. 17, 50.126 and 50.234. See also the discussion in Myres 1969, 132–6.

[4] Illington 102.

[5] W 90, however, was apparently made by the potter of Illington 281 and 286.

[6] Myres 1969, 135, and Map 10 show the rather limited distribution of products from this prolific workshop.

period at Caistor is shown by E 7 and W 30 (pls. VI*b* and VII*a*, fig. 44), products of the remarkable animal-stamp workshop which also made an urn for Lackford.[1] The association of these urns with other related pieces was recorded in such detail by F. R. M., and their intrinsic interest is so great, that it has been thought desirable to discuss them and the circumstances of their discovery at some length.

Five urns, E 7, E 8 (fig. 44), E 10, E 11 (fig. 57), and E 12 (fig. 45), were found together in contact with one another in circumstances which make it reasonably certain that they were buried at the same time. They lay 30 in. (75 cm.) deep under the roots of a fir tree, mixed up with numerous large flints. The disturbance due to the roots of the tree was so great that the relation of the flints to the pots could not be exactly ascertained, but most of the flints were resting on the pots which had been badly crushed by them. A few inches south of this group and at a slightly lower level was the base of another pot containing a few burnt bones and a fused bead. This makes it fairly clear that the E 7 group was intrusive and had partly destroyed an earlier cremation. A further source of disturbance had been caused by a rabbit burrow which led to a nest immediately below these pots, and it is probable that the missing parts of them had long since disappeared down this burrow. Extensive digging was carried out in search of these missing parts but without success. There were no associated objects with any of these pots,[2] a fact which is consistent with the other evidence for the late date of the whole group.

It is worth stressing the circumstances in which these urns were found because of the remarkable character of some of them and of other urns with which they can be closely associated both at Caistor and elsewhere. To take the least interesting members of the group first, E 12 is a striking example of the final stage in the decadence of the biconical style of ornament (see p. 53). Its form has become globular and has entirely lost the angular character appropriate to this type of decoration. The enclosed zone of linear decoration has been pushed up onto the neck and shoulder and reduced to a meaningless jumble of lines and dots. E 10, which is by the same potter (XI) as E 11 and two other urns, R 1 and R 4, is a shoulder-boss urn of a similar late globular form; its decoration is also thoroughly decadent, consisting of a random scatter of small stamps over the bosses and in the space to the right of each, with a group of diagonal lines awkwardly filling the rest of each panel. A single impression of a larger stamp has been added to the right of each boss, after the ground had been peppered with the smaller stamp, impressions of which can be seen underlying it. Somewhat similar treatment is shown on E 11 and on the other two urns by this potter, R 1 and R 4 (fig. 57). This random use of stamped ornament is characteristic of the final phase of its popularity in the pagan period. E 8 is stamped in the same random manner and has small vestigial solid shoulder bosses, and linear ornament confined, apart from neck-lines, to brief vertical groups on each side of the bosses and to flat unsymmetrical arcading emphasized by stamps, suggesting a remote memory of the *Buckelurne* style. These four urns, E 8, E 10, E 11, E 12, could be treated almost as type specimens of the final decadence to which the earlier decorative motifs had been reduced by the end of the sixth or early seventh century.

[1] Lethbridge 1951, fig. 31, 48.2487.
[2] The presence of a fused bead is noted by F. R. M. in his note on E 12, but in view of his positive statement that there were no objects with any of the E 7 group, it seems likely that this bead is the one recorded by him as remaining in the base of the urn destroyed by the burial of these pots; this urn is otherwise unrecorded by F. R. M.

It is against this background of late associations that the remarkable urn E 7 (pl. VIb) must be considered. In itself it might be thought to bear no obvious signs of late date, with its sharply biconical form, prominent hollow bosses, and carefully executed scheme of decoration. The use of swastika stamps, of 'wyrm' stamps (see p. 63) interlocked to form a continuous cable, and of the large animal stamps might also be thought to indicate a time when classical motifs were being eagerly copied in the German world, and realistic animal ornament had not yet broken down into the meaningless complexities of the zoomorphic Style I. It could indeed be argued that E 7 was a valued antique at the time of its burial, for it had been extensively mended with lead in its lower part in ancient times. On any showing, however, it was an exceptional piece, both in the exaggeration of its biconical form, the excellence and regularity of its workmanship, and the unusual size and special character of its stamped ornament. Such an urn might well be thought worth mending, even if the damage occurred within a few days or hours of its creation.

Typologically, however, its scheme of decoration places it in the shoulder-boss group of urns with stamped panels and so it is unlikely to antedate the sixth century. In view of its associations it seems best to regard it as a late piece in this series like the urns buried with it, and to account for its apparently early features as a case of deliberate archaism. That Anglo-Saxon potters in the later part of the sixth century were fully capable of harking back to the fashions of the past, when occasion called for a specially distinctive urn, is a well-established fact.[1] Moreover E 7 does not stand alone: W 30, of which unfortunately only fragments remain (pl. VIIa), was evidently an even more remarkable example of the same kind. Although its form is different, being much larger, more globular in shape, and apparently without bosses, it shows a similar combination of a cabled collar produced by interlocking 'wyrm' stamps, swastika stamps (two forms), and large animal stamps (three varieties). None of these stamps is identical with those on E 7, but the combination of three such exceptional features is unmistakable evidence for a common origin. The full combination is recorded elsewhere only on the urn from Lackford already mentioned.[2] This has a cabled collar made apparently from the same 'wyrm' stamp as that on W 30, a different complex swastika stamp, and an animal stamp which, though not identical with any on W 30, is like one of them in showing a backward-biting beast. It is noteworthy that the animal stamps on W 30 and on Lackford 48.2487 both possess large round eyes, while the less elaborate animal stamp on E 7 has no eye; there is a similar contrast between the simple swastika stamp of E 7 and the complex varieties on W 30 and the Lackford pot. There are, in fact, two separate varieties within the group of animal-stamp pots. They all include elements of the combination of a cabled interlace, swastikas, and animal stamps, but the forms these elements take are different in the two varieties. In one, comprising W 30 and

---

[1] The Illington/Lackford potter whose later work may be almost contemporary with the E 7 group also produced elaborately bossed urns with raised collars like Lackford 48, 2475 (Lethbridge 1951, fig. 18). Another by the same hand came from St. John's, Cambridge (Myres 1969, fig. 48), and parts of several more from West Stow Heath. See also the work of a Girton potter discussed in Myres 1937b, 396–8 and fig. 9.

[2] Lackford 48.2487 (Lethbridge 1951, fig. 31). One of

the Castle Acre, Norf., urns is similar in style to E 7 and carries similar complex swastika stamps to those of this group, but as its upper part is missing it is impossible to say whether it had a cabled collar or animal stamps. Newark 208 has animal stamps and these are combined on Newark 257 with 'wyrm' stamps that could have been used to form a cabled collar. But the style of these pots is not the same.

Lackford 48.2487, the interlace is composed of simple wyrm stamps, the animals face left and have eyes, and the swastikas are complex; in the other, the wyrm stamps are ribbed, the animals are eyeless and face right and the swastikas are simple. Urns sharing one or more of these features with E 7 are N 83 (eyeless animals) and Newark 257 (ribbed wyrm stamps and eyeless animals). The significance of these differences is far from clear at present but they are in all likelihood contemporary.

In commenting on Lackford 48.2487 Lethbridge suggested that the animal type might be compared with that on the Brighthampton sword, thus linking it with products of the so-called Quoit Brooch style of the fifth century.[1] But, as he also pointed out, a far closer comparison can be made with the backward-biting beasts on such seventh-century illuminations as those of the Book of Durrow, and this comparison is the more significant because in these manuscripts there is the same combination of such animals with complex swastikas and with cabled interlace. On these grounds Lethbridge dated Lackford 48.2487 'probably not earlier than A.D. 600'. This is undoubtedly correct, and carries with it a similar date for W 30, though E 7, as noted above, is of the other variety.

The artistic link thus provided between the latest pagan pottery of East Anglia and the earliest known Hiberno-Saxon manuscripts of the Christian age raises fascinating speculations which cannot be pursued here. But it can hardly be unconnected with the religious syncretism of the East Anglian royal family at this time, to which Bede bears witness. One is bound to wonder what kind of service books the pagan worshipper in Rædwald's temple saw in use at the Christian altar which he installed there, perhaps about 615–20;[2] and what kind of service books St. Fursa the Irishman used in his monastery in the Saxon shore fort at Burgh Castle, barely 15 miles down the valley from Caistor, between about 636 and 644.[3]

Something further should be said at this point about N 83 (pl. VIIb and fig. 44). This was discovered in fragments on the surface, having been thrown out and broken up by rabbiters, and there is no stratigraphical evidence of its date or indication of its contents. Of the two animal stamps used on it, the larger is eyeless and not unlike the animal on E 7, but the smaller is a much less realistic affair with only two legs and a large rump: it could even be intended for a bird. N 83 has neither swastika stamps nor a cabled collar; in form it bears a general resemblance to R 13 (fig. 15) and like it has an arrangement of chevron lines below the main zone of stamped decoration, which is probably intended to suggest the '↑' rune, and so in all likelihood a devotion to the god Tiw.[4]

But if N 83 may have only an indirect association with the E 7 group, it is possible to link another remarkable urn, R 9/10 (pl. VIa and fig. 44), more closely with it. This is also fragmentary and was an accidental discovery, whose findspot is not known. It is the upper part of a very large urn[5] with a narrow neck and flaring rim, and is decorated with four stamps of

[1] Op. cit. 31. For general discussion of the animal ornament in the Quoit Brooch style see Evison 1965, 46–78. There are in fact significant differences between the animal types of the Quoit Brooch style and those of the W 30/Lackford 48.2487 potter.

[2] Hist. Eccles. ii. 15.

[3] Ibid. iii. 19. The late Professor Francis Wormald suggested to me that elaborate stamps of the kind used on this group of pots would have been equally appropriate as bookbinder's tools for use on the covers of contemporary service books or on the leather budgets or satchels in which they were habitually carried. The satchel in which the Book of Armagh has long been kept, though probably much later, is decorated with roundels containing animals and confused interlace that could indicate a tradition going back to the seventh century (Waterer 1968, pls. VI B and VII).

[4] See pp. 66–8 for a discussion of the Caistor pots bearing runes or rune-like signs.

[5] By Potter XII.

which three are identical with stamps on E 8. It must have been made by the same potter and, like E 8, its decoration includes flat linear arcading emphasized by stamps, but it has no bosses. The remarkable feature of this urn is the freehand drawing of a wolf or dog with a long tail, apparently barking at a retreating boat. Both the animal and the boat are drawn in outline only, but the attitude of the former, with its open or bristling jaws, and the position of the prow and steering paddle on the latter, leave no room for doubt that a specific incident or scene, evidently of some topical significance, is here portrayed.[1] It cannot be without interest that this unique and spirited drawing, perhaps the oldest recorded illustrative picture from Anglo-Saxon times, should occur on a pot made by a potter another of whose products was directly associated with one of the few known urns bearing animal stamps. It would seem that at the very end of the pagan period at Caistor potters were feeling their way towards the use of this medium for naturalistic representation of current and traditional scenes. It is tantalizing that nothing more should be known of this group of urns than that in all probability they date from late in the sixth or early in the seventh century.

There is, however, some reason to believe that R 9/10 was not the only urn at Caistor with an animal drawing on it. A note by F. R. M. may fitly conclude this account. He writes:

'The Rev. J. W. Corbould-Warren has informed me that there used to be an urn in the garden at Caistor Hall which had on it a drawing of an animal with very long ears. This urn stood in a certain spot in the garden for years and was eventually broken up by boys throwing stones at it. I made a long search for fragments of this urn but without success.'[2]

If the dating here proposed for the animal-stamp potter whose work provides a direct link between Caistor and Lackford is correct, it may be illustrative of the growing political consolidation that was binding all parts of East Anglia together in the early years of the seventh century under the rule of the Wuffingas. This is the age of Rædwald who, before his death early in the second quarter of the seventh century, had not only succeeded to the political predominance among the Anglo-Saxon kingdoms held previously in succession by Ceawlin of Wessex and Æthelbert of Kent but, as noted above, had begun the tentative flirtation with Christianity which soon led under his descendants to the end of pagan burial customs in the great East Anglian cemeteries.

The work of the other more prolific potters at Caistor, such as Potters II (figs. 49, 50) and III (figs. 51, 52), also belongs for the most part to this final phase in the cremation period. Potter II commonly made pots of ovate form with wide (X 36) or narrow mouths (G 3, X 37) decorated in the unbossed panel style with groups of vertical lines extending almost to the base forming panels of which the upper parts only are outlined with stamps, four or five (including a swastika stamp) being used on each. Potter III also made pots of this kind, M 31, M 32, M 57 (fig. 52), but in this case the upper parts of the panels are filled with stamps, some of which are exceptionally large; on P 33 (fig. 51), a more wide-shouldered form, the stamps are arranged as pendent triangles, but without enclosing lines, a clear indication of the final phase in the stamped panel style.[3] But it is of interest that both these potters on

[1] See p. 118 for discussion of the suggestion made by Miss V. I. Evison, F.S.A., that it may be intended to represent a version of the Naglfar/Fenrir story, the earliest literary evidence for which belongs to a period long after the seventh century.

[2] However, there is always the possibility that this vessel was a Castor ware beaker with barbotine decoration of hare and hounds.

[3] An urn from Barton Seagrave, Northants. (B.M. 91. 3–19.2) which is decorated with similarly undemarcated

occasion turned out bossed urns. N 64 (fig. 50) has groups of three shoulder bosses enclosed by hanging swags outlined by stamps; that it is by Potter II is clear both by its use of the same five stamps as appear on X 36, and by the fact that the groups of bosses are separated from one another by vertical lines running to near the base and outlined in the upper part only by stamps, exactly as in the more normal products of this potter. P 16 (fig. 51) is a biconical urn with small hollow bosses, alternately vertical and circular, on the carination. There is a zone of stamped biconical ornament on the neck, and the circular bosses are covered by single-line *stehende Bogen*, the whole composition being strongly reminiscent of the last phase of the *Buckelurne* style. Yet it was certainly made by Potter III, for its five stamps all appear on other products of this potter: two of them indeed on P 30, a large globular urn which, though without bosses, shares with P 16 the feature of large single-line *stehende Bogen*. It is possible that the wide range of styles exhibited by these two potters may indicate that their workshops were in operation over a considerable part of the sixth century. A similar explanation could apply to the variety shown in the work of Potters V, VI, and VII, but not enough examples of their output have survived to establish their normal range of designs.

Internal evidence for the date of these workshops is provided, in the case of Potter II, by the fact that G 3, one of its standard products, was intrusively buried with G 4 (fig. 29), a plain barrel-shaped pot of late type, over G 5 (not illustrated), apparently a plain urn with paired bosses which, however, contained a brooch which was either a Group I cruciform or a small–long brooch of the early sixth century. This suggests a date for G 3 not earlier than 550. Similar dating evidence for the standard work of Potter III comes from the fact that P 33 was apparently intrusive upon P 32 (fig. 58), a stamped shoulder-boss urn not likely to be later than the first half of the sixth century.

Some Special Types

Among the Caistor urns are a number decorated in ways which do not closely conform to any of the standard schemes normally used on the continental or English pottery. Most of these display freehand designs of one kind or another, varying from what look like nothing more significant than random doodles to attempts at the portrayal of specific objects, or even perhaps of some pictorial scene that may have a meaningful intent. Among the specific objects represented are symbols that had long carried a religious significance in northern art and mythology such as the swastika and the legless serpent or 'wyrm'. There are also attempts, some more convincing than others, at the portrayal of runes. A few of these are recognizable as such but others are rather rune-like signs intended to convey to an illiterate public not so much an exact message, or even some magic formula, but rather a general impression of mysterious power. A number of these symbols occur on the pottery not only as freehand drawings, but also formalized as stamps, and it is impossible to consider them wholly in the one medium without reference to the other. The relation between the two indeed is a matter of some interest.

The urn which carries perhaps the boldest of these freehand linear designs is N 69 (fig. 1). In form also it is unusual, a wide hollow-necked biconical bowl with flaring rim.[1] It is

stamped panels, shows two stamps very similar to, if not identical with, ones used by Potter III. Although it has shoulder bosses, unlike the Caistor products of Potter III, it must have come from the same, or a closely related, workshop.

[1] The late Professor G. Bersu informed me that pottery of this kind is known from the North Frisian islands off the west coast of Schleswig, but I have not been able to establish a really close parallel.

decorated, below four strong grooves on the neck, with a series of reversed S curves in strong multiple grooves, set on their sides and interlocking to produce a continuous scroll pattern. This running design is interrupted not, as so often happens on Anglo-Saxon pottery, by a jumbled misfit of lines arising from initial failure to space the design round the pot before carrying it out, but by a deliberate composition consisting of three arched grooves or *stehende Bogen* set between two groups of three vertical grooves. The impression created is thus of a moving procession of curvilinear creatures confronted by a stationary object that could be either a door in a building or a fenced mound.

This impression may not be wholly fanciful: indeed it would be doing the potter an injustice to suppose that he cannot have intended to produce precisely this effect. The drawing is quite firm and deliberate, and there is no suggestion of indecision or bungling about it. Moreover there is plenty of contemporary evidence to show that the S curve was commonly used at this time to indicate a zoomorphic form, the legless serpent or 'wyrm'. The zoomorphic intent is obvious where, as sometimes happens, the S curve is provided with an eye at one end,[1] or indeed, for good measure, at both ends,[2] but even when this detail is omitted[3] there is no doubt what is meant. Nor does N 69 stand alone in the suggestion of a continuous procession of wyrm-like creatures running round the pot. A well-known urn from Kettering, Northants., has a continuous interlocking series of such creatures, very much in the manner of N 69, but more neatly and realistically drawn, in that each is provided with a large finger-tip eye.[4] The motif is occasionally reduced to a purely schematic statement, and used as a pattern for breaking up zones of stamped biconical decoration as, for example, by one of the sixth-century potters at Sancton.[5]

The unusual feature of N 69 is thus not so much the 'wyrm' procession in itself, but its relation to the static feature that looks like a door or a fenced mound and appears to be of interest to the creatures as they approach it. The combination of the two motifs on one pot is not entirely unparalleled; it occurs, for example, on one of the Sancton *Buckelurnen*, but in that case there is no obvious organic relationship between the two objects,[6] as there is on N 69. Whether the static object is intended for a door or a mound—it could well be meant to suggest both—one is forcibly reminded of the scene in *Beowulf* in which a ferocious 'wyrm' or dragon acts as the guardian or protector of the tomb treasure in a mound. It may well be that the potter of N 69 was weaving with this spirited design a sort of pictorial spell by which the grave containing the urn and its contents would be protected by supernatural forces against disturbance.

There seems no doubt that the 'wyrm' design as it appears on Anglo-Saxon pottery is

---

[1] Several examples with eyes from Beetgum and other Dutch sites are in the museums at Leeuwarden and Groningen. An English example is Lackford 48.2473 (Lethbridge 1951, fig. 28), which also has a suggestion of jaws.

[2] One of the *Buckelurnen* from Sancton, now at Hull, by a potter who specialized in these freehand designs, shows a 'wyrm' with a stamped eye at both ends (Myres 1969, fig. 46, 2025). Lackford 50.47 (Lethbridge 1951, fig. 30) carries a 'wyrm' stamp with a head at both ends. That on N 28 (fig. 42) has notches to indicate bristles down the back.

[3] As on the urn from West Keal, Lincs.: Myres 1969, fig. 49, 511.

[4] This urn has been frequently reproduced: Baldwin Brown 1915, pl. CXXXIV. 5; Plettke 1920, Tafel 51.6; Myres 1969, fig. 49. 779. Another procession of this kind is on Newark 364, where the potter's intention is further emphasized by the prominent use of a large 'wyrm' stamp.

[5] Myres 1969, fig. 49.66 and 2279.

[6] Myres 1969, fig. 46.2275. See also Westerwanna 1167 (Zimmer-Linnfeld *et al.* 1960), a remarkable fourth-century urn on which the same combination occurs, along with other related cult objects, swastikas, rosettes, and so on. But here too the objects are portrayed individually: there is no attempt to make them tell a story, as on N 69.

thus intended as a protective device. This is its purpose, whether drawn freehand or impressed with a stamp. 'Wyrm' stamps became one of the commonest of all, and they can perhaps be taken as a good illustration of that combination of the imaginative and the practical which has always marked the Anglo-Saxon character. To cover a pot with numerous impressions of a simply made 'wyrm' stamp appealed to them as at once less laborious, quicker, and more effective than to draw out one or two such creatures freehand. Caistor is typical of the cremation cemeteries in its ready adoption of this popular labour-saving device.[1]

There is an obvious relationship between the 'wyrm' and the swastika as magical or religious symbols, if only for the practical reason that swastikas are most easily made by imposing one 'wyrm' at right angles upon another.[2] Large freehand swastikas appear as part of the biconical design on N 17 (fig. 13) and a single swastika has been added among the chevron lines on Y 22 (fig. 2). There are also a few cases of swastika stamps. The animal-stamp potter of E 7 and W 30 uses them, and so do Potters II and III, the latter infrequently. Apart from these, the device hardly occurs on the Caistor pottery. There seems no doubt that the swastika was particularly the symbol of Thor, and its ostentatious use on N 17 and Y 22 may well indicate a special devotion to him. But there is little to suggest that this cult was generally popular at Caistor.

Less easy to interpret are the freehand scrawls which make up the decoration on M 9, W 24, W 44 (all fig. 21), or W 2 (fig. 18). Of these, there is too little left of W 44 to conjecture the scheme, if any; it is unfortunate that W 24 also is too fragmentary to restore the full design which was evidently vigorous and elaborate; the jumble of lines in the surviving panel of W 2 has no obvious significance. M 9, however, is complete, but the meaning of the four scenes in the panels between the groups of vertical lines is far from clear. One has simply horizontal lines and a row of dots; one is a composite criss-cross design; the third might be some kind of schematic animal; and the fourth is probably intended for a comb. Pictures of combs and other grave goods, or stamps representing them, are sometimes found on urns,[3] presumably as an alternative to placing the object itself inside. Such a symbolic practice seems to indicate a stage in the decline of the belief that grave goods were of positive benefit to the dead. There is no direct evidence for the date of M 9.

Then there are the urns carrying runes or rune-like signs. No urn at Caistor carried any group of such signs that could be properly termed an inscription, or was intended to look like one. The nearest to such a group are the marks on the neck of X 11 (fig. 27), a plain urn of late appearance that contained with the burnt bones many pieces of decorated bone strips, probably derived from the mountings of a box.[4] But it is not certain that these marks, which are very indistinct, and bear no relation to any true rune forms, were deliberately made at all: at best they are probably no more than idle doodles.

---

[1] 'Wyrm' stamps are found on at least fourteen of the stamped urns here published, as well as a large number of sherds that were not worth illustrating.

[2] A two-headed 'wyrm' stamp is thus used to produce swastikas on Lackford 50.47 (Lethbridge 1951, fig. 30); there are other instances.

[3] The groups of vertical lines under a horizontal line and some dots on W 51 (fig. 21) could be intended for a comb;

so could some of the designs in the panels of the elaborately decorated P 17 (fig. 35). Stamps representing combs occur on the exceptional stamped urn from the Galgenberg near Cuxhaven (Waller 1938, 50 and Tafel 34.1), and on several English urns. There is a drawing of a pair of shears on an urn from Garwerd in the Biologisch-archaeologisch Institut at Groningen.

[4] See p. 85 and pls. XX, XXI.

The clearest use of runes on the Caistor pottery concerns a few urns on which the '↑' rune has been either drawn freehand as part of the decorative scheme, or has been scratched, or impressed in the form of a stamp. R 13 (fig. 15) is the best case of the first method; it is a sub-biconical urn of relatively early type, which carries, below a group of strong neck-lines, seven '↑' runes conspicuously set on the maximum diameter, two of which are separated by a single group of four diagonal lines. Other less certain but probable cases of the same kind are M 33 (fig. 22), which displays very large two-line '↑' runes on the shoulder, and the fragmentary N 104 (fig. 18), a shoulder-boss urn with groups of bosses in the panels between which are large two-line chevrons with a single vertical line depending from the apex, which may be intended for '↑' runes. A similar case is Y 43 (fig. 22), a wide-mouthed jar whose sole decoration consists of three- or four-line chevrons some of which have a single vertical line depending from the apex, possibly intended to make them look like '↑' runes.[1] One certain instance in which the '↑' rune has been deliberately scratched (twice) is the single sherd which is all that remains of M 5(b) (fig. 46); it is very unfortunate that one cannot say what relation the runes bore to the decorative design of the pot. There is also one certain case of the '↑' rune as a stamp: this is on P 36(c) (fig. 40), also unfortunately only a fragment. The stamp is used to fill the lowest of at least two stamped zones set low on the neck, above three-line pendent swags containing two groups of three vertical lines; the stamp is circular and carries a raised '↑' rune.

Caistor is not the only cemetery which has produced urns decorated with the '↑' rune. The phenomenon was first noticed by Dr. K. R. Fennell at Loveden Hill, Lincs. where, as at Caistor, it occurs both in freehand and in stamped form.[2] Examples have since been noted elsewhere, both in this country[3] and on the Continent.[4] There can be little doubt that the use of this particular rune by itself on pottery is due to the fact that it stands for the god Tiw or Tig, the popularity of whose cult in the early Anglo-Saxon period is shown not only by his name appearing in a number of place-names,[5] but by the allocation of a weekday, Tuesday, to his special protection. It is therefore safe to assume that a devotion to the cult of Tiw is indicated by these '↑' rune pots: as a war-god belonging apparently to an older mythological stratum than Woden he may have been thought an especially potent figure in the earlier stages of the invasion.

Three Caistor pots carry signs that may be intended to represent a wider range of runes. These are N 25 (fig. 18), P 7 and W 51 (fig. 21). N 25 is a wide shoulder-boss urn with tall conical neck; in the panels between the seven bosses are designs which may be intended for the 'ᚷ' rune (three times), the '✳' rune (twice upside down), and the 'ᚫ' rune (twice up-

---

[1] Another case where one only of a group of two-line chevrons has been made to look like a '↑' rune by adding vertical lines depending from the apex is P 10 (fig. 22). It is difficult to see what other purpose can have been served in doing this, but it may be just due to carelessness.

[2] A small sherd 61/B 17 C has a small '↑' very similar to those on M 5(b); there are several drawn freehand with other runes on 62/C8/305, and with stamps on C1/298.

[3] The small hollow-necked jar from Kempston, Beds., in the British Museum (91.6–24.32) is a possible case: but the rune may be 'ᛌ' not '↑'.

[4] The earliest I have noticed is the third-century one from the Galgenberg (Waller 1938, Tafel 8.5); there are a number at Westerwanna (Zimmer-Linnfeld et al. 1960, 870, 1364 (both with rosettes); 270, 1244, 1251, 1311, 1385, 1406, 1526); Duhnen-Wehrberg (Waller 1959) Tafel 48.53, is another; Altenwalde (Waller 1957), Tafel 2.17 is a possibility, but the device between the stehende Bogen may be just decorative; Tafel 17.152 is a clear case; Tafel 15.127 and 129 are probables.

[5] e.g. Tuesley (Surrey), Tewin (Herts.), or Tysoe (Warwicks.).

side down as '⋎'). Since the 'ꞡ' rune would look the same if drawn upside down, it seems probable that the pot was decorated in this way when standing in an inverted position, with the result that, when it was put the right way up, all the runes were really upside down. These runes have no obvious significance in combination, so it was probably of little consequence to the potter or his client which way up they appeared on the finished product: they were probably treated simply as vague symbols of indefinite and mysterious power. It is of some interest that Lackford 50.101[1] is similar to N 25 in form, fabric, and design and may well come from the same workshop. It also carries what seems to be the 'ꞡ' rune, the '⋏' rune (upside down as '⋎'), and possibly the '✳' rune (once as '✳' and once as '⋆'); in addition it has what may be the 'ꞡ' rune (twice). Here too it seems likely that the decoration was carried out with the pot inverted, but the potter's lack of skill as a rune-master is more obviously shown in the bungled attempts to portray the '✳' rune.

P 7 has linear designs which may be intended to represent a further series of runes, 'Ⲩ', '⋀', and '⧣', the latter being on its side as 'W'. Since the first two are the right way up, it is perhaps more likely that the last is not meant for 'S', but is a variant form for 'Ᏸ', the 'Þ' rune, which occurs at an early date.[2] Here again there is no obvious sense in the combination, and the signs are probably used at random as individual symbols of mysterious power.

W 51 is unfortunately only a fragment; it comes from a globular urn with corrugated neck. Below this, on the only surviving piece, are designs suggesting the 'ꞡ' and 'Ⲩ' runes separated by a group of vertical lines depending from a horizontal line, which could be taken to indicate a comb with very long teeth (see p. 65).

Whether the series of runes which appear to be used on this group of pots is a random selection by the potters or their masters, or is based on some deliberate principle of choice, it is at least of interest that a number of them seem to recur on pots from other sites both in this country and in Germany. Thus a shoulder-boss urn from North Elmham, Norfolk, carries the 'ꞡ' and '⧣' runes alternately in its panels, both being set sideways, so that in this case the pot was probably decorated in that position.[3] The '⧣' rune also may appear once along with 'Ᏸ' and 'ᚱ' in the panels of a shoulder-boss urn from Ingham, Suffolk.[4] On the Continent, it would seem that '⧣' and '⋏' (perhaps for '⋀') occur along with 'Ᏸ' on a fine *Buckelurne* from Westerwanna,[5] and '✳' is repeated several times as the main decoration on a pot from Hemmoor Warstade.[6]

Attention may finally be called to one or two cases at Caistor where stamps carrying designs that closely resemble runes are used. The 'Ⲧ' rune stamp on P 36(c) (fig. 40) has already been mentioned as a certain instance. The '⋀' set in a lozenge-shaped stamp on A 3 (fig. 38) is difficult to explain as anything except the symmetrical form of the '⋀' rune,[7] and the same is true of the '⋀' set in a triangular stamp on X 13(d) (fig. 45), and perhaps those on W 94 (fig. 39) and W 85 (fig. 42). There is, however, a very large class of triangular stamps related to these where the base of the triangle is open, as on that used by

[1] Not illustrated in the Lackford report; but see Myres 1969, fig. 51, 2987.

[2] Information from Dr. R. I. Page to whom I am greatly indebted for help on this difficult subject. He is in no way responsible for any views expressed in this part of the report.

[3] Myres 1969, fig. 51, 718.

[4] Now at the Society of Antiquaries: Myres 1969, fig. 51, 1038.

[5] Westerwanna 796 (Zimmer-Linnfeld *et al.* 1960).

[6] Waller 1959, Tafel 16 Gr. 24.

[7] It is always used on A 3 this way up, not upside down as drawn on fig. 38.

Potter II on X 36, X 37, N 64 (figs. 49 and 50), or where the outline is notched, as on that used by Potter III on M 23(a) or P 16 (fig. 51), or otherwise elaborated. For these it would be unwise to claim a runic significance,[1] especially as they are frequently impressed to point indifferently in any direction. This is the case with the two such stamps used by the E 8, R 9/10 Potter (fig. 44), which are much closer than most of this class to the simple form of the 'ᚦ' rune. It would certainly be hazardous to think of any of the numerous cross motifs used on stamps in terms of the 'ᚷ' rune, for the device is far too common to be other than simple decoration in the great majority of cases. If they have any deeper significance it is more likely to be related to that of the star and rosette motifs which have a long history in the mythology of northern Europe as solar symbols, and appear on the Caistor pottery also in a wide variety of forms.

Undecorated Pottery

Caistor, like most English cemeteries of this period, has produced a considerable quantity of undecorated pottery (figs. 24–31). Some of the more distinctive types among these plain wares, such as the Anglian globular forms (figs. 24–5) and the hollow-necked group of northern antecedents (fig. 28), have already been discussed (pp. 46, 50), as have also the few pieces such as Y 15 and M 46 that seem to show the influence of Roman or sub-Roman models (fig. 33). It remains to say something of the remainder.

Most of this is indistinguishable from the range of domestic cook-pots which are found in quantity, and generally in fragments, among the domestic rubbish of Anglo-Saxon occupation sites. The forms are often irregular and of low technical competence, the fabrics being crude and rough. One should not expect to obtain much information, either typological or chronological, from such simple cook-pot types as K 6(b), N 33, N 90, N 91, Y 14, or Y 32 (fig. 24), which doubtless had a long life and were intended to serve a variety of unchanging household needs. K 6(b), for example, whatever its original purpose, may well have ended up as a lid for K 6(a) (fig. 32), itself a cook-pot of a different kind. N 90 and N 91 were closely associated in the ground with N 89 (fig. 24), a plain globular urn of early Anglian type, and may be contemporary with it.[2] Few of these simple cook-pots contained any associated objects, a fact which supports the probability that the use of domestic pots as cinerary urns was more prevalent among the poorer members of the community than among those whose status might demand something more distinctive as a container. One or two vessels of domestic character from the cemetery may not have served any funerary purpose at all, since they neither contained burnt bones, nor were associated with inhumations; this was the case with N 33 (fig. 24) and N 13 (fig. 31). They may have been left on the site after use in a funeral ritual or meal, or as containers for offerings.

Some of the plain urns can be roughly grouped in categories which fall between these crude domestic wares and the more distinctive types discussed on pp. 46, 50. Such, for example, are the broad-shouldered forms on figs. 26 and 27, M 35, N 5, X 34. The type occurs in Schleswig: an example from Borgstedt[3] contained objects datable to the end of the fifth century. It has been noted also in this country, as at Elkington, Lincs., and Lack-

---

[1] These were termed 'slot' stamps by F. R. M. who thought that they might represent the spoor of a hooved animal.

[2] N 90 is in fact very similar to a fourth-century pot from Nybølle, Fünen: Albrectsen 1968, Tavle 130a.

[3] Genrich 1954, Tafel 7D.

ford, Suffolk, the latter with an early sixth-century cruciform brooch.[1] M 35 contained iron tweezers and part of a comb, which are consistent with this dating. Related to this hump-shouldered type are the more simple shouldered urns on figs. 29 and 30, some of which (X 18, Y 46) are approaching the biconical contour. Of the shouldered urns N 45 (fig. 29) contained the remains of a cruciform brooch of the early sixth century while G 1 (fig. 29) was intrusive, disturbing a previous cremation, and thus not likely to be early. No others are closely datable, and the forms are of such common occurrence that there is no need to list parallels from other English or continental cemeteries.

Of the undecorated bowls not already discussed perhaps the most interesting are N 55 and X 5 (fig. 29) whose straight rims sloping inwards recall a type known in Holstein in the late fourth and early fifth centuries.[2] It also occurs in Fünen, apparently in the fourth century.[3] It would thus appear from the continental parallels that these urns must be placed among the earlier groups of Caistor pottery.

Among the latest should probably be placed N 41(b) and X 30 (fig. 31). The cylindrical neck, bulging slightly in the middle, of N 41(b) was unique at Caistor, as was its bright brown fabric. Both may owe something to continental fashions in wheel-made pottery, but exact parallels are hard to find.[4] The profile of X 30 is not far removed from that of the tall-necked round-bottomed pottery that is characteristic of early seventh-century cemeteries.[5] The excavator's note on this pot suggests that there may have been more of these at Caistor than the surviving material suggests;[6] if so they would be among the last types of urns likely to have been in use there before cremation was finally abandoned as a burial rite.

Vessels with Pierced and Solid Lugs

Wide-mouthed cook-pots with three horizontally pierced lug-handles are a common feature of Anglo-Saxon cemeteries both in England and on the Continent. The type derives from the so-called *Dreiknubbentopf* characteristic of the proto-Saxon culture of Holstein in the second and third centuries A.D.[7] Examples with a well-moulded footring, very like the Caistor piece K 6(a) (fig. 32), have been published from Westerwanna; a closer parallel from this country is that from Kempston, Beds.:[8] they do not seem to be closely datable. An example from an inhumation burial at Abingdon, Berks., was accompanied by two gilt-bronze button brooches, and also, as in the case of K 6(a), by a wide-mouthed round-bottomed cook-pot, which may have served it as a lid.[9] The small models of this type with three pierced or solid bosses and a footring, found in N 39 (fig. 3) and N 71 (fig. 32), are worthy of note.

The more biconical form without footstand, having three pierced lugs set on or near the carination, is less common in England. The damaged Caistor example X 15 (fig. 32) may

[1] Myres 1969, fig. 4, where the details are given.

[2] e.g. Genrich 1954, 28, no. 21 from Hammoor.

[3] Albrectsen 1968, Tavle 124d from Fravdegård, datable between 325 and 400, is very like N 55; Tavle 134e from Næsby is closer to X 5, but not closely datable.

[4] An English parallel to the neck and rim is Sancton 59 (Hull Museum). For the form compare a wheel-made pot from Rathewitz Gr. 14; for the swollen neck one from Reppichau, both apparently late sixth century: Schmidt 1961, Abb. 53a and b. It could be a simplified version of

a rilled neck, as on the pot from Westheim Gr. 1 of the seventh century (Dannheimer 1962, Tafel 33c).

[5] e.g. Shudy Camps (Lethbridge 1936, pl. 1, Graves 18 and 25).

[6] F. R. M. wrote: 'Judging from fragments this type of pot was not uncommon in the cemetery, but this is the only restorable one that I have found.'   [7] Tischler 1937, 17.

[8] Tischler 1954b, 65, Abb. 16. The Kempston piece (B.M. 91.6–24.30) is illustrated in Myres 1969, fig. 12, 1977.

[9] Leeds and Harden 1936, 40, B 51, and fig. 6.

be compared with one from Beringstedt, Holstein, which contained a late fourth-century brooch.[1] A less angular example from Lackford was apparently found in association with pots of the second half of the sixth century.[2] The type evidently had a long life and there is no evidence to date X 15 within these limits.

In addition to vessels of the cook-pot type with three lugs pierced for suspension there are a number of undecorated vessels with three solid lugs (fig. 32). Most of these are shouldered bowls with upright or only slightly everted rims (E 6, N 26, N 48, N 65, P 54, Y 42) and they form at Caistor a distinctive group, not easy to parallel from other English cemeteries.[3] The purpose of the three small solid bosses is no doubt primarily practical (to facilitate suspension by a cord) and not decorative, and to that extent they should be classed rather with the cook-pots with pierced lugs than with the main series of shoulder-boss urns.[4] But the shoulder-boss bowl with upright rim, often with numerous small solid bosses, is not uncommon in East Holstein from the middle of the fourth century onwards,[5] and the Caistor type of E 6, N 65, etc., could well have arisen by a drastic simplification of this form under influence from the three-knobbed cook-pot. Only one of the Caistor knobbed bowls contained grave goods (N 48, with part of a comb, and three fused beads), though M 12(a), a plain round-shouldered urn with three applied knobs now lost (fig. 32), which is somewhat similar to a Dutch urn from Rijnsburg, now at Leiden, may have contained a pair of iron shears and a knife. There is not enough evidence to date any of these vessels with precision.

Undecorated Shoulder-boss Urns (fig. 31)

Like most English cemeteries Caistor produced a number of urns decorated with shoulder-bosses only. These conform to the usual shoulder-boss forms, whether bowls (P 8), biconical types (M 12(b)), or shouldered jars (A 1). There is also one example (N 99) of a large wide bowl with tall flaring lip, which can be paralleled from Loveden Hill, Lincs.,[6] and also from Anderlecht in Belgium. A 1, P 8, and M 12(b) all contained grave goods and P 8, which had five glass beads and part of some bronze objects, also had two pecked holes of the 'open window' type, one in the bottom and one in the lower part of the side.[7]

These may all be taken as signs of fairly early date. Jankuhn is quoted by Lethbridge[8] as stating that urns of this sort are 'typical of the Angles of Schleswig', and that one of biconical form from Lackford, not unlike M 12(b), 'might have been found in Angeln'. There is, however, little evidence to show how long the fashion for plain shoulder-boss urns may have persisted in England. It may well cover the same range of time as the bossed panel style, of which it is the undecorated equivalent. Most of the Saxon pottery from Anderlecht, which produced a close parallel to N 99, is of the sixth century or later.[9]

[1] Genrich 1954, Tafel 1D. Illington 147 c is comparable to X 15.   [2] Lethbridge 1951, fig. 19, 50. 95 A, and p. 19.

[3] A fragmentary urn from Elkington (15, not illustrated in the report) may have been of this kind, but it seems to have had at least four solid applied bosses.

[4] The distinction is interestingly illustrated by a hybrid example from Loveden Hill NE 23. This is similar in form to Caistor E 6 or N 65 but instead of the usual three solid bosses has four solid bosses and one hollow one, thus approximating both in number of bosses and in their technique to the normal shoulder-boss urn.

[5] Late fourth- or early fifth-century examples from Hammoor are illustrated by Genrich 1954, Tafeln 15A and 16B; and from Borgstedt, Tafel 4E.   [6] Urn NE 6.

[7] It may be only a coincidence that Elkington 71, another undecorated shoulder-boss urn with an 'open window' in the side, also contained fused beads: but such coincidences are worth noting (Webster and Myres 1951, 41, fig. 12. 71).

[8] Lethbridge 1951, 20.

[9] Cumont 1908, 301: he does not illustrate the vessel similar to N 99.

Cremations of Children

The following note is based on a summary analysis made by F. R. M. of information about the child cremations at Caistor.

Twenty-six urns certainly contained the cremated remains of children,[1] recognizable either from the nature of the bone (especially skull) fragments or (in thirteen cases) from the presence of milk teeth. In two cases (E 5, X 11) the urns, both large, contained adult remains as well. Of the twenty-four which contained children only the height ranged from 7·5 to 3·5 in. (19·0 to 8·9 cm.), with an average of 5·2 in. (13·2 cm.). Since this is very much below the normal size for Anglo-Saxon cremation urns, it seems clear that small urns were very often used for child cremations. Five of the twenty-four urns were undecorated, a proportion considerably below that for the cemetery as a whole, and not less than sixteen contained grave goods, about twice the average for the cemetery; the objects included four manicure sets (or parts of sets), four bone combs (or parts of them), and a few things, such as a translucent pebble, pieces of iron pyrites, or the base of a Samian ware cup, which might have been included as toys.

If it can be assumed that the child cremations are spaced in the same proportion as the adult cremations over the whole period in which cremation was in use at Caistor, the higher proportion both of decorated urns and of associated objects suggests that more care on the average was taken over the burial of children than of adults. It may be that the ritual appropriate to child funerals remained conservative at a time when the belief in its value to adults (e.g. the deposit of grave goods with the ashes) was breaking down. Another explanation is that it was only the children of well-to-do, and therefore conservative, families that were accorded the distinction of individual urn burial at all. Families too poor or too casual to afford a decorated urn or grave goods for adult burials may not have spared even a plain household pot for the cremated bones of their children. Such deposits, if buried without a container, or in a perishable container such as a bag or basket, would very easily disappear or escape notice in the disturbed soil of the cemetery.

---

[1] Dr. Wells has identified a further four cases, but these do not affect the conclusions given here. Two of them (N 34 and N 45) also contained adult bones, and may represent joint cremations of mother and child. See pp. 121–2.

SUMMARY LIST OF ASSOCIATED URNS

By J. N. L. Myres

F. R. M. was fully conscious of the need to record whenever possible any significant associations between two or more urns that he noticed in the course of his excavations. In a number of cases he illustrated such associations with pencil sketches, and the best of these are here reproduced (pls. XII–XV). The disturbed condition of the ground (see p. 3) made the interpretation of such relationships unusually difficult, and it was not always clear whether the juxtaposition was evidence for contemporary or successive burial. But in a number of instances his record leaves little room for doubt and, in view of the importance of these associations for determining the relative chronology of the different types of pottery in the cemetery, the more significant are here summarized in tabular form. For convenience of reference they have been grouped under five headings as follows:—

A are 'Encisted groups', whose contemporary burial is made certain by their enclosure within a surround of large flints or tiles, or by their being jointly covered by a spread of such materials clearly related to them.

B are groups that are probably contemporary, although not so enclosed or covered.

C are instances where one burial overlies or has disturbed another in such a way as to make it reasonably certain that a lapse of time separated the two deposits.

D are cases in which the remains of two or more urns are so intermingled as to make it probable that one has disturbed another, although it may be uncertain which is the earlier.

E are what F. R. M. termed 'grave-diggers' dumps', assemblages of broken urns probably resulting from disturbance and reburial, either to make way for a later urn, or more probably for one of the inhumation graves that are a feature of the final period of the cemetery's use. Such assemblages are of course only of chronological significance to the extent that, while they may comprise urns of various dates, these must all be earlier than the burial that caused their disturbance.

In a few cases it may not be certain in which of these categories an associated group of urns should be placed, and occasionally a group may include elements that require mention under more than one heading, as when, for example, an encisted group had disturbed a previous cremation. Details of all these, and of some other less certain associations, can be found in the Inventory. Page references are given in the Table to other parts of this report where the significance of some of them is further discussed.

A. Encisted groups

E 7, E 8, E 10, E 11, E 12 (see pp. 59–61 and C below).

F 1, F 2.

N 52, N 53 (see pp. 45–6).

P 17, P 18.

Y 9, Y 10, Y 11(a), Y 11(b), Y 12 (see pl. XVb, p. 56 and C below).

B. Other probably contemporary groups

N 1, N 2, N 3, N 4. See pl. XIVa and p. 50.

N 16, N 17, and an unnumbered urn (see pl. XIVb and p. 52).

N 43, N 44.

N 58, N 59, N 60.

N 88, N 89, N 90, N 91 (see p. 68).

P 39, P 40.

X 23, X 24 (but see pp. 47, 49).

X 27(a), X 27(b).

Y 13, Y 14, Y 15, Y 16.

Y 18, Y 19, Y 20, Y 21 (see pp. 56–7).

Y 40, Y 41 (see p. 45).

C. Deposits separated by a lapse of time

1. *One urn above another*

M 6, and probably M 10, overlay M 11 (see p. 51).

M 18 overlay M 19 (see pp. 46, 58).

M 47 (with Group II cruciform brooch) overlay M 46 (see p. 57).

M 49(a) overlay M 48(a) and M 48(b) (see pp. 48–9, 53).

X 1 overlay X 2 (see pl. XII*c* and p. 47).

X 3 overlay X 4 (see p. 56).

Y 5 overlay Y 4 (see pl. XII*a* and pp. 74–6).

2. *One urn intrusive upon another*

The E 7 group (see *A* above) disturbed an un-numbered urn (see pp. 59–61).

G 1 intrusive upon G 2 (see p. 69).

G 3 and G 4 (both by Potter II) intrusive upon G 5 (with early brooch) (see p. 63).

M 3(b) crushed M 3(a).

M 15 (by Potter IV) probably intrusive upon several unnumbered urns (see p. 57).

M 16(a) (by Potter I) probably broke up M 16(b) (see p. 57).

N 81(a) crushed N 81 (see p. 58).

P 33 (by Potter III) cut away part of P 32 (see p. 63).

X 12 (by Potter I) probably intrusive upon X 13 and possibly X 13(b), (c) and (d) (see p. 57).

X 15 apparently intrusive upon X 14 and perhaps other urns.

The Y 9 group (see *A* above) probably disturbed Y 11(c) and (d) (see pl. XV*b* and p. 56).

3. *Urns damaged by Inhumation Graves*, other than 'Grave-diggers' dumps' (see *E* below)

K 7 broken by Grave 6.

N 87 cut in half by Grave 35.

Z 4 broken by Grave 7 (see p. 53).

D. Disturbed groups possibly of several dates

M 26, M 27, M 28 (see pp. 49, 55).

M 44(a), M 44(b) (see p. 52).

M 54, M 55 (see p. 47).

X 9(a) (= W 92), X 9(b)–(f).

E. 'Grave-diggers' dumps'

M 21 possibly disturbed and reburied by diggers of Grave 20.

M 22(a), M 22(b).

M 24(a), (b), (c) possibly a dump from Grave 24.

M 29, M 31, M 32 (both by Potter III), M 33.

N 5, N 7 disturbed and reburied by diggers of Grave 30: see also N 11.

N 54 probably disturbed by, and reburied in, Grave 32.

N 62 and a quantity of broken sherds possibly a dump from Grave 38.

P 8(a), (b), (c) and other broken sherds.

P 36(a)–(f).

X 18, X 19, X 36, X 37 (both by Potter II) possibly a dump from Grave 17.

ROMAN POTTERY USED FOR ANGLO-SAXON CREMATIONS

By T. H. McK. Clough and J. N. L. Myres

SIX Roman coarse pottery vessels are described in the Inventory as having been found in the cemetery (N 6, P 43, P 48, Y 4 (fig. 33), N 72, and P 45 (fig. 58)). All of these except P 45 and N 72 are known to have contained cremations. P 45 was found badly broken, but all the surviving fragments were close together and the pot is nearly complete;[1] no burnt bones were found in association with the sherds and it is therefore uncertain whether this pot was used as a cremation urn, even though it was found not far from P 43 and P 48. F. R. M. suggested that it might have come from the burnt Roman building (Structure D) close to which it was found. The other pot, N 72, was found complete and appeared to contain nothing but earth until closer examination revealed a few minute fragments of bone (nowhere said to be burnt) which suggested to F. R. M. that the pot could possibly have contained the remains of a very young infant. Since the bones do not survive, it is not possible to check this and N 72 is also best left aside as unlikely to have contained a cremation.

It must be decided whether the four pots which did contain burnt bones represent random cremations of Roman origin or Anglo-Saxon cremations placed in Roman pots. One important piece of evidence here is that of P 43, which contained with the cremated bones an unburnt fragment of a bone comb analogous with those accompanying undoubted Anglo-Saxon burials (pp. 91–6). The perforation of a small hole through the base of the pot reflects an occasional Anglo-Saxon practice found elsewhere in this and other cemeteries. The other three Roman pots, N 6, P 48, and Y 4, all contained burnt bones without any accompanying objects.

For the date of these burials the most significant point is that P 43, P 45, and P 48 were all buried in the loam layer which, as indicated above (pp. 19, 30), represents the result of clearing and levelling the site after it had gone out of use as a habitation area early in the third century. These three burials cannot therefore be earlier than the third century. Cremation as a burial rite had fallen out of fashion with most of the Romanized population by this date, and this strengthens the case for regarding them as an integral part of the Anglo-Saxon cemetery.

They are moreover placed in close association with Anglo-Saxon cremation urns. Both P 43 and the Anglo-Saxon P 54 stood on the floor of Structure D, while two more Anglo-Saxon pots, P 42 and P 44, were found in holes dug through or into the floor (see p. 20). N 6 was found near Structure M in the southern part of the cemetery; P 48 was close to Structure D; and Y 4 was found north-west of Structure B with the Anglo-Saxon Y 5 nearly above it and separated from it by three inches of earth (pl. XIIa). It is thus stratigraphically possible that Y 4, which is also typologically different from the other Roman cremation pots, could have been buried in the Roman period since it certainly antedates Y 5, which is probably of

[1] Cf. Atkinson's Type S 19 (Atkinson 1937, 217).

the fifth century. But the character of the site and the recorded information leave one with the impression that it also forms part of the Anglo-Saxon cemetery.

Another cremation without grave goods but in a Roman pot deserves mention. This does not come from the cemetery itself, but from the berm outside the south wall of the Roman town, close to bastion 3; it was found during Professor Atkinson's excavations in 1934 (Inventory, p. 207). Since this site lay within an inhabited *insula* before the construction of the town wall, the insertion of a cremation here before the town was remodelled to exclude this occupied area is most unlikely. On the other hand numerous instances could be quoted of Anglo-Saxon cremation burials being found immediately outside the walls of Romano-British towns. At Caistor the defences visible today were constructed either in the mid-third century with the addition of bastions in the fourth century, or else in a single building phase at the later date (p. 17, note 5). In either case one can reasonably interpret this particular burial as a further instance of the use of Roman pots for funerary purposes by the Anglo-Saxon inhabitants, especially as its general character is similar in type to P 43 and P 48. It may be mentioned that there is in Norwich Castle Museum (accession number 121.944) another complete jar of almost identical form and fabric which must be seen as a contemporary product; this is also reported to have been found at Caistor, although no further details about its findspot or any contents it may have held are recorded.

If, therefore, it can be taken as fairly certain that, with the possible exception of Y 4, these cremations in Roman pots took place no earlier than the third century and must be regarded as an integral part of the Anglo-Saxon cemetery, it remains to inquire whether any indication of their date can be obtained from an examination of the pots themselves.[1] Unfortunately the scarcity of securely dated Roman coarse pottery in Norfolk, especially of vessels certainly attributable to the third century or later, makes this a somewhat inconclusive inquiry. It is, however, immediately apparent that, again with the exception of Y 4, these pots, including that from the berm of the south wall, form a closely homogeneous group; P 43, P 48, and the south berm pot in particular are all jars with short necks, swollen and everted but not undercut rims, rounded profiles with no offset between neck and sloping shoulder, and slightly angled bases.

Jars of this general type have been published from the village site at Needham, Norfolk, and are there dated in the first half of the second century.[2] But perhaps the closest parallels are to be found at Caistor itself, where the pottery kilns underlying Building 4 produced a quantity of jars of much the same kind though perhaps typologically rather earlier. These kilns were dated in the first half of the second century by Atkinson, and had gone out of use after serving as a rubbish tip, some time before Building 4 was put up in the third century.[3]

It is of some interest that these kilns underlay Building 4 for this structure survived, as has been noted above (pp. 33-4), to become the scene of some gruesome activity at the very end of the Roman period. If these cremation pots are all as early as the second century, even the later part of it, some explanation must be found for their use in an Anglo-Saxon context.

---

[1] We are greatly indebted to Mr. Hugh Thompson for assistance in this part of the discussion. He is in no way responsible for our conclusions.

[2] Frere and Clarke 1945; P 43 is quite close to fig. 4. 51.

[3] Atkinson 1932; P 43 is not unlike pl. VIII B2: P 48 is nearer pl. VIII C4. But the wares from these kilns seem typologically earlier: they have more pronounced shoulders and for the most part a definite offset between neck and shoulder, giving a more elegant profile than our pieces.

It is most natural to suppose that they came from a single source, a deposit of complete pots of second-century date that came to light during the overlap between the Roman and Anglo-Saxon control of *Venta Icenorum*. Now one of the kilns underlying Building 4 contained a deposit of exactly this kind. It had apparently collapsed during firing and was abandoned while still full of its last load of coarse ware jars. Professor Atkinson stated that he was able to excavate only those kilns in this area that he encountered in the actual course of clearing Building 4: he hinted that it was quite likely that there were others of the same period in its immediate vicinity.[1] Moreover, he noted the presence of later rubbish pits that penetrated to the level of the kilns: what more likely than that the diggers of one such pit may have encountered another collapsed kiln and so revealed a welcome cache of serviceable second-century pottery, some of which found its way into the hands of undertakers supplying the needs of the newly established barbarian cremation cemetery?

Some such explanation is required on the assumption that the cemetery pots are really a century or more older than the earliest date at which they are likely to have been used for Anglo-Saxon cremations. It has the additional attraction of hinting at a possible link between the earlier users of the cemetery and exactly that part of *Venta Icenorum* which is known to have been still in some kind of occupation towards the end of the fourth century and has produced several of the bits of belt fittings that suggest the presence of barbarian mercenaries at that time. But in the absence of securely dated types of Roman coarse pottery in this area later than the second century, it cannot be taken as certain that the cemetery pots are necessarily as early as that. It has already been noted that their profiles are slacker and less sharply detailed than those of that date from the Caistor kilns. If it should turn out that they belong rather to the third or even the early fourth century, they would be much nearer in date to the earliest days of the cemetery's use: indeed they could then become an important piece of evidence for the date of its beginning.

Y 4 is a different case from the other Roman pots used in the cemetery. Not only is it stratigraphically possible that its burial antedates the inception of the cemetery's use, for it directly underlay an Anglo-Saxon urn Y 5 that is probably of fifth-century date, but its form is quite different from the others. Local second-century parallels both for its form and its decoration can be adduced from Grimstone End, Pakenham, Suffolk,[2] Needham, and from Caistor itself,[3] but it could be argued that its sharply offset and widely everted rim is closer to standard fourth-century cavetto rim types.[4]

---

[1] Atkinson 1932, 39. In 1822 another Roman kiln still containing its last load of pots was found on the site of the Markshall cemetery, which suggests another possible source of supply: see p. 234. As these pots have not survived it is of course impossible to date the kiln.

[2] Brown *et al.* 1955, fig. 26. 8 (first quarter of second century).

[3] Frere and Clarke 1945, fig. 3. 34 (Trajan/Hadrian); and Atkinson 1937, 218 and S 30 (first half of second century).

[4] As, e.g., Kenyon 1948, fig. 26. 20, or Wheeler and Wheeler 1932, fig. 26. 34. But neither of these is local, and the rim of Y 4 does not completely oversail the shoulder as occurs with many late fourth-century examples.

THE GRAVE GOODS FROM THE CREMATIONS

By Barbara Green

INTRODUCTION

GRAVE goods are recorded from 155 of the Caistor urns, that is from about 50 per cent of the more or less complete urns. An iron knife (No. 11) and a piece of fused bronze (No. 9) are recorded from an unurned cremation while a further eleven objects, all almost certainly from broken-up urns, were preserved by F. R. M. It is difficult to be certain if this represents a true percentage. The nature of the site, the condition of many of the urns, and the method of recovering the grave goods suggest that it may be too low.

F. R. M. emptied most of his urns in the field and sorted out the grave goods there, usually throwing away immediately the rest of the contents of each urn (see p. 4). It is quite possible that a number of small objects were lost in this process. It is a common experience that material can still be recovered after several careful sievings of an urn's contents in the laboratory. Moreover, most of the urns were more or less broken or collapsed when found and it is notoriously difficult in such cases to be certain either that all associated objects are recovered or that those that are recovered are genuine associations. This is not to denigrate F. R. M.'s achievement. He retained all he found and was careful to keep together as a single group the urn and its associated grave goods. Unfortunately, with a few notable exceptions, this has not been a common practice in the older excavations of Anglo-Saxon cemeteries, as is obvious from the limited number of references quoted in the following pages.

In fact, F. R. M.'s care in preserving all objects which he recorded as found in urns has led to problems. He did not keep the cremated human bones nor did he normally record whether the grave goods were found under, in, or above the bone mass. The amount of cremated bones can vary very much from urn to urn, as does the amount of soil which gets into an urn. A number of the Caistor urns were encisted (see p. 72) or had had a flint or tile placed over the mouth which would have prevented the entry of much soil. They were, moreover, buried in an abandoned Roman domestic site. It is quite possible that certain objects, for example iron nails, were not grave goods but had fallen into the urns from the surrounding soil. Some Roman objects, however, do seem to be deliberate inclusions, for example the piece of Samian cup from P 34 and the coin, perforated for suspension, from Y 40. The large translucent pebbles (e.g. in N 71) could have come from the surrounding glacial deposits and may also be accidental inclusions. Such items are rarely recorded from Anglo-Saxon urns, but it is difficult to be certain if this is due to less meticulous recording. If F. R. M. had noted the presence of these items in or under the bone mass then their presence in the urn would probably be the result of a deliberate act. But even this is by no means certain; we do not know where the bodies were burnt, or how carefully the ashes and grave goods were sorted and placed in the urn. Items possibly from earlier cremations could have been scraped up from the pyre site with the ashes and genuinely associated objects. All doubtful associations of this kind are noted as such in the Inventory, in the hope that this may be a useful guide to excavators in recording the contents of other cremation cemeteries. Other associations are noted as doubtful when the pieces could have come from one of several urns.

The grave goods are described in detail in the Inventory, but their distribution and associations are tabulated on pp. 80–4. The commonest objects are knives, shears, tweezers, combs, and beads. Brooches, scrap bronze, glass, ivory bag rings, gaming pieces, dress rings, buckles, a wrist clasp, a bronze needle, bone casket fittings, spindle whorls, and miniature urns are also recorded. Most of these categories of object are discussed separately below. A number of unidentifiable pieces of iron and bronze were also found and have been noted in the chart.

It is uncertain how many urns contained animal bones. F. R. M. did not recognize any until November 1936.[1] Except for a fragment of bird bone recorded from A 3, the earliest noted is in M 47. In all they have been recorded with seventeen urns. It is not certain how many of these records refer to bones actually found inside the urn. F. R. M. did count as associations bones which in some instances were outside the vessel.[2] Because of the disturbed condition of the site it is difficult to be certain how good an association such a find represents.

Animal bones are known from inhumation graves,[3] but they have only rarely been recorded from cremations.[4] This may well be due to poor recording rather than to genuine absence, as the cremated bones have very rarely been preserved. Most of the animal bones show signs of having been burned and are thus not readily distinguishable. Only if the animal bones were distinctive, e.g. bird bones, are they likely to have been recorded.

In many instances the objects found in the urns are not only fragmentary but are also incomplete. This may in part be due to the way F. R. M. collected the material, but even when grave goods have been removed from urns under ideal conditions many of the objects are found to be both broken and incomplete. Lethbridge has suggested that there may be some magical reason for this in the case of combs[5] but such an explanation is difficult to accept for objects such as brooches, tweezers, shears, or knives. Combs, though often fragmentary, are not always deliberately broken, e.g. E 13B.

The grave goods can be divided into two groups—those that show signs of burning and those that are unburned. It is impossible to be certain in the case of iron objects if they have been burned or not, but some of the bronze, bone, and glass objects do show signs of burning. Most of these, such as beads and brooches, are likely to have been on the body at the time it was burned, and their burnt state suggests that the dead were normally cremated in their clothes. In fact this explanation probably accounts for the signs of burning on all those objects which do show it.

It has been noted above how the amount of cremated bone varies from urn to urn both at Caistor and elsewhere. Presumably the bones and remains of objects worn on the body were collected and placed in an urn when the fire had died down. The pieces of bone vary in size very considerably from urn to urn and it is quite probable that, especially when cremation had not been very thorough, large pieces were broken up so that they could more conveniently be placed in the urn. If only a token quantity of bone was put in an urn, only

---

[1] See footnote, p. 119.
[2] Ibid.
[3] e.g. Burwell, Lethbridge 1931.

[4] e.g. Castle Acre, Norf., Housman 1895, 103; Sutton Hoo, Barrow No. 3, Green 1963.
[5] Lethbridge 1951, 12–13.

part of the grave goods on the body at the time of the fire might be included. This may help to account for the incompleteness of some of the items, for instance the occurrence of brooch pins without their brooches (e.g. in A 3). But some of the apparently unburnt objects, especially combs, had certainly been deliberately broken and were already incomplete when put in the urn. Did the Anglo-Saxon undertakers keep a stock of old, broken objects ready to put into a pot or did members of the family produce unwanted and broken trifles from the house for inclusion?

There is another problem which only the careful excavation and recording of cremation cemeteries can solve. If only a part of a burnt body and its personal possessions were placed in an urn, what happened to the rest? Were the unburied remains distributed to the four winds, or were they left on the site of the funeral pyre to become associated perhaps with the remains of subsequent cremations on the same site? In view of such possibilities it would be unwise to assume that all the objects associated with a cremation are necessarily contemporary.

A comparison of the cremation grave goods with those found in inhumation graves shows that many of the same items were included in both types of burial, for instance brooches, beads, ivory rings, buckles, spindle whorls, sheet bronze (if the identification suggested on p. 112 is correct), and tweezers. Many of these are items indicative of women's burials if found with inhumations. The normal absence from cremations of distinctively male objects such as spears, shield bosses, or swords has been noted before.[1] But this absence may be simply because such items can only rarely be fitted into burial urns. The possibility that objects burnt with one body could find their way into the urn of another suggests that great care should be taken in guessing the sex of any burial from such associations. However, there are some instances where the number of objects makes such a suggestion acceptable.

At Caistor as elsewhere a higher proportion of the earlier urns (i.e. fifth and early sixth century) contain grave goods than do the later. Some of the very earliest urns, e.g. E 5 and N 52 (fig. 1) and E 14 (fig. 2), large Saxon vessels dated on continental parallels to the late fourth or opening years of the fifth century, and N 14 (fig. 4), an Anglian corrugated urn of comparable date, contain objects most appropriate to women, suggesting that the earliest Germanic settlers brought their women with them.

The contents of E 14 are of additional interest in that some of the grave goods show signs of the fire (the comb fragments Bi and the beads C) while the others do not. Surprisingly, the second group includes a portion of another comb (Bii) and a bronze expanding ring (E). Admittedly not all the beads (C) are badly affected by the fire, and it is possible that some fell between an arm and the side of the body and were thus to some extent protected. However, the state of the comb fragment (Bii) and the ring (E) does suggest that some additional objects were placed with the remains after their cremation.

Some of the grave goods appear to be more commonly associated with cremations than inhumations, such as combs, and manicure sets of knife, shears, and tweezers. It will be seen from the Table that the majority of the manicure sets occur in urns of Anglian origin. It is quite possible that they indicate male burials. Some other less obvious associations can also be seen from the Table.

[1] Leeds 1936, 32; Myres 1969, 123.

Abbreviations used in the Table of Grave Goods

A	Anglian urns of various types
ad or a.d.	association doubtful
A/S	Anglian/Saxon hybrid urns
bz	bronze
F	present, fired
frag.	fragment
HN	urns with hollow necks and carinated shoulders
m	missing
S	Saxon urns of various types
X	present, not definitely fired
?	identification uncertain

This Table shows the associations of the urns found with grave goods at Caistor-by-Norwich. Only four groups of urns have been specified under the heading 'Urn Type': pots which have distinctively Anglian features (plain globular urns, and those with corrugated or bossed and corrugated decoration, etc.); pots which have Saxon features (*Buckelurnen*, urns decorated with *stehende Bogen*, etc.); pots with hollow necks and carinated shoulders; and a few which are distinctive Anglian/Saxon hybrids. All illustration numbers refer to figs. unless otherwise stated.

Urn number	Urn type	Urn illustration	Grave goods illustrations	Manicure sets			Comb	Brooch	Brooch pin	Beads	Glass	Gaming piece	Sheet bronze	Spindle whorl	Ivory ring	Buckle	Animal bone	Miscellaneous
				Shears	Knife	Tweezers												
A 1	—	31	—															Iron object, m; burnt clay, m
A 3	—	38	38						X							F		
A 4	HN	28	28	X														Iron nail
A 8	S	17	17				X		F									
A 9	A	25	25	X	?													
A 12	—	10	10					X										
D 1	—	30	—															
D 3	—	m	59										X					Iron nail a.d.
D 5	—	—	59				X											
D 7	—	38	38										X					
D 8	?A	11	11	X	X													Pebble a.d.
D 9	—	41	41	—X—			X											Iron clip?
D 10	—	m	59				X											
D 11	—	19	19												X			
E 1	—	—	59				F											
E 3	—	23	—															Comb case F
E 4	?A	18	18										X					bz frag. F a.d.
E 5	S	1	1		m	X			F									
E 9	A	8	8		X													
E 13	S	16	16				X											
E 14	S	2	2				X F	X	F									Silver ring; Iron ring
E 15	—	35	35		X				F									
E 16	A	8	8		X													
E 19	—	—	59						F	X								Cone beaker (pl. XIXa)
E 20	?A	10	10	X										F				
F 4	—	m	59															bz wrist clasp a.d.

Urn number	Urn type	Urn illustration	Grave goods illustrations	Shears	Knife	Tweezers	Comb	Brooch	Brooch pin	Beads	Glass	Gaming piece	Sheet bronze	Spindle whorl	Ivory ring	Buckle	Animal bone	Miscellaneous
G 5	—	m	59					F										
H 1	?A	35	35	X	X	?												
K 1	—	m	59															Iron frag.
K 5	A	7	7						F									
K 7	S	3	3							X								
M 7	—	—	—														F	
M 8	A	4	4	X	?	X												Iron frags. m
M 9	—	21	21						F									
M 11	A/S	15	15	X	?	X												
M 12 a or b	—	32)31/	59	X	?													
M 13	—	14	59				Fad ad											
M 17	—	m	59	X													F	
M 19	—	25	—														F	
M 22 a or b	—	20)23/	59					X		—F—								
M 28	—	17	59				Fad											
M 31	—	52	52	X														
M 32	—	52	52	X	X	X												
M 33	—	22	59				mad	Fad										
M 35	?A	26	26		X	X	X											
M 39	—	14	14			X												
M 41	A	7	7					?F										
M 42	—	18	18		?			F		—F—								
M 43	A	25	25	?	X	X												
M 44 a or b	—	10)21/	59	X														
M 47	—	34	34					F									F	
M 49 a	—	14	14							F		F						
M 51	A	7	7	X	X	X												
M 52	A	8	8	X	X													
M 53	HN	28	28				X											
M 57	—	52	52									X F						
N 1	—	41	—														F	
N 10	—	13	13					F		F	F							bz ring; astragalus, F.
N 12	A	7	7	X	X	X												Iron ring (?from manicure set)
N 14	A	4	4							F							F	Clay ring
N 15	A/S	3	3							X								
N 16	—	13	—	m	m	m												
N 17	—	13	13							X								
N 18	A	25	25	X	?	X												
N 19	A/S	3	3							X							F	
N 22	A	8	8							F								
N 23	A	26	26		X											X		
N 25	—	18	—														m	
N 28	—	42	59				ad											
N 30	A	9	9	?	X													

Urn Number	Urn type	Urn illustration	Grave goods illustrations	Manicure sets			Comb	Brooch	Brooch pin	Beads	Glass	Gaming piece	Sheet bronze	Spindle whorl	Ivory ring	Buckle	Animal bone	Miscellaneous
				Shears	Knife	Tweezers												
N 31	—	19	19							F								
N 34	A/S	3	3							F						m		
N 35	—	—	59		?								F					
N 36	—	20	20	X	X													bz needle; bz frag.; quern frag. a.d.
N 37	—	9	—						m									
N 39	A/S	3	3										F					Miniature urn
N 41 b	—	31	31	X	?													
N 45	HN	29	29					F	X	F								
N 47	—	—	—															Iron frag. a.d.
N 48	—	32	32				X			F								
N 49	—	m	59	X	X	X												
N 50	—	2	—														m	
N 52	S	1	1							F	F				F		m	Iron ring; iron clip
N 56	S	34	34	X	X	X	X						X					Astragalus, F
N 59	A	5	5	X	X	X							F					Astragali, 1 runic, F
N 63	A	25	25	X	X												m	
N 64	—	50	—														m	
N 68	—	30	—															Pebble, m, a.d.
N 70	—	13	13															Iron ring; bz strips, F
N 71	—	—	32															Miniature urns; pebble a.d.
N 74	—	12	12							?F								
N 76 a or b	—	50) —)	59	X	X													Iron frag.
N 77	—	35	59															Iron nail a.d.
N 86	A	6	6	X														
N 87	HN	28	28	X	?													
N 90	—	24	24					?F		F								bz frag.
N 92	S	16	16				X										m	
N 93	—	42	42			X				?F							F	
N 94	A	6	—															Iron nail a.d.
N 95	A	4	4			X												Miniature urn
N 96	A	4	4	X	X	X												Iron pyrites, m, a.d.
N 101	—	23	59													ad		
N 102	A	10	10			X	X											
N 103	A	9	9															Fused bronze
N 104	—	18	59															Iron knife a.d.
P 1	—	—	59					F		?F								
P 3	A	9	9							F								
P 8	—	31	31							F				F				
P 9	—	—	59		?												F	
P 11	—	—	59											F			F	
P 12	—	22	22												F			
P 13	—	42	—														F	
P 14	S	2	2	X	X													
P 20	HN	28	28				m			F				F			m	
P 24	—	—	59															
P 25	—	11	11												F			
P 26	—	53	59											X				Iron nail a.d.

Urn Number	Urn type	Urn illustration	Grave goods illustrations	Manicure sets			Comb	Brooch	Brooch pin	Beads	Glass	Gaming piece	Sheet bronze	Spindle whorl	Ivory ring	Buckle	Animal bone	Miscellaneous
				Shears	Knife	Tweezers												
P 32	—	58)																
P 33	—	51)	59									m	X					Iron hinge
P 34	—	53	53				X						m					Samian frag.
P 38	—	55	59															Iron nail a.d.
P 41	—	53	53															Iron nail
P 42	A	25	25				X											
P 43	—.	33	33				X											
P 46	—	43	59								ad							
P 51	—	—	59														mad	Iron nail a.d.
P 53	—	2	—												F			
R 12	S	16	16				X											
R 17	—	19	—															Fused material
X 1	—	40	—														F	
X 3	—	38	38								F							
X 5	—	29	29							F								Bronze edging
X 11	—	27	27															Casket fittings, F Bronze frag., F
X 22	—	12	12							F								
X 23	A	9	9	X	X	X	X											
X 24	S	17	17										F					
X 25	—	m	59															Bronze strip F, iron nail
X 27 a or b	HN	23) 29)	59					F	?F									
X 28	S	12	12	X	X	?												
X 29	—	—	59				ad							ad				
X 31	A/S	3	3															Iron blade
X 32	—	m	59	X														
X 35	S	1	1										X					
X 38	—	40	59															Iron knife a.d.
Y 3	—	14	14										F					
Y 8	S	16	16			?	F											
Y 17	HN	28	28				X											
Y 19	—	11	11							F								
Y 22	S	2	2				X						F					
Y 23	A	11	11				X											
Y 26	HN	28	28	X	X	X												
Y 28	A	9	9							F								Fused material
Y 36	—	33	33										X					
Y 40	A	12	12				X											Roman coin
Y 41	S	11	11			?												
Z 2	—	m	59	X														
Z 6	—	—	59					F										Iron blade a.d.
Berm pot	—	33	·—														F	
Stray finds																		
1			60					F										
2			60												F			
3			60				F											
4			60										X					

Urn number	Urn type	Urn illustration	Grave goods illustrations	Manicure sets			Comb	Brooch	Brooch pin	Beads	Glass	Gaming piece	Sheet bronze	Spindle whorl	Ivory ring	Buckle	Animal bone	Miscellaneous
				Shears	Knife	Tweezers												
Stray finds (cont.):																		
5			60							X								
6			60							X								
7			60									F						
8			60															Fused bronze
9			60															Fused bronze
10			60							F								(possibly from E 12)
11			60		X													
12			60					X										
13			60			X												
14			60								F							

BEADS

A 8 (fig. 17); E 5 (fig. 1); E 14 (fig. 2); E 15 (fig. 35); E 19 (fig. 59); K 5 (fig. 7); M 9 (fig. 21); M 49(a) (fig. 14); N 14 (fig. 4); N 22 (fig. 8); N 31 (fig. 19); N 34 (fig. 3); N 37 (not fig.); N 45 (fig. 29); N 48 (fig. 32); N 52 (fig. 1); N 74 (fig. 12); N 90 (fig. 24); N 93 (fig. 42); P 1 (fig. 59); P 3 (fig. 9); P 8 (fig. 31); P 20 (fig. 28); X 5 (fig. 29); X 22 (fig. 12); X 27 (fig. 59); Y 28 (fig. 9); No. 5 (fig. 60); No. 6 (fig. 60); No. 10 (fig. 60).

Beads have been identified in twenty-six burial urns; one other urn, N 74, contains fused glass which may represent beads and three strays were found in the cemetery (Nos. 5, 6, and 10). Eighteen urns containing beads also contained other grave goods. Five of these were found with certain or probable brooches or brooch pins (E 14, N 45, N 90, P 1, X 27), an association which strongly suggests that these were women's cremations. The other associations are varied: A 8 also contained a comb fragment, E 5 tweezers and a possible knife, E 14 (in addition to the brooch pin) comb fragments, a finger- and an ear-ring, E 15 fragment of tweezers, E 19 glass, M 49(a) sheet bronze, N 14 an animal bone and a clay ring, N 34 animal bones, N 48 a comb fragment, N 52 glass, an ivory ring, an animal bone, an iron ring, and an iron clip, N 93 tweezers and animal bones, P 8 sheet bronze, P 20 a comb, sheet bronze, and an animal bone, and X 5 bronze edging. N 52 contains an ivory ring, an object which, it is suggested, is found only in a woman's burial (p. 101). But none of the other urns contains items which one can assign exclusively to either sex. Though beads occur twice with tweezers (E 5, E15) they do not seem to occur with a full manicure set. If, as seems probable, beads indicate women's cremations, this is one of the reasons for thinking that manicure sets were mainly for men.

All the beads identified from the Caistor cremations are of glass and practically all are badly distorted and discoloured by fire, so badly that it is only rarely that the size, shape, and colour of the beads can be determined; sometimes it is even impossible to be sure of the number of beads which go to make up the mass. Perhaps the best group is that from E 14.

This urn contained probably eighteen beads of which eleven are reasonably identifiable. It is possible to identify certain types—the melon bead (Cxi), the horned bead (e.g. Cix), and the globular bead which is the main type and which varies considerably in size. X 22Bi is a disc bead, a type not represented in urn E 14. Some are apparently of a single colour but others are of two or three, being decorated with marvered trails and spots. Opaque white, red, blue, and yellow colours have all been identified. These can be paralleled with those found in inhumation cemeteries such as Little Wilbraham, Cambs.,[1] Holywell Row, Suffolk;[2] Chamberlains Barn, Leighton Buzzard, Beds.;[3] Finglesham, Kent;[4] and Ipswich, Suffolk.[5] None of the long cylindrical or cuboid beads, or the biconical beads found so commonly in inhumation cemeteries have been identified. The actual number at Caistor of which the type can be recognized is so small that it is perhaps dangerous to attempt to draw conclusions. Unfortunately, little attention has been paid to beads from cremations and few are illustrated in reports. However, those which have been examined do conform to the same general types.

Two beads, Nos. 5 and 6, which are strays from the cemetery, are more likely to come from inhumation graves. Neither is distorted or discoloured and No. 5, a translucent clear green glass bead, is unlike any other from a cremation. Amber beads too have not been identified, but this is of course only to be expected if the beads found in urns were actually on the corpse when it was buried, as amber melts readily at a low temperature (about 360° C.).

Nothing can be said of the dates of the beads in isolation from the suggested dates of the urns. They are found in vessels which typologically range from the late fourth/early fifth centuries (e.g. E 14 and N 52) through the fifth century (e.g. M 49, K 5) into the sixth century (e.g. M 9).

One interesting association is found in E 14, where some eighteen beads are associated with a brooch pin and two rings. One ring, E 14F, has a coiled bezel and is similar in form to the rings found in association with beads as parts of necklets in seventh-century cemeteries.[6] However, these are of silver while E 14F is of iron and is presumably correctly identified as a finger-ring.

There is apparently no tendency for beads to occur in particular urn types, but they are missing, as are grave goods in general, from the sixth-century stamped urns. They are found in the large early Saxon urns (e.g. E 14 and N 52), in a *Buckelurne* (A 8), in Anglian urns of the corrugated (N 14) and bossed and corrugated types (K 5, N 22), and in the hollow-necked and carinated shoulder type (N 45), to mention but a few.

BONE CASKET FITTINGS

X 11 (fig. 27 and pls. XX, XXI)

Thin decorated bone plates and strips which were used as inlay for a wooden box are recorded from only one urn at Caistor, X 11. This is a barrel-shaped urn, undecorated save for some marks on the neck which may have been intended to look like runes. Apart from the bone mountings, only a bone peg and some bronze globules are recorded from the urn.

---

[1] Neville 1852.
[2] Lethbridge 1931.
[3] Hyslop 1963.
[4] Chadwick 1958.
[5] Layard 1907.
[6] Evidence summarized in Hyslop 1963, 161–200.

Such casket fittings are not common but are recorded from both Roman and post-Roman sites in Britain and on the Continent. The motifs used for decorating the fragments are those found on other late provincial Roman bone objects, particularly combs, i.e. groups of parallel lines, compass-drawn circles, 'bull's-eyes', and motifs made of interlocking circles or segments of circles. A plate decorated with a guilloche (pl. XX*c*) occurs at Richborough[1] among other casket fittings found in a fourth-century context near the bottom of the inner stone fort ditch. This design was found also on casket fittings from Heilbronn,[2] which were probably of the same date, and another found in 1902 in a grave at Zweins near Franeker.[3] The 'wave-with-a-bull's-eye' motif (pl. XX*b*) is found on casket fittings from a Frankish cemetery at Maroeuil, Belgium,[4] while the 'wave', but without the 'bull's-eye', occurs on the Zweins casket.[5]

Richborough, Kent, provides parallels to other pieces. Fittings from Pit 281[6] included some trapezoidal pieces, three of which formed sides of a hollow square. Four of the Caistor pieces are almost identical in size and shape (pl. XXI). The other two Caistor trapezoidal pieces are comparable with the two other Richborough pieces illustrated on the same plate.

The triangular pieces (pl. XX*k*) can be paralleled at Lydney where they are likely to be of fourth-century date.[7] The half-round strips (pl. XX*a*) from Caistor are not easy to parallel, but a very similar piece came from site 1 at Richborough.[8]

The fittings from Pit 281 at Richborough are difficult to date.[9] The pit is a fourth-century excavation, but second-century rubbish, said to include the bone fittings, had been thrown into the top. However, it is quite possible that the bone pieces are later than the rest of the material with which they were found. On the Continent other comparable examples seem to belong to the late fourth or early fifth centuries, for example one from a *Laetengrab* at Fécamp (Seine-Maritime),[10] which was dated to about 400. This was compared by Werner to late Roman examples from Vermand and Paris (Quartier Saint Marcel) and to another from a Frankish woman's grave at Envermeu dating to the late fifth century.[11] Other Frankish examples include that mentioned above from Maroeuil, Belgium,[12] and Weilbach, West Germany.[13]

A late fifth-century date is probable for cremation burial 38 at Abingdon, Berks.,[14] which contained pieces of bone inlay in addition to three beads and a small plate of bronze. Casket fittings were found in urn 172 at Illington, Norfolk,[15] together with some bronze globules (cf. Caistor X 11) and perhaps some pieces of bone comb. Unfortunately only the lower part of this urn survives and this is plain. Some pieces of what are said to be ivory were found in the seventh-century cremation burial at Asthall Barrow, Oxon.,[16] but the decoration on these pieces is quite unlike that on the examples cited already. Pieces of another casket which Kendrick dates to the late fourth or early fifth century come perhaps from a cemetery at Dover, Kent.[17]

[1] Bushe-Fox 1949, 152 and pl. LVII, 276 g.
[2] Ibid.
[3] Roes 1963, pl. LXIII. 8 and 9.
[4] de Loë 1939, 161–3, fig. 132.
[5] Roes 1963, pl. LXIII. 10.
[6] Cunliffe 1968, 106 and pl. LXI.
[7] Wheeler and Wheeler 1932, 91 and pl. XXXI A and B, 147 and 155.

[8] Bushe-Fox 1926, 47 and pl. XV. 34, upper.
[9] Cunliffe 1968, 34.   [10] Werner 1962, 145–54.
[11] Ibid. 153, footnotes 12 and 13.
[12] de Loë 1939, 161–3.   [13] Schoppa 1953, 44 ff.
[14] Leeds and Harden 1936, 18; Biddle *et al.* 1968, 39 and fig. 9.
[15] Unpublished, in N.C.M.
[16] Leeds 1924, 118 and fig. 4.
[17] Kendrick 1937, 448 and pl. XCVII.

It would seem likely that such caskets were made in the late fourth and early fifth centuries. It is unfortunate that X 11 is undecorated and that its form gives no clear indication of its date. These caskets, wherever made, could well be treasured as heirlooms and it is possible that those found in burials of the later fifth or early sixth centuries were old when deposited. So little normally survives that it is impossible to determine if the caskets were old when buried. The Caistor example may well have belonged to one of the early mercenaries but there are no means of knowing when it came to rest in X 11.

BROOCHES

A 3 (fig. 38); A 12 (fig. 10); E 14 (fig. 2); G 5 (fig. 59); M 22 (fig. 59); M 33 (text-fig. 1 and fig. 59); M 41 (fig. 7); M 42 (fig. 18); M 47 (fig. 34); N 45 (fig. 29); N 90 (fig. 24); P 1 (fig. 59); X 27 (fig. 59); Y 19 (fig. 11); Z 6 (fig. 59); No. 1 (pl. XIXc, text-fig. 2, and fig. 60); No. 12 (fig. 60).

Brooches or parts of brooches are recorded from thirteen Caistor urns. In addition there are two stray brooches from the Caistor cemetery and two pieces of bronze from urns N 90 and X 27 which may be brooches. Three of the twelve are represented only by pins. All have been affected by fire, some only slightly (in particular A 12B), while others such as M 47B and C, N 45B, P 1B, X 27B, Y 19B, are so distorted as to make identification very difficult.

Caistor is not unusual in producing so few brooches. They are apparently rare finds at other cremation cemeteries and, as at Caistor, are frequently fragmentary. For instance, at Abingdon, Berks., three urns out of eighty-two produced brooches,[1] at South Elkington, Lincs., four out of over 200 urns contained brooch fragments[2] and at Illington, too, only four urns out of over 200 produced brooches.[3] However, at Lackford, Suff., the proportion was somewhat higher, with 14 out of the 226 urns illustrated (about half the urns recovered in the excavations) containing brooch fragments.[4]

The brooches are not concentrated in any particular group of urns. Only A 3, E 14, M 42, M 47, N 45, N 90, P 1, and X 27 contained objects other than brooches. Of these, three contained only beads (N 45, P 1, and X 27) and two others (E 14 and N 90) beads in addition to other objects.

In only two instances does a more or less complete brooch seem to have been buried (N 45B and No. 1); a substantial part of G 5B survives, but the foot is missing. It does seem likely that the brooches were in many instances damaged before the burnt bones and accompanying objects were placed in the burial urns (see p. 78).

The commonest type of brooch was the bow brooch, only two plate brooches (Nos. 1 and 12) being recorded. Where the type of bow brooch can be determined with any degree of certainty, it is the cruciform with a zoomorphic foot. One or two could be cruciform small-long brooches. M 33C is exceptional in being almost certainly a square-headed brooch of Kenninghall II type.

None of these bow brooches are typologically very early. G 5B is perhaps a Group I cruciform of advanced type comparable with one from Barrington A (Malton), Cambs.,[5]

---

[1] Leeds and Harden 1936.
[2] Webster and Myres 1951, 25 ff.
[3] Records in N.C.M. We are indebted to the late Gp.

Capt. G. Knocker and to the Dept. of the Environment for permission to cite this unpublished material.
[4] Lethbridge 1951.   [5] Åberg 1926, 36 and fig. 55.

a pair from Grave XII, St. John's, Cambridge,[1] and one from West Stow Heath, Suff.[2] These may be dated to the last quarter of the fifth century. Unfortunately, the foot of G 5B is missing and the surviving part is also closely paralleled by a pair of cruciform small-long brooches from a woman's inhumation burial at Glen Parva, Leics.[3] In addition to this pair of brooches, that burial contained a Group I cruciform brooch, a pair of 'girdle-hangers', two bronze rings of uncertain use, a faceted and perforated crystal, fragments of a cone beaker, beads, fragments of an ivory bag ring, and the bone plates of a knife-handle. This burial is dated about 500. Unfortunately only a few sherds of urn G 5 survive.

The foot fragment from M 42 is probably part of a developed Group I brooch, but it could well come from a Group II. The urn M 42 is of considerable interest (see pp. 51–2) and was probably old when buried.

Urn M 47 contained parts of two cruciform brooches and two fragments of animal bone. Only one of the brooches can be identified with any degree of certainty. It has two swollen nostrils, separated by the tip of the nose, a ridge down the centre of the face and prominent eyes. These features are found on a more elaborate specimen from Islip, Northants.[4] The separate swollen nostrils are present on a brooch from Lackford found in a plain urn with a number of other objects. This brooch Lethbridge dates about 500.[5] The nearest parallel to the M 47 Group II brooch is one from Little Wilbraham Grave 73;[6] this grave contained a pair of cruciform brooches, five beads, and iron knife, and a small bronze buckle. A slightly more elaborate cruciform brooch was found in Grave 143 at the same cemetery[7] together with a square-headed small-long brooch and ten beads. A date of 500 or a little later can be suggested for all these brooches. M 47 is a shoulder-boss urn with a single line of stamps on the neck and almost empty panels. Its association with a Group II cruciform is a useful pointer to the date of this stage of the bossed panel style (see p. 57).[8]

The remains of two Group III cruciform brooches—N 45B and A 12B—can be identified with some degree of certainty. Although N 45B is very warped by fire it is one of the very rare examples at Caistor of what seems to have been an almost complete brooch being buried in an urn. The nose parts are very similar to those on Group III brooches from Barrington A[9] and Hornsea, Yorks.[10] With N 45B was an iron pin (D), probably from this brooch, and a fused glass bead. This undecorated urn (see p. 50) is a developed example of the northern group with hollow necks and carinated shoulders. This group is mainly fifth century in date, but N 45B shows that it persisted in modified form well into the sixth century.

A 12B is a fragment consisting only of the foot of a cruciform brooch. It is very similar to a brooch of this type from a terp site at Achlum[11] and to another from Grave 79 at Holywell Row, Suff.[12] With the latter were a rather more advanced Group III cruciform, a Group IV cruciform, two small-long brooches, girdle hangers, a wire wrist-clasp,[13] belt ornaments, a plain pot, and an ox jaw.[14] Lethbridge considered that the simpler Group III brooch was probably later than those figured by Åberg from East Shefford, Berks., and Barrington A,[15]

[1] Fox 1923, pl. XXVII. 3.
[2] Åberg 1926, 186, no. 16.
[3] Leicester Museum (n.d.), figs. 14 and 15, pp. 19–20.
[4] Åberg 1926, 3, fig. 56.
[5] Lethbridge 1951, 18, fig. 14, 50.71.
[6] Neville 1852, 18 and pl. 8.
[7] Ibid. 22 and pl. 8.

[8] Myres 1969, 56–7.
[9] Åberg 1926, 39, fig. 65.
[10] Sheppard 1913, fig. XXXe, 265.
[11] Boeles 1951, 536 and pl. XXXV. 3.
[12] Lethbridge 1931, 35 and fig. 16.3.
[13] Leeds 1945, 60–1.
[14] Lethbridge 1931, 32–7 and fig. 16.
[15] Åberg 1926, 39, figs. 64 and 65.

the latter being the parallel cited for N 45B. But one would not expect the urn A 12 to be as late as these parallels suggest and there is no typological reason for such simple Group III brooches being as late as the mid-sixth century. Although fragmentary, this piece is still sharp and was probably not old when buried.

It is unfortunate that the two brooch fragments M 33 B and C can only doubtfully be associated with their urn. M 33 was one of a group of at least four urns, probably disturbed by a grave-digger (see p. 73), and all were fragmentary. These two are typologically the most advanced of the brooches from this cemetery. These pieces were examined by Leeds who was uncertain if they were parts of a single cruciform brooch similar to one from Sancton, Yorks.,[1] or if they were parts of two separate brooches. The latter does seem more likely. If these two pieces were parts of a single brooch the foot would be very long, much longer than that of any other example of this group.

M 33B, the fragment of horse's head with prominent eyes and well-defined eyebrows (text-fig. 1), is similar to a Group IV brooch from Londesborough, Yorks.[2] The eyebrows of this beast are apparently plain while those of M 33B are filled with hatching. Such moulding as survives above the head is similar to that on the Londesborough brooch. Another parallel is a Group V brooch from Barrington B, Cambs.[3] It has the same broad animal head with well-defined eyebrows, prominent eyes, and simple mouldings above the head.

Insufficient survives of M 33C for it to be certain if this is part of the foot of a Group V cruciform brooch or if it is part of a square-headed brooch. The spade-shaped foot bordered by birds' heads with curved beaks enclosing a central beaked head, very much more anthropomorphic than the majority of such heads found on brooches, is very similar to the foot of Leeds's type specimen for his Kenninghall II or C 2 square-headed brooches.[4] The beaked head on this brooch is unusually anthropomorphic with a long nose. The birds' heads have crested foreheads as do nearly all examples of this type of beast. The birds' heads on M 33C are not crested and the closest parallels to them are to be found on another Kenninghall II brooch from Staxton, Yorks.,[5] although the shape of the terminal is different and the birds do not enclose a head. Leeds points out the affinities between these square-headed brooches and the Group V cruciforms.[6] Leeds would date this group of square-headed brooches to the seventh century.[7] Even if this dating is too late and the brooch should be placed rather in the late sixth century, the burial from which it came must be among the latest of the Caistor cremations. M 33 is part of a group of urns which F. R. M. suggested was moved by grave-diggers. Graves 24 and 25 lie immediately to the north of the group with Grave 27 to the south. Unfortunately only Grave 25 contained grave goods and these were three pieces of rusty iron (fig. 62 and p. 226).

The bow brooches from Caistor that can be dated thus have a chronological range from the late fifth to the late sixth centuries. It may seem curious that there are no examples of the earliest cruciform brooches such as have been found for instance in north-west Suffolk and at St. John's, Cambridge.[8] But the total number of brooches is so small in relation to the number of burials that their absence does nothing to invalidate the arguments here put forward (pp. 43–8) for the very early date of a number of the urns.

[1] Leeds 1913, fig. 13, middle of lower row.
[2] Åberg 1926, 46, fig. 76.
[3] Fox 1923, pl. XXIX. 1, centre of upper row.
[4] Leeds 1949, 79 ff. and fig. 130.
[5] Ibid., fig. 131.   [6] Ibid. 80.   [7] Ibid. 121.
[8] Åberg 1926, 34, figs. 44–8.

It is extremely unfortunate that the one really early brooch from the cemetery (text-fig. 2), a cast saucer brooch decorated in the chip-carved manner with five running spirals (No. 1), was a stray find from the cemetery site.[1] This brooch has been figured more than once in the literature[2] together with a very similar but apparently slightly more elaborately decorated brooch from Westerwanna[3] found in an urn[4] of Tischler's 'Cuxhaven/Galgenberg Typ',[5]

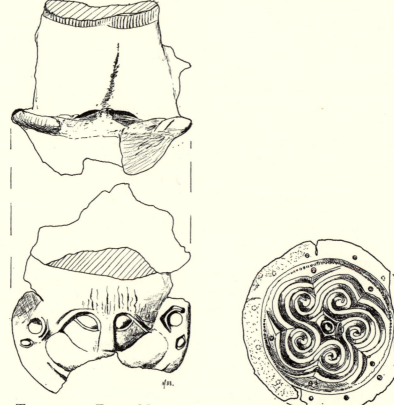

TEXT-FIG. 1. Foot of bronze brooch, possibly from urn M 33 (scale $\frac{2}{1}$).

TEXT-FIG. 2. Bronze saucer brooch (scale $\frac{1}{1}$).

which is dated to the late fourth and early fifth centuries. The parallels and dating evidence for this group of brooches from both England and the Continent are conveniently summarized by Bidder and Morris.[6] It is a type of specifically Saxon origin stemming from the lower Elbe valley. The tooling of the Caistor brooch is strong and it is perhaps closer to the continental pieces than to other British examples. In fact a continental origin would not be unreasonable; the brooch may well have been brought to Caistor by one of the earlier Saxons who settled at the site.

[1] *Not*, as stated in Bidder and Morris 1959, 82, from an urn.
[2] e.g. Leeds 1936, 39 and pl. XI*b*.
[3] Ibid., pl. XI*a* and *c*.
[4] Ibid., pl. XI*d*.
[5] Tischler 1954b, 48 and Abb. 8; Myres 1969, 42.
[6] Bidder and Morris 1959, 80–3.

COMBS (pls. XXII, XXIII)

A 8 (fig. 17); D 5 (fig. 59); D 9 (fig. 41); D 10 (fig. 59); E 1 (fig. 59); E 13 (fig. 16); E 14 (fig. 2); M 13 (fig. 59); M 35 (fig. 26); M 53 (fig. 28); N 10 (fig. 13); N 15 (fig. 3); N 17 (fig. 13); N 19 (fig. 3); N 48 (fig. 32); N 56 (fig. 34); N 92 (fig. 16); N 102 (fig. 10); P 20 (fig. 28); P 34 (fig. 53); P 42 (fig. 25); P 43 (fig. 33); R 12 (fig. 16); X 23 (fig. 9); Y 8 (fig. 16); Y 17 (fig. 28); Y 23 (fig. 11); No. 3 (fig. 60).

Combs are recorded from 27 urns, while another fragment (No. 3) had obviously come from an urn. Thus after beads and manicure sets, or parts thereof, combs are the commonest type of grave goods. In addition, a comb was originally recorded by F. R. M. from M 33 (see Inventory).

The majority of the combs are the large triplex type, with centre-plates made up from a number of plates, with side-plates of one or two pieces of bone and the whole riveted together. Four types can be recognized at Caistor—the triangular, the round-backed, the double-sided, and the single-sided Frisian type. In addition there are two miniature combs (R 12B and X 23E), each made from a single piece of bone. Two of the large combs are more or less complete, D 9C being a round-backed comb and E 13B a triangular comb; substantial remains of a round-backed comb D 5B and Frisian combs E 1B, M 53B, and Y 17B also survive. The rest are fragmentary and often no more than a single fragment was recorded from an urn.

Thirteen of the urns contained grave-goods other than comb fragments; one of them, E 14, contained fragments of two types of comb—a double-sided and a piece of either a triangular or a round-backed comb. X 23 contained a miniature comb in addition to a manicure set, while A 8 (with beads), N 48 (with beads), and N 56 (with manicure set and a fragment of sheet bronze) all contained pieces of triangular combs. It was impossible to classify the other fragments with any degree of certainty. By contrast, in only one instance (P 42) out of the fourteen urns which contained only combs was it impossible to be certain of the comb type. One urn (M 13) may have contained parts of probably two triangular combs.

Of those urns which contained grave goods in addition to combs four (A 8, E 14, P 20, and N 48) contained beads, two (N56 and X 23) contained full manicure sets of knife, shears, and tweezers, and three (M 35, N 102, and Y 8) contained one or two elements of the set. Three urns (N 56, P 20, and P 34) contained sheet bronze fragments, and P 20 contained animal bones.

When the urns containing combs are arranged typologically the only pattern to emerge is that four of the five urns (W 64 is fragmentary) of the 'Cuxhaven/Galgenberg Typ' decorated with *stehende Bogen* contain combs (fig. 16). However, the type of comb found is not consistent. E 13 contains an almost complete triangular comb, R 12 a miniature comb, Y 8 pieces of a probably Frisian comb, while the fragments from N 92 are almost certainly pieces of triangular combs. In addition Markshall IX (fig. 16) is perhaps accompanied by a comb fragment (p. 249).

This striking coincidence of combs with urns decorated with *stehende Bogen* at Caistor is not unparalleled elsewhere. One of the urns of this type from Loveden Hill, Lincs., contained a comb[1] as did urn 150 from Sancton, Yorks., and urn 50.125 from Lackford, Suff.[2] However,

[1] We are indebted to Dr. K. R. Fennell for permission to quote unpublished data from this site.
[2] Lethbridge 1951, 16 and fig. 5.

at South Elkington, Lincs.,[1] no combs at all were recorded, while at Abingdon, Berks.,[2] where combs were found in thirteen urns, none came from the five urns decorated with *stehende Bogen*.[3] At Mahndorf[4] six combs were found in cremation urns, but none was found in those urns of the 'Cuxhaven/Galgenberg Typ' recorded from the cemetery.

Two Frisian combs were found in urns with hollow necks and carinated shoulders (Y 17 and M 53). Another urn of this group, P 20, contained a comb but this unfortunately is missing and the type unrecorded.

There are six instances of combs having been affected by fire—E 1B, C and D, E 14Bi (Bii not affected), M 13B, N 10B, Y 8B and No. 3. At Lackford, Suff., Lethbridge[5] found that the combs were 'invariably unburnt'. Sometimes at Caistor (e.g. A 8) the combs are unburnt while associated objects have been badly affected by fire. At Mahndorf[6] and in Frisia[7] the comb fragments were normally burnt.

Perhaps the most interesting group are the *barred Frisian combs*. These are single-sided combs, each with a small central handle and with the side-plates formed on one side from a single thin flat plate and on the other from two plano-convex bars. Projections from the upper ends of the centre-plate, which curve inwards towards the central grip, are carved to represent animal heads, although some of these are very degenerate and hardly recognizable as such. The combination of flat plate and half-round bars seems to be diagnostic of this type of comb; no certain double-sided comb showing this feature has been noted. However, there are comb-cases which have been made in this way; many are associated with Frisian combs and it is quite possible that all cases of this type belonged to Frisian combs.

At Caistor sufficient survives of both Y 17B and M 53B for there to be no doubt of their classification as Frisian. It is uncertain if the fragments in urn E1 represent a single comb with a comb-case, or two combs. The identification of Y 8B as Frisian is less certain, but there is a single fragment of a thin plate decorated with incised parallel lines in addition to pieces of centre-plate and plano-convex bars.

These combs are found typically in Frisia, and Roes[8] could quote only one example from outside that area, a comb found at York in the mid-nineteenth century. Unfortunately the find spot and circumstances of discovery are not recorded.[9] Another English example was found in 1965 in what was probably an Anglo-Saxon hut at Grimstone End, Pakenham, Suff.[10] Two other possible examples come from the cremation cemetery at Spong Hill, North Elmham, Norf.[11] and from urn 49.6 at Lackford.[12] This latter is described as part of a double-sided comb, and it is accompanied by what is probably part of a comb-case.

The side-plates of the Lackford comb are both apparently made up from plano-convex bars. The upper edges of these bars do not show the nicks normally found along toothed edges. The length of this comb when complete was at least 3·9 in. (10 cm.). The comb-case would only have taken a comb 3·7 in. (9·4 cm.) long. This was made up from a flat plate and plano-convex bars; a part of one bar survives. The width of this bar is less than half the width of

---

[1] Webster and Myres 1951, 25–64.
[2] Leeds and Harden 1936.
[3] Biddle *et al.* 1968.
[4] Grohne 1953.
[5] Lethbridge 1951, 12.
[6] Grohne 1953, 155.
[7] Boeles 1951, 334.
[8] Roes 1963, 12.

[9] *V.C.H. Yorks* vol. ii, frontispiece, no. 15. Mr. G. F. Willmot informs me that the comb is no. 145 in the Cook Coll. MSS. catalogue and was found during excavation carried out 1845–55, within and outside the city walls.
[10] Owles and Smedley 1966, 194 and fig. 25.
[11] Unpublished. In the East Dereham Museum.
[12] Lethbridge 1951, 16 and fig. 1.

the flat plate, but is the same as the width of the bars on the comb fragment. It is difficult to be certain quite how these pieces should be interpreted. It is thus uncertain if the reconstruction is accurate. A careful examination of the pieces does suggest that the 'comb-case' is part of a comb of Frisian type. The urn in which these pieces were found is a *Buckelurne* of Myres Group II[1] and dates to the second half of the fifth century.

Few of these combs come from a datable context. One very similar to Y 17B with an openwork grip, was found at Hoogebeintum in a grave with a fifth-century cruciform brooch (pl. XXIIIa, b).[2] Boeles implies[3] that similar combs were found at Furfooz, but it has not been possible to trace any record of such combs among the material from the site.[4]

The engraved decoration on all the combs is very simple. The thin flat plates are decorated with groups of parallel lines and sometimes 'bull's-eye' motifs. The plano-convex bars on the other hand usually carry panel style decoration. In Frisia a common style is plain panels alternating with panels filled with close-set vertical parallel lines.[5] Those from Lackford, York, Pakenham, and Caistor Y 8 are decorated in the same manner. However Y 17B, M 53B, and the Spong Hill, North Elmham, fragments differ in having panels divided diagonally; one half is filled with close-set vertical lines while the other half is plain. This style of decoration echoes the 'hatched triangle' motif common on continental pottery of the third and fourth centuries and surviving occasionally in England (see Y 40, N 11, N 102, and W 9, and discussion p. 44). E 1B has a number of panels decorated in this manner, but they are separated by groups of vertical lines, and in addition there are panels filled with a St. Andrew's cross.

The majority of the grips which survive on these combs are solid and mushroom-shaped. That of M 53B is very close to one from Frisia,[6] but the decoration on the bars is quite different. The Frisian example is unusual in that it is not in panel style. The openwork grips of Y 17B and the comb from Hoogebeintum are unusual. The association of the latter piece with a fifth-century brooch is consistent with the date suggested for urn Y 17 and other urns of this group with hollow necks and sharply carinated shoulders (see p. 50). M 53B, also from an urn of this group, is likely to be of a similar date. It is unfortunate that the comb recorded by F. R. M. from urn P 20 is missing and the type unrecorded. The Group II *Buckelurne* from Lackford[7] strengthens the suggestion that this type of comb is of fifth-century date.

It is possible that these combs were being produced over a period of more than fifty years. In the majority of examples where the curved projections from the centre-plate survive, the animal heads are hardly recognizable as such. However, those on an example from Frisia[8] are truly zoomorphic. The animals each have a rounded head with a mane, a large round eye, and gaping jaws. These heads are closely paralleled by the pair at either end of the hinge bar of the bronze buckle from Catterick, Yorks., of Hawkes and Dunning Type IVB.[9] This buckle was found on the floor of a building below an occupation level dated by a stratified coin to the late fourth or fifth century.[10] Other similar heads are found at either end of the

---

[1] Myres 1969, 144.
[2] Boeles 1951, 533, pl. XXVII. 10; Roes 1963, pl. XII. 4.
[3] Boeles 1951, 335.
[4] Nenquin 1953. I am grateful to Dr. Nenquin for checking the material for me.
[5] Roes 1963, pl. XIII.
[6] Ibid., pl. XIII. 2.
[7] Lethbridge 1951, 16 and fig. 1.
[8] Roes 1963, pl. XIII. 4.
[9] Hawkes and Dunning 1961, 61, fig. 22.
[10] Ibid. 62.

loop of a buckle from Grave 321 at Vermand (Aisne),[1] a Type IIIA bronze buckle from Icklingham, Suff.,[2] and a Type IIA buckle from a Romano-British villa at North Wraxall, Wilts.[3]

The much simplified head on the comb from Finkum[4] has a small triangular ear and a squared-off snout. This is similar to heads found on buckles of Types IIIA and IIIB[5] and is closest perhaps to the heads on a IIIB buckle from Grave 57, Long Wittenham, Berks.[6]

The *round-backed combs* are very difficult to parallel satisfactorily. The end sections of the centre-plates of D 5B, D 9 C (pl. XXIIa, b), and E 14 Bi (this latter more likely to be round-backed than triangular) continue the curve of the back well beyond the corners of the side-plates. M 35D, a fragment which is not certainly from such a comb, shows something of the same character. The majority of examples of round-backed combs both from England and the Continent are different; the centre-plate does not project beyond the corners of the side-plates and has vertical ends.[7] However, there are a few exceptions. In one or two Frisian examples the ends of the centre-plate do slope, continuing the curve of the back, and project beyond the ends of the centre-plate. Two further examples come from the inhumation ceme-tery at Reuden, Kr. Zeitz, in central Germany.[8] The curve of the back is flatter than that of the Caistor combs and the decoration on the example from Grab 14 somewhat simpler. These are dated to the late fifth century.[9]

The curvature too of D 5B and D 9C is rather different from the majority of examples, and tends to be somewhat shallower. There are parallels in Frisia.[10] These are decorated in the same manner as the Caistor examples, that is with simple engraved lines, 'bull's-eyes', and concentric circles. This type of decoration is also found on other English round-backed combs from Lackford,[11] found in a probably early sixth-century stamped urn, from urn 181 at Girton, Cambs.,[12] and from two urns at Little Wilbraham, Cambs.[13] Roes points out that in Frisia many of the combs are decorated by techniques commonly used on metals.[14] A similar type of decoration is used on certain Danish combs, for example from Nydam, Vimose, and Gotland, and this, she considers, is a characteristic of 'very early combs', presumably of the late fourth and early fifth centuries. Roes also considers that decoration on both sides of the comb is an early feature; combs having one plain side are later.[15]

At Hemmoor-Warstade examples of both the simple engraved designs[16] and those produced by metal-working techniques[17] are found. The shape of the combs in all cases is apparently similar, with a rather shallowly curved back and vertical ends to the centre-plates. The spring of a brooch, possibly of late fourth-century or early fifth-century date, came from Grab 7. This would suggest that the two decorative styles are roughly contemporary on the

[1] Evison 1965, fig. 26c.
[2] Hawkes and Dunning 1961, 60 and fig. 20d.
[3] Ibid. 52 and fig. 18b.
[4] Roes 1963, pl. XIII. 1.
[5] Hawkes and Dunning 1961, fig. 20.
[6] Ibid. 60 and fig. 20g.
[7] e.g. examples from Frisia, Roes 1963, pl. II; Hem-moor, Waller 1959, Tafel 11, 12; Gleschendorf, Kr. Eutin, Genrich 1954, Tafel 11 D; Lackford, Lethbridge 1951, fig. 33.
[8] Schmidt 1961, Taf. 55a (Grab 6) and Abb. 56, 6, p. 142 (Grab 14).

[9] Ibid., 141–4.
[10] Roes 1963, pl. V. 5 particularly, also pl. V. 4 and 6.
[11] Lethbridge 1951, 21 and fig. 33, 50.106.
[12] In Museum of Archaeology and Ethnology, Cambridge, not listed in Hollingworth and O'Reilly 1925.
[13] Neville 1852, pl. 23.
[14] Roes 1963, 8–9.
[15] Ibid. 8.
[16] Waller 1959, Tafel 10, Grab 7.
[17] Ibid., Tafel 11, Grab 10; Tafel 12, Grab 11, Grab 12.

Continent; the simple engraved motifs are of course found on triangular and double-sided combs as well as on other bone objects. This style can be dated to the later fourth century and it certainly continues in and through the fifth.

The Caistor examples are perhaps hybrids, made in this country by comb makers familiar with the continental round-backed forms but who preferred the more elegant curved projections of the centre-plate normally found on triangular combs. The urns in which these combs were found at Caistor are varied. The earliest is E 14 (fig. 2), one of the group of early Saxon urns related to Plettke's types A 3–5 (p. 45), which are dated to the late fourth or very early fifth century. M 35 (fig. 26), which contains a comb fragment possibly of this type, is a large undecorated hump-shouldered urn with a short upright rim, of Anglian derivation and perhaps dating to about 500. D 9 (fig. 41) is an elaborately stamped urn which can perhaps be dated to the second half of the sixth century. This urn is probably later than the bossed and stamped urn 50.106 from Lackford which contained a round-backed comb of continental type.[1] D 5 was found with urns D 3 and D 4 in Roman pit 10; unfortunately only the lower parts of all three were recovered.

The commonest type of comb from this cemetery, as apparently from most other cremation cemeteries in England, is the large, triplex *triangular comb*. Nine urns contained pieces which can be certainly identified as of this type (A 8, E 13, M 13 (probably two combs), N 15, N 17, N 48, N 56, P 43, and Y 23) while a further six urns (E 14, N 10, N 19, N 92, N 102, and P 42) contained fragments which could be parts of triangular or round-backed combs. Of the certain pieces of triangular combs, all are fragmentary except for E 13B (pl. XXIIc); this is almost complete and lacks only the end sections of the centre-plate and most of the teeth. This comb comes from an urn of the early fifth-century 'Cuxhaven/Galgenberg Typ' with *stehende Bogen* decoration, a type which (see p. 91) often contains combs. A large part of the centre-plate of M 13B survives, together with another small piece of centre-plate, M 13C, which almost certainly comes from a different but very similar comb (see p. 138). Unfortunately these pieces were only doubtfully associated with the fragmentary urn.

N 92, another urn of the 'Cuxhaven/Galgenberg Typ', contained a fragment which is almost certainly from a triangular comb, in addition to a red deer metapodial. Other urns of Saxon type which contained pieces of this type of comb are A 8, a *Buckelurne* of Myres Group IV which probably dates to the late fifth century and also contained beads; and N 56, a fifth-century stamped bowl related to urns produced by Potter VIII (see p. 55); this urn also contained a manicure set and a fragment of sheet bronze. The fragment of comb found in E 14, a large early Saxon urn, may be from a triangular comb, but is more likely to come from a round-backed comb.

Two fifth-century Anglian urns, decorated with chevrons filled with corrugation, contain a certain fragment (Y 23B) and a possible fragment (N 102B) of this type of comb. An Anglian plain globular urn, again of fifth-century date, P 42, also contains a possible fragment. None of these urns, in contrast to the Saxon urns, contain any other grave goods.

N 17B comes from a biconical urn with line-and-dot decoration. This urn was buried at the same time as N 16, an urn of the same type. The latter contained a manicure set which is now lost. On typological grounds these urns could be of early fifth-century date (p. 52). Another urn of this type, N 10, contained a comb fragment which could be of the triangular

---

[1] Lethbridge 1951, 21 and fig. 33.

type. The urn also contained a gaming piece, a sheep's astragalus, part of a bronze ring, and fragments of a glass vessel.

The other three certain triangular comb fragments come from N 15, an early Anglo-Saxon urn with groups of vertical lines; from N 48, a plain shoulder-boss urn with three solid nipple-bosses, which also contained beads; and from P 43, a Roman jar. This is the only Roman vessel from Caistor used as a cremation urn which contained any grave goods (p. 74). N 19, another early Anglo-Saxon urn with groups of vertical lines, contained, in addition to a pig bone, a comb fragment which may be of triangular type.

It is unfortunate that the side-plates of E 13B and M 13B and C, the only combs from which substantial remains of the side-plates survive, are decorated only with groups of incised parallel lines. Commonly, these combs are decorated also with concentric circles and 'bull's-eyes'.[1] Leeds[2] considered that the presence of these combs in a burial was indicative of an early date and Lethbridge[3] pointed out how similar the combs from urns 49.19 and 48.2490 at Lackford, Suff., are to those found on Roman sites. At Caistor many such combs are found in urns which can, on stylistic grounds, be dated to the fifth century, but in a number of instances, e.g. N 48, the urns cannot be closely dated. Moreover, P 34, a probably mid-sixth-century urn by Potter IV, contains a piece which has been repaired. Mr. S. E. West tells us that, in the settlement site at West Stow, Suff., he has found good, fresh examples of this type of comb in levels which he believes to be of the late sixth or early seventh centuries, which suggests that the form and style of decoration may have had a long life in at least that part of East Anglia.[4]

There is, however, one type of triangular comb which does seem to have a fairly limited chronological range. In this type the upper edge of the centre-plate projects above the side-plates and is ornate. Many, if not all, of these combs seem to have been made at Trier.[5] They are found in cemeteries on the Continent such as Furfooz[6] and Gudendorf,[7] and on occasion in this country in cemeteries[8] and domestic sites.[9] This type would seem to belong to the late fourth or first half of the fifth century, but a detailed study of them is needed.[10] It is possible that N 10B and N 102C belong to this type. Both urns have very early stylistic features (see pp. 44–5, 52) and could well belong to the years around 400.

The other type of composite comb found at Caistor is the *double-sided comb*. This is poorly represented, only two examples being recorded. Both are unburnt fragments of centre-plate, D 10B, with coarse and fine teeth, and E 14Bii, with similar teeth on either side. E 14 is one of the large early Saxon jars which can be paralleled on the Continent by urns containing late fourth- and early fifth-century brooches (see p. 45). D 10 is fragmentary and too little survives for the type to be determined. This type of comb ranges from late Roman to medieval times and is commonly found in Anglo-Saxon cremation urns.[11]

The final type found at Caistor is the *miniature comb*, two examples of which are recorded,

[1] e.g. Eye, Suff., Akerman 1855; Lackford, Suff., Lethbridge 1951, 17, fig. 6, 49.19 and 48.2490; Girton, Cambs., Hollingworth and O'Reilly 1925, pl. V. 2.

[2] Leeds 1936, 31.

[3] Lethbridge 1951, 17.

[4] West 1969, 13–15 and fig. 10.

[5] We are indebted to Dr. Gose for this information.

[6] Nenquin 1953, 69–72, pls. IX–X.

[7] Waller 1959, Tafel 34, Grab 27.

[8] e.g. Pensthorpe and Castle Acre, Norf., both early cremation cemeteries.

[9] Sutton Courtenay, Berks. Leeds 1927, pl. VII. 2c.

[10] They are briefly discussed, in connection with the example found in a very late Roman context under the Old Minster at Winchester, in Biddle 1970, 313.

[11] Waterman 1959, 87 ff.

R 12B and X 23E. These are made from a single piece of bone and could not have been used. It is possible that they were made specially for funerary purposes, although one has turned up in a domestic context at West Stow, Suff.[1]

R 12B (pl. XXIII*e*) has a round back and is slightly waisted. Urn R 12 is a typical example of the 'Cuxhaven/Galgenberg Typ' with *stehende Bogen* and finger-tipped rosettes, dated to the late fourth or very early fifth century (see p. 48). The shape of X 23E (pl. XXIII*c*) is an irregular hexagon; it was found together with a small manicure set in an Anglian bossed and corrugated urn; X 24, a *Buckelurne* of Myres Group II, was found on its shoulder. Typologically both urns date to the mid-fifth century.

Miniature combs are known on the Continent,[2] but are apparently rare. They are not common in England, but have been recorded from a number of cemeteries, notably Loveden Hill,[3] Lincs., Bidford-on-Avon, Warwicks.,[4] Castle Acre, Norf.,[5] Abingdon, Berks.,[6] and Lackford, Suff.[7] Abingdon has produced from the cremation urns the largest concentration in this country. They vary in shape, some being round-backed, others triangular and one even more or less rectangular. At Abingdon some are the only grave goods in the urn (e.g. C 12),[8] others are found with miniature manicure sets (e.g. C 9 and 13)[9] and yet others are found with articles such as needles.

Two good parallels to R 12B occur at Abingdon, one from C 58, a large undecorated urn[10] and another from C 82, a *Buckelurne* of Myres Group II.[11] In addition to the comb, this urn contained a fused bead, a bronze pin, a bronze needle, and a pot sherd. Another Group II *Buckelurne*, urn 57/34 from Loveden Hill, Lincs.,[12] also contained a comb of this type. A further example from the same cemetery comes from a Group V *Buckelurne*, urn 59/151, together with part of a large triangular comb.[13] Another comes from urn 49.25A at Lackford, Suff.[14] This was found with a very similar urn; both are unstamped urns with pairs of vertical grooves flanking vertical bosses and plain panels between. Lethbridge considered these to be derived from the Hanover region and they are certainly fifth century in date.

DRESS RINGS

E 14 (fig. 2); N 10 (fig. 13); N 70 (fig. 13).

N 10D is a small fragment of a bronze ring which from its curvature and diameter is almost certainly part of either a finger-ring or an 'ear-ring'.

The two most complete dress rings are E 14E and F. E is a bronze expanding ring of the type known from inhumations and usually identified as ear-rings.[15] Many of them are of silver. It is unlikely that they could have been worn hanging from a pierced ear; they might have been hung by threads round the ear, or caught on to a net or fabric drape worn over

[1] We are indebted to Mr. S. E. West for this information.
[2] Roes 1963, 6–7, pl. I, 5, 6; Westerwanna urn 155 in iron (Zimmer-Linfeld *et al.* 1960, Taf. 20).
[3] We are indebted to Dr. Fennell for this information.
[4] Humphreys *et al.* 1923, pl. XVI, fig. 2c.
[5] In N.C.M.
[6] Leeds and Harden 1936, pls. III and IV.
[7] Lethbridge 1951, figs. 1, 11, 15, 27, 28, 35.

[8] Leeds and Harden 1936, 15, pl. III.
[9] Ibid. 14–15, pl. III.   [10] Ibid. 20 and pl. III.
[11] Ibid. 23, urn, fig. 4; comb, pl. III.
[12] Myres 1969, 143. Dr. Fennell kindly supplied information on the contents.
[13] Myres 1969, 146, and Dr. Fennell.
[14] Lethbridge 1951, 17–18 and fig. 11.
[15] e.g. Faussett 1856, xxvii.

the head. Lethbridge's suggestion that some were used for suspending strings of beads[1] seems a much more plausible interpretation. That they were sometimes worn elsewhere Lethbridge showed at Burwell, where in Grave 26 such a silver ring formed part of a pendant,[2] while in Grave 42 some formed part of a chatelaine.[3] The association of such a ring in E 14 with beads does suggest that it may have formed part of a necklace.

It is uncertain if the iron ring E 14F is also part of the necklace or if it is a finger-ring. Such rings with a flat bezel made by twisting the wire into a flat coil are almost invariably of silver when found in Anglo-Saxon cemeteries. The majority are probably finger-rings[4] but they do occur as parts of necklaces. These latter are perhaps rather larger than the finger-rings. The silver examples occur in Kent, Bedfordshire, and Cambridgeshire[5] and they seem to date from the mid-sixth to seventh centuries. They develop from Roman prototypes and it is possible that E 14F is in fact Roman. Another possible example from Caistor is N 70B; it is fragmentary but the twists on the fragments suggest that they form part of such a ring rather than part of an iron expanding ring. N 70 is a biconical urn with line-and-dot decoration, while E 14 is one of the large heavy Saxon urns which can be paralleled at Westerwanna where they contain brooches dated to the late fourth or very early fifth centuries (see p. 45). The presence of such rings cannot be used as an argument against the early date of those urns, for they are of a different material from those of the late sixth or seventh centuries. It may well be that the rings with coiled bezel from Caistor can be best linked with the Danish and German examples which were not regarded by Mrs. Hyslop as influencing the later English form.

GAMING PIECES

N 10 (fig. 13); N 35 (fig. 59); N 59 (fig. 5); No. 7 (fig. 60).

Three Caistor urns contained plano-convex bone counters and there was a stray from the cemetery (No. 7). All showed clear indications of having been burnt. N 35 contained a single counter and a fragmentary iron blade, probably part of a knife or shears. N 10 also contained a single counter, together with comb fragments, pieces of a glass vessel, a fragment of a bronze ring, and a sheep's astragalus. N 59, however, contained thirty-three counters of which twenty-two were of bone (and white) and eleven were of a dark material, possibly shale. In addition to a manicure set funerary type of (see p. 104) there were over thirty-six (? thirty-nine) astragali. Of these one was clearly quite distinct, being larger, of dark brown colour, and having on one face a runic inscription. It was roe deer. One other certain roe deer astragalus was identifiable among the others, which were all more or less warped and crackled by fire; of these fifteen were certainly sheep while the others were either sheep or roe deer. The runic astragalus and its possible significance in this remarkable assemblage is discussed by Dr. R. I. Page below (pp. 114–17).

Gaming pieces are not uncommon in burials whether by cremation or inhumation. These plano-convex counters are, however, found more commonly in cremations than in inhumations. It is difficult to be certain how closely allied they are to those made from horses'

---

[1] Lethbridge 1931, 2.
[2] Ibid. 51.
[3] Ibid. 54–5, fig. 27.

[4] Chadwick 1958, 39.
[5] Hyslop 1963, 198–9.

teeth found at sites such as Taplow, Bucks., and Faversham, Kent,[1] or even to those bone counters decorated with incised circles on the upper surface such as were found at Sarre, Kent, and Cold Eaton, Derbyshire.[2] Those from the latter site were found with an unurned cremation in a barrow, but it was not possible to date it closely.[3] Baldwin Brown[4] did not consider that these circles had any numerical significance, nor perhaps do the small hollows found on the underside of some undecorated plano-convex examples. These can be one, two, or three in number, but they are by no means always present. If they are merely holes for holding the counters on a lathe it is difficult to see why the numbers vary;[5] most are certainly turned on a lathe. Mrs. Ozanne[6] considers that this indicates that some at least were imported from abroad, certainly those that were found in urns of fifth-century type. Continental parallels can be found from sites such as Hemmoor-Warstade,[7] Gudendorf,[8] and Wehden in Germany,[9] and Maagaard, Denmark.[10] Similar ones, but later in date, are known from Birka.[11] Gaming pieces of stone are known from Mahndorf,[12] and from Castle Acre, Norf., where in urn 48 three small quartz pebbles were found of approximately the same size as the three bone counters from the same urn.[13] Glass counters are also recorded in continental burials: for instance at Hemmoor-Westersode five black and five white plano-convex glass pieces and a bone die were found in Grave 10 accompanying a Roman bronze cauldron;[14] this burial was probably fourth century in date. Mrs. Ozanne[15] lists some of the East Anglian cremation cemeteries in which they were found. This undecorated plano-convex type is certainly common in East Anglia, but they are also recorded from Sancton, Yorks.,[16] and South Elkington, Lincs.[17] Loveden Hill, Lincs., has the largest number from one site, with at least thirteen urns containing them: three of these urns contained forty-five, forty-three, and thirty-one counters respectively.[18]

Gaming pieces are of little value for dating purposes, though the largest groups seem to occur mainly in early urns. N 59 is one of the earliest urns from Caistor (see p. 46) while Sancton 5, with fourteen counters, and Loveden Hill 11, with seventeen, are both of the fifth century. N 10 is not much later than the middle of the fifth century (see p. 52). Probably contemporary with this is urn 48.2485 from Lackford, Suff.,[19] which contained at least two dozen counters. On the other hand Lackford 48.2474 is probably sixth century, and so is Loveden Hill 8, which had no less than forty-five. The records from inhumations cited by Mrs. Ozanne show that they continue as grave goods into the seventh century.[20]

The association of a plano-convex counter with an astragalus in N 10 is surely not fortuitous in view of the assemblage in N 59; no other astragali were recorded from the cemetery

[1] British Museum 1923, 48 and fig. 50.
[2] Baldwin Brown 1915, 413 and pl. XCVII. Decorated pieces are also on record from Loveden Hill, Lincs.
[3] Ozanne 1962–3, 37.
[4] Baldwin Brown 1915, 413.
[5] Urn 11 from Loveden Hill, Lincs., for example, contained seventeen counters of which four had three holes and one of similar type had none; eight had two holes; and four of a slightly different type from the others had no holes. This suggests that they could have had some scoring value in a game.   [6] Ozanne 1962–3.
[7] Waller 1959, Grab 2, Taf. 6; Grab 3, Taf. 7; Grab 7, Taf. 10; Grab 9, Taf. 11.
[8] Waller 1959, Grab 27, Taf. 34.

[9] Waller 1961, Taf. 49, 407c and 332.
[10] Norling-Christensen 1957, 72–3 and fig. 23.
[11] Arbman 1940, Taf. 150.1, Grave 197.
[12] Grohne 1953, 166–7.
[13] N.C.M. unpublished, 50.962, from 1961 excavations.
[14] Waller 1959, 11 and Tafel 3.
[15] Ozanne 1962–3, 37.
[16] Unpublished; we are grateful to Mr. J. Bartlett for this information.
[17] Webster and Myres 1951.
[18] We are indebted to Dr. Fennell for this information.
[19] Lethbridge 1951, 17 and fig. 8.
[20] Ozanne 1962–3, 37.

apart from the fragment in N 56. Astragali are not recorded from the urns containing counters in other cemeteries but, as animal bones are so rarely recorded, their absence may be apparent rather than real. We do not know what particular purpose these gaming pieces served. Details of a number of Roman board games survive[1] but whether any such games were in use in the Anglo-Saxon period in Britain is unknown. Nor can much be said about continental board games at this period. Bell describes a game *hnefatafl*[2] which was known in Denmark about 400, in which forty-eight white pieces were used against twenty-four black. The proportions of white to black are the same as those of pieces from N 59 (itself an Anglian urn) but the counters are different from those illustrated. Leeds in a letter to F. R. M.[3] suggested that the large number of pieces from N 59 reminded him of a Chinese board game, *Wei Ch'i*, the principle of which was to enclose your adversary's men.

This mixture of black and white pieces is not restricted to Caistor, although records are not common. Two white and two black pieces come from urn 175 at Illington, Norf.;[4] 48.2485 from Lackford, Suff., contained, according to Lethbridge,[5] 'more than two dozen badly burnt ivory playing men'. A careful examination of the two dozen in the Museum of Archaeology and Ethnology in Cambridge suggests that eleven were meant to be black and thirteen white.

GLASS

E 19 (pl. XIX*a*); M 42 (fig. 18); M 57 (fig. 52); N 10 (fig. 13); N 52 (fig. 1); X 3 (fig. 38).

Little can be said about the glass fragments found in five of the Caistor urns. The only complete vessel is the cone beaker found in E 19; this has been fully discussed by Harden.[6] Fragments of another possible cone-beaker were identified by Dr. Harden in N 52D and he considered it uncertain if other fragments (E) came from this vessel or another, perhaps Roman, piece. The ten fragments in M 57 (an urn from the workshop of Potter III) certainly came from a Roman vessel of third/fourth-century date. The pieces from the other three urns could not be identified.

These fragments are perhaps associated with women's burials, for E 19 also contained beads, M 42 a cruciform brooch, and N 52, among other objects, beads and fragments of an ivory ring. Cremation burial 10 at Abingdon, Berks., also contained beads with a glass.[7]

Harden points out that nearly all glass from cemeteries comes from inhumation graves,[8] and lists cremation sites known to have produced glasses. All except Abingdon were in East Anglia—Caistor and Castle Acre, Norf., Lackford, Suff., and Girton, Cambs. Since then another complete cone-beaker has been found in an urn from Loveden Hill, Lincs.[9]

IVORY RINGS

N 52 (fig. 1); P 12 (fig. 22); P 25 (fig. 11); P 53 (fig. 2); No. 2 (fig. 60).

Fragments of burnt elephant ivory are recorded from five burials at Caistor. These fragments are parts of rings which have a D-shaped section.

[1] Bell 1960.
[2] Ibid. 79–80 and fig. 66.
[3] 1937: in N.C.M.
[4] N.C.M., unpublished.
[5] Lethbridge 1951, 17 and fig. 8.
[6] Harden 1956, 132–67. He records a claw beaker fragment from Caistor on p. 159; this is almost certainly a bluish waste glass fragment with bronze stuck to it from Atkinson's excavations.
[7] Leeds and Harden 1936, 14.
[8] Harden 1956, 133–4.
[9] S 8.142. Information kindly supplied by Dr. Fennell.

In two instances, N 52B and P 25B, it was possible to reconstruct the approximate diameters of the rings; the first was about 4 in. (about 10 cm.) and the second approximately 4·25 in. (about 10·8 cm.). These rings are obviously identical with those found in inhumation cemeteries. So far these rings have been identified at more than forty cemeteries or single burials in this country.[1] They have also been recorded from two domestic sites, at Waterbeach, Cambs.,[2] and from House IV at Sutton Courtenay, Berks.[3]

These rings vary from about 4 in. (10 cm.) to about 6 in. (15 cm.) in diameter. In every case where they have been examined by the writer they could be shown to have been cut from the upper part of an elephant's tusk as a complete ring. Some writers have wrongly suggested that they were made up from a number of small sections stuck together as, for instance, in the report on that from Mitcham Grave 221.[4] Elephant ivory splits naturally into cuboid pieces when exposed to heat or dampness and drying out. Unfortunately, too little of the cross-section of the tusk survives in any ring for a determination of the species of elephant to be made. These rings must have been imported, for to make them from fossil elephant tusks derived from glacial deposits in this country would not be practicable.[5] Similar rings are found on the Continent, but there they usually encircle bronze open-work discs. Examples include a ring from Meckenheim in Rhenish Hesse,[6] Dangolsheim (Bas-Rhin) where the ring was found in a Merovingian grave, at Cividale, and in Alamannic graves at, for example, Oerlingen, Bölach, and Ingersheim (Württemberg).[7] It is very likely that these came into western Europe and England from the Mediterranean, perhaps from Byzantium. Merchants there would have been able to obtain ivory from both African and Indian elephants, but it is not possible to determine if these rings are made of ivory from one species or from both. The numbers recorded from cemeteries suggest a flourishing trade in the finished rings, for if whole tusks were traded more ivory objects might be expected to survive.

In inhumation graves these rings are found with women. At Illington ten of the eleven cremations which contained these rings were of women; it was not possible to determine the sex of the eleventh cremation with any certainty. Examples from cremations from the Spong Hill, North Elmham, cemetery in every case have come from women's burials.[8] These rings therefore are a useful indicator of sex. They appear to have been in use more or less throughout the pagan period from the fifth to the seventh century. The ring from Mitcham came from Grave 221 together with an iron knife and two saucer brooches.[9] These brooches are

[1] Abingdon, Berks.; Alfriston, Sussex; Barrington A, Cambs.; Barrington B, Cambs.; Bidford-on-Avon, Warwicks.; Brighthampton, Oxon.; Brightwell Heath, Suff.; Caistor-by-Norwich; Cassington, Oxon.; Castle Acre, Norf.; Chatham Lines, Kent; Devizes, Wilts.; Dover, Kent; Driffield, Yorks.; Fairford, Glos.; Girton, Cambs.; Glen Parva, Leics.; Harnham Hill, Wilts.; Holdenby, Northants.; Holywell Row, Suff.; Hornsea, Yorks.; Howletts, Kent; Illington, Norf.; Kempston, Beds.; Kingston, Kent; Kirton-in-Lindsey, Lincs.; Lackford, Suff.; Limbury (Leagrave Common), Beds.; Little Eriswell, Suff.; Long Wittenham, Berks.; Loveden Hill, Lincs.; Luton, Beds.; Markshall; Mitcham, Surrey; Nassington, Northants.; North Elmham, Norf.; Petersfinger, Wilts.; Shudy Camps, Cambs.; Sleaford, Lincs.; Soham, Cambs.; Staxton, Yorks.; Willoughby-on-the-Wolds, Notts.; Woodyates, Dorset, etc.

[2] Lethbridge 1927, 144, fig. 4, no. 8.

[3] Leeds 1923, 158 and pl. XXVIII, fig. 1. H.

[4] Bidder and Morris 1959, 74 and pl. XVII. 221.

[5] The writer has had six years' experience of trying to conserve and consolidate fossil elephant tusks found in glacial deposits. They start fracturing in a very short time after removal from the ground.

[6] Baldwin Brown 1915, 400 and pl. XCI. 5.

[7] Vogt 1960. I am indebted to Dr. Hayo Vierck for drawing my attention to this article.

[8] I am indebted to Dr. Calvin Wells for examining this material for me.

[9] Bidder and Morris 1959, 74, 117–18, and pl. XVII. 221.

decorated with a 'sharply cut "Star of David" ', unique in England but 'closely matched by a brooch from Germany, Galgenberg inhumation 18, found with an urn and an "Arm-brustfibel" ancestral to the fifth century equal-arm types . . .'.[1] It is suggested that the Mitcham brooch belonged to the earliest settlers and thus is no later than the early fifth century. A similar late fourth- or very early fifth-century date is suggested for two of our urns that contain these rings, N 52B and P 53B. Both can be paralleled at Westerwanna,[2] N 52 (fig. 1) being comparable with Westerwanna 11 which contained a fourth-century brooch and P 53 with Westerwanna 1347 which also contained a fourth-century brooch (see p. 45, n. 8). P 53B was the only object recorded from the urn, but N 52 contained a number of objects in addition to the ivory ring—an iron clip and iron ring (both of which might be associated with the ivory ring), some beads, fragments of a glass vessel, and a sheep's rib. Two other rings, P 25B and P 12B, come from urns with simple linear decoration of early type (figs. 11 and 22); both were the only grave goods recorded. The dating of these rings at Caistor is thus consistently early. Elsewhere these rings have been noted in late fifth- or sixth-century contexts.[3] A few may have been buried as late as the seventh century, for example that from Grave 19 at Shudy Camps which also contained silver pendants identical with those from Burwell, Cambs., Grave 121.[4]

Vogt has convincingly shown that the rings and open-work plaques found in Alamannic graves are bag rings.[5] He suggests that a small pouch was fixed inside the ring and that this bag was closed by a draw thread; the bronze plaque covered this but could be lifted. The bags were attached to a chatelaine.

In England there are no records of the associated bronze discs. Some writers have suggested that the rings were bracelets, others that they formed part either of a chatelaine or of a bag. The latter interpretation is most probably correct. There are very few, if any, certain records of these rings being found actually on the arms of skeletons. For instance, although the Mitcham ring is stated to have been 'on the left forearm', it is also said to have been 'Found where the left arm should have been'.[6] Normally they are found beside the hip or below the waist.

There are many instances of these rings being found with girdle hangers or other parts of a chatelaine,[7] which strongly suggests that they belonged to a pouch or bag. There have been suggestions that the ivory rings sometimes bear the impressions of canvas.[8] This may be so, but transverse sections of elephant ivory do show a criss-cross pattern which could be mistaken for the weave of fabric. The type of bag suggested by Vogt can be shown to work satisfactorily in practice. But perhaps the simplest and most likely method was to attach the ring just inside the mouth of a long purse. This could then be suspended from the belt by

[1] Bidder and Morris 1959, 91. The so-called 'urn' with Galgenberg 18 is a small carinated bowl of early fifth-century type.

[2] No such ivory rings have been identified at Wester-wanna nor am I aware of any from the Elbe/Weser area. The absence of these rings may be apparent rather than real because, when broken, it is easy to overlook their fragments in a mass of cremated bones.

[3] e.g. Glen Parva (Leicester Museum (n.d.), 19–20 where wrongly described as bone), late fifth/early sixth century; Lackford, 50.71 (Lethbridge 1951, 18 and fig. 14) with a

cruciform brooch, about 500; Little Eriswell Grave 28 (Hutchinson 1966, 10–11), late sixth century; Barrington B Grave 75 (Fox 1923, 255), late sixth–seventh century.

[4] Lethbridge 1936, 23.

[5] Vogt 1960, 70 ff. and figs.

[6] Bidder and Morris 1959, 74, 117.

[7] e.g. Petersfinger Grave VIII (Leeds and Shortt 1953, 8 f. and fig. 3); Sleaford, Graves 78, 86, 143, 151, 207 (Thomas 1887, 386 ff.); Driffield Grave 18 (Mortimer 1905, 279).

[8] Sleaford, Grave 151 (Thomas 1887, 399).

a single thong attached to the ring at one point so that it hung vertically, thus closing the bag. Thus secured, a bag about twice as long as the diameter of the ring would remain closed under normal conditions, but any item could be removed easily and quickly without the need to untie and retie any draw threads (text-fig. 3).

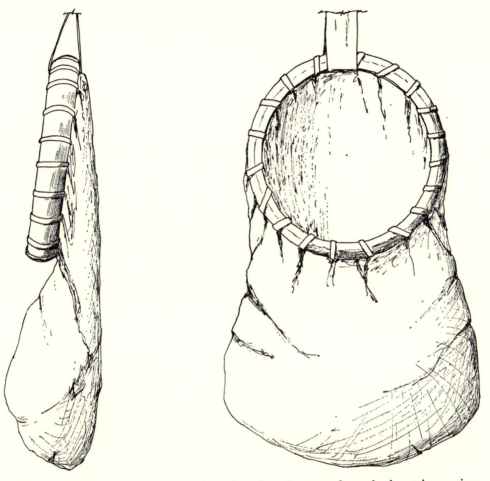

TEXT-FIG. 3. Reconstruction of a bag showing the use of an elephant-ivory ring.

MANICURE SETS

1. Urns with full set:

H 1 (fig. 35); M 8 (fig. 4); M 11 (fig. 15); M 32 (fig. 52); M 43 (fig. 25); M 51 (fig. 7); N 12 (fig. 7); N 16 (not fig.); N 49 (fig. 59); N 56 (fig. 34); N 59 (fig. 5); N 96 (fig. 4); X 23 (fig. 9); X 28 (fig. 12); Y 26 (fig. 28).

2. Urns with two elements only:

A 9 (fig. 25); D 8 (fig. 11); M 35 (fig. 26); M 52 (fig. 8); N 18 (fig. 25); N 26 (fig. 32); N 63 (fig. 25); N 76 (fig. 59); N 87 (fig. 28); P 14 (fig. 2).

3. Urns with single element only:

A 4 (fig. 28); D 9 (fig. 41); E 5 (fig. 1); E 9 (fig. 8); E 15 (fig. 35); E 16 (fig. 8); E 20 (fig. 10); K 7 (fig. 3); M 12 (fig. 59); M 17 (fig. 59); M 28 (fig. 59); M 31 (fig. 52); M 39 (fig. 14); M 44 (fig. 59); N 23 (fig. 26); N 28 (fig. 59); N 30 (fig. 9); N 41(b) (fig. 31); N 86 (fig. 6); N 93 (fig. 42); N 95 (fig. 4); N 102 (fig. 10); N 104 (fig. 59); X 29 (fig. 59); X 32 (fig. 59); Y 22 (fig. 2); Y 40 (fig. 12); Z 2 (fig. 59); No. 11 (fig. 60); No. 13 (fig. 60).

4. Urns with possibly a single element:

M 42 (fig. 18); N 35 (fig. 59); P 9 (fig. 59); X 38 (fig. 59); Y 8 (fig. 16); Y 41 (fig. 11); Z 6 (fig. 59).

At Caistor a manicure or toilet set consists of a pair of iron shears, an iron knife, and a pair of bronze or iron tweezers. Full sets are recorded from 15 urns. Two elements only are recorded from ten urns, although it is possible that N 18 contains three rather than two pieces. A single element has been identified with certainty from 28 urns, another (No. 11) apparently from an unurned cremation, with yet another (No. 13) being a stray find from the cemetery; four of these (E 5, M 12, N 30, and N 41(b)) may each contain two elements. A further seven urns contain iron fragments which may be part of one of these objects.

Toilet implements are the commonest type of grave goods from the cemetery, occurring certainly in fifty-three urns out of the 155 from which associated objects other than cremated human bone are recorded. In addition there are Nos. 11 and 13 and the seven possible pieces, giving a total of sixty-two burials associated with such implements. This is a very high proportion; even at Abingdon,[1] an English site renowned for its manicure sets, only ten out of the thirty-five urns containing grave goods held manicure sets or parts thereof.

At Caistor, as at a number of other cremation cemeteries in both Germany and England,[2] some of the toilet implements are miniature, non-functional ones (e.g. Altenwalde, Sancton, Yorks., Castle Acre, Norf.[3]). At some sites tweezers and shears, and occasionally knives, are cut from sheet bronze, but at Caistor only tweezers are made in this manner—E 5B, N 30B, N 59D, N 95C, and No. 13—and only one of these, N 95C, was found in a full set. N 30B was associated with a piece of iron which could well be a small knife or part of a small pair of shears, but the other examples were accompanied only by beads (E 5B), or a miniature urn (N 95), while No. 13 was a stray find. At Caistor there are twelve examples of funerary sets where all three implements are made of iron. These funerary sets are distinguished by the small size of the pieces (in eight urns all of the implements are less than two inches (5 cm.) long, and in the remaining four all are under 2·5 in. (6·35 cm.) long). The shape of the shears and knives is also distinctive. In some instances they are small copies of the large functional objects found in some of the urns and on domestic sites; but many of the knives in particular take quite distinctive forms not found in functional tools. As these objects are made of iron, and are therefore rusted, and many are broken, it is not always possible to determine the original form and size of the piece. In addition to the special funerary types of implements, and the rarer occurrence of large functional knives, shears, and tweezers in the urns, there are four examples of very stylish bronze tweezers, almost certainly Roman in origin.

[1] Leeds and Harden 1936, 11–23.   [2] Leeds 1936, 30–1; Baldwin Brown 1915, 391–4.
[3] Baldwin Brown 1915, pl. LXXXVII, 6, 7, 8.

Before considering further the associations of these implements, their types must be discussed. This typology is meant as a convenience; there is not yet sufficient evidence to determine if it has any significance.

Tweezers

Four types of tweezers can be distinguished at Caistor: I, functional bronze tweezers of Roman type; II, small bronze tweezers cut from sheet bronze; III, small iron tweezers; IV, large iron tweezers.

I. There are three certain examples of this type, K 7B, M 28B, and N 28B. These tweezers are stout and well made with the upper ends of the arms constricted to form a terminal loop. Sometimes a bronze or iron ring is linked to this, e.g. K 7B, so that the tweezers can be suspended from a belt or chatelaine. The distal ends are often expanded. The upper parts of the arms and the terminal loop are usually decorated with groups of incised horizontal lines and notches; in addition, the edges sometimes are faceted. K 7B is decorated merely with lines, but M 28B and N 28B are also notched. Such tweezers are found in cremation urns at cemeteries such as Little Wilbraham, Cambs.,[1] Lackford, Suff.,[2] Heworth, Yorks.[3] and Spong Hill, North Elmham, Norf.[4] A small pair was found in Abingdon C 9[5] in addition to a small pair of iron tweezers, iron shears and knife, and miniature bone comb. They are also recorded from inhumation burials, as for instance at Holywell Row, Suff.,[6] Petersfinger, Wilts.,[7] and Girton, Cambs.[8] It is difficult to be certain if any of these tweezers were actually of provincial Roman workmanship, acquired by purchase or picked up on a Roman site, or if Anglo-Saxon bronze workers produced such objects in the Roman tradition and decorated in the Roman manner. Lethbridge could match a pair from Lackford urn 48.2490 exactly at Roman Chesterford.[9] Lethbridge also considered that these tweezers must be early (i.e. fifth century).[10] One of the five pairs of bronze tweezers recorded from Galgenberg bei Cuxhaven is a very stylish example of this type,[11] found with an elaborate *Buckelurne* with a foot.[12] Other examples are known from the German cemeteries, for instance Hemmoor-Warstade[13] and Quelkhorn,[14] but unfortunately these are stray finds. A plainer pair from Duhnen-Wehrberg was found with a brooch of late fourth-century type.[15] Unfortunately, the evidence for Caistor adds little information about dating. Certainly K 7B is from an early Saxon wide-mouthed bowl (fig. 3) of the type dated to the late fourth or early fifth century (see p. 50), but M 28B and N 28B are only doubtfully associated with their urns. So unfortunately is X 29C, a small undecorated but very well-made pair of bronze tweezers which probably also fits into this group. M 28 and N 28 are both stylish and relatively early urns; X 29 is too fragmentary for a date to be suggested.

Lethbridge[16] states that these bronze tweezers were 'invariably unburnt when they were placed in the funerary urn', but M 28B has certainly been through the fire.

[1] Neville 1852, pl. 11.
[2] Lethbridge 1951, figs. 2, 5, 6, 12, 22, 35.
[3] Baldwin Brown 1915, LXXV, 1.
[4] Unpublished, in N.C.M.
[5] Leeds and Harden 1936, pl. III. 9.
[6] Lethbridge 1931, Grave 50, 28 and fig. 14. F and Grave 63, 33 and fig. 14. H.
[7] Leeds and Shortt 1953, pl. VIII.

[8] Hollingworth and O'Reilly 1925, pl. IV. 1 C.
[9] Lethbridge 1951, 17 and fig. 6.   [10] Ibid. 16.
[11] Waller 1938, 43 and 55 and Tafel 34. 5.
[12] Ibid. and Tafel 34. 6.
[13] Waller 1959, Tafel 22, Grab 64 and Grab 75.
[14] Ibid., Tafel 30, 76.
[15] Ibid. 28 and Tafel 41, 8a and b.
[16] Lethbridge 1951, 12.

II. As mentioned above five examples cut from sheet bronze are recorded—E 5B, N 30B, N 59D, N 95C, and No. 13. Two (N 95C and No. 13) are well made with a terminal loop formed by constricting the arms, and with inturned distal ends. However, neither is robust enough to have been used, even to pull out a small splinter. E 5B and N 30B are reasonably well made, but N 59D is very crude. The outline of this last pair was drawn on the sheet with a pointed instrument and the tweezers then seem to have been torn rather than clipped out. All the edges are rough and in one place the sheet did not tear along the line, leaving the scratched outline. The distal ends are inturned, but the two arms are separate. They may have been broken at the time they were made. There is no doubt that these at least were only token tweezers, possibly supplied at the last moment to complete a manicure set from which the original tweezers were missing. This pair is the only one of the five to be part of a full funerary set. In addition, this urn, one of the very early corrugated Anglian pots (see p. 46, fig. 5) contained a set of black and white gaming pieces and astragali of sheep and roe deer one of which, N 59F, bears a runic inscription (see pl. XIX*b* and p. 114). N 30B, which was found with two fragments of iron, perhaps to be identified as part of a knife or pair of shears, and N 95C, accompanied by a miniature urn, both come from Anglian vessels. N 95 (fig. 4) is a biconical corrugated urn, with a tall neck, very similar to N 59, but N 30 (fig. 9) is probably a little later as the vertical corrugation is not as regular and close-set. E 5B was accompanied by fused glass beads and comes from a large early Saxon vessel which can be dated also to the late fourth or early fifth century (see p. 45 and fig. 1).

Similar tweezers come from Sancton urn 12.[1] This is a fifth-century wide-mouthed shouldered urn decorated with three deeply tooled grooves on the neck above groups of three vertical grooves on the shoulder. The tweezers were accompanied by bronze shears and a knife. Another but better-made example from Sancton is from urn 9,[2] a large urn with stamped swags by a Sancton professional potter,[3] probably dating from the later sixth century. An example from Altenwalde, accompanied by miniature bronze shears and comb, and miniature iron knife, comes from a rather globular urn,[4] decorated with *stehende Bogen* and 'wyrm' stamps and dating probably from the first half of the fifth century.

III. By far the largest number of tweezers from Caistor, twenty-two in all, belong to this group of small iron pairs. Some may have been functional, but the rust has destroyed fine detail.

These can be divided into four groups:

(*a*) clearly well made with proximal loops and sharply angled distal ends—E 15C (with glass beads), M 35C (with iron knife and fragment of a large bone comb), M 32C (with iron knife and shears), and N 56D (with iron knife and shears, fragment of bone comb and fragment of sheet bronze). These tweezers could perhaps have been used.

(*b*) hardly any proximal loop but distal ends sharply inturned; again these might have been functional. The examples are N 93B (with two probable glass beads and a sheep's bone), N 102B (with fragment of bone comb), N 63C (with iron shears and two pieces of pig's ribs), N 76B (with probable shears and a fragment of iron which may be part of the

---

[1] Sheppard 1909, i, 57 and fig. 12b; ii, pl. V. fig. 12; Myres 1969, fig. 26. 143.

[2] Ibid. i, 54–5 and fig. 9c; ii, pl. IV. fig. 9.

[3] Myres 1969, fig. 30. 149.

[4] N.C.M. 27.95. Presented by H. W. Feilden.

tweezers), M 43C (with a miniature knife and probable shears), and X 23D (with knife and shears and a miniature bone comb).

(c) tweezers with some loop and the distal ends only gently angled—M 8D (with iron shears, a probable knife, and three fragments of iron now missing) and N 96D (with shears and knife).

(d) very crude tweezers with no loop and with no real angling of the distal ends—A 9C (with miniature shears), M 11D (with functional shears and a probable knife) and M 51D and N 49D (both with knife and shears). Y 26D (with knife and shears) had hardly any loop but the distal ends were broken, while D 8C (with shears and a water-worn quartz pebble which was only doubtfully associated), E 16B (with no additional grave goods), M 52C (with shears), H 1D (with knife and shears) and N 12D (with knife, shears, and iron ring possibly from the tweezers) are too fragmentary to classify.

It is interesting that the only certain associations of groups (c) and (d), which cannot have been functional, are with knives and shears, and that in eight of these cases the full set is present.

IV. There are very few examples of the certainly functional large tweezers from Caistor. The only complete example is M 39B; the distal ends of the arms are slightly expanded and inturned, and the proximal ends are constricted to form a loop which is linked to an iron ring. This is the only object recorded from the urn, a biconical vessel decorated with a zone of irregular three-line chevrons above linear swags. P 14C, which was accompanied by a large knife, has lost the distal ends of the arms, and the proximal ends were not apparently constricted to form a loop. The urn (fig. 2) is a Saxon type, decorated with neck grooves and three-line chevrons, which can probably be dated to the early years of the fifth century (see p. 45). X 28D is even more fragmentary; only part of one arm, perhaps rusted to a suspension ring, survives. The urn, which also contained a large knife and large shears, is a sharply biconical form with a cabled carination and *stehende Bogen*, and probably dates fairly early in the fifth century (see p. 53 and fig. 12). The other two pairs, N 18C and M 35C, are either small examples of this group or large examples of group IIIa. Both are well made with terminal loops. Urn N 18 is a plain globular urn with upright neck of Anglian type (fig. 25). N 18C was accompanied by a large pair of shears and probably a knife tang. M 35C was found with a knife and a fragment of bone comb. Urn M 35 (fig. 26) is a plain hump-shouldered vessel comparable with Lackford 50.71 which contained a late tutulus brooch and a cruciform brooch c. 500[1] (see p. 69). The association of these large functional iron tweezers would thus seem to be mostly with urns of markedly early type, and of both Anglian and Saxon derivation.

This high proportion of iron tweezers from urns is interesting for, except at Abingdon, Berks.,[2] they are apparently less common than bronze ones. They are recorded, however, from Castle Acre, Illington, and Spong Hill, North Elmham in Norfolk,[3] S. Elkington, Lincs.,[4] Lackford, Suff.,[5] and Little Wilbraham, Cambs.[6] It may be that they genuinely are rare; Baldwin Brown states: 'Tweezers, almost always of bronze, are a very common but rather a puzzling accompaniment of burials . . .'[7] However, it is possible that when in a

[1] Lethbridge 1951, fig. 14.
[2] Leeds and Harden 1936, 11–23 and pl. III.
[3] All in N.C.M. Unpublished.
[4] Webster and Myres 1951.
[5] Lethbridge 1951.
[6] Neville 1852, pl. 38.
[7] Baldwin Brown 1915, 392.

rusted and fragmentary state they have not been recognized. They are rare, too, on the Continent; for instance, only a single pair is recorded from Gudendorf,[1] and this unfortunately comes from a fragmentary urn.

Shears

All shears from Caistor are of iron. Only two examples are large and certainly functional —N 18B and X 28C. In both pairs the arms are about as long as the blades and the over-all length is more than 3·5 in. (8·9 cm.). X 28C was found with a large functional knife and a piece of iron which is probably part of a large pair of tweezers. N 18B was associated with a pair of iron tweezers almost two inches long and a fragment of iron, possibly a knife tang. The other pairs are all small. Some are like the two large pairs in having arms as long as, or a little longer than the blades, e.g. X 23C, N 56C, and it is possible that these were functional pairs; their size suggests that in strength they were something like modern embroidery scissors which are only suitable for cutting sewing threads. However, there are other pairs with long blades and short or very short arms. On A 9B for instance the arms are no more than a curve of iron joining the blades together. This is the ultimate in shortness of arm but other pairs also have very short arms, e.g. M 51C, M 8C, D 8B, and Z 2B. None of these can have been functional and surely must have been made merely as tokens. N 86B, despite its long arms and comparatively short blades, also seems to be a funerary pair as it is asymmetrical, one arm being appreciably shorter than the other. Although it is fragmentary, M 52B seems to be another example of this type. These short-armed shears grade into the long-armed functional types. A few examples of the short-armed type are found elsewhere in this country, e.g. Illington (urn 91) and Castle Acre, Norf.,[2] and in bronze at Loveden Hill, Lincs. However, at Abingdon they all seem to be of the long-armed type.[3] On the Continent short-armed bronze shears with kite-shaped blades have been found, for example at Altenwalde[4] and at Galgenberg bei Cuxhaven.[5] At the latter cemetery there was one very corroded pair of iron shears and five pairs of bronze shears.[6] All except the bronze pair cited are similar to the functional type with long arms and slender tapering blades. This type, whether large or miniature, in bronze or in iron, is that commonly found in German cemeteries.

Knives

Five or six of the iron knives from Caistor urns are ordinary domestic knives of the *sax* type with a straight-backed blade, angled shoulders and tapering tang and, originally, a wooden haft. Of these only one, X 28B, comes from a manicure set, and the shears and tweezers (if such X 28D represents) are large and functional. The biconical urn is decorated with a cabled carination and *stehende Bogen*; it is probably early fifth century in date (see p. 53, fig. 12). P 14B was associated with a large pair of probable iron tweezers. P 14 is one of the large late fourth-/early fifth-century Saxon urns which can be closely paralleled at

[1] Waller 1959, 26 and Tafel 37.
[2] In N.C.M.
[3] Leeds and Harden 1936, pl. III.
[4] Waller 1957, Tafel 1. 5.
[5] Waller 1938, 55–6 and Tafel 25. 6.
[6] Ibid. 55–6, where fig. refs. given.

sites such as Westerwanna (see p. 45), as is Y 22 (fig. 2) which contains another of these large knives, this time in association with three fragments of sheet bronze. N 23B was found in a plain globular urn of Anglian type (see p. 46, fig. 26) in association with an iron buckle. N 104B and X 38B were both only doubtfully associated with their urns.

The other knives, which are small, are quite different and were probably never meant to be used. Few, if any, had wooden hafts, even if they apparently have tangs. A number of types can be distinguished, although it is a little difficult to classify them all because many are broken or too rusty.

I. Long blade with the line of the haft continued along the back of the blade; the lower shoulder is curved. The back of the blade may be straight, e.g. N 96B, or curved, e.g. N 59B. The fragment of tang M 8B may belong to this group.

II. Short curved blade with no handle, but a small loop projecting above the back of the blade, e.g. N 12B. E 9B may be of this type.

III. Similar but with the loop below the back, e.g. P 9B. This is very close to one from C 13 at Abingdon.[1] X 23B, from Caistor, is probably similar, but the haft is broken.

IV. Knives with long, more or less parallel-sided blades and small loops instead of handles, e.g. Y 40B and H 1B. Y 40B has a long oval loop, and was accompanied only by a Roman coin which had been pierced for suspension. H 1B, with a very small loop, forms part of a full manicure set, as does Y 26B which is almost certainly of the same type.

V. Long iron handles forming an obtuse angle with the short curved and pointed blade. Two of these can be identified at Caistor—M 43B (the end of the handle is broken) and N 56B which has a shorter and flat handle with a hole at the end made simply by piercing the strip. This type is found at Abingdon, e.g. C 19, C 20, C 66.[2] Sometimes they can be difficult to distinguish from a single arm of a pair of shears, and it is likely that they are more widely distributed than has been realized.

It is possible that two of the 'knives' at Caistor were originally parts of shears—M 51B and N 36B. It is quite possible that M 51B, which is associated with a pair of shears and tweezers, was deliberately prepared from a pair of shears and added as a 'knife' to complete a full manicure set.

These small knives have been identified from other cremation cemeteries, for instance, types III and V from Spong Hill, North Elmham;[3] there is the well-known example of type III from Eye, Suff., found with a pair of iron shears, bronze tweezers, and a triangular bone comb in a fifth-century urn with a pedestal base, neck grooves, and long bosses flanked by pairs of vertical grooves.[4] A type I knife, very similar to N 59B but larger, was found at Sancton in urn 10, a *Buckelurne* of Myres Group II.[5] A number of these types are also found on the Continent, as for instance at Altenwalde,[6] Westerwanna[7] and Oberjersdal.[8] All these come from late fourth- or fifth-century urns of undoubted Saxon type. In England also, where the urns containing miniature sets of these implements can be dated, they can usually be assigned to the fifth century.

[1] Leeds and Harden 1936, pl. III. 13.
[2] Ibid., pl. III.
[3] In East Dereham Museum—unpublished.
[4] Akerman 1855, 43 f., pl. XXII.
[5] Sheppard 1909, 56 and fig. 10a, pl. IV. 10; Myres 1969, fig. 23. 128.

[6] Type III: Waller 1957, 7970, Tafel 2. 12, and 7947, Tafel 1. 5. Type IV: ibid., 1884, Tafel 14. 110.
[7] Type III: Zimmer-Linnfeld *et al.* 1960, 1184, Tafel 148. Type V: ibid., 1091, Tafel 134.
[8] Type III: Tischler 1955, Tafel 17, Grab IX.

Discussion

At Caistor the occurrence of manicure sets in urns of Anglian origin, notably in plain globular, in corrugated, and in bossed and corrugated urns, is very striking. Of the 13 urns which contained complete special funerary sets, eight can be classified as Anglian and only one as Saxon, i.e. N 56 (fig. 34), a fifth-century urn which can be paralleled in Holstein and the lower Elbe area and which may well come from the same workshop as N 54 and P 44 (see p. 55). In addition to the manicure set the urn contained a piece of bone comb and a fragment of sheet bronze. Other non-Anglian urns are M 11 (fig. 15), a carinated urn decorated with horizontal grooves and probably dating to the early fifth century, N 49 which is fragmentary, and Y 26 (fig. 28), a fifth-century urn of northern type with hollow neck and carinated shoulder. The latest urn to contain a set is M 32 (fig. 52) which comes from the workshop of Potter III. Typologically the urns of this potter would belong to the sixth century or even the early seventh (see p. 62); the products of this workshop are one of the only two professional potter groups from Caistor which contain grave goods. M 31 contains a small pair of shears with very short arms; M 57 contains scraps of sheet bronze. At least three other products of this potter are very fragmentary.

Of the other urns containing one or two elements of a special funerary set, eleven out of twenty-five are Anglian. Of the others the grave goods are only doubtfully associated with N 76 and M 12, urns M 17 and X 32 are missing, M 31 is, as mentioned above, by Potter III, N 87 and A 4 are the northern type with hollow necks and carinated shoulders, and E 5 is one of the large late fourth-/early fifth-century Saxon urns; the rest cannot really be classified more specifically than as Anglo-Saxon.

The urns containing large sets, or one or two elements thereof, are more varied. N 18, M 35, and N 23 (figs. 25 and 26) are plain globular urns of Anglian origin. P 14, Y 22, and K 7 (figs. 2 and 3) are late fourth-/early fifth-century Saxon urns, while X 28 (fig. 12) is a fifth-century Saxon urn decorated with *stehende Bogen*.

This association of manicure sets predominantly with urns of Anglian antecedents rather than with those of Saxon origin is especially surprising because, on the Continent, Anglian urns of the plain globular or corrugated types rarely contain any grave goods. Unfortunately, these types of urns are not common in this country[1], so that it is difficult to be certain if Caistor is unique in this respect. At Sancton, where there is the most closely comparable group of early Anglian forms, no similar concentration of manicure sets is apparent. But the contents of many urns from the earlier excavations there are ill-recorded.

The social implications of this are of considerable interest. On the Continent these manicure sets, particularly those of special funerary type, seem to occur mainly in pots of the fourth and early fifth centuries, the period at which it is suggested the earlier Saxon settlers were to be found at Caistor.[2] The Anglian urns which contain these funerary sets at Caistor are on typological grounds and continental dating (see pp. 45–7) contemporary in the main with the Saxon series. This suggests fusion at Caistor of Angle and Saxon funerary customs, and thus possibly a merging of their separate social organizations, at a period when the

[1] Myres 1969, 53.
[2] It is a remarkable fact that east of the Elbe in Mecklenburg the use of manicure sets in cremation burials went out of fashion altogether by the fourth century: it is only in the Saxon lands further west that it lasted long enough to be brought to Britain by the earliest settlers (Schach-Dörges 1970, Abb. 1).

ceramic traditions of the two peoples were still recognizably distinct. It is noticeable that only a few of the distinctively Saxon urns contain even one element of a manicure set, and that the majority of these are large functional pieces. It could even be suggested that if, as seems probable, manicure sets are an indication of male burials, their common association here with the earlier Anglian urns might indicate a special issue to a group of men jointly engaged on some similar task. None of the large long tanged knives with small washers on the ends of the tangs, found at a number of German sites but particularly at Westerwanna,[1] have been found at Caistor. Examples of this type such as have been found in late Roman military burials at Winchester[2] have not been recognized in cremation urns in England.

SCRAP BRONZE

D 3 (fig. 59); D 7 (fig. 38); E 4 (fig. 18); E 20 (fig. 10); M 49(a) (fig. 14); N 39 (fig. 3); N 56 (fig. 34); P 8 (fig. 31); P 11 (fig. 59); P 20 (fig. 28); P 32/33 (fig. 59); P 34 (fig. 53); X 24 (fig. 17); X 25 (fig. 59); X 35 (fig. 1); Y 3 (fig. 14); Y 22 (fig. 2); Y 36 (fig. 33).

The most puzzling grave goods are the pieces of scrap bronze found in eighteen urns at Caistor. The number of pieces in each urn varies from one to thirty-three. In every case except D 7, M 49(a), and X 25 the fragments are pieces of bronze sheet broken or clipped out of a larger piece. Some pieces could have come from broken-up cauldrons; the thickness of the sheet is consistent with this, and E 14 contains a piece with four rivets of the type found in cauldrons. This could be part of a patch. D 7 also contained two irregularly shaped fragments, but the bronze is slightly thicker than the rest. M 49(a) and P 8 both contained bronze strips. One of the pieces in M 49(a) had small rivet holes in it with one pin-like rivet still in position. These might be part of a binding, perhaps from a girdle. The two in P 8 (which probably originally joined) are less distinctive, but could also be a piece of binding. Nine of the urns contained pieces which were warped and distorted by fire, which might perhaps indicate that they were in fact part of an object worn by the dead person at the time of the cremation. P 8 and P 20 also contained beads which would indicate women's burials, but the latter urn contained thirty-three pieces and they were not parts of a pair of brooches or fragments of wrist clasps. The pieces, except for the effects of fire, differed little from unburnt examples. P 34 was a child's cremation and contained, in addition to the bronze fragment, a bone comb and the base of a Samian Form 33 cup. In all, eleven of the urns contained grave goods additional to the bronze; E 20 had a pair of shears, N 56 a funerary manicure set and a comb fragment, N 39 a miniature urn, X 25 an iron nail, P 8 beads, P 20 beads, a comb fragment, and animal bones, P 11 perhaps a fragment of burnt animal bone, while P 32 or 33 (see p. 175) contained an iron hinge which may be associated with the bronze.

The urns themselves show a considerable variation in type and date range, although certain urns of Saxon type can be identified (N 56, X 35, and Y 22), while no distinctively Anglian vessels contained pieces.

Parallels are not easy to find although one suspects that this lack may be apparent rather than real, in that such scrap pieces are usually not illustrated and are only rarely mentioned in published reports. A larger number of such pieces were found in a Sancton urn and Sheppard thought they were part of a bronze cup or box.[3] An elaborately stamped and bossed

[1] e.g. Zimmer-Linnfeld et al. 1960, Tafel 20. 155.   [2] Clarke, G. 1970, figs. 4–6.   [3] Sheppard 1909, 65.

bowl from Nassington, Northants,[1] contained a number of fragments 'including one of waisted elliptical shape, L. 1 in., perforated at either end'. Other grave goods were a bone spindle whorl or toggle, a piece of an iron key, a small bronze ring, and a fragment of ivory ring, indicating a woman's burial. They are known also from Abingdon, Berks.,[2] South Elkington, Lincs.,[3] and in Norfolk at Castle Acre,[4] Spong Hill, North Elmham, and Illington.[5] At North Elmham fragments were found in urns 23 (with a gaming piece and a possible bone bead; ? young adult male[6]), 28 (with a burnt bone ring, part of a brooch, glass beads, and a bronze rivet; ? young adult female), and 38 (with bronze tweezers, fragment of iron, possibly a knife, glass bead; child). All three urns on typological grounds date to ± 500. There were a number of examples from Illington, at least seven groups appearing to be just scrap metal. Urns 41/41A and 47 had beads in addition while urns 47, 101, and 130 all contained cruciform brooches (47 ?Group II, 101 Group II, and 130 Group II or III). These would indicate again the association with women's burials, in some instances at least.

Where these fragments can be associated with females (two children's burials are noted above), it is possible that they come from bronze work-boxes similar to those found, for example, at Barton-on-Humber, Yorks.,[7] Burwell,[8] or Little Wilbraham, Cambs.[9] These were carried on the person and sometimes at least hung from a chatelaine. That many of the fragments were on the body is suggested by the burnt condition of nine of the groups. The piece from E 14 is difficult to fit onto a bronze work-box, but it could perhaps be a patch. The bronze clip found in Illington urn 101 could be part of such a box.

It is not impossible that scrap bronze was used at this period as an irregular sort of token currency. Bronze had a value as the raw material for jewellery and small tools, and a collection of such scraps could be useful whether for disposal to a metal-worker in return for finished goods or as small change in the absence of a minted coinage.

SPINDLE WHORLS

P 24 (fig. 59); X 29 (fig. 59); No. 4 (fig. 60).

The two spindle whorls recorded from urns are of different materials. X 29B was made from a grey ware Roman potsherd; it was possibly associated with a small, well-made, plain pair of bronze tweezers which, like it, came from a mass of sherds which represented several urns. P 24B is of bone, with concentric incised lines, probably lathe marks, and was found with the fragmentary remains of a plain urn.

Spindle whorls are known from both cremation and inhumation burials, but some examples seem more like large beads and may have served as such. Clay spindle whorls have been recorded from German cemeteries at Galgenberg,[10] Wehden[11] (bone also) and Mahndorf.[12] A plain bone spindle whorl comes from C 29 at Abingdon, Berks., with a saucer

---

[1] Leeds and Atkinson 1944, 103.
[2] Leeds and Harden 1936.
[3] Webster and Myres 1951, 29.
[4] N.C.M. unpublished, 1961 excavations.
[5] N.C.M. unpublished.
[6] We are indebted to Dr. Calvin Wells for reporting on the cremated human material.

[7] Sheppard 1940, 258–60 and fig. on p. 261; 46–7 and fig. 18.
[8] Lethbridge 1931, Gr. 121, fig. 36.1; Gr. 42, fig. 28 and pl. III.   [9] Neville 1852, Gr. 42, pl. 15.
[10] Waller 1938, 57–8, Tafel, 15, 8. 9 and 31, 8.
[11] Waller 1961, 25–6, Tafel 51.
[12] Grohne 1953, 159–62, Abb. 59.

brooch fragment[1] of the sixth century. A second bone spindle whorl, decorated in a similar manner to P 24B comes from Inhumation 61 at Abingdon.[2] This child's burial was a rich one and again dates from the sixth century. Another bone example is recorded from Sleaford, Lincs., Grave 55,[3] in company with a cruciform brooch and a small long brooch of the panelled square-head type,[4] obviously a sixth-century grave. Again a sixth-century date is suggested by the example from Inhumation 71, at Girton, Cambs.[5] The nearest parallel in form comes from Falcon Inn, Petty Cury, Cambridge. It was found in 1904 possibly associated with part of a shale bracelet, part of a double-sided bone comb and four glass beads.[6] It is not certain if these come from a burial.

The parallels cited suggest a sixth-century date for the bone piece P 24B. Spindle whorls made from Roman potsherds are known from both Roman and Saxon domestic sites. Examples similar to X 29B were found in the Roman town at Caistor so that it must remain uncertain if this is a Roman piece or of contemporary Anglo-Saxon manufacture.

No. 4, a clay object, is a stray from the cemetery area. It is not certainly a spindle whorl, nor is it certainly from an Anglo-Saxon burial; it was found beneath urns E 7 and 8. It is similar to a clay whorl from Lackford.[7] The latter is, however, only half as thick. No. 4 shows no sign of having been in a cremation fire, and it could perhaps be a Roman piece. If it is not a spindle whorl it is perhaps some type of weight, intended to hold a thread taut.

WRIST CLASP

F 4 (fig. 59).

It is unfortunate that the only identifiable wrist clasp could not be certainly associated with any urn. It does come from a cremation as it was found in a bone mass (see p. 133). Only half the clasp survives, the eye half, and this is incomplete, the ends and the bar being broken. One other wrist clasp is recorded from the cemetery, from Grave 10 (see p. 222); it may come from a disturbed cremation. It is of the same simple type, but rather flimsier.

F 4B is made from sheet bronze and decorated with a line of punched circles parallel with the edges. It belongs to the simplest type without any strengthening bars, the type illustrated by Baldwin Brown from near Welbourn, Lincs., Holdenby, Northants., and Rothley Temple, Leics.[8]

The typology and distribution of these objects have been discussed by a number of authors,[9] almost entirely in relation to their occurrence with inhumation burials. Such clasps are, however, recorded from cremation burials at Sancton, Yorks., where it was misidentified as a belt-clasp,[10] and at Lackford, Suff.[11] The clasp in urn 50.127 was accompanied by the foot of an early sixth-century cruciform brooch, while that in urn 48.2483 was found with a mount from a drinking horn which Lethbridge dated to the later sixth century. This dating is consistent with that suggested by the evidence from inhumation burials.

[1] Leeds and Harden 1936, 17 and pl. IV.
[2] Ibid. 43 and pl. XIII.
[3] Thomas 1887, 392.   [4] Leeds 1945, 32–6 and 105.
[5] Hollingworth and O'Reilly 1925.
[6] Museum of Archaeology and Ethnology, Cambridge, no. 1904.299.   [7] Lethbridge 1951, 22 and fig. 35, 50.209B.
[8] Baldwin Brown 1915, pl. LXXVIII, 1, 2, 3.

[9] e.g., op. cit., 362–6; Leeds 1945, 53–61; Lethbridge 1931, 78–9. The most recent study is in an unpublished Oxford B.Litt. thesis by Hayo Vierck.
[10] Sheppard 1909, 62, fig. 20b.
[11] Lethbridge 1951, urn 50.127, p. 18 and fig. 14; urn 48.2483, p. 19, fig. 20; urn 48.2472, p. 19, fig. 20; urn 50.95A, p. 20, fig. 24.

I

THE RUNIC INSCRIPTION FROM N 59

By R. I. Page

THE following abbreviations are used:

Gmc	Germanic
nom.	nominative
OE	Old English
OHG	Old High German
ON	Old Norse
PrOE	Primitive Old English
PrON	Primitive Old Norse
sg.	singular

One of the astragali from N 59 was found to bear a runic inscription (pl. XIX*b*). This bone was originally identified and has been published as sheep, as were all the other astragali from this urn. Recently, however, a re-examination has shown that the runic astragalus is in fact roe deer and not sheep; of the other thirty-five or more astragali, one can be identified as roe deer and fifteen as sheep. Identification of the remainder is uncertain (Inventory, p. 160, F and G).

The Caistor-by-Norwich runemaster used a sharp instrument to cut or scratch his six letters on one of the broad faces of this large astragalus. He set them out in a single line so that they occupy most of the available space. The main staves, 11–14 mm. high, run from just below the top down to the base, which is rather worn as though with frequent handling. Letters are shaped with some care, though inevitably on a small object like this there is clumsiness—stems may be crooked and joins not cleanly made, while there seems to be a graver slip at rune 3. Yet there is no difficulty of identification, and the intended lines are clearly distinguishable from chance scratches or breaks. There is no other sign of working anywhere on the astragalus.

The runes are

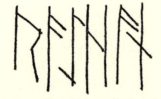

TEXT-FIG. 4. Runic inscription (scale $\frac{2}{1}$)

Using Professor Bruce Dickins's system of transliteration for Anglo-Saxon runes,[1] these are

'r æ ჳ h æ n'
1 2 3 4 5 6

[1] Dickins 1932; see in general Marquardt 1961.

However, since that system of transliteration is probably misleading in the case of Caistor-by-Norwich, it is better to define the runes by their rune-names. These are

1. OE *rad*, ON *reið*, Gothic *reda*, apparently 'riding, the act of riding'.

2 and 5. OE *æsc*, 'ash-tree', though with the form of the Germanic *a*-rune whose name, recorded in Gothic as *aza* (<Gmc * *ansuz*, 'god, spirit'), developed into OE as *os*, into ON as *óss*.

3. OE *eoh*, *íh*, 'yew-tree', no ON equivalent known; the Gothic equivalent may have the name *ezec*.

4. OE *hægel*, ON *hagall*, Gothic *haal*, 'hail'.

6. OE *ned*, *nyd*, ON *nauðr*, 'need, necessity', Gothic *noicz*.

Only rune 4 is typologically interesting. If this is the *h*-rune, and I cannot see what else it can be, it is of unusual form for England for it has the single cross-bar typical of North and East Germanic inscriptions. The only comparable English examples are on the Ash (Gilton) pommel, the Loveden Hill urn and the Sandwich/Richborough stone, but in none of these is the form clear or the identification certain. Hickes's transcript of the lost Cotton MS. Otho B X shows a single-barred *h*-rune, but he may be inaccurate or have copied from a faded exemplar. Otherwise, Anglo-Saxon and Continental West Germanic inscriptions have exclusively the two-barred *h*-rune, ᛡ, amply evidenced. The single-barred *h*-rune is widespread in Scandinavia where its southernmost examples are on the Torsbjerg, Angeln, shield-boss and the Gallehus, Tønder, golden horn. South and west of this line is an area with no surviving runes until we come to the Frisian inscriptions, which use the double-barred type.[1] Thus it looks as though the Caistor-by-Norwich runes are to be linked to the Scandinavian ones, particularly since the cemetery shows other influence from South Jutland/Fyn. The inscription is then likely to be nearer North than West Germanic or, if such terms are appropriate to the Caistor-by-Norwich date, nearer PrON than PrOE.

The point is important in considering what phonetic values the runemaster attached to the runes ᚨ (2, 5) and ᛁ (3). In North Germanic the old *a*-rune remained the symbol for the low back vowel. In OE it was used for the fronted sound (given in written texts by *æ*) which developed under certain circumstances from earlier *a*, and for related front sounds. So it received the new rune-name *æsc*. For the surviving back vowel, and related sounds, the Anglo-Saxons used a new rune ᚪ, given the name *ac*, 'oak'. On Caistor-by-Norwich I think it likely that ᚨ retains the value *a*. ᛁ is a rare rune, and it is hard to establish its phonetic value. I have argued in detail elsewhere that this rune originally represented a high front vowel in the region of *i*, even though in later Anglo-Saxon inscriptions it appears for the spirant [x]. Thus the inscription is to be read *raihan*.

As the bibliography shows, the late Professor C. L. Wrenn was active in examining this legend.[3] He recognized the problems arising from the very early date of the material and our uncertainty as to its context of thought, and so he admitted that his interpretations could only be conjectural. To me they have seemed, not merely conjectural, but also most unlikely. I have argued specifically against them elsewhere,[4] and here I am content to sum up my arguments. Professor Wrenn began by assuming that the Caistor-by-Norwich runes

---

[1] The Hailfingen *sax* has a pair of very dubious single-barred forms among other curious pseudo-runic characters; see Arntz and Zeiss 1939, 242–5.

[2] Page 1968.

[3] Wrenn 1959, 1962, 1965.

[4] Page 1968.

were magical, though he never said why. He made the suggestive comment that this Anglo-Saxon burial ground was close to the Roman town of *Venta Icenorum*, whose ruins had 'magical associations' for the Anglo-Saxons. Certainly, later generations seem to have regarded ancient works with awe, but the attitude of the Anglo-Saxons of this cemetery to the nearby Roman site is unknown. We are not even sure what was the state of the Roman town in the fifth century, whether it was still occupied, and if so by whom. There is some evidence—equivocal, however—of a massacre on the site no earlier than 400,[1] and the Anglo-Saxons may well have regarded *Venta Icenorum* more as a devastated enemy stronghold than as *orðanc enta geweorc*, 'a skilfully wrought structure of giants'. In any case such a superstitious view would not explain a magical inscription on an object connected, not essentially with the cemetery itself, but with the activities of someone cremated and buried there. Presumably Wrenn's assumption is based on the thesis that runes were in essence magical. This thesis is contested by many modern runologists.[2]

Wrenn added two details to support his case: (i) the group of astragali were probably used in gaming, and perhaps this activity had magical implications, as in the divination and lot-casting which Tacitus describes as customary among the Germani. There seems, however, no reason to assume that Anglo-Saxon gaming was necessarily linked to magic, especially since Tacitus tells how the Germani were addicted to gambling, which surely implies non-magical games; (ii) the number of astragali in urn N 59 was thirty, which was a magical number. Certainly, thirty, like other multiples of three, was probably a magical number among the Anglo-Saxons. Unfortunately we do not know the exact number of astragali in urn N 59; there were at least thirty-five others (p. 160).

I therefore reject Wrenn's various magical interpretations of the Caistor-by-Norwich legend (as well as rejecting his reading, *rah(w)han*, with rune ᛇ taken as a labial spirant). It is proper that I suggest an alternative, though the material is inadequate for more than conjecture. Two roots could give *raihan*:[3] (i) **rei-*, 'scratch, cut, tear', which gives, with the *-k(h)-* suffix, OHG *riga*, 'line', *rihan*, 'set in line', ON *rá*, *rámerki*, 'landmark, boundary', and, with suffix differentiation, OE *raw*, *ræw*, 'row'; (ii) **rei-*, 'dappled, coloured'. With a *-ko-* suffix this gives OE *raha*, *ra*, 'roebuck', *ræge*, 'roe'. Each of these could form a weak masculine *nomen agentis*, (i) meaning 'inscriber, ?runemaster, ?one who sets things in line', (ii) perhaps meaning 'stainer, colourer', whose connection with runic inscriptions could be that, both in fact and fiction, runes were often painted: cf. the ON verb *faihido*, 'painted', on the Einang, Valdres, stone, *faþi* on that from Valby, Vestfold. Thus **raiho* could mean 'painter, i.e. runemaster'. In a discussion of the place-name Teversall, Notts., E. Ekwall considered the element *tiefrere*, *tefrere*, derived from OE *teafor*, 'raddle used as a pigment'. The word's cognates, ON *taufr*, OHG *zouber* mean 'magic', and Ekwall suggests that *tiefrere* might mean 'sorcerer'.[4] By a similar semantic process **raiho*, 'colourer', might gain this meaning. Caistor-by-Norwich *raihan* can hardly retain the very primitive *-an* ending of the nom. sg. of a *nomen agentis*; it must rather be an oblique ending as in PrON *wita(n)dahalaiban* on the Tune, Ostfold, stone. The text could then mean something like '(this belongs) to **raiho*' or '(the property) of **raiho*'. **raiho* could have developed into a personal name as did such words as

[1] For the supposed massacre, see pp. 33–4.

[2] For a sceptical view based on the Anglo-Saxon material see Page 1964.

[3] Pokorny 1959, i. 857–9.

[4] Ekwall 1960.

OE *Beta, Wealda, Hunta, *Ridda*. Possibly *raiho* could apply to the astragalus itself and mean something like 'that which marks', with the oblique case implying '(acting as) a marker'.

A final suggestion relates together both the astragali and the gaming pieces from urn N 59. The latter probably and the former possibly were used in some board game such as flourished in classical times and was taken up by the Germanic peoples, ON *tafl*, OE *tæfl* (< Latin *tabula*).[1] The astragali form a group of about thirty-five, one of which seems distinguished from the others by its size, its inscription, and perhaps its colour. There are thirty-three gaming pieces, forming by their colours two groups, one twice the strength of the other. These two characteristics occur in a game recorded often in medieval Norse literature under the name *hnefatafl*, a version of which was played in later Anglo-Saxon England. The game takes place between two sides of unequal size, the smaller occupying the centre of a chequered board, the larger its edges. The king (ON *hnefi*, OE ?*cyningstan*), a piece different in some way from the others, is put at the centre surrounded by defenders. The attacking side tries to capture the king, the defenders to open up a way to the board's edge. *raihan* could be some sort of distinguishing name for the king. Alternatively, the astragali could be pieces in a board game based on the chase, where one piece is pursued by a number of others, though I know of no evidence that the Anglo-Saxons knew chase games. In these the pieces are usually called by animal names, fox and geese, fox and lambs, wolf and sheep, etc. It is a long shot, but *raihan* could be such an animal name, related to Gmc *raiho*, whence OE *raha, ra*, 'roebuck'.

[1] On these see Pauly-Wissowa 1894, s.v. *lusoria tabula*; Austin 1934–5, 24–34, 76–82; Murray 1952, 55–64.

THE WOLF AND BOAT DRAWING ON R 9/10 (text-fig. 5, fig. 44 and pl VI*a*)

By Barbara Green

THE urn fragment (described on p. 180) shows a wolf or dog with long curving tail and open jaws apparently barking at a retreating boat which is shown with high prow, stern paddle, and thirteen vertical strokes representing either oars or the upright spears of the crew. We are greatly indebted to Miss V. I. Evison, F.S.A., for the suggestion that the scene depicted on this sherd may have been a representation of an incident in a northern myth, a much later written version of which has survived in Snorri Sturlusson's *Edda, Gylfaginning*. The suggested scene depicted is from the day of the Doom of the Gods. If this interpretation is correct, the boat is *Naglfar*—the ship made of dead men's nails—and the wolf *Fenrir*, one of Loki's offspring.

And Naglfar will flee on this raging sea, and a giant called Hrymr will steer Naglfar. And the wolf Fenrir will go along with a gaping mouth, his lower jaw towards the earth and his upper jaw towards the heaven; it would gape more if there were room.[1]

A steering oar is clearly shown towards the stern of the boat and the jaws of the animal are gaping. Such a scene, taken from a Doom story, would be appropriate for a burial urn.

TEXT-FIG. 5. The wolf and boat drawing on urn R 9/10 (scale ½)

The association of ships with the dead at this period is well known, andt he practice of ship-burial in seventh-century East Anglia is attested at Sutton Hoo and Snape. The discovery in the Middle Saxon (*c.* 650–850) cemetery at Caister-on-Sea of parts of boats laidover the bodies[2] shows that the association of boats with the dead was not the prerogative of royalty.

The suggestion of a fifth-century date for this piece cannot stand.[3] R 9/10 is by the same potter as E 8, and this urn was part of the E 7 group. E 7 is not likely to be much earlier than 600 and was old when buried with a group of urns that are all stylistically decadent (see p. 59). An early seventh-century date would not be unreasonable for E 8 and R 9/10. The potter would therefore be working in Norfolk not much before the time when ship-burial was certainly being practised in the area.

The wolf on R 9/10, with its long snout, long lean body, and the line dividing the tail from the haunch, is unlike the naturalistic animals of the fifth-century Quoit Brooch style.[4] It is much nearer in feeling to the wolves shown on the left-side panel of the Franks casket,[5] though these are of course later in date than R 9/10.

---

[1] We are much indebted to Mrs. Elizabeth Okasha for this translation. The text used was Gordon 1927, 17–18.

[2] Green 1963, 57.

[3] Gelling and Davidson 1969, 156 and fig. 76.

[4] Evison 1965.

[5] British Museum 1923, pl. VIII.

HUMAN REMAINS

INTRODUCTION By J. N. L. Myres

AT the time when the excavation of the Caistor cemetery took place, little attention was commonly paid by excavators to the study of the cremated bones in the urns. It was not generally appreciated how much information might be obtained from them regarding the age, sex, stature, or pathology of the individuals concerned, the presence or absence of extraneous matter such as animal or bird bones, the possibility of double or even multiple cremations and so on. In consequence very few collections of cremated bones from older excavations of Anglo-Saxon cemeteries have survived for osteological analysis.

The Caistor cemetery is unfortunately no exception to this general rule. F. R. M. did not normally preserve from the contents of the urns which he excavated anything except the associated grave-goods, whether of metal, glass, bone, or occasionally pottery. He noted the exceptional occurrence of mineral objects, such as translucent pebbles or pieces of iron pyrites. The rest he threw away. He was, however, interested in signs indicating the cremation of children and retained some evidence for this practice, mainly in the form of milk teeth and skull bones. He also records that in November 1936 he became aware of the presence of animal bones in some urns, and from that point he seems to have kept a number of bones which he recognized as proof of this practice.[1]

In consequence of this selective treatment, the small groups of surviving bones from the cremations, which come from only thirty-seven urns in all, cannot be regarded as a fair sample even from this small number of deposits. Any attempt to use them statistically would prove very misleading. While it is very unfortunate that F. R. M. kept so little of this material, it must be remembered that genuinely uncontaminated deposits would only have occurred in those urns that were still reasonably complete in the ground. Since the great majority were already crushed or collapsed or partly missing there could never have been anything like the quantity of closed deposits available for osteological study as might be implied by the very large number of urns that were eventually capable of reconstruction.

Dr. Calvin Wells has kindly examined this disappointing group of material and has reported on it as follows. Where he has been able to provide any significant information on the contents of individual urns it has been added at the appropriate points in the Inventory.

[1] F. R. M.'s note on animal bones is worth quoting. He wrote: 'In Nov. 1936 I noticed for the first time an animal bone in one of the urns among the human burnt bones . . . Since my attention was called to the matter by the finding of this bone, I have carefully looked for animal bones . . . and frequently found them. This makes it certain that I must previously have overlooked scores of similar cases. . . . I think the most likely explanation of the presence of the animal bones in the urns is that pieces of cooked meat were placed in them . . . probably as provision for the journey to the next world. With one exception [the bird bones in A 3] all those . . . have belonged either to sheep or pigs . . . . On two or three occasions I have found urns actually standing on bones. In one of these cases the urn was resting on large pieces of the nasal and frontal bones of . . . probably an ox or horse. . . . I have also found portions of the ribs of a large animal placed on the shoulder of one of the urns. . . . I now think that at least 15% of the urns had animal bones.'

THE CREMATIONS By Calvin Wells

THIS potentially valuable series of cremations is almost worthless for the osteologist, owing to the scanty amount of material which has been preserved. It seems likely that at least 90 per cent of the contents even of the thirty-seven urns here considered were jettisoned at the time of excavation. Of these surviving specimens only four could not have fitted into a pocket matchbox. Some of them consist of no more than three or two or even a single fragment of bone. Yet F. R. M.'s notes clearly show that in some of these instances very substantial amounts of bone were originally present. He seems to have selected children's cremations in preference to adults' and teeth in preference to other skeletal fragments. One may wonder, therefore, if any purpose can now be served by a scrutiny of the few osteological crumbs which survive. To examine and pronounce on them incurs the hazard of misinterpretation; to ignore them is defeatist. It has been decided to present a brief account of what still survives and to treat the material on its present merits, but any conclusions reached must be handled with the greatest caution. This is all the more lamentable because, slight though the material is, it seems probable that it may originally have presented some unusual features and raised interesting problems.

To determine the age at death of each individual was quite impossible with such deficient remains. Only three categories of age were adopted: Infant (under two years), Child, and Adult. It is likely that all 'Child' cremations were under 13 years of age: no adolescents were recognized. Of the twenty-eight surviving specimens containing human remains thirteen (46·4 per cent) were children or infants. This high figure contrasts with what I have found in other cemeteries, using the same criteria of age. It is almost certainly due to F. R. M.'s special interest in child cremation. Even so he identified only twenty-six examples, a proportion that is significantly low in relation to what might be expected from the total number of surviving urns. Table 1 shows the incidence of under 13-year-old burials from a few other Anglo-Saxon urnfields.

TABLE 1

Site	Date	Total cremations	Infants and children		Underfired		Surviving petrous temporals		Cremations with animal bones	
			n	%	n	%	n	%	n	%
Caistor-by-Norwich	A-S	28	13	46·4	1	3·6	13	23·2	5	17·8*
Loveden Hill, Lincs.[1]	A-S	66†	10	15·1	6	9·0	5	3·5	11	16·9
Illington, Norfolk[2]	A-S	104	18	17·3	28	26·9	30	14·4	22	21·1
North Elmham (Spong Hill), Norfolk[1]	A-S	40	10	25·0	11	27·5	18	22·5	11	27·5

* Of the twenty-eight cremations containing human remains five (17·8 per cent) also contained animal bone. Nine cremations contained only animal bone, making a total of fourteen (37·8 per cent) out of thirty-seven. This probably is the result of selection by the excavator.

† This sample is not greatly more representative than that from Caistor, for nearly 350 cremation urns are recorded from the Loveden Hill cemetery.

[1] Wells (unpublished).   [2] Wells (1960).

At Illington it was possible to record not only the frequency with which animal bones accompanied the cremations but also to recognize a pattern of distribution according to the age and sex of the individuals and the species of animal found with them. At Caistor we face the tantalizing recognition that, even among these scanty remnants, at least fourteen cremations contained animal remains. As indicated above F. R. M. began to take an interest in the animal bones from his urns only after he had been excavating the cemetery for some time. This explains how it comes about that in addition to the twenty-eight urns with human remains, the material which he kept from nine urns consisted only of animal bones.[1] It seems certain that here we have the result of a selection by F. R. M. of animal remains and the discarding of any human fragments that accompanied them.

In the Markshall Anglo-Saxon cremations (see p. 245) 43 per cent showed some degree of underfiring. At Loveden Hill 9 per cent, at Illington 27 per cent, at North Elmham (Spong Hill) 27·5 per cent were similarly recorded as being inefficiently cremated to some extent. At Caistor-by-Norwich only one specimen (3·6 per cent) gave evidence of inadequate firing. This is not to be interpreted, however, as a demonstration of unusual efficiency. It is no doubt nothing more than another reflection of the inadequate sample.

Determination of sex is virtually impossible with these meagre fragments. Two burials were tentatively estimated as females and three as males. No cremation showed any evidence of containing more than one individual. The only pathology detected was the ante-mortem loss of three teeth in Y 16 and dental irregularity and overcrowding in the urnless burial.

A feature of some interest is that, despite the perfunctory preservation of this material, no fewer than thirteen petrous temporal bones survive out of the fifty-six possible in the twenty-eight individuals which are represented. This 23·2 per cent survival rate might at first be thought to be due to another haphazard whimsy of selection on the part of the excavator. But in fact it is nearly identical with the petrous temporal survival rate at North Elmham (Spong Hill), a completely reliable series, where the frequency was 22·5 per cent. This figure is by no means uncommon in urnfields although rates ranging from 12–16 per cent, as at Welwyn and Illington, are more usual. The very low 3·8 per cent at Loveden Hill may also be due to the inadequacy of the sample.

[1] Apart from the bird bones in A 3, the collection includes no non-human bones in urns before the early part of the M series. This was probably the point at which F. R. M. began to notice their presence.

INVENTORY OF CREMATION POTTERY AND ASSOCIATED GRAVE GOODS

By J. N. L. Myres and Barbara Green

The four-figure number to the right of the Inventory number is that under which the urn will appear in J. N. L. Myres, *Corpus of Anglo-Saxon Pottery* (forthcoming). Where such a number is not given, the urn in question will not be illustrated in the *Corpus*.

A 1 (fig. 31) 1790

Found in fragments.

Depth 22 in. (56 cm.).

Shoulder-boss urn, neck and rim missing: thick gritty smoothed brown ware.

Decorated with four/six vertical hollow bosses.

Contents

A. Burnt bones.
B. Small iron object—F. R. M.'s notes, missing.
C. Fragments of burnt clay—F. R. M.'s notes, missing.

A 1 was partially covered by the base of another urn (not illustrated), which had apparently been used as a lid. Fragments of an urn (apparently not preserved) were found nearby.

A 2 (fig. 29) 1773

Found collapsed.

Depth 22 in. (56 cm.).

Biconical urn with wide mouth and everted rim: gritty brown ware, surface red/brown.

Undecorated.

Contents

A. Burnt bones.

A 3 (fig. 38) 1840

Found broken.

Depth 26 in. (66 cm.).

Broad-shouldered urn with short upstanding rim: smooth soft brown ware.

Decorated with a flat collar of diagonal lines demarcated above and below with two firm lines: below are single vertical lines of stamps demarcated on each side by a single vertical line and separating panels containing three-line chevrons bordered below by a single line of stamps: a single stamp is set on each side at the head of each vertical line of stamps.

One stamp is used.

Contents

A. Burnt bones of an adult. Dr. Wells reports: 'Two tooth roots are all that survive. One is from a maxillary, the other from a mandibular molar. Both are fully formed. Firing efficient. A few small bones of an unidentifiable bird are present.'
B. Two iron pins, one certainly part of a brooch pin; the other may be part of the same pin or a separate piece.
C. Small bird bones, see A above (not shown on fig. 38).

A 3 was lying on its side with a few large flints and a lump of baked clay (6×3 in., 15×8 cm.) just above it.

A 4 (fig. 28) 1762

Found almost complete.

Depth 25 in. (64 cm.).

Small biconical urn with sharp carination and upright rim: hard gritty pinkish grey ware.

Undecorated.

Contents

B. Arm of a miniature pair of iron shears. The arm is beginning to curve and the original length would not have been much more. Surviving length 1·6 in. (4·1 cm.).
C. Iron nail, curved with flattened head and of square section. Tip apparently broken. Surviving length 1·4 in. (3·5 cm.).

No burnt bones recorded by F. R. M. (so perhaps not a cremation).

A 4 was found on patch of light shingly gravel with A 5 and A 6.

A 5 (not illustrated)

Found in fragments.

Depth 25 in. (64 cm.).

A few fragments of the side of a pot containing burnt bones, others being scattered near by.
Urn missing.
A 5 was found with A 4 and A 6. Nine inches (23 cm.) to the east was a denarius of Septimius Severus (rev. inscription **VICT. AVGG. COS. II · P.P.**) issued A.D. 198: F. R. M. suggested coin possibly associated with urns.

A 6 (not illustrated)

Found broken.

Depth 25 in. (64 cm.).

Base only, containing burnt bones.
Urn missing.
A 6 was found with A 4 and A 5.

A 7 (pl. XII*d* and fig. 35) 1821

Found almost complete.

Depth 26 in. (66 cm.).

Globular shoulder-boss urn with tall neck and well-moulded everted rim: hard gritty pinkish grey ware.

Decorated with four strong neck-lines above two rather irregular lines of stamps: in the lower row the impressions are much more widely spaced than in the upper. After the stamped impressions were dry, four solid applied bosses were added over the stamped area. These subsequently became detached, and only two were found, both having negative impressions of the stamps on their undersides.
One stamp is used.

Contents
A. Burnt bones.

A 8 (pl. XIII and fig. 17) 1671

Found broken.

Depth 26 in. (66 cm.).

Globular *Buckelurne* with narrow neck and short upright rim: gritty smoothed dark ware.

Decorated with three faintly drawn neck-lines, between which are two slightly raised collars, the lower of which carries a single-line diagonal cross at intervals: below are six hollow shoulder-bosses faintly feathered: between the bosses is irregular linear decoration, and there is a single arched line over some of the bosses. Below one of the bosses there is a single impression of a stamp. All the decoration is extremely careless and irregular.

Contents
A. Burnt bones, possibly female (F. R. M.).
B. Section of centre-plate of triangular bone comb, with two iron rivets.
C. Five small glass beads, distorted by fire: (i) red with white dot decoration, (ii) white with marvered red stripes, (iii) green with yellow dot decoration (these three fused together), (iv) blue, (v) red and white stripes.

Four inches above the urn was a layer of large flints and sixteen pieces of Roman tile covering an area about 18 in. (45 cm.) square.

A 9 (fig. 25) 1744

Found collapsed.

Depth 22 in. (56 cm.).

Globular urn, with short upright rim: rough red/brown ware, very thick-walled.
Undecorated.

Contents
A. Burnt bones.
B. Miniature pair of iron shears 1·5 in. (3·8 cm.) long.
C. Probably miniature pair of iron tweezers; the distal ends of the arms are apparently missing. Surviving length 0·9 in. (2·3 cm.).

A 10 (not illustrated)

Found in fragments.

Depth 22 in. (56 cm.).

Fragments of urn, apparently of globular form with short everted rim: light brown ware, no complete profile 'but enough goes together to give a good idea of its shape' (F. R. M.).
Decorated with two neck-lines from which depend about six groups of four vertical lines to the maximum diameter.
Urn missing.

Contents

A. Burnt bones.

A 10 had the base of another urn (apparently not preserved) containing bones resting on the top of it: no trace of the rest of the upper pot was found.

A 11 (fig. 7) 1590

Found almost complete.

Depth 22 in. (56 cm.).

Shoulder-boss urn with tall conical neck and flaring rim: smooth dark grey ware, once burnished.

Decorated with continuous horizontal corrugation on the neck, above twelve small hollow shoulder-bosses, the panels between which are filled with vertical corrugation.

Contents

A. Burnt bones.

A 11 was found half-buried in gravel; several large flints and part of a burnt Roman tile were found just above it.

A 12 (fig. 10) 1616

Found broken.

Depth 23 in. (58 cm.).

Shouldered urn with tall conical neck and short upright rim: corky red/brown ware.

Decorated at the base of the neck with four close-set sharp lines above irregularly tooled three-line chevrons between the upper points of which are two slightly looped lines.

Contents

A. Burnt bones.
B. Foot of bronze cruciform brooch of Åberg Group III, in good condition and little, if at all, affected by fire. The animal head is simple with protuberant eyes and scroll nostrils. The nose is pointed and projects just below the line of the nostrils.

Several large flints were found above the urn.

A 13 (not illustrated)

Found broken.

Depth 23 in. (58 cm.).

Lower part only of large urn: smooth dark grey/brown ware.

No decoration appears.

Contents

A. Burnt bones.

A 14 (not illustrated)

Found in fragments.

Depth 23 in. (58 cm.).

Fragments of rather large urn of uncertain form: reddish/brown ware.

Decorated with two neck-lines above a zone of semi-circular arcading.

Urn missing.

Contents

A. Burnt bones.

A 15 (not illustrated)

Found in fragments.

Depth 23 in. (58 cm.).

Many small fragments of an urn in grey/brown ware.

Undecorated.

Urn missing.

Contents

A. Burnt bones.

A 15 was found on a gravel patch beneath a Roman tile, also broken up.

A 16 (fig. 3) 1556

Found broken.

Depth 23 in. (58 cm.).

Lower part of large bowl: gritty pitted grey ware.

Decorated with at least one line on the maximum diameter above four/five line chevrons.

Contents

A. Burnt bones.

Apparently the upper part of A 16 was missing when the burial took place, for no part of it was found. Instead many fragments from the lower part of another bowl of darker brown/grey ware were mixed with the burnt bones. It is suggested that this damaged bowl was used as a lid for the cremation in the lower part of A 16. Alternatively it might have been the base of an urn subsequently buried, the deposition of which removed the whole of the upper part of A 16. But the dimensions fit A 16 so well that it seems most likely to have served as a lid, and it is shown as such on fig. 3.

B 1 (fig. 55) 1916

Found broken.

Depth 15 in. (38 cm.) (but not *in situ*).

Globular urn with wide mouth and upright rim: smooth grey ware, once burnished.

Decorated with three neck-lines above four lines of stamps of which the first two are separated by a single line: the two lower rows of stamps are very irregularly set out.

Two stamps are used.

B 1 is by Potter X

Contents

A. A few burnt bones.

B 1 was found on its side and had apparently been dug out by a rabbiter.

B 2 (pl. VIII*a* and fig. 8) 1600

Found in fragments.

Depth 30 in. (76 cm.).

Biconical shoulder-boss bowl with short everted rim: smooth chestnut-brown ware with high black burnish.

Decorated on the neck with continuous horizontal corrugation over which are set two raised collars linked by four/six vertical raised ribs. On the shoulder are twenty-four small bosses alternately plain and feathered, the former being vertical and solid, the latter round and hollow. The panels are filled with vertical corrugation.

Contents

A. A few burnt bones lay among the sherds.

B 2, dug out by rabbiters, had been broken up and the fragments widely scattered.

C 1 (fig. 17) 1668

Found broken.

Depth 20 in. (51 cm.).

Large globular *Buckelurne* with conical neck, rim missing, and well-moulded footstand: smooth grey/brown ware, well fired.

Decorated with at least three broad neck-lines above ten hollow bosses, alternately vertical and horizontal, carrying three/four vertical and horizontal lines respectively. Small two-line 'V's are set between the bosses. Below one horizontal boss is a large fracture which has been mended by lead in ancient times.

Contents

A. Burnt bones.

D 1 (urn fig. 30; grave goods not illustrated) 1778

Found collapsed.

Depth 15 in. (38 cm.).

Small shouldered urn with short upright rim: smooth red ware, burnished dark brown.

Undecorated.

Contents

A. A few small fragments of burnt bones and two milk teeth. Dr. Wells reports: 'Infant. A fragment of a petrous temporal bone; seven flakes of long bone, the largest 21 mm. long; two damaged deciduous molar crowns, probably unerupted. Firing efficient. No animal remains.'

B. Head of iron nail (association doubtful; F. R. M. notes 'probably from Roman Pit 10').

D 1 was found in black soil containing Roman sherds and objects (Roman Pit 10). A large tile and a few large flints were immediately above it, a large flint being inside the pot.

D 2 (fig. 3) 1560

Found broken.

Depth 7 in. (18 cm.).

Small globular bowl with wide mouth and everted rim: smooth brown ware, with high black polish.

Decorated with two faintly burnished neck-lines above single-line burnished chevrons.

Contents

A. A few small fragments of burnt bone and one milk tooth.

D 2 was found in Roman Pit 10 (see p. 24).

D 3 (urn not illustrated; grave goods fig. 59)

Found broken.

Depth 13 in. (33 cm.).

Lower part of large thick-walled urn: grey/brown ware burnt brick-red inside.

No decoration appears.

Urn missing.

Contents

A. Burnt bones.

B. Three fragments of sheet bronze (F. R. M. notes, one fragment now missing). The fragments have sharp irregular edges and are much twisted; apparently broken off a larger sheet.

D 3 was found in Roman Pit 10 in the same group as D 4 and D 5 (sketch plan in F. R. M.'s notes).

D 4 (not illustrated)

Found in fragments.

Depth 13 in. (33 cm.).

Numerous fragments of base of grey urn.
No decoration appears.
Urn missing.

Contents

A. Burnt bones.

D 4 was found in Roman Pit 10 in the same group as D 3 and D 5 (sketch plan in F. R. M.'s notes).

D 5 (urn not illustrated; grave goods pl. XXII*a* and fig. 59)

Found broken.

Depth 13 in. (33 cm.).

Lower part of large urn: light brown ware.
No decoration appears.

Contents

A. Burnt bones. F. R. M. records that these were in larger pieces than usual and less burnt; 'must have been male'.

B. Half of a round-backed bone comb with iron rivets. The centre-plate projects slightly above the tops of the side-plates and is rounded; it curves gently outwards at the end. Both side-plates are decorated with segments of large compass-drawn circles and 'bull's eye' decoration within a border of incised parallel lines; the designs on the two plates are different. Original height about 2·2 in. (5·6 cm.). This comb lay beneath the burnt bones on the bottom of the pot. N.B. Fig. 59 shows both sides of the comb.

D 5 was found in Roman Pit 10, in the same group as D 3 and D 4 (sketch plan in F. R. M.'s notes).

D 6 (fig. 38) 1843

Found collapsed.

Depth 20 in. (51 cm.).

Biconical urn with sharply everted rim: brownish-grey ware, once burnished black.

Decorated with three strong grooves below a thin neck-line: below are wide chevrons of one strong groove with a thin line on each side. There is a horizontal line of stamps below the neck grooves, and the lower edges of the chevrons are also outlined with a row of stamps.

One stamp is used.

Contents

A. Burnt bones.

Several large flints were close beside this urn, apparently part of cist around D 7.

D 7 (pl. XV*a* and fig. 38) 1841

Found broken.

Depth 24 in. (61 cm.).

Broad-shouldered urn with wide mouth and everted rim: smooth grey/brown ware.

Decorated with a horizontal line of stamps on the neck, demarcated above and below by three strong lines: below are three-line chevrons, the upper edges of which are bordered by a line of stamps. From the points of the chevrons depend irregular vertical groups of lines and stamps, one space being left blank.

Three stamps are used.

Contents

A. Burnt bones.

B. Two fragments of sheet bronze—with irregular outlines; they are slightly curved and slightly thicker than the majority of such fragments.

D 7 was in a cist made of flints and tiles with three tiles arranged over it as a roof 2–3 in. (5–8 cm.) above the urn. It was standing on scattered burnt bones which extended beneath the tiles and flints, indicating that a previous cremation had been disturbed when the cist was built.

D 8 (fig. 11) 1625

Found in fragments.

Depth 21 in. (53 cm.).

Part of a globular urn with tall conical neck, rim missing: rough corky pink/grey ware.

Decorated with at least four neck-lines above a raised slashed collar. Below are blocks of varying numbers (six/fifteen) of diagonal and vertical lines.

Contents

A. Burnt bones.
B. Miniature pair of iron shears, tip of blade broken. Surviving length 1·5 in. (3·8 cm.). Rusted on to C.
C. Miniature pair of iron tweezers; broken and upper part missing.
D. Pebble of water-worn milky quartz crystal, probably from the surrounding Drift deposits; it could have got into the urn with the infill (association doubtful).

   B and C bear textile impressions, possibly from a bag (see p. 232).

D 8 was found 7 in. (18 cm.) from the wattle-marked daub of a Roman hut, Structure K. The urn contained some daub and Roman sherds.

D 9 (pl. XXII*b* and fig. 41) 1865

Found broken.

Depth 24 in. (61 cm.).

Large ovate urn with short neck and everted rim: smooth grey/black ware.

Decorated with three groups of four neck-lines separating two single lines of stamps. Below are wide rounded four/five line pendent swags each containing a horizontal line of four/six stamps. Below the gaps between these panels are four-line pendent chevrons with a single stamp in each angle.

Three stamps are used.

Contents

A. Burnt bones.
B. Part of an iron knife, or pair of iron shears, tip of blade missing. The shape of the handle suggests that the identification of this piece as one arm of a pair of shears is more likely to be correct.
C. About two-thirds of a round-backed bone comb with iron rivets. Upper part of centre-plate flat and flush with the side-plates. The centre-plate curves gently beyond the side-plates; the end is truncated. The decoration on both side-plates consists of a series of four incised lines parallel with the lower edge while a row of large 'bull's-eye' decoration follows the curve. Maximum height 1·4 in. (3·6 cm.), original length 3·6 in. (9·1 cm.).

D. Two fragments of iron, one of which is curved. These may form part of a single object, perhaps a clip, and have been shown as such.

D 9 was found in black soil, with large pieces of wattle-marked daub (Structure K) near to it. Two large pieces of iron and Samian ware sherds (not preserved) were found close to the base of the urn.

D 10 (urn not illustrated; grave goods pl. XXIII*d* and fig. 59)

Found in fragments.

Depth 24 in. (61 cm.).

A few fragments of the base of an urn in dark ware. No decoration appears. Urn missing.

Contents

A. Burnt bones.
B. Section of centre-plate of a double-sided bone comb with iron rivet. This comb had coarse teeth on one side and fine teeth on the other.

Fragment of glass found beneath D 10 but probably from Roman Structure K.

D 11 (fig. 19) 1687

Found collapsed.

Depth 14 in. (36 cm.).

Large shoulder-boss urn with conical neck: rim and upper part of neck missing: soft smoothed brown/grey ware.

Decorated on the neck with a very prominent solid slashed raised collar demarcated above by at least two and below by four neck-lines, a line of large dots and two more neck-lines. On the shoulder are four hollow vertical bosses carrying a vertical line of smaller dots demarcated on each side by three/five lines. The panels contain a large three-line chevron.

Contents

A. Burnt bones.
B. Large semi-circular bronze buckle with iron tongue. The buckle is somewhat crudely made, and the cross-section varies from round to sub-oval. Length 1·4 in. (3·6 cm.).

On the shoulder of D 11 were the lower parts of another urn (apparently not preserved), decorated with numerous bosses. F. R. M. suggested that this may have served as a lid, but it is perhaps more likely to be the remains of an intrusive burial which has destroyed the upper part of D 11. These urns were found in Roman Pit 10.

E 1 (urn not illustrated; grave goods fig. 59)

Found in fragments.

Depth 10 in. (25 cm.).

Fragments of base of urn: reddish ware.
No decoration appears.

Contents

A. Burnt bones.
B. Fragments of a probable single-sided, barred, Frisian bone comb, with iron rivets; this identification is indicated by the nature of the side-plates. One side-plate is formed of a single flat piece of bone decorated with pairs of parallel incised lines running the length of the plate, and a central row of 'bull's-eye' decoration. The half-round bars of bone form the other side-plate. These are decorated with groups of vertical incised lines separated by panels. The panels contain crosses or are half-filled with diagonal lines. Only a fragment of the centre-plate remains riveted in position. This comb is slightly warped by fire. Surviving length 4·4 in. (11·2 cm.).
C. Curved bone plate, broken on one side; one end is notched and decorated on one side with two 'bull's-eyes'. A small piece of flat bone plate decorated with two pairs of incised horizontal lines probably goes with this. This flat plate is obviously not part of B as the spacing of the decoration is different. The shape of the curved plate suggests that it comes from a comb case rather than a comb. With these two pieces may go D.
D. Two pieces of a half-round bone bar with iron rivets and holes for other rivets. The decoration is similar to that on the other two half-round bars (B); D (0·25 in., 0·6 cm.) is narrower than B (0·3 in., 0·8 cm.). The two pieces of D have been shown on fig. 59 as joining, but a careful examination of the decoration indicates that they are either two ends of a longer bar with at least four rivets or parts of two bars. The former interpretation is the more likely as C and D are probably parts of a comb case for B. D would then be the lowest bar of the case; further evidence for this

interpretation comes from the length of the iron rivets (B 0·35 in., 0·9 cm.; D 0·45 in., 1·1 cm.).

All these comb and case fragments have been affected by fire.

E 2 (fig. 18) 1677

Found shattered.

Depth 15 in. (38 cm.).

Shoulder-boss urn with hollow neck and wide mouth, rim missing: soft smoothed dark grey/brown ware.
Decorated on the neck with continuous three-line wavy meander in broad tooling, with one or two large dots below each wave. On the shoulder are five hollow bosses irregularly outlined with dots and separating panels containing either three groups of vertical lines separated by a vertical line of two dots, or three-line chevrons similarly separated.

Contents

A. Burnt bones.

E 3 (urn fig. 23; grave goods not illustrated)

Found in fragments.

Depth 28 in. (71 cm.).

Part of side of a shouldered urn: smoothed dark brown ware.
Decorated on the neck with a low slashed collar demarcated above by one and below by two lines, above groups of vertical, diagonal and horizontal lines, apparently irregular in arrangement.

Contents

A. Burnt bones.
B. Small fragment of burnt bronze, bent and with irregular edges, apparently decorated with a raised ridge (association doubtful, as not mentioned or illustrated in F. R. M.'s inventory; not shown on fig. 23).

E 4 (fig. 18) 1678

Found in fragments.

Depth 30 in. (76 cm.).

Shoulder-boss urn with hollow neck, rim missing: light smooth buff/grey ware, burnished: thin-walled and well-made.

Decorated on the neck with a flat collar demarcated above by three fine lines and below by four, and carrying a line of dots. On the shoulder are six hollow bosses in three groups of two: each boss is outlined with dots and the smaller panels between them have a vertical line of dots demarcated on each side by groups of two/three neat vertical lines. The larger panels are entirely filled with close-set vertical lines.

Contents

A. Burnt bones.
B. Fragment of riveted sheet bronze, possibly broken from a rectangular piece. Four large-headed bronze rivets remain which are beaten flat onto the metal on one side but stand proud on the other. Perhaps a patch from a bowl or cauldron.

E 5 (fig. 1) 1540
Found complete.

Depth 30 in. (76 cm.).

Large heavily-made shouldered urn with short conical neck, wide mouth, and well-moulded rim: red ware, with black surface burnish.

Decorated with four deep neck-grooves above continuous two-line pendent triangles in deep grooving, one of which is replaced by a one-line diagonal cross: in two places one and two finger-tips respectively are set between the triangles.

Contents

A. Burnt bones of an adult and a child, aged 6–8 years (F. R. M.).
B. Miniature pair of bronze tweezers, cut from sheet bronze and obviously never intended for use. The end of one arm has been lost. Iron-stained. Length 0·65 in. (1·65 cm.). (Not listed in inventory but shown in F. R. M.'s photograph with beads.)
C. Five glass beads, all distorted by heat.

  (i) Half of a large barrel bead, divided into apparently alternating blue and green panels, each defined by a fine marvered trail of opaque white glass; within each panel a yellow 'daisy'. Length of axis 0·75 in. (1·9 cm.).

  (ii) Opaque reddish-brown ring bead with a plain perforation; small white spots spaced round the middle of the bead perhaps central to a larger spot of dark opaque glass. Diameter 0·5 in. (1·3 cm.).

  (iii) Two fragments of a large opaque white bead with opaque reddish-brown marvered interlacing trails and yellow 'bars'.

  (iv) A small badly distorted semi-translucent white bead.

  (v) Opaque red barrel bead with a plain perforation and opaque yellow spots spaced round the middle of the bead. Diameter 0·45 in. (1·1 cm.).

There were fragments of other urns and an iron knife numbered E 5 by F. R. M. Now missing.

E 6 (fig. 32) 1804
Found complete.

Depth 24 in. (61 cm.).

Shoulder-boss bowl with conical neck and short upright rim: red/brown ware, smoothed black.
Decorated only with three solid nipple bosses.

Contents

A. Burnt bones. Dr. Wells reports: 'Adult. ?Female. Fifty-three fragments of bone, all small and much eroded. Identifiable are a few scraps of cranial vault and pieces of long bones. Moderately well fired. No animal remains were detected but they could not be definitely excluded.'

E 7 (pl. VIb and fig. 44) 1883
Found in fragments.

Depth 30 in. (76 cm.).

Biconical bossed urn with short everted rim: sandy red ware, smoothed dark brown.

Decorated on the neck with two wide zones of stamps separated and demarcated above and below with two deeply tooled lines. On the carination are five sharp hollow bosses, each surrounded with a zone of stamps demarcated on both sides by two deeply tooled lines. The intervening panels contain a single horizontal line of stamps demarcated above and below by two deeply tooled lines.

Four stamps are used, including an animal stamp.

Contents

A. Burnt bones.

E 7 has been mended in the lower part with lead in ancient times. It was in contact with E 8, E 10, E 11, and E 12, with many large flints and tiles above them. See note on E 7 group (pp. 59–61).

E 8 (fig. 44) 1880

Found badly broken.

Depth 30 in. (76 cm.).

Shoulder-boss urn with wide mouth and well-moulded everted rim: red/brown ware, smoothed dark brown.

Decorated on the neck with three lines above two lines of stamps separated by a single line. Below is a chaotic medley of stamps with various attempts at patterned groups not systematically carried out. On the shoulder are three small solid bosses demarcated on each side by three short vertical lines. In the panels below the shoulder are two vaguely set arches of stamps outlined above and below by a single line.

Five stamps are used.

E 8 is by Potter XII (pp. 61–2).

Contents

A. Burnt bones.

E 8 is one of the E 7 group (q.v.).

E 9 (fig. 8) 1598

Found complete.

Depth 30 in. (76 cm.).

Wide-mouthed shoulder-boss bowl with hollow neck and everted rim: coarse grey ware, now badly weathered but formerly burnished dark.

Decorated on the neck with continuous horizontal corrugation above eight hollow shoulder-bosses. These carry diagonal corrugation and separate panels filled with vertical corrugation.

Contents

A. Burnt bones of an infant.
B. Small iron knife, broken; part of rectangular tang survives with fragments of iron-impregnated wooden haft. Distal end of blade curves upwards. Length of blade 1·2 in. (3 cm.).

E 10 (fig. 57) 1930

Found shattered.

Depth 30 in. (76 cm.).

Shoulder-boss urn with short conical neck, rim missing: smooth red/brown ware, possibly once burnished black.

Decorated with two close-set grooved neck-lines, above eight vertical hollow shoulder-bosses. The

bosses and a triangular space to the right of each are closely covered with stamps, the rest of the panels between the bosses being filled with diagonal grooved lines.

Two stamps are used, one of which occurs once only in the triangular space to the right of each boss, and was applied after the ground had been covered with the smaller stamp, impressions of which can be seen under it.

E 10 is by Potter XI (p. 59).

Contents

A. Burnt bones.

E 10 is one of the E 7 group (q.v.).

E 11 (fig. 57) 1929

Found in fragments.

Depth 30 in. (76 cm.).

Part of a globular or sub-biconical urn, rim and part of side missing: smooth red/brown ware, perhaps once burnished.

Decorated with at least two grooved neck-lines from which depend groups of diagonal grooves and three-line arched oval panels, all closely covered with stamps.

Three stamps appear.

E 11 is by Potter XI (p. 59).

Contents

A. Burnt bones.

E 11 is one of the E 7 group (q.v.).

E 12 (fig. 45) 1885

Found in fragments.

Depth 30 in. (76 cm.).

Globular urn with narrow neck and everted rim: rough, sandy red ware.

Decorated from shoulder to rim with a random arrangement of lightly drawn vertical, diagonal, and horizontal lines and groups of jabs mostly forming a series of narrow vertical panels divided horizontally, and demarcated below by a horizontal line.

Contents

A. Burnt bones.
B. Fused glass bead mentioned in F. R. M. note, but he states elsewhere that there were no associated objects with any urn of the E 7 group. In view of this it seems likely that this bead is the one recorded by him as remaining in the base of the

urn destroyed by the burial of the E 7 group. This bead is apparently missing, but No. 10 (fig. 59) could be it.

E 12 is one of the E 7 group (q.v.).

E 13 (pls. IIIb, XXIIc and fig. 16) 1658
Found complete.

Depth 30 in. (76 cm.).

Shouldered urn with upstanding rim: hard, smoothed dark brown/grey ware, well made.

Decorated with four strong neck-lines above continuous three-line arcading.

Contents

A. Burnt bones of an infant (F. R. M.). Dr. Wells reports: 'Child. Broken fragments of the crowns of four deciduous molars. Well fired. No animal remains.'
B. Large triangular bone comb, with bronze rivets. The centre-plate projects above the upper edges of the side-plates, and is rounded. The side-plates are decorated with sets of incised lines, parallel with the edges. The centre-plate originally projected beyond the side-plates but the ends are missing. Some teeth survive in centre to full length, but the majority are only stumps and the comb was presumably old when put in the urn. Height 1·9 in. (4·8 cm.), surviving length 5·4 in. (13·7 cm.).

E 14 (fig. 2) 1546
Found almost complete.

Depth 22 in. (56 cm.).

Shouldered urn with conical neck, heavy everted rim, and well-moulded base: thick burnished dark grey ware.

Decorated with four widely spaced burnished grooves on the neck above continuous diagonal grooving on the shoulder.

Contents

A. Burnt bones.
B. Fragments of at least two bone combs, (i) affected by fire, (ii) unburnt.
   (i) It seems probable that four of the fragments formed part of the centre-plate of a three-layered round-backed or triangular comb with iron rivets. Three other fragments, decorated with 'bull's-eye' and compass-

drawn circles, probably form part of the side-plates or a comb case.
   (ii) Fragment of centre-plate of a double-sided comb, with coarse teeth on one side and fine teeth on the other. Parts of two iron-stained rivet-holes survive.
C. About eighteen glass beads, some only slightly affected by fire.
   (i) Opaque reddish-brown barrel bead.
   (ii) Opaque white bead, with clear blue marvered interlacing trails and red opaque spots.
   (iii) Half of a five-horned bead, cf. (v), badly affected by fire so that colour has been lost.
   (iv) Standard bead, badly affected by fire so that colour has been lost.
   (v) Half of an opaque white, five-horned bead, with the 'horns' defined by opaque red marvered interlacing trails, and in the centre of each 'horn' an opaque red spot.
   (vi) Opaque reddish-brown and yellow standard bead, badly distorted by fire.
   (vii) Opaque yellow and perhaps red bead, badly distorted by fire.
   (viii) Fragment badly distorted by fire so that shape and colour have been lost.
   (ix) Opaque white five-horned bead similar to (v). Diameter 0·5 in. (1·3 cm.).
   (x) Opaque blue bead with white opaque marvered 'wisps'. Diameter 0·45 in. (1·2 cm.).
   (xi) Small melon bead, probably originally pale blue, but colour lost in burning. Diameter 0·45 in. (1·2 cm.).
   (xii) Fragments of probably seven beads, all considerably altered by fire so that form and colour have been lost.
D. Part of an iron pin, probably from a brooch.
E. Silver ring of expanding type. The end twists have been hammered or crushed almost flat. Maximum diameter 1·1 in. (2·8 cm.).
F. Iron finger or thumb ring made from length of wire. The ends have been twisted round each other to make an almost flat bezel and then twisted round the loop on either side of the bezel. Diameter 1 in. (2·5 cm.).

E 15 (fig. 35) 1822
Found shattered.

Depth 22 in. (56 cm.).

Large globular shoulder-boss urn with short upright rim: smooth dark ware, burnished black.

Decorated with one sharp neck-line above a raised cabled collar below which is a line of stamps demarcated above and below by a sharp line. On the shoulder are three groups of three vertical hollow bosses, each boss demarcated on each side with two sharp lines. In the panels are large three-line chevrons irregularly fitted to the space.

One stamp is used.

Contents

A. Burnt bones.
B. Mass of fused glass beads. This must represent several beads, but only one, of opaque dark blue glass, can be distinguished.
C. Pair of iron tweezers, which are much corroded, with the distal end of one arm missing. The arms are constricted near the proximal end to form a terminal loop. Length 1·35 in. (3·5 cm.).

E 16 (fig. 8) 1594

Found broken.

Depth 18 in. (46 cm.).

Very small shoulder-boss urn with upright rim and hollow pedestal foot: rough dark red ware, once burnished bright brown.

Decorated with three grooves on the neck above eight/ten solid vertical bosses carrying diagonal grooves, and separating panels filled with two or three vertical grooves.

Contents

A. One fragment of bone, probably of an infant.
B. One arm of a miniature pair of iron tweezers broken through the loop. Length 0·75 in. (1·9 cm.).

E 17 (not illustrated)

Found in fragments.

Depth 20 in. (51 cm.).

A few fragments only of an urn: reddish-brown ware. Undecorated.

Contents

A. Burnt bones.

E 18 (not illustrated)

Found in fragments.

Depth 20 in. (51 cm.).

Fragments of a coarse thick-walled urn: brown/red ware with smoothed surfaces.

No decoration appears.

Contents

A. Burnt bones.

E 19 (urn not illustrated; grave goods, B, pl. XIX*a*, C, fig. 59)

Found broken.

Depth 12 in. (30 cm.).

Lower part of a large thin-walled urn.

No decoration appears.

Contents

A. Burnt bones.
B. Cone beaker, of pale green glass, Harden's type IIId (Harden 1956). The corrugations are twisted on the body and the trails on the neck are of material similar to the rest of the glass. The rim is flared and is not a true circle. The corrugations begin about 0·5 in. from the base of the beaker; the lower part is plain. Part of the base is missing, but it was apparently flat. There is an eccentric hole in the base (diameter 0·2 in. (0·5 cm.) apparently made in antiquity. Length 5·9 in. (15 cm.). Maximum diameter of rim 3 in. (7·6 cm.). Diameter of base 0·9 in. (2·3 cm.).
C. Five fused glass beads. These are all extremely distorted and it is impossible to determine their original shapes and dimensions. Two were probably red, but the colour of the others cannot be determined.

This urn had been disturbed, probably by rabbiters. Its lower part was lying nearly upside down but still contained bones and the glass vessel which had apparently stood upright in the urn surrounded by bone fragments and partly filled with them.

E 20 (fig. 10) 1611

Found in fragments.

Depth 20 in. (51 cm.).

Large sub-biconical urn with very short upright rim: smoothed gritty brown ware.

Decorated on the neck with two groups of three grooves above one group of four resting on the maximum diameter. Below are five-line chevrons.

Contents

A. Burnt bones.
B. Pair of iron shears, with the tip of one blade missing. Length 2·4 in. (6·2 cm.).

C. Two fragments of sheet bronze, of irregular form and probably clipped from a large sheet; distorted by fire.

E 21 (not illustrated)
Found in fragments.

Depth 20 in. (51 cm.).

Fragments of small urn.
Undecorated.
Urn missing.

Contents
A. Burnt bones.

E 22 (fig. 9) 1608
Found broken.

Depth. Not recorded.

Small shoulder-boss urn, rim missing: very soft red/brown ware.
Decorated low on the neck with horizontal corrugation above numerous hollow shoulder-bosses separating panels filled with vertical corrugation.

Contents. None recorded.

F 1 (fig. 23) 1720
Found broken.

Depth 21 in. (53 cm.).

Lower part of an urn of uncertain form: smooth grey ware.
Decorated with at least one line on the maximum diameter, crossed by two close-set diagonal lines.

Contents. Unknown.

F 1 was in contact with F 2, and was surrounded by numerous large flints and small pieces of wattle-marked daub. (No Roman structure marked on plan in this area.)

F 2 (fig. 30) 1781
Found broken.

Depth 21 in. (53 cm.).

Globular urn with wide mouth and upright rim: smoothed dull grey ware.
Undecorated.

Contents
A. Burnt bones.

F 2 was in contact with F 1, and was surrounded by numerous large flints and small pieces of wattle-marked daub. (No Roman structure marked on plan in this area.)

F 3 (fig. 43) 1878
Found broken.

Depth 21 in. (53 cm.).

Biconical urn with narrow neck and flaring rim: smooth grey/brown ware, burnished dark.
Decorated with two firm neck-lines under the rim above a zone of widely spaced triangular groups of stamps. Below is a wider zone of two/three-line chevrons running to the carination which is marked by two/three horizontal lines. In one triangle of the chevron zone are two isolated stamps.
Two stamps are used.

Contents
A. Burnt bones.

A small unburnt green bead was found very near this pot but apparently not associated with it (it is possible that No. 5, fig. 60 and p. 207, is this bead).

F 4 (urn not illustrated; grave goods fig. 59)
Found in fragments.

Depth 15 in. (38 cm.).

Fragments, probably the remains of at least two urns: one with polished black surface, the other dark grey with shallow grooves.
Urns missing.
To the north of the urn sherds was a bone mass containing a piece of bronze and the remains of a pot, perhaps the top of an urn. There is no certain association between the sherds described and the bone mass.

Contents
A. A mass of burnt bones.
B. Part of a bronze wrist clasp badly warped and crackled by fire. Made from sheet bronze and decorated with a single row of punched dots parallel with the edges. The outer bar of the eye, into which the hook on the other plate would have fitted, is missing, as are the two ends. Surviving width 0·62 in. (1·6 cm.), surviving length 1 in. (2·5 cm.). Association doubtful.

G 1 (fig. 29) 1777

Found in fragments.

Depth 19 in. (48 cm.).

Globular urn with wide mouth and everted rim: rough grey/brown ware.
Undecorated.

Contents

A. Burnt bones.

G 1 was found on top of G 2, both being collapsed (sketch in F. R. M.'s notes).

G 2 (not illustrated)

Found in fragments.

Depth 22 in. (56 cm.).

Fragments of a large urn with everted rim: light brown ware.
Decoration not apparent.
Urn missing.

Contents

A. Burnt bones.

G 2 was apparently destroyed by the insertion of G 1 (sketch in F. R. M.'s notes).

G 3 (fig. 50) 1897

Found shattered.

Depth 24 in. (61 cm.).

Tall ovate urn with narrow neck and everted rim: smooth red/brown ware, perhaps once burnished.
Decorated with three neck-lines from which depend six groups of three/four vertical lines almost to the base: the top and upper part of the sides of the panels so formed are outlined with a single line of stamps. At least four stamps are used.
G 3 is by Potter II (pp. 62–3).

Contents

A. Burnt bones.

G 3 was intrusive upon G 5 (q.v.).

G 4 (fig. 29) 1774

Found in fragments.

Depth 24 in. (61 cm.).

Barrel-shaped urn with everted rim: brown/grey ware.
Undecorated.

Contents

A. A few fragments of burnt bone were adherent to it.

G 4 was intrusive upon G 5 (q.v.).

G 5 (urn not illustrated; grave goods fig. 59)

Found in fragments.

Depth 24 in. (61 cm.).

A few fragments, in two groups about a foot apart, of a russet-brown urn.
Decorated with small hollow bosses in pairs.
Urn missing.

Contents

A. Burnt bones.
B. Part of a bronze brooch, warped by fire; the foot is missing so that it is uncertain if this is part of a cruciform brooch or a cruciform small-long brooch. A single, separately cast full-round knob survives, which has a stay projecting on to the front of the plain rectangular head plate which is without wings; the knob is decorated with a single groove, while the stay is decorated with a number of grooves. The bow is distorted, but there is some evidence to suggest that it was faceted with a median ridge. Surviving length 1·7 in. (4·45 cm.).

G 5 was apparently destroyed by the intrusion of G 3 and G 4.

H 1 (fig. 35) 1820

Found in fragments.

Depth 27 in. (69 cm.).

Globular shoulder-boss urn with short everted rim: smooth grey/brown ware once burnished.
Decorated low on the neck with three firm lines above a line of stamps. Below are fourteen small hollow shoulder-bosses separating panels filled with vertical lines.
One very small stamp is used.

Contents

A. Burnt bones.
B. Miniature iron knife with comparatively long blade and small looped handle. The blade tapers slightly to a rounded end. The loop appears to be closed, but this may be due to corrosion. Length 1·9 in. (4·8 cm.).

C. Miniature pair of iron shears, the tip of one blade and part of one arm missing; the blades are comparatively long and taper to a point. Length 1·75 in. (4·5 cm.).
D. Probably arm of pair of iron tweezers. This piece of iron is much corroded, but it tapers to one end, and the broader end curves slightly. The association of this with the knife and shears makes this identification probable. Surviving length 1·1 in. (2·8 cm.).

K 1 (urn not illustrated; grave goods fig. 59)
Found in fragments.

Depth 20 in. (51 cm.).

Fragments of undecorated urn.
Urn missing.

Contents
A. Burnt bones.
B. Bent piece of iron. F. R. M. suggested that it formed part of a pair of shears, but it is impossible to identify this fragment with certainty.

K 2 (fig. 15) 1656
Found broken.

Depth 15 in. (38 cm.).

Biconical urn with upright rim: smoothed but gritty grey/brown ware.
Decorated above the carination with four strong lines.

Contents
A. Burnt bones.

K 3 (not illustrated)
Found in fragments.

Depth 15 in. (38 cm.).

Fragment of base of urn.
Urn missing.

Contents
A. Burnt bones.

K 3 was found near K 4.

K 4 (not illustrated)
Depth 15 in. (38 cm.).

Urn destroyed by post-hole of modern fence.
Urn missing.

Contents
A. Burnt bones.

K 4 was found near K 3.

K 5 (fig. 7) 1593
Found in fragments.

Depth 15 in. (38 cm.).

Shoulder-boss urn with high conical neck and narrow upright rim: rough grey/black ware, once burnished.
Decorated with continuous broad horizontal corrugation on the neck, above ten hollow shoulder-bosses, separating panels filled with broad vertical corrugation.

Contents
A. Burnt bones.
B. Parts of probably three glass beads, fused together and greatly distorted by heat. Two probably opaque white, and one large bead, dark in colour with white marvered interlacing and opaque blue decoration; it is possible that the blue decoration may be part of a fourth bead.

K 6 (figs. 32, 24) 1805, 1740
K 6(a) and K 6(b) were recovered together in fragments: it was not realized that two vessels were concerned until they were mended. K 6(b) was probably used as a cover for the contents of K 6(a) but, if so, it must have rested on the burnt bones, as it is too small to cover the mouth of the urn.[1]

(a) (fig. 32) 1805
Depth 15 in. (38 cm.).

Large cook-pot with slightly constricted neck, wide mouth, upright rim, and well-made, slightly hollowed footring: smooth brown/black ware, with traces of surface burning.
Decorated on the shoulder with three pierced lugs.

[1] Cf. Waller 1938, Tafel 7.4 for a continental example of a pot used as a lid but too small for the purpose.

Contents

A. Burnt bones.

(b) (fig. 24)   1740

Depth 15 in. (38 cm.).

Hemispherical cook-pot with wide mouth, straight rim and round bottom: hard smoothed light-brown ware with traces of burning.

Undecorated.

Contents. None.

K 7 (fig. 3) 1555

Found in fragments.

Depth 12 in. (30 cm.).

Wide-mouthed biconical bowl with tall neck and slightly everted rim: dark brown/grey ware.

Decorated with three neck-lines from which depend widely spaced groups of three vertical lines.

Contents

A. Burnt bones.
B. Pair of bronze tweezers, well made and functional, of Roman type. The top of the tweezers is expanded to form a loop. Threaded through this loop is a D-shaped loop of wire. The arms of the tweezers are decorated with groups of horizontal incised lines. Length 2·9 in. (7·4 cm.). The tweezers were stuck to a piece of the base of the urn.

K 7 was touching the south-west edge of Grave 6, and had been broken up, probably in digging the grave.

M 1 (fig. 34) 1812

Found almost complete.

Depth 26 in. (66 cm.).

Large globular urn with tall hollow neck, wide mouth and slightly everted rim: red/brown ware, burnished black; very well made.

Decorated low on the neck with a raised slashed collar demarcated above and below with three firm lines. Below are wide groups of diagonal lines, grooves and rows of dots separating spaces some of which are filled with a horizontal line of stamps above one/three horizontal lines, some with rosettes carried out in finger tipping and dots, or dots and stamps, some with both.

Two stamps are used.

Contents

A. Burnt bones.

M 2 (fig. 23)

Depth 22 in. (56 cm.).

Apparently parts of three pots, all found in fragments.

(a) (fig. 23) Upper part of a shouldered urn with upright neck and swollen rim.

Decorated with two lines on the neck above diagonal lines on the shoulder.

M 2(a) has been mended with lead.

(b) (not illustrated) A small brown pot, undecorated.

(c) (not illustrated) An urn in black polished ware, decorated with lines and three stamps.

Contents

A. Burnt bones. Dr. Wells reports: 'Adult. Four fragments of long bone; the biggest is 24 mm. long. Well fired. No animal remains.'

M 3 (figs. 3, 27) 1559, 1756

M 3 comprised two urns of which M 3(a) had been crushed by the insertion of M 3(b) which was itself covered by a large flint.

(a) (fig. 3)   1559

Depth 25 in. (64 cm.).

Small globular urn with wide mouth and everted rim: smooth brown ware.

Decorated low on the neck with two slight lines from which depend widely spaced pairs of vertical lines.

Contents

A. Burnt bones.

(b) (fig. 27, where wrongly labelled M 3(a)) 1756

Depth 23 in. (58 cm.).

Sub-biconical urn with wide mouth and everted rim: smoothed brown ware.

Undecorated.

Contents

A. Burnt bones.

M 4 (fig. 43) 1873

Found in fragments.

Depth 17 in. (43 cm.).

Shouldered urn with tall hollow neck and everted rim: smooth light brown ware with dark patches.

Decorated with six lines of stamps demarcated above and below and separated by single lines.
Two stamps are used.

Contents

A. A few burnt bones.

This is one of a group of five urns, M 4, M 6, M 10, M 11, M 17.

M 5 (fig. 46)

M 5 comprises fragments of at least two urns.

Depth 22 in. (56 cm.).

(a) (fig. 46)

Upper part of a shouldered urn with upright neck, rim missing: soft brown ware.
Decorated with a narrow flat slashed collar above a line of stamps demarcated above and below by two lines. On the shoulder is a diagonally slashed zone above a single horizontal line.

Contents

A. A few burnt bones.

(b) (fig. 46)

Fragments showing random stamping without lines.
One stamp appears. There are also two scratched '↑' runes.
F. R. M. says 'iron knife just above' but this is now missing.

M 6 (fig. 54) 1912

Found in fragments.

Depth 17 in. (43 cm.).

Wide globular urn with conical neck and short everted rim: rough brick-red/brown ware.
Decorated with six neck-lines above a line of stamps, separated by a single line from a continuous line of stamps arranged as chevrons under each of which is placed a stamp.
Two stamps are used.
M 6 is by Potter VI (p. 56).

Contents

A. Burnt bones.

M 6 is one of the M 4 group (q.v.).

M 7 (not illustrated)

Found in fragments.

Depth 15 in. (38 cm.).

Fragments mainly of the base of an urn in dark brown ware.
No decoration appears.

Contents

A. A few pieces of burnt bone. Dr. Wells reports: '? Adult. Two very small fragments of long bone. Well fired.'
B. Animal bone. Dr. Wells reports: 'Part of a posterior thoracic or anterior lumbar vertebra of a sheep or goat, less than six months old.'

M 8 (fig. 4) 1567

Found in fragments.

Depth 18 in. (46 cm.).

Part of side and base of sub-biconical urn with tall neck, rim missing: soft brown ware, very badly baked.
Decorated on the neck with horizontal corrugation above vertical corrugation on the shoulder.

Contents

A. Burnt bones.
B. Possibly part of a miniature iron knife, corroded and broken at both ends.
C. Pair of iron shears, corroded; blade missing from one arm, and part of blade missing from other. Surviving length 1·5 in. (3·8 cm.).
D. Pair of iron tweezers corroded and snapped in one place. Length 1·3 in. (3·3 cm.).
E. Three other pieces of iron. F. R. M.'s notes, missing; not shown on fig. 4.

M 9 (fig. 21) 1705

Found 'much broken'.

Depth 22 in. (56 cm.).

Globular urn with wide mouth and slightly everted rim: sandy red/brown ware, badly fired.
Decorated with three wide neck-lines above groups of thin vertical lines between which are various freehand designs in line-and-dot, including a sketch of a comb, a complex cruciform arrangement, and what may be intended for an animal: but all extremely rough.

Contents

A. Burnt bones.
B. Part of a large fused glass bead, whose original size, shape, and colour cannot be determined. It partly encloses a fragment of bone.

M 10 (fig. 7) 1589

Found in fragments.

Depth 20 in. (51 cm.).

Large shoulder-boss urn with wide mouth and short upright rim: heavy dark brown ware, badly fired.

Decorated with three or four hollow shoulder-bosses demarcated on each side by a vertical groove, and separating panels filled with horizontal corrugation.

Contents

A. Burnt bones.

M 10 is one of the M 4 group (q.v.).

M 11 (fig. 15) 1657

Found broken.

Depth 23 in. (58 cm.).

Biconical urn with wide mouth and short everted rim: heavy dark ware, burnished black, well made.

Decorated with three strong grooves above the well-marked carination.

Contents

A. Burnt bones.
B. Possible fragment of blade of iron knife, much corroded.
C. Functional pair of iron shears, somewhat corroded; the blades taper very little. Length 2·8 in. (7·1 cm.).
D. Pair of iron tweezers, corroded; the distal ends of the arms are only slightly curved, while the proximal ends of the arms are not expanded into a loop but have apparently been squeezed tightly together for about a quarter of the length of the arms. It is difficult to be certain if these were functional or made for funerary purposes. Length 2·15 in. (5·5 cm.).

M 11 is one of the M 4 group (q.v.).

M 12 (figs. 32, 31; grave goods fig. 59) 1792

M 12 comprises fragments of two urns.

Depth 20 in. (51 cm.).

(a) (urn fig. 32)

Lower part of a large round-shouldered urn: hard gritty red/buff ware.

Undecorated, but on the shoulder is a horizontal scar apparently marking position of an applied lug or boss: the corresponding part opposite is lost.

(b) (urn fig. 31)   1792

Shoulder-boss urn with conical neck and everted rim: corky grey ware, once burnished black.

Decorated with eight vertical hollow bosses.

Contents

A. Burnt bones.
B. Pair of iron shears, corroded. Length 2·05 in. (5·2 cm.).
C. Fragment of iron which may be part of an iron knife; much corroded, but one end does appear to be part of a blade.

These grave goods come either from M 12(a) or M 12(b).

M 13 (urn fig. 14; grave goods fig. 59)

Found in fragments.

Depth 18 in. (46 cm.).

Crumbled remains of an urn: dark grey ware.

Decorated with three faint lines between two zones of diagonal or chevron lines.

Contents

A. Burnt bones including 'many teeth'.
B. Fragments of a triangular bone comb with iron rivets, some fragments warped and crackled by fire. The back of the centre-plate projected above the side-plates and was rounded. Side-plate fragment decorated with incised lines parallel with the edges. The comb must have been more than 4 in. (10 cm.) long.
C. Two pieces of side-plate of a triangular bone comb with iron rivets and decorated with incised lines parallel with the edges. This plate may come from one side of B, but the angles at the outer corners are different from the attached piece. In addition, the incised lines are differently grouped and cut much more shallowly.

Association doubtful as the urn was so fragmentary and there were other broken urns near by.

M 14 (fig. 24) 1739

Found 'nearly whole'.

Depth 19 in. (48 cm.).

Globular urn with wide mouth, short upright rim and round bottom: smooth brown ware. There is a 0·50 in. (1·3 cm.) hole in the centre of the bottom.
Undecorated.

Contents

A. Burnt bones.

M 15 (fig. 53) 1911

Found shattered.

Depth 22 in. (56 cm.).

Shoulder-boss urn with wide mouth and everted rim: smooth thick dark brown ware.

Decorated on the neck with a raised stamped collar, demarcated above and below by three light lines. On the shoulder are three pairs of solid flat-topped bosses separated and demarcated on each side by three/four vertical lines. The panels between the grouped bosses contain a horizontal line of stamps demarcated above by two and below by four lines.

Two stamps are used.
M 15 is by Potter IV (p. 57).

Contents

A. Burnt bones.

There is also a bag of fragments labelled M 15 to which the following note by F. R. M. presumably refers:

'Fragments of perhaps six pots. No profile amongst them. One pot decorated with lines and dots, another with lines and a stamp resembling that on M 57 but not the same.'

It is possible that these fragments represent urns broken up by the intrusion of M 15.

M 16 (figs. 47, 23) 1887

M 16 comprises fragments of at least two urns, of which M 16(b) was probably broken up by the intrusion of M 16(a).

Depth 20 in. (51 cm.).

(a) (fig. 47) 1887
Shoulder-boss urn with hollow neck and everted rim: soft smoothed red/brown ware, perhaps once burnished dark.

Decorated on the neck with a line of stamps demarcated above and below by three lines. Below is a slightly raised slashed collar, and another zone of stamps demarcated above and below by a single line. On the shoulder are twelve long vertical hollow bosses, demarcated on each side by two lines. The intervening panels contain a single line above two horizontal lines of stamps each demarcated below by one/two lines. Four panels are missing: nine stamps appear.

M 16(a) is by Potter I (p. 57).

Contents

A. Burnt bones.

(b) (fig. 23)
Upper part of a shouldered urn with short upright neck and rim: brown ware.

Decorated on the neck with three widely spaced grooves above widely spaced groups of three vertical grooves at the shoulder.

Contents. Unknown.

M 17 (urn not illustrated; grave goods fig. 59)

Depth 22 in. (56 cm.).

No details recorded.
Urn missing.

Contents

A. Burnt bones.
B. Miniature pair of iron shears, corroded. Length 1·6 in. (4·1 cm.).

M 17 is one of the M 4 group (q.v.).

M 18 (fig. 39) 1849

Found in fragments.

Depth 20 in. (51 cm.).

Wide-mouthed biconical bowl, rim missing: smooth light grey ware.

Decorated on the neck with three fine sharp close-set lines below which are three/four-line pendent triangles filled with stamps. The groups of lines appear to have been made simultaneously perhaps with the teeth of a small comb.

Two stamps are used.

Contents

A. Burnt bones.

M 18 overlapped M 19 which must have been deposited earlier.

M 19 (fig. 25) 1743

Found in fragments.

Depth 20 in. (51 cm.).

Globular urn, rim missing: smooth heavy brown ware.
Undecorated.

Contents

A. Burnt bones, see B.
B. Animal bone. Dr. Wells reports: 'A single fragment of a third molar tooth of an ox, about 4–5 years old, is all that is present here.' (Not shown on fig. 25.)

M 19 was overlapped by M 18 which must have been deposited later.

M 20 (fig. 38) 1845

Found in fragments.

Depth 22 in. (56 cm.).

Large globular urn with short slightly everted rim: coarse thick brown ware with traces of dark burnish.
Decorated on the neck with a line of stamps demarcated above and below by two firm lines. Below is a zone demarcated below by a single line in which groups of vertical lines alternate with two stamps set vertically. Below are irregular groups of chevron lines with a few scattered stamps. At least two stamps are used, one being a plain rectangle.

Contents

A. A few burnt bones.

M 21 (fig. 4) 1570

Found in fragments.

Depth 22 in. (56 cm.).

Wide-shouldered urn with tall conical neck, rim missing: smooth brown ware.
Decorated with three shallow grooves on the neck above continuous vertical grooves on the shoulder.

Contents

A. Burnt bones.

M 21 was 4 in. (10 cm.) from left ankle of skeleton in Grave 20 and might have been reburied by the grave-digger. F. R. M.'s photograph shows M 21 broken but sherds not scattered.

M 22 (urns figs. 20, 23; grave goods fig. 59)

M 22 comprises parts of several urns, perhaps a grave-digger's dump.

Depth 19 in. (48 cm.).

(a) (in error, drawings of different sherds from this urn appear on figs. 20 and 23) 1696

Upper part of a shoulder-boss urn: thick heavy red/brown ware.
Decorated with three widely spaced grooves on the neck above hollow shoulder-bosses separating panels containing three/four-groove chevrons.

(b) (fig. 23)

Part of side of a shouldered urn: smooth dark ware.
Decorated with four neck-lines above four-line chevrons on the shoulder.

Contents

B. Iron brooch pin, much corroded, with a hinged spring. A small fragment of fused bronze adheres to the pin. F. R. M. thought it might have come from a saucer brooch, but it is impossible to be certain. Association doubtful as it is uncertain from which urn this comes.

M 23 (fig. 51)

M 23 comprises fragments of two urns.

Depth 18 in. (46 cm.).

(a) (fig. 51)

Part of an urn decorated with two neck-lines above vertical and diagonal groups of lines and stamps.
Seven stamps appear.
M 23(a) is by Potter III (p. 68).

Contents

A. Burnt bones.

(b) (not illustrated)

No significant details recorded.

M 24 (figs. 20, 49) 1893

M 24 comprises parts of at least three pots, found near Grave 24 and possibly disturbed by grave-diggers.

Depth 24 in. (61 cm.).

(a) (fig. 20)

Fragments of shoulder-boss urn.

Decorated with two raised collars, the upper carrying a line of dots, the lower small single-line chevrons above hollow bosses carrying a vertical line of dots demarcated on each side by three lines and separating panels containing groups of vertical and diagonal lines.

Contents

A. Burnt bones.

(b) (not illustrated)

No significant details recorded.

(c) (fig. 49) 1893

Part of side of a shoulder-boss bowl.

Decorated with one line at the base of the neck above widely spaced groups of two vertical lines descending almost to the base, and bordered on each side for part of the way by vertical lines of stamps. Some of the panels so formed are empty save for a horizontal line of stamps at the top: others contain three slight vertical hollow bosses demarcated on each side by two vertical lines and separated from each other by a vertical line of stamps.

At least three stamps are used.

M 24(c) is by Potter II (pp. 62–3), the scheme being very similar to that of N 64 (fig. 50).

Contents

A. Burnt bones.

M 25 (not illustrated)

Found in fragments.

Depth 20 in. (51 cm.).

Much broken decorated urn.
Urn missing.

Contents. None recorded.

M 26 (fig. 31)

Found in fragments.

Depth 18 in. (46 cm.).

Fragments of several urns, one decorated with hollow shoulder-bosses only.

Contents. None recorded.

M 26 was part of a group including M 27, M 28, all confused and broken up.

M 27 (fig. 43) 1879

Found in fragments.

Depth 18 in. (46 cm.).

Parts of a large shouldered urn: rough brown ware.
Decorated with three faint neck-lines above a line of stamps, interrupted by faint two-line arches outlined below by a line of stamps. Between the arches are more stamps.

At least one stamp is used, very faintly applied.

Contents

A. Burnt bones.

There is also the lower part of a bossed urn.
M 27 is part of the M 26 group (q.v.).

M 28 (urn fig. 17, grave goods fig. 59) 1664

Found in fragments.

Depth 18 in. (46 cm.).

Large *Buckelurne* with hollow conical neck and slightly everted rim: smooth soft brown ware, poorly fired.
Decorated with four grooves on the neck above ten hollow shoulder-bosses, alternately vertical and horizontal, each covered by an arch of three light lines.

Contents

A. Burnt bones.
B. Pair of bronze tweezers, distorted by heat, of Roman type. The arms are notched and decorated with incised horizontal lines. The ends of the arms are slightly constricted to form a small loop, and decorated with two incised lines. Length 2·8 in. (7·1 cm.).

Association with this urn is doubtful, as the sherds were confused with those of M 26 and M 27.

M 29 (fig. 27) 1757

Found in fragments.

Depth 20 in. (51 cm.).

Large sub-biconical urn with wide mouth and heavy flaring rim: rough gritty red ware.
Undecorated.

Contents

A. Burnt bones.

M 29 was one of a group, M 29, M 31, M 32, M 33, thought to have been taken out and reburied by

Anglo-Saxon grave-diggers. M 29 had been deposited in fragments, for many pieces overlapped and two large sections of the upper part lay one inside the other with no soil between. There were also bones beneath the base, presumably spilt when the pot broke during reburial.

M 30

No urn is recorded under this number.

M 31 (fig. 52) 1904

Found in fragments.

Depth 20 in. (51 cm.).

Lower part of globular urn, neck and rim missing: smoothed dark grey/brown ware.

Decorated below the neck, which is missing, with eight groups of three vertical lines running to the base. In upper part of the panels so formed are large stamps.

At least two stamps are used.

M 31 is by Potter III (pp. 62–3).

Contents

A. Burnt bones.
B. Miniature pair of iron shears, with long blades and very short arms. Length 1·3 in. (3·3 cm.). Found in lower part of urn.

M 31 is part of the M 29 group (q.v.).

M 32 (fig. 52) 1903

Found in fragments.

Depth 20 in. (51 cm.).

Lower part of globular urn similar in form, fabric, and decoration to M 31. Three neck-lines are preserved above the vertical lines.

At least one stamp is used.

M 32 is by Potter III (pp. 62–3).

Contents

A. Burnt bones.
B. Miniature iron knife, corroded, with apparently a roughly triangular blade; no break is visible, but it is likely that part has been lost. Length 1·0 in. (2·5 cm.).
C. Miniature pair of iron tweezers, corroded, distal end of one arm missing. Length 1·2 in. (3·0 cm.).
D. Miniature pair of iron shears, corroded; blades curve slightly inwards. Length 1·65 in. (4·2 cm.)

M 32 is part of the M 29 group (q.v.).

M 33 (urn fig. 22; grave goods fig. 59 and text fig. 1) 1711

Found in fragments.

Depth. Unknown.

Large shouldered urn, neck and rim missing: smooth brown ware.

Decorated with two strong neck-lines above two-line chevrons from the points of at least some of which depend two vertical lines, possibly intended to represent the '↑' rune.

Contents

A. Burnt bones.
B. Part of the foot of a large bronze cruciform brooch, warped by fire. Only the upper part of the animal head survives, defined above by a horizontal moulding decorated with fine horizontal lines. The eyes are round and prominent and set beneath gently arching eyebrows. These are formed by two grooves, the space between being filled by fine, close-set vertical lines. This probably is part of an Åberg Group IV brooch, but possibly from a Group V.
C. Part of the foot of a large bronze square-headed or cruciform brooch distorted by fire. The end of the foot is spade-shaped, the edges of the spade being beasts with long curved beaks, oval eyes, but without crests. Part of the body of one survives and is solid except for a single longitudinal groove; it is only this groove which indicates where the body ends and the head begins. The upper part of the spade is partly filled with a naturalistic human head with a long nose. One eye is round and one oval; this may be the result of heat distortion. Eyebrows are defined by grooves. Faint wavy vertical lines on the upper part of the head were probably part of the original design and meant to represent hair. On the upper part of the surviving fragment, a series of close-set short vertical lines curves across the brooch in two spans at the broken end. Either a Kenninghall II square-headed brooch or, less likely, an Åberg Group V cruciform brooch.
D. Bone comb, missing; listed in F. R. M.'s original note but omitted from F. R. M.'s inventory.

Association doubtful, and improbable in view of the comparatively early date likely for the urn.

M 33 is part of the M 29 group (q.v.).

M 34 (not illustrated)

Fragments of two or more urns, one decorated with incised lines. One of them may have had a Roman smooth brown ware lid, a piece of which was found in association with them.

M 35 (fig. 26) 1754

Found in fragments.

Depth 20 in. (51 cm.).

Large hump-shouldered urn with short upright rim: rough dark ware. A small hole has been bored on the shoulder.
Undecorated.

Contents

A. Burnt bones.
B. Iron knife, corroded, tip of blade missing, blade apparently concave on the cutting edge but in all probability broken; part of the wooden haft, impregnated with rust, survives. Surviving length 2·25 in. (5·7 cm.).
    In box with the other grave goods, but not listed in F. R. M.'s inventory.
C. Iron tweezers, corroded, distal part of one arm missing; proximal ends of arms constricted to form a loop. Length 1·45 in. (3·7 cm.).
D. Fragment of the end of a centre-plate of a possible round backed bone comb. There is a slight horizontal ridge on either side marking the original position of the side-plates; rivet holes survive and the bone shows considerable iron staining. It is likely that the back of the centre-plate was flush with the backs of the side-plates. The major part of this fragment projected below and beyond the lower corner of the side-plates. This projection is decorated with two incised lines parallel with the upper edge.

M 35 is very similar to Lackford 50.71 (Lethbridge 1951, fig. 14) which contained part of a late tutulus brooch and a cruciform brooch of about A.D. 500.

M 36 (not illustrated)

Found broken.

Depth 26 in. (66 cm.).

Lower parts of two apparently undecorated urns.

Contents

A. Burnt bones.

M 37 (fig. 19) 1685

Less than half found.

Depth 24 in. (61 cm.).

Shoulder-boss urn with hollow neck and heavy everted rim: smoothed gritty red/brown ware, very heavily built especially at the base.
Decorated with six sharp neck-lines between the lowest two of which is a line of dots. On the shoulder are about twelve small solid bosses carrying a scatter of dots and separating panels containing two horizontal lines of dots.

Contents

A. Burnt bones.

M 38 (not illustrated)

Found in fragments.

Depth 24 in. (61 cm.).

Fragments of rough brown pot, mostly base, decorated with lightly tooled single chevrons.

Contents

A. Burnt bones.

M 39 (fig. 14) 1640

Found badly broken and much missing.

Depth 22 in. (56 cm.).

Biconical urn with narrow neck and sharply flaring rim: smooth grey ware.
Decorated with a single lightly tooled neck-line, below which are large three-line chevrons, between which some triangles are divided centrally by one or two vertical lines: below the carination are wide two-line swags, rather out of step with the chevrons above.

Contents

A. Burnt bones.
B. Iron tweezers, corroded. The proximal ends of the arms form a loop which is linked with a small iron ring of circular section; this ring was obviously for suspension. No decoration appears. Length of tweezers 2·4 in. (6·2 cm.). Diameter of iron ring 0·6 in. (1·5 cm.).

M 40 (fig. 7) 1588

Found broken.

Depth 30 in. (76 cm.).

Large shoulder-boss urn with conical neck and everted rim: heavy reddish ware, burnished dull black, well made.

Decorated high on the neck with a zone of two-line chevrons above continuous corrugation: on the shoulder are seven hollow bosses separating panels filled with continuous vertical corrugation.

Contents

A. Burnt bones.

M 40 may come from the same workshop as N 24 (q.v.).

M 41 (fig. 7) 1591

Found in fragments.

Depth 28 in. (71 cm.).

Shoulder-boss urn with tall conical neck, rim missing: rough brown/grey ware, once burnished black.

Decorated on the neck with continuous horizontal corrugation, above at least eight solid shoulder-bosses separating panels of continuous vertical corrugation.

Contents

A. Burnt bones.
B. An irregularly shaped fragment of fused bronze, possibly part of a brooch.

M 42 (fig. 18) 1676

Found badly shattered.

Depth 14 in. (36 cm.).

Two-handled bowl with conical neck, wide mouth and slightly everted rim: smooth dark ware burnished black.

Decorated low on the neck with two light grooves above panels of light diagonal lines and irregular groups of faint dots some apparently arranged as triangles. There had been two vertical pierced handles on the shoulder (both broken off) below each of which were three horizontal grooves. The urn was irregularly made and had been very badly shattered so that much of the design is uncertain.

Contents

A. Burnt bones. Dr. Wells reports: 'Adult. One damaged 3rd molar tooth. Well fired. No animal remains.'
B. Fragment of bronze cruciform brooch slightly distorted by heat, possibly late Åberg Group I but more probably Group II. Only part of the horse's head remains, the nostrils are missing. The

eyes are prominent, the forehead plain; the upper part of the foot, which is broken just above the head, is decorated with three horizontal mouldings. Only a small part of the catch-pin remains. Length 1·25 in. (3·2 cm.).
C. Amorphous mass of translucent fused glass, originally greenish in colour. It may be part of a vessel, as there is an indication of trail decoration, or a bead.
D. Fragment of iron, much corroded, possibly part of the blade of a knife.

M 42 lay on the south-west corner of a clay floor connected with a Roman oven or hearth (Roman Structure C): it had been flattened out under several large flints. An undecorated urn (not preserved) was associated with it.

M 43 (fig. 25) 1747

Found in fragments.

Depth 18 in. (46 cm.).

Small globular urn with short upright rim: smoothed coarse thick grey/brown ware.
Undecorated.

Contents

A. Burnt bones, possibly of child.
B. Miniature iron knife, corroded. The blade is at an obtuse angle to the haft. The end of the haft is broken and probably had a small loop at the end. The haft tapers away from the blade. Surviving length 1·7 in. (4·3 cm.).
C. Iron tweezers, corroded. The distal ends of the arms were curved. Length 1·75 in. (4·5 cm.).
D. Possibly blade of iron shears, corroded. The tip of the blade is missing. A small fragment of an arm of the shears remains. Surviving length 1·3 in. (3·3 cm.).

M 44 (urns figs. 10, 21 and grave goods fig. 59) 1707

It would appear that M 44(a) and M 44(b) were found together. If they were not buried simultaneously M 44(a) is likely to be the later since more of its upper part is preserved, while the lower part of M 44(b) is more in evidence. Both found in fragments.

Depth 18 in. (46 cm.).

(a) (fig. 10)

Part of a shouldered urn, rim and lower part missing: thick smooth brown ware.

Decorated with seven firmly tooled neck-lines above groups of five/six-line chevrons, the triangles between which are either outlined, or partly or wholly filled with sharply impressed dots. In one panel there is an attempt at a circular pattern of dots.

M 44(a) could be from the same workshop as N 32.

(b) (fig. 21) 1707

Biconical urn, rim missing: heavy dark ware burnished black, well made.

Decorated on the neck with a broad groove demarcated on each side by two sharp lines, above widely spaced vertical groups of grooves and lines, similarly arranged.

Contents

A. Burnt bones.
B. Small pair of iron shears, corroded. These are a functional pair. The proximal end is broad and the arms taper towards the blades. The tips of both blades are missing. Surviving length 2·2 in. (5·6 cm.).

The shears could come from either M 44(a) or M 44(b).

M 45 (fig. 26) 1751

Found broken.

Depth 20 in. (51 cm.).

Shouldered urn with wide mouth and upright rim: hard rough light brown ware.
Undecorated.

Contents

A. Burnt bones.

M 46 (fig. 33) 1808

Found in fragments.

Depth 24 in. (62 cm.).

Hump-shouldered urn with short deeply hollowed neck, wide mouth and well-moulded everted rim: smooth red/brown/buff ware.
Undecorated.

Contents

A. Burnt bones.

The rim and the fabric of M 46 are reminiscent of Roman wheel-made wares. It underlay M 47 and is thus prior to the Group II cruciform brooch which the latter contained.

M 47 (fig. 34) 1816

Found almost complete.

Depth. Not recorded but on top of M 46 which was 24 in. (61 cm.) deep.

Shoulder-boss bowl with tall conical neck, rim missing: smooth dark grey/brown ware, perhaps once burnished.

Decorated on the neck with a single line of stamps demarcated above and below by two lines: below are seven vertical hollow bosses, demarcated on each side with a shallow groove and three lines, the rest of the panels being blank.

Two stamps are used.

Contents

A. Burnt bones, including milk molar, of child 5–6 years old (F. R. M.). Dr. Wells reports: 'Child. One damaged maxillary molar tooth; one small middle phalange of a finger. Well fired.' See D below.
B. Part of bronze cruciform brooch, Åberg Group II. Part of the bow, foot, and catch-pin remain; all show slight decrepitation. The lower part of the bow and the foot are ornamented with pairs of incised horizontal lines and, immediately above the animal head, with horizontal mouldings. The animal head is well developed. The eyes are prominent, the temples curve over them and meet to form a central vertical ridge down the nose. The nostrils are swollen, oval and free. The lower part of the catch pin is missing.
C. Part of bronze cruciform brooch. Part of the bow and foot remain. The fragment shows considerable decrepitation and distortion. It is decorated with two sets of four horizontal incised lines or mouldings. Although the two brooches were of approximately the same size, the details of the decoration show that they were not from the same mould.
D. Two fragments of a slightly burnt metapodial epiphysis of a young sheep or goat (not shown on fig. 34).

M 47 overlay M 46.

M 48 (fig. 17) 1666, 1669

The fragments of M 48(a) were associated with those of M 48(b) and both underlay M 49(a).

Depth 22 in. (56 cm.).

(a) (fig. 17)   1669

Fragments of a shoulder-boss urn with wide upright neck, rim missing, and a constricted base with foot-stand: smoothed rough dark ware.

Decorated with two grooves at base of the neck and numerous plain vertical hollow bosses.

Contents. Unknown.

(b) (fig. 17)   1666

Small globular *Buckelurne* with hollow neck, everted rim and base with well-made footstand: heavy reddish-brown ware, burnished black.

Decorated on the neck with a solid raised collar carrying a line of jab stamps above pairs of vertical slashed or jabbed solid bosses: in the panels between these bosses are small circular hollow bosses each carrying one impression of a stamp and surrounded by three other similar impressions, the whole set within diagonal groups of one groove demarcated on each side by two sharp lines to form a broken arch. Below is a horizontal line of dots demarcated top and bottom by a fine line, and below this are two-line chevrons extending to the constriction above the base with a single stamp in each triangle.

Two stamps are used.

Contents

A. Burnt bones and milk teeth of a child.

M 49 (figs. 14, 18) 1649, 1681

Two urns were given this number and their relationship is not recorded.

(a) (fig. 14)   1649

Found broken.

Depth 22 in. (56 cm.).

Biconical urn, rim missing: smooth brown/buff ware.

Decorated with two zones of continuous two-line chevrons separated by two lines and demarcated above and below by a single line, the latter on the sharp carination.

Contents

A. Burnt bones.
B. At least four fused glass beads—much distorted by heat. It is impossible to determine the original shapes, number and colour of these beads. Fragments of cremated bone have become incorporated in the melted glass.

C. Two fragments of sheet bronze. One is a plain strip, broken at either end and 0·5 in. (1·3 cm.) wide. The surface of the other piece has been partly destroyed by heat. Along each edge of the strip are two small rivet holes. One bronze pin-like rivet remains, and stands proud of the sheet. The strip is 0·35 in. (0·9 cm.) wide.

M 49(a) overlay M 48(a) and M 48(b).

(b) (fig. 18)   1681

'Not seriously broken.'

Depth 20 in. (51 cm.).

Shoulder-boss urn with wide mouth and upright rim: smooth reddish ware burnished dark; strongly made.

Decorated low on the neck with three strong grooves above five solid curved bosses on the shoulder, two with ends upwards and three with ends downwards: one of the former has broken off. The bosses are demarcated by groups of two/four vertical grooves from the intervening panels which each contain a triangular group of three dots: two dots also occur over the two bosses whose ends point upwards.

Contents

A. Burnt bones.

M 50 (fig. 6) 1583

Found in fragments.

Depth 20 in. (51 cm.).

Globular urn with narrow neck and short upright rim: rough brown ware with pitted surface.

Decorated on the neck with light continuous corrugation above panels of light vertical corrugation alternating with vertical feathered corrugation extending below the maximum diameter.

Contents

A. Burnt bones.

M 51 (fig. 7) 1587

Found in fragments.

Depth 22 in. (56 cm.).

Lower part of a large shoulder-boss urn, rim missing: smooth dark ware, burnished black.

Decorated with a broad groove low on the neck above (probably) ten small solid shoulder-bosses set in widely spaced pairs. In the smaller spaces between the bosses are one or more vertical grooves, and in the main panels a grooved circle (or square with rounded corners) demarcated on each side by vertical corrugation filling the rest of the panel.

Contents
A. Burnt bones.
B. Iron knife, part of tang missing. The cutting edge of the knife is horizontal for over half its length and then slopes quite steeply towards the tang. The back of the knife is nearly parallel to the cutting edge and then curves down to meet it. In shape it is very like the blade of a pair of shears, and may, as there is a small pair of shears in the urn, be the blade of a large pair broken off and placed in the urn to represent a knife. Length of blade 1·75 in. (4·5 cm.).
C. Small pair of iron shears, corroded, length 1·85 in. (4·7 cm.).
D. Small pair of iron tweezers, with unusually wide arms, much corroded. Length 1·4 in. (3·6 cm.).

M 52 (fig. 8) 1596
Found in fragments.

Depth 22 in. (56 cm.).

Biconical shoulder-boss bowl with short everted rim: smooth dark ware, once burnished black.
Decorated on the neck with a flat collar demarcated above and below by a groove and containing panels of vertical corrugation separated by panels containing a single large depression. On the shoulder are about twelve vertical hollow bosses, separating panels filled with vertical corrugation.

Contents
A. Burnt bones.
B. Small pair of iron shears, corroded, part of one blade missing. Length 1·55 in. (3·9 cm.).
C. Central part of arm of a pair of iron tweezers, corroded.

M 53 (fig. 28) 1760
Found almost complete.

Depth 22 in. (56 cm.).

Sharp-shouldered urn with tall concave neck and flat-topped upright rim: smoothed grey/brown ware. Undecorated.

Contents
A. Burnt bones.

B. Part of a single-sided barred bone comb, with iron rivets; most of the centre-plate and parts of the side-plates are missing. One side-plate is formed of two parallel plano-convex bars, with panel decoration. On the upper bar each panel is divided diagonally by an incised line, and the upper triangles thus formed are filled with incised parallel vertical lines, while the lower triangles are plain. The decoration on the lower bar appears to be a mirror image of that on the upper. The other side-plate is a single thin flat bone plate decorated with two sets of incised parallel horizontal lines, the upper of five lines, the lower of four. The centre-plate is flush with the top of the bar and side-plates. This comb has a central solid handle, formed by a projection from the centre-plate and two separate side-plates. The top of the handle is convex and the sides notched. There is a detached piece of an end section of a centre-plate which appears to belong to this comb but does not join.

M 54 (pl. IVa and fig. 8) 1597
Found complete.

Depth 22 in. (56 cm.).

Wide-mouthed shoulder-boss bowl with conical neck and everted rim: dark brown ware, once burnished brown.
Decorated on the neck with continuous horizontal corrugation, above eight slight hollow shoulder-bosses, separating panels filled with continuous vertical corrugation.

Contents
A. Burnt bones and several pieces of M 55 (q.v.).

M 55 (fig. 7) 1592
Found in fragments.

Depth 22 in. (56 cm.).

Shoulder-boss urn with tall conical neck and everted rim: smooth heavy dark ware, burnished black/light brown.
Decorated on the neck with a raised slashed collar demarcated above and below by a strong groove, above twelve solid vertical shoulder-bosses, separating panels filled with continuous vertical corrugation.

Contents. 'No bones seen' (F. R. M.).

M 55 was found in fragments above, around and inside M 54. F. R. M. therefore considered that M 55 was probably buried above M 54, but it is equally possible that M 55 was broken by the insertion of M 54. The similarity of type suggests that the two are contemporary.

M 56 (not illustrated)

Found in fragments.

Depth 21 in. (53 cm.).

Many fragments of an urn with tall upright rim: reddish-brown ware with smooth surface.
Undecorated.

Contents

A. Burnt bones.

M 57 (fig. 52) 1905

Found almost complete.

Depth 24 in. (61 cm.).

Globular urn with hollow neck and flaring rim: smooth dark ware, burnished.
Decorated with three firmly tooled neck-lines from which depend nine groups of three vertical lines reaching almost to the base: the upper parts of the panels so formed are filled with large stamps.
Three stamps are used.
M 57 is by Potter III (p. 62).

Contents

A. Burnt bones.
B. Ten fragments of third-/fourth- century Roman glass vessel—two fragments are somewhat distorted by heat. One rim fragment remains, showing it to be slightly flared. The diameter at the rim was probably about 2·5 in. (6·4 cm.). It is difficult to be certain whether the glass was originally clear or translucent.

M 58 (not illustrated)

Found in fragments.

Depth 22 in. (56 cm.).

'A few fragments of pot decorated with lines, bosses and stamps' (F. R. M.).
Urn missing.

Contents

A. A few burnt bones.

N 1 (fig. 41) 1864

Found almost complete.

Depth 23–4 in. (58–61 cm.).

Sub-biconical urn with flaring rim: smooth red/brown ware.
Decorated with two neck-lines from which depend seven groups of three vertical lines to the maximum diameter. In the panels are three/five stamps.
One stamp is used.

Contents

A. Burnt bones, see B.
B. Two parts of a pig's right scapula, slightly burnt.

N 1 had N 2 and N 3 on its shoulder and was in contact with N 4. F. R. M. writes: 'This group of pots was only three feet south [plan shows south-east] of Grave 30 and may be a grave-diggers' dump, but I am inclined to think it a family group. About the group were a few scattered flints and bits of tile. It was surrounded by rabbit holes in every direction. The group was in hardened yellow sand with no signs of disturbance.' (See pl. XIVa).
Whereas N 2, N 3, and N 4 are early urns of the same type and could well have been a family group, N 1 looks later, a fact which might be taken to favour the idea that the early urns in the group may have been shifted by a grave-digger from Grave 30 and deposited with N 1. But see p. 50, n. 6.

N 2 (fig. 6) 1579

Found shattered.

Depth about 17 in. (43 cm.).

Large sharp-shouldered bowl with tall hollow neck, wide mouth and flaring rim: thin smooth red/brown ware, perhaps once burnished.
Decorated with rather carelessly drawn horizontal corrugation on the neck, above groups of vertical corrugation on the shoulder. In two (? three originally) places parts of the vertical corrugation run up the neck through the horizontal corrugation, nearly to the rim.

Contents

A. Burnt bones only, but in unusually large fragments: several large pieces of the vault of the skull were arranged above the rest of the bones almost covering them: some of these pieces were packed together like saucers. F. R. M. notes that the bones were those of a small person but appeared to be adult, perhaps a woman.

N 2 and N 3 were on the shoulder of N 1 (q.v.).

N 3 (fig. 6) 1585

Found in fragments.

Depth 17 in. (43 cm.).

Shouldered urn with hollow neck and upright rim: thin smooth red/brown ware, perhaps once burnished.

Decorated with five or six carelessly tooled neck-lines, above continuous but widely spaced vertical lines on the shoulder.

Contents

A. Burnt bones.

N 3 and N 2 were on the shoulder of N 1 (q.v.) (see pl. XIV *a*).

N 4 (fig. 6) 1581

Found in fragments.

Depth about 17 in. (43 cm.).

Shouldered urn with hollow neck and upright rim: thin smooth dark ware, perhaps once burnished.

Decorated with three neck-lines above a flat slashed collar: on the shoulder is continuous vertical corrugation interrupted in several places by a narrow panel of diagonal or feathered corrugation.

Contents

A. Burnt bones.

N 4 was in contact with N 1 (q.v.) and had part of a tile on top of it as a cover.

N 5 (fig. 26) 1753

Found in fragments.

Depth 21 in. (53 cm.).

Large hump-shouldered urn with short neck and swollen everted rim: rough thick gritty buff/grey ware.

Undecorated.

Contents

A. Burnt bones. Dr. Wells reports: 'Child. The crowns of two deciduous mandibular molars. Well fired. No animal remains.'

N 5 and N 7 were in a dump reburied by the diggers of Grave 30, N 5 being on its side. F. R. M.'s sketch shows position 3½ ft. (107 cm.) south-west of Grave 30.

N 6 (fig. 33) 1811

Found broken and incomplete.

Depth 15 in. (38 cm.).

Roman coarse ware vessel, probably flagon, neck and handle missing. F. R. M. writes: 'some rim present but does not fit on', but no rim sherds can now be found; light grey fabric with traces of smooth or possibly burnished finish; slight grooving at base of neck. Iron stain inside shows that it probably once contained an iron object, but there was no sign of this among the bones.

Undecorated.

Contents

A. Burnt bones.

N 6 was found near Structure M.

N 7 (fig. 3) 1552

Found broken.

Depth 21 in. (53 cm.).

Sub-biconical bowl with wide mouth and short straight rim, possibly cut down in ancient times: thin dark grey smoothed ware.

Decorated with three lightly tooled neck-lines from which depend groups of three light lines to the maximum diameter, separating panels containing three light horizontal lines.

Contents

A. Burnt bones.

N 7 was with N 5 (q.v.) in a dump reburied by the diggers of Grave 30. Some pieces of N 7 remained in the filling of Grave 30.

N 8 (not illustrated)

Found in fragments.

Depth 16 in. (41 cm.).

A few fragments of the lower part of a crude thick-walled urn with smooth brown surface.

Undecorated.

Contents

A. Burnt bones.

N 9 (fig. 19) 1688

Found broken.

Depth 24 in. (62 cm.).

Upper part of a large biconical shoulder-boss urn with short upright rim: smooth grey/light brown ware probably once burnished.

Decorated on the neck with a wide zone containing a confused pattern of very faint dots demarcated above by a single line and below by a raised hollow collar, partly slashed, partly carrying a line of dots. Below the collar are a few groups of dots above two neck-lines and about ten hollow shoulder-bosses separating panels containing a confused pattern of faint vertical grooves and groups of dots.

Contents

A. Burnt bones.

N 10 (fig. 13) 1638

Found broken.

Depth 24 in. (62 cm.).

Large biconical urn with short upright neck and well-moulded rim: dark ware, originally with waxy burnish (still preserved on neck which had fallen inside the pot—see pl. XII*b*), well made.

Decorated with a raised slashed collar, demarcated above by two and below by one strong groove, below which is a zone of continuous one two-groove chevrons, each triangle containing one large dot. Below this are two strong grooves, a line of large dots, another groove and large two-groove chevrons with one large dot in each triangle. There is a circular hole 0·50 in. (1·3 cm.) across cut in the bottom of the pot, asymmetrically, from the outside after baking.

Contents

A. Burnt bones (see F below).
B. Two fragments of a bone comb, possibly triangular, warped by fire. Both fragments are of the centre-plate and retain the stumps of teeth. One has a wavy upper edge which projected above the side-plates (a faint line on either side of the centre-plate marks the upper limit of the side-plates). A small fragment of the lower part of a side-plate remains attached by a large iron rivet; the only decoration visible is a pair of incised horizontal lines parallel with the lower edge. The other fragment is probably part of the end of the centre-plate which projected beyond

the corners of the side-plates; part of an iron-stained rivet-hole survives.
C. Bone gaming-piece, slightly affected by heat, plano-convex, with two small holes in the centre of the base. Diameter 0·6 in. (1·5 cm.)
D. Fragment of bronze ring, circular in section: slightly bent, so impossible to determine diameter, but probably part of a finger ring.
E. Eleven fragments of a glass vessel, much distorted by heat; clear green glass. Several pieces have fragments of cremated bone attached.
F. Sheep's astragalus. This may have been used in gaming—see N 59.

N 11 (fig. 12)

Found in fragments.

Depth 16 in. (41 cm.).

Upper part of an urn with angular shoulder, conical neck, and short upright rim: rough brown ware.

Decorated immediately below the rim with two faint neck-lines below which are triangular panels hatched with groups of diagonal lines at right angles to one another.

Contents

A. Burnt bones.

N 11 lay 4½ ft. (137 cm.) south of Grave 30 and may have been broken up and reburied by the diggers of that grave.

N 12 (fig. 7) 1586

Found almost complete.

Depth 30 in. (76 cm.).

Small shoulder-boss urn with short conical neck and everted rim: smooth brown ware, well made.

Decorated with three strong grooves on the neck above eight small solid vertical bosses, separating panels filled with strong vertical corrugation.

Contents

A. Burnt bones of a child with milk teeth. Dr. Wells reports: 'Child. Damaged fragments of two petrous temporal bones; three deciduous molar crowns; a dozen tiny scraps of long bone, the biggest 26 mm. long. Well fired. No animal remains.'
B. Miniature iron knife, the handle of which curves upwards and forms a loop. The blade is also curved. Length 1·5 in. (3·8 cm.).

C. Small pair of iron shears, tips of blades missing, much corroded. Surviving length 1·5 in. (3·8 cm.).
D. Parts of the arms of a pair of iron tweezers.
E. Small iron ring, corroded, resembling a washer, roughly square in section. This may have been attached to the tweezers, but is rather smaller than those found in other urns. Diameter 0·5 in. (1·3 cm.).

N 13 (fig. 31) 1788

Found broken.

Depth 30 in. (76 cm.).

Upper part of a small globular urn with flaring rim, base missing: corky brown ware.
Undecorated.

Contents. No bones were associated with this pot, which may not have been a cremation urn.

N 14 (pl. IV*b* and fig. 4) 1564

Found in fragments.

Depth 28 in. (71 cm.).

Wide-mouthed bowl with angular shoulder, tall conical neck and thickened rim: smooth dark ware, probably once burnished.
Decorated with continuous horizontal corrugation from the rim to the base of the neck, and continuous vertical corrugation on the shoulder.

Contents
A. Burnt bones (see D below).
B. Six glass beads, all more or less affected by fire.
  (i) Possibly an opaque white bead with marvered trail (? interlaced) and red spot decoration, discoloured and distorted by heat.
  (ii) Blue standard barrel bead, slightly distorted by heat. Maximum diameter 0·65 in. (1·7 cm.).
  (iii) Disc bead, slightly distorted by heat; probably originally blue. Diameter 0·45 in. (1·1 cm.).
  (iv) Long cylinder bead, reddish-brown with yellow marvered decoration, somewhat distorted by heat. Length of axis 0·5 in. (1·3 cm.).
  (v) Bead of two colours, one of which is red, considerably distorted by heat.
  (vi) Bead considerably distorted by heat, probably blue.

C. Incomplete grey clay ring, very crudely made and lightly baked. It is uncertain if it was ever complete, but if so it would have been oval; smooth on inside, rough on outside. Perhaps a child's plaything. Maximum internal diameter 0·6 in. (1·5 cm.).
D. Proximal portion of left femur of small sheep and fragment of long bone.

N 15 (fig. 3) 1561

Found almost complete.

Depth 32 in. (81 cm.).

Small sub-biconical urn with everted rim: smooth brown ware, probably once burnished.
Decorated with three grooved neck-lines, from which depend eight groups of five vertical grooves.

Contents
A. Burnt bones of a child with milk teeth. Dr. Wells reports: 'Child. Fragments of two petrous temporal bones; one small fragment of vault; four tiny slivers of long bone. Well fired. No animal remains.'
B. Fragment of triangular bone comb, with iron rivets. The sloping edge of the centre-plate is flush with the edges of the side-plate. The side-plates are decorated with sets of incised lines parallel with the edges.

N 16 (fig. 13) 1634

Found broken.

Depth 28 in. (71 cm.).

Small shouldered urn with hollow neck and everted rim: smoothed red/brown ware.
Decorated under the rim with a zone of 'match-end' jabs in groups of five demarcated top and bottom by a single firm line, below which is a line of single small dots, interrupted in one place by two groups of five lines, and demarcated below by two lines. On the shoulder are groups of three deep vertical notches above a single line and continuous single-line chevrons.

Contents
A. Burnt bones of a child with milk teeth.
B. Manicure set, in F. R. M.'s original note, not in inventory, and now missing (not shown on fig. 13).

N 16 and the base of an undecorated urn (apparently not preserved) similar to D 1 and containing adult burnt bones, were on the shoulder of N 17. The three urns were probably buried at the same time. They were by the hearth in Roman Structure M. Sketch by F. R. M. (pl. XIV*b*).

N 17 (fig. 13) 1637

Found broken.

Depth 32 in. (81 cm.).

Large sub-biconical urn with tall neck and everted rim: thick rough red/buff ware.

Decorated with two sharply drawn neck-lines above a wide zone containing six large two-line swastikas drawn freehand: between some of these at the bottom are triangles, which point upwards, filled with small dots: other groups of dots, generally three set as a triangle, occur irregularly among the swastikas. The zone is demarcated below by two sharply drawn horizontal lines between which is a line of dots.

Contents

A. Burnt bones, large, probably a man.
B. Two fragments of a triangular bone comb, both are fragments of the centre-plate and show the stumps of teeth. One fragment has an indented upper edge which projected above the side-plate (cf. N 10, fig. 13); the line marking the upper limit of the side-plate is clearly visible; iron rivets.

N 17 had N 16 (q.v.) on its shoulder (pl. XIV*b*).

N 18 (fig. 25) 1742

Found in fragments.

Depth 24 in. (61 cm.).

Globular urn with tall narrow neck and upright rim, base and part of side missing: smooth dark ware. Undecorated.

Contents

A. Burnt bones.
B. Pair of iron shears, corroded. This pair is larger than those normally found in these cremation urns, and obviously functional. The blades are relatively long; part of the loop is missing. Surviving length 3·55 in. (9·0 cm.).
C. Pair of iron tweezers, corroded. The distal tip of one arm is missing. The proximal ends of the arms are constricted to form a terminal loop. Length 1·95 in. (5·0 cm.).
D. Fragment of iron, corroded. This thin strip of iron may be part of a knife tang, but it is impossible to be certain.

N 19 (fig. 3) 1558

Found complete.

Depth 24 in. (61 cm.).

Wide-mouthed globular urn with short neck and everted rim: smooth dark ware, probably once burnished.

Decorated with three strong grooves on the neck from which depend nine groups of four vertical grooves: three panels so formed contain a large diagonal grooved cross, the other five being blank.

Contents

A. Burnt bones (see C below).
B. Part of the sloping end of the centre-plate of a bone comb, possibly round-backed. On both sides it is just possible to make out where the lower angles of the side-plates had covered the centre-plate. There is part of a small rivet hole with iron staining.
C. Incomplete right ilium of pig (not shown on fig. 3).

N 20 (not illustrated)

Found in fragments.

Depth 26 in. (66 cm.).

A few fragments of an urn in smooth grey/brown ware.

Decorated on the shoulder with small vertical solid bosses.

Contents

A. Burnt bones.

N 21 (fig. 6) 1582

Found complete.

Depth 24 in. (61 cm.).

Shouldered urn with hollow neck and upright rim: smooth dark ware, probably once burnished black, well made.

Decorated with six sharply tooled neck-lines above continuous vertical corrugation on the shoulder, interrupted in four places by vertical panels of feathered corrugation.

Contents

A. Burnt bones.

N 22 (fig. 8) 1599

Found almost complete.

Depth 22 in. (56 cm.).

Wide-mouthed shoulder-boss bowl with upright neck and rim: thin smooth red/brown ware.

Decorated with a light groove at the base of the neck above eighteen long hollow vertical shoulder-bosses separating panels filled with vertical corrugation.

Contents

A. Burnt bones.
B. Opaque dark blue glass bead, distorted by fire.

N 23 (fig. 26) 1750

Found in fragments.

Depth 22 in. (56 cm.).

Lower part of a globular urn with wide mouth, rim missing: heavy smoothed light brown ware.
Undecorated.

Contents

A. Burnt bones.
B. Large iron knife, corroded. Tip of blade and haft missing. Surviving length 3·0 in. (7·6 cm.).
C. Part of large kidney-shaped iron buckle, corroded; the tongue is missing. Length 1·7 in. (4·3 cm.).

B and C are not recorded in F. R. M.'s inventory but are shown on a photograph with this urn number.

N 24 (fig. 4) 1562

Found in fragments.

Depth 22 in. (56 cm.).

Upper part of a shouldered urn with high conical neck, rim missing: very heavy red/brown ware with black surface burnish.

Decorated high on the neck with a zone of lightly scratched two-line chevrons, below which is continuous horizontal corrugation above continuous vertical corrugation on the shoulder, the latter divided into four panels by four groups of three broader grooves.

Contents

A. Burnt bones.

N 24 may come from the same workshop as M 40 (fig. 7) (q.v.).

N 25 (fig. 18) 1675

Found almost complete.

Depth 22 in. (56 cm.).

Shoulder-boss urn with conical neck and upright rim: smooth brown ware, once burnished, well made.

Decorated low on the neck with six close-set fine lines above seven hollow vertical shoulder-bosses, separating panels outlined on each side with three fine vertical lines and filled with three variations of a linear design including a two-line diagonal cross. The cross occurs three times alone, twice bisected by two vertical lines, and twice with a two-line 'V' below it. These designs may be intended to suggest runes (see pp. 66–7).

Contents

A. Burnt bones.
B. A few pieces of unburnt animal bones, indeterminate (not shown on fig. 18).

N 26 (fig. 32) 1798

Found broken.

Depth 22 in. (56 cm.).

Shoulder-boss bowl with short everted rim: thin smoothed dark grey/brown ware.

Decorated with (probably three) small solid nipple-bosses of which only one remains.

Contents

A. Burnt bones.

N 27 (not illustrated)

Found in fragments.

Depth 32 in. (81 cm.).

Fragments of a large, apparently globular, urn: heavy brown ware with smoothed surface.
Undecorated.

Contents

A. Burnt bones.

N 28 (urn fig. 42; grave goods fig. 59) 1869

Found badly broken.

Depth 32 in. (81 cm.).

Biconical urn with tall hollow neck and slightly everted rim: rather coarse red/brown ware burnished black.

Decorated under the rim with a line of jabs demar-cated above by one/two and below by two/three lines. Below is a zone of four/five-line chevrons above two more lines, another line of jabs, and a further line. Below is a line of stamps above three more lines, another line of jabs, another line, and a line of stamps. On the carination are two lines, and below are con-tinuous three/five-line chevrons.

Two stamps are used.

Contents

A. Burnt bones.
B. A pair of bronze tweezers, of Roman type. The distal ends of the arms are greatly expanded and the proximal ends are constricted to form a terminal loop. The arms are ornamented with incised parallel horizontal lines and notches; in this zone and round the loop the edge is faceted. Length 2·3 in. (5·8 cm.).

Association doubtful as N 28 was reconstructed from a mass of sherds; parts of at least two other urns, both coarse and undecorated, were present, and the tweezers may have come from any of the three.

N 29 (not illustrated)

N 29 comprises a few fragments belonging to two different urns.

Depth 18 in. (46 cm.).

(a) A thin-walled shoulder-boss urn or bowl: smooth brown ware.

Decorated with two faint grooves at base of neck above a continuous row of small round hollow shoulder-bosses giving a wavy outline to the shoulder.

Contents

A. Burnt bones.

(b) A heavy urn with upstanding rim: smooth brown ware.

Decorated with at least six faint grooves on the neck.

Contents

A. Burnt bones.

N 30 (fig. 9) 1602

Found almost complete.

Depth 22 in. (56 cm.).

Small tub-shaped urn with wide mouth and flaring rim: red/brown ware burnished black.

Decorated with five grooves on the neck forming broad continuous corrugation, above four groups of four/seven shallow vertical grooves on the shoulder: one of the intervening spaces contains a single 'V'.

Contents

A. Burnt bones of an infant.
B. Miniature pair of bronze tweezers, made from a piece of sheet bronze, cut and bent to shape. The distal end of one arm is missing. Length 0·8 in. (2·0 cm.).
C. Two fragments of iron, which apparently join; possibly part of an iron knife or iron shears; corroded.

B was found stuck to C.

N 31 (fig. 19) 1686

Found complete.

Depth 32 in. (81 cm.).

Shoulder-boss urn with horizontal humped shoul-der, short hollow neck and everted rim: smooth soft pitted fawn/buff ware.

Decorated on the neck with three tooled lines, on the horizontal shoulder with four close-set corded lines, above four prominent narrow vertical hollow bosses, each surrounded by four lines; in the panels are large three-line arches running nearly to the base. There is a large ancient hole in the base, part or all of which may be intentional.

Contents

A. Burnt bones.
B. At least three fused glass beads. It is impossible to determine their original size, shape, and colour, but they were all large beads.

N 32 (fig. 10) 1613

Found broken.

Depth 22 in. (56 cm.).

Large shouldered urn with tall conical neck, upper part of neck and rim missing: smooth brown ware.

Decorated on the lower part of the neck with a line of dots above five tooled lines: on the shoulder are six/seven-line chevrons, the triangles between which are outlined with dots.

Contents

A. Burnt bones.

N 32 could be from the same workshop as M 44(a) (fig. 10) (q.v.).

N 33 (fig. 24) 1735

Found complete.

Depth 30 in. (76 cm.).

Small tub-shaped cook-pot: very rough coarse pitted buff/brown ware.
Undecorated.

Contents. None.

F. R. M. notes that N 33 was 'not cinerary: very close to it were found two curiously shaped pieces of iron [missing]. No grave or any pot found near it.'

N 34 (fig. 3) 1550

Found almost complete.

Depth 33 in. (84 cm.).

Sharply carinated biconical bowl with short upright rim: hard well-made smoothed light brown ware.
Decorated low on the neck with six sharply tooled lines, above six groups of seven deeply cut diagonal notches on the carination, between which are groups of four dots set three above the carination and one below it.

Contents
A. Burnt bones, including a milk tooth of a child. The urn was unusually full of bones; possibly more than one body (F. R. M.). Dr. Wells reports: 'Adult. One damaged tooth root, possibly a canine. Well fired.'
B. Glass bead, distorted and discoloured by fire.
C. Fragment of animal rib (not shown on fig. 3).

N 35 (urn not illustrated; grave goods fig. 59)

Found in fragments.

Depth 25 in. (64 cm.).

A few fragments of a shoulder-boss urn: smooth dark ware, probably once burnished.
Decorated with small hollow bosses and probably three-line chevrons in the panels.

Contents
A. Burnt bones.
B. Fragment of iron blade, corroded. One end tapers to a rounded tip, the other end is broken. From the size and shape it could well be part of an iron knife.

C. Bone gaming-piece, plano-convex, no holes in base; cracked by heat. Diameter 0·75 in. (1·9 cm.).

N 36 (fig. 20) 1699

Found broken.

Depth 25 in. (64 cm.).

Lower part of a biconical shoulder-boss urn, neck and rim missing: smooth soft crumbly buff/brown ware.
Decorated on the carination with a continuous thickened bulge, on which are set about eight small solid vertical bosses.

Contents
A. Burnt bones. Dr. Wells reports: 'Child. Two damaged petrous temporal bones; three molar crowns and one root; a few dozen flakes of vault and long bones, none larger than about 20×14 mm. Well fired. No animal remains.'
B. Small iron knife, part of blade and tip of tang missing; corroded. Surviving length 2·15 in. (5·5 cm.).
C. Small pair of iron shears, one blade missing; corroded. Length 1·7 in. (4·3 cm.).
D. Part of bronze needle or bodkin, pointed end missing; made from very thin sheet bronze folded into three and beaten flat so that it is subrectangular in section; eye crudely jabbed out. Surviving length 1·05 in. (2·7 cm.).
E. Small bronze globule, diameter 0·25 in. (0·64 cm.).
F. Two fragments of Niedermendig lava, association doubtful as they could well be Roman rubbish which entered urn with infill (not shown on fig. 20).

N 37 (fig. 9) 1609

Found almost complete.

Depth 33 in. (84 cm.).

Shoulder-boss urn with wide mouth and flaring rim: smooth red/brown ware, perhaps once burnished.
Decorated on the neck with two light grooves above three narrow vertical hollow bosses separating panels partly filled with vertical lines.

Contents
A. Burnt bones.
B. Three fused glass beads in F. R. M.'s notes—now missing (not shown on fig. 9).

N 38 (not illustrated)

Found in fragments.

Depth 31 in. (79 cm.).

Fragments of a very heavily built urn with short upright rim: coarse red ware.
Undecorated.

Contents

A. Burnt bones.

N 39 (fig. 3) 1553, 1554

Found 'shattered and crumbled'.

Depth 26 in. (66 cm.).

Wide-mouthed shouldered bowl with upright rim: very crumbled rough brown ware.
Decorated with three tooled neck-lines from which depend vertical lines to the shoulder; at ? four points a one-line diagonal cross replaces about three vertical lines.

Contents

A. Burnt bones of an adult.
B. Miniature urn with splayed sides and hollow pedestal base: rough flinty red ware. Decorated with ? three horizontally pierced vertical lugs. Found lying on top of bones. 1553.
C. Two fragments of sheet bronze, warped and cracked by fire, apparently cut from a larger sheet.

N 40 (fig. 2) 1545

Found broken.

Depth 22 in. (56 cm.).

Wide-mouthed sub-biconical urn with tall neck and slightly everted rim: strong smooth brown ware.
Decorated with four firm lines at base of neck above three/five-line chevrons, the triangles between which are entirely filled with small jabs, except one which is filled with larger plain sunk circles.

Contents

A. Burnt bones.

N 41 (figs. 31, 40) 1789, 1858

N 41 comprises two urns. N 41(a) was found in fragments scattered over a considerable area between N 40 and N 41(b): it may have been disturbed by a rabbiter.

(a) (fig. 40)   1858

Depth. Not recorded.

Upper part of an urn with tall conical neck, narrow mouth, and slightly everted rim: smooth brown ware, well made, once burnished.
Decorated on the neck with four groups of strong grooves, the uppermost of four, the others of two, separating three plain flat collars: below a single chevron line demarcates groups of four or more widely spaced and carelessly applied stamps.
One stamp is used.

Contents. None seen.

(b) (fig. 31)   1789

Depth 22 in. (56 cm.).

Ovoid urn with tall thickened cylindrical neck and sharply everted and flattened rim: smooth burnished bright brown ware.
Undecorated.
The form and fabric of this urn are without parallel at Caistor. For parallels elsewhere, see p. 69, n. 4.

Contents

A. Burnt bones.
B. Small pair of iron shears, corroded. The blades, of which most of one and the tip of the other are missing, are comparatively long, and the diameter of the proximal loop is unusually great. It is difficult to see how these could have been used efficiently. Surviving length 2·15 in. (5·5 cm.).
C. Iron fragment, corroded and broken, possibly part of an iron knife.

N 42 (fig. 13) 1636

Found badly shattered.

Depth 19 in. (48 cm.).

Biconical urn with narrow neck and everted rim: hard smoothed sandy brown ware.
Decorated on the neck with a zone of dots demarcated above and below by two sharp lines, then another line of dots demarcated above and below by a single line. Below is a wide zone demarcated below by a single line on the carination, and containing a series of single-line arches separated from one another by two vertical lines enclosing a line of dots. The panels under the arches are divided vertically by two single

lines into three spaces, each of which contains a vertical or diagonal line of dots. There are also diagonal lines of dots in the spandrels above the arches.

Contents

A. Burnt bones.

N 43 (not illustrated)

Found in fragments.

Depth 22 in. (56 cm.).

A few fragments of a shouldered urn with short upright neck and slightly swollen rim: smooth brown ware, once polished.
Undecorated.

Contents

A. Burnt bones.

N 43 was in contact with N 44.

N 44 (fig. 5) 1578

Found broken.

Depth 22 in. (56 cm.).

Upper part of a globular urn with wide mouth, upright neck and slightly everted rim; smooth dark brown ware, once polished.

Decorated on the neck with continuous horizontal corrugation above alternate panels of horizontal and vertical corrugation on the shoulder.

Contents. No bones seen.

N 44 was in contact with N 43.

N 45 (fig. 29) 1768

'Nearly half missing'.

Depth 26 in. (66 cm.).

Shouldered urn with conical neck, wide mouth, and everted rim: sandy grey/brown ware.
Undecorated.

Contents

A. Burnt bones, including a milk tooth (F. R. M.). Dr. Wells reports: 'Adult. The root of a ?3rd mandibular molar. Well fired. No animal bones.' Perhaps a double burial.
B. Bronze cruciform brooch, bent double and part melted by the fire; probably Åberg Group III because of the scroll-shaped nostrils and apparent

lack of lappets. A clearly defined vertical ridge runs down the centre of the nose of the animal's head, which does not appear to project beyond the nostrils. The upper part of the foot is decorated with horizontal mouldings. The bow has a central vertical ribbed moulding.
C. Fused glass bead. It is impossible to determine the original size, shape, and colour of this bead, but it was probably a large one.
D. Part of an iron brooch pin. This probably belonged to the bronze cruciform brooch.

N 46 (fig. 36) 1824

Found badly shattered.

Depth 26 in. (66 cm.).

Large shoulder-boss urn with tall conical neck, rim missing: smooth badly-fired dark brown ware.

Decorated with three fine neck-lines above a line of dots and two lines of stamps separated from one another by three similar lines. Below are two more lines. On the shoulder are six small hollow bosses, demarcated on each side by two vertical lines, the panels between which contain three-line chevrons irregularly spaced. Below the bosses and panels are two more lines.

Two stamps are used.

Contents

A. Burnt bones.

N 47 (not illustrated)

Found in fragments.

Depth 24 in. (61 cm.).

A few fragments of a wide-mouthed urn with short upright rim: red/brown ware with smoothed surface.
Undecorated.

Contents

A. Burnt bones.
B. Fragment of iron, corroded, possibly part of an iron blade, but impossible to determine. Not in F. R. M.'s inventory, association doubtful.

N 48 (fig. 32) 1795

Found complete.

Depth 30 in. (76 cm.).

Shoulder-boss bowl with tall hollow neck and thickened upright rim: smoothed brown/grey ware, well made.

Decorated with three solid nipple-bosses.

Contents
A. Burnt bones, apparently of a very large person.
B. Section of the centre-plate of a large triangular bone comb, with iron rivets, two of which remain; teeth survive to full length. The upper edge of the centre-plate was apparently flush with the side-plates.
C. Three fused glass beads—probably all barrel beads, but it is not possible to be certain. One bead was red.

N 48 had about a quarter of a Roman tile over it as a lid which had excluded all earth.

N 49 (urn not illustrated; grave goods fig. 59)

'Found mostly reduced to mud.'

Depth 2 in. (5 cm.).

A few fragments of an urn : brown ware with surface burnish.
No decoration appears.
Urn missing.

Contents
A. Burnt bones of an adult.
B. Part of a small iron knife, corroded. Most of the tang is missing, but a small impression of the wooden haft remains. The blade is broken, but was apparently sub-triangular in shape.
C. Miniature pair of iron shears, corroded. The tips of both blades are missing. Surviving length 1·1 in. (2·8 cm.).
D. Small pair of iron tweezers, corroded; the distal ends of the arms are missing. Apparently a simple pair with no pronounced terminal loop and no expansion of the distal ends. Surviving length 1·25 in. (3·2 cm.).

N 50 (fig. 2) 1548

Found broken.

Depth 22 in. (56 cm.).

Globular urn with short upright neck, wide mouth and slightly everted rim: hard red/grey ware with sandy surface once smoothed. The fabric and rim look sub-Roman. A neat 0·50 in. (1·3 cm.) circular hole has been pecked from outside in the bottom of the pot.
Decorated with five faintly tooled neck-lines above large four-line pendent triangles.

Contents
A. Burnt bones.
B. Sheep's bone (recorded in F. R. M.'s notes, now missing).

N 51 (pl. V*a* and fig. 9) 1606

Found complete.

Depth 30 in. (76 cm.).

Shoulder-boss urn with conical neck, wide mouth, and upright rim: smooth dark ware, once burnished.
Decorated with six firm neck-lines above eight small solid applied bosses, four of which have come off, separating panels filled with close-set vertical lines.

Contents
A. Burnt bones.

N 52 (fig. 1) 1542

Found badly shattered and much missing.

Depth 31 in. (79 cm.).

Large wide-mouthed urn with sloping shoulder, upright neck, and slightly everted rim: smooth dark red/brown ware, once burnished.
Decorated low on the neck with four lightly tooled lines, above very faint three-line pendent triangles.

Contents
A. Burnt bones.
B. Two fragments of burnt elephant ivory ring. Original diameter about 4 in. (10 cm.).
C. Three fused glass beads, two fused together.
    (i) Pale green or opaque white disc bead, distorted by heat.
    (ii) Blue disc bead, somewhat distorted by heat and fused to (iii). Maximum diameter 0·4 in. (1·0 cm.).
    (iii) Bead greatly affected by fire, fused to (ii); impossible to determine original colour.
D. Four fragments of fused clear glass, possibly part of a cone beaker. Several fragments show the characteristic ridging.
E. Four fragments of fused glass, some of which may belong to D.
F. Incomplete iron ring. Minimum diameter 1·15 in. (2·9 cm.).
G. Two fragments of rectangular iron clip, 1·05 × 0·4 in. (2·7 × 1·0 cm.). Corroded at one corner only.
H. Sheep's rib (recorded in F. R. M.'s notes, now missing).

N 52 was in contact with N 53 under a large heap of big flints, broken Roman tiles, and a piece of Niedermendig lava.

N 53 (fig. 5) 1577

Found almost complete.

Depth 31 in. (79 cm.).

Small shouldered bowl with wide mouth and everted rim: smooth buff/brown ware, once burnished black.

Decorated with continuous light horizontal corrugation on the neck above continuous light vertical corrugation on the shoulder.

Contents

A. Burnt bones of a child.

N 53 was in contact with N 52 and both were covered by a large heap of big flints and broken Roman tiles.

The presence of an ivory ring with N 52 suggests that these were an associated burial of mother and child (see p. 45).

N 54 (pl. II*b* and fig. 56) 1926

Found complete.

Depth 38 in. (97 cm.).

Large wide-mouthed bowl with concave neck and everted rim: well-made dark ware with burnished surface.

Decorated with a raised stamped collar on the neck, demarcated above and below by four firm lines: below is continuous four-line arcading, the central lines enclosing a line of stamps: there are three/six stamps in the spandrels above the arcading: one of the arches has three instead of two lines below the stamped zone.

Two stamps are used.

N 54 is by Potter VIII (p. 55).

Contents

A. Burnt bones.

N 54 was found unbroken at the bottom of Grave 32, 1 foot to the north of the nearest bone, at the same depth as the interment. It may have been buried with the body, though it is typologically much earlier than the probable date of Grave 32. Perhaps it was found by the grave-diggers and reburied in Grave 32.

N 54 is not shown on the cemetery plan (map 2).

N 55 (fig. 29) 1772

Found almost complete.

Depth 29 in. (74 cm.).

Small globular urn with wide mouth and upright rim: smooth grey ware.

Undecorated.

Contents

A. Burnt bones.

N 55 was found in contact with, but outside, the heap of stones and tiles which covered N 52 and N 53.

N 56 (fig. 34) 1814

Found complete.

Depth 34 in. (86 cm.).

Sub-biconical bowl with upright neck and slightly everted rim: dark ware once burnished black.

Decorated low on the neck with a raised stamped collar demarcated above by three and below by two firm lines. Below is an irregular arrangement of linear chevrons and stamps, the chevron line of stamps being generally demarcated above by three and below by two lines. But in two places a horizontal line of stamps with one or two lines below it takes the place of the chevrons, and in one place there is a three-line chevron with no stamps.

Two stamps are used.

N 56 is related to the work of Potter VIII (fig. 56 and p. 55).

Contents

A. Burnt bones. Dr. Wells reports: 'Adult. Seventy-six small fragments, including pieces of cranial vault; vertebrae and long bone fragments; and a damaged left patella. Slight underfiring on a few of the bones.' (See G below.)

B. Small iron knife, corroded. The iron haft is enlarged at the end and an oval hole has been made in it. The blade is curved. Length 2·35 in. (6·0 cm.).

C. Small pair of iron shears, corroded; the tip of one blade is missing. Length 2·1 in. (5·3 cm.).

D. Small pair of iron tweezers, corroded. The distal end of one arm is missing. The proximal ends of the arms have been constricted to form a terminal loop. Length 1·55 in. (3·9 cm.).

E. End section of centre-plate of triangular bone comb, with iron rivets, of which one remains. The upper edges of the side-plates were apparently flush with the edge of the centre-plate. The lower part of this piece projected below and beyond the side-plates. Just below the position of the lower corner of one side-plate is a single piece of decoration—two compass-drawn concentric circles.

F. Small fragment of sheet bronze, slightly twisted and with rough edges.

G. Fragment of sheep astragalus (not shown on fig. 34).

Above N 56 was part of a Roman tile which had excluded earth from the contents.

N 57 (not illustrated)

Found in fragments.

Depth 24 in. (61 cm.).

Fragments of a heavy urn: smooth brown ware. Undecorated.

Contents

A. Burnt bones.

N 58 (not illustrated)

Found shattered.

Depth 19 in. (48 cm.).

Fragments of an urn with carinated shoulder: badly baked brown ware with smoothed surface.

Decorated with three or four lightly tooled lines widely spaced on the neck from which groups of three or four lines run diagonally to the carinated shoulder.

Contents

A. Burnt bones.

N 58 was in contact with N 59 and N 60.

N 59 (pl. XIX*b* and fig. 5) 1573

Found broken.

Depth 19 in. (48 cm.).

Large globular urn with tall conical neck, rim missing: burnished black ware.

Decorated with continuous horizontal corrugation on the neck above continuous vertical corrugation on the shoulder; the latter divided into four panels by four groups of three broader grooves.

Contents

A. Burnt bones.

B. Iron knife, corroded, tang bears impression of wooden haft. Tips of blade and tang missing. Surviving length 2·85 in. (7·3 cm.).

C. Half of small pair of iron shears, tip of blade missing. Surviving length 1·85 in. (4·75 cm.).

D. Miniature pair of bronze tweezers, broken at top, roughly cut from sheet bronze. Along part of one arm the maker did not follow the incised cutting line and the rough projection has not been trimmed, so obviously not intended for use. Length 1·1 in. (2·8 cm.).

E. 33 gaming pieces, all plano-convex. Eleven are black: opinions vary on the material from which they were made, but possibly black shale. Twenty-two pieces are white, all probably of bone. All pieces have been more or less affected by fire, the bone pieces being more distorted than the black. Maximum diameters 0·65 in. (1·7 cm.) to 0·85 in. (2·15 cm.).

F. Roe deer's astragalus with runic inscription (pp. 114–17).[1] This piece is larger than any of the other astragali from this urn (G) and is dark brown. It appears to have a polish which none of the others have, but it is difficult to be certain if this is original or due to much handling since excavation. Maximum length 1·1 in. (2·85 cm.).

G. 35+ astragali, some complete, some fragmentary; there may have been as many as thirty-eight. One is certainly roe deer, fifteen are sheep; it is not possible to determine if the rest are sheep or roe deer, but a number are probably the latter. These vary very much in size and degree of cracking and warping by fire.

N 59 was in contact with N 58 and N 60 and appears to be from the same workshop as N 82 (8 ft. (2·5 m.) to the west of it) (fig. 5) and N 75 (4½ ft. (137 cm.) north-west of it) (fig. 5).

N 60 (fig. 41) 1862

Found in fragments.

Depth 19 in. (48 cm.).

Lower part of heavy globular urn, neck and rim missing: smooth brown ware.

---

[1] This was originally identified, and has been published, as sheep, as were all of G. Mr. J. Goldsmith of N.C.M. suggested the new identification and this was confirmed by Mr. Eric Higgs of the Museum of Archaeology and Ethnology, Cambridge, who also kindly re-examined the other astragali (G).

Decorated with a series of diagonal or curving lines separating alternate lines of shallow oval dots and small stamps.

One stamp is used.

Contents

A. Burnt bones.

N 60 was in contact with N 58 and N 59.

N 61 (fig. 25) 1745

Found 'badly broken'.

Depth 26 in. (66 cm.).

Globular urn with short upright rim: rough sandy buff/grey ware.
Undecorated.

Contents

A. Burnt bones.

N 61 is very similar to N 63 (fig. 25) and could be from the same workshop.

N 62 (fig. 19) 1684

Found in fragments.

Depth. Not recorded.

Shoulder-boss urn with conical neck, narrow mouth, and flattened rim: thin smooth brown ware.

Decorated on the neck with a plain collar demarcated above by one and below by two lightly tooled lines above about eight vertical hollow bosses demarcated on each side by two lines and separating panels containing groups of diagonal lines.

Contents. None recorded.

N 62 was reconstructed from a collection of fragments which included parts of several urns. These may have been a grave-digger's dump from Grave 38.

N 63 (fig. 25) 1746

Found almost complete.

Depth 22 in. (56 cm.).

Globular urn with short upright rim: rough sandy red/brown ware.
Undecorated.

Contents

A. Burnt bones. Dr. Wells reports: 'Adult, probably male. Two contiguous fragments, 124 mm. long,

of a sturdy shaft of an ulna. Well fired. No animal remains.'

B. Small pair of iron shears, top of one blade missing; corroded. Length 2·3 in. (5·8 cm.).

C. Miniature pair of iron tweezers, corroded. Length 1·2 in. (3·0 cm.).

D. Two pieces of pig's rib, missing, not shown on fig. 25.

N 63 is very similar to N 61 (fig. 25), and could be from the same workshop.

N 64 (fig. 50) 1896

Found in fragments.

Depth 23 in. (58 cm.).

Shoulder-boss bowl with upright neck and rim: thin red/brown ware, burnished brown.

Decorated with two faintly tooled grooves at base of the neck, above three or four groups of two firmly tooled vertical lines descending almost to the base, and bordered on each side in the upper part by vertical lines of stamps. In each of the panels so formed is a pendent semicircular line above a line of stamps, enclosing a group of three small vertical hollow bosses, demarcated on each side by two vertical lines and separated from each other by a vertical line of stamps.

Five stamps appear.

N 64 is by Potter II (p. 68), the scheme being very similar to that of M 24(c) (fig. 49).

Contents

A. Burnt bones, including animal bone.

N 65 (fig. 32) 1796

Found badly broken.

Depth 22 in. (56 cm.).

Small shoulder-boss bowl with upright rim: smooth burnished brown ware, well made.

Decorated with two or three very slight solid bosses.

Contents

A. A few pieces of burnt bone, probably an infant.

N 66 (fig. 46)

Found in fragments.

Depth 13 in. (33 cm.).

A few fragments of a shouldered urn: coarse brown ware with red surface.

Decorated apparently with one or two strong grooves on the neck above a medley of vertical and diagonal grooves and stamps, not enough of which are preserved to show the design, if any.

Two stamps appear.

Contents

A. Burnt bones.

N 67 (fig. 5) 1576

Found broken.

Depth 22 in. (56 cm.).

Lower part of a globular urn: smoothed dark grey ware.

Decorated with continuous light vertical grooves extending nearly to the base.

Contents. None recorded.

N 68 (fig. 30) 1779

Found badly shattered.

Depth 22 in. (56 cm.).

Shouldered jar with upright neck and slightly everted rim: smoothed red/brown ware. A hole has been pecked in the side just above the base.

Undecorated.

Contents

A. Burnt bones. Dr. Wells reports: 'Child. One fragment of a damaged petrous temporal bone; five small fragments of molar crowns. Well fired. No animal remains.'
B. A translucent pebble, possibly a carnelian (F. R. M's notes), now missing. This association is doubtful as the pebble could have entered with the earth.

N 69 (fig. 1) 1539

Found complete.

Depth 22 in. (56 cm.).

Large wide-mouthed bowl with tall concave neck and flaring well-moulded rim: very well made hard dark ware with high black burnish.

Decorated with four strong neck-grooves above two long panels of freehand running spirals in three strong grooves: at each end of the long panels are short panels demarcated by three strong vertical grooves and containing a single group of three grooved arches.

The possible significance of this unusual decoration is discussed on pp. 63–4.

Contents

A. Burnt bones.

N 70 (fig. 13) 1635

Found almost complete.

Depth 24 in. (61 cm.).

Globular urn with conical neck, rim missing: smoothed dark ware once burnished black.

Decorated with at least four strong corrugated neck-lines above a continuous zone of three/five-groove chevrons, demarcated below by a single groove. Below are blocks of vertical corrugation separating panels containing horizontal corrugation, groups of dots and diagonal crosses.

Contents

A. Burnt bones.
B. Fragment of an iron ring, probably a finger ring with a flat bezel of twisted wire; cf. E 14 (fig. 2).
C. Two bronze strips of plano-convex section, from a mounting decorated with groups of horizontal parallel mouldings; cracked and warped by fire. Two bronze rivets survive.

N 71 (urn not illustrated; grave goods fig. 32)

Found in fragments.

Depth 15 in. (38 cm.).

Fragments of lower part of an urn (probably biconical): dark brown/black ware, probably originally burnished.

Decorated apparently with at least two light grooves on the neck above a zone of diagonal grooves or chevrons.

Contents

A. Burnt bones, possibly of a child.
B. Miniature cook-pot with wide mouth and hollow footring: rough flinty buff/brown ware. Decorated with three solid nipple-bosses.
C. Miniature dish with thick handle: rough flinty buff/brown ware. Undecorated.
D. A translucent pebble—not mentioned in F.R.M.'s inventory, association doubtful.

N 72 (fig. 58)

Found complete.

Depth 15 in. (38 cm.).

Roman coarse ware jar; medium grey fabric.
Decorated only with a single horizontal groove immediately below the neck.

Contents

A. Four or five very small fragments of bone found after a careful search of the earth with which the pot was filled. The bones do not survive.

N 72 was found about 17 ft. (5.2 m.) south-west of Structure E.

N 73 (fig. 5)

Found in fragments.

Depth 12 in. (30 cm.).

Upper part of a globular urn with upstanding neck and everted rim: smoothed dull grey ware.
Decorated with continuous light horizontal corrugation on the neck above vertical corrugation on the shoulder.

Contents

A. Burnt bones.

N 74 (fig. 12)

Found in fragments.

Depth 20 in. (51 cm.).

Upper part of a thick-walled globular urn with a short upright rim: smoothed dark brown ware.
Decorated on the maximum diameter with two faintly tooled lines above groups of faint vertical and diagonal lines.

Contents

A. Burnt bones.
B. Piece of fused glass, probably one or two beads.

N 75 (fig. 5) 1572

Found almost complete.

Depth 19 in. (48 cm.).

Globular urn with short conical neck and everted rim: burnished black ware.

Decorated with continuous horizontal corrugation on the neck above vertical corrugation on the shoulder, the latter divided into four panels by four groups of three broader grooves.

Contents

A. Burnt bones.

N 75 appears to be from the same workshop as N 59 (fig. 5) and N 82 (fig. 5).

N 76 (urn fig. 50 and grave goods fig. 59)

N 76 was a collection of fragments from at least two urns.

Depth 13 in. (33 cm.).

(a) (fig. 50) 1898

Upper part of wide-mouthed urn with everted rim: smooth sandy brown ware.
Decorated low on the neck with two slight grooves above a line of stamps which is interrupted by the points of large two-line chevrons.
One stamp appears.
N 76(a) is by Potter II (pp. 62–3).

(b) (urn not illustrated)

Fragments of a wide-mouthed urn with upstanding neck and everted rim: smooth brown ware.
Decorated probably with groups of solid bosses, stamps, and lines. At least three stamps are used.

Contents

A. Burnt bones.
B. Small pair of iron tweezers, distal ends of arms broken.
C. Probably part of blade and arm of a small pair of iron shears, but may be part of a small knife.
D. Fragment of iron, possibly part of iron tweezers but does not join.

Association doubtful, as these could have come from either urn.

N 77 (urn fig. 35; grave goods fig. 59) 1819

Found badly shattered.

Depth 22 in. (56 cm.).

Small shoulder-boss urn with conical neck and upright rim: rough pitted dark grey ware.
Decorated with four neck-lines above three groups of three small hollow bosses, with two more horizontal

lines above each group. The groups of bosses are demarcated on each side by two/four vertical lines and separate panels containing a three/four-line chevron or a group of diagonal lines. Single stamps are set in some of the triangles above and below the chevrons.

One stamp is used.

Contents
A. Burnt bones.
B. Large iron nail (association doubtful).

N 77 is recorded as found on top of another urn, apparently not preserved.

N 78 (not illustrated)

N 78 comprises fragments of two urns.

Depth 24 in. (61 cm.).

(a) Fragments of a coarse thick-walled cook-pot: red/brown ware.

(b) Fragments of a thin-walled brown urn.
Both undecorated.

Contents
A. Burnt bones.

N 79 (fig. 15) 1655

Found almost complete.

Depth 23 in. (58 cm.).

Sub-biconical urn with hollow neck and everted rim: smoothed red/brown ware, perhaps once burnished.

Decorated with a zone containing groups of three vertical and diagonal lines demarcated above and below by a single horizontal line, above large three-line chevrons.

Contents
A. Burnt bones.

N 80 (not illustrated)

N 80 comprises fragments of two urns.

Depth 21 in. (53 cm.).

(a) Part of an urn with upstanding neck, everted rim and carinated shoulder: thin smooth red/brown ware.

(b) Part of an urn with widely everted rim: smoothed dark brown/black ware.

Both undecorated.

Contents
A. Burnt bones.

N 81 (fig. 22) 1713

Found shattered.

Depth 15 in. (38 cm.).

Shouldered urn with narrow neck and slightly everted rim: thin smooth grey ware: two holes have been pecked in the side, one near the base, the other half-way up.

Decoration was apparently intended but never carried out, perhaps because the pot became too dry: there are traces, very lightly drawn, of two widely spaced neck-lines with dots possibly for stamps between, and below faint traces of large three-line chevrons.

This is the only case known at Caistor of decoration laid out but not executed.

Contents
A. Burnt bones.

N 81 was found crushed under N 81(a).

N 81(a) (fig. 46)

Found in fragments.

Depth 15 in. (38 cm.).

Numerous small fragments of a thin-walled urn: smoothed dark brown ware.

Decorated with two lines of stamps each demarcated below by three fine lines. Below are faint two-line pendent triangles containing stamps in the upper part.

At least three stamps are used.

Contents
A. Burnt bones.

N 81(a) was found over N 81.

N 82 (fig. 5) 1574

Found badly broken.

Depth 16 in. (41 cm.).

Lower part of large wide-shouldered urn, neck and rim missing: burnished black ware.

Decorated with continuous corrugation on the neck above vertical corrugation on the shoulder, the latter divided into four panels by four groups of three broader grooves.

Contents

A. Burnt bones.

N 82 is from the same workshop as N 59 (fig. 5) and N 75 (fig. 5).

N 83 (pl. VII*b* and fig. 44) 1881

Found in fragments.

Depth. Unknown.

Shouldered urn with tall conical neck and everted rim: smooth dark brown ware, well made and probably once burnished.

Decorated with three horizontal zones of stamps, demarcated below by three, two, and two firm lines respectively: the third zone contains two rows of stamps. Below are chevrons of five/six sharply drawn lines with a vertical line through the apex.

Three stamps are used, two being animal stamps.

Contents

A. A few fragments of burnt bone in the base.

N 83 was reconstructed from fragments found on the surface over several square yards, having been thrown out by recent rabbit digging.

N 84 (fig. 11) 1623

Found broken.

Depth 25 in. (64 cm.).

Sharp-shouldered urn with tall conical neck, rim missing: well-made smooth grey/brown ware, once burnished.

Decorated low on the neck with seven close-set firm lines above a continuous zone of neat three/four-line chevrons.

Contents

A. Burnt bones of young infant with milk teeth (F. R. M.). Dr. Wells reports: 'Child. One fragment of a damaged petrous temporal bone; one fragment of a deciduous molar crown. Well fired. No animal remains.'

N 85 (not illustrated)

Found in fragments.

Depth 19 in. (48 cm.).

Fragments of large shouldered urn: smoothed dark brown ware.
Undecorated.

Contents

A. Burnt bones.

N 86 (fig. 6) 1584

Found broken.

Depth 24 in. (61 cm.).

Shouldered bowl with conical neck, wide mouth and everted rim: thin smooth burnished black ware.

Decorated with continuous horizontal corrugation on the neck above continuous vertical corrugation on the shoulder.

Contents

A. Burnt bones.
B. Iron shears, tip of one blade missing. One blade starts 0·3 in. (0·8 cm.) above the other, and this does not appear to be due to distortion. Length 2·55 in. (6·5 cm.).

N 87 (fig. 28) 1763

Found broken.

Depth 24 in. (61 cm.).

Bag-shaped urn with tall conical neck and upright rim: hard burnished dark brown ware, well made.
Undecorated.

Contents

A. Burnt bones.
B. Fragment of small iron knife blade, badly corroded.
C. Small pair of iron shears, one blade missing. Surviving blade too short and narrow for B to belong to it. Length 1·4 in. (3·6 cm.).

N 87 was found in the side of Grave 35, 2 ft. (60 cm.) from the nearest part of the skeleton. The urn was lying on its side with about half of it missing, having evidently been cut in two when the grave was dug. Fragments of another urn (apparently not preserved) were found in the grave.

N 88 (fig. 14)

Found in fragments.

Depth 20 in. (51 cm.).

Side of biconical urn, rim and base missing: heavy soft smoothed brown ware.

Decorated with at least two neck-lines above a zone of three-line chevrons demarcated below by a faint line on the carination.

Contents

A. Burnt bones.

N 88 was associated with N 89, N 90, N 91. The four urns stood in a line running north and south one foot north of Grave 36, separated by only one or two inches from one another. F. R. M. wrote: 'I think it is likely that they were reburied by Saxon grave-diggers.' But in view of the similarity of the three plain urns (N 89, N 90, N 91) it seems more probable that they are connected burials from one household.

N 89 (fig. 24) 1741

Found in fragments.

Depth 20 in. (51 cm.).

Globular cook-pot with upright rim and round bottom: red/brown ware.
Undecorated.

Contents

A. Burnt bones.

N 89 was one of the N 88 group (q.v.).

N 90 (fig. 24) 1733

Found almost complete.

Depth 20 in. (51 cm.).

Cook-pot with wide mouth and slightly everted rim: smoothed red/grey ware.
Undecorated.

Contents

A. Burnt bones.
B. At least four fused glass beads, one a white disc bead, others too distorted to identify type or colour.
C. Two fragments of bronze, badly warped and distorted by heat, one of which *may* be part of a cruciform brooch with full-round knob.

N 90 was one of the N 88 group (q.v.).

N 91 (fig. 24) 1737

Found almost complete.

Depth 20 in. (51 cm.).

Barrel-shaped cook-pot with inturned rim: smoothed red/grey ware.
Undecorated.

Contents

A. Burnt bones.

N 91 was one of the N 88 group (q.v.).

N 92 (fig. 16) 1660

Found almost complete.

Depth 27 in. (69 cm.).

Wide globular urn with hollow neck and slightly everted rim: smoothed sandy red/brown ware.

Decorated with four grooved neck-lines above continuous wide-grooved arcading. The arches are separated by a vertical groove and there is one large oval dot under each.

Contents

A. Burnt bones of a child.
B. Fragment of centre-plate of a large bone comb with iron rivets, one rivet remaining, probably from a triangular comb.
C. Fragment of red deer metapodial, wrongly identified as sheep on fig. 16.

N 93 (fig. 42) 1870

Found almost complete.

Depth 26 in. (66 cm.).

Biconical urn with short everted rim: smooth buff/brown ware.

Decorated close under the rim with two neck-lines from which depend six groups of three/four vertical lines forming panels demarcated below by four lines on the carination, the space between the upper two lines being diagonally slashed for most of the space under one panel. All the panels, except one which is blank, contain vertical lines of stamps, two having two lines, one four, one five, and the other (much restored) being apparently entirely filled with stamps.

Two stamps are used.

Contents

A. Burnt bones (see D below).
B. Small pair of iron tweezers, distal end of one arm missing; corroded. Length 1·3 in. (3·3 cm.).

C. Probably two glass beads, too distorted and dis-coloured by fire to determine shape.

D. Sheep bone, F. R. M.'s inventory, but now missing. Dr. Wells reports: 'One fragment of a posterior cervical vertebra of an ox. Somewhat underfired. Also a fragment of a metapodial, ?red deer.' (not shown on fig. 42.)

N 94 (fig. 6) 1580

Found shattered.

Depth 27 in. (69 cm.).

Shouldered urn with upright neck and short straight rim: dark ware, once burnished black.

Decorated with three strong grooves on the neck above panels of alternate vertical and horizontal corrugation on the shoulder.

Contents

A. Burnt bones.

B. Part of iron nail, tip and head missing (association doubtful).

N 95 (fig. 4) 1568, 1569

Found almost complete.

Depth 24 in. (61 cm.).

Wide-shouldered urn with tall conical neck and swollen rim: well-made smooth dark ware which has had a high black burnish.

Decorated on the neck with continuous horizontal corrugation above continuous vertical corrugation on the shoulder.

Contents

A. Burnt bones of a large adult.

B. Beneath and in contact with urn was a miniature egg-shaped pot. It was lying on its side and filled with earth. Undecorated.   1568.

C. Bronze tweezers cut from sheet bronze; the prox-imal ends of the arms have been constricted so that a small loop was formed; although these are much better made than others cut from sheet bronze, they are not functional. Length 1·15 ins. (3·0 cm.).

N 95 is very like N 96, but somewhat smaller.

N 96 (fig. 4) 1563

Found broken.

Depth 22 in. (56 cm.).

Wide-shouldered urn with tall conical neck, rim missing: well-made smooth dark ware which has had a high black burnish.

Decorated on the neck with continuous horizontal corrugation above continuous vertical corrugation on the shoulder.

Contents

A. Burnt bones.

B. Iron knife, part of tang missing; long tapering blade; corroded. Surviving length 2·25 in. (5·7 cm.).

C. Arm of a small pair of iron shears; upper part of blade remains, showing that B could not be part of this.

D. Small pair of iron tweezers, part of one arm miss-ing, corroded. Length 1·5 in. (3·8 cm.).

E. A piece of iron pyrites is recorded in F. R. M.'s notes as coming from this urn, but is now missing. It could have been an erratic in the surrounding Drift, which entered the urn with the infill.

N 96 is very like N 95 but somewhat larger.

N 97 (fig. 39) 1851

Found broken.

Depth 23 in. (58 cm.).

Globular urn with short neck and everted rim: thick soft red/brown ware.

Decorated on the neck with a groove above two slightly raised collars diagonally slashed in opposite directions and demarcated from one another and the decoration below by single grooves. Below, vertical bands of corrugation separate four panels, each of which contains a central carelessly applied vertical line of stamps.

Three stamps are used.

Contents

A. Burnt bones.

N 98 (not illustrated)

Found in fragments.

Depth 24 in. (61 cm.).

Fragments of upper part of an urn with sloping shoulder and everted rim: sandy red/brown ware.

Undecorated.

Contents

A. Burnt bones.

N 99 (fig. 31) 1791

Found complete.

Depth 24 in. (61 cm.).

Shoulder-boss urn with tall hollow neck, wide mouth and flaring rim: corky buff/grey ware.

Decorated with six hollow bosses with a deep groove on each side as if pinched up laterally: they are spaced irregularly, two being very close together.

Contents

A. Burnt bones.

N 100 (fig. 35) 1818

'Found broken up and scattered.'

Depth. Not known.

Small shoulder-boss urn with conical neck and flaring rim: dark ware, highly burnished.

Decorated with three tooled neck-lines between the upper two of which is a single line of stamps. On the shoulder are four vertical hollow bosses two of which carry a single vertical line: the bosses are alternately covered with a three-line arch and demarcated on each side by four/five vertical lines. The panels each contain a single large rosette stamp (p. 57).

Two stamps are used.

Contents. Not known.

N 101 (urn fig. 23; grave goods fig. 59)

Found in fragments.

Depth 26 in. (66 cm.).

Lower part of an urn with very thick base: coarse buff/red ware, heavily built.

Decorated apparently with pairs of short diagonal lines widely spaced on the maximum diameter.

Contents

A. Burnt bones.
B. A kidney-shaped iron buckle, too badly corroded to determine if top is flat or curved. Iron tongue remains. Length 1·75 in. (4·5 cm.). Association doubtful. Cf. N 23 (fig. 26).

N 102 (fig. 10) 1612

Found broken.

Depth 27 in. (69 cm.).

Shouldered urn with tall conical neck, rim missing: smooth dark ware, once burnished black: well made.

Decorated with continuous heavy corrugation on the neck, interrupted near the bottom by a horizontal row of large dots: on the shoulder is a single chevron line, the spaces above and below which are filled with diagonal corrugation set at right angles giving a basketry effect. On one side this regular pattern becomes a confused medley of vertical and diagonal grooves which F. R. M. thought might be intended to look like an inscription in runes (but see p. 45).

Contents

A. Burnt bones.
B. Small pair of iron tweezers, distal end of one arm missing; corroded. Length 1·25 in. (3·2 cm.).
C. Fragment of end section of the centre-plate of a bone comb; it is not possible to determine original shape. No rivet holes present. The upper edge presumably projected beyond the side-plates and seems to have been notched.

N 103 (fig. 9) 1605

Found shattered.

Depth 27 in. (69 cm.).

Globular urn with short neck and everted rim: rather rough dark ware, probably once smoothed or burnished.

Decorated with five broad corrugated lines on the neck divided into panels by a single vertical groove, above continuous broad vertical corrugation.

Contents

A. Burnt bones.
B. Small mass of fused bronze. It is impossible to say whether this is part of a bronze object which has been affected by the cremation fire, or whether it is a scrap of bronze waste.

N 104 (urn fig. 18; grave goods fig. 59)

Found in fragments.

Depth 27 in. (69 cm.).

Upper part of a shoulder-boss urn: thick smoothed brown ware.

Decorated with three neck-lines above groups of at least two small hollow shoulder bosses: between the two bosses of each pair are three firm vertical lines and in the panels between the groups are firmly drawn two-line chevrons with a vertical line below the apex. These could be intended for '↑' runes.

Contents
A. Burnt bones.
B. Large iron knife, tang bent and end broken. Very much larger than those usually found in the urns. Surviving length 4·7 in. (12 cm.). Association doubtful.

P 1 (urn not illustrated; grave goods fig. 59)

Found in fragments.

Depth 10 in. (25 cm.).

Fragments of lower part of an urn: smooth well-made dark ware once burnished black.
No decoration appears.

Contents
A. Burnt bones.
B. Two fragments of bronze brooch, greatly warped and distorted by fire, one piece decorated with raised horizontal lines, the other with a line of raised dots in a groove. Possibly parts of a small-long or cruciform brooch.
C. Probable remains of three glass beads distorted and discoloured by fire.

P 2 (fig. 29) 1775

Found almost complete.

Depth 24 in. (61 cm.).

Sub-biconical urn with everted rim: rough corky red/brown ware.
Undecorated.

Contents
A. Burnt bones.

P 3 (fig. 9) 1604

Found in fragments.

Depth 23 in. (58 cm.).

Part of a shouldered urn with high conical neck, rim and base missing: heavy, light grey/brown ware, very much weathered and pitted.
Decorated low on the neck with three corrugated grooves above continuous vertical corrugation on the shoulder, interrupted at several points by blank spaces marked by slight hollows on the inner surface as though intended to be shoulder-bosses which were not completed.

Contents
A. Burnt bones.
B. Blue glass disc bead slightly distorted by fire.

P 4 (not illustrated)

Depth 24 in. (61 cm.).

An urnless cremation.
A large quantity of burnt bones, much more than are usually found in an urn, mixed with and resting on a heap of large flints, which had probably originally covered the deposit. No associated objects, but one of the flints was heavily iron-stained.
Presumably there was a perishable container, such as a bag or basket, in which the burnt bones were buried. The burnt bones of an adult, probably male, from an 'urnless cremation', survive; these may be from this burial (p. 207).

P 5 (not illustrated)

Found in fragments.

Depth 34 in. (86 cm.).

Fragments of an urn: smooth dark ware.
Undecorated.

Contents
A. Burnt bones.

P 6 (not illustrated)

Found in fragments.

Depth 22 in. (56 cm.).

A few fragments of a badly baked urn: rough red ware with smooth surface.
Undecorated.

Contents
A. Burnt bones.

P 7 (fig. 21) 1703

Found shattered.

Depth 24 in. (61 cm.).

Shouldered urn with short conical neck and everted rim: smoothed red/brown ware.
Decorated with four neck-lines, between the third and fourth of which there is a widely spaced line of dots. Below are groups of three or four vertical or

diagonal lines extending far down the side. In each panel between them is a short horizontal groove and below it a deep circular depression: below this in some panels there is a 'V' bisected by a vertical line rising to the depression, in others there is a 'W' with the middle point below the depression. These figures may have been meant to look like runes (see p. 67).

Contents

A. Burnt bones.

P 8 (fig. 31) 1793

Found broken.

Depth 29 in. (74 cm.).

Shoulder-boss bowl with everted rim: smooth grey/brown ware.

Decorated with five hollow bosses. Two circular holes have been pecked, one in the base and one low on the side.

Contents

A. Burnt bones.
B. Five glass beads, all distorted by fire.
    (i) Red bead with marvered white and blue spots.
    (ii) Large bead, apparently red, with marvered yellow and green stripes.
    (ii) Yellow bead.
    (iv) Opaque white bead with marvered blue trail decoration.
    (v) Large bead of clear glass.
C. Two small fragments of sheet bronze, warped and cracked by fire, one fragment attached to B (iv). Originally these two pieces may have been joined.

Heap of sherds from near P 8 (figs. 36, 45) 1828

This heap, which may have been a grave-digger's dump, contained parts of at least three decorated urns: no burnt bones found.

P 8(a) (fig. 36) 1828

Upper part of a large shoulder-boss urn with conical neck and upright rim: smooth red/brown ware.

Decorated with five neck-lines above a double row of stamps below which is another row of stamps demarcated above and below by three more lines. On the shoulder are about eighteen short vertical hollow bosses the panels between which are filled by vertical lines.

Three stamps appear.

P 8(b) (fig. 45)

Part of neck of a shouldered urn: smooth red/brown ware.

Decorated on the neck with vertical and diagonal lines enclosing lines of stamps. On the shoulder is a line of stamps demarcated above by one and below by two lines.

One stamp appears.

P 8(c) (fig. 45)

Part of side of a rounded urn: burnished black ware.

Decorated apparently with three-line pendent triangles sparsely filled with stamps.

Two stamps appear.

P 9 (urn not illustrated; grave goods fig. 59)

Found in fragments.

Depth 30 in. (76 cm.).

Fragments of an urn: pitted red ware.

Decorated with corrugated neck-lines and very slight shoulder-bosses, the panels between which are filled with vertical corrugation.

Contents

A. Burnt bones.
B. Probably a miniature iron knife with a looped handle. The tang curls round almost to the base of the blade. It is narrower here than above the blade and cannot be part of a pair of shears.
C. Animal bone, perhaps hare.

P 10 (fig. 22) 1714

Found broken.

Depth 24 in. (61 cm.).

Sub-biconical urn with narrow neck and flaring rim: hard smooth grey/black ware.

Decorated with five sharply tooled neck-lines above two/three-line chevrons, one of which has two vertical lines from the apex, perhaps intended to represent the '↑' rune (see p. 66).

Contents

A. Burnt bones.

P 10 was found under several large flints.

P 11 (urn not illustrated; grave goods fig. 59)

Found in fragments.

Depth 26 in. (66 cm.).

Fragments of an urn: soft smooth brown ware, very much disintegrated.

Decoration uncertain. F. R. M. says 'incised lines' but all surviving fragments seem undecorated.

Contents

A. Burnt bones. Dr. Wells reports: 'Five minute fragments of bone, almost certainly not human. Somewhat underfired.'
B. Three fragments of sheet bronze, slightly crackled by fire, one piece probably clipped, and the others broken, from a larger sheet.

P 12 (fig. 22) 1709

Found almost complete.

Depth 31 in. (79 cm.).

Globular urn with wide mouth and short everted rim: smooth highly burnished grey/black ware, well made.

Decorated with three neck-lines above large three-line chevrons.

Contents

A. Burnt bones.
B. Numerous fragments of a burnt elephant ivory ring; it is not possible to determine its diameter.

P 13 (fig. 42) 1866

Found in fragments.

Depth 23 in. (58 cm.).

Shouldered urn with tall conical neck, rim missing: rough grey ware, once smoothed but now very pitted and worn.

Decorated with a line of stamps demarcated above by at least three and below by five neck-lines: below are pendent two/four-line triangles filled with stamps and demarcated below by two lines, above continuous four-line chevrons.

One stamp is used, very carelessly impressed.

Contents

A. Burnt bones.
B. Fragment of a probable tibia of a small sheep.

With P 13 was the base of a crudely made pot (apparently not preserved) which may have been used as a cover.

P 14 (fig. 2) 1547

Found broken.

Depth 30 in. (76 cm.).

Large globular urn with narrow concave neck and flaring rim: smooth grey ware.

Decorated with four grooved neck-lines above large faintly drawn three/four-line chevrons.

Contents

A. Burnt bones.
B. Part of iron knife, part of tang and tip of blade missing. Too corroded for type to be determined. Length 2·5 in. (6·4 cm.).
C. Iron tweezers, broken at top, distal end of one arm missing. The distal ends of the arms are expanded, proximal ends constricted to form a terminal loop; corroded. Length 2·3 in. (5·8 cm.).

P 15 (pl. II*a* and fig. 12) 1626

Found complete.

Depth 26 in. (66 cm.).

Wide-mouthed biconical bowl with bead rim: hard smoothed grey/brown ware, very well-made.

Decorated with a zone of three-line chevrons demarcated above by three and below by four firmly tooled lines. On the sharp carination is a line of nicks and below are continuous shallow three-line swags; all the decoration is executed with unusual precision and regularity.

Contents

A. Burnt bones.

F. R. M. writes: 'in my opinion some sort of wheel must have been used' in making this very carefully formed urn (see also p. 43).

One large flint was found inside P 15 and several others were in contact with it.

P 16 (fig. 51) 1901

Found badly broken.

Depth 33 in. (84 cm.).

Biconical shoulder-boss urn with short narrow neck and upright rim: smooth grey/brown ware, once burnished.

Decorated on the neck with a zone of single-line chevrons, in the lower triangles of which are three stamps, the zone demarcated above by one and below by two lines. On the carination are four narrow vertical hollow bosses each outlined on each side by a single line of stamps. In each panel is a wide single-line arch covering a small nipple-boss, wholly or partly surrounded by stamps. All these nipple-bosses have been restored but the one which is preserved has a single stamp on it, forming the centre of the rosette. There is an external cross on the base.

Five stamps are used.

P 16 is by Potter III (pp. 62–3).

Contents

A. Burnt bones.

Two large flints and a large piece of sandstone were found on the top of P 16 which was badly crushed under their weight.

P 17 (fig. 35) 1823

Found broken.

Depth 36 in. (91 cm.).

Biconical shoulder-boss urn with narrow neck and sharply everted rim: smoothed dark brown ware.

Decorated with an indistinct line of small stamps on the underside of the lip above a raised slashed collar demarcated above and below by three corrugated grooves. Below is a larger raised slashed collar from which depend vertical raised slashed bands which expand on the carination into seven feathered hollow bosses. The panels contain a vertical line of diagonal slashing on each side of the vertical raised bands, and this merges with the feathering on the bosses. At the top of the panels is a slashed band above a line of dots and below this three lines forming a single broken pointed arch outlined below with dots: the bottom of the panels is closed with a zone of vertical lines. It is possible that the design in the panels is intended to represent a comb (see p. 65).

One stamp is used.

Contents

A. Burnt bones.

Touching the shoulder of P 17 was P 18 which had been crushed by large flints.

P 18 (fig. 37)

Found in fragments.

Depth 33 in. (84 cm.).

Part of a large shoulder-boss urn with tall conical neck, rim and base missing: rough red ware.

Decorated on the neck with a zone of stamps demarcated above by three and below by four lightly tooled lines. Below is another zone of stamps above four/five further lines. On the shoulder are solid vertical bosses demarcated on each side by two/four vertical lines. At the top of the panels is a horizontal line of stamps above three/four horizontal lines.

One stamp appears, very indistinctly impressed.

Contents

A. Burnt bones.

P 18 was touching the shoulder of P 17 and had been crushed by large flints.

P 19 (fig. 20)

Found in fragments.

Depth 36 in. (91 cm.).

Part of side of a shoulder-boss urn, rim and base missing: sandy red ware.

Decorated with a raised slashed collar demarcated on each side by two lines: below are solid shoulder-bosses, at least one of which was feathered: in the panels was apparently a confused design of light lines and dots, which also run onto and below the lower part of the bosses.

Contents

A. Burnt bones.

P 20 (fig. 28) 1765

Found broken.

Depth 30 in. (76 cm.).

Large biconical urn with tall hollow neck and upright rim: smoothed dark ware.

Undecorated.

Contents

A. Burnt bones.
B. Three glass beads, distorted by fire.
    (i) Blue and white.
    (ii) Possibly reddish brown.
    (iii) Yellow disc bead.
C. Thirty-three fragments of sheet bronze, some badly, and others only slightly, crackled and warped by fire. These fragments vary considerably in size and shape.
D. Fragment of bone comb (F. R. M.'s inventory, now missing).

E. Two or three animal bones (F. R. M.'s inventory, now missing).

P 20 was standing on numerous fragments of burnt animal bones extending for some inches beyond it: they were not associated with any other pottery, and could not have escaped from P 20 which though broken was well preserved.

P 21 (fig. 53) 1907

Found badly broken.

Depth 30 in. (76 cm.).

Shoulder-boss urn with wide mouth and everted rim: grey/brown smooth ware.

Decorated on the neck with a raised stamped collar demarcated above by three and below by two lines. On the shoulder are three pairs of small solid flat-topped bosses demarcated on each side by three vertical lines. The panels between the grouped bosses contain a horizontal line of stamps demarcated above by two/three and below by three/four lines.

Two stamps are used.

P 21 is by Potter IV (p. 57).

Contents

A. Burnt bones.

P 21 had as a cover a piece of Roman tile.

P 22 (fig. 48) 1891

Found in fragments.

Depth 28 in. (71 cm.).

Lower part of a large shoulder-boss urn, most of neck and rim missing: thin smooth grey ware, well made.

Decorated with three neck-lines above a raised slashed collar, below which is a line of stamps and two or three more neck-lines.[1] On the shoulder are ? twelve hollow vertical shoulder-bosses bordered by two vertical lines: in the panels is a horizontal zone of stamps demarcated above and below by two lines above a vertical line of stamps demarcated on each side by two or three vertical lines.

At least six stamps are used (but only two are shown on fig. 48).

P 22 is by Potter I (p. 57).

Contents

A. Burnt bones.

P 23 (fig. 1) 1543

Found badly broken.

Depth 26 in. (66 cm.).

Large shouldered urn with wide mouth and everted rim: smooth dark grey/brown ware.

Decorated on the neck with three faintly tooled grooves above long three-line chevrons one of which is replaced by a three-line diagonal cross.

Contents

A. Burnt bones.

P 23 is very distorted, the present maximum diameter being ovoid, and has been badly restored, the only portion of rim remaining being set too low.

P 24 (urn not illustrated; grave goods fig. 59)

Found in fragments.

Depth 28 in. (71 cm.).

Fragments of a thick-walled urn: heavy brown ware. Undecorated.

Contents

A. Burnt bones.
B. Bone spindle whorl decorated with three incised concentric circles, broken on one side. Diameter 1·7 in. (4·3 cm.).

P 25 (fig. 11) 1621

Found shattered.

Depth 26 in. (66 cm.).

Biconical urn, rim missing: thick red/brown ware, once smoothed, now gritty.

Decorated with at least four firm neck-lines above continuous two-line chevrons outlined on each side by a row of dots.

Contents

A. Burnt bones.
B. Fragments of burnt elephant ivory ring, D-shaped in section. Diameter approx 4·25 in. (10·8 cm.).

P 26 (urn fig. 53; grave goods fig. 59) 1910

Found badly broken.

Depth 26 in. (66 cm.).

Large shoulder-boss urn with wide mouth and short slightly everted rim: smooth dark brown ware.

---

[1] Evidence for the upper part of P 22 was not found until after the drawing on fig. 48 had been made.

Decorated on the neck with a raised stamped collar demarcated above by four and below by seven light lines. On the shoulder are three pairs of small flat-topped solid bosses demarcated on each side by groups of vertical lines. The panels between the grouped bosses contain a horizontal line of stamps demarcated above by one and below by five lines.

Three stamps are used, one of them appearing in one impression only on the raised collar.

P 26 is by Potter IV (p. 57).

Contents

A. Burnt bones.
B. Large iron nail, corroded, badly twisted (association doubtful).

P 27 (fig. 54) 1914

Found in fragments.

Depth 24 in. (61 cm.).

Part of shouldered urn, rim and lower part missing: smoothed dark brown ware.

Decorated on the neck with at least two lines above a line of stamps separated by three lines from another line of stamps below which are four more lines.

Two stamps are used.

P 27 is by Potter V (p. 63).

Contents

A. Burnt bones.

P 28 (figs. 37 and 60 no. 15)

Found in fragments.

Depth 22 in. (56 cm.).

Part of a large shoulder-boss urn, rim and base missing: smooth brown ware.

Decorated on the neck with a line of stamps demarcated above by three and below by four firm lines. On the shoulder are vertical hollow bosses, demarcated on each side by two vertical lines. In the panels is a horizontal line of stamps.

Two stamps appear.

Contents

A. Burnt bones.

F. R. M. records that P 28 had been mended with lead: this sherd was stored separately and is fig. 60 no. 15.

P 29 (not illustrated)

Found broken.

Depth 22 in. (56 cm.).

Most of lower part of an urn with well-formed base: smooth red/brown ware.

Undecorated.

Contents

A. Burnt bones.

P 30 (fig. 51) 1900

Found in fragments.

Depth 26 in. (66 cm.).

Large globular urn, with conical neck and upright rim, base missing: smooth buff/brown ware.

Decorated on the neck with two light grooves above very large single-line arches extending almost to the base, and covering two vertical lines. In the spandrels are groups of stamps.

Three stamps appear.

P 30 is by Potter III (pp. 62–3).

Contents

A. Burnt bones.

P 31 (fig. 58) 4118

Found shattered.

Depth 26 in. (66 cm.).

Large biconical urn with tall neck, everted rim and sagging base: smooth brown ware.

Decorated low on the neck with a line of stamps demarcated above and below by four fine lines: on the shoulder is a continuous zone of three/four line chevrons, the spaces above and below which are filled with stamps.

One stamp is used.

Contents

A. Burnt bones.

P 32 (urn fig. 58: grave goods fig. 59) 4119

Found in fragments.

Depth 24 in. (61 cm.).

About half a globular shoulder-boss urn with short hollow neck and everted rim: rough brown ware, perhaps once smoothed.

Decorated with four lines on the hollow neck above a flat slashed collar with a line below it. On the maximum diameter were four slight hollow bosses covered with feathering which extends beyond them. Above and between the bosses are irregularly set three/four-line chevrons bordered above and sometimes outlined internally with a line of dots, or possibly blurred stamps.

Contents
A. Burnt bones.
B. Three fragments of sheet bronze clipped from a larger sheet. Association doubtful as these may have belonged to P 33.
C. Possibly an iron hinge with fused glass on it (F. R. M.'s notes; glass now missing). Association doubtful because an iron stain on P 33 indicates that C may be associated with that urn.

It would appear that P 32 was half dug away for the burial of P 33, whose fragments were mixed with it. P 32 is probably by the same potter as W 40 (fig. 58).

P 33 (urn fig. 51; grave goods fig. 59)
Found in fragments.

Depth 24 in. (61 cm.).

Part of a globular or shouldered urn with tall hollow neck, rim and base missing: smooth dark ware.
Decorated with three grooves on the neck from which depend groups of three vertical grooves. In the panels so formed are stamps set in triangular groups.
At least two stamps are used.
P 33 is by Potter III (pp. 62–3).

Contents
A. Burnt bones.
B. Three fragments of sheet bronze: see P 32.
C. Possible iron hinge: see P 32.

It is uncertain whether these grave goods belong to P 32 or P 33, and they are described under P 32. It would appear that P 33 was buried against P 32 and destroyed half of it.

P 34 (fig. 53) 1908
Found broken.

Depth 24 in. (61 cm.).

Small biconical urn with everted rim: red/brown ware.

Decorated on the neck with a line of stamps demarcated above by three and below by three/five lines. From the latter depend three vertical bands of three/four stamps demarcated on each side by three lines. In each panel so formed is a horizontal line of stamps demarcated above by one and below by three lines.
One stamp is used.
P 34 is by Potter IV (p. 57).

Contents
A. Burnt bones of a child with milk teeth.
B. Fragment of centre-plate of an iron-stained bone comb repaired with a bronze strip held by two rivets, one bronze and one iron.
C. The base of a Samian cup, Form 33, with stamp PISTILLI (potter Pistillus of Lezoux A.D. 140–50 (Oswald 1931, 241 (not illustrated)) perhaps used as a plaything.
D. A fragment of sheet bronze—F. R. M.'s inventory, now missing.

P 35 (not illustrated)
Found in fragments.

Depth 30 in. (76 cm.).

Fragments of a shoulder-boss urn: rough red/brown ware, perhaps once smoothed.
Decorated with horizontal corrugation on the neck, and numerous small hollow bosses on the shoulder between which is continuous vertical corrugation.
Urn missing.

Contents
A. Burnt bones.

P 36 (figs. 19, 35, 40, 46) 1683, 1817, 1853
P 36 comprises parts of at least six urns and large lumps of burnt bones which were found in a pit nearly 48 in. (122 cm.) deep. There were no small objects. Among the fragments were:

(a) (fig. 35) 1817
Upper part of a shoulder-boss urn with wide mouth and everted rim: smoothed dark ware.
Decorated on the neck with five sharp lines above three groups of three small solid bosses demarcated on each side by five/seven vertical lines. Over each group of bosses are placed four pairs of jabs. In the panels are irregular groups and vertical lines of stamps separated by two/four vertical lines.
One stamp is used.

(b) (fig. 19)   1683

Large shoulder-boss urn with conical neck and slightly everted rim: smooth dark grey ware.

Decorated under the rim with three lines above two collars, the upper raised and notched, the lower flat and slashed. Below are four more lines and on the shoulder groups of two vertical slashed bosses separated by groups of vertical lines. The panels are loosely filled with vertical lines. Below the bosses is a single horizontal line.

(c) (fig. 40)   1853

Parts of a shouldered urn, rim and base missing: smooth dark ware, well made.

Decorated on the neck with at least two lines of stamps below each of which are three lines. On the shoulder are three-line pendent swags containing two groups of three vertical lines.

Two stamps appear, one of which carries the '↑' rune (see pp. 66–7).

(d) (fig. 46)

Parts of a globular urn, rim and base missing: smooth dark ware.

Decorated with at least three strong grooves on the neck above groups of chevron grooves interspersed with lines of stamps. Below are vertical grooves.

One stamp appears.

P 36(d) is similar in style to W 35 (fig. 56) which is by Potter IX and may come from this workshop.

(e) (not illustrated)

Fragments of a small urn: red/brown ware. Undecorated.

(f) (not illustrated)

One fragment of an urn decorated with grooves.

P 37

No urn appears to be recorded under this number.

P 38 (urn fig. 55; grave goods fig. 59)   1917
Found shattered.

Depth 34 in. (86 cm.).

Shouldered urn with wide mouth and upright rim: thin brown ware, once burnished dark.

Decorated at the base of the neck with two sharp lines above a line of stamps, three more lines, another line of stamps and two more lines.

Two stamps are used.

P 38 is probably by Potter X; but the four-point stamp is not identical with that on the other pots by this potter.

Contents
A. Burnt bones.
B. Part of a large iron nail (association doubtful).

P 39 (fig. 27)   1758
Found almost complete.

Depth 34 in. (86 cm.).

Large shouldered urn with wide mouth and everted rim: heavy dark brown ware.
Undecorated.

Contents
A. Burnt bones.

P 39 was in contact with P 40.

P 40 (fig. 54)   1915
Found badly shattered.

Depth 34 in. (86 cm.).

Sub-biconical urn with everted rim, shape much distorted: soft red/brown ware.

Decorated on the neck with three faint lines above a zone of three-line chevrons, the spaces above and below which are filled with stamps, except one space which is filled with diagonal lines.

Three stamps are used.

P 40 is by Potter V (p. 63).

Contents
A. Burnt bones.

P 40 was in contact with P 39.

P 41 (fig. 53)   1906
Found almost complete.

Depth 24 in. (61 cm.).

Small shoulder-boss urn with conical neck and everted rim: brown ware.

Decorated on the neck with a raised slashed collar demarcated above by four/five lines and below by three/four lines. On the shoulder are three groups of two solid flat-topped bosses, separated and demarcated on both sides by three/five vertical lines. In the panels between the grouped bosses is a horizontal line of stamps demarcated above and below by four horizontal lines.

One stamp is used.

P 41 is by Potter IV (p. 57).

Contents

A. Burnt bones. Dr. Wells reports: 'Child. Crowns of one maxillary medial incisor and of two canines. Well fired. No animal remains.'
B. An iron nail, corroded. Length 1·8 in. (4·6 cm.).

P 42 (fig. 25) 1748

Found complete.

Depth 26 in. (66 cm.).

Globular urn with short upright rim: red ware, smoothed dark surface.

Undecorated.

Contents

A. Burnt bones.
B. Fragment of end-section of centre-plate of bone comb, iron-stained; some teeth survive to their full length.

P 42 was found in a hole dug through the floor of Roman Structure D to sand.

P 43 (fig. 33)

Found almost complete.

Depth 24 in. (61 cm.).

Roman coarse ware jar with slightly undercut rim; centre of base neatly perforated by hole approximately 0·4 in. (1 cm.) in diameter; smoothly finished fine fabric ranging from dark to light grey.

Decorated with one burnished line and a thin incised line which spirals upwards from it to encircle the pot at least three times.

Contents

A. Burnt bones.
B. Section of centre-plate of triangular bone comb with one complete rivet hole and part of another; the back of the centre-plate projected above the side-plates and is rounded.

P 43, which is the only Roman pot found with an associated object, was found near the edge of Roman Structure D. Two other Roman pots, P 45 and P 48, were found just outside Structure D, while P 54 lay on the floor and P 42 was in a hole dug through the floor.

P 44 (fig. 56) 1925

Found in fragments.

Depth 29 in. (74 cm.).

Upper part of a large shoulder-boss urn with wide mouth and upstanding everted rim: smooth heavy brown ware, well made.

Decorated on the neck with a raised jabbed collar demarcated above by three and below by four firm lines. On the shoulder are three groups of three small solid bosses separated and demarcated on each side by groups of vertical lines; in the panels are irregular groups of three/four-line chevrons, the spaces above and below which are partly filled with stamps.

One true stamp is used, the jabs being probably made with the end of a bird bone.

P 44 is by Potter VIII (p. 55).

Contents

A. Burnt bones.

P 44 was standing in a hole in a burnt clay floor of a Roman hut (Roman Structure D), so that its base had rotted away from continually standing in water.

P 45 (fig. 58)

Found broken and incomplete.

Depth. Not recorded.

Roman coarse ware bowl; medium grey fabric with traces of smooth finish.

Decorated only with a single horizontal groove.

Contents

None recorded and there is no evidence to suggest that this pot contained a cremation.

P 45 was found just outside Structure D.

P 46 (fig. 43) 1874

Found almost complete.

Depth 22 in. (56 cm.).

Biconical urn with short sharply flaring rim: thin red/brown ware.

Decorated on the neck with three light lines above a line of stamps, two more lines, another line of stamps and three more lines on the carination.

Two stamps are used, both very indistinct.

Contents

A. Burnt bones of a child about eight years old.
Dr. Wells reports: 'Child. The crown of a first

permanent molar; a deciduous canine; and a damaged incisor. Well fired. No animal remains.'

B. A small piece of unburnt Roman green glass (association doubtful).

Part of a Roman tile was used as a cover to P 46.

P 47 (not illustrated)

Found in fragments.

Depth 22 in. (56 cm.).

Lower part of a large urn: sandy brown ware with smooth surface.
No decoration appears.

Contents

A. Burnt bones.

P 48 (fig. 33)

Found shattered and incomplete.

Depth 18 in. (46 cm.).

Roman coarse ware jar; fine grey fabric, smoothly finished.
Decorated with slight grooving at neck.

Contents

A. Burnt bones.

P 48 was found outside Structure D.

P 49 (fig. 54) 1913

Found in fragments.

Depth 20 in. (51 cm.).

Globular urn with upright rim: smooth brown ware.
Decorated on the neck with four light lines above three zones of stamps separated from each other by single lines. Below is a band demarcated above and below by a single line, and containing stamps, which rises and falls to form a continuous curve or zigzag the upper points of which interrupt the two lower zones of stamps, while the lower reach the maximum diameter.
Three stamps appear.
P 49 is by Potter VI (p. 63).

Contents

A. Burnt bones.

P 50 (fig. 30) 1782

Found shattered.

Depth 18 in. (46 cm.).

Shouldered urn with hollow neck and upright rim: dark ware, once burnished.
Undecorated.

Contents

A. Burnt bones.

P 51 (urn not illustrated; grave goods fig. 59)

Found broken.

Depth 20 in. (51 cm.).

Base of an urn: smoothed grey/brown ware.
No decoration appears.

Contents

A. Burnt bones.
B. Part of an iron nail, badly corroded.
C. Animal bones.

Association of B and C doubtful, as not noted in F. R. M.'s inventory.

P 52 (not illustrated)

Found in fragments.

Depth 21 in. (53 cm.).

Fragments of an urn: smooth brown ware.
Undecorated.

Contents

A. Burnt bones.

P 53 (urn fig. 2) 1544

Found shattered.

Depth 22 in. (56 cm.).

Large biconical urn with tall neck and heavily moulded rim: thick smooth dark brown ware.
Decorated low on the neck with a continuous arcade of dots above four broadly tooled lines. Below are four/ten-line chevrons mostly bordered above and below with lines of dots.

Contents

A. Burnt bones.
B. Pieces of burnt elephant ivory ring, too fragmentary to determine diameter (not illustrated).

P 54 (fig. 32) 1799

Found badly broken.

Depth 24 in. (61 cm.).

Shoulder-boss bowl with short everted rim: rough pitted brown ware.

Decorated with three solid nipple-bosses.

Contents

A. Burnt bones.

P 54 lay on the floor of Roman Structure D.

R

The R series has been formed from the urns accumulated by the Revd. J. W. Corbould-Warren in his private collection at Caistor Hall, and from some other chance discoveries made by rabbiters. For this reason the depth at which they were found is not known, and their contents are mostly unrecorded. Most of these urns do not appear on the plan since no information has been preserved of their exact findspots. With the exception of R 9/10, R 11, and R 13–16, they were found complete or almost complete.

R 1 (fig. 57) 1927

Globular urn with hollow neck and everted rim: smooth pitted brown ware, once burnished.

Decorated on the neck with a line of stamps above three grooved lines. Below are groups of vertical or diagonal grooves demarcating panels each of which contains a three-groove arch, the spandrels above and the spaces below which are mostly filled with stamps.

One stamp is used.

R 1 is by Potter XI (p. 59).

Contents

Unknown, but when presented to Norwich Museum it contained a few fragments of iron, which may be associated. The original size and shape of the object or objects cannot be determined.

R 2 (fig. 15) 1651

Biconical urn with short slightly everted rim: smooth dark brown ware burnished.

Decorated on the shoulder with a flat slashed collar demarcated above and below by three lines. At one point the slashing on the collar is interrupted by a blank space.

R 2 had been dug by rabbiters out of the same hole as R 13 (fig. 15).

R 3 (fig. 42) 1871

Sub-biconical urn with short slightly everted rim: smooth brown ware, once burnished.

Decorated with a wide zone of two-line chevrons demarcated above and below by two light lines. In the triangles are stamps arranged in various patterns, some cruciform, some outlining the panel with a single central stamp.

Four stamps are used.

R 4 (fig. 57) 1928

Shouldered urn with hollow neck and everted rim: heavy smooth ware.

Decorated on the shoulder with a zone containing four horizontal lines of stamps demarcated above by three and below by two lines.

Two stamps are used.

R 4 is by Potter XI (p. 59).

R 5 (fig. 21) 1706

Biconical urn with everted rim: well-made burnished dark ware.

Decorated on the neck with two firm lines above a strong groove, below which are groups of three vertical lines separating spaces containing two diagonal lines.

R 6 (fig. 55) 1918

Globular round-bottomed urn with wide mouth and upright rim: smooth ware.

Decorated on the neck with two firm lines from which depend two-line pendent triangles filled with stamps.

Two stamps are used.

R 6 is by Potter X.

R 7 (fig. 29) 1770

Globular urn with upright rim: smooth ware. Undecorated.

R 8 (pl. V*b*)

Shoulder-boss urn with short conical neck and everted rim: burnished dark ware.

Decorated on the neck with horizontal corrugation above ? eight vertical hollow bosses demarcated on each side by two grooves and separating panels containing curvilinear corrugation.

Urn missing.

R 9/10 (pl. VI*a* and fig. 44) 1882

Upper part of a large biconical urn with narrow neck and flaring rim: smooth brown ware.

Decorated on the neck with three lines of stamps each demarcated above and below by a firm line. On the carination are single arches of stamps demarcated above and below by a single line: in the spandrels between the arches are one/two stamps and sometimes a single horizontal line. At one point above the arches are freehand drawings of a wolf or dog with long curving tail and open jaws apparently barking at a retreating boat which is shown with high prow and stern paddle, and thirteen vertical strokes representing either oars, or the upright spears of the crew. (see p. 118).

Four stamps appear.

R 9/10 is by Potter XII (pp. 61–2).

R 11 (fig. 32) 1803

Large shoulder-boss urn with wide mouth and upright rim, base missing: smooth brown ware, once burnished.

Decorated with three solid applied nipple-bosses (two broken away).

R 12 (pl. III*a* and fig. 16) 1659

Globular urn with tall hollow neck and slightly everted rim: hard smooth black ware, very well made.

Decorated on the base of the neck with a flat slashed collar demarcated above and below by three firm lines. Below are five three-line arches with two horizontal lines across their bases. The spandrels between the arches contain rosettes composed of seven or eight dots surrounding a circular depression.

This urn is exceptionally well made and the decoration is very regular in design and execution (p. 48).

Contents
A. Burnt bones.
B. Miniature round-backed bone comb, perfect, and unaffected by fire; flared lower edge. Too small for use. Height 1·45 in. (3·7 cm.) (pl. XXXIII*e*).

R 13 (fig. 15) 1653

Sub-biconical urn with slightly everted rim: smooth black ware, once burnished.

Decorated on the neck with five strong lines below which on the carination are seven widely spaced chevrons each with a vertical line from the apex forming freehand '↑' runes, and one group of four short diagonal lines (see p. 66).

Contents Unknown, but found on the surface in fragments surrounded by burnt bones.

R 13 had been dug by rabbiters 'out of the same hole as R 2' (F. R. M.).

R 14 (fig. 19) 1689

Small biconical shoulder-boss urn with everted rim and well-moulded foot-ring; polished black ware.

Decorated on the neck with a flat slashed collar demarcated above by three and below by two grooves. On the shoulder are five small vertical solid bosses separating panels filled with short vertical grooves.

R 14 was reconstructed from fragments found in a large rabbit hole that ran from the plantation past Grave 1.

R 15 (fig. 37) 1830

Shoulder-boss urn, rim missing: smooth dark grey ware, once burnished.

Decorated on the neck with five sharp lines above a line of stamps. On the shoulder are probably four groups of two vertical bosses pinched up from deep grooves between and on each side of them. In each panel is a tall single-line arch rising through the horizontal line of stamps and covering a vertical line of stamps.

One stamp is used.

'Reconstructed from fragments found near Grave 1 and in Z trench' (F. R. M.).

R 16 (not illustrated)

Fragments of a broken-up pot.

Depth 11 in. (28 cm.).

Urn missing.

R 17 (fig. 19) 1690

Large shoulder-boss urn with conical neck and everted rim: dark grey ware, once burnished.

Decorated with three broad grooves on the neck, above five large hollow bosses on the shoulder, separating panels containing a vertical line of dots demarcated on each side by two/four vertical grooves.

Contents
A. Burnt bones. Dr. Wells reports: 'Adult. Parts of two tooth crowns and eight roots. Two tiny flakes of long bone are partly embedded in a fused

material [B] similar to that found at Illington (Wells 1960). Well fired. No animal remains.'

B. Fragment of fused material preserved. This has not been analysed but is superficially very similar to fused material from Illington, Norfolk. Analyses of this have failed to establish with any certainty whether the material is the remains of fused glass, or sand, etc., from beneath the funeral pyre.[1] The material from Illington is not apparently the same as the German *Urnenharz*. See also Y 28.

R 18 (fig. 43) 1876

Sub-biconical urn with tall neck and everted rim: smooth brown ware, probably once burnished.

Decorated on the neck with a line of stamps demarcated above and below by four firm lines: below is a line of stamps above five three-line arches, the spandrels between which are filled with stamps.

W

The W series has been formed from what appeared to be the more significant broken-up or incomplete urns, of which large quantities of sherds were collected by F. R. M. either on the surface or in the course of his excavations. Most of these come from urns destroyed in earlier times by grave-diggers, rabbits, tree roots, or rabbiters, and, since very few are sufficiently preserved to present a complete profile, it is not usually possible to indicate the dimensions, or even in some cases the forms or complete schemes of decoration. The depth at which such disturbed fragments occurred was not held to be significant and is consequently unrecorded. Many of these sherds were thrown together by F. R. M. in what he termed 'Junk Bags', and most of these have no, even approximate, provenance: others were roughly classified by him as derived from certain parts of the cemetery. But it has not been possible to record them on map 2, since the original positions of the urns from which they come are not known. In the course of sorting these sherds, some missing bits of urns in other parts of the numbered series were found (thus W 31 was part of R 9/10), and these have been placed with the urns to which they belong. In a few cases urns wholly missing from the numbered series were identified, generally as fragments, among sherds to which W numbers had already been provisionally allotted (thus W 3 turned out to be the

missing K 7). This accounts for some of the gaps in the W numbering. The remaining gaps are due either to the realization that different W numbers had been given to two or more sherds from one urn, or to the decision that some provisionally numbered sherds were not worth illustrating. It should be emphasized that the mass of sherds from which the W series has been formed must represent a very much larger number of urns than those to which W numbers have here been allotted.

W 1 (fig. 55)

Upper part of a large sub-biconical urn with short everted rim: black ware, well made.

Decorated on the neck with five slightly raised collars of which the second and fifth are slashed: below are two-line chevrons, in the upper triangles of which are three large dots.

W 1 appears to be from the same workshop (Potter VII) as Y 30 (fig. 55).

'Found among wattle and daub in D Trench' (F. R. M.).

W 2 (fig. 18)

Upper part of a large shoulder-boss urn with hollow neck and slightly everted rim: burnished dark ware.

Decorated on the lower part of the neck with continuous horizontal corrugation, above widely spaced solid shoulder-bosses; the only preserved panel between them has an irregular arrangement of diagonal corrugated grooves, which might be intended to look like runes.

'Among flints on Grave 3' (F. R. M.).

[W 3 = K 7 q.v.]

W 4 (fig. 32)

Upper part of a wide-mouthed cook-pot, probably similar in shape to K 6(a) (fig. 32): rough grey ware.

Decorated on the sloping shoulder with (probably three) horizontally pierced lugs.

'From X and Y region near Grave 12' (F. R. M.).

---

[1] Reports in N.C.M. records from the Laboratorium der Farbwerke, Hoechst (West Germany), and the British Museum Research Laboratory.

W 5(a) (fig. 30) 1780

Shouldered jar with slightly everted rim: smoothed buff-brown ware.
Undecorated.

'Broken up in Grave 36' (F. R. M.).

W 5(b) (fig. 23)

Part of shoulder of a shouldered or globular urn: buff-brown ware.
Decorated with at least four firm neck-lines above groups of at least five diagonal or chevron lines.
'Broken up in Grave 36' (F. R. M.).

W 6 (fig. 22)

Upper part of a globular urn with short upright rim: smoothed buff-brown ware.
Decorated with four close-set neck-lines above seven-line chevrons on the shoulder.
'Broken up in Grave 36' (F. R. M.).

W 7 (fig. 41)

Upper part of a shouldered urn with upright neck and everted rim: smooth dark ware.
Decorated on the neck with two rows of stamps separated and demarcated above and below by two lines: below are four-line pendent triangles partially filled with stamps.
Two stamps appear, similar to, but not identical with, those on W 23 (fig. 37).
'M area' (F. R. M.).

W 8 (fig. 43)

Upper part of a biconical urn with upright rim: smooth dark ware.
Decorated with two lines of stamps separated and demarcated above and below by a single line.
Two stamps appear.
'M area' (F. R. M.).

W 9 (fig. 12)

Upper part of urn with short everted rim: rough grey ware.
Decorated with a single neck-line above a zone of triangular panels hatched with groups of diagonal lines at right angles to one another.
'M area' (F. R. M.).

W 10 (fig. 45)

Rim sherd: smooth dark ware.
Decorated with a line of stamps on the neck, demarcated above and below by two lines: below are single lines chevrons and stamps.
Two stamps appear.
'M area' (F. R. M.).

W 11 (fig. 17)

Part of neck and side of a large *Buckelurne*: smooth dark ware.
Decorated with at least seven close-set neck-lines above a zone of dots, a single line, a double line of small dots and another line. This lower line of dots is interrupted by widely spaced hollow bosses below which is a continuous line of large dots. On the shoulder are further hollow bosses set asymmetrically with the upper bosses and separating panels which contain five close-set lines above two lines of dots of different sizes each demarcated below by a single line. Below are two further lines of larger dots.
'M area' (F. R. M.).

W 12 (fig. 20)

Part of side of a shoulder-boss urn: smooth brown ware.
Decorated with at least three neck-lines above slashed hollow shoulder-bosses separating panels filled with vertical grooves.
'M area' (F. R. M.).

W 13 (fig. 37)

Part of side of a shoulder-boss urn: smooth dark ware.
Decorated with a zone of at least two rows of stamps demarcated below by two close-set lines, above solid vertical bosses carrying a vertical line of stamps. The panels contain a zone of diagonal lines demarcated below by two lines above what appear to be two-line pendent triangles filled with stamps.
Two stamps appear.
'M area' (F. R. M.).

W 14 (fig. 20 where wrongly called P 14)

Part of side of a shoulder-boss urn: smooth dark ware.
Decorated with a vertical hollow feathered boss demarcated on each side by a vertical line. The panels contain diagonal line-and-groove, or line-and-groove chevrons.
'M area' (F. R. M.).

W 15 (fig. 45)

Part of side of a biconical urn: heavy dark ware.

Decorated with a line of jabs demarcated above by at least one and below by two firm lines: below is part of a freehand linear design and one impression of a stamp.

'M area' (F. R. M.).

W 16 (fig. 11)

Part of side of a shouldered urn: smooth dark ware.

Decorated with at least four faint and interrupted neck-lines above two-line chevrons outlined above, and partly also below, with dots, and crossed with faint diagonal lines.

'M area' (F. R. M.).

W 17 (fig. 37)

Part of side of a shoulder-boss urn: rough grey ware.

Decorated with slight bosses apparently demarcated on each side by two vertical lines: in the panels are at least two horizontal lines of stamps.

One stamp appears.

'M area' (F. R. M.).

W 18 (fig. 58)

Part of side of a shoulder-boss urn.

Decorated with vertical hollow bosses demarcated by ?three vertical lines separating panels containing at least two horizontal lines of stamps separated by three lines.

One stamp appears.

W 18 is similar to the work of Potter IV, but has hollow not solid bosses, and a stamp not known to have been used by that potter.

'M area' (F. R. M.).

W 19 (fig. 56)

Part of side of a (probably biconical) urn: smooth dark ware.

Decorated with a line of stamps demarcated above by at least three, and below by three lines, above groups of three vertical lines and stamps.

Two stamps appear, one of which is somewhat larger than that on other pots by this potter.

W 19 is by Potter IX.

'M area' (F. R. M.).

W 20 (fig. 45)

Part of side of a shouldered urn: smooth buff ware.

Decorated with at least six close-set neck-lines above a line of stamps, two more lines, another line of stamps and five more close-set lines on the carination: below is an apparently random arrangement of stamps.

Two stamps appear.

'M area' (F. R. M.).

W 21 (fig. 46)

Part of side of a biconical urn with thickened carination: smooth dark ware.

Decorated with at least three lines of stamps not demarcated by lines.

Two stamps appear.

'M area' (F. R. M.).

W 22 (fig. 49)

Part of side of an urn of uncertain shape: smooth dark ware.

Decorated with at least two lines of stamps and three/five vertical lines.

Two stamps appear, both used by Potter II (pp. 62–3).

'M area' (F. R. M.).

W 23 (fig. 37) 1832

Part of side of a shoulder-boss urn: rough buff ware.

Decorated with at least two lines of stamps demarcated below by two and one line respectively. On the shoulder are nine/ten vertical hollow bosses, separating panels containing one three-line chevron covering a vertical and horizontal line of stamps: in some panels the chevron is also outlined above by stamps.

Two stamps appear, similar to, but not identical with, those on W 7 (fig. 41).

'Sherds from Rev. J. W. Corbould-Warren's collection' (F. R. M.).

W 24 (fig. 21)

Part of side of a large shouldered urn: heavy dark ware.

Decorated with a flat slashed collar demarcated above and below by three firm lines. Below is freehand decoration consisting of a broad five-line wavy band, the spaces above which appear to be filled alternately with two strong vertical grooves intersecting with two horizontal lines to form a double cross, and with groups of horizontal or diagonal grooves.

'From rabbit burrow by F Trench' (F. R. M.).

W 25 (fig. 23)

Rim and neck of a large urn of uncertain shape: smooth dark ware.

Decorated with a flat slashed collar demarcated above by three lines and below by one line.

W 26 (fig. 40)

Upper part of a globular urn with short upright rim: rough grey ware.

Decorated under the rim with five neck-lines, below which are large irregular single-line chevrons, the spaces above and below which are confusedly set with stamps.

One stamp appears.

W 27 (fig. 20)

Part of side of a shoulder-boss urn of *Buckelurne* type: smooth dark ware.

Decorated with a raised slashed collar demarcated below by two lines. On the shoulder are diagonally slashed vertical hollow bosses demarcated on each side by two vertical lines. In the only remaining panel is a two-line chevron covering a plain vertical hollow boss.

W 28 (fig. 46)

Part of side of a shoulder-boss urn: smooth brown ware.

Decorated with small hollow bosses below a group of stamps, the whole demarcated on each side by three vertical lines. The panels include four horizontal lines.

One stamp appears.

[W 29 = X 39 q.v.]

W 30 (pl. VIIa and fig. 44) 1884

Part of a large globular urn with tall conical neck, rim and base missing: smooth dark ware, well made.

Decorated with a narrow notched collar demarcated above and below by two lines. Below is a zone of continuous cabling composed of interlocking stamps, and two more lines. Covering most of the side were at least two diamond-shaped areas each outlined by a notched line demarcated on each side by two/four sharp lines and containing a zone of large stamps, two more lines, a plain zone and apparently a central stamp. Animal stamps are set below the cabled zone on each side of the upper angle of the diamond-shaped area and possibly elsewhere.

Six stamps appear, three being animals, two developed swastikas, and one for the cabling.

W 30 is related to E 7 (fig. 44) and Lackford 48.2487 (Lethbridge 1951, fig. 31): stamps of the same unusual types are used on all three urns, though none are identical (see p. 60).

[W 31 = R 9/10 q.v.]

W 32 (fig. 23)

Part of a round-shouldered urn with tall neck, rim and base missing: very rough, thick grey ware.

Decorated with at least two neck-lines above a flat slashed collar: on the shoulder are groups of seven/eight diagonal lines arranged as chevrons.

W 33 (fig. 14)

Upper part of a small shouldered urn with everted rim: smooth grey ware.

Decorated with two widely spaced neck-lines between which are two-line chevrons: on the shoulder are three-line chevrons.

'XY area' (F. R. M.).

W 34 (fig. 15)

Lower part of a biconical urn, rim missing: smooth red/brown ware.

Decorated with two groups of four neck-lines separated by a blank space.

'XY area' (F. R. M.).

W 35 (fig. 56)

Upper part of a biconical bossed urn with everted rim: thick rough grey ware.

Decorated on the carination with four solid bosses, each covered by three/four pointed arched zones of stamps demarcated above and below and separated by a single line. In the panels above the carination are four flat arched zones of stamps each demarcated above and below by one/two lines and separated by a single line. Below the carination are vertical groups of lines between some of which are stamps.

One stamp appears.

W 35 is by Potter IX.

'XY area' (F. R. M.).

W 36 (fig. 23)

Upper part of a biconical urn with hollow neck and upright rim: dull brown ware.

Decorated above the carination with three neck-lines above two-line pendent swags.
'XY area' (F. R. M.).

[W 37 = Y 7(c) q.v.]

W 38 (fig. 10)

Part of a small biconical urn: rough brown ware.
Decorated with at least four neck-lines above three-line chevrons running to the carination, on which there is a line of finger-tips.
'XY area' (F. R. M.).

W 39 (fig. 41)

Part of side of a biconical urn: smooth grey ware.
Decorated with at least three neck-lines above a line of stamps and two more lines just above the carination. Below are two-line chevrons filled with stamps.
Two stamps appear.
The type of stamps on W 39 and its general arrangement suggest that this urn may be related to the work of the Illington/Lackford potter (see p. 58).
'XY area' (F. R. M.).

W 40 (fig. 58)

Part of side of a shoulder-boss urn: rough grey ware.
Decorated with a flat slashed collar above small vertical bosses separating panels containing five-line pendent triangles outlined internally, and perhaps also externally, with a line of dots.
W 40 is probably by the same potter as P 32 (fig. 58).
'XY area' (F. R. M.).

W 41 (fig. 37)

Part of side of a shoulder-boss urn: smooth grey ware.
Decorated with four grooves on the neck above a slightly raised slashed collar and a double line of very small stamps like dots. On the shoulder are widely spaced small hollow bosses, the panels between which are filled with vertical corrugation.
'XY area' (F. R. M.).

W 42 (fig. 45)

Upper part of a globular urn with short everted rim: smooth dark ware.
Decorated with a double line of stamps irregularly set and demarcated above and below by three neck-lines: below are more stamps.
One stamp appears.
'XY area' (F. R. M.).

W 43 (fig. 45)

Tall upstanding rim of a large urn: smooth red/brown ware.
Decorated at the base of the neck with four faint lines above a line of stamps.
One stamp appears.
'XY area' (F. R. M.).

W 44 (fig. 21)

Upper part of an urn with sloping shoulder and upright rim: smooth brown ware.
Decorated with four firm neck-lines above two wavy lines and traces of further freehand decoration below.
'XY area' (F. R. M.).

W 45 (fig. 45)

Upper part of a shouldered urn with everted rim: smooth grey ware.
Decorated with a line of stamps demarcated above and below by three neck-lines: on the shoulder is a group of four diagonal lines.
One stamp appears.
'XY area' (F. R. M.).

W 46 (fig. 4)

Part of side of a shouldered urn: polished black ware.
Decorated with six lines of horizontal corrugation on the neck above continuous vertical corrugation on the shoulder.
'XY area' (F. R. M.).

W 47 (fig. 23)

Upper part of a shouldered urn with short upright neck: smooth black ware.
Decorated with three strong neck-lines above groups of vertical lines on the shoulder.
'XY area' (F. R. M.).

W 48 (fig. 45)

Upper part of a small shouldered urn with upright rim: smooth dark brown ware.
Decorated with a line of stamps demarcated above by three and below by two neck-lines. On the shoulder are groups of vertical lines.
One stamp appears.
'XY area' (F. R. M.).

W 49 (fig. 46)

Part of side of a sub-biconical urn: smooth red/brown ware.

Decorated above the maximum diameter with groups of vertical lines separating panels containing at least two horizontal lines of stamps.

One stamp appears.

W 49 could be related to the work of Potter III. 'XY area' (F. R. M.).

W 50 (fig. 40)

Part of side of an urn with sloping shoulder: grey ware.

Decorated with two lines of stamps separated and demarcated above and below by three lines.

Two stamps appear.

'From Grave 13' (F. R. M.).

W 51 (fig. 21) 1701

Side of a globular urn with conical neck: smooth dark ware.

Decorated with at least six close-set neck-lines above an irregular freehand design comprising groups of vertical lines below a line of dots and a short horizontal line alternating with large two-line X and V forms, the latter bisected by a single vertical line, possibly intended to look like runes (see p. 67). There is a row of dots between the upper points of each.

'Round about Graves 21–25' (F. R. M.).

W 52 (fig. 4)

Part of side of a shouldered urn with conical neck: smooth buff-brown ware.

Decorated with faint horizontal corrugation on the neck above vertical corrugation on the shoulder.

'Round about Graves 21–25' (F. R. M.).

W 53 (fig. 23)

Upper part of a small shouldered urn with everted rim: smooth dark ware.

Decorated with five sharp neck-lines above three-line chevrons on the shoulder.

'Round about Graves 21–25' (F. R. M.).

W 54 (fig. 10)

Part of side of an urn with sloping shoulder: smooth grey ware.

Decorated with a flat slashed collar demarcated above by two and below by three grooves.

'Round about Graves 21–25' (F. R. M.).

W 55 (fig. 15)

Part of side of a large biconical urn: thick smooth grey ware.

Decorated above the carination with a zone of two-line chevrons demarcated above and below by two lines.

W 56 (fig. 14)

Part of side of a biconical urn: smooth grey ware.

Decorated with a zone of three-line chevrons demarcated above by at least two and below by two lines on the carination.

W 57 (fig. 14)

Upper part of a large biconical urn with upright swollen rim: smooth dark ware.

Decorated with a raised slashed collar demarcated above and below by three lines, above a zone of single-line chevrons demarcated below by two lines on the thickened carination. The chevrons are outlined below by dots and the upper triangles are bisected by a vertical line of dots. Below the carination are pendent three-line triangles bisected by a vertical line.

W 58 (not illustrated)

Part of side of a biconical urn: grey/brown ware.

Decorated with a wide groove demarcated above by two lines and below by one resting on the carination; below are vertical/diagonal lines.

W 59 (fig. 20)

Part of side of a shoulder-boss urn: smooth dark ware.

Decorated with at least three neck-lines above small hollow shoulder-bosses, separating panels filled with vertical lines.

W 60 (fig. 23)

Part of side of a biconical urn: heavy grey ware.

Decorated with continuous horizontal corrugation above the carination and three-line chevrons below.

W 61 (fig. 23)

Small part of side of an urn of uncertain shape: heavy dark ware.

Decorated with at least one neck-line above pendent triangles outlined by a feathered zone and filled with two smaller triangles and a short vertical line.

W 62 (fig. 46)

Rim of a small urn of uncertain shape: thin smooth grey ware.

Decorated with two fine neck-lines above a zone of at least two lines of stamps.

One stamp appears.

W 63 (fig. 46)

Part of side of an urn of uncertain shape: thin smooth grey ware.

Decorated with a zone of two line chevrons demarcated above and below by at least three lines: some of the triangles appear to contain groups of horizontal and vertical lines, and others a single stamp.

One stamp appears.

W 64 (fig. 16) 1662

Lower part of an urn with well-made hollow foot-ring: smooth grey ware.

Decorated with the lower ends of groups of four/five diagonal lines, probably from chevrons.

W 65 (fig. 32) 1797

Lower part of a small urn with crude foot-ring: rough grey ware.

No decoration appears: probably from a cook-pot with lugs of a type similar to K 6(a) (fig. 32).

W 66 (fig. 45)

Part of side of a biconical urn: smooth grey ware.

Decorated with at least three lines above a line of large stamps on the carination.

One stamp appears.

W 67 (fig. 45)

Part of side of a globular urn: rough buff/grey ware.

Decorated with vertical and horizontal bands of stamps set in pairs and unaccompanied by lines.

Three stamps appear.

W 68 (fig. 45)

Part of side of a globular urn: hard buff/brown ware.

Decorated with a double line of stamps, demarcated above by two and below by at least three lines.

One stamp appears.

W 69 (fig. 45)

Part of side of an urn with tall conical neck: rough grey ware.

Decorated with an irregular arrangement of stamps unaccompanied by lines.

Two stamps appear.

W 70 (fig. 46)

Sloping shoulder of an urn with tall neck: grey ware.

Decorated with a single neck-line above pairs of vertical lines, the spaces between which are filled with a vertical line of stamps.

One stamp appears.

W 70 is related to the work of Potter III (pp. 62–3).

W 71 (fig. 49)

Small part of side of an ovate or globular urn: grey ware.

Decorated with two neck-lines above a line of stamps.

One stamp appears.

W 71 is by Potter III, similar to G 3 (fig. 50).

W 72 (fig. 46)

Part of shoulder of an urn of uncertain shape: smooth brown ware.

Decorated with at least five light neck-lines above a line of stamps and three-line chevrons.

One stamp appears.

W 73 (fig. 46)

Part of side of a biconical urn: grey/brown ware.

Decorated with a sharp line on the carination above which are vertical columns of stamps.

Two stamps appear.

W 74 (fig. 45)

Part of side of an urn with tall conical neck: smooth grey ware.

Decorated with at least two lines above a broad zone divided by three-line diagonal or chevron lines into spaces filled with stamps.

Two stamps appear.

W 75 (fig. 37)

Part of side of a globular urn: smooth brown ware.

Decorated low on the neck with at least four lines

above an irregular line of stamps, perhaps intended to be set as chevrons, and two more close-set lines. Below are long three-line pendent triangles filled with stamps. Two stamps appear.

[W 76 is part of Y 7(a) q.v.]

W 77 (fig. 48) 1890

Upper part of a shoulder-boss urn: smooth brown ware.

Decorated with a line of stamps demarcated above and below by three fine lines. On the shoulder are vertical hollow bosses demarcated on each side by one line: the panels contain a horizontal line of stamps demarcated below by two lines above groups of stamps demarcated on each side by two/three lines.

Four stamps appear.

W 77 is by Potter I (p. 57). See note after W 83.

W 78 (fig. 45)

Part of rim of an urn, probably of shoulder-boss type: smooth brown ware.

Decorated with an irregular zone of stamps demarcated above by three and below by two lines, above a slashed collar.

One stamp appears.

W 78 is in the manner of Potter I, probably similar to M 16(a) (fig. 47), but the stamp is not otherwise recorded for that workshop.

W 79 (fig. 48)

Upper part of a small shoulder-boss urn: smooth brown ware.

Decorated with a line of stamps demarcated above by three and below by two lines. Below are vertical hollow bosses carrying vertical and short diagonal lines, and separating panels filled with stamps.

Two stamps appear.

W 79 is by Potter I (p. 57). See note after W 83.

W 80 (fig. 48)

Part of side of a shouldered urn: smooth brown ware.

Decorated with two lines of stamps each demarcated below by four fine lines. Below are four-line pendent triangles filled with stamps.

Three stamps appear.

W 80 is by Potter I (p. 57). See note after W 83.

W 81 (fig. 48)

Part of side of a shoulder-boss urn: smooth brown ware.

Decorated with a raised slashed collar above a line of stamps demarcated above and below by two close-set lines. On the shoulder are vertical hollow bosses demarcated on each side by a single line, the panels between which contain two lines above at least one line of stamps.

One stamp appears.

W 81 is by Potter I, very similar to M 16(a) (fig. 47). See note after W 83.

W 82 (fig. 48)

Part of side of a shouldered urn: smooth brown ware.

Decorated with at least two lines of stamps demarcated above and below and separated by two close-set lines. Below are three-line pendent triangles filled with stamps.

Three stamps appear.

W 82 is by Potter I, probably very similar to W 80 (fig. 48). See note after W 83.

W 83 (fig. 48)

Small part of side of a shoulder-boss urn: smooth brown ware.

Decorated with a line of stamps demarcated above and below by two lines, above a line of diagonal dabs and two more lines. Below is the top of a boss, and the adjacent panel is plain. One stamp appears.

W 83 is by Potter I, perhaps somewhat similar to X 39 (fig. 48).

W 77 and W 79–83 all carry one or more stamps used by Potter I, and are from urns bearing decoration in the manner of that workshop. But the sherds are individually too small to show either the full scheme of decoration or the full range of stamps likely to have been displayed by each urn. It is possible that two or more of them may derive from a single urn, but there are significant differences in detail between them which make this unlikely.

W 84 (fig. 42) 1867

Upper part of a biconical urn with upright rim: smooth grey ware.

Decorated with a wide zone of three-line chevrons demarcated above and below by three lines, and containing stamps in the upper triangles. Below the carination is a line of stamps demarcated above and below by three lines, and lower still are two-line chevrons which must reach near the base of the urn.

Two stamps appear.

W 85 (fig. 42)

Greater part of side of a biconical urn, rim, and base missing: grey ware.

Decorated on the neck with a broad zone containing stamps arranged in chevrons and demarcated on each side by two lines above a line of stamps demarcated above by two and below by three lines on the carination.

Two stamps appear.

W 86 (fig. 37)

Upper part of a shoulder-boss urn with tall neck and flattened everted rim: burnished dark ware.

Decorated on the neck with a wide line of stamps demarcated above and below by two lines. Below are small hollow shoulder-bosses carrying a group of vertical lines, and separating panels containing at least one line of stamps.

Three stamps appear.

W 87 (fig. 46)

Neck and shoulder of a barrel-shaped urn: smooth brown ware.

Decorated with a line of stamps demarcated above by four and below by one line. Below are long panels demarcated by one/three vertical lines with a single stamp at the top of each.

Two stamps appear.

W 88 (fig. 45)

Part of side of a shouldered urn: grey ware.

Decorated with two lines of stamps separated and demarcated above and below by three lines.

Two stamps appear.

W 88 may come from the workshop of Potter VII (fig. 55).

W 89 (fig. 58)

Part of side of a shoulder-boss urn with conical neck: grey ware.

Decorated with at least two lines of stamps on the neck below each of which are three lines. On the shoulder are vertical hollow bosses above which are groups of stamps: the panels are filled with vertical lines.

Three stamps appear.

W 90 (fig. 39) 1847

Upper part of a small shouldered urn with short upright rim: brown ware.

Decorated with a line of stamps demarcated above by five and below by four close-set lines. Below are groups of stamps arranged as pendent triangles and short vertical bands unaccompanied by lines.

Three stamps appear.

W 90 is by the potter who made Illington 281 and 286, which are related to the work of the Illington/Lackford potter (see p. 58).

W 91 (fig. 46)

Part of side of an urn of uncertain shape: brown ware.

Decorated with a line of stamps demarcated above and below by two irregular lines. Below are groups of close-set horizontal and vertical lines.

One stamp appears.

[W 92 (fig. 46) = part of X 9(a) (fig. 39) q.v.]

W 93 (fig. 46)

Piece of side of a shouldered urn with tall neck: smooth brown ware.

Decorated high on the neck with at least one line above a single line of stamps.

Two stamps appear.

W 94 (fig. 39)

Upper part of a small round-shouldered urn with short upright rim: smooth grey ware.

Decorated with a line of stamps demarcated above and below by three fine lines. Below are two-line pendent triangles filled with stamps.

Three stamps appear.

X 1 (fig. 40)

Found in fragments.

Depth 18 in. (46 cm.).

Upper part of a globular urn with short upright rim: soft red/brown ware.

Decorated immediately below the rim with three fine lines above a broad zone of two-line chevrons, the spaces between which have (mostly vertical) lines of stamps. Below are three more lines above a further zone of two/three-line chevrons separating vertical lines of stamps.

Two stamps appear.

Contents

A. Burnt bones.
B. Fragment of a burnt horse tooth (not shown on fig. 40).

X 1 partly overlay X 2, F. R. M.'s sketch (pl. XII*c*).

X 2 (fig. 5) 1571

Found whole.

Depth 30 in. (76 cm.).

Wide-mouthed shouldered bowl with conical neck and everted rim: red/brown ware with high black polish, well made.

Decorated with continuous horizontal corrugation on the neck above continuous vertical corrugation on the shoulder, the latter divided into four panels by four groups of three broader grooves.

Contents

A. Burnt bones.

X 2 was partly beneath X 1, F. R. M.'s sketch (pl. XII*c*).

X 3 (fig. 38) 1844

Found broken.

Depth 18 in. (46 cm.).

Globular urn, neck and rim missing: smooth grey/brown ware.

Decorated on the neck with a line of stamps demarcated above by one and below by two firm lines. Below are large three-line chevrons with the triangles above and below partly or wholly filled with stamps.

Two stamps are used.

Contents

A. Burnt bones.
B. Fragments of fused, thick glass vessel.

X 3 overlay X 4.

X 4 (fig. 9) 1603

Found in fragments.

Depth 23 in. (58 cm.).

Shouldered urn with wide mouth and upright neck and rim: smooth dark ware burnished black, very well made 'with by far the most successful polish that I have found' (F. R. M.).

Decorated on the neck with seven faint grooves above small three-line chevrons on the shoulder.

Contents

A. Burnt bones.

Only half of X 4 was found underlying X 3, other fragments were found scattered.

X 5 (fig. 29) 1776

Found broken.

Depth 32 in. (81 cm.).

Biconical urn with wide mouth and upright rim: smooth brown ware.
Undecorated.

Contents

A. Burnt bones.
B. Fragment of sheet bronze edging, made by folding a piece of sheet bronze over the edge of some material (perhaps wood or leather) and securing it by bronze rivets. One rivet remains, and a broken hole for another. Thickness of material *c.* 0·1 in. (0·3 cm.).
C. Glass bead, completely distorted and discoloured by fire.

'This pot may have been mended with lead, for a largish lump . . . was near it when found. But there were fragments of a stamped pot [apparently not preserved] with it also and this pot may have had the mend.' (F. R. M.)

X 6 (fig. 24) 1734

Found in fragments.

Depth 18 in. (46 cm.).

Barrel-shaped urn with wide mouth and swollen rim: smooth brown ware.
Undecorated.

Contents. None.

X 6 was possibly an accessory vessel from an inhumation.

A lead mend was found close to X 6 and X 7; it is uncertain from which urn it came.

X 7 (fig. 36) 1825

Found broken.

Depth 19 in. (48 cm.).

Shoulder-boss urn with hollow conical neck and swollen upright rim: hard smooth grey ware.

Decorated immediately below the rim with two firm lines above three successive lines of stamps each bordered by two lines. On the shoulder is a further double line of stamps interrupted at intervals by six small hollow bosses. In the panels below are two-line pendent triangles, the upper part of each being filled with stamps.

Five stamps are used.

Contents

A. Burnt bones.

A lead mend was close to the fragments of this pot and to those of X 6. F. R. M. thought it belonged to X 7 which has a hole it would fit.

X 8 (not illustrated)

Found in fragments.

Depth 19 in. (48 cm.).

Fragments of an urn apparently globular in form with upright rim: smooth brown ware.
Undecorated.

Contents

A. Burnt bones.

X 9 (figs. 11, 29, 39, 46)

Found in fragments.

X 9 was apparently a dump containing parts of at least seven urns and a lead mend. It seems possible that X 9(a) was intrusively buried amongst X 9(b), X 9(c) and perhaps other urns, for it alone seems to have preserved some of its contents.

Depth 19 in. (48 cm.).

(a) (fig. 39) = W 92 (fig. 46)

Part of a large biconical urn, rim and base missing: polished black ware.

Decorated on the neck with a raised stamped collar demarcated above and below by four sharp lines. Below are three-line pendent semi-circular panels containing irregular groups of vertical lines and stamps: one panel includes a finger-tipped rosette encircled by stamps. From other fragments identified since fig. 39 was drawn, it appears that there were further finger-tip rosettes and some stamps between the panels. See W 92 (fig. 46).

Two stamps appear.

Contents

A. Burnt bones.

(b) (fig. 11)

Upper part of a globular urn with upright rim: soft black ware.

Decorated with four neck-grooves above a series of vertical grooves mixed with dots, some of which are arranged as rosettes.

X 9(b) is probably by the same potter as Y 41 (fig. 11).

(c) (fig. 29)

Upper part of an urn with sharp shoulder, hollow neck and upright rim: hard dark ware.
Undecorated.

(d) (not illustrated)   Boss from a pot in grey ware.

(e)
(f)   (fig. 46) Fragments from three different
(g)   stamped urns.

X 10 (not illustrated)

Found in fragments.

Depth 26 in. (66 cm.).

Fragments of a very heavily made urn in coarse brown ware.
Undecorated.

Contents

A. Burnt bones.

X 11 (pl. XX, XXI and fig. 27) 1759

Found broken.

Depth 25 in. (64 cm.).

Barrel-shaped urn with wide mouth, slightly flaring rim and round bottom: smoothed hard grey ware.

Undecorated except for some marks on the neck possibly intended to look like a runic inscription (see p. 65).

Contents

A. Burnt bones. Dr. Wells reports: 'Mostly adult, but including one bicuspid tooth of a child aged 6–7. Well fired. No animal remains.'

B. Numerous pieces of decorated bone strips, mountings from a wooden casket, warped and cracked by fire. These cannot be fitted together. There are two types of strip—(i) narrow half-round bars with upper surface carved into cable decoration (pl. XX*a*), and (ii) thin flat plates (pl. XX*b–f, h–o*).

(i) Four fragments of the half-round bar, each having a mitred end, indicating that these were probably edging pieces for a square or rectangular surface, perhaps a lid. On three pieces the cable decoration runs in two directions from a vertical groove (pl. XX*a*), again suggesting that these fragments form a border for a single-plane surface. One side must be at least 9 in. (23 cm.) long.

(ii) The plates vary considerably in width, shape, and decoration and possibly fitted together like a jig-saw. A number of pieces are apparently undecorated, but the majority bear engraved ornament, a range of which is shown on fig. 27 and plate XX. The commonest patterns are a guilloche with 'bull's-eye' (pl. XX*c*) and a wave with a 'bull's-eye' within each wave (pl. XX*b*). There are many fragments of a narrow strip with engraved St. Andrew's crosses, each separated by a pair of vertical lines (pl. XX*e*). Other motifs are 'bull's-eye', pairs of incised lines, and concentric circles. These fragments are pierced by rivet holes. F. R. M. records that a bone peg was found *in situ*. A bone peg 0·85 in. (2·2 cm.) long was found among the pieces (pl. XX*g*).

C. Two bronze 'globules' attached to human bone fragments, not shown on fig. 27.

X 12 (fig. 47) 1886

Found broken.

Depth 17 in. (43 cm.).

Large shoulder-boss urn with hollow neck and short upright rim: hard smooth red/grey ware.

Decorated on the neck with four light lines above three lines of stamps all demarcated below by three lines. On the shoulder are twelve long hollow bosses each carrying a vertical line of stamps. Eight of the panels contain a diagonal cross of three/four lines, the top and sometimes the bottom spaces being filled with stamps; three of the remaining four panels (every third) contain a vertical line of stamps demarcated on each side by a group of vertical lines; the fourth is empty.

Six stamps are used.

X 12 is by Potter I (p. 57).

Contents

A. Burnt bones.

X 12 was in contact with X 13, perhaps intrusively.

X 13 (fig. 21)

Found in fragments.

Depth 17 in. (43 cm.).

Upper part of a globular bowl with upright rim, base missing: polished black ware.

Decorated on the neck with two zones of line-and-groove ornament. Below are irregular line-and-groove chevrons and arcading with an indistinct stamp in some of the spaces.

Two stamps appear.

Contents

A. Burnt bones.

Fragments of at least three other urns were associated with X 13:

X 13(b) (not illustrated)

Part of the neck and shoulder of a large urn: grey ware. Decorated with horizontal corrugation on neck and bands of vertical corrugation on shoulder.

X 13(c) (not illustrated)

One boss of an urn apparently decorated only with small hollow shoulder-bosses.

X 13(d) (fig. 45)

Parts of the conical neck and shoulder of a large urn with upright rim: brown ware.

Decorated with two lines above a zone of stamps above two more lines above another zone of stamps. Below are one or two zones of single-line chevrons, a narrow line of jabs on the maximum diameter and further chevron lines below. See p. 57.

At least four stamps appear.

X 14 (not illustrated)

Found in fragments.

Depth 15 in. (38 cm.).

Fragments of several undecorated urns.

Contents

A. Burnt bones.

'Parts of base of X 15 on top of X 14' (F. R. M.).

X 15 (fig. 32) 1807

Found in fragments.

Depth 15 in. (38 cm.).

Lower part of biconical cook-pot: hard sandy brown ware.

Decorated with three applied perforated lugs, one of which is missing.

Contents

A. Burnt bones.

X 15 was found 'mixed up with others: remains of two others were with it—one a plain pot with rim foot [*sic*], the other a few sherds of a decorated pot' (F. R. M.). Parts of the base of X 15 were on top of X 14.

X 16 (fig. 26) 1752

Found in fragments.

Depth 17 in. (43 cm.).

Shouldered urn with short everted rim: rough light red ware.

Undecorated.

Contents

A. Burnt bones.

X 17 (fig. 34) 1815

Found in fragments.

Depth 17 in. (43 cm.).

Shouldered urn with wide mouth and upright rim: smoothed grey/brown ware.

Decorated on the neck with a line of stamps demarcated above by one and below by two firm lines. Below are three-line chevrons, the triangles above and below which are filled with stamps.

One stamp is used.

Contents

A. Burnt bones.

X 18 (fig. 30) 1786

Found in fragments.

Depth 25 in. (64 cm.).

Sharp-shouldered urn with straight inturned rim: smooth black ware, once burnished.

Undecorated.

Contents

A. Burnt bones.

X 18, X 19, X 36, and X 37 were part of a group of urns 'broken and confused', possibly a gravedigger's dump from Grave 17.

X 19 (not illustrated)

Found in fragments.

Depth 21 in. (53 cm.).

Fragments of a large urn: soft red/brown ware with smoothed surface.

Decorated only with an uncertain number of slight vertical hollow bosses.

Contents

A. Burnt bones.

X 19 is part of the X 18 group (q.v.).

X 20

'Cannot trace this pot—probably due to a mistake in numbering' (F. R. M.).

X 21 (not illustrated)

Found almost complete.

Depth 18 in. (46 cm.).

Wide-mouthed bowl: burnished black ware.

Decorated with horizontal corrugation on the neck and continuous vertical corrugation on the shoulder.

Urn missing.

Contents

A. Burnt bones.

X 22 (fig. 12) 1628

Found almost complete.

Depth 20 in. (51 cm.).

Sub-biconical bowl with tall neck and everted rim: smooth grey ware, once burnished.

Decorated above the maximum diameter with three lightly tooled lines, above which are groups of three scratched lines linked above by a single scratched line. All the decoration above the three tooled lines 'looks as if it was done as an afterthought with a pin' (F. R. M.).

Contents
A. Burnt bones.
B. Three fused glass beads.
   (i) Blue disc bead.
   (ii) Yellow bead.
   (iii) Small blue bead.

X 23 (pl. XXIIIc and fig. 9) 1607

Found broken.

Depth 21 in. (53 cm.).

Large shoulder-boss urn with tall conical neck and slightly everted rim: rough light grey ware.

Decorated with two broad grooves on the neck above a zone of diagonal grooves below which are three further grooves. On the shoulder are four vertical bosses, slightly hollow and built up externally, separating panels filled with faint broad vertical corrugation.

Contents
A. Burnt bones.
B. Part of small iron knife, most of tang missing, tip of blade turns sharply upwards making an angle of about 125° with the back. Surviving length 1·3 in. (3·3 cm.).
C. Pair of iron shears, tip of one blade missing, length 2·15 in. (5·5 cm.).
D. Fragments of a pair of iron tweezers, corroded, the distal end of one arm missing, and the other arm broken. It is impossible to be certain of the true length but probably c. 2 in. (5 cm.) long.
E. Undecorated miniature bone comb in the form of an irregular hexagon (pl. XXIIIc), cut from a single piece of bone, the points of the teeth forming the longest side. Maximum length 1·35 in. (3·4 cm.). Height 1·2 in. (3·0 cm.).

X 23 had X 24 standing on its shoulder and itself stood on a large piece of animal bone, possibly frontal bone of horse or ox (bone missing). F. R. M.'s note.

X 24 (fig. 17) 1667

Found broken.

Depth 18 in. (46 cm.).

Large globular *Buckelurne* with upright neck and everted rim: smooth pitted grey/brown ware.

Decorated on the neck with ?4 solid nipple-bosses above three tooled lines; on the shoulder are four large hollow bosses of which two are round and carry

two vertical and one horizontal line crossing: above are irregular groups of dots. The other two bosses are vertical and carry a group of vertical lines with a horizontal line crossing the upper part and some more dots. In each panel between the large bosses is a hollow nipple-boss with a horizontal line of dots above and interrupted by it.

Contents
A. Burnt bones.
B. Fragment of sheet bronze considerably warped and crackled by fire.

X 24 rested on the shoulder of X 23 and was probably buried at the same time, but could be later (see p. 47).

X 25 (urn not illustrated; grave goods fig. 59)

Found in fragments.

Depth 20 in. (51 cm.).

Fragments of a dark grey/brown urn.
Decorated with incised lines.
Urn missing.

Contents
A. Burnt bones.
B. Fragment of bronze strip, warped by fire.
C. Iron nail (association doubtful).

X 26 (fig. 15) 1652

Found complete.

Depth 18 in. (46 cm.).

Small shouldered urn with hollow neck and everted rim: smooth grey ware, well made.
Decorated on the neck with two faint grooves.

Contents
A. Burnt bones of a young child.

X 26 was found on the edge of Grave 17.

X 27 (urns figs. 23, 29; grave goods fig. 59)

X 27 comprises parts of two urns, found on the edge of Grave 17, apparently associated.

Depth 34 in. (86 cm.).

(a) (fig. 23)

Part of a straight-sided urn: thick smooth grey ware.
Decorated with a zone of three-line chevrons demarcated above by two and below by three/four fine

lines. On the shoulder are three-line arches covering three vertical lines, apparently alternating with a different linear design.

(b) (fig. 29)

Part of a shouldered urn: smooth grey ware. Undecorated.

Contents

A. Burnt bones.
B. Amorphous mass of fused glass and bronze from which an iron pin protrudes. The bronze is apparently the remains of a brooch. The glass is probably several beads.

It is uncertain to which urn these objects belong.

X 28 (fig. 12) 1633

Found broken.

Depth 20 in. (51 cm.).

Upper part of a large biconical urn with everted rim: thick red/brown ware.

Decorated on the carination with a raised slashed cordon, above which is a continuous line of grooved arcading below a single horizontal groove.

Contents

A. Burnt bones.
B. Large iron knife, with long tang; tip of blade curves upwards, corroded. Length 4·5 in. (11·4 cm.).
C. Large pair of iron shears, corroded but complete; functional. Length 3·8 in. (9·7 cm.).
D. Iron strip, probably an arm of a pair of tweezers, with, perhaps, an iron ring attached, but badly corroded.

X 28 was found touching X 29.

X 29 (urns not illustrated; grave goods fig. 59)

X 29 comprises a collection of fragments from several urns, one showing linear decoration.

Depth 18 in. (46 cm.).

Contents

A. Burnt bones.
B. Spindle whorl made from a Roman potsherd. Maximum diameter 1·9 in. (4·8 cm.).
C. Small pair of bronze tweezers, distal ends of arms expanded, proximal ends constricted to form a

terminal loop. Though these tweezers are small they are functional. Length 1·55 in. (4·0 cm.).

It is uncertain from which urn these grave goods come.

X 29 was found touching X 28.

X 30 (fig. 31) 1787

Found broken.

Depth 22 in. (56 cm.).

Globular urn with conical neck, everted rim and round bottom: heavy dark grey ware, once burnished. Undecorated.

Contents

A. Burnt bones.

'Judging from fragments, this type of pot was not uncommon in the cemetery but this is the only restorable one that I have found.' (F. R. M.)

X 31 (fig. 3) 1551

Found in fragments.

Depth 21 in. (53 cm.).

Upper part of a shouldered bowl with upstanding neck and everted rim: smooth grey ware.

Decorated with three faintly tooled neck-lines above three-line chevrons on the shoulder.

Contents

A. Burnt bones.
B. Probably part of a large iron blade, roughly square. Both ends have been broken, and it shows quite considerable corrosion. Found in midst of bones.

'The bottom of this pot had disintegrated but I have a good idea of the size and shape of the pot from the bone mass.' (F. R. M.)

X 32 (urn not illustrated; grave goods fig. 59)

Found broken.

Depth 18 in. (46 cm.).

Wide-mouthed globular urn with slightly everted rim: heavy smooth brownish grey ware. Undecorated.

Urn missing.

Contents

A. Burnt bones.
B. Small pair of iron shears, corroded. Length 2 in. (5·1 cm.). Association doubtful. F. R. M. notes: 'Broken empty urn found among a few bones and a small pair of shears beneath.'

X 33 (fig. 12) 1627

Found broken.

Depth 34 in. (86 cm.).

Biconical urn with short upright rim: soft grey ware.
Decorated on the neck with two thin grooved lines above single-line chevrons reaching to the carination.

Contents

A. Burnt bones.

X 34 (fig. 27) 1755

Found broken.

Depth 20 in. (51 cm.).

Hump-shouldered urn with short upstanding rim: heavy pitted grey ware.
Undecorated.

Contents

A. Burnt bones.

'This pot was built in with the usual array of flints and tiles. Among them, in actual contact with the pot, was a long red tile or brick measuring roughly 15 × 4 × 3 in. (38 × 10 × 7·6 cm.). One side of it was weathered and has an inscription?, the other trowelled for mortar. Corbould-Warren has the brick.' (F. R. M.)
This brick never reached N.C.M.

X 35 (fig. 1) 1541

Found complete.

Depth 24 in. (61 cm.).

Large shouldered urn with wide mouth, slightly everted rim and well-made base: smooth dark ware, once burnished.
Decorated on the neck with three grooves from which depend seven groups of three/four vertical grooves running below the shoulder.

Contents

A. Burnt bones.
B. Fragment of sheet bronze, clipped from a larger sheet, one end curled over.

'This pot was covered by a great heap of large flints. One of these was inside it and had caused the fracture. This was the second largest pot.' (F. R. M.)

X 36 (fig. 49) 1894

Found broken.

Depth Not recorded.

Wide-mouthed ovoid urn with short flaring rim: smooth grey ware.
Decorated on the neck with two grooves from which depend seven pairs of vertical lines reaching almost to the base. The top and upper part of the sides of the panels so formed are outlined with stamps.
Five stamps are used.
X 36 is by Potter II (p. 62).

Contents None recorded.

X 36 came from a grave-digger's dump a few feet east of Grave 17, together with X 37 and part of a coarse plain urn, apparently not preserved. See also X 18, X 19.

X 37 (fig. 49) 1895

Found in fragments.

Depth Not recorded.

Tall narrow-necked ovoid urn, rim missing: smooth grey ware.
Decorated on the neck with two grooves from which depend six groups of three vertical grooves reaching almost to the base. The top and upper part of the sides of the panels so formed are outlined with stamps.
Five stamps appear.
X 37 is by Potter II (p. 62).

Contents None recorded.

X 37 came from a grave-digger's dump a few feet east of Grave 17, together with X 36 and part of a coarse plain urn, apparently not preserved. See also X 18, X 19.

X 38 (urn fig. 40; grave goods fig. 59)

Found in fragments.

Depth 20 in. (51 cm.).

Fragments of a shouldered urn with hollow neck, rim and base missing: smooth brown ware.
Decorated on the neck with at least two light lines below which is a zone of irregular three-line chevrons

and criss-cross lines enclosing vertical and horizontal lines of stamps.

One stamp is used.

Contents

A. Burnt bones.
B. Part of an iron knife, short, pointed tang, blade broken. F. R. M. suggests that this may come from an inhumation (association doubtful).

Associated with X 38 was:

X 38(a) (not illustrated)

Fragments of an urn in heavy grey ware. Undecorated.

X 39 (fig. 48) 1892

Found in fragments.

Depth Not recorded.

Upper part of large shoulder-boss urn: smooth brown ware.

Decorated on the neck with three lines of stamps demarcated above and below and separated from one another by three lines. On the shoulder are sixteen small vertical hollow bosses separating blank panels.

Three stamps appear.

X 39 is by Potter I (p. 57).

Contents None recorded.

Y 1 (fig. 36) 1827

Found broken.

Depth 24 in. (61 cm.).

Shoulder-boss urn with high wide conical neck and slightly everted rim: thin smooth, well-fired grey/brown ware.

Decorated below the rim with seven/eight sharp close-set lines above a line of stamps below which are three more lines, another line of stamps, and two more lines. On the shoulder are six hollow bosses demarcated on each side by groups of three/five vertical lines, the panels between them containing four/six-line pendent triangles. Below the bosses and pendent triangles are two/three sharp lines running continuously round the pot.

One stamp is used.

Contents

A. Burnt bones.

Y 2 (figs. 14, 22, 45)

Y 2 comprises a collection of fragments of several urns.

Depth 16–24 in. (41–61 cm.).

Among these are:

(a) (fig. 14)

Upper part of a globular urn with upright rim: smooth grey/brown ware.

Decorated on the neck with three sharp lines above two zones containing four/five-line chevrons, separated and demarcated below by single lines. Faint bosses (not shown on fig. 14) are set between the chevrons in the lower zone.

Y 2(a) is probably from the same workshop as Z 4 (fig. 14).

(b) (fig. 22)

Part of rim and side of a globular urn with short everted rim: smooth brown ware.

Decorated on the neck with three grooves above a deep zone of three-line chevrons.

(c) (fig. 45)

Part of side of a sharply shouldered urn: smooth brown ware.

Decorated at the base of the neck with three lines above a zone of three-line chevrons interspersed with stamps.

Two stamps appear.

(d) (not illustrated)

Rim of a Romano-British grey ware lid.

(e) (not illustrated)

Fragment of a biconical urn decorated with a zone of two/three-line chevrons demarcated above by three and below by two horizontal lines.

Y 3 (fig. 14) 1643

Found broken.

Depth 15 in. (38 cm.).

Shouldered urn, rim missing: smooth black ware.

Decorated low on the neck with a zone of continuous one-line chevrons, each triangle divided by a central vertical line, demarcated above and below by two sharp lines.

Contents

A. Burnt bones.

B. Seven small fragments of sheet bronze, apparently broken from a larger sheet, all warped and crackled by fire.

Y 4 (fig. 33)

Found complete.

Depth 27 in. (69 cm.).

Roman coarse ware jar with everted rim: fine grey fabric smoothly finished.

Decorated with many vertical and one (possibly three) horizontal burnished lines.

Contents

A. Burnt bones. Dr. Wells reports: 'Adult, possibly male. A few hundred fragments, almost all small. Identifiable are fragments of vault with unfused sutures; pieces of cranial base; vertebral, pelvic, and rib fragments; many slivers of long bone. Well fired. No animal remains.'

Y 4 lay under Y 5, with about 3 in. (7·6 cm.) of soil between them, as shown in F. R. M.'s drawing (pl. XII*a*).

Y 5 (fig. 26) 1749

Found broken.

Depth 17 in. (43 cm.).

Globular urn with short upright neck and straight rim: smooth buff ware.

Decorated on the shoulder with four zones separated by single lines: the upper two zones contain a line of dots, the third a line of close-set small jabs, the fourth is blank except for a short space containing ten vertical lines of three or four small jabs.

Contents

A. Burnt bones.

Y 5 overlay Y 4 with about 3 in. (7·6 cm.) of soil between them (see pl. XII*a*).

Y 6 (fig. 39) 1852

Found broken.

Depth 17 in. (43 cm.).

Globular urn with wide mouth and everted rim: smooth brown ware.

Decorated on the neck with two irregular sharp lines above a line of stamps and a single line. Below are pendent one-line swags outlined below with stamps and containing a certral vertical line of stamps. One panel also has a line of stamps along the top edge.

Five stamps are used.

Contents

A. Burnt bones.

'This pot . . . was surrounded above and at sides by several large flints and two pieces of Roman tile. It was burst open and the bones scattered by weight of stones on top of it. Many fragments of a plain pot [apparently not preserved] were round it' (F. R. M.).

Y 7 (figs. 36, 41) 1826, 1863

Y 7 comprises fragments of several urns found together 3 ft. (91 cm.) south of Y 5, disturbed by rabbit burrows.

Depth. Unrecorded.

Among the decorated pieces are:

(a) (fig. 36)   1826

Upper part of a biconical bossed urn with upright neck and flaring rim: smooth brown ware.

Decorated with four light neck-lines above a line of stamps, three more lines, another line of stamps, and three more lines. Cutting into these lines are solid bosses on the carination demarcated on each side by three vertical lines. The panels between them contain a horizontal line of stamps and two more lines above short two-line chevrons with stamps in the spaces above and below them.

One stamp appears.

(b) (fig. 41)

Part of a shouldered bowl with wide mouth, rim and base missing: smooth brown ware.

Decorated on the neck with four lines, a line of stamps, and three more lines. On the shoulder is a zone of criss-cross lines above small three-line pendent triangles containing three stamps.

One stamp appears.

(c) (fig. 41)   1863

Upper part of an urn with conical neck and upright rim: smooth brown ware.

Decorated on the neck with a line of stamps demarcated above and below by three lines; on the shoulder are groups of three vertical lines separating groups of diagonal lines and stamps.

Two stamps appear.

Y 8 (fig. 16) 1661

Found in fragments.

Depth 17 in. (43 cm.).

Globular urn with narrow neck and everted rim: heavy smooth dark grey ware.

Decorated on the neck with four corrugated grooves above continuous two-groove flat arches in the spandrels between which are two or three large dots.

Contents

B. Fragments of a bone comb, affected by fire. Two fragments of centre-plate with bronze rivets survive. A small piece of thin sheet decorated with incised lines also survives. Several pieces of half round 'bar' decorated with groups of incised vertical lines may be part of a comb case or belong to the comb. If the latter, the comb is probably of the barred type; cf. Y 17, M 53.
C. Fragment of iron, possibly part of a small pair of tweezers.

Burnt bones are not recorded.
Y 8 was surrounded by several large flints.

Y 9 (fig. 43) 1875

Found almost complete.

Depth 20 in. (51 cm.).

Wide-mouthed sub-biconical urn with everted rim: smooth dark grey ware.

Decorated with a single line above three lines of stamps separated by single lines. The top line of stamps is interrupted at one point by three impressions of a seven-toothed comb arranged like a reversed N: in the second row is also one similar comb mark.

Two stamps are used.

Contents

A. Burnt bones.

Y 9 formed one of a group of several urns (Y 9, Y 10, Y 11 (at least four urns), Y 12) found together surrounded with large flints and a Roman tile (see pl. XVb and pp. 56–7).

Y 10 (fig. 22)

Found collapsed.

Depth 20 in. (51 cm.).

Upper part of a globular urn with short upright neck and rim, base missing: smooth sandy brown ware.

Decorated on the neck with three grooves above large two-line chevrons on the shoulder.

Contents

A. Burnt bones.

Y 10 was part of the Y 9 group (q.v.).

Y 11 (figs. 20, 39) 1698

Y 11 comprises a collection of sherds forming parts of at least four decorated urns, which contained burnt bones.

Depth 18–20 in. (46–51 cm.).

(a) (fig. 39)

Upper part of a shouldered urn with slightly everted rim: smooth brown ware.

Decorated on the neck with a line of stamps demarcated above and below by a single fine line; below are pendent two/three-line triangles partly filled with stamps very carelessly applied.

One stamp appears.

(b) (fig. 20) 1698

Lower part of a shoulder-boss urn, neck and rim missing: smooth brown ware.

Decorated with numerous applied vertical shoulder-bosses separating panels some of which contain vertical lines.

(c) (not illustrated)

Fragments of an urn in smooth grey ware with a zone of linear decoration bounded below the maximum diameter by two horizontal lines.

(d) (not illustrated)

One piece of an urn or bowl in rough grey ware with continuous horizontal corrugation on the neck and vertical corrugation below.

There is also part of a heavy brown base possibly from Y 11(a).

Two Y 11 urns are recorded by F. R. M. as part of the Y 9 group, presumably Y 11(a) and Y 11(b). It would seem possible that Y 11(d) and possibly Y 11(c) also, were earlier burials disturbed by the intrusion of the Y 9 group (see pl. XVb and pp. 56–7).

Y 12 (fig. 28) 1761

Found collapsed.

Depth 20 in. (51 cm.).

Sharp-shouldered urn with hollow neck and upright rim: heavy grey ware.

Undecorated.

Contents

A. Burnt bones.

Y 12 was part of the Y 9 group (q.v.).

Y 13 (not illustrated)

Depth 15 in. (38 cm.).

Urn missing.

Contents

A. Burnt bones.

Y 13 was found in a group with Y 14, Y 15, Y 16.

Y 14 (fig. 24) 1732

Found broken.

Depth 15 in. (38 cm.).

Bag-shaped cook-pot with wide mouth, upright rim, and narrow base: coarse red/brown ware. Undecorated.

Contents

A. Burnt bones.

Y 14 was part of the Y 13 group (q.v.).

Y 15 (fig. 33) 1809

Found broken.

Depth 15 in. (38 cm.).

Sub-biconical urn with wide mouth, everted rim, and well-moulded foot: smooth red/brown ware. Undecorated.

Contents

A. Burnt bones.

The foot of Y 15 suggests that it was made by some-one familiar with the manufacture of wheel-turned pottery.

Y 15 was part of the Y 13 group (q.v.).

Y 16 (fig. 43) 1872

Found broken.

Depth 15 in. (38 cm.).

Sharp-shouldered urn with hollow neck and up-right rim: smooth grey/brown ware.

Decorated on the neck with three firm lines above a zone of vertical and diagonal lines separating spaces containing stamps. On the sharp shoulder is a raised cordon demarcated above and below by a single line above a line of stamps with widely spaced (apparently four) linear crosses at the points of the arms of which are single stamps. Parts of only two of these crosses remain.

One stamp is used.

Contents

A. Burnt bones. Dr. Wells reports: 'Adult. Three fragments of mandible. The right I_1, M_1, and M_2 had been lost ante mortem; the right I_2, C, P_1, P_2 and the left I_1, I_2, C, and P_1 had been lost post mortem. Well fired. No animal remains.'

Y 16 is part of the Y 13 group (q.v.).

Y 17 (pl. XXIII*a* and fig. 28) 1766

Found collapsed.

Depth 15 in. (38 cm.).

Biconical bowl with hollow neck and slightly everted rim: smooth polished grey/black ware. Undecorated.

Contents

A. Burnt bones of a young child with milk teeth. Dr. Wells reports: 'Child. Crowns of three deciduous teeth. Well fired. No animal remains.'

B. Part of a single-sided barred bone comb. The side-plates are formed of a single, thin, flat sheet of bone on one side and two horizontal plano-convex bars on the other, fastened with iron rivets. The thin plate is decorated with small concentric circles and groups of parallel incised lines. The bars forming the other side-plate have panel decoration, each panel being divided by a diagonal line and the lower triangle thus formed being filled with vertical incised lines; the upper triangle is plain. The upper part of the centre-plate curves beyond the side-plates, and carries 'bull's-eye' decoration on one side and faint overlapping circles on the other. The lower projection of the centre-plate is also decorated on one side with 'bull's-eye' patterns. The loop handle is sub-rectangular in form and is a projection of the centre-plate. It too bears 'bull's-eye' decoration. This comb has evolved from those decorated with hippocamp heads. Height 1·8 in. (4·6 cm.). 'This comb appeared to be whole when seen in the earth on top of the bones but really it was in hundreds of pieces' (F. R. M.). See pl. XXIII*a*.

Y 17 was found under a heap of twenty-five large flints and Roman tiles.

Y 18 (fig. 18) 1679

Found in fragments.

Depth 22 in. (56 cm.).

Shoulder-boss urn with wide mouth and upright rim: smooth black ware, once burnished.

Decorated on the neck with five fine lines between the lowest two of which are widely spaced vertical lines. On the shoulder are eight/nine vertical hollow bosses, which interrupt the lowest horizontal line.

'The lines are very carelessly done and give the impression of having been done when the pot was too dry before firing' (F. R. M.).

Contents

A. Burnt bones.

Y 18 was found in a group with Y 19, Y 20, Y 21. See pp. 56–7.

Y 19 (fig. 11)

Found in fragments.

Depth 22 in. (56 cm.).

Upper part of a shouldered urn with swollen upright rim: black ware, once polished.

Decorated with three firm lines on the neck above a zone of irregular three/four-line chevrons, the triangles being filled with deeply impressed dots.

Contents

A. Burnt bones.
B. Twisted fragment of bronze brooch, distorted and expanded by heat, probably part of a bow of a simple cruciform brooch.

Y 19 was part of the Y 18 group (q.v.).

Y 20 (fig. 29) 1769

Found broken.

Depth 22 in. (56 cm.).

Shouldered bowl with upright rim: smooth smoky-grey ware.
Undecorated.

Contents

A. Burnt bones.

Y 20 was part of the Y 18 group (q.v.).

Y 21 (not illustrated)

Found in fragments.

Depth 20 in. (51 cm.).

Fragments of a shouldered urn with conical neck: very ill-baked grey ware.
Undecorated.

Contents

A. Burnt bones.

Y 21 was part of the Y 18 group (q.v.).

Y 22 (fig. 2 and text-fig. 6) 1549

Found in fragments.

Depth 20 in. (51 cm.).

Wide-mouthed globular urn with heavy flaring rim: thick grey/brown ware, burnished.

Decorated on the neck with three deep grooves above large four-groove pendent triangles. In one of these is a swastika scratched after firing and in the next space to it some impressions, probably accidental, perhaps made by a wrist clasp (text-fig. 6).

Contents

A. Burnt bones.
B. Large tanged iron knife, tip of tang missing, badly corroded; blade may be complete. Surviving length 4·3 in. (11·0 cm.).
C. Three fragments of sheet bronze, two somewhat cracked; and warped by fire; all have been clipped or broken from a larger sheet.

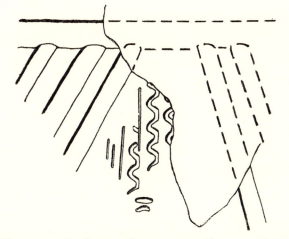

TEXT-FIG. 6. Impression on urn Y 22, perhaps made by a wrist-clasp (scale $\frac{1}{1}$).

Y 23 (pl. XXIII*f* and fig. 11) 1624

Found shattered.

Depth 18 in. (46 cm.).

Large biconical urn, rim missing: pitted grey ware, perhaps once burnished.

Decorated with at least four corrugated lines on the neck above irregular groups of four-line chevrons, some of the upper triangles being divided with a pair of vertical lines bordered by horizontal corrugation, others containing diagonal corrugation parallel with the chevron.

Contents

A. Burnt bones.
B. End section of centre-plate of a triangular bone comb; one rivet hole and parts of two others remain; all unstained by metal. Lines marking the bases of the side-plates are visible on both sides. The end of the centre-plate projected beyond the side-plates (pl. XXIII*f*).

Y 24 (fig. 9) 1610

Found collapsed.

Depth 22 in. (56 cm.).

Shoulder-boss urn with tall conical neck, wide mouth, and widely flaring rim: smoothed brown ware.

Decorated on the neck with nine lightly tooled lines above four groups of three vertical solid bosses on the shoulder, separating panels each containing a widely spaced three-line chevron.

Contents

A. Burnt bones.

Y 25

No urn appears to be recorded under this number.

Y 26 (fig. 28) 1764

Found collapsed.

Depth 18 in. (46 cm.).

Biconical urn with tall hollow neck, rim missing: brown ware.
Undecorated.

Contents

A. Burnt bones.
B. Small iron knife with long blade, most of tang missing, corroded. Surviving length 2·4 in. (6·1 cm.).

C. Part of small pair of iron shears, one blade broken and the other missing, corroded. Surviving length 1·7 in. (4·3 cm.).
D. Part of pair of iron tweezers, both distal ends missing. Surviving length 1·6 in. (4·1 cm.).

Y 27 (fig. 34) 1813

Found complete.

Depth 22 in. (56 cm.).

Wide-shouldered urn with tall conical neck and everted rim: hard grey/brown ware, well made.

Decorated low on the neck with three wide grooves, between the lower two of which are four groups of stamps alternating with blank spaces. On the shoulder are continuous one-line chevrons, the upper and lower triangles being filled in some places with stamps and in others being divided with two/three vertical grooves.

One stamp is used.

Contents

A. Two sets of burnt bones separated by a layer of earth, the upper set containing also some pieces of a brown plain urn, Y 27(a) (not described), which was buried over Y 27 and was subsequently shattered.

Y 28 (fig. 9) 1601

Found complete.

Depth 22 in. (56 cm.).

Shoulder-boss urn with conical neck and everted rim: black ware, once burnished.

Decorated at the base of the neck with five close-set firm lines above eight slashed vertical hollow bosses on the shoulder separating panels filled in the centre with a group of close-set vertical lines leaving a blank space on each side of the bosses.

Contents

A. Burnt bones of a young child.
B. At least one fused glass bead. There are two pieces of fused material incorporating bone fragments preserved. These have not been analysed but are superficially very similar to fused material found in a number of urns from Illington, Norfolk. Analyses of this have failed to establish with any certainty whether the material is the remains of fused glass, or sand, etc. from beneath the

funeral pyre.[1] The material from Illington is not apparently the same as the German *Urnenharz*. See also R 17.

Y 29 (fig. 3) 1557

Found almost complete.

Depth 29 in. (74 cm.).

Wide-mouthed shouldered bowl with everted rim: hard burnished black ware, very well made.

Decorated on the neck with three strong grooves above continuous diagonal grooves on the shoulder.

Contents

A. A few fragments of burnt bone probably of a child.

Y 29 was under a large heap of tiles and faced flints.

Y 30 (fig. 55) 1920

Found broken.

Depth 28 in. (71 cm.).

Sub-biconical urn with tall neck, rim missing: smooth brown ware, once burnished.

Decorated on the neck with five raised collars, of which the second and fifth are finger-tipped, separated by grooves. On the shoulder are irregular grooved chevrons, in an attempt at 'line-and-groove' technique, alternating with a pair of deep vertical grooves. The spaces above and below the chevrons each contain a larger finger-tip dot.

Y 30 is by Potter VII (p. 52).

Contents

A. Burnt bones.

Y 31 (fig. 56) 1923

Found in fragments.

Depth 28 in. (71 cm.).

Sub-biconical urn with wide mouth and upright rim: soft red/brown ware.

Decorated on the neck with two light lines above a wide zone divided into panels by groups of three diagonal lines which are carried down through all the lower decoration to form wide chevrons. The panels are filled with stamps. Above the maximum diameter this upper zone is closed below by three horizontal lines, and on it is a zone of small single-line chevrons. Below this the diagonal lines of the upper zone are carried down to form empty panels demarcated below by a horizontal line.

Two stamps appear.

Y 31 is by Potter IX.

Contents

A. Burnt bones.

Y 32 (fig. 24) 1738

Found broken.

Depth 28 in. (71 cm.).

Bag-shaped cook-pot with wide mouth and upright rim: smoky grey/buff ware.

Undecorated.

Contents

A. Burnt bones.

Y 33 (fig. 30) 1784

Found collapsed.

Depth 28 in. (71 cm.).

Biconical urn with short upright rim: rough grey ware.

Undecorated.

Contents

A. Burnt bones.

Y 34 (fig. 8) 1595

Found collapsed.

Depth 28 in. (71 cm.).

Wide-mouthed shoulder-boss urn with everted rim: smooth black ware, burnished.

Decorated on the neck with three strong grooves above eight vertical hollow bosses on the shoulder separating panels filled with vertical corrugation.

Contents

A. Burnt bones.

[1] Reports in N.C.M. records from the Laboratorium der Farbwerke, Hoechst (West Germany), and the British Museum Research Laboratory.

Y 35 (fig. 38) 1842

Found in fragments.

Depth 28 in. (71 cm.).

Globular urn with short neck and everted rim: smooth grey ware.

Decorated on the neck with three light lines above large two-line chevrons outlined on both sides and along the top of the panels with a line of stamps.

One stamp is used.

Contents None.

Y 36 (pl. I*a* and fig. 33) 1810

Found broken.

Depth 24 in. (61 cm.).

Biconical urn with wide mouth and swollen everted rim: hard fine burnished light grey ware, extremely well made.

Decorated on the neck with a line of close-set stamps, demarcated above and below by four sharp lines. Below, extending to the carination, is a zone of three-line trellis pattern in finer lines. The decoration is all carried out very neatly and is very much reminiscent, as is the fabric, of Romano-British technique.

Two stamps are used, both very clearly applied. See p. 54.

Contents

A. Burnt bones.
B. Fragment of sheet bronze, broken from a larger piece; one edge is straight and probably represents the original edge.

Y 37 (not illustrated)

Found in fragments.

Depth 28 in. (71 cm.).

A few fragments of a base: heavy brown ware.

Contents

A. Burnt bones.

Y 38 (fig. 17) 1665

Found broken.

Depth 18 in. (46 cm.).

Tall *Buckelurne* with well-moulded, slightly dished footstand, with several circular perforations in the base: grey/brown ware, once burnished.

Decorated on the neck with a line of dots demarcated above and below by a fine line. On the shoulder were probably sixteen hollow bosses of which four were circular and surrounded by dots to form rosettes, and the rest were vertical and set in threes between them. The central boss of each group of three carries a vertical line or a line of dots. Between the bosses are faint vertical lines.

Contents

A. Burnt bones.

Y 39 (fig. 53) 1909

Found broken.

Depth 22 in. (56 cm.).

Miniature shoulder-boss urn with everted rim: rough brown ware.

Decorated on the neck with a raised slashed collar demarcated above and below by three/four light lines. On the shoulder are four groups of two vertical solid bosses separated and demarcated on each side by groups of vertical lines. The panels between the grouped bosses contain a single horizontal line of stamps with two horizontal lines above and three below.

One stamp is used.

Y 39 is by Potter IV (p. 57).

Contents

A. Burnt bones of a very young child (F. R. M.). Dr. Wells reports: 'Infant. Fragments of two petrous temporal bones; ten minute unidentifiable fragments. Well fired. No animal remains.'

Y 40 (fig. 12) 1632

Found broken.

Depth 18 in. (46 cm.).

Biconical urn with upright rim: dark grey/brown ware once burnished.

Decorated on the neck with two firm lines above a zone of single-line chevrons, the triangles filled with close-set diagonal lines, set at right angles, giving an over-all basketry pattern. Below are three more lines above the carination.

'On restoring the pot it became evident that it was moulded in two parts which were afterwards joined together along the carination' (F. R. M.).

Contents
A. Burnt bones.
B. Iron knife with long curved blade and looped handle apparently joined to the cutting edge, but corroded. Length 2·8 in. (7·1 cm.).
C. Perforated Roman coin, very worn but perhaps an antoninianus of Valerian I, A.D. 253–9.

Y 40 was in contact with Y 41. See p. 44.

Y 41 (fig. 11) 1619

Found in fragments.

Depth 18 in. (46 cm.).

Large sub-biconical urn with tall neck and upright rim: heavy black ware probably once burnished.

Decorated on the neck with four grooves above an irregular pattern of wavy lines, the spaces being partly filled with large dots.

Y 41 is probably by the same potter as X 9(b) (fig. 11).

Contents
A. Burnt bones.
B. Fragment of a probable pair of iron tweezers, distal end expanded.

Y 41 was in contact with Y 40. See p. 45.

Y 42 (fig. 32) 1800

Found broken.

Depth 15 in. (38 cm.).

Shoulder-boss urn with tall conical neck, rim missing: smooth dark grey ware, once burnished.
Decorated with ?three small applied nipple-bosses.

Contents
A. Burnt bones.

Y 43 (fig. 22) 1712

Found broken.

Depth 27 in. (69 cm.).

Shouldered urn with wide mouth and everted rim: brown ware, once burnished.
Decorated below the shoulder with light multiple-line chevrons, carelessly drawn; some have a vertical

line from the apex, perhaps intended to represent the '↑' rune (see p. 66).

Contents
A. Burnt bones.

Y 44 (fig. 56) 1922

Found broken.

Depth 27 in. (69 cm.).

Biconical bowl with everted rim: smooth brown ware.
Decorated on the neck with a line of stamps demarcated above by one and below by three light lines. Below the carination are four large three-line swags, each enclosing three short vertical lines.
One stamp is used.
Y 44 is by Potter IX.

Contents
A. Burnt bones.

Y 45 (fig. 36) 1829

Found broken.

Depth 26 in. (66 cm.).

Biconical shoulder-boss urn with upright rim: smooth brown ware, once burnished.
Decorated on the neck with a line of stamps demarcated above and below by three light lines, then another line of stamps and two more lines. On the shoulder are eleven slight hollow bosses, the panels between which contain three-line pendent triangles filled with stamps, small dots, or triangular jabs.
Three stamps are used.

Contents
A. Burnt bones.

Y 46 (fig. 30) 1785

Found almost complete.

Depth 26 in. (66 cm.).

Sharp-shouldered urn with hollow neck and upright rim: smooth dark brown ware, once burnished.
Undecorated.

Contents
A. Burnt bones.

Y 47 (figs. 24, 30, 37) 1736, 1783

Y 47 comprises a collection of fragments from several urns.

Depth 18 in. (46 cm.).

(a) (fig. 30)   1783

Shouldered urn with conical neck and upright rim: heavy brown ware.
Undecorated.

(b) (fig. 24)   1736

Shouldered cook-pot, rim missing: smooth brown ware.
Undecorated.

(c) (fig. 37, where wrongly labelled Y 47(b))

Part of a biconical bossed urn, rim and base missing: smooth heavy dark ware.
Decorated on the neck with at least five sharp lines above two lines of stamps separated by a single line. On the carination are a number of solid lug bosses.
One stamp appears.

Contents

A. Burnt bones.

Z 1 (not illustrated)

Found in fragments.

Depth 13 in. (33 cm.).

A few fragments of grey ware urn, decorated with incised lines.
Urn missing.

Contents

A. Burnt bones.

Z 2 (urn not illustrated; grave goods fig. 59)

Depth 13 in. (33 cm.).

'This pot was almost completely disintegrated to form a reddish mud' (F. R. M.).
Urn missing.

Contents

A. Burnt bones.
B. Part of a small pair of iron shears with very long blades; most of one blade and the tip of the other missing. Surviving length 1·85 in. (4·7 cm.).

Z 3 (not illustrated)

Found in fragments.

Depth 15 in. (38 cm.).

Part of base of large urn: dark brown ware.
No decoration appears.
Urn missing.

Contents

A. Burnt bones.

Z 4 (fig. 14) 1647

Found in fragments.

Depth 12 in. (30 cm.).

Shouldered urn with upright rim: smooth brown ware.
Decorated on the neck with four faint lines above a broad zone of four-line chevrons. Below the shoulder is a broad zone of horizontal feathering demarcated above and below by two light lines.

Contents

A. Burnt bones.

Z 4 was probably broken up in the digging of Grave 7. It is probably from the same workshop as Y 2(a) (fig. 14).

Z 5 (fig. 14) 1639

Found broken.

Depth 20 in. (51 cm.).

Biconical urn with everted rim: smooth brown ware, once burnished.
Decorated on the neck with large single-line chevrons below each of which is a vertical line of dots and a horizontal line of dots linking the lower points. On the carination is a single line below which are large carelessly drawn single-line chevrons extending nearly to the base.

Contents

A. Burnt bones.

Z 6 (urn not illustrated; grave goods fig. 59)

Found broken.

Depth 12 in. (30 cm.).

Base only.

Contents

A. Burnt bones.
B. Fragment of bronze brooch; a piece of fused bronze remains attached to the iron spring and pin; it is impossible to determine the type of brooch.
C. Part of iron blade, badly corroded, possibly part of small knife or shears. Association doubtful as found loose in Grave 11.

Found 9 in. (23 cm.) west of skull in Grave 11 and disturbed by it.

B.M. 1870. 12–6.1 (fig. 17) 1663

Biconical *Buckelurne* of Group II, original rim missing: smooth grey ware.

Decorated with a row of oval hollow bosses on the neck, demarcated above by at least three and below by two lines. On the carination are further oval hollow bosses demarcated on each side by four/five lines. The original rim has been lost in ancient times and a new rim formed along the top surviving neckline.

Contents None recorded.

Urn in the Wisbech Museum (fig. 58) 3675

Small biconical urn with wide mouth and everted rim: red/brown ware.

Undecorated.

This urn is similar in form and fabric to A 2 (fig. 29) but smaller and less heavily made. It came to the Wisbech Museum from William Peckover in 1835.

Urn from Caistor-by-Norwich Roman town (fig. 33)

Found complete.

Roman coarse ware jar, fine grey fabric.
Undecorated.

Contents

A. Burnt bones. Dr. Wells reports: 'Adult. ?Male. Several dozen fragments, almost all very small. Identifiable are: pieces of cranial vault; one petrous temporal bone; small fragments of vertebrae and pelvis; many fragments of ribs, long bones, metacarpals and phalanges. Well fired. Four pieces of animal bone were present: three of unidentifiable bird, one of thoracic vertebra of an ox.'

This pot was found near bastion 3 on the berm of the south wall.

Five further urns, known only from old illustrations, are not described here; they are shown on pls. XVI–XVIII.

Urnless Cremation

A box of burnt bones, labelled 'Urnless Cremation', was found with the other human remains from this cemetery. These presumably represent either the urnless cremation P 4, the cremated bones near N 26 which contained fragments of an applied brooch (fig. 60, no. 12, and p. 208), or any of the other urnless cremations recorded by F. R. M. in his field notebook.

Dr. Wells reports: 'Adult. ? Male. A few hundred small fragments. Identifiable are small pieces of vault, with endocranial fusion of sutures; fragments of base and face; part of a maxillary alveolus, showing irregularity and overcrowding of the (now lost) teeth; the dens and body of an axis; other vertebral fragments; many small pieces of long bone, including a few articular surfaces of humeral head and femoral condyle; many unidentifiable fragments. Well fired. No animal bones.'

Stray finds, probably from cremations (fig. 60)

1. Cast bronze saucer brooch with a 'chip carved' ornament of five running spirals around a beaded circlet which contains a small central boss. The spirals are enclosed within a beaded circlet, the inner edge of which is bevelled. On this, corresponding with the five V's between the spirals, are five punched dots. On the border traces of punched dots and vertical and diagonal lines can be seen, although too little survives for the pattern to be determined. Part of the border, pin, spring, and catch-pin are missing. Diameter 1·8 in. (4·6 cm.). Text-fig. 2 and pl. XIXc.
2. Fragment of burnt elephant ivory ring.
3. Fragment of centre-plate of bone comb with an iron rivet; slightly affected by burning.
4. Under E 7 and E 8: large cylindrical clay spindle-whorl; not very well made, sides taper slightly, perforation not central. Thickness 1·1 in. (2·8 cm.), diameter 1·7 in. (4·3 cm.).
5. Small clear green glass bead, perhaps not from a cremation. This is perhaps the bead found near F 3 (p. 133). Length 0·4 in. (1 cm.).
6. Small opaque white glass bead with blue marvered 'trail' decoration. Unaffected by fire;

possibly from an inhumation. Length 0·3 in. (0·7 cm.).

7. Bone gaming piece, plano-convex, with two small holes in base, warped by fire. Maximum diameter 0·6 in. (1·5 cm.).

8. Piece of fused bronze.

9. In Grave 17, possibly from disturbed cremation: fragment of fused bronze.

10. Fused glass bead, distorted by fire but apparently of greenish translucent glass.

11. In Grave 17, possibly from disturbed cremation: part of small iron knife, tip of blade missing, remains of wooden haft survive. Surviving length 1·9 in. (4·8 cm.).

12. From cremated bones near N 26: fragments of an applied brooch. The pin, catch-pin, and a few fragments of a bronze disc with, apparently, an applied silver face survive, but it is too fragmentary to reconstruct. The pin has a silvery appearance. Tests carried out in the Museum in the 1950s left dark stains on the pin suggesting that silver had been used. It has not been possible to repeat this result despite several tests.

13. Pair of miniature bronze tweezers, apparently cut from sheet bronze but well made; proximal ends of arms constricted to form terminal loop; top of one arm missing. Length 0·75 in. (1·9 cm.).

14. Five fragments of green glass, all more or less affected by fire. These may be grave goods or may be Roman rubbish. (One fragment only illustrated.)

15. Potsherd with lead mend belonging to P 28 (q.v).

III

THE CAISTOR-BY-NORWICH CEMETERY— INHUMATIONS

THE INHUMATION BURIALS AND THEIR GRAVE GOODS

By Barbara Green

INTRODUCTION

THE thirty-nine graves at Caistor contained the remains of about sixty bodies; in addition loose skulls were found south of Roman Pit 2 and south-west of Grave 1. Many of the graves had been disturbed by rabbits, rabbiters, tree roots, and perhaps earlier archaeologists. Because of this it was usually impossible to define a grave with any degree of certainty and they have thus been shown conventionally on the plan (map 2). It was also difficult to determine how many single burials were disturbed by the insertion of later burials, as for example seems likely in Grave 3. However, in a number of cases the relative positions of the bodies do strongly suggest that multiple burial was a feature of this cemetery, for example Graves 2, 4 (upper skeletons), 8, and 12. This practice is known elsewhere, for example, at Holywell Row, Suff.,[1] Little Wilbraham, Cambs.,[2] and Kingston, Kent.[3] Some of the 'graves', however, seemed to be no more than pits into which the bodies had been thrown, for example Grave 6.

Most of the bones were either missing or in the last stages of decay, '. . . some of them being represented by a mere line of bone dust. . .'. Because of this only a very few bones were preserved (see pp. 217–18) and little could be done to determine the age and sex of the individuals interred here.

The majority of the bodies were orientated with heads to the west, but one had its head to the east (Grave 27), two to the north-west (Graves 30 and 36), and two or three to the south-west (Graves 20, 37, and ?26).

The graves are fairly generally distributed throughout the area excavated, and a large number of cremation vessels were disturbed and destroyed when the graves were dug. F. R. M. thought that on some occasions grave-diggers had carefully reburied some urns or parts of urns which they had disturbed (see p. 72). Occasionally, these urns were preserved and numbered but often F. R. M. noted such assemblages merely as 'grave-diggers' dumps' 'several urns', 'vast quantities of sherds', or 'a great number of sherds'. Consequently, it is impossible to determine how many were thus disturbed; the absolute minimum is thirty-eight urns.

One of the features of at least ten of the graves was the piles of flints and Roman tiles found over the bodies. In a number of cases, but not invariably, these were recorded together

---

[1] Lethbridge 1931, 2.   [2] Op. cit. 73.   [3] Faussett 1856.

with disturbed cremation urns, and it is therefore possible that some represent disturbed flint and tile cists (see p. 72 and pl. XV). However, a number of instances are recorded where no urn sherds are noted; also in some instances the numbers of flints and tiles involved are very high. It may be that these were deliberately placed over the grave perhaps to mark it (we do not know the Saxon ground level or the level of the flints and tiles) or perhaps to keep the spirits in. However, except in the cases of Graves 8 and 16 and perhaps 12, the graves have been disturbed and therefore the flints and tiles over them must also have been disturbed. This feature must remain a puzzle.

The grave goods are comparatively few in number and are not of great interest or very helpful for dating purposes. In general they suggest dates in the late sixth or seventh centuries. Objects are recorded from thirteen graves with a further six containing possible associations. However, it is impossible to be certain how many of the objects were deliberately placed in the graves. Many of the iron objects are so rusty that their original shape and purpose cannot be determined. As the graves are dug through Roman occupation levels, it is difficult to be certain how many of the nondescript items are Roman. Further complications arise from the post-Saxon disturbance of the site and from the number of cremation burials destroyed when the graves were dug; a few of the grave goods almost certainly come from disturbed urns. These disturbances by rabbits, rabbiters, tree roots, and early archaeologists make it difficult to determine from which grave certain objects came. It is particularly disappointing that Grave 13 which probably contained among other things a wheel-made pot of Frankish affinities (pl. XXIVa) should have been so badly disturbed. If the objects attributed to it come from the grave it would seem to be the latest on the site, dating perhaps from the second half of the seventh century, but some of the objects seem much earlier than this. F. R. M. suggested that a Coptic bronze bowl (No. 9, pl. XXIVb), found somewhere at Caistor about 1860, possibly came from this grave but there is no evidence to support this.

The burials do in the main seem to represent the latest phase of Anglo-Saxon activity on the site, but there was almost certainly some overlap between the two burial practices.

The sketch plans reproduced on text-figs. 6 and 7 are based on the records F. R. M. made to clarify the layout within some of the graves.

BEADS

Grave 1 (fig. 60); Grave 7 (fig. 60); Grave 16 (fig. 62); No. 11 (fig. 63); No. 12 (fig 63).

Very few beads are recorded from the inhumation burials at Caistor. The highest number recorded from a single grave was five from Grave 1; one of these is now missing.

All the beads except one (i.e. Grave 1 A) are of glass and of these all except Grave 1 C can be matched in sixth- and seventh-century burials at, for example, Little Wilbraham, Cambs.,[1] Hadleigh Road, Ipswich,[2] Holywell Row,[3] Suff., Leighton Buzzard, Beds.,[4] Finglesham,[5] Orpington,[6] Coombe,[7] and Westbere,[8] Kent. None of the types seems to have

[1] Neville 1852, pls. 18–21.
[2] Layard 1909, pls. V, VI, and VII.
[3] Lethbridge 1931, 1–45.
[4] Hyslop 1963, 161–200.
[5] Chadwick 1959, 9, fig. 5.

[6] Tester 1968, Grave 41 and fig. 8; 1969, Grave 58 and fig. 4.
[7] Davidson and Webster 1967, fig. 5 and p. 34.
[8] Jessup 1946, 16 and pl. II.

a restricted date range. The only glass bead not matched in these Anglo-Saxon cemeteries is Grave 1 C, which has an opaque white helical spiral; the glass looks as though it has been sprinkled with gold dust. Beck, who examined the beads from Grave 1,[1] stated that it was '. . . unlike a Saxon bead and much more resembles a Roman one'. The golden sparkle is due to decomposition of the glass. Baldwin Brown drew attention to this 'nacrous lustre' when describing some segmented beads from Broadstairs, Kent.[2] It is also a well-known result of the decomposition of certain glass vessels.[3]

Beck[4] thought that the large amber bead (A) from Grave 1 was an earlier bead, possibly of Bronze Age date, which had been reused. This opinion appears to be based on the type of corrosion as well as on the form of the bead. This bead is certainly more carefully made and of a more symmetrical shape than the large majority of Anglo-Saxon amber beads. However, a number of similar beads are recorded from other Anglo-Saxon cemeteries, for instance from Little Wilbraham,[5] Hadleigh Road, Ipswich,[6] Guildown, Surrey,[7] and probably Gilton, Kent.[8] These would suggest that this amber bead is contemporary with the other beads recorded from the cemetery.

BRONZE RIVETS

Grave 7 (fig. 60); Grave 10 (fig. 61).

The two round-headed bronze rivets in Grave 10 are certainly from a shield. A piece of lime wood remains attached to one of the rivets. No certain shield boss survives, but it is possible that the piece of iron (E) is part of a boss. As neither rivet shows any trace of iron-staining they may have held the ends of a leather grip rather than have fastened a boss, if such existed, to the shield. These disc-headed studs, whether of iron, bronze, or silvered, are known from a large number of cemeteries. Miss Evison lists a number in the Holborough cemetery report[9] and others can be added such as those from Orpington[10] and Finglesham[11] in Kent.

The diamond-headed rivet from Grave 7 is not likely to have come from a shield, although such a shaped shield rivet was found at Holborough in Kent.[12] But there the rivet was of iron with a bronze-plated head and a small dome in the centre. The Caistor rivet was found in the neck region of the skeleton with some fragments of sheet bronze; a bead in the bottom of the grave indicates that this may be a woman's burial. A disc-headed rivet of unknown function was found in Grave 16 at Holywell Row, Suff., a woman's burial dated to the late sixth or early seventh century.[13]

BROOCHES

Grave 8 (fig. 60); Grave 16 (fig. 62); Grave 32 (fig. 62).

The only brooches recorded from the inhumation graves are the bronze annular brooches of the type recorded from so many East Anglian cemeteries and discussed by Leeds in 1945.[14]

[1] MS. note in N.C.M.
[2] Baldwin Brown 1914, 432–3 and pl. CIV. 1.
[3] Op. cit., 485.   [4] MS. note in N.C.M.
[5] Neville 1852, pl. 22.   [6] Layard 1909, pl. VII.
[7] Lowther 1931, pl. IX, four from Grave 85.
[8] Faussett 1856, pl. V.

[9] Evison 1956.
[10] Tester 1968, 139. fig. 6.
[11] Chadwick 1959, 29–30, figs. 13, 14 d.
[12] Evison 1956, fig. 17, Grave 8.
[13] Lethbridge 1931, 12 and fig. 6.
[14] Leeds 1945, 45–9 and 106.

Recent finds such as those from the cemetery at Little Eriswell, Suff.,[1] confirm Leeds's conclusions. Pairs of such brooches were found in Graves 16 and 32. These brooches, where found in a datable context, usually belong to the sixth century. No evidence for iron chatelaines is recorded from these graves, which strengthens the case for a sixth-century date. The single brooch from Grave 8 is discussed on p. 213: it is almost certainly an old piece that was used as part of a chatelaine.

BUCKLES

Grave 17 (fig. 62); Grave 32 (fig. 62); No. 13 (fig. 63).

The iron buckle from Grave 32 is rather nondescript but can be paralleled at Holywell Row in Graves 43 and 93. Grave 93[2] contained a male burial with spear, carinated shield boss, clips, bronze binding, and a knife. Grave 43[3] contained a woman's burial with, in addition, amber beads, a pair of annular brooches, three iron keys, an ivory ring, and a gilt object set with a garnet. Both these graves can perhaps be dated to the sixth century, Grave 43 being late in the century.

The two bronze buckles, Grave 17 B and No. 13, probably belong to the same general type although they differ in their decoration. Buckles with oval loops and more or less square chapes are found in a number of East Anglian cemeteries. Lethbridge[4] says that these buckles 'are so alike as to suggest distribution from a centre in this district'. These buckles are found at Holywell Row and Burwell[5] in contexts which indicate a late sixth- or seventh-century date. Two buckles decorated with an inverted V defined by two incised lines, were found in Graves 67 and 87 (both male burials) at Shudy Camps;[6] Lethbridge comments that the ornamentation is unusual. The buckle from Grave 17 is very close to these, particularly to that from Grave 67.

A similar seventh-century date is indicated for No. 13. This is a simpler version of an unassociated buckle from Finglesham, Kent.[7] The loop of the Caistor buckle is plain but the lower edge of the plate is decorated with a row of notches and above it is a row of rivets. Other parallels given to the Finglesham buckle are Watts Avenue, Holborough Grave 18, and Bekesbourne Grave 32, all in Kent, and Burwell, Cambs., Grave 72.

CHATELAINES

Grave 8 (fig. 60); Grave 13 (fig. 61); ?Grave 31 (fig. 62).

The remains of two linked iron rings in Graves 8 (D), 13 (D), and 31 (B) (part of one ring only survives) are almost certainly parts of chatelaines. The rings in Grave 31 were found above the chest, but the chatelaine could have been displaced at the time of burial or later; F. R. M. identified the skeleton as that of an old woman. The other objects found in Grave 8 suggest that one at least of the skeletons was female. Such chatelaines composed of iron chains are a feature of later sixth- and seventh-century graves in a number of cemeteries. Roach Smith in his introduction to *Inventorium Sepulchrale*[8] notes '. . . that in the graves of

[1] Hutchinson 1966.
[2] Lethbridge 1931, 42 and fig. 13 F. 1.
[3] Op. cit. 23 and Fig. 13A.
[4] Op. cit. 78.
[5] Ibid.
[6] Lethbridge 1936, 21, 23, and fig. 1.
[7] Chadwick 1959, 27, 39, and fig. 6 d.
[8] Faussett 1856, xxvii–xxviii.

females there is frequent mention of small iron chains, or links of small chains, decomposed, or oxidized into a mass'. They are recorded from graves at Gilton, Kingston, Sibertswold, Barfriston, Bekesbourne, and Crundale, all in Kent. Lethbridge noted their occurrence in a number of graves at both Shudy Camps[1] and Burwell,[2] Cambs.; and Grave 70 at Holywell Row, Suff., contained such a piece.[3] This latter grave Lethbridge dated to the seventh century. Such chatelaines are used by Lethbridge to link these two Cambridgeshire cemeteries with Faussett's Kentish group and are, he considers, indicative of a late date.[4]

The iron key (F) in Grave 8 is an object often found with the links of such a chatelaine in graves of the sixth and seventh centuries. They are recorded from Shudy Camps,[5] Burwell and Holywell Row,[6] Leighton Buzzard, Beds.,[7] Finglesham, Kent,[8] and at Thornham, Norf.[9] Some of these keys are 'T-shaped' while others have a single hook, but they appear to be contemporary. The bronze annular brooch (A) found in Grave 8, lay with iron objects on a level with the hips (see text-fig. 6). In Graves 76 and 83 at Burwell[10] annular brooches were found as parts of chatelaines; these graves would seem to date from the seventh century when the wearing of brooches as such was no longer fashionable.

Grave 83 at Burwell contained, as part of the chatelaine, a large, rather crudely made bronze ring which fastened with a 'hook and eye'. A similar ring occurred in Grave 16 at Chartham, Kent.[11] In Grave X at Thornham,[12] a number of beads were strung on another which was part of an iron chatelaine; also suspended from this was an escutcheon from a hanging bowl of Fowler's Group II.[13] These three, which are all parts of chatelaines, provide the best parallels for the ring (A) in Grave 13. This latter, which was described by F. R. M. as a bracelet, is over 4 in. in diameter. It is too large to be worn as a bracelet except high up on the arm of a fat person. Six small bronze rings of the expanding type were apparently strung on it, and their presence makes it unlikely that the large ring was part of a bracelet. Such small rings are found as part of chatelaines. This grave was very much disturbed, but the presence of parts of an iron chain strengthens the identification of the ring as part of a chatelaine. These elaborate chatelaines do seem to appear in the later sixth century and perhaps replace bags with ivory rings which had previously been the fashionable receptacle for small items such as knives, shears, needles, etc. (see pp. 100–3 and text-fig 3).

Another large bronze ring (B) has also been attributed to this grave. It is flat and of rectangular section, and it would be extremely uncomfortable to wear as an armlet. It has a 'hook and eye' fastening; the cross-and-pellet decoration can be matched on late Roman and early Anglo-Saxon objects of the fourth and fifth centuries. Miss Evison has drawn attention to somewhat similar objects, perhaps infants' necklaces, from Gotland;[14] there is also one from West Stow. Mrs. Hawkes in correspondence has suggested a possible Lombardic origin.

[1] Lethbridge 1936.
[2] Ibid. 1931, 47–70.
[3] Op. cit. 34.
[4] Lethbridge 1936, 27–9.
[5] Ibid., 17, 23.
[6] Ibid. 1931, number of refs. in index.
[7] Hyslop 1963, 179 and fig. 12J.
[8] Chadwick 1959, Grave D 3, p. 17.
[9] In N.C.M. unpublished. Grave XIV. Also in the grave was a buckle of the type described on p. 212.
[10] Lethbridge 1931, 61–5, figs. 32 and 33.
[11] Faussett 1856, pl. XVI. 11.
[12] N.C.M. unpublished.
[13] Fowler 1968, 307.
[14] Nerman 1935, Tafel 43, 414.

PINS

Grave 16 (fig. 62); Grave 31 (fig. 62).

The two bronze pins from the cemetery are very different. Grave 16 G is about 6½ in. long, the upper part of the shaft is quite elaborately decorated, and the round flat head is pierced for suspension; a fragment of the iron loop survives. This pin was found on the thorax of the skeleton. The other pin is much shorter and plainer; it 'was found exactly where the mouth would have been' (text-fig. 8, Grave 31 C).

Bronze pins are quite common in Anglo-Saxon burials, either singly or in pairs. The use of pairs of linked pins for fastening garments is discussed by Mrs. Hyslop in her report on the Leighton Buzzard cemeteries.[1] The pin from Grave 31 is very similar to these in form, but it is of bronze and lacks the garnet set in the head. The nearest parallel in bronze is the pin from Grave 6 at Burwell[2] which would be contemporary with those discussed by Mrs. Hyslop. This has an oval head but is otherwise very close to Grave 31 C. The Burwell pin was found on the breast of the skeleton and Lethbridge suggested it was used for securing a shroud.

The pin from Grave 16 is very close in form to a much shorter pin from Grave 42 at Harnham Hill, near Salisbury.[3] It was found on the right side of the skeleton. Also in the grave were a pair of applied saucer brooches each with a blue bead set in the centre and further decorated with a raised star.

A long pin about 6½ in. long was found at Leagrave, Beds.,[4] in a woman's burial which had two disc brooches, a gilt pendant, and a bronze pin with two (originally three) spangles (triangular pieces of bronze) attached to its head. This pin was found on the left clavicle. It was compared with pins from Kempston and Searby, Lincs. Other examples of bronze pins with a pierced head and loop for suspension were found at Driffield, Yorks. (sixth- or early seventh-century graves),[5] Broadway Hill, Worcs.,[6] Brighthampton,[7] and Great Wigston, Leics.[8] These are all much shorter than the Leagrave and Caistor pins.

POTTERY, by J. N. L. Myres

Pl. XXIVa and figs. 60–2.

Three of the inhumation burials (Graves 8, 13, 17) were accompanied by pottery. There is some doubt about the pot in Grave 8, which is recorded as lying 'outside the grave bed' and some 20 in. south of the southern skull in the grave and linked with it by a line of food bones (text-fig. 7). The pot in Grave 17 lay at the feet of the skeleton (text-fig. 8). That in Grave 13 contained a small piece of animal bone, and may thus have been used to hold some sort of meat stew at the time of the burial.

All these pots are consistent with the late date postulated for the inhumation burials at Caistor as a whole. Two of them (Graves 8, 17) are plain vessels of a kind familiar from late sixth- or seventh-century burials elsewhere. That in Grave 8 recalls the pot from Shudy

[1] Hyslop 1963, 198.
[2] Lethbridge 1936, 49 and fig. 22. 7.
[3] Akerman 1853, 263, pl. XII.
[4] British Museum 1923, 75, fig. 87.
[5] Mortimer 1905, 280, No. 19 and pl. XCIX, fig. 787; 281, No. 24 and pl. CI, fig. 807; 292, No. 11, pl. CXIII, fig. 887.
[6] Cook 1958, 70 and fig. 9. 12.
[7] Akerman 1860, 85.
[8] Smith 1852, 167, pl. XLII, 14.

Camps, Cambs., Grave 52.[1] The rather sharp-shouldered form of the pot from Grave 17 can be paralleled in some Kentish examples such as a little pot from Sittingbourne in the British Museum.

The only decorated vessel from an inhumation (Grave 13) carries five horizontal lines of rouletting similar to that commonly found on bottle vases in Kent. The upper part of the pot has fourteen slight vertical undulations, which scarcely amount to bosses of the normal Anglo-Saxon kind. This type of decoration is clearly related to the ribbed or fluted ornament which occurs frequently on pottery of the sixth and seventh centuries in Holland and Belgium as well as in the south-east of England.[2] Alike in form, fabric, and decoration this pot belongs to a late phase quite distinct from the tradition which produced the earlier cremation urns of the pagan period.

SILVER RING

Grave 8 (fig. 60).

The ring in Grave 8 is of silver and on it is strung a terracotta coloured bead. Such silver rings are well known from inhumation graves of the late sixth and early seventh centuries; these sites are listed by Mrs. Ozanne in her paper on 'The Peak Dwellers'.[3]

Rings of this kind are commonly called 'ear-rings' but they are unlikely to have been used for this purpose; the use of such rings has been discussed on p. 98 in connection with a bronze ring of this type found in urn E 14.

SPEARHEADS

Grave 3 (fig. 60); Grave 10 (fig. 61); Grave 26 (fig. 62).

All three are very corroded and it is difficult to be certain of the form, but they seem to be of the normal pagan types found in many cemeteries. That from Grave 10 was of interest in that it had a ferrule and a broad iron band which encircled the shaft near the base of the socket. This band seems to have been decorated. The spearhead from Grave 62 at Finglesham[4] was also accompanied by an iron collar, though here it seems to have gone over the split end of the socket. Such bands are unusual in English cemeteries.

WHETSTONE

Grave 10 (fig. 61).

The whetstone from Grave 10 is long and tapering and is broken at the narrower end so that the original length is not known. It is made of a fine-grained mudstone.[5]

The occurrence of whetstones in Anglo-Saxon graves was discussed by Miss Evison in 1956 in connection with such a piece from Holborough, Kent.[6] Miss Evison points out that while the majority are made from rough-textured rock a small number, among which is the Holborough find, are small and made from fine-grained rock. The Holborough whetstone, unfortunately a stray in the cemetery, is also of mudstone.

[1] Lethbridge 1936, 19 and pl. 1.
[2] See the examples given in Myres 1937a, 432–7.
[3] Ozanne 1962–3, 29.
[4] Chadwick 1959, 28 and fig. 14 b–c.
[5] Report by S. Ellis on p. 222.
[6] Evison 1956, 105–7.

Both the Holborough whetstone and one from Grave 136, Guildown, Surrey,[1] are pierced for suspension, the latter at the broad end. This is very similar to the Caistor whetstone except that this is not so pierced. Although the narrow end of the Caistor stone is broken, probably very little is actually missing. The Guildown whetstone was in a boy's grave, together with a spear and knife. Caistor Grave 10 seems to have contained only one skeleton, and the associated spear, shield, and knife suggest that this is a man's grave. The Guildown cemetery is almost certainly datable within the sixth century,[2] but the examples listed by Miss Evison indicated that these whetstones have a fairly wide date range.[3]

WRIST CLASP

Grave 10 (fig. 61).

Only the 'eye' half of a simple plate type of wrist clasp was recovered from near the grave. It is very similar to that found in urn F 4, and it may come from one of the broken-up urns found near the grave, although it is unburnt. References and parallels are given on p. 113.

DISCUSSION

These thirty-nine inhumation graves share a number of characteristics with one another and with the group of late cemeteries discussed in 1963 by Mrs. Hyslop.[4] The common features are (a) the scarcity of brooches in general and the absence of square-headed and cruciform brooches in particular, (b) the scarcity of beads, (c) the presence of small buckles with plain oval loops, (d) the relative scarcity of weapons, (e) the consistency of west-east orientation, (f) the presence of undecorated pottery vessels of more or less globular forms with tall necks and of squat, wide-mouthed vessels, (g) the high proportion of graves containing no associated objects and, it might be added, (h) the presence of iron chatelaines. The Caistor inhumations did not, however, produce some of the more sophisticated objects characteristic of these late cemeteries such as (a) linked silver or gold pins, (b) pendants, (c) thread boxes, and (d) wooden chests. Nor was there any evidence that the interments were covered by barrows. Despite these discrepancies the inhumations at Caistor seem to be closely allied to those in these late cemeteries, albeit as rather poor relations.

The iron chatelaines, the buckles, the pin from Grave 31, the bronze rings and pot from Grave 13, and the use of an annular brooch as part of a chatelaine, together with the absence of both cruciform and square-headed brooches and long strings of beads, and the comparative scarcity of grave goods, all point to the inhumations being of late sixth- or seventh-century date. Further evidence for a late date is that several of the graves disturbed earlier cremations: thus the diggers of Grave 17 apparently disturbed urns X 18, X 19, X 36, and X 37. X 36 and X 37 are both by Potter II whose products cover a long period of the sixth century and may extend into the early seventh century (see p. 62). Cremation, however, was not wholly superseded by inhumations at this time.

Some of the urns, e.g. E 7, W 30, may be as late as the early seventh century (see p. 61). Thus in the final phase of the cemetery's use cremation and inhumation were practised contemporaneously. But the latest burials are probably inhumations, and of these the latest of

[1] Lowther 1931, 1–50.
[2] Ibid.
[3] Evison 1956, 105–7.
[4] Hyslop 1963, 189–94.

all are almost certainly Grave 13, and the burial, if such it was, which contained the Coptic bowl.

HUMAN REMAINS, by Calvin Wells[1]

Grave 1

Adult. Sex uncertain.

This consists of five small fragments of cranial vault and three mandibular teeth: an M_1, M_2, and M_3. The M_1 is severely eroded on the occlusal surface; the M_2 has three roots.

Grave 2

Adult. Sex uncertain, probably male.

This consists of fragments of maxillae and mandible bearing the following teeth *in situ*:

$$R \frac{8\ 7\ 6\ ?\ ?\ ?\ ?\ ?\ |\ ?\ ?\ ?\ ?\ 5\ 6\ 7\ 8}{8\ 7\ 6\ 5\ ?\ ?\ ?\ ?\ |} L$$

The teeth are very heavily worn and there are large caries cavities on the occlusal surfaces of both maxillary M_1 teeth.

Grave 3

Adult. Sex uncertain.

This consists only of a very small fragment of the L. side of a mandible with the canine and P_1 teeth *in situ*; and two broken crowns of incisors. Erosion of the occlusal surfaces is extensive.

Grave 4

Child or young adolescent. Sex uncertain.

This consists of: one tiny facial fragment; part of a molar tooth; a small fragment of rib; and two damaged phalanges.

Grave 13

Adult. Probably male.

This consists of part of a damaged mandibular body. It carries :

$$R \frac{|}{?\ 7\ 6\ 5\ 4\ 3\ 2\ 0\ |\ 1\ 0\ 3\ 4\ 5\ 6\ 7\ 0} L$$

Dental attrition is heavy. Caries absent.

Grave 27

This consists of about ninety fragments of bone from at least three persons.

One is a young adult, probably male; another is a female about 17–18 years of age; the third is an adult about 40–55 years of age but of uncertain sex.

[1] Some of the few fragmentary human inhumations which reached N.C.M. were labelled A, D, J, K; they may have come from numbered graves (Lot A *may* correspond to Grave 37), but there is no reference to such a lettered series in F.R.M.'s notes.

Lot A, possibly from Grave 37[1]

Adult, age 40–50. Male.

This consists of about thirty cranial fragments which can be reconstructed to form most of the vault; the complete maxillae; and most of the mandible.

It is a strongly built skull with no unusual features. The following teeth survive:

$$R \; \frac{8 \; 7 \; 6 \; 5 \; 4 \; 3 \; 2 \; 1 \; | \; 1 \; 2 \; 3 \; 4 \; 5 \; 6 \; 7 \; 8}{- \; 7 \; 6 \; 5 \; 4 \; 3 \; 2 \; 1 \; | \; 1 \; 2 \; 0 \; 4 \; 5 \; 6 \; 7 \; 8} \; L$$

Dental attrition is heavy. Caries is absent. There is evidence that a periodontal abscess existed around the maxillary R. M_3.

A few tiny fragments of vertebrae also survive here.

Lot D

Adult. Male.

This consists of the R. ramus and part of the body of a heavily built mandible containing:

$$\frac{}{8 \; 7 \; 6 \; 5 \; 4 \; ? \; ? \; ?} \Big|$$

All teeth except the M_3 are heavily eroded. There is some evidence of periodontal abscess or osteitis in the region of this tooth.

Lot J

Adult. Female.

This consists of nine small fragments of cranial vault; the L. and R. petrous temporal bones; part of a L. mandibular condyle; and crowns of two maxillary molars. Little can be said about these few scraps.

Lot K

Adult. Male.

This consists of about two dozen small cranial fragments and four fragments which can be united to form much of a mandible containing:

$$R \; \frac{? \; 7 \; 6 \; 5 \; ? \; ? \; ? \; ? \; | \; ? \; ? \; 3 \; 4 \; 5 \; 6 \; 7 \; 8}{8 \; 7 \; 6 \; 5 \; 4 \; 3 \; 2 \; 0 \; |} \; L$$

Attrition of the occlusal surfaces is extensive. No caries is present.

Comments

Very little can profitably be said about these much damaged and defective remains. No unusual anomalies or anatomical features were found. The only pathology is the extensive dental attrition, two caries cavities, and some periodontal disease.

[1] See footnote, p. 217.

INVENTORY OF THE INHUMATIONS AND ASSOCIATED GRAVE GOODS

By Barbara Green

GRAVE 1 (fig. 60)

D. 21 in. (53 cm.) to flints.

Grave much disturbed. Skull fragments were found among a spread of sixteen large faced flints and pieces of Roman tile. Scattered beneath these were five beads (A, B, C) and, according to the field notes, an iron knife (D), now missing. Other fragments of human bones were found *c.* 4 ft. (1·2 m.) and *c.* 6 ft. (1·8 m.) to the west of the first find, and at depths of 12 in. (30 cm.) and 14 in. (35 cm.) respectively.

Sherds with a stamped decoration were found among the main group of flints and tiles, while at a slightly higher level F. R. M. found the base of an urn with a few fragments of burnt bone adhering to it—all that remains of a cremation urn or urns disturbed when the grave was dug (no number and sherds apparently not kept).

Grave Goods

A. Amber bead, large ring shaped. Perforation shows wear. Report by Beck:[1] 'It appears to have been originally perforated so as to be worn on a large string such as a leather thong. At a later date it has been worn on a small string which has cut the surface on both sides of the bead.'
Diam. 1·15 in. (2·9 cm.).

B. i and ii. Two glass melon beads, dark green in colour, opaque; coarse gadrooning.
Diam. i, 0·65 in. (1·65 cm.); ii, 0·625 in. (1·6 cm.). A third bead is now missing.

C. Iridescent glass barrel bead with opaque white marvered spiral trail which goes four times round the bead; large perforation.
Diam. 0·5 in. (1·25 cm.).

D. F. R. M. notes that there was a 'Saxon knife 7 ins. long', but this is not in his inventory and is now missing.

GRAVE 2

D. *c.* 2 ft. 4 in. (70 cm.) to skeletons.

Grave disturbed. One skull and lower parts of two skeletons survived; other bones were probably dug away by rabbiters. Photographs show that the legs were undisturbed. About 4 in. (10 cm.) of soil separated the two sets of leg bones, which lay one above the other. Both were apparently extended burials, on their backs with heads to the west. A few tiles, several large flints, and Anglo-Saxon potsherds were found around the bones of the upper skeleton.

Upper skeleton: adult, possibly female (F. R. M.). Pelvis, femora, and about three-quarters of the tibiae and fibulae survived.

Lower skeleton: adult, possibly male (F. R. M.). Perfect from feet to second lumbar vertebra, rest missing.

F. R. M. thought that part of a skull found west of the other bones belonged to the upper skeleton. However, Dr. Wells (see p. 217) has identified it as probably that of a middle-aged man.

An iron nail was found among flints and tiles, but this is probably Roman rubbish.

GRAVE 3 (plan, text-fig. 7; grave goods fig. 60)

D. *c.* 2 ft. (60 cm.).

Grave disturbed but outline clearly defined. Unburnt bone fragments including a light femur were found among a heap of over seventy large flints (some faced) and Roman tiles, an iron knife (B), sherds of at least five cremation urns, and fragments of burnt bones. These covered skeleton 1 of which the bones of the left leg and part of the pelvis remained. A skull, found about 3 in. (7·5 cm.) higher and about 3 ft. 6 in. (1·05 m.) to the west of the pelvis, is probably part of the same body; a lower jaw lay *c.* 1 ft. (30 cm.) to the north of the skull. An iron spearhead (A) was found near the skull. Perhaps a crouched burial with head to the west. F. R. M. thought that the bone fragments found above belonged to this burial. A second skull and lower jaw were found lying in the bend of the knee of skeleton 1.

Grave Goods

A. Iron spearhead, angular blade, split socket. Length 18 in. (46 cm.).

B. Iron knife. Length 6 in. (15·5 cm.).

[1] MS. note in N.C.M. dated 1933.

GRAVE 4

D. 24 in. (60 cm.) to bottom of grave.

Grave disturbed. Contained parts of three skeletons, the two upper lying side by side 1 ft. (30 cm.) above the third. When examining the upper skeletons F. R. M. found 'no signs of a grave' but 'a few signs of a grave were present in the case of the lower skeleton'.

Upper skeletons: Two skulls 'very small and round', both possibly female, found to west. One, lying on its left side with hand bones beneath, was probably associated with pelvis and leg bones in flexed position, indicating a crouched burial. Skull 2 was found lying on its occipital region south of skull 1 and separated from it by 1 in. (2·5 cm.) of soil. Skull 2 was probably associated with leg bones found beneath the flexed legs; probably an extended burial. Apart from a few fragments of humerus no parts of either upper skeleton survived. These two skulls overlay the legs of the lower skeleton midway between knee and ankle and were separated by one foot of soil.

Lower skeleton: Extended burial on back, head to west. Part of lower jaw, pelvis, and leg bones to *c.* 4 in. (10 cm.) above ankles survive; must have been about 5 ft. 6 in. (1·65 m.) tall. The bones were 'in the last stages of decay'.

Some bones are preserved perhaps from both upper skeletons (see p. 217). F. R. M. thought these were possibly two burials.

Two pieces of iron, probably nails, were found near the upper skulls, but association doubtful. No large flints nearby.

GRAVE 5

D. *c.* 18 in. (45 cm.) at feet. Six feet from south edge of Grave 3.

Slight traces of a grave. Skeleton on back, adult. Skull leaning over right shoulder; left arm fully flexed at elbow. Traces of right scapula, humerus, and a few vertebrae survived, also pelvis and leg bones to ankles. Extended burial.

No associated objects.

GRAVE 6

D. 27 in. (67·5 cm.); *c.* 6 ft. (1·8 m.) long × 3 ft. (90 cm.) wide.

Fragments of base of Urn K 7 touching S.W. edge of grave.

F. R. M. found no evidence that the grave was disturbed except for a rabbit burrow across its upper part. Contained five skulls 'and a large quantity of bones, probably enough for five skeletons'; the majority were much decayed. 'I got the impression that a hole had been dug, and five bodies thrown in, anyhow.' Three of the skulls were lying at the end of the grave and two more along the edge. '. . . Speaking generally the skulls had other bones over and under them. The other bones were so mixed up that it was not possible to make out the individual skeletons, but bones like tibia and fibula and ulna and radius were generally together, which points to there having been no general disturbance.'

A piece of iron, two inches long, with traces of wood or bone on it, possibly a knife, found in grave.

GRAVE 7 (fig. 60)

D. to feet 15 in. (38 cm.)

Skeleton on left side in crouching position with head to east. The bones were much decayed but most were present. In the region of the neck were several small pieces of thin bronze (B) and a stud (A). A bead (C) was found at the bottom of the grave. Base of urn Z 4 was 6 in. (15 cm.) above and 1 ft. (30 cm.) south of skull.

Grave Goods

A. Bronze stud, with diamond shaped head, undecorated, tips broken. Length 0·9 in. (2·3 cm.).
B. Three fragments of thin sheet bronze strip with a row of small punched diamonds along each side; one piece has the remains of a rivet hole. Width 0·4 in. (1 cm.).
C. Small cylindrical glass bead, dark red with marvered yellow blotches and trails. Large perforation at one end, but very small at other. Length 0·3 in. (0·8 cm.). Diam. 0·2 in. (0·5 cm.).
D. Fragment of worked bone very heavily iron-stained; possibly part of a comb. This may have come from Urn Z 4.

GRAVE 8 (plan, text-fig. 7; grave goods fig. 60)

D. to skulls 9 in (22·5 cm.), D. to feet 18 in. (45 cm.).

Two skeletons, 'one immediately on top of the other, pelvis to pelvis, with no intervening earth between them.' Heads to west. The skeletons lay on a bed of gravel raised about 3 in. (7·5 cm.) above the rest of the grave, which extended about 4 ft. further south than the gravel bed. The grave must therefore have been more than 9 ft. (2·7 m.) long (but no measurements given). 'Twenty five large flints and

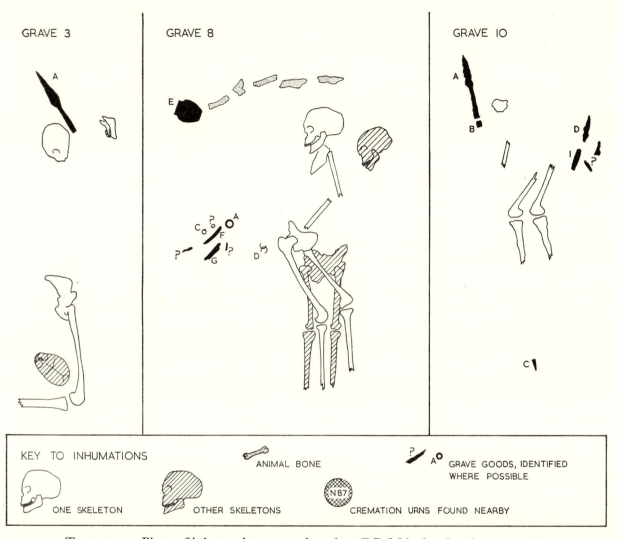

GRAVE 3   GRAVE 8   GRAVE 10

KEY TO INHUMATIONS   ANIMAL BONE   ? A○ GRAVE GOODS, IDENTIFIED WHERE POSSIBLE

ONE SKELETON   OTHER SKELETONS   N87   CREMATION URNS FOUND NEARBY

TEXT-FIG. 7. Plans of inhumation graves based on F.R.M.'s sketches (not to scale).

tiles were found about the grave, nearly all of these were over the feet in a single layer.' The lower skeleton was an extended burial on its back, the upper a crouched burial on its left side. Both skulls, which were separated by about 6 in. (15 cm.), lay on right cheeks facing south. F. R. M. thought they might have been turned over by the plough. Only fragments of the skeletons survived although the legs were in good condition.

At the west end of the grave was a line of animal bone fragments, and a pot lying on its side (E). About 1 ft. (30 cm.) south of the gravel bed on a level with the hips of the upper skeleton were scattered a number of iron and bronze objects. The remains of

two iron rings (D) were found on the edge of the gravel bed. A small iron object was found to the north of the grave. It is uncertain if this is H(i) below or was discarded.

Grave Goods

A. Bronze annular brooch, pin missing. Two concentric circles of 'bull's eye' decoration on both sides. On the front this is divided into four sections by three shallow grooves each flanked by two pairs of incised parallel lines and by the lines alone where the pin was attached. Two holes in addition to hole for pin pierced through brooch. Diam. 1·8 in. (4·6 cm.).

B. Fragments of sheet bronze, three very irregular and the fourth roughly triangular pierced by a small hole, possibly part of a work-box (see p. 112). Another small fragment of bronze embedded in the rust of F.

C. Silver 'ear-ring'; expanding wire ring from which is suspended a single reddish brown glass bead. Diam. 0·85 in. (2·15 cm.).

D. Remains of two interlocking iron rings, part of a chatelaine.

E. Tall shouldered pottery jar with upright rim; rough red/grey ware; undecorated.

F. Iron key with single hook and loop for suspension; part of iron ring from which it hung survives in hole. Fragment of bronze embedded in rust of shaft.

G. Iron knife, part of blade and tip of tang missing.

H. (i) Iron nail with large head, tip of shank missing.
   (ii) Iron hook pointed at one end and expanded at other; rectangular section.

These two items may be Roman rubbish and not grave goods.

GRAVE 9

D. to skull 20 in. (50 cm.)

Grave much disturbed by rabbits and rabbiters. Probably contained two skeletons with heads to west. One skull was found in two pieces, about 8 in. (20 cm.) apart. A second skull was found 2 ft. (60 cm.) to north. A few scattered fragments of bone lay east of the skulls. A large number of big flints were associated with the grave.

No associated objects.

GRAVE 10 (plan, text-fig. 7; grave goods fig. 61)

D. 26 in. (65 cm.)?—field notes 2 ft. 8 in. (80 cm.)

Grave much disturbed, bottom much harder than surrounding soil, apparently with clay in its composition. A very large quantity of sherds from broken-up urns and a few large flints were found in trenches about the grave. A bronze wrist-clasp (H) was found 'near broken urns and also near grave'. A few bones of one skeleton, head to west, survived; the only bones in position were lower parts of femora and

upper parts of tibiae; the legs 'appear to have been flexed at an obtuse angle'. A piece of skull vault lay 2 ft. (60 cm.) west of knees; a fragment of humerus survived. A spearhead (A) and collar (B) lay 6 in. (15 cm.) south of skull; 7 ft. (2·1 m.) east of the spear tip was an iron ferrule (C). Slightly above the level of the skeleton 'near where the skull should have been' was a bronze stud embedded in wood (F). Near the knees was an iron ring with bronze loop (G), also an iron object (not identified). A knife (D), whetstone (I), and pieces of iron (one probably E) lay near where the hips would have been. Several other iron pieces lay about the grave (possibly some not kept).

Grave Goods

A. Iron spearhead, angular blade, split socket; fragments of wooden shaft survive. Length 14·3 in. (36·7 cm.).

B. Iron collar from spear; very rusted but apparently decorated with ribbing. Diam. 0·4 in. (1·7 cm.).

C. Iron spear ferrule, cylindrical and pointed at one end. Length 3·6 in. (9·1 cm.).

D. Iron knife, tip of tang missing, very corroded. Length 5·9 in. (15 cm.).

E. Fragment of sheet iron, bent. This may be part of a shield boss.

F. Two bronze studs from a shield; one still has wood (lime, *Tilia* sp.) attached.[1] Studs have long thin shanks and flat undecorated circular heads. Diam. 0·85 in. (2·2 cm.). Length 0·7 in. (1·8 cm.).

G. Strap terminal—an iron ring with a strip bronze loop, held to strap by an iron rivet; the bronze has irregular lines of small punched circles on both sides. Diam. ring 0·9 in. (2·35 cm.). Length bronze loop 0·95 in. (2·4 cm.).

H. Sheet bronze wrist-clasp, 'eye' half only. The loop and the lower corners are broken, but traces of two rivet holes survive. Decorated with three rows of punched circles.

I. Long whetstone of rectangular section tapering more to one end than to the other. S. E. Ellis reports:[2] 'This is a very fine-grained quartz-sericite-chlorite mudstone. It contains tests of foraminifera which are indeterminable but indicate an age not older than Carboniferous. . . . It has not yet been matched. Possible sources are the Yoredale series of the Northern Pennines, in the neighbourhood of the Whin Sill (i.e. Teesdale), or the Culm Measures of Devon.

[1] We are grateful to Mr. P. W. Lambley of N.C.M. for his identification.

[2] We are grateful to Mr. Ellis of the British Museum (Natural History) for his report, dated May 1958.

GRAVE 11

D. at least 16 in (40 cm.)

F. R. M. thought that this grave might have been part of Grave 8 as '. . . only 42 inches separated the respective skeletons, and the bottom of the grave had the appearance of being continuous with the raised gravel bed on which the skeletons in Grave 8 lay'. Extended burial on back with head to west; skeleton '. . . in the last stages of decay and largely missing: the skull was in two separate pieces six inches apart. . .'.

The base of urn Z 6 was found 6 in. (15 cm.) west of the skull and several sherds, representing one or more urns, were found in the grave. F. R. M. thought that the blade of a pair of shears found in the grave came from Z 6.

No other objects recorded.

GRAVE 12 (plan, text-fig. 8)

D. up to 5 ft.

This grave lay over the northern part of Roman Pit 6 (see p. 23) 'and had partially subsided into it. . . . This grave was entirely in very hard loam which also filled the pit beneath.' The grave contained two extended burials, with heads to west, one immediately over the other. Some burnt clay from Structure B (see p. 19) was found at a level some 8 in. (20 cm.) above the skeletons. F. R. M.'s notes are confused on the relationship of the grave to the structure. 'At least 150 large flints and tiles were over and around this grave and there were fragments of many broken urns in and around it.' It is uncertain if these flints and tiles were part of Structure B or associated with the grave, as was noted elsewhere on the site. However, as it is likely that Pit 6 was dug after the destruction of Structure B the flints and tiles were more probably associated with the burial. A large decorated Anglo-Saxon sherd was found touching the jaw of the upper skeleton. It is difficult to be certain how much of the skeletons survived, although the sketches suggest that they were unusually well preserved.

A few scattered iron objects were found but they were not apparently associated and they were not kept.

GRAVE 13 (pl. XXIVa and fig. 61)

D. 3 ft. (90 cm.).

This grave had been robbed or dug out at some time. The chin part of a lower jaw was found '2 ft. S. of the grave and at about 1 ft. above its level' (see p. 217). No bones were found in the grave. The grave had a hard floor covered with a little black earth. In the black earth at the north end of the grave several bronze objects were found together. These included a decorated bronze ring (B) and another bronze ring (A) on which were strung four small bronze expanding rings. The clasp of the large ring was undone and F. R. M. thought that two other expanding rings lying close by had originally been strung on it (as shown on fig. 61). A pair of iron shears (C) and an iron knife (E) 'were found close to the grave. Among the roots of a tree which grew on the west margin of the grave was a remarkable food vessel' (F). The pot was estimated as lying about 18 in. (45 cm.) west of the grave and at a depth of 2½ ft. (75 cm.). It contained a fragment of animal bone (not kept). A large brass coin of Lucius Verus was found 'near the grave and probably belonged to it'. It is not pierced for suspension and its association with the grave must be regarded as doubtful. The grave was covered by a pile of Roman tiles and flints, and many others were scattered around; 125 in all were counted. The remains of three cremation urns were found when excavating the grave; two were in contact 3 ft. (90 cm.) east of the grave at a depth of 18 in. (45 cm.). The third was found at about the same depth and distance south-east of the grave (none were numbered nor do they seem to have been kept).

Grave Goods

A. Bronze ring of circular section, rather crudely made from wire which tapers towards the hook and the eye. This ring has a simple hook-and-eye fastening, the eye being made by bending back one end of the wire and twisting it round the main wire. From the ring hang six small bronze rings of the expanding type, very crude, some made from wire of circular section and two of rectangular section. F. R. M. identified this as a bracelet, but it is too large and is almost certainly part of a chatelaine. Diam. large ring 4·1 in. (10·5 cm.), small rings *c.* 1·3 in. (3·3 cm.).

B. Bronze ring made from a piece of bronze wire most of which has been beaten flat so that it has a rectangular section; the ends are left circular. These have been twisted to make a hook-and-eye fastening. The flat part has incised panel decoration with St. Andrew's crosses in the panels each with 'bull's-eyes' in the angles; each panel separated by groups of incised parallel lines: it was probably reused as a chatelaine. Max. diam. 3·45 in. (8·8 cm.).

C. Part of a large pair of iron shears with short arms and a flat terminal loop.

D. Parts of two interlocking iron rings, probably part of a chatelaine.

E. Iron knife, very corroded but the blade and tang both seem narrower in relation to the length than is usual; tip of tang missing. Length 4·55 in. (11·6 cm.).

F. Wheel-made bulbous pottery jar with upstanding neck and everted rim with internal bevel; rough hard light grey ware. Decorated with five widely spaced rouletted lines round the body from the base of the neck to a little below the maximum diameter. The upper part of the pot is decorated with fourteen slight vertical hollows (pl. XXIV*a*). It contained a small piece of animal bone.

GRAVE 14

D. 2 ft. 6 in. (75 cm.)

Grave cut into loam, 'almost completely destroyed by rabbits which had burrowed through it in all directions'. The only surviving bones were the upper half of the right femur and the shaft of the left femur. Head perhaps to west.

No associated objects.

GRAVE 15

D. 26 in. (65 cm.)

This grave, cut in gravel, perhaps extended west under the plantation fence, but it was not noticed when the trench outside the fence was dug.

Three skulls, 'in a very decayed condition, were arranged in a row in a N. and S. direction on a sort of rough ledge about 3 in. higher than the rest of the grave'. A pelvis, with parts of the femora in position, was found about 3 ft. (90 cm.) east of the skulls. Between the skulls and pelvis numerous fragments of leg bones were scattered irregularly; no other bones were present. Very few flints were found in the grave.

No associated objects.

GRAVE 16 (fig. 62)

D. 4 ft. (1·2 m.).

F. R. M. says this grave was not disturbed. It was cut in gravel, contained black earth and had twenty or thirty large flints above it. Extended burial with head to west, arms folded across abdominal region, skull resting on its base.

'Several broken fragments of cinerary urns about grave.'

Two annular bronze brooches (A and B) were found beneath the crossed arms, a large bronze pin (G) was found on the north side of the thorax, three beads (D) were found in the black earth; several iron objects (E, H, K, and perhaps all the other associated objects) lay to the north of the skeleton in the region of the hips. A piece of decorated bronze strip (C) and a fragment of sheet bronze (L) are shown on one of F. R. M.'s photographs of the grave goods, but neither is mentioned in either the field notes or inventory. The sheet bronze could well have come from a broken up cremation.

Grave Goods

A. Annular bronze brooch, divided into four undecorated segments by three grooves each flanked by two pairs of incised lines and the attachment groove for the iron pin (mainly missing). An impression in rust of textile (see p. 232) occurs on the underside. Diam. 1·75 in. (4·5 cm.).

B. Annular bronze brooch similar to A except that the notch for the attachment of the pin (missing) is flanked by two pairs of incised lines. Diam. 1·65 in. (4·25 cm.).

C. Bronze strip with pairs of notches alternating with pairs of horizontal incised lines; slightly curved. This seems to be unbroken; there is no indication as to how it was attached. This was not listed in F. R. M.'s notes and may not be part of the grave goods. Length 1·5 in. (3·8 cm.).

D. Three glass beads:
   (i) Yellow cylindrical bead with marvered red interlacing trails; the diameter of the perforation at one end is greater than at the other. Length 0·325 in. (0·8 cm.).
   (ii) Small green disc bead. Length 0·105 in. (0·3 cm.).
   (iii) Blue dumb-bell shaped bead; the diameter of the perforation is greater at one end than the other. Length 0·375 in. (0·95 cm.).

E. Probably a large iron knife, very rusted. The 'tang' seems to have had a circular section and to be pierced. It is possible that this is part of a leaf-shaped spearhead. (If the latter identification is correct it has been shown upside down on fig. 62.)

F. Part of an iron blade, possibly part of a knife. It seems to be thicker on one side than the other, although this may be due to rust.

G. Bronze pin with flat rounded head pierced for suspension; part of an iron link survives. The upper part of the shaft is rectangular in section and decorated with three pairs of horizontal incised lines; the rest of the shaft is circular in section. The pin is bent in the middle.

H. Piece of iron, broken, circular head with iron rivet through.

I. Three pieces of iron, two probably parts of nails.

J. Two iron nails.

K. Iron rod bent over at one end to form a loop. This might be part of an iron key.

It is uncertain how many of these iron objects are genuine grave goods; they could be Roman rubbish.

L. Fragment of sheet bronze, not listed in F. R. M.'s notes. This could have come from one of the disturbed cinerary urns.

GRAVE 17 (section, text-fig. 8; grave goods fig. 62)

D. 3 ft. (90 cm.).

This grave contained two adult extended burials, one on top of the other, with heads to the west, and perhaps a child's burial at their feet; '. . . a piece of bone probably part of a child's femur . . .' was found in some black earth at the feet of the adults, also 'a bronze bracelet, in two pieces, which was much too small for an adult [A], a small knife [?D], and a tiny bronze buckle with leather still adherent' (B).

Of the upper skeleton only the skull and two or three pieces of the tibiae remained. Three inches of soil separated the skull of this burial from that of the lower skeleton. The latter was 'fairly well represented up to the pelvis; above this nothing remained of it but the skull'.

An empty food vessel (I) was found on its side at a depth of 30 in. (75 cm.) between the possible child's burial and where the feet of the adults should have been. 'In the adult part of the grave several iron objects were found, including a knife [?E]. There were also 2 roman coins, a 2nd Brass of Commodus and a 2nd Brass of Trajan' (K).

'There were vast quantities of broken up urns about the grave. Two urns with burnt bones in them were actually in the grave itself. One of these was X 26 [p. 194, found on the south side of the grave at 18 in. (45 cm.) deep] . . . containing the burnt bones of an infant. This pot was so small that rabbits could easily have pushed [it] into the grave.' The number of the other urn is not given; it may have been X 27 (p. 194) or an urn which was not numbered or kept.

Grave goods

A. Bronze bracelet made from undecorated bronze strip; the ends overlap slightly. F. R. M.

thought it was a child's bracelet. Diam. 1·9 in. (4·85 cm.).

B. Bronze buckle, kidney shaped with bronze tongue; attached to it is a broken buckle-plate of sheet bronze through which is a dome-headed rivet and which is decorated on the front with an inverted V defined by two parallel incised lines. Width of buckle 0·7 in. (1·8 cm.). No leather now survives.

C. Curved piece of iron, fragmentary and corroded.

D. Iron knife with sharply angled blade and long tang, tip of which is missing. Length 5·1 in. (12·95 cm.).

E. Iron knife similar to D, but tip of blade and tip of tang missing; tang shorter and broader than that of D. Length 4·7 ins. (11·9 cm.).

F. Fragment of iron.

G. Curved bronze strip, broken at both ends, of rectangular section.

H. Curved piece of iron, broader at one end than the other, possibly a bent nail of which most of the head is missing.

I. Wide-mouthed pot with sharply carinated shoulder and short slightly everted rim: smooth dark brown burnished ware. Undecorated.

J. Fragment of fused bronze—almost certainly this came from one of the broken urns.

K. Two Roman bronze coins:

(i) Sestertius of Trajan, very worn, identified as *R.I.C.* 519.

(ii) Sestertius of Commodus, *R.I.C.* 608.

Both are probably stray Roman objects and not true grave goods; the pieces of iron (C, F, H) and bronze fragment (G) are perhaps in the same category.

GRAVE 18

D. 26 in. (65 cm.).

A single burial which was probably lying on its back with head to the west. Only the shafts of the femora, part of the pelvis and some bones of the left hand survived.

No associated objects.

GRAVE 19

D. 28 in (70 cm.).

A single crouched burial with head to the west. 'Bones very soft and largely missing'. The skull was damaged and displaced. 'Fragment of urn' is shown on sketch plan near the surviving humerus shaft, presumably from a disturbed cremation.

No associated objects.

GRAVE 20

D. to top of bones 18 in. (45 cm.).

Extended burial on its back with head to the south-west. The skull was missing and F. R. M. thought that it had been destroyed by rabbits as he found a large rabbit hole at the south-west end of the grave. 'The bones of the left forearm lay across thorax, leg and foot bones unusually perfect.' Distance from head of femur to ankle was 33½ in. (83·7 cm.).

Urn M 21 was found 'separated from the left ankle joint by 4 in.'

No associated objects.

GRAVE 21

D. 28 in. (70 cm.).

A single skeleton was found lying face downward with feet to the east. The skull was lying on its right cheek facing south-east with the occiput in contact with the head of the left femur. The bones were better preserved than usual and the foot bones were present.

No associated objects found.

A food vessel was found 'near Grave 21' and a glass bead about 1 ft. (30 cm.) south of the grave and 3 in. (7·5 cm.) below the level of the bottom of the grave (see fig. 63, nos. 12 and 14 and p. 230).

GRAVE 22

D. 28 in. (70 cm.).

'This grave was found beneath the roots of a tree. The roots had caused so much disturbance of the bones that it was not possible to make much of it. The skull lay to the east of the tree and the leg bones to the west. . . . A great number of broken up urns found around this Grave.'

No associated objects.

GRAVE 23

D. 28 in. (70 cm.)

The grave cut through Structure G (p. 21). A single extended burial, face downward, with head to west. The skull was found lying on its left cheek. The skull, the shafts of a radius and ulna, the pelvis, and leg bones survived. The pelvis was slightly deeper than the skull or feet.

No associated objects.

GRAVE 24

D. 30 in. (75 cm.).

The grave cut through the south end of Structure G (see p. 21). 'Practically nothing left of this skeleton except the skull and larger leg bones. Skull lying on its left side facing north. . . .' Crouched burial, on left side with head to west.

No associated objects.

GRAVE 25 (plan, text-fig. 8; grave goods fig. 62)

D. 30 in. (75 cm.).

The grave contained two skeletons with heads to west, lying more or less side by side. The northern skeleton lay partly on its right side with its skull resting on its occipital region with the chin pointing north-east. No ribs or vertebrae survived. Two iron nails (A and ?B) were found near the skull. The southern skeleton lay partly on its left side with its skull lying on its left cheek. Two iron objects were found with this skeleton, one lying in the upper thoracic region, a 'butt end of spear' (apparently missing), and the other in the pelvic region (probably C). A flint scraper (not preserved) was found in the grave 'at level of bones'.

Grave goods

A. Head and part of shank of an iron nail or stud. It is very rusted but the nail seems to have a smaller and more dome-shaped head than the usual type found on the site.
B. Fragment of iron, square section.
C. Fragment of very rusty iron.

GRAVE 26 (fig. 62)

D. at pelvis of upper skeleton 30 in. (75 cm.).

'This grave contained two skeletons, partly super-imposed, only the lower part of the under skeleton could be exposed as the rest lay under the roots of a tree.' The sketch plan shows that the upper skeleton, of an extended burial, lay at an angle across the tibiae of the lower and with head to the west. The pelvis of the upper skeleton was deeper than the skull or tibiae. The upper part of the body was missing; the skull was lying on its right cheek. 'More than a foot of earth separated the skull of the top skeleton from the legs of the lower skeleton.'

A small spearhead (A) was found upright 2 ft. (60 cm.) south of the pelvis at grave level.

Grave goods

A. Iron spearhead, very corroded so that blade shape cannot be determined with certainty; split socket. Length 8·1 in. (20·8 cm.).

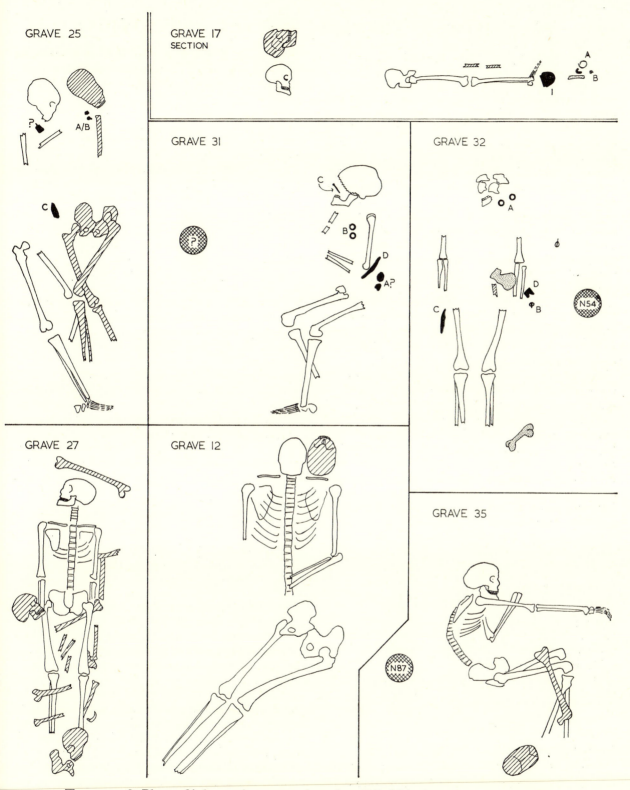

TEXT-FIG. 8. Plans of inhumation graves based on F.R.M.'s sketches (not to scale).
For key, see text-fig. 7, p. 221.

GRAVE 27 (plan, text-fig. 8)

D. of grave 28 in. (70 cm.).

The grave had been cut through the northern end of Structure C (p. 20).

The grave contained at least four skeletons, 'Two of which could be made out without difficulty' (the two lower).

The lowest skeleton was a crouched burial, with right hand beneath skull which was 'much broken up' and looking north; the rest of the skeleton was 'mainly there'. Immediately above this was an extended skeleton, on its back, with head to the west and arms by its sides. The pelvis of this skeleton 'lay immediately over, and touching, the bent knees of the lower skeleton'. To the south of the upper skeleton lay a skull on its left cheek with the teeth touching the right side of the pelvis. Another skull, looking south-east, lay over the foot of the upper skeleton. Over the two skeletons were numerous bones presumably belonging to the two skulls. It is difficult to reconcile F. R. M.'s description with his sketch plan of Grave 27.

A piece of animal bone was found beneath the right clavicle of the upper skeleton, while sherds of one or more urns were found beneath the skull.

The two more or less complete skeletons could represent a later burial disturbing an earlier one. However, as no stray human bones are recorded in the lower part of the grave, it seems quite likely that the two upper skeletons were disturbed by ploughing and were perhaps contemporary with the two lower burials.

No associated objects.

GRAVE 28

D. of grave 10 in. (25 cm.).

'How this grave escaped being ploughed out is a mystery.' It contained a single skeleton lying on its back with head to west. 'Fairly complete, but in the last stages of decay.'

No associated objects.

'This is the only grave in the north part of the cemetery.'

GRAVE 29

D. 28 in. (70 cm.).

Disturbed by rabbit burrow. It contained the remains of a single extended burial with head to west; practically all that remained were skull and leg bones.

No associated objects. A small Roman bronze coin was found in grave '. . . Gloria Exercitus, but it probably had no connection with it.'

GRAVE 30

D. 36 in. (90 cm.).

Grave cut into the north-west corner of Structure M (p. 22) and was 3 ft. (90 cm.) south of N 1 group.

'Remains of a skeleton lying on a very hard gravel infiltrated with clay, about a hundred large flints and tiles were over and around the grave, and also numerous pieces of wattle and daub and wall plaster. It is doubtful whether the flints are really connected with the grave as similar conditions extended fanwise from the grave eastward for several yards as far as the last trench, and presumably extended further'.

'Skull lying on Vertex. Sutures completely closed. . . Presumably skeleton of an old man.'

Two iron objects were found near the skull and a third near the lower end of the right femur. One of these was probably a nail, the other was unidentifiable. Their association with the burial must be considered doubtful as they could well have come from Structure M. A large lump of wall plaster (not preserved) was found between the femora.

Two sherds of urn N 7 were found in the grave, one in contact with the left tibia. Both sherds could be joined to the rest of N 7 which, with N 5, was 'found dumped 3½ ft. S.W. of this grave at depth 21 in.'

GRAVE 31 (plan, text-fig. 8; grave goods fig. 62)

D. about 30 in. (75 cm.).

Skeleton lying on sand, 'Presumably lying on right side with right hand beneath skull, but no trace of this hand could be found. The right side of the skull had completely gone and probably the hand also. . . . The few teeth and stumps remaining were badly decayed. . . . Probably the skeleton of an old woman.'

A bronze pin (C) 'was found exactly where the mouth would have been'. Two iron rings were found above the chest at a slightly higher level; part of one ring survives (B). An iron knife (D) lay near the left elbow, near to two pieces of iron which joined (A).

The base of an urn containing burnt bones (no number, not kept) was found, at a depth of 24 in. (60 cm.), 3 ft. (90 cm.) to the north of the skeleton.

Grave goods

A. Two joining pieces of rusty iron.
B. A curved piece of iron, apparently of circular section; it is possibly part of an iron ring, perhaps part of a chatelaine.
C. Bronze pin with flat circular head with a loop set at right angles; an expanding ring of very thin bronze wire is attached. The shaft is circular in section and has three horizontal grooves immediately below the head. Length 2·5 in. (6·4 cm.).
D. An iron knife, tip of blade and tip of tang missing.

GRAVE 32 (plan, text-fig. 8; grave goods fig. 62)

D. 3 ft. 2 in. (95 cm.).

The grave cut into the fill of Roman Pit 1 (see p. 22). An extended burial on its back with head to the west; little was left of the skeleton.

Near the remains of the skull were two bronze brooches (A); a knife (C) was found beside the right femur, while a buckle (B) and an iron object (D) lay beside the left lower arm. Animal bones, Roman potsherds, and an enamelled fly brooch (pp. 26–7, fig. 63, 2) were found in the black earth filling of the pit; the brooch was about 1 ft. (30 cm.) from the skeleton. F. R. M. thought that these pieces were from Roman levels and had been disturbed by the cutting of the grave; it is possible that the iron object (D) also belongs to this category.

About 1 ft. (30 cm.) to the north of the skeleton a complete cremation urn (N 54) containing burnt bones was found. 'It seems likely that this urn was found when the grave was dug, and reburied at the side of the grave. The whole grave (urn included) was under a pile of larger flints, 170 were counted and fragments of two urns found among them' (not numbered, apparently not kept).

Grave goods

A. (i) and (ii). Pair of bronze annular brooches each decorated with three pairs of incised parallel lines which, with the pin, divide the brooches up into four unequal plain segments. Part of the pin of (i) survives. Diam. (i) 1·75 in. (4·5 cm.), (ii) 1·7 in. (4·3 cm.). For textile, see p. 232.
B. Kidney-shaped iron buckle with iron tongue. Length 1·125 in. (2·85 cm.).
C. Iron knife. Length 5·25 in. (13·3 cm.).
D. Rectangular piece of iron; it is uncertain if the irregular curve of one side is the result of a break or was part of the design.

GRAVE 33

D. 26 in. (65 cm.).

This grave contained portions of two skeletons. 'The bones crumbled at a touch.' Skulls, leg bones, and part of one pelvis survived. 'The legs of one skeleton were flexed at the knee and lay between the extended leg bones of the other skeleton. The flexed legs appeared to belong to the skull at the west end of the grave and were considerably smaller than the extended leg bones.' Another skull lay to the east of the leg bones near the upper ends of the femora of the extended legs, while a lower jaw lay between the tibiae of this skeleton.

No associated objects.

GRAVE 34 (fig. 62)

D. 31 in. (77 cm.).

Extended single burial, on its back, with head to west; arms straight down by sides. Skull, arm bones, pelvis, and leg bones survived. An iron knife (B) lay with tip just above the head of the left femur, while 'in about the centre of the skeleton was a small bronze object' (A).

Many fragments of an urn were found in the grave fill but apparently discarded.

Grave goods

A. Strip of bronze, oval section, flattened and rounded at one end, broken at the other.
B. Iron knife. Tip of tang and part of blade missing.

GRAVE 35 (plan, text-fig. 8)

D. 36 in. (90 cm.).

'The grave contained two skeletons probably belonging to men in the prime of life. The upper skeleton, judging from the length of the femurs, must have belonged to an unusually tall man. The position of the two skeletons gave the impression of having been flung in anyhow.' The bones of the lower skeleton 'appeared to have been scattered by some sort of disturbance. The skull and most of the bones lay 6 in. deeper than those of the upper skeleton [a crouched burial], but the right femur of the lower lay, detached, across the knees of the upper'. Perhaps this represents an earlier burial disturbed by a later.

Urn N 87 was found on the south side of the grave, 2 ft. (60 cm.) from the nearest bone. About half the urn was missing, presumably cut away when the grave was dug. Some sherds found in the grave fill could not be fitted on to N 87.

No associated objects.

GRAVE 36

D. 41 in. (1·03 m.).

'An exceptionally narrow grave' which had been cut through Structure H (p. 21).

A single extended burial, head to north-west and turned onto right side; lower arms crossed just above pelvis. Probably a male; length of skeleton 5 ft. 11 in. (1·78 m.). Skull sutures not closed. 'An unusually well preserved skeleton except for the skull and feet.'

Broken-up urns were found in the grave fill (perhaps W 5(a) and (b), and W 6), and four urns (N 88, 89, 90, and 91) were found standing in a line at the foot of the grave separated from each other by an inch or two: possibly reburied by grave diggers.

The orientation of the grave, its relation to Structure H, and the relationship of the urns to the grave as shown in a sketch in the inventory are not as shown on F. R. M.'s cemetery plan.

No associated objects.

GRAVE 37

D. 38 in. (95 cm.).

'This grave . . . was merely a hole in the ground. The upper parts of the skeleton were under many bones of the ox and pig, so it was dug out before it was recognised as human.' The legs were recognized and were lying extended with feet to the north-east. The skull and lower jaw were lying, the skull on its right cheek, on the west side of the knees. 'The head must have been cut off to get in the position it was found in. There was a fracture of the lower jaw that looked antemortem.' F. R. M. considered the bones those of a large muscular young man.

The animal bones (not kept) were the only objects associated with the burial.

GRAVES 38 AND 39

No details are known of these two graves other than their positions.

STRAY FINDS FROM INHUMATION BURIALS (fig. 63, 10–14)

10. Iron knife with long sharply angled blade. Length 6·25 in. (16·1 cm.).

11. Long heptahedral green glass bead with large perforation, roughly same diameter right through. Length 0·35 in. (0·9 cm.). Found near urn F 3.

12. Large glass ring bead, opaque white with dark blue marvered trail. Large central perforation. Diam. 0·55 in. (1·4 cm.). Found about 1 ft. (30 cm.) south of Grave 21 and about 3 in. (7·5 cm.) below the bottom of the grave.

13. Oval bronze buckle, with bronze tongue and remains of rectangular bronze buckle plate. A row of close-set dome-headed rivets runs parallel with lower edge of plate, which is decorated with a row of short vertical grooves. Length of buckle 1 in. (2·5 cm.).

14. Barrel-shaped pottery beaker with straight upright rim: rough black burnished ware. Undecorated. There is a small hole in the lower part of the side. Found near Grave 21.

THE COPTIC BOWL (pl. XXIVb and fig. 63, 9)

Cone-shaped bronze bowl, rim thickened to a triangular section with a flattened top and vertical external facet. Open-work foot with thickened base, and with row of upright and inverted triangles, rather roughly and crudely cut out. A small right-angled triangle fills a large gap resulting from the inaccurate spacing of the other triangles. Two opposing pairs of loops just below the rim for handles which are missing. Parts of rim and foot are missing. Max. diam. 11 in. (28 cm.). Height 3·5 in. (8·8 cm.).

Found *c.* 1860 at Caistor.[1] R. A. Smith[2] thought that it probably came from a field just north of the Roman town, but the reason for this is not stated. No burials are recorded from this field. It is perhaps more reasonable to suggest that it came from one of the inhumation burials at Caistor whose existence was not known at this date; Grave 13 at least seems to be of seventh-century date which would suit this bowl.

In Britain the majority of these bowls are found in the Kentish cemeteries.[3] However, three others are recorded from East Anglia, all from Suffolk, and all old finds.[4] One was found 6 ft. deep at Wickham Market,[5] another at Chilton Hall, Sudbury,[6] and a third, which was accompanied by a hanging bowl, from Needham Market or Badley.[7]

These bowls must have reached Britain by trade from the Mediterranean in the later sixth and seventh centuries.[8]

[1] Exhibited by Robert Fitch at the Society of Antiquaries, 8 March 1860. *Proc. Soc. Antiq.* i (1859–61), 106. Presented to N.C.M. 1894, acc. no. 76.94(386).

[2] *V.C.H. Norfolk*, i (1901) 334.

[3] Conway 1917–18, 81–3; Åberg 1926, 102–3, 207–8; British Museum 1923, 76–7.

[4] The Coptic bowl from the great ship burial at Sutton Hoo, Suffolk, is of a rather different type (Bruce-Mitford 1972, pl. B).

[5] Whitwell 1918, 179–80 and plate.

[6] Leeds 1936, pl. XVI C.

[7] Smith 1907–9, 69–70; Fowler 1968, 307.

[8] Leeds 1936, 35.

TEXTILE REMAINS

By B. Chambers

TWO of the graves yielded bronze ring brooches with fragments of textile remaining on them: one in Grave 16 and two in Grave 32. In each case the textile was under the iron pin, which had distorted the fabric it pierced, and the fibres were completely mineralized by the oxidation of the iron. The brooch from Grave 16 also showed a narrow strip of fabric on the under-side with a fairly clear weave pattern. The only other certain textile remains were on three fragments of iron shears and tweezers from D 8, and these fibres, too, were completely mineralized. A few tiny fragments from M 42 were at first thought to be textile fibres, but could not be identified as such.

Grave 16

Material: a vegetable fibre, probably linen.
Spinning: both systems Z-spun, fairly tightly.
Weave: 2 × 2 twill; count 45–50 × 40.

One side of the fragment on the under side appears to be a selvedge, and assuming this to be the side of the piece of fabric rather than the beginning or end, the higher count is that of the warp threads. Most of the weft threads have been displaced so that they are not at right angles to the warps, probably due to the pull of the brooch pin on the fabric when fastened.

Grave 32

(*a*) Brooch without pin—part of the hinge end of the iron pin remains, showing a few threads in an apparent chevron pattern, probably part of a twill cloth, but it was not possible to identify the fibres or weave.

(*b*) Brooch with broken pin—a small fragment of textile remains beside the hinge, and a mass in the space between pin, hinge, and underside of brooch, folded in such a way as to suggest that fabric was pleated under the pin against the back of the brooch.

Material: probably linen.
Spinning: one system Z-spun, the other S. Only a few threads were of sufficient length to show the direction of spinning.
Weave: 2 × 2 twill: the areas where the weave pattern was visible were too small to make a count with any certainty, but the threads and weave both appeared similar to those on the brooch from Grave 16.

Cremation D 8

Material: probably linen.
Spinning: both systems Z-spun, fairly tightly twisted.
Weave: 2 × 2 twill; count 24 × 20.

Each of the three fragments of metal (B and C) bore fragments of mineralized cloth, which appeared to be from the same piece of fabric.

The cloths described here are all of types commonly found on Saxon sites, for example at Laceby, Lincs., Mildenhall, Suff., Icklingham, Suff., and Finglesham, Kent. Those attached to brooch pins no doubt formed part of cloaks or tunics, and are quite finely woven, while the coarser one found on the shears and tweezers may have formed part of a bag, in which they were carried, or of a heavy outer garment.

IV

THE MARKSHALL CEMETERY

INTRODUCTION

By Barbara Green

THIS cemetery, which lies on White's Hill on the west side of the river Tas and some 300 yards from the north-west corner of the walled area of *Venta Icenorum*, was discovered in 1815. In that year four of the urns were exhibited at the Society of Antiquaries and subsequently published in *Archaeologia*.[1] Many urns were found while preparing the ground for planting trees. Further discoveries were followed by the excavation of 120 square yards in 1822 by Charles Layton.[2] He found remains of urns '. . . so near the surface that most of them had been broken by the plough . . . they were arranged in regular rows in the quincunx order, and distant about six feet one from another. . . . In making this excavation I discovered the bottom of a kiln or Furnace,[3] with some urns actually in it, as they were placed for burning. . . .' A few other finds are reported later in the nineteenth century, but no further archaeological excavation is recorded until 1948 when G. P. Larwood under the auspices of the Norfolk Research Committee[4] carried out trial excavations to see if any portion of the cemetery had survived earlier investigations. Work had just been resumed on the Caistor cemetery report and it was felt that a comparison between the Caistor and Markshall material could be of great value. Sufficient material was recovered for further work to be carried out in 1949.

The results obtained indicated that the total area of the cemetery had been about 70 ft. (21 m.) east to west by 40 ft. (12 m.) north to south. The general depth of the soil was about 2 ft. 6 in (75 cm.) and urn potsherds were scattered throughout this depth. Only four urns, (I, II, III, and IV) were found in anything approaching a complete state; one or two urns later proved to be reconstructable. The base of urn II rested at about 2 ft. (60 cm.) and that of urn IV at 2 ft. 7 in. (78 cm.) from the modern surface. The fragmentary condition of the other urns can be attributed to the nineteenth-century excavators and to ploughing.

The remains of over a hundred urns were recovered during these excavations. Only five of those found during the nineteenth century are known to survive, one in the Ashmolean Museum, Oxford[5] (urn X, fig. 65) and four in N.C.M.[6] The 1948–9 excavators recovered

---

[1] *Arch.* xviii (1817), 436–7 and pl. XXVII.

[2] *Arch.* xxii (1829), 412–14. Letter 12 May 1822.

[3] A Roman pottery kiln, ibid., pl. XXXVI; no identifiable vessels survive.

[4] Thanks are due to Mr. J. Skinner and Mr. G. Daniels for permission to excavate. The finds from these two seasons were presented to N.C.M., accession numbers 203.948 and 51.949.

[5] No. 1885.604.

[6] 50.25 (urn IX, fig. 16), 65.47a (urn VIII, fig. 71), 65.47b (urn VII, fig. 71) and 65.47c (urn VI, fig. 70).

cremated bones from eight urns (see p. 245) and associated objects with four only (urns I, III, IV, and V). Urn IX, presented to Norwich Museum in 1825, has been illustrated (fig. 16) as containing a collection of grave goods, including a knob from an early cruciform brooch and, most surprisingly, a fragment of amber. A careful study of the early records indicates that the only certain association is with a single pair of bronze tweezers, either the pair illustrated on fig. 16 or another pair[1] (see p. 248): the other objects may have come from other burials found at this time. Dr. Wells has identified the remains of at least three individuals amongst the cremated bones apparently associated with urn IX (see p. 246), which may be taken as further evidence for the amalgamation of several burials.

There are no records of any inhumation burials being found on White's Hill. The fragment of amber mentioned above is unlikely to be from a cremation, and a 'glass goblet' mentioned by Layton has been taken as 'pretty certain proof of an inhumation in that cemetery'.[2] But this could as well have come from a cremation urn as from an inhumation burial. In the Squire MSS.[3] is a sketch of a bronze 'ewer' found in 1813, supposedly in an urn. Squire's drawings are crude and give no idea of size. The vessel is taller than it is broad and wider at the base than the top. The bottom is rounded and it is supported on three small curved feet. It has two simple curved handles. It is an anomalous piece whether from a cremation or an inhumation.

[1] N.C.M. 27.26; N.C.M. 1909, no. 459.   [2] Myres 1942, 332 f.   [3] In N.C.M., 47.97.

GENERAL NOTE ON THE POTTERY

By J. N. L. Myres

AS is apparent from the circumstances in which it was recovered, the pottery from the Markshall cemetery is preserved with far less completeness and coherence than that from Caistor. It represents the debris of several hundred urns of which less than a dozen are complete, or survive in sufficient fragments to permit the reconstruction of a complete profile. About a hundred items in all seemed to justify individual illustration and description, and of most of these there only remain pieces too small to allow either the shape or the scheme of decoration to be fully ascertained. Yet the cemetery may well have contained as much material as that of Caistor, from which four or five times as many urns, mostly more or less complete, are available for comparison.

In these circumstances it would clearly be unwise to base any firm conclusions upon apparent similarities or contrasts between the surviving pottery of these neighbouring cemeteries. It is only possible to note the facts that emerge from a comparison of the two groups as they here present themselves, without placing any undue emphasis upon differences which may well be the result of pure chance. Such apparent differences are indeed remarkable and must be noted, but whether they are historically significant must remain open to doubt.

It can, however, be stated at once that the two cemeteries are roughly contemporary. Markshall, like Caistor, was certainly in use from the later part of the fourth century until at least the end of the sixth. The presence of a few pieces of Ipswich ware (XXIX–XXXI, fig. 58) may suggest indeed that it lasted well into the seventh century, but it is not known whether these pieces came from graves or had been left casually on the site after its disuse. Of its earliest days there are no examples, as there are at Caistor (p. 54), of pots illustrating the transition from Roman to barbarian methods of manufacture, nor do there seem to be any notable examples of the early Anglian corrugated technique which form such a distinctive element among the Caistor urns, though LXIII (fig. 70) approaches that style. Perhaps the earliest piece is XCVI (fig. 65), which appears to be the pedestal foot from a carinated bowl of a type exceedingly rare in this country[1] but common in the late fourth- and early fifth-century pottery on both sides of the lower Elbe and the adjacent parts of East Holstein and the Saxon lands westward to the Weser. This piece provides the clue to the continental origins of the first users of the Markshall cemetery, for the surviving pottery is remarkable for the high proportion of vessels it includes which are strikingly similar to those in vogue in the Saxon homelands in the generations before and after 400. While such pieces are not unknown at Caistor—see the discussion (p. 48) of R 12 and related examples on fig. 16— parts of early urns of this character form a larger proportion among the Markshall collection than they do in the much greater quantity of pottery from Caistor. The connections are

[1] The only complete one comes from Mitcham Gr. 205 (Bidder and Morris 1959, pl. XIX); fragments are known from Ham (Surrey), Dorchester (Oxon.), and the settle- ment sites of Sutton Courtenay (Berks.), Mucking (Essex), and West Stow Heath (Suffolk). The type is discussed in *Ant. J.* xlviii (1968) 224–6 and Myres 1969, 77–80.

particularly close with such Saxon cemeteries in the Elbe/Weser area as Wehden, Mahndorf, Altenwalde, Gudendorf, and Westerwanna.[1]

Among the earliest vessels of this kind at Markshall should probably be counted XXI and XXXVIII (fig. 65) both unstamped examples of the 'Cuxhaven/Galgenberg Typ' of Tischler,[2] with their characteristic round-bellied or round-shouldered forms and decoration of standing arches (stehende Bogen), deep grooves, and finger-tips. With them goes XXIV (fig. 65) with massed line-and-groove ornament and continuous interlocking S curves that recall the 'running wyrm' design of Caistor N 69 (fig. 1). LXII (fig. 67) is very similar indeed to Borgstedt 156, a fine example of Genrich's Nordseekustengruppe, dated by its contents to the later part of the fourth century.[3] Not much later may be the stamped examples XIII, XXV, and LXXXIII (fig. 65) of which XXV retains the early feature of finger-tipped rosettes between the arches and, along with XIX and LXXXIX (fig. 70), is probably from the same workshop (Potter VIII) that produced Caistor N 54, P 44 (fig. 56). LXXXIII has an unusual type of stamp, reminiscent of the Roman planta pedis. Another stamp of this form was used by a potter who worked for the early cemeteries at Castle Acre, Rushford, and North Elmham. Stamps of this kind are also found on continental urns from Altenwalde, Westerwanna, Mahndorf, Brinkum, and the Galgenberg near Cuxhaven,[4] but they are very rare indeed in this country. There is a similar correspondence between the Markshall vessels with other types of linear and groove-and-dot designs, most of which are on figs. 66 and 67, and the same group of continental Saxon cemeteries, a correspondence which would certainly be more obvious if more of the Markshall pieces were sufficiently well preserved to show the complete form and decorative scheme of the pots.[5]

More remarkable still are the parallels between the earlier Buckelurnen, which succeed to, and no doubt overlap in date with, the unbossed types hitherto under consideration. The interesting case of Markshall IX (fig. 16) has been discussed above (p. 48). The earliest types of Buckelurnen are comparatively ill-represented at Caistor, where most of the examples (fig. 17) are not markedly continental in character. But at Markshall parts of nearly a dozen survive, in addition to Markshall IX, and they include several which can be very closely matched abroad. Of these by far the most remarkable is LXX (pl. X) of which unfortunately only fragments remain. But they are enough to show not only that it is the only known English example on which some of the bosses take the form of a human face, but that the whole scheme of decoration, and especially the treatment of the face, is so closely similar to the well-known face-urn 58 from Wehden (pl. XI), itself unique in the German cemeteries, as to suggest most strongly a common origin. The two are placed side by side on fig. 68. It is indeed difficult not to believe that these two urns are the work of the same potter. But

[1] Cp., e.g., XXXVIII with Wehden 204 and 538, and with Westerwanna 1272 and 1277c, XXI with Altenwalde 17 and 116, Wehden 112, Galgenberg Tafel 24.6, and with Westerwanna 1390 and 1448: XXV with Westerwanna 1095. (Waller 1938, 1957, and 1961, Zimmer-Linnfeld et al. 1960).

[2] Tischler 1954b, 48 and Abb. 8: see further p. 47 above.

[3] Genrich 1954, 31 and Tafel 8 F.

[4] e.g. Waller 1957, Altenwalde 149; Zimmer-Linnfeld et al. 1961, Westerwanna 998 (fragments only), and the elaborately stamped Galgenberg urn (Waller 1938, Abb.

13): see also the examples from Mahndorf and Brinkum in Grohne 1953, 92, Abb. 30B.

[5] Cp., e.g., LXII with Wehden 504 and Westerwanna 763: XLIV with Wehden 120, 205, and Westerwanna 475: LXVII with Altenwalde 57: XV with Wehden 707: L with Westerwanna 755: XL with Westerwanna 10, 16, 83, 826, 1424: LXVI with Westerwanna 199, 1296, Wehden 696, Altenwalde 2, Quelkhorn 87, and many others: LXXXVIII with Westerwanna 1, 6, and Altenwalde 56. (Waller 1957, 1959, and 1961: Zimmer-Linnfeld et al. 1960).

whether this means that Markshall LXX is a direct import from the Wehden area, or that Wehden 58 is a direct export from Markshall, or that the craftsman emigrated from Wehden to Markshall and continued his professional work in his new home, cannot of course be determined. It may or may not be significant that Markshall LXX is not only rather larger than Wehden 58 but seems to show a more confident and careful handling of the facial details, especially of the eyes and mouth, which might indicate a somewhat greater maturity. Whatever the relationship of these two very stylish urns may be, they provide, like the similar correspondence between Caistor B 2 and its Anglian counterparts from Hammoor and Süderbrarup (see pls. VIII and IX and p. 47), a personal link of the most intimate kind with the actual process of migration across the North Sea. It is of some interest that in each case the date must be around the middle of the fifth century, the traditional period of the *Adventus Saxonum in Britanniam*, the mass movement of invasion which finally overwhelmed the sub-Roman regimes of eastern Britain. It would seem that in Norfolk at any rate some distinct elements both of pure Angle and of pure Saxon cultural antecedents played a part in the process side by side.

Another unusual *Buckelurne* of continental type is LXXXIV (fig. 69). This too survives only in shattered fragments whose arrangement is uncertain, but it was evidently of the sharply biconical form. The elaborately decorated panels of the upper half, which are so flat that they were at first mistaken for parts of a dish or tray, were apparently made separately and subsequently luted together with the help of vertical slashed strips, the whole being then fitted on to the lower half along the carination. No close parallel to this technique has so far been noted,[1] nor is the general design easy to match in this country. But a very similar style of decoration does occur on biconical *Buckelurnen* in some continental Saxon cemeteries as at Gudendorf or Mahndorf.[2] In the latter case the urn was associated with an equal-armed brooch of the fifth century. More normal perhaps but still markedly continental in character is XLIII (fig. 65), which must be part of an urn very similar to Westerwanna 796.

Markshall, like Caistor, has produced a full range of stamped pottery, most of which must belong to the sixth century. It includes some fine examples of the bossed panel style in all its stages (e.g. VI, XVI, LXXXIX, fig. 70), one of which, VI, has a feature common in the continental Saxon area, a cross on the outside of the base. There are also many varieties of stamped pots without bosses (mostly fig. 71), including one very large urn, XIII (fig. 65), which combines stamps with massed necklines and linear arcading (*stehende Bogen*): this urn has the unusual feature of widely spaced lines of stamps set vertically in isolation just above the base, a treatment which can be matched on one of the Wehden urns, though this is of quite different character.[3] One urn, LXXVIII (fig. 71) is decorated in a very late phase of the devolution of the stamped panel style and may well belong to the years around 600 or even later: it also carries the exceptional feature of a group of random jabs eccentrically placed on the outside of the base. It has already been noted that the presence of some pieces of Ipswich ware (XXIX–XXXI, fig. 58) may indicate the continued use of the cemetery well into the seventh century (see pp. 240–2).

No vessels certainly by any of the more prolific potters whose products occur in the Caistor

---

[1] But see now p. 255, n. 1.
[2] Waller 1959, Tafel 34.15: Grohne 1953, 112, Abb. 37A.
[3] Waller 1961, Tafel 22, 559, an elaborately stamped biconical *Buckelurne* with a foot and diagonal bosses on the carination.

cemetery have been identified at Markshall except, as noted above, XIX, XXV, and LXXXIX, which may come from the workshop of the early Potter VIII. But little significance should be attached to this apparent lack of contact in view of the fragmentary nature of the surviving material. There are, however, as at Caistor, some examples of the rare animal stamps (XI, XCI, fig. 44). These are not identical with any noted at Caistor and unfortunately occur on sherds too small to indicate the type or types of urn that carried them. As suggested above (p. 61) they may well belong to the period of overlap between pagan and Christian fashions of ornament in the early part of the seventh century. A link with another Norfolk cemetery is provided by the stamped fragment XCIV (fig. 71) which is by the potter who made Illington 163 and another urn, of which only a sherd remains, for that community.

MIDDLE SAXON POTTERY (IPSWICH WARE)

By J. G. Hurst

THE cooking-pots XXIX–XXXI (fig. 58) are typical Ipswich ware;[1] the simple upright rims are of group I[2] and the smooth sandy thick fabric is one of four common types.[3] The date range of Ipswich ware is still very uncertain as so few middle Saxon sites are datable precisely and many of the finds from sites in East Anglia are unstratified. In very general terms it may be suggested that it was made at various centres in East Anglia between 650 and 850. It marks a considerable change from the earlier hand-made wares which were made in rough clamps, as Ipswich ware was turned on a slow wheel and fired in proper kilns where the air flow could be controlled.[4]

Fifteen years ago a starting-date of c. 650 was suggested based on evidence from three sites. (1) At Burgh Castle, Suffolk, where the monastery was founded about 635, Ipswich ware was found on the surface.[5] (2) At Bradwell, Essex, where St. Cedd's chapel was built about 654, Ipswich ware was found over the Roman levels.[6] (3) At Framlingham, Suffolk, a complete Ipswich ware cooking-pot was found associated with a seventh-century Frankish open-work disc.[7] It is now realized that the Framlingham disc was dated too closely and it cannot be said whether it is seventh or eighth century. The first two examples, however, still hold and have been confirmed. A large area of the Saxon monastery at Burgh Castle was excavated between 1958 and 1960.[8] This produced several monastic buildings and large quantities of Ipswich ware. At neither Burgh nor Bradwell were any hand-made sherds found, suggesting that Ipswich ware must have been in full production, and had completely supplanted the hand-made wares, at least on coastal sites, by c. 650.

It was suggested that, as there was no Ipswich ware associated with Sutton Hoo in c. 650, and there was the hand-made bottle,[9] a date later in the seventh century was more likely for the start of pottery made on a slow wheel. The position has now changed with the revised dating of the main Sutton Hoo ship burial to c. 625.[10] The recent careful excavation of the mound and the old ground surface has shown only rough brown sandy hand-made sherds[11] so it would be fair to suggest that Ipswich ware was not current, or at least common, by 625. The recent reinterpretation of the small drinking-horns as maplewood bowls[12] likewise helps to explain the lack of pottery in the burial deposit and has important implications for our ideas on containers of the period and the frequency of pottery on settlement sites.

In 1938, however, Mr. Basil Brown excavated another boat burial at Sutton Hoo, barrow 2,[13] and in the fill between the boat and the mound he found a single rim of sandy Ipswich

[1] Hurst and West 1957, 29–42.

[2] West 1963, 248 (I simple, II internal hollow, III external beading).

[3] Hurst 1959, 14 (a. smooth sandy, b. sandy, c. rough sandy, d. pimply).

[4] Smedley and Owles 1963, 311 (Kiln V).

[5] Proc. Cambs. Antiq. Soc. li (1957) 64.

[6] Hurst and West 1957, 34; J.R.S. xxxviii (1948) 91–2.

[7] Dunning 1956.

[8] Excavations by the late Mr. C. Green in 1958–60 for the Ministry of Works, unpublished except for short note in Med. Arch. iii (1959) 299.

[9] Bruce-Mitford 1968, 53 and pl. 20 a.

[10] Ibid. 45–51.

[11] Information from Mr. P. Ashbee.

[12] Information from Dr. R. L. S. Bruce-Mitford.

[13] Bruce-Mitford 1968, 15–17.

ware associated with friable brown hand-made sherds comparable with those found by Mr. Ashbee under the main Sutton Hoo barrow. The dating of the finds from barrow 2 is still uncertain, and has not been reassessed since the back-dating of the main find. They are not, however, likely to be long after 650. This find, together with the lack of hand-made sherds at Burgh Castle which was founded *c*. 635, does strongly suggest that Ipswich ware may in fact have started a decade or two before 650.

Excavations at Caister-by-Yarmouth[1] produced a series of twelve burials covered by sections of boats. Five of these were placed on either side of the Roman road leaving the town at a time when this was still respected. Later burials gradually encroached on it. These burials seem to be the humbler version of the royal ship burials and are not likely to be later than the seventh century. This cemetery was associated with the huts in the Roman town which contained Ipswich ware only and also *sceattas* of the late seventh and early eighth century.

Another very important recent find has been the Ipswich sherd stamped with human faces from the Cox Lane kiln area in Ipswich.[2] These have remarkable similarity with the faces on the Sutton Hoo whetstone and the leg of the bird-mount on the Sutton Hoo shield, all being set within the same pear-shaped frame. This sherd surely cannot be dated much later than the middle of the seventh century.

Unfortunately, neither the simple rim form nor the smooth sandy ware of the Markshall sherds can be used as an early dating feature. Besides the fact that there must have been regional variations, random groupings of the various fabrics and rims have been found associated on several sites. At the moment there are too few stratified sites and, although in the long term it may be possible to differentiate, recent experience in trying to classify and date the development of Thetford ware, between the ninth and twelfth century, has not been very promising. Likewise there may not be any simple logical development of Ipswich ware between the seventh and ninth centuries.

There, therefore, seems to be no reason why Ipswich ware should not have reached Markshall by *c*. 650, especially as it is not very far away from Burgh Castle. It must, however, be stressed that these finds were not complete burial pots but unstratified sherds. It is quite possible that they are later than the cemetery though there is no other sign of later occupation in the immediate vicinity and it would be more reasonable to suggest that they were contemporary with the cemetery.

It has been remarked that if Ipswich ware did start in the second quarter of the seventh century it is odd that pots of this kind are not found in other cemeteries. There are two possible reasons for this. In the first place it is clear that the earliest Ipswich ware had an eastern distribution along the North Sea coast and may not have penetrated far inland, or to the area round the Wash, till later in the seventh century. Recent excavations at North Elmham, Norfolk, on the middle Saxon village[3] suggest a considerable overlap period for Ipswich ware and the hand-made wares. There are few pagan Anglo-Saxon cemeteries in this eastern part of East Anglia; the main concentration is further west[4] in areas where Ipswich ware may not have penetrated before 700, by which time the cemeteries will have been out of use. Secondly, Ipswich ware was a quite new product linked with continental

---

[1] Excavation by the late Mr. C. Green in 1954, unpublished, but see note in Hurst and West 1957, 34–5.

[2] Smedley and Owles 1967.

[3] Wade-Martins 1969.

[4] Map 3 and p. 258.

trade and contacts in a period of intense missionary activity and christianization. It is likely that the later cremations were of those people who still clung to their pagan ways and would wish to be buried in the traditional type of burial urn. It is, therefore, hardly surprising that Ipswich ware burial urns are not found in the late pagan cemeteries; this lack cannot be taken as proof that pottery made on a slow wheel did not reach East Anglia till the cemeteries went out of use. The only three possible connections are at Markshall, Framlingham, and Sutton Hoo barrow 2, where these may be domestic vessels dropped by those concerned with the burials.

GRAVE GOODS FROM THE CREMATIONS

By Barbara Green

THE grave goods from this cemetery are of little interest and importance compared with the pottery, largely because there are so few. Objects are recorded from only eight urns since most of those now associated with urn IX are probably the result of nineteenth-century conflation with the contents of other urns (see p. 249). But the objects do almost certainly come from the Markshall cemetery.

The objects which survive are:

manicure or toilet implements—tweezers: III C (fig. 70), VIII D (fig. 71), IX C (fig. 16), N.C.M.
    (not fig. 27.26); shears: III B (fig. 70), VIII C (fig. 71); knife: VIII B (fig. 70)
comb fragments—I D (fig. 71), V C (fig. 66), IX D (fig. 16)
bronze rivet—IX G (fig. 16)
gaming pieces—I C (fig. 71), V B (fig. 66)
glass beads—I B (fig. 71), II B (fig. 67), IX F (fig. 16)
clay spindle whorl—IV B (fig. 69)
knob from bronze brooch—IX B (fig. 16)
ivory bag ring—IX E (fig. 16)
mammoth tooth fragment—VII B (not fig.)

It is very unlikely that the amber fragments (IX H) come from a cremation urn. Beads, and probably this was an amber bead, are almost invariably distorted by fire; amber would have burnt in the cremation fire if it had been on the body. It is possible that it comes from an inhumation burial (see p. 235).

Little need be said about the grave goods, and the parallels are cited in the appropriate section in the Caistor report.

Manicure or toilet implements (see p. 103): one complete manicure set is recorded, that from urn VIII. The size and type of implements suggest that this is a special funerary set. The pair of shears has long blades and short arms. The knife is perhaps Caistor type III with a curved blade and an iron handle curved down into a loop—cf. P 9 B (fig. 59). However, the blade is rather long and it is in fact very similar to a pair of shears from Caistor, Z 2 B (fig. 59). It is possible that we have here an example of a 'knife' having been made from a pair of shears for funerary purposes as was suggested in the case of M 51 B and N 36 B. In view of the concentration of toilet implements in urns of Anglian origin at Caistor, it is interesting to note that urn VIII is a very unusual corrugated type, perhaps of mid-fifth-century date.

The shears and tweezers found in urn III are also of the funerary type, although the arms of the shears are almost as long as the blades.

The two pairs of tweezers, one pair of which comes from urn IX, are both of Caistor type I, being of bronze and functional. The pair illustrated with urn IX is decorated with horizontal incised lines just below the terminal loop. The other pair is slightly smaller and plain.

It has already been noted that at Caistor K 7 B came from a Saxon vessel, while on the Continent such types are found in the Elbe–Weser cemeteries. Urn IX is a Saxon urn transitional between the 'Cuxhaven/Galgenberg Typ' and *Buckelurnen* (see p. 48) and dating perhaps to the mid-fifth century.

Combs (see p. 91): all the pieces are of large triangular combs, I D being an end section and V C and IX D being central sections. The lack of certain associations between IX D and urn IX must be stressed here, as the other four urns with *stehende Bogen* illustrated on fig. 16 do contain comb fragments. The *bronze rivet* IX G almost certainly comes from another large comb.

Gaming pieces (see p. 98): urn I contains two white bone pieces, one being slightly smaller than the other, while urn V contains one white bone piece with two holes in the base. They are comparable with the Caistor examples.

Glass beads (see p. 84): these usually indicate women's burials, as do the pieces of *ivory bag ring* (see p. 100) and the *clay spindle whorl* (see p. 112). This latter is unlike the Caistor examples, being rather bun-shaped.

The brooch knob is one of the pieces now known not to be certainly associated with urn IX with which it was illustrated. It is uncertain if it is the terminal knob from the head plate of an advanced type of Åberg Group I cruciform brooch, comparable with (but more elaborate than) that on G 5 B (fig. 59) and others such as one from Barrington A (Malton) Cambs.[1] (see p. 87). As with G 5 B, this could alternatively be part of a cruciform small-long brooch such as those found at Glen Parva, Leics.[2]

Perhaps the most interesting object from these urns is the fragment of *mammoth tooth* from urn VII. This urn was found in the nineteenth century and the piece may have been wrongly placed in the urn; but it could perhaps have entered the urn with topsoil at or after burial, although its large size makes this unlikely. It is iron-stained and sand has been cemented to the *lamellae*; almost certainly it comes from the local glacial gravels, if not of the cemetery itself then from somewhere near by. Mammoth remains are recorded from Markshall[3] as well as other places in the area, but no other record of association with an Anglo-Saxon cremation has been found.

[1] Åberg 1926, 36, fig. 55.   [2] Leicester Museum (n.d.), figs. 14 and 15, pp. 19–20.
[3] Woodward 1881, 144.

HUMAN REMAINS

By Calvin Wells

THE Markshall pottery found in the 1948 and 1949 excavations was so fragmentary that only four urns were recovered containing their bone mass. A group of burnt bones found during the 1948 excavations cannot be attributed to any urn. Urn IX, found in 1815, contained more than one burial; this was almost certainly the result of the amalgamation of the contents of several urns (see pp. 235, 249) found at that time or later.

Bones not associated with any urn (1948).

Infant.

A few dozen tiny fragments including minute scraps of cranial vault; part of a damaged petrous temporal bone; and some tiny slivers of long bone. Well fired. No animal remains.

One small fragment of an adult cranial vault, with endocranial fusion of a suture, is also present.

Urn I

Adult, 30–40 years. Female.

Several dozen fragments, almost all small. Identifiable are: pieces of cranial vault, with early endocranial fusion of sutures; a damaged petrous temporal bone and other fragments of cranial base; a fragment of superior orbital margin; part of the left maxilla showing that all teeth back to and including the first molar were present at death. Behind this the alveolus is defective. A mandibular condyle and an alveolar fragment; the damaged root of a premolar tooth.

Post-cranial remains include: a few fragments of vertebrae, pelvis, and ribs; many small pieces of long bone, including the trochlear region of a humerus; the medial third of a clavicle; part of a talus; metacarpal and metatarsal fragments.

Firing is somewhat inefficient on a few vertebral fragments. Only one individual appears to be present. No animal remains.

Urn II

Adult, 30–40 years. Male.

Many hundreds of fragments, almost all small but a few pieces of long bone up to 85 mm. in length. Many fragments are identifiable, including: pieces of cranial vault, with unfused or very early fusion of sutures; a damaged petrous temporal and other frag-ments of base, such as the glenoid fossae, pieces of face, including small lengths of alveoli from both jaws (at least eight teeth were present at death; none was detected as having been lost ante mortem); six tooth roots also survive.

Post-cranial remains include many fragments of vertebrae, including the dens of the axis, and parts of the bodies and articular facets of several vertebrae; pelvic and rib fragments; pieces of scapulae and clavicles; many fragments of long bone, including part of the linea aspera, articular surfaces from the head of a humerus, a radius, femoral head and femoral condyles; a right patella; fragments of talus, metacarpals, metatarsals, and phalanges.

Most have been well fired but small areas of underfiring occur, especially on lumbar vertebrae. Collection of the remains has been efficient—right down to terminal phalanges of feet. Only one individual is identifiable. No animal remains.

Urn III

Child, 6–7 years.

Several hundred fragments, all very small. Identifiable are: many fragments of cranial vault and a few of base and face; four damaged tooth crowns. Vertebral, pelvic and rib fragments; many slivers of long bones and a few articular surfaces with unfused epiphyses; pieces of small bones of hands and feet. Well fired. Efficiently collected. Two fragments of bird bone and one of animal tooth are present here.

Urn IV

Adult, 30–40 years. Male.

A few hundred fragments, mostly small. Identifiable are: fragments of cranial vault with early endocranial fusion of sutures; one petrous temporal and other pieces of base; a few facial fragments. Post-cranial remains include vertebral, pelvic and rib fragments; many pieces of long bones including proximal and distal articular fragments of humerus, femur, and tibia; a few small elements from hands and feet. These remains are mostly well fired but there is definite underfiring of distal tibial and metatarsal areas. This might suggest that the legs and feet were on the periphery of a somewhat inadequate pyre. Lumbar vertebral and femoral head fragments, both deeply placed anatomically, are also underfired. Only one body is identifiable. A proximal fragment from a horse metatarsal and another piece of unidentifiable animal bone are present here.

Urn VII

Infant.

A few minute flakes of cranial vault and long bone. Well fired. No animal remains.

Urn VIII

Adult. ?Female.

Many dozens of fragments, mostly small. Identifiable are: fragments of cranial vault with endocranial fusion of sutures; a few pieces of base and face; many vertebral and pelvic fragments and many splinters of long bones. Well fired. Only one individual indentified. No animal remains.

Urn IX

1. Adult. Female.
2. Adult. ??Male.
3. ?Adolescent. ?Sex.

Several thousand fragments, almost all very small. Identifiable are: pieces of cranial vault with some advanced sutural fusion; small fragments of cranial base and a few facial elements; part of the L. side of a mandible showing ante-mortem loss of the second molar, apparently with developmental absence of the third molar; a fragment of the R. alveolus of a mandible showing that P_1 to M_2 were present in the jaw at death.

Post-cranial fragments include: a fragment of atlas and many other vertebrae; pieces of pelvis and ribs; many small splinters from all long bones; a number of articular surfaces and various distinctive features such as the linea aspera, deltoid insertion, bicipital groove, etc. Small fragments of metacarpals, talus, navicular, and other bones of hands and feet.

Two small fragments of the trochlear surface of a ?R. humerus appear to come from different bones but the presence of at least three individuals here is proved unequivocally by finding three L. petrous temporals. There are also two R. petrous temporals which probably pair with two of the L. ones. The sex of these individuals cannot be determined with certainty. One is almost certainly female, as shown by the smallness of articular surfaces, despite epiphyseal union to indicate full adult status. A fragment of mastoid process further supports this, as does the general gracility of many fragments. A few somewhat more sturdy pieces suggest the presence of a male, but this remains doubtful. A few fragments of long bone appear to show traces of unfused epiphyses and suggest an adolescent rather than a child. This tentative diagnosis should be accepted with much caution: the fragments throughout are small, eroded, and ambiguous.

Virtually all elements have been well fired. In view of the fact that there are three individuals here the collection of the bones has been somewhat perfunctory, in spite of the fact that pieces have been retrieved from all parts of the body. No animal remains were detected.

Only urn IX contained more than one burial. Of the ten individuals, three were probably male, three probably female, and four unsexable juveniles. This figure of 40 per cent for children's burials is only slightly less than that at the Caistor-by-Norwich site. Estimation of the age at death of the six adults depends on the uncertain evidence of cranial sutures and the condition of a few teeth. All would seem to have died fairly young, none more than about 35 years, perhaps.

Nine (45·0 per cent) out of a possible 20 petrous temporal bones survive. This again emphasizes the survival capacity and diagnostic value of this feature.

The presence of animal bones is interesting but the series is too small to permit any useful inferences to be drawn about their association with age or sex.

In general these cadavers were efficiently cremated, although some evidence of underfiring is noted above in three cases.

INVENTORY OF CREMATION POTTERY AND ASSOCIATED GRAVE GOODS

By J. N. L. Myres and Barbara Green

Urns XXXIX, LVII–LIX, LXI, LXXII, XCV, and C do not merit illustration and have been omitted from the Inventory.

The four-figure number to the right of the Inventory number is that under which the urn will appear in J. N. L. Myres, *Corpus of Anglo-Saxon Pottery* (forthcoming). Where such a number is not given, the urn in question will not be illustrated in the *Corpus*.

I (fig. 71) 1501

Shouldered urn with short conical neck and upright rim: rough grey ware.

Decorated with a zone of indistinct stamps on the neck above three firm lines: there is another zone of stamps on the shoulder from which depend large three-line chevrons.

Two stamps appear.

Contents

A. Burnt bones of a woman, 30–40 years (see p. 245).
B. At least three fused glass beads, only one opaque white, probably with red spots, illustrated.
C. Two plano-convex bone gaming-pieces.
   (i) maximum basal diameter 0·55 in. (1·4 cm.); has been in fire.
   (ii) maximum basal diameter 0·65 in. (1·7 cm.); unburnt.
D. End section of the centre-plate of a triangular bone comb with two iron rivets.
E. Fragment of burnt animal bone (not shown on fig. 71).

II (fig. 67) 1502

Shouldered urn with conical neck and flaring rim on well-moulded footring: smooth dark grey ware.

Decorated with four grooves on the neck above a zone of large dots, another groove, another zone of dots and another groove. From the shoulder depend groups of three strong lines, in the spaces between which are one/two large dots.

Contents

A. Burnt bones of male, 30–40 years (see p. 245).
B. Mass of fused glass beads, only two recognizable as such.

III (fig. 70) 1503

Upper part of shoulder-boss urn with short everted rim: rough red/brown ware.

Decorated with three lines on the neck above a flat slashed collar and two more lines. On the shoulder are slashed vertical hollow bosses demarcated by two lines. In the panels are diagonal zones of stamps demarcated by two lines and below are roughly drawn three-line chevrons.

One stamp appears.

Contents

A. Burnt bones of a child, 6–7 years (see p. 245).
B. Pair of iron shears, the tip of one blade is missing. The loop is flattened while the arms are apparently rectangular in section. Length 1·8 in. (4·6 cm.).
C. Small pair of iron tweezers; the ends of the arms are slightly expanded. These could have been used. Length 1·4 in. (3·5 cm.).

IV (fig. 69) 1936

Globular urn with short upright rim: thick rough grey/brown ware.

Undecorated.

Contents

A. Burnt bones of male, 30–40 years (see p. 245).
B. Bun-shaped clay spindle-whorl, rough, undecorated surface. Maximum diameter 1·7 in. (4·3 cm.). Diameter of hole 0·45 in. (1·1 cm.).

V (fig. 66)

Part of side of shouldered urn or bowl with tall conical neck; rim and base missing: thick smooth grey ware.

Decorated with at least five strong lines on the neck above three-line chevrons on the shoulder.

Contents

B. Plano-convex bone gaming-piece with two roughly square holes in base; has been in fire. Maximum basal diameter 0·7 in. (1·8 cm.).
C. Fragment of centre-plate of a triangular bone comb, part of rivet hole with iron stain survives.

Association doubtful as these were found in an area in which disturbed broken sherds were concentrated; only a single sherd of this urn survives and no bones were recorded.

VI (fig. 70) 3984

Large shoulder-boss urn with tall conical neck and short everted rim: smooth grey/brown ware, once burnished.

Decorated with four sharp close-set neck-lines above a zone of stamps, three more lines, another zone of stamps, and three more lines. On the shoulder are seventeen short vertical hollow bosses, the panels between which are filled with four/seven close-set vertical lines. On the outside of the base is a deeply grooved cross.

One stamp is used.

Contents: none recorded.

Accession No. 65c.47.

VII (fig. 71) 3980

Sub-biconical bowl with everted rim: smooth dark ware, burnished black.

Decorated with a single zone of stamps demarcated above and below by two strong lines.

One stamp is used.

Contents

A. Burnt bones of an infant (see p. 246).
Apparently associated with this urn:
Two plates of a mammoth (*Mammuthus primigenius*) tooth. Iron-consolidated sand adheres to one surface showing that the tooth was broken when recovered from the glacial gravels. Mammoth teeth have been recorded from this area.[1]

Accession No. 65b.47.

VIII (fig. 71) 3987

Shoulder-boss urn with tall neck, wide mouth, and upright rim: smooth dark ware, burnished black.

Decorated on the neck with three low collars each demarcated (and formed) by a broad groove: the first is plain, the second carries a continuous line of jabs, the third is intersected by the broad vertical grooves which demarcate (and form) a continuous zone of thirty-four small vertical bosses on the shoulder, thus breaking it into sections each carrying one or two jabs.

Contents

A. Burnt bones of an adult, ? female (see p. 246).
B. Small iron knife with curved blade and thin curved handle, end broken off. Extreme tip of blade missing. This type almost certainly did not have a wooden handle and was probably made for funerary purposes. Surviving length 1·9 in. (4·8 cm.).
C. Small pair of iron shears with flattened loop and short handles and long tapering blades. Length 2·25 in. (5·7 cm.).
D. Iron tweezers, very corroded, ends of arms missing, but apparently expanded. Length 1·75 in. (4·4 cm.).

IX (fig. 16) 1674

Globular urn with tall conical neck and footring base, rim missing: smooth grey ware probably once burnished.

Decorated low on the neck with five close-set corrugated grooves above a single sharp line, below which are continuous line-and-groove arches (a groove demarcated by two sharp lines) carelessly set out and executed.

Contents

A. Burnt bones of at least three individuals (see p. 246).
B. Knob from a bronze brooch, full-round in section, decorated with two pairs of horizontal grooves; the stay (now broken) which projected across the head-plate is also grooved. This knob is one of the side-knobs to which the brooch spring was attached. It could come from either a Group I or II cruciform or from a cruciform small-long brooch.
C. Pair of bronze tweezers of Roman type. The pair illustrated on fig. 16 may not be the pair recorded from this urn despite the fact that they were presented, together with other objects, at the same time. These tweezers have a loop made by

[1] e.g. Woodward 1881, 144.

constricting the two arms; the arms expand below this. The arms are decorated on either side by three and then two engraved horizontal lines set just below the loop. Length 2·75 in. (7 cm.).

A smaller and more elaborately decorated pair of tweezers, presented to N.C.M. in 1826, is said to be associated with this urn.[1] These tweezers have a terminal loop and expanded arms which are faceted and decorated with six groups of engraved horizontal lines. Length 2·2 in. (5·6 cm.).

D. Fragment of centre-plate of triangular bone comb, with iron-staining around remains of rivet hole; teeth broken.

E. Six fragments of burnt elephant ivory ring. The pieces are too small for any reconstruction to be attempted.

F. Large fused glass bead.

G. Bronze rivet, rectangular section, slightly tapering. Length 0·4 in. (1 cm.).

H. Four fragments of amber, presumably from a bead, unburnt.

This urn was found with twenty others in 1815 and came into N.C.M. collections in 1825. In 1847 it was exhibited at a meeting of the Archaeological Institute.[2] It was said to contain burnt bones and a pair of bronze tweezers. The other objects, B and D–H, are not mentioned. The burnt bones now said to have come from this urn contain the remains of at least three individuals. It seems very likely that bones and objects from other urns have become associated with this pot at a later date. It is not recorded on fig. 16 that these associations are doubtful.

X (fig. 65) (= Ashmolean 1885.604) 1095

Large *Buckelurne* with conical neck and slightly everted rim: smooth grey/brown ware, probably once burnished.

Decorated with three large hollow shoulder bosses, each set under an arch of dots demarcated above by a plain line and below by a notched line, and by two inner sets of four/five arched lines. Between the arches are circular hollow bosses each surrounded by a circular line and carrying two groups of four lines intersecting at right angles to form a cross.

XI (fig. 44)

Part of shoulder of small urn, form uncertain: smooth grey ware with burnished surface.

Decorated with an animal stamp above two sharp lines: below were groups of diagonal lines or chevrons on the shoulder.

XII (fig. 70)

Part of neck and shoulder of large shoulder-boss urn: smooth dark ware.

Decorated on the neck with at least three grooved lines above a zone of stamps and three more grooves. On the shoulder are numerous vertical hollow bosses, the panels between which are filled with vertical grooves.

One stamp appears.

XIII (fig. 65) 3989

Large biconical urn with short everted rim, base missing: burnished buff/brown ware.

Decorated on the neck with eight close-set strong lines above a groove and four more lines: below are a zone of stamps, five more strong lines, and wide three-line arches extending to the maximum diameter. A stamp is set in some of the spandrels. On the lower part there are further vertical or diagonal lines of stamps widely spaced and running to the base.

One stamp is used.

XIV (fig. 66) 1509

Large sub-biconical urn with narrow neck and swollen everted rim: burnished buff/brown ware.

Decorated on the neck with six strong lines above large four-line chevrons extending just below the maximum diameter. A single vertical line drops from the point of each chevron, and between each there is a three-line swag hanging from the lowest neck-line.

XV (fig. 67)

Part of side of shouldered urn: thick burnished grey/brown ware.

Decorated with at least three strong neck-lines, above diagonal groups of line-and-groove separated by single impressions of a stamp.

One stamp appears.

XVI (fig. 70) 3983

Lower part of large shoulder-boss urn: smooth grey/brown ware.

Decorated with about six vertical hollow shoulder-bosses, each demarcated by four vertical lines, the

---

[1] Norwich Castle Museum 1909, 51, no. 459.

[2] *Proc. Arch. Inst.*, Norwich 1847, xxix.

panels between which contain a horizontal zone of stamps demarcated above and below by two lines: beneath are three-line chevrons, the spaces above and below which are filled with stamps.

Two stamps appear.

XVII (fig. 66) 3981

Part of side of urn with tall conical neck, rim and base missing: red/brown ware burnished black.

Decorated on the upper part with a wide zone of three-line chevrons, demarcated above and below by three strong grooves. Below are groups of six/seven strong vertical lines.

XVIII (fig. 69) 1935

Hollow-necked biconical urn with upright rim: rough corky brown ware with smoothed surface.
Undecorated.

XIX (fig. 70) 3977

Part of side of shoulder-boss urn: thick grey ware with smooth dark surface.

Decorated on the neck with at least four close-set lines above a solid stamped collar below which are five close-set lines. On the shoulder are widely spaced small vertical partly hollow bosses each demarcated by a wide group of close-set lines: the panels apparently contained two horizontal lines above a zone of stamps.

Two stamps appear.

XX (fig. 71)

Upper part of urn with tall conical neck and everted rim: smooth brown ware.

Decorated low on the neck with seven sharp lines above a zone of three-line chevrons the spaces above and below which are filled with stamps.

One stamp appears.

XXI (fig. 65)

Upper part of wide shouldered urn with short upright rim: smooth grey/brown ware.

Decorated on the neck with a groove demarcated above and below by a single line. On the shoulder are large single arches in similar line-and-groove technique, separated by a vertical group of line-and-groove.

XXII (fig. 66) 3982

Upper part of large globular urn with narrow neck and slightly everted rim: smooth buff/brown ware.

Decorated low on the neck with four strong grooves below which are irregular single-line tall arches with a single vertical line in each. At one point at least a single-line diagonal cross fills the upper space between two chevrons.

XXIII (fig. 71)

Rim and neck of well-made urn with narrow neck and everted rim: smooth dark ware with burnished surface.

Decorated on the neck with three fine lines above a zone of widely spaced stamps below which are at least two more lines.

One stamp appears.

XXIV (fig. 65) 3986

Part of side of large globular urn: thick dark ware with smooth black surface.

Decorated on the neck with a wide zone of alternate line-and-groove (six lines and five grooves), below which are two undulating zones of line-and-groove (a groove demarcated above and below by a line), forming 'S' curves which interlock to produce a cabled effect.

XXV (fig. 65) 3978

Part of side of globular urn: smooth grey/brown ware, burnished.

Decorated with at least three irregular neck-lines above a solid raised collar carrying a zone of stamps. Below is another zone of stamps and four more lines. On the shoulder are three/four-line arches in the spandrels between which are irregular rosettes formed of deep jabs surrounding a circular depression.

Two stamps appear, both also on LXXXIX.

XXVI (fig. 71)

Rim and neck of well-made urn with flaring rim: smooth black ware, burnished.

Decorated with a solid raised collar bearing a zone of stamps demarcated above by three and below by at least two strong lines.

One stamp appears.

XXVII (fig. 65)

Upper part of urn with tall conical neck and everted rim: smooth dark ware, once burnished.

Decorated low on the neck with a flat slashed collar demarcated above and below by two lines, below which is a zone of stamps and another line. On the shoulder are irregular small flat slashed arches between which are groups of stamps.

Two stamps appear.

XXVIII (fig. 67)

Part of side of urn, form uncertain: rough grey/brown ware.

Decorated with two faint neck-lines and single-line arches below, the whole scattered with jabs.

XXIX (fig. 58)

Body sherd from near the neck of Ipswich ware cooking pot; smooth fine grey ware; undecorated.

XXX (fig. 58)

Sherds from upper part of Ipswich ware cooking pot with everted squared-off rim; smooth fine grey ware; undecorated.

XXXI (fig. 58)

Sherds from lower part of Ipswich ware cooking pot, showing angle between side and sagging base; smooth fine grey ware; undecorated.

XXXII (not illustrated)

Body sherds from Ipswich ware cooking pot; smooth fine grey ware, one sherd with pinkish tone; undecorated.

XXXIII (not illustrated)

Small body sherd from Ipswich ware cooking pot; smooth fine grey ware; undecorated.

XXXIV (fig. 65)

Part of side of biconical urn: smooth buff/brown ware.

Decorated on the neck with at least two solid raised slashed collars, and on the carination with a continuous raised slashed band undulating to form a series of arches or chevrons. The full design does not appear, but was probably similar to that on LXVIII.

XXXV (fig. 65)

Part of side of a globular urn: smooth grey/brown ware.

Decorated apparently with a raised collar above large raised and slashed arches: the full design does not appear.

XXXVI (fig. 67)

Part of shoulder of large urn, form uncertain: smooth brown/black ware, burnished.

Decorated with a slightly thickened slashed collar demarcated above and below by a zone of corrugated grooves (at least three above and four below). On the shoulder are groups of diagonal corrugated grooves.

XXXVII (fig. 70)

Part of shoulder of shoulder-boss urn: smooth grey/brown ware.

Decorated low on the neck with a flat slashed collar demarcated above and below by a single groove. On the shoulder are round hollow bosses demarcated by two vertical grooves: the panels appear to have been partly filled with groups of diagonal grooves.

XXXVIII (fig. 65)

Part of side of globular urn: smooth buff/brown ware, burnished.

Decorated with two solid raised collars, the upper plain, the lower slashed with large oval depressions. Below are two-groove arches with a single large circular depression in the spandrels between them.

XL (fig. 66)

Upper part of globular urn with short upright rim: smooth grey ware.

Decorated with two grooved neck-lines, below which are three-line chevrons.

XLI (fig. 71)

Part of side of urn, form uncertain: smooth red/brown ware.

Decorated on the neck with at least two lines above a zone of stamps, below which are three more lines, and three-line chevrons running at least to the maximum diameter.

XLII (fig. 70)

Part of side of small shoulder-boss urn: thin dark grey ware, once burnished.

Decorated with a flat slashed collar demarcated above and below by two fine lines. Below are very slight vertical hollow bosses demarcated by three fine lines: at the top of the panels is a single zone of stamps.

One stamp appears.

XLIII (fig. 65)

Part of side of globular *Buckelurne* with conical neck: hard thin black ware, burnished.

Decorated with a slightly thickened flat collar demarcated above and below by a single line. On the belly were vertical hollow bosses, some large and decorated with sharp lines in various patterns, others small and plain. In the panels were elaborate designs in sharp lines and occasional dots of which not enough remain to make an accurate description of the whole scheme possible.

XLIV (fig. 67)

Part of side of large urn, form uncertain: thick heavy buff/brown ware, once burnished.

Decorated apparently with at least two horizontal grooves below which are groups of deep vertical grooves separated by vertical lines of large dots.

XLV (fig. 66)

Part of side of globular urn, with slight bosses: thin corky grey ware.

Decorated apparently with a zone of fine diagonal lines and groups of dots above three fine lines. Below there are very slight bosses, in the panels between which are two diagonal lines linked by faint diagonal slashing. Not enough decoration remains to make the design clear.

XLVI (fig. 66)

Lower part of side of shoulder-boss urn: smooth dark ware.

Decorated with narrow vertical shoulder-bosses, demarcated by two strong grooves. In the panels are three-line chevrons of similar grooves.

XLVII (fig. 67)

Part of side of biconical urn: dark ware, with smooth black surface.

Decorated with at least four grooves on the neck above a zone of stamps which was apparently interrupted at intervals below by diagonal or chevron lines.

One stamp appears.

XLVIII (fig. 65)

Lower part of side of large urn, form uncertain: thick dark ware with burnished black surface.

Decorated apparently with large two/three line pendent swags.

XLIX (fig. 66)

Part of side of biconical shoulder-boss urn: pitted, corky grey ware.

Decorated above the carination with groups of fine diagonal or chevron lines above four fine lines. From the carination fall slight vertical hollow bosses, some slashed with horizontal lines. In the panels is a confusing jumble of fine lines: possibly there were swags intersecting with vertical lines in some panels, but not enough remains to show what the potter's intention was.

L (fig. 67)

Part of side of urn, form uncertain: smooth sandy brown ware.

Decorated with groups of strong vertical grooves, between which are groups of diagonal grooves with a single large dot in the spaces above and below.

LI (fig. 67)

Part of side of shoulder-boss urn: smooth black ware.

Decorated with at least one groove above a zone of large dots and two more grooves: on the shoulder are narrow vertical hollow bosses demarcated by two sharp lines: the panels have two sharp lines above a filling of dots.

LII (fig. 69)

Part of side of urn, form uncertain: smooth brown ware.

Decorated with three strong grooves on the neck, below which are vertical and diagonal groups of line-and-groove, not enough of which remains to show the design. Some diagonal lines appear to be lightly slashed.

LIII (fig. 67)

Part of side of urn, form uncertain: smooth dark ware.

Decorated with at least two fine neck-lines above a zone of small dots, below which are three more fine lines. Below are groups of vertical lines.

LIV (fig. 70)

Part of side of shoulder-boss urn: rather rough dark brown/grey ware.

Decorated low on the neck with a zone of stamps above a single line: on the shoulder are hollow bosses carrying vertical grooves, the panels between which are filled with similar grooves and stamps.

One stamp appears.

LV (fig. 71)

Part of shoulder of urn, form uncertain: smooth brown/black ware, burnished.

Decorated with at least one fine neck-line, above groups of three-line chevrons, the spaces below which are filled with stamps.

One stamp appears.

LVI (fig. 71)

Part of side of urn, form uncertain: smooth grey ware.

Decorated with a zone of stamps on the neck demarcated above and below by two firm lines. Below are groups of chevron lines, the spaces between which are filled with stamps.

One stamp appears.

LX (fig. 67)

Part of side of ?wide-mouthed bowl: rough grey ware.

Decorated with a zone of stamps above four firm neck-lines and wide three-line chevrons.

One stamp appears.

LXII (fig. 67) 3988

Upper part of large biconical urn: smooth buff/brown ware.

Decorated with three strong grooves on the neck above a zone of single-groove chevrons extending to the carination. Below the point of each chevron is a large single dot.

LXIII (fig. 70) 3985

Upper part of large shoulder-boss bowl: smooth dark grey ware.

Decorated with two slight collars, demarcated by grooves, the upper plain, the lower slashed. On the shoulder are about fifteen round hollow bosses, the panels being filled with vertical corrugation.

LXIV (fig. 65)

Part of neck, probably of *Buckelurne*: dark ware, burnished.

Decorated with a strongly slashed solid applied collar demarcated above and below by two strong lines.

LXV (fig. 67)

Part of neck and shoulder of wide shouldered urn: smooth grey ware.

Decorated low on the neck with three firm lines: below on the rather sharp shoulder are deep vertical grooves demarcated by two firm lines: in the panels are apparently groups of diagonal lines, and some small jabs.

LXVI (fig. 66)

Part of neck and side of urn, form uncertain: smooth grey ware.

Decorated on the neck with a firm groove demarcated above by one and below by two firm lines. Below are four-line chevrons.

LXVII (fig. 67)

Part of side of urn, form uncertain: grey ware, with dark burnished surface.

Decorated with at least two grooves above three-groove chevrons, the spaces between which contain one or two annular depressions bordered by a line of dots.

LXVIII (fig. 65)

Upper part of small *Buckelurne* with tall conical neck: smooth grey/brown ware, burnished.

Decorated low on the neck with three solid raised collars, the upper one plain, the two lower slashed. Below are solid raised semicircular slashed arches, apparently covering small plain bosses.

LXIX (fig. 67)

Upper part of bowl with tall neck and short upright rim: red/brown ware, burnished black.

Decorated with a line of dots above four close-set grooves: below are groups of three/four short close-set vertical grooves on the shoulder.

LXX (pl. X and fig. 68) 1969

Part of side of large *Buckelurne*: hard black ware, burnished inside and out.

Decorated with at least one small solid raised collar, slashed and dotted, demarcated above and below by two strong lines. Below are narrow vertical hollow bosses (some in pairs), slashed in line-and-groove and dotted; the panels between them contain diagonal line-and-groove with large dots in the angles; at the bottom of one panel is a boss in the form of a human face with hair indicated in diagonal lines bordered by two horizontal lines, eyes by punched circles with raised centres, and mouth by a double curved line and a dimple on the chin. At the bottom of the adjacent boss is part of a hollow split oval horizontal boss.

LXXI (fig. 70)

Part of neck and side of shoulder-boss urn: smooth dark grey ware.

Decorated with a zone of jabs, demarcated above and below by a firm groove. Below are small vertical hollow bosses, demarcated with two grooves; the panels between which contain three-groove chevrons.

LXXIII (fig. 67)

Part of side of shouldered bowl: fine hard grey ware, burnished.

Decorated low on the neck with three sharp lines between the lower two of which are widely spaced diagonal jabs: on the shoulder are widely spaced diagonal oval depressions.

LXXIV (fig. 71)

Part of side of shouldered urn: buff/brown ware with burnished dark brown surface.

Decorated with at least one firm neck-line from which depend groups of vertical lines, the panels between which are largely filled with stamps.

One stamp appears.

LXXV (fig. 66)

Part of neck of large urn, probably biconical: thick grey ware with burnished black surface.

Decorated with a wide zone demarcated above by at least two and below by four fine lines and containing three-line chevrons. In the spaces are free-hand crosses or stars formed of two/three short intersecting lines.

LXXVI (fig. 67)

Part of side of large shouldered urn with tall neck: rough light grey ware with smoothed surface.

Decorated with a zone of large dots demarcated above and below by two wide grooves. Below are groups of three vertical grooves separating panels containing diagonal grooves and lines of large dots apparently arranged as chevrons.

LXXVII (fig. 70)

Part of rim and side of shoulder-boss urn with everted rim: smooth light buff/brown ware.

Decorated on the neck with at least one zone of stamps demarcated above and below by a groove. On the shoulder are vertical hollow bosses, of which the surface has scaled, but which apparently carried a vertical line of stamps: in the panels are vertical grooves.

One stamp appears.

LXXVIII (fig. 71) 4106

Lower part of globular urn with conical neck: smooth sandy grey/brown ware.

Decorated on the neck with a zone of stamps above two faint lines, below which are several zones of stamps possibly arranged as pendent triangles but without linear demarcation. On the outside of the base is a group of crescentic jabs irregularly arranged.

Two stamps appear.

LXXIX (fig. 67)

Part of side of urn, form uncertain: smooth light buff ware.

Decorated apparently with two light lines above a double zone of dots and three more lines. Below are groups of two or more diagonal lines, possibly arranged as chevrons, the spaces between which are filled with dots.

LXXX (fig. 69)

Upper part of large shouldered urn with sloping neck and everted rim: thick rough corky buff ware with smoothed surface.

Decorated on the neck with three grooves, below which are groups of vertical grooves, the panels between which contain groups of three diagonal grooves.

LXXXI (fig. 70)

Part of side of shoulder-boss urn: dark ware, with burnished black surface.

Decorated with numerous long vertical hollow bosses, each demarcated by a single line: one of the narrow panels contains a single impression of a stamp.

One stamp appears.

LXXXII (fig. 71)

Part of side of large urn: grey ware with black smoothed surface.

Decorated with at least two neck-lines above a double zone of stamps; below are three more lines, another zone of stamps, and three more lines.

Three stamps appear.

LXXXIII (fig. 65)

Part of side of shoulder-boss urn with tall conical neck: smooth dark grey ware, with burnished black surface.

Decorated under the rim (missing) with at least eight close-set fine lines, above a zone of very blurred stamps, and another twelve close-set fine lines, the zone interrupted in one place by two oval dabs. On the shoulder are three-line arches, covering small plain bosses. Between the arches are single blurred impressions of the same stamp, with an oval dab on each side.

One stamp appears.

LXXXIV (fig. 69) 1931

Parts of large biconical *Buckelurne* with foot-ring base: hard grey ware, with burnished dark surface.

Decorated above the carination with eight flat vertical panels separated by narrow vertical raised slashed strips and containing different designs. Two panels had a small boss on the carination surmounted by a series of concentric arched lines, one or two of which separate a zone of oval depressions: the outermost line is emphasized by a narrow raised slashed strip which joined the vertical strips demarcating the panel. Three panels had small circular hollow bosses, set in two rows above or below a group of horizontal lines. One panel had a small circular vertically-slashed hollow boss on the carination with a zone of depressions on each side and above it at least eight horizontal lines, between the fourth and fifth of which is a zone of oval depressions. The design of the seventh panel is fragmentary: it apparently had on each side a vertical zone of oval depressions demarcated by two lines and in the middle a further group of oval depressions. The eighth panel is missing. Below the carination were short vertical lines.

It would appear from the fractures that the panels were made separately and subsequently luted to one another and to the rest of the urn, a procedure which might have involved a second firing.[1]

LXXXV (fig. 67)

Upper part of large urn with conical neck, and everted rim: rough corky ware, with burnished dark surface.

Decorated with four strong neck-lines, the three flat collars between which contain widely spaced large dots set alternately. Below are single-line arches with at least two large dots in the spandrels between them.

LXXXVI (fig. 71)

Part of side of urn, form uncertain: smooth brown ware, burnished.

Decorated with a zone of stamps, demarcated above and below by two fine lines.

One stamp appears.

LXXXVII (fig. 71)

Part of side of urn, form uncertain: smooth dark ware, burnished.

Decorated with three-line chevrons, the lower spaces containing stamps.

One stamp appears.

LXXXVIII (fig. 66)

Part of side of large globular urn: fine thin black ware, once burnished.

Decorated with continuous chevrons in well-executed line-and-groove.

LXXXIX (fig. 70) 3976

Upper part of large shoulder-boss urn, rim and base missing: red/brown ware, with burnished dark brown surface.

Decorated on the neck with four close-set firm lines, a solid raised collar carrying a zone of stamps, four more lines, a similar raised collar carrying a zone of stamps, four more lines, a third collar carrying jabs, and five more lines. Below are groups of five solid vertical bosses separated and demarcated by close-set lines; the panels between them are partly filled with vertical lines and partly with a horizontal zone of stamps above two spaced lines, a zone of jabs, and three more spaced lines.

Three stamps appear, two of them also on XXV.

XC (fig. 71)

Part of side of urn, form uncertain.

Decorated with four neck-lines above vertical and diagonal groups of three lines, the spaces between which are filled with stamps.

One stamp appears.

XCI (fig. 44)

Sherd with impression of stamp showing swan or goose.

---

[1] Dr. P. Schmid has kindly drawn my attention to a sherd from Feddersen Wierde (F461 Ea) which is from an urn of very similar form and decoration and appears to exhibit the same unusual technique. It would seem very likely that the same workshop produced both vessels.

XCII (fig. 71)

Lower part of side of urn, form uncertain.

Decorated with two-line chevrons or pendent triangles, outlined on the lower side with stamps.

One stamp appears.

XCIII (fig. 71)

Upper part of side of urn, form uncertain.

Decorated with a zone of stamps, demarcated above by three and below by at least one line.

One stamp appears.

XCIV (fig. 71)

Upper part of side of urn, form uncertain.

Decorated with a double zone of stamps, demarcated above by at least one, and below by two lines: below is a group of two vertical lines separating panels one of which is blank and the other filled with stamps.

Three stamps appear.

XCVI (fig. 65)

Part of pedestal foot, probably from a carinated bowl: smooth sandy brown ware, once burnished.

Decorated just above the constriction with a slightly raised cordon demarcated above and below by a line.

XCVII (fig. 65)

Upper part of side of urn, form uncertain: smooth dark ware, once burnished.

Decorated with applied vertical and horizontal hatched strips, of which not enough remains to show the design.

[XCVIII is part of LXX (fig. 68) q.v.]

XCIX (fig. 66)

Upper part of side of urn, form uncertain: smooth grey ware.

Decorated with a single neck-line above groups of diagonal lines intersecting at right angles: not enough remains to show the design, but the treatment is similar to that on XLIX and CI.

CI (fig. 66)

Part of side of urn, form uncertain: smooth grey ware.

Decorated with a single neck-line above groups of diagonal lines intersecting at right angles; the treatment is similar to that on XLIX and XCIX, and it could be part of the latter.

CII (fig. 70)

Part of neck of a small urn, form uncertain: smooth dark ware, burnished.

Decorated with a flat slashed collar demarcated above and below by two sharp lines.

A further urn, known only from an old illustration, is not described here; it is shown on pl. XVI*b*.

V

APPENDICES

1. NOTES ON THE MANUFACTURE OF ANGLO-SAXON POTTERY

By J. N. L. Myres

F. R. M. spent a good deal of time on experimental attempts to produce hand-made pottery similar in fabric, form, and decoration to the commoner types of urns found in the Caistor cemetery. He was anxious to ascertain by trial and error the processes of manufacture that were used, and to try out various theories which he had on the methods employed in producing finished pots of different types. So far as I know, he had no previous experience of pot-making, and was probably as ignorant as the Anglo-Saxon potters themselves of the chemical processes involved, or the technical factors that determined success or failure in achieving the desired results. Perhaps for this reason his observations may be worth recording, for he approached the problem much as primitive man would have done. He discussed his experiments with me on several occasions, and there is also preserved a long letter which he wrote to Professor Donald Atkinson on 3 May 1935 reporting his conclusions on several aspects of Anglo-Saxon pot-making. In what follows the verbal quotations are taken from this letter.

F. R. M. was very dissatisfied with his earlier efforts to produce vessels at all similar to genuine Anglo-Saxon pots. These had been based on clay prepared with a good deal of care, and fired in various types of specially constructed furnace. Both the fabric and the finish of the pots so made were quite unlike the models he was trying to follow, and he soon found that much more primitive and haphazard procedures were required to produce the desired effects.

'You remember that bag of river mud . . .', he wrote to Atkinson, 'I have done a good deal of experimenting with it as pot-making material. It isn't quite the right stuff. There are not enough flints in, the vegetable matter in it is too decayed, and it contains too many water snail shells. For all that it is very like the stuff some of the Caistor pots were made of . . .' By improving somewhat on this un-promising raw material, working into it various quantities of flint grits, pounded potsherds, and finely chopped grass or leaves, and removing the larger sticks and beetles, he found that this river or pond mud was the best basis for most of the fabrics he was trying to imitate. With it he soon found he could make, by the mud-pie process, quite plausible forms of bowls or cups. But taller forms defeated him until he realized the practical convenience of bosses. 'I think the most interesting discovery I have made', he wrote, 'is the fact that the bosses are not merely ornaments. They are also buttresses, and without their aid it is, in my experience, an absolute impossibility to make a jar-shaped pot using river mud. If a plain jar is wanted the bosses have to be made first and afterwards pressed down.' He tried to overcome the difficulty of forming large vessels without bosses by using what he terms the 'coiled snake method'. But his river mud would not co-operate: 'it is impossible to make a snake with it: it won't hold together for a second'.[1]

---

[1] In this F. R. M. was less successful than some Anglo-Saxon potters, who certainly used the coil method in forming large vessels.

Then there was the question of firing. No type of kiln, however primitive, seemed to produce the right effect, especially the sharp differences often seen in the degree of firing to which different parts of the same pot had been subjected. Eventually he found that a garden bonfire gave the best results. 'After numerous experiments', he wrote, 'I think the Saxons most likely fired their pots by covering them thickly with green herbage of some sort and then lighting a big fire on the top of them. The fire must be kept going until all the greenstuff is carbonized but not burnt away. You then get the characteristic colour of Saxon pots, sometimes nearly black. If the fire gets directly to the pots they are burnt red or buff colour. This often happens to the necks of the pots . . . with this process the base of the pot is commonly much less well fired than the rest—again like the genuine urns.'[1] He also found that surface treatment of the fired pots was necessary before they had cooled. 'All my pots are beeswaxed when hot out of the fire. They don't look like the real thing until they have undergone this process: and also they will then hold water: untreated they are porous.'

With regard to decoration he found that 'the pots have to be stamped within 24 hours of making, otherwise they get too dry to take a good impression. The incised lines can be put on 2 or 3 days after making, if necessary. After 3 or 4 days the pots can be freely handled without any fear of damaging them. In fact they are surprisingly tough. Their appearance can then be considerably improved by cutting off bumps with a knife and afterwards smoothing down with a wet finger. Such improvements may be continued as long as you like, even when the pot is quite dry.' F. R. M. thought it quite likely that the more elaborate Saxon urns were improved in this way over a long period, being kept perhaps for months for finishing before being fired. He believed that most of the ordinary stamps, especially those of circular, rectangular, or triangular outline were simply cut on the ends of sticks, and discarded when worn out, being replaced, if necessary, by others of similar form. This would help to explain the numerous cases where pots, obviously from the same workshop, are found to be decorated by similar but not identical stamps. F. R. M. became very expert in the rapid cutting of stamps in this way: he had a large collection of them for use on the pots that he made, and their impressions are certainly indistinguishable from those on genuine Anglo-Saxon pottery. Indeed by following the principles here described, which were all the result of personal experiment, he could, towards the end of his life, turn out, if the bonfire behaved properly, some very plausible Anglo-Saxon pots indeed. Readers can, however, rest assured that no Mann-made urns are published in this book.

2. GAZETTEER OF ANGLO-SAXON CEMETERIES AND BURIALS IN EAST ANGLIA

By T. H. McK. Clough and Barbara Green

The area covered is that shown on map 3.

The classification of these sites follows, in a simplified form, that used by the Ordnance Survey in *Britain in the Dark Ages* (1966). Deviations from, or additions to, the Ordnance Survey gazetteer are indicated, and the list, which was closed in September 1970, also amends and adds to the information given in Meaney 1964.

Abbreviations

*	Classification differs from that of the Ordnance Survey
†	Additions to the Ordnance Survey list

---

[1] F. R. M. noted a number of urns from the cemetery of which the upper part is well preserved but the base or lower part entirely disintegrated. Since the sandy soil drains very readily this could not be due simply to the bottoms of the urns becoming more waterlogged than the rest.

(C)	Cambridgeshire
(E)	Essex
(He)	Hertfordshire
(Hu)	Huntingdonshire
(N)	Norfolk
(S)	Suffolk
I.C.	Predominantly inhumation cemetery
C.C.	Predominantly cremation cemetery
M.C.	Mixed cemetery
I.B.	Inhumation burials up to three in number
C.B.	Cremation burials up to three in number
V/VI/VII	Starting-date of the cemetery where known
D	There is some doubt that the site is Anglo-Saxon

Anglo-Saxon Cemeteries

Site	Grid Reference	Type	Starting Date
1. Hunstanton—Hunstanton Park (N)	TF 696411	I.C.	Early VI
2. Thornham (N)	TF 725425	I.C.	VII
3. Holkham—Howe Hill (N)	TF 877450 approx.	I.C.	?VI
4. Langham (N)	TG 020411	I.B.	?VI
5. Snettisham (N)	TF 683344	C.B.	?V
6. Sedgeford (N)	TF 7136	C.C.	prob. V
7. Little Walsingham (N)	TF 930364	I.B.	VI
8. Great Walsingham (N)	TF 938375 approx.	C.C.	?V
†9. Fakenham (N)	TF 9230	I.B.	VI
10. Little Snoring (N)	TF 953322	I.B.	
*11. Kettlestone—Pensthorpe (N)	TF 950295	C.C.	V
12. Wolterton—Mannington Hall (N)	TG 147323	C.C.	?VI
†13. Mundesley (N)	TG 318362	C.C.	Late V.
†14. Smallburgh (N)	TG 337240	I.B.	?VI
15. North Elmham—Spong Hill (N)	TF 983195	C.C.	V
16. Castle Acre—Priory Field (N)	TF 797156	C.C.	V
17. Narford (N)	TF 770140	I.B.	?VI
18. Narford—Bradmoor (N)	TF 775145	C.C.	D
†19. Grimston (N)	TF 721224	I.C.	VI
*20. North Runcton—churchyard (N)	TF 646159	M.C.	c.500
21. Tottenhill (N)	TF 635108	M.C.	?VI
22. Wallington—Stow Bridge (N)	TF 6007	C.B.	VI
†22a. Downham Market (N)	TF 6103	C.B.	V
23. Wisbech—Corn Exchange (C)	TF 463096	I.B.	
24. Hilgay—churchyard (N)	TL 622981	I.B.	?VI
†25. Wereham (N)	TF 681015 approx.	C.C.	?V
26. Wretton (N)	TF 696007	I.B.	
†27. Methwold (N)	TL 7394	I.B.	?VI
28. Northwold—nr. watermill (N)	TL 770961	I.C.	VI
29. Mundford (N)	TL 802935	I.C.	?VI
*30. Mundford—nr. Round Plantation (N)	TL 8093	I.B.	
31. Foulden (N)	TL 781994	I.C.	?VII
†32. Swaffham—The Paddocks (N)	TF 818086	I.C.	VI
33. Sporle—Petygards Farm (N)	TF 854075	I.C.	?VI
*34. Watton (N)	TL 919008	I.B.	?VI
35. Drayton—nr. Lodge (N)	TG 188131 approx.	C.C.	V

Anglo-Saxon Cemeteries (cont.):

Site		Grid Reference	Type	Starting Date
36.	Norwich—Catton, Eade Road (N)	TG 227099	C.C.	V
37.	Thorpe St. Andrew (N)	TG 254087	I.B.	
38.	Markshall (N)	TG 229039	C.C.	Late IV/V
*39.	Caistor-by-Norwich (N)	TG 235032	M.C.	Late IV/V
40.	Poringland (N)	TG 271020	I.B.	
41.	Brundall Gardens (N)	TG 322084 approx.	C.C.	Late IV/V
*42.	Brundall—St. Clement's (N)	TG 330079	I.B.	?VI
43.	Caister-on-Sea (N)	TG 517123	I.C.	VII
44.	Burgh Castle (S)	TG 476045 approx.	C.C.	?V
†45.	Burgh Castle (S)	TG 476045	I.C.	VII
46.	Pakefield—Gisleham (S)	TM 519897	I.B.	VI
47.	Stockton (N)	TM 380940	I.B.	D
48.	Kirby Cane—Pewter Hill (N)	TM 373933	I.B.	D
49.	Broome (N)	TM 340930	I.B.	
50.	Earsham (N)	TM 326888	C.C.	?VI
51.	Bungay—Joyce Road (S)	TM 347891	I.C.	
52.	Bungay—Stow Park (S)	TM 327879	C.C.	D
53.	Gissing (N)	TM 1585	I.B.	VI
†54.	Hoxne (S)	TM 180775 approx.	M.C.	V
55.	Eye (S)	TM 156748	C.C.	V
56.	Thorndon—White Horse Farm (S)	TM 136701 approx.	I.C.	
57.	Finningham—railway (S)	TM 066684 approx.	C.C.	
58.	Badwell Ash (S)	TM 002693	M.C.	?VI
59.	Rickinghall Inferior (S)	TM 0275	I.B.	
†60.	Botesdale (S)	TM 0475	C.B.	?VI
61.	Redgrave—Moneypot Hill (S)	TM 046787	C.C.	?VI
62.	Kenninghall (N)	TM 034861	I.C.	Early VI
*63.	Hargham/Old Buckenham (N)	Not known	C.C.	V
64.	Rockland All Saints—Mount Pleasant (N)	TL 995947	C.C.	V
65.	Shropham (N)	TL 984927	C.C.	V
66.	Wretham—Illington (N)	TL 948898	C.C.	V
*67.	Brettenham (N)	TL 939845	I.C.	VI
68.	Brettenham—Shadwell/Rushford (N)	Not known	C.C.	V
†69.	Thetford—Bury Road (N)	TL 8682	I.B.	
70.	Thetford Warren (N)	TL 8383	I.B.	
71.	Thetford—modern cemetery (N)	TL 864825	I.C.	
72.	Barnham Heath (S)	TL 887797	I.B.	VI
†73.	Fakenham (S)	TL 906772	I.B.	?VI
74.	Fakenham Heath (S)	TL 890769	C.B.	V
75.	Stanton Chair (S)	TL 955742	I.B.	
76.	Bardwell (S)	TL 943728 approx.	I.B.	?VI
77.	Ixworth Thorpe (S)	TL 925720	I.B.	
78.	Ixworth—Cross House (S)	TL 935701	I.C.	?V
79.	Pakenham—Grimstone End (S)	TL 936693	I.C.	V
80.	Bury St. Edmunds—Hardwick Lane (S)	TL 852629	I.B.	
81.	Bury St. Edmunds (S)	TL 846658	I.C.	?VI
82.	Fornham St. Genevieve (S)	TL 834690	I.C.	
83.	Culford (S)	TL 833703	C.B.	V
84.	West Stow (S)	TL 795714	M.C.	V
85.	Icklingham—Mitchell's Hill (S)	TL 778723	I.C.	?VI

Site		Grid Reference	Type	Starting Date
86.	Lackford (S)	TL 776713	C.C.	V
87.	Risby—Poor's Heath (S)	TL 792685	C.B.	VI
88.	Barrow—Barrow Bottom (S)	TL 773661	I.B.	
89.	Tuddenham (S)	TL 741704 approx.	M.C.	VI
90.	Mildenhall (S)	TL 710740	I.B.	VI
*91.	Mildenhall—Warren Hill (S)	TL 745741	I.C.	VI
92.	Mildenhall—Holywell Row (S)	TL 714766	I.C.	c. 500
93.	Eriswell—Foxhole (S)	TL 733778	I.B.	VI
94.	Eriswell—Lakenheath Base (S)	TL 731803	I.C.	VI
95.	Wangford (S)	TL 750831	I.B.	
96.	Lakenheath (S)	TL 729830	M.C.	VI
97.	Ely—Trinity/Newbarns Road (C)	TL 548812	I.C.	VI
98.	Little Downham—Baptist Church (C)	TL 523838	I.C.	
99.	Chatteris (C)	TL 394860	I.C.	
100.	Mepal—Mepal Fen (C)	TL 430820	C.B.	
101.	Somersham (Hu)	TL 360778	C.B.	V
102.	Ely—Fields Farm (C)	TL 522777	I.C.	?Late V
103.	Soham—Parish Church (C)	TL 593731	I.C.	?VI
104.	Soham—new cemetery site (C)	TL 599723	I.C.	?VI
105.	Soham—waterworks (C)	TL 614715	I.C.	?VI
106.	Chippenham—Freckenham Road (C)	TL 660712	I.C.	?VI
107.	Burwell (C)	TL 590665	I.C.	Late VI
108.	Exning—Windmill Hill (S)	TL 625658	I.C.	?VI
109.	Bottisham—Allington Hill (C)	TL 576590	I.B.	VII
110.	Little Wilbraham (C)	TL 560577	M.C.	Late IV/V
111.	Chesterton—Swan's gravel pit (C)	TL 475605	I.B.	
112.	Girton—Girton College (C)	TL 423609	M.C.	V
113.	Oakington (C)	TL 415645	I.C.	
114.	Cambridge—St. John's College (C)	TL 441588	M.C.	Late IV/V
115.	Cambridge—Rose Crescent (C)	TL 449585	M.C.	V
116.	Cambridge—St. Giles (C)	TL 448592	C.C.	
117.	Cambridge—Barton Road (C)	TL 440575	I.C.	
118.	Cambridge—Jesus Lane (C)	TL 451588	I.B.	
119.	Cambridge—various	Various	I.B.	
120.	Grantchester (C)	TL 431556	I.B.	
121.	Trumpington—Dam Hill (C)	TL 450550	I.C.	
122.	Cherry Hinton (C)	TL 484555	I.C.	?VI
123.	Balsham—Fleam Dyke (C)	TL 5754	I.B.	
124.	Babraham—Worstead Street (C)	TL 500530	I.B.	
125.	Sawston—Huckeridge Hill (C)	TL 480504	I.C.	?V
126.	Little Shelford (C)	TL 459509	I.C.	
127.	Hauxton (C)	TL 432528	I.C.	c. 500
128.	Haslingfield—Cantelupe Farm (C)	TL 413520	M.C.	V
129.	Barrington A (C)	TL 372496	I.C.	V
130.	Barrington B—Hooper's Field (C)	TL 387497	M.C.	V
131.	Foxton (C)	TL 407488	I.B.	
132.	Melbourn—Street Way (C)	TL 382438	I.C.	?VI
133.	Therfield—Therfield Heath (He)	TL 340403	I.B.	
134.	Great Chesterford (E)	TL 501435	M.C.	V
135.	Saffron Walden (E)	TL 535382	I.C.	?VII
136.	Wendens Ambo—Myrtle Hill (E)	TL 529363	I.B.	

Anglo-Saxon Cemeteries (cont.):

Site	Grid References	Type	Starting Date
137. Hildersham—Furrey Hills (C)	TL 552487	M.C.	
138. Linton A (C)	TL 564468	M.C.	
139. Linton B (C)	TL 583486	I.C.	?L. V
140. Shudy Camps (C)	TL 605444	I.C.	Late VI
†141. Sudbury—Chilton Hall (S)	TL 890427	I.B.	VII
142. Badley—Gate Ford/Needham Market (S)	TM 079561	I.B.	VII
143. Bramford (S)	Not known	?C.B.	VI/VII
144. Ipswich—Hadleigh Road (S)	TM 146445	M.C.	?VI
145. Akenham (S)	TM 159496	?I.B.	?VI
146. Kesgrave (S)	TM 2246	C.B.	VI
147. Brightwell—Brightwell Heath (S)	TM 241444	C.B.	?VI
148. Martlesham—Martlesham Heath (S)	TM 245461	I.B.	
149. Waldringfield (S)	TM 282442	C.B.	V
150. Sutton Hoo (S)	TM 288487	M.C.	?VI
*151. Ufford (S)	TM 294520	I.B.	VI
152. Rendlesham—Hoo Hill (S)	TM 331535	C.C.	?VI
153. Wickham Market (S)	TM 302567	I.B.	VII
154. Parham—Fryer's Close (S)	TM 309605	I.B.	
†155. Framlingham (S)	TM 287637	I.C.	VII
156. Snape (S)	TM 402597	C.C.	V

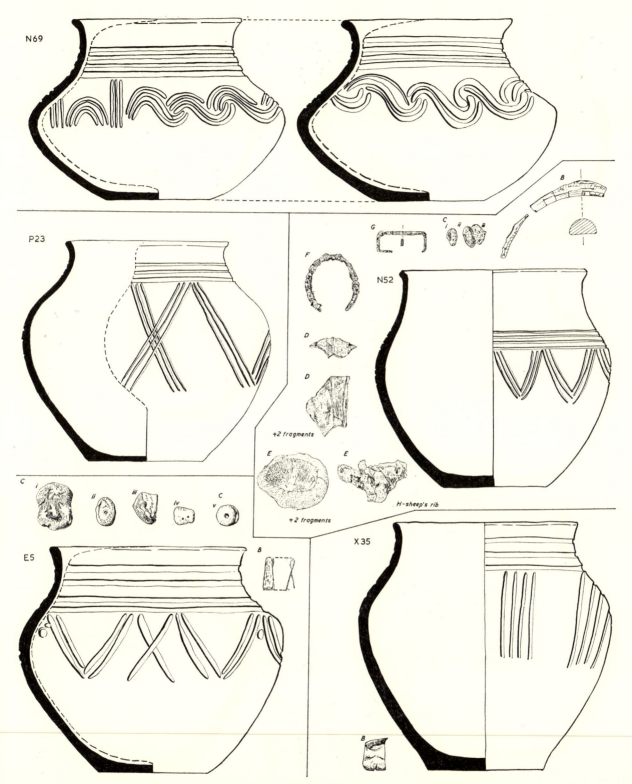

FIG. 1. Urns from Caistor-by-Norwich (scales: urns ¼, grave goods ½).

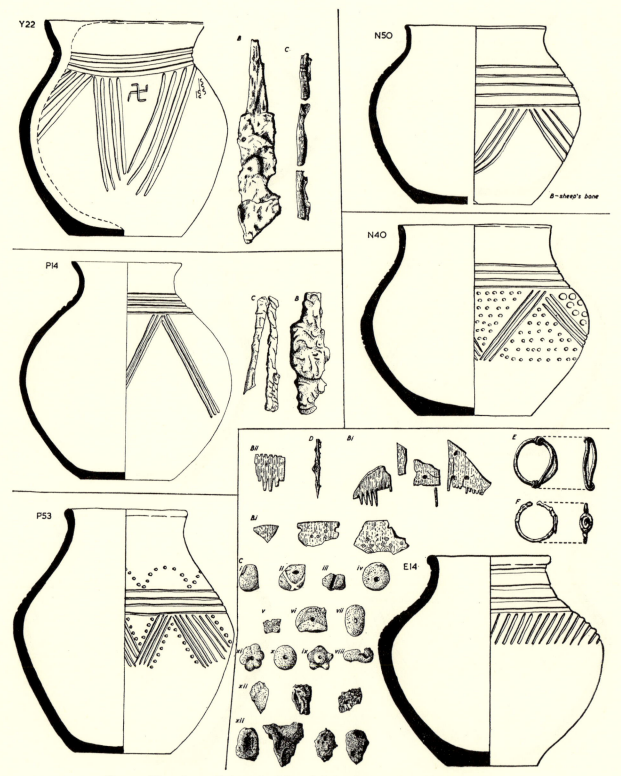

FIG. 2. Urns from Caistor-by-Norwich (scales: urns ¼, grave goods ½).

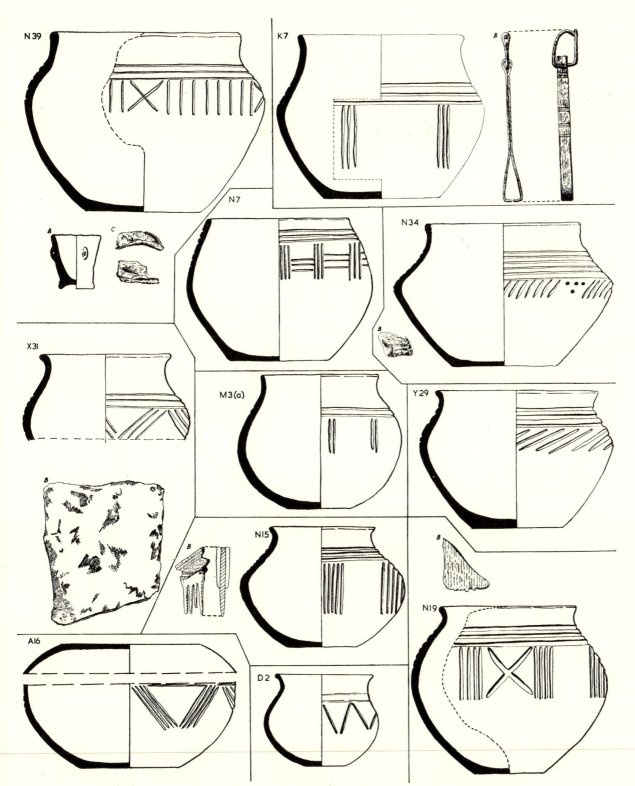

Fig. 3. Urns from Caistor-by-Norwich (scales: urns ¼, grave goods ½).

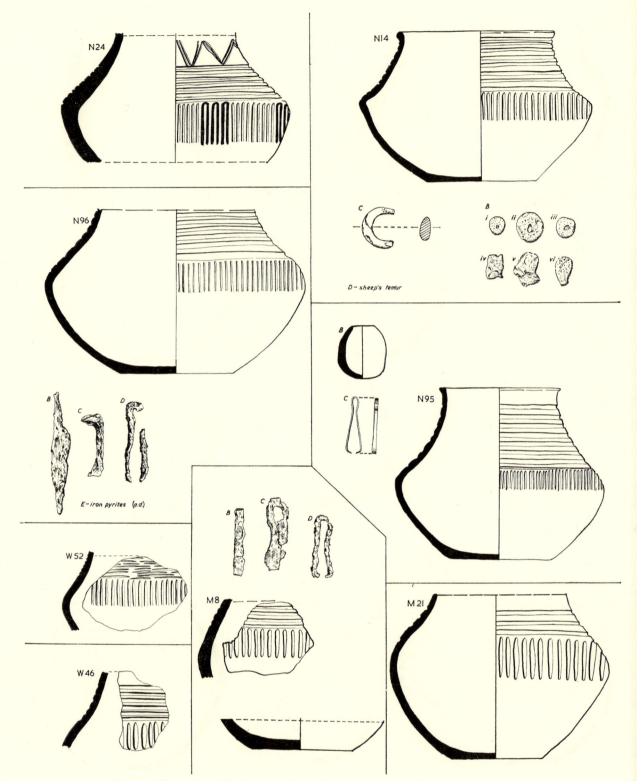

FIG. 4. Urns from Caistor-by-Norwich (scales: urns ¼, grave goods ½).

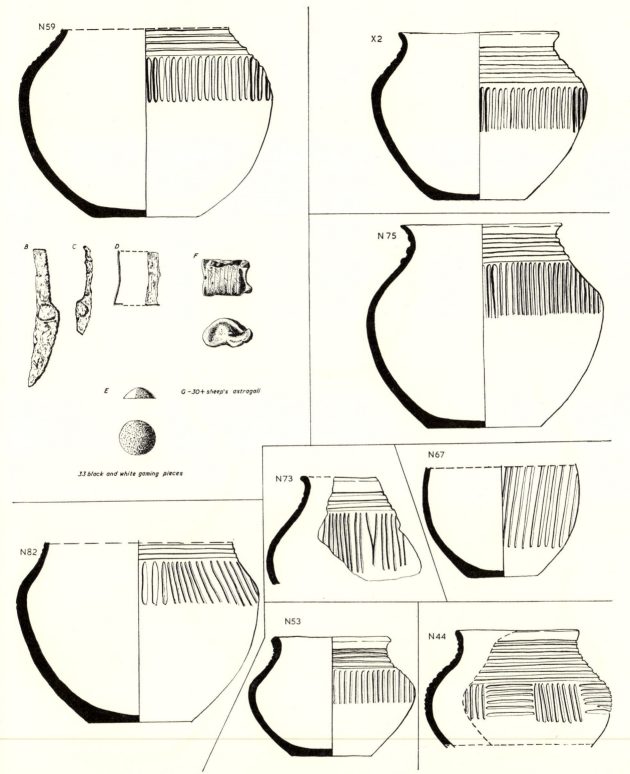

FIG. 5. Urns from Caistor-by-Norwich (scales: urns ¼, grave goods ½).

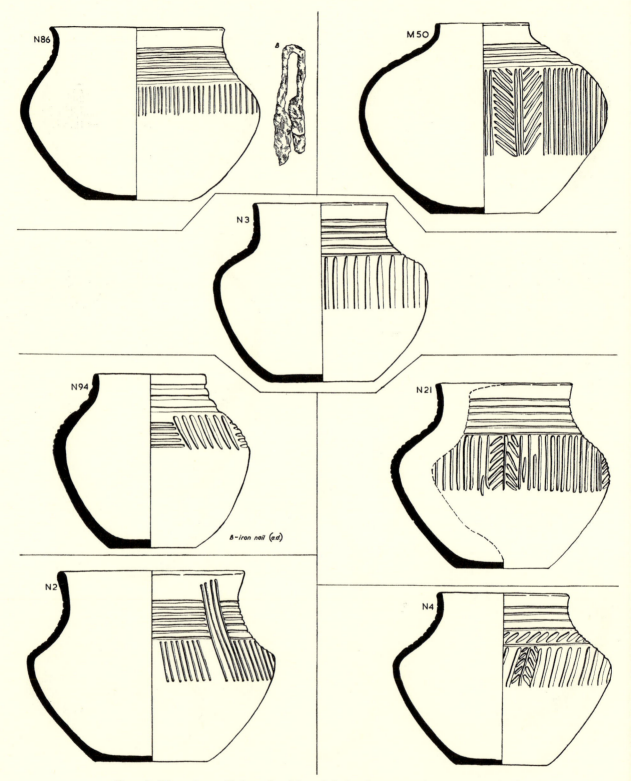

FIG. 6. Urns from Caistor-by-Norwich (scales: urns ¼, grave goods ½).

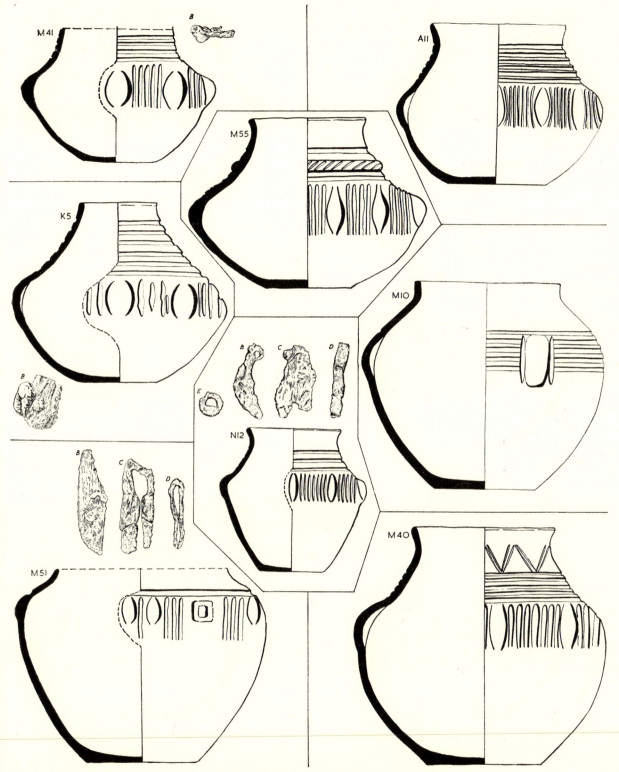

Fig. 7. Urns from Caistor-by-Norwich (scales: urns ¼, grave goods ½).

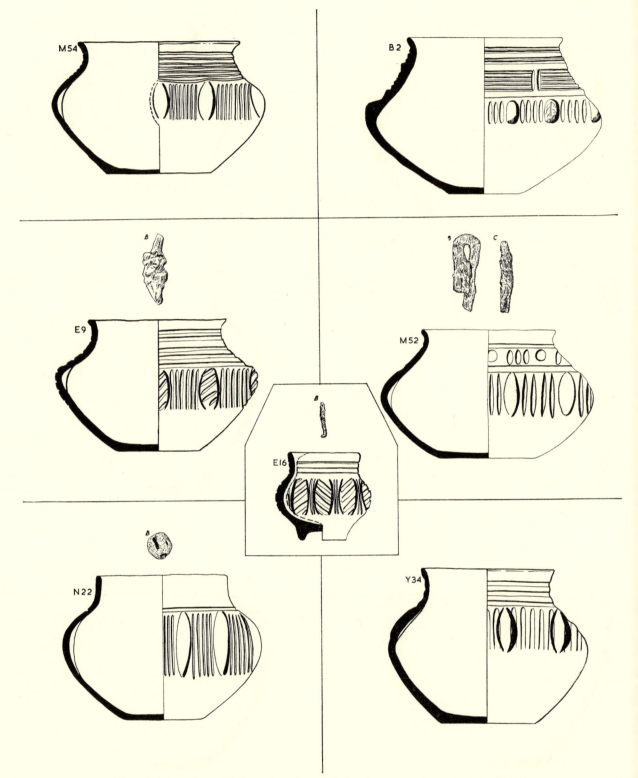

FIG. 8. Urns from Caistor-by-Norwich (scales: urns ¼, grave goods ½).

FIG. 9. Urns from Caistor-by-Norwich (scales: urns ¼, grave goods ½).

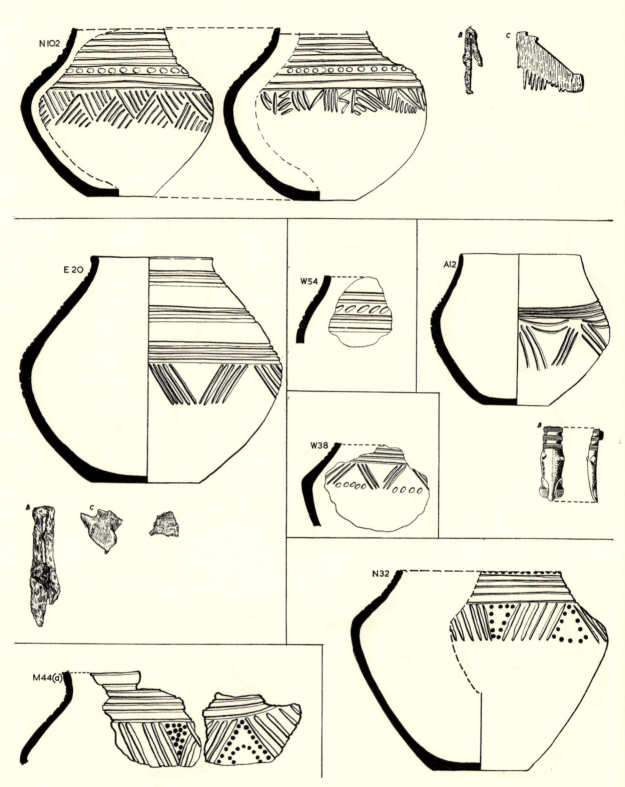

FIG. 10. Urns from Caistor-by-Norwich (scales: urns ¼, grave goods ½).

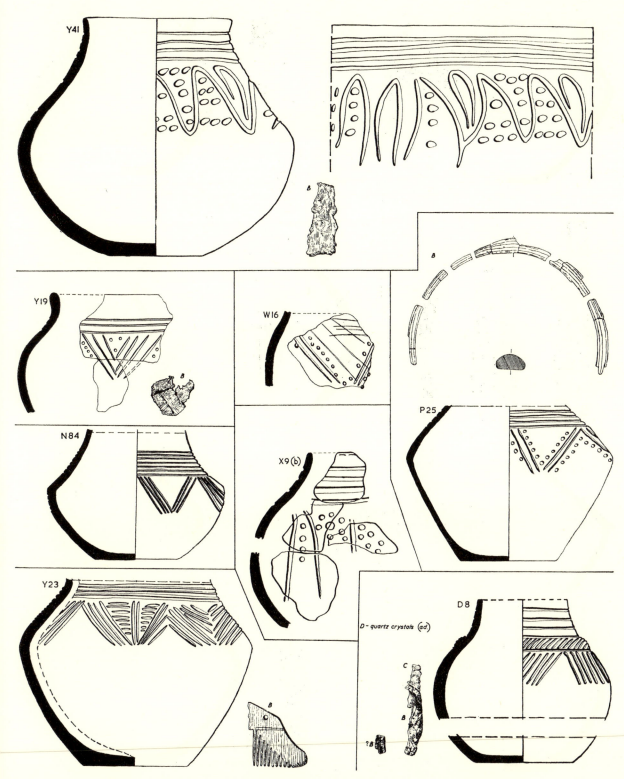

FIG. 11. Urns from Caistor-by-Norwich (scales: urns ¼, grave goods ½).

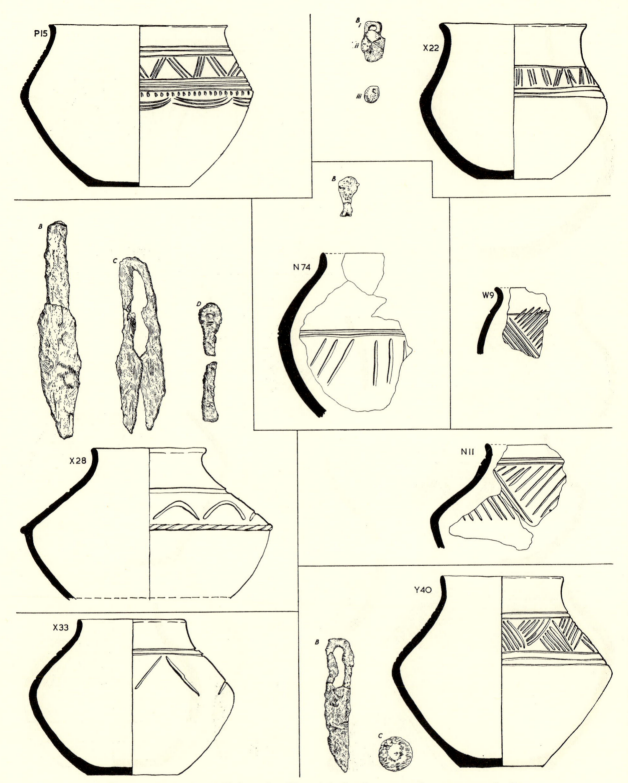

FIG. 12. Urns from Caistor-by-Norwich (scales: urns $\frac{1}{4}$, grave goods $\frac{1}{2}$).

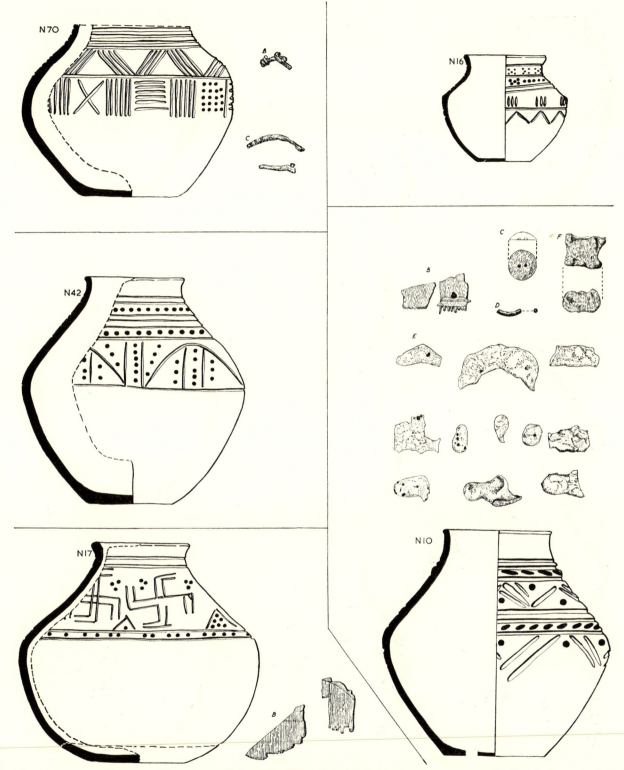

FIG. 13. Urns from Caistor-by-Norwich (scales: urns ¼, grave goods ½).

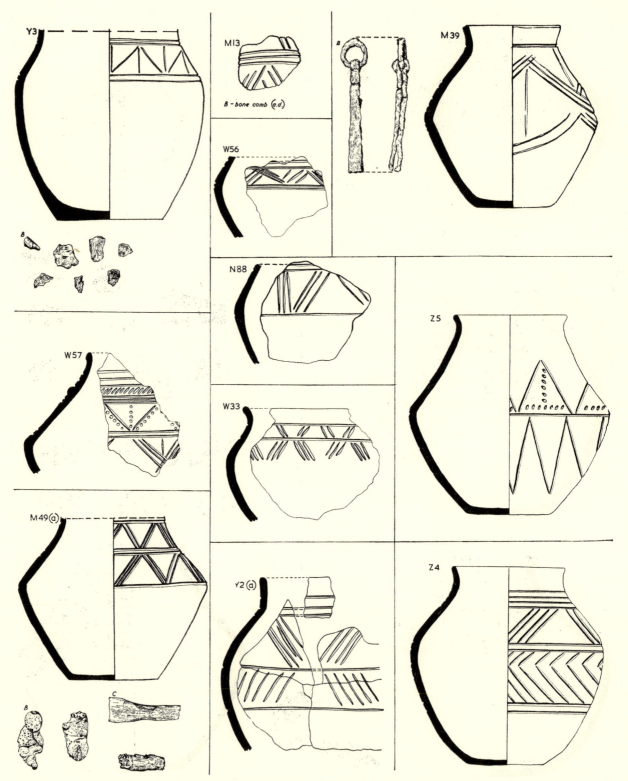

FIG. 14. Urns from Caistor-by-Norwich (scales: urns ¼, grave goods ½).

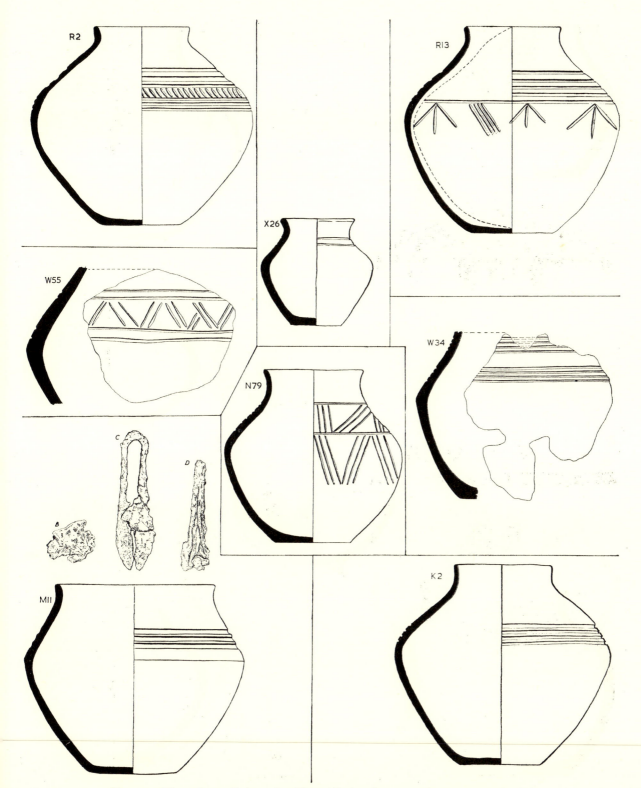

FIG. 15. Urns from Caistor-by-Norwich (scales: urns $\frac{1}{4}$, grave goods $\frac{1}{2}$).

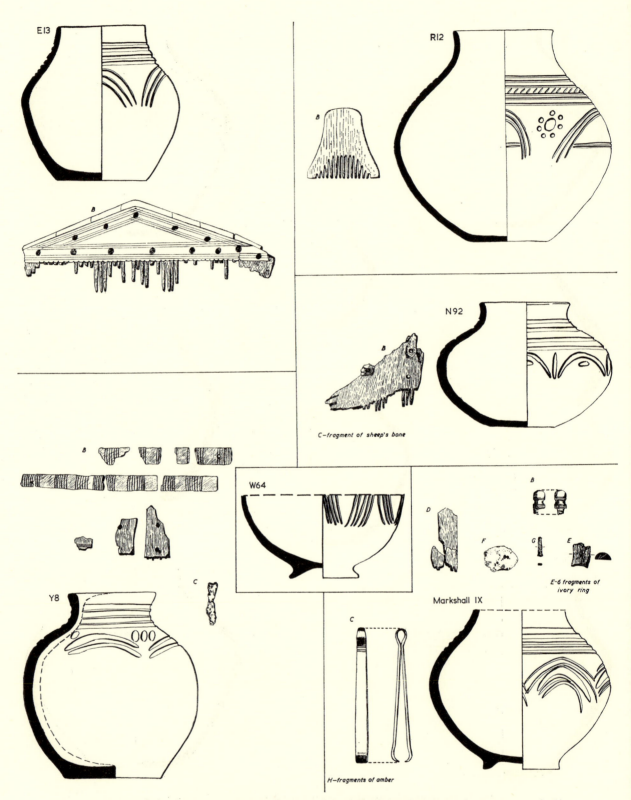

FIG. 16. Urns from Caistor-by-Norwich and Markshall (scales: urns ¼, grave goods ½).
For Markshall IX grave goods, see pp. 248–9.

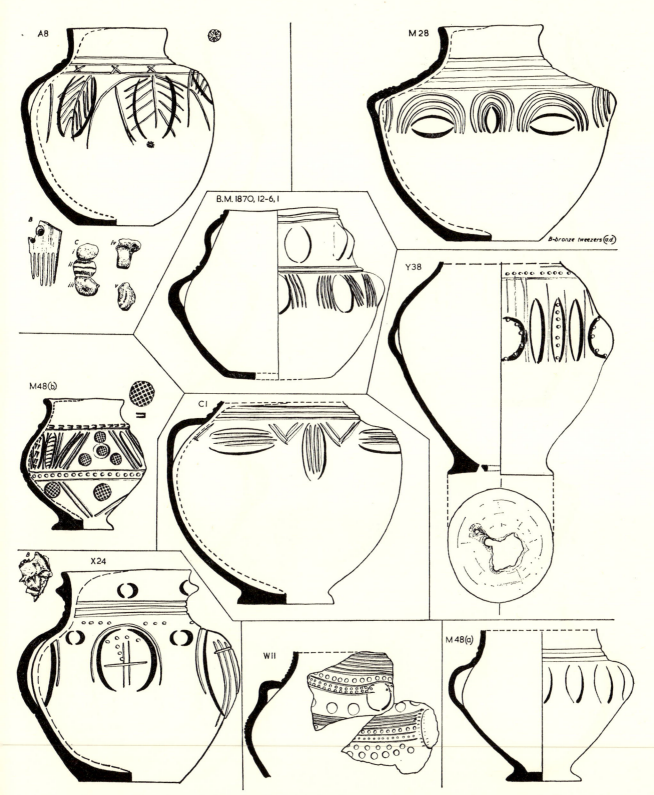

FIG. 17. Urns from Caistor-by-Norwich (scales: urns ¼, stamps and grave goods ½).

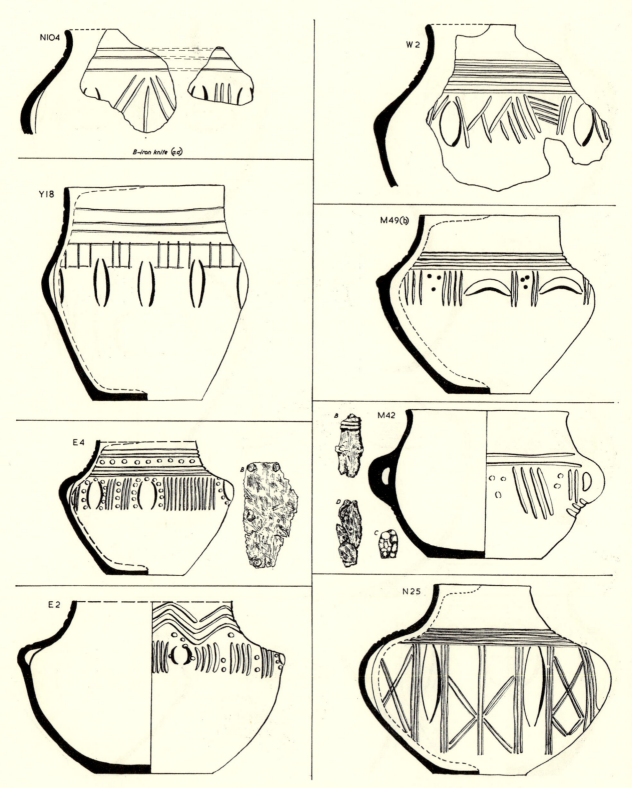

FIG. 18. Urns from Caistor-by-Norwich (scales: urns ¼, grave goods ½).

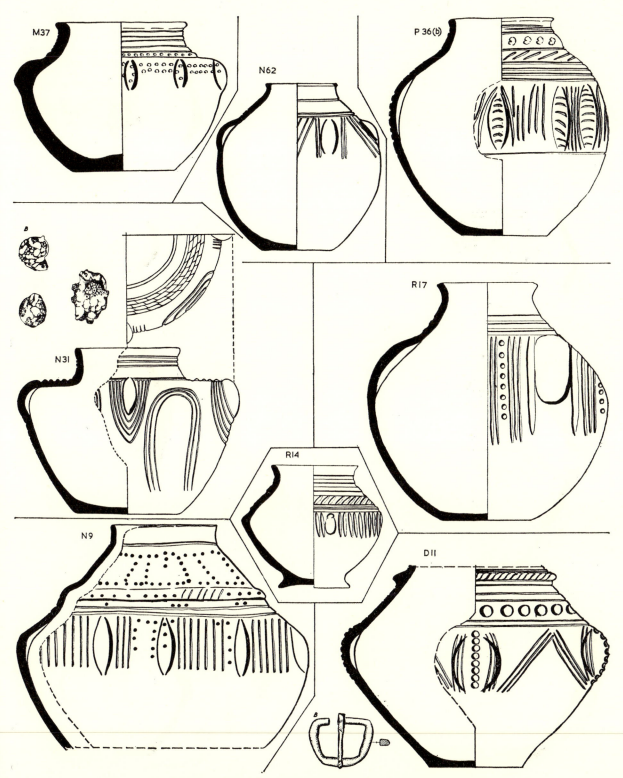

FIG. 19. Urns from Caistor-by-Norwich (scales: urns ¼, grave goods ½).

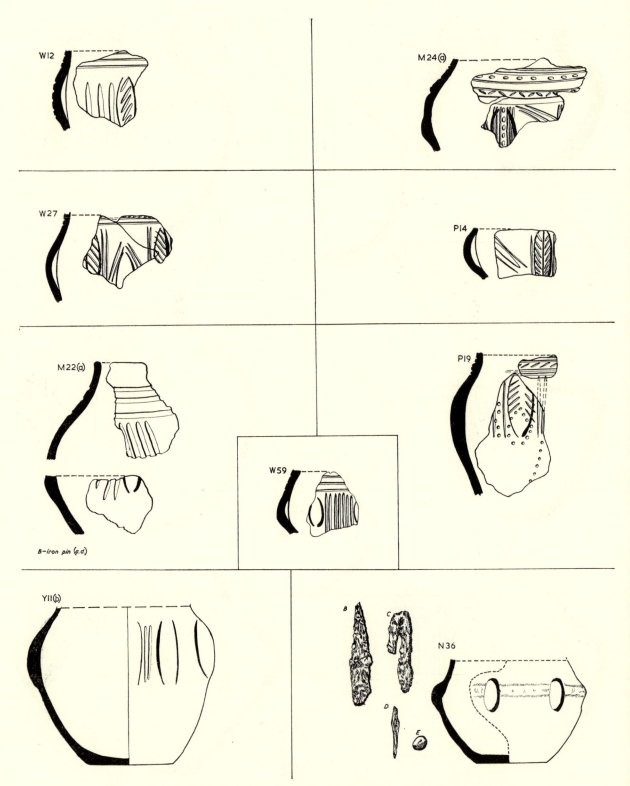

W12 M24(a)

W27 P14

M22(a) P19

B-iron pin (a.d.)

W59

Y11(b) N36

B C D E

Fig. 20. Urns from Caistor-by-Norwich (scales: urns ¼, grave goods ½).
For M22(a) see also fig. 23; for P14, read W14.

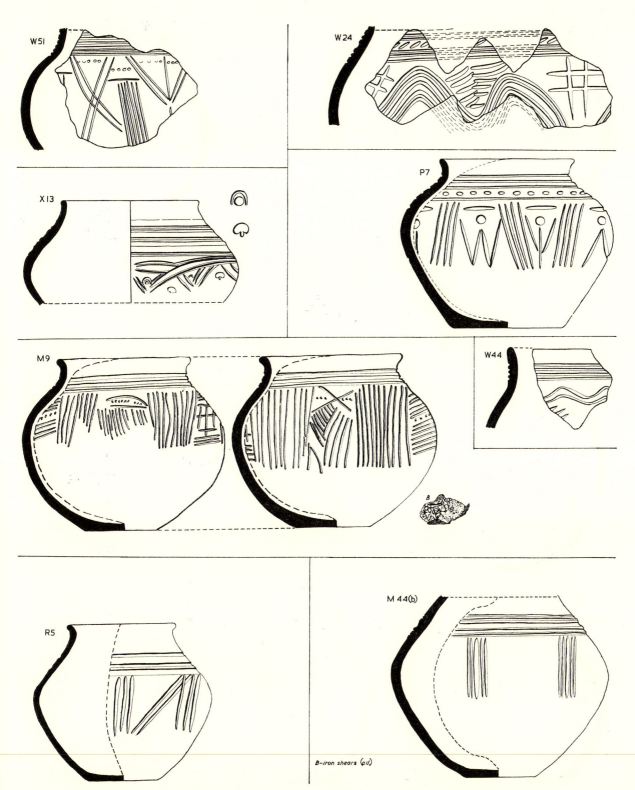

FIG. 21. Urns from Caistor-by-Norwich (scales: urns ¼, stamps and grave goods ½).

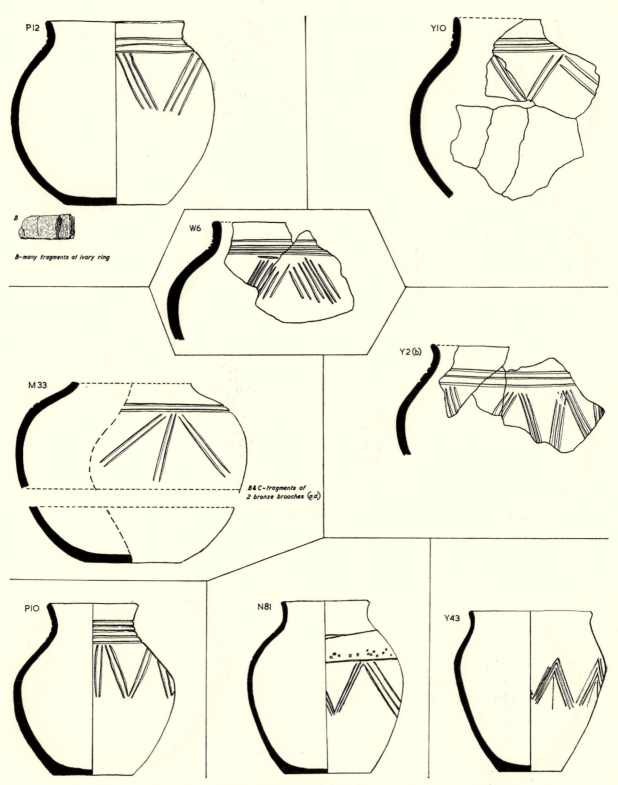

FIG. 22. Urns from Caistor-by-Norwich (scales: urns ¼, grave goods ½).

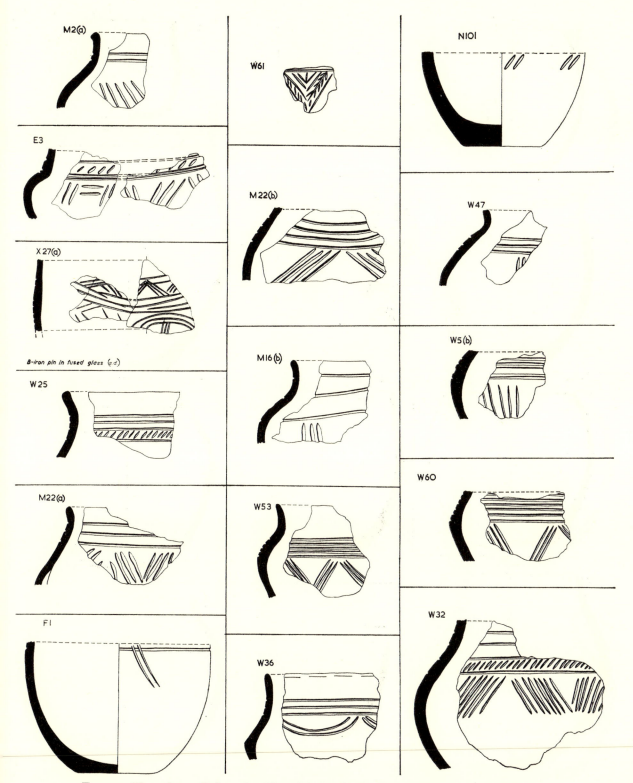

FIG. 23. Urns from Caistor-by-Norwich (scale ¼). For M22(a) see also fig. 20.

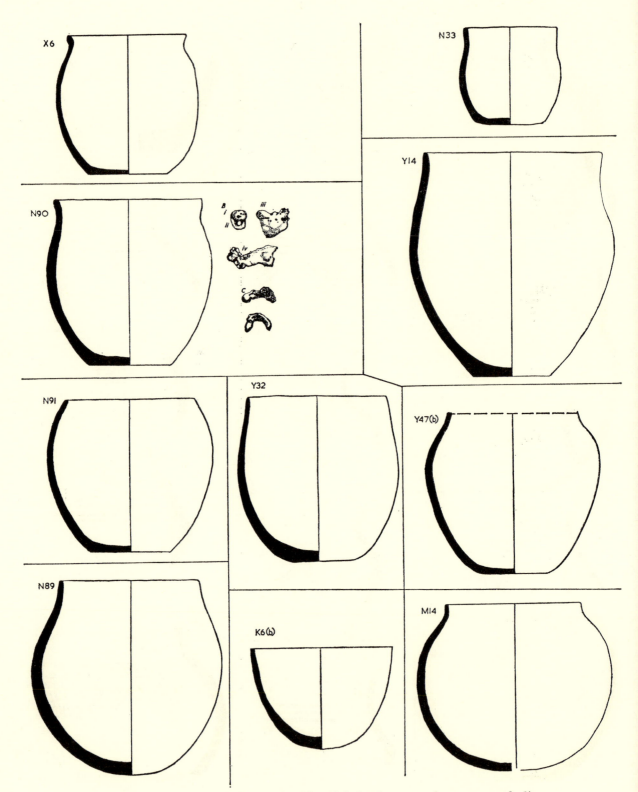

FIG. 24. Urns from Caistor-by-Norwich (scales: urns $\frac{1}{4}$, grave goods $\frac{1}{2}$).

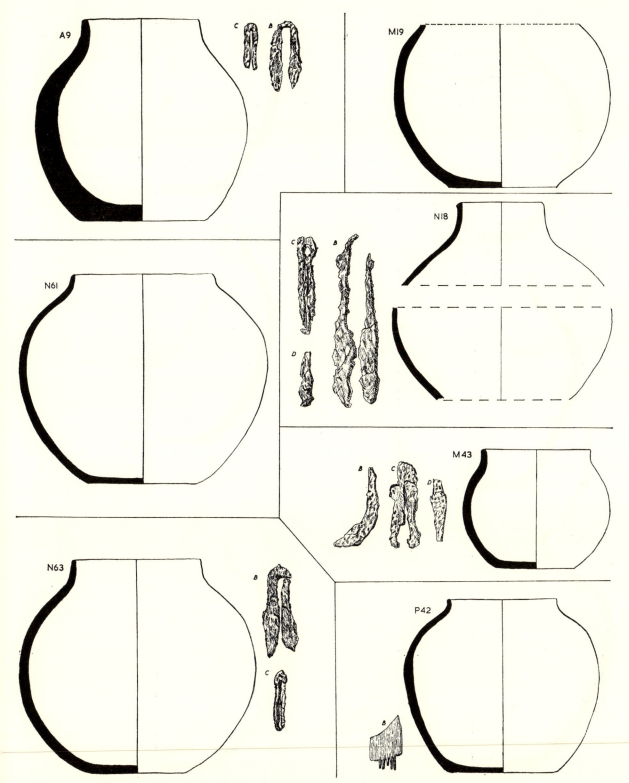

FIG. 25. Urns from Caistor-by-Norwich (scales: urns ¼, grave goods ½).

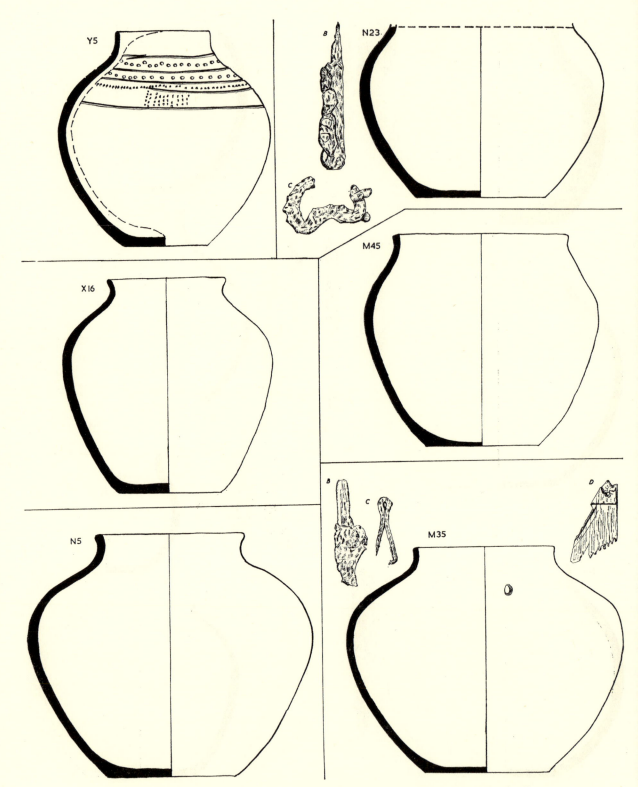

FIG. 26. Urns from Caistor-by-Norwich (scales: urns ¼, grave goods ½).

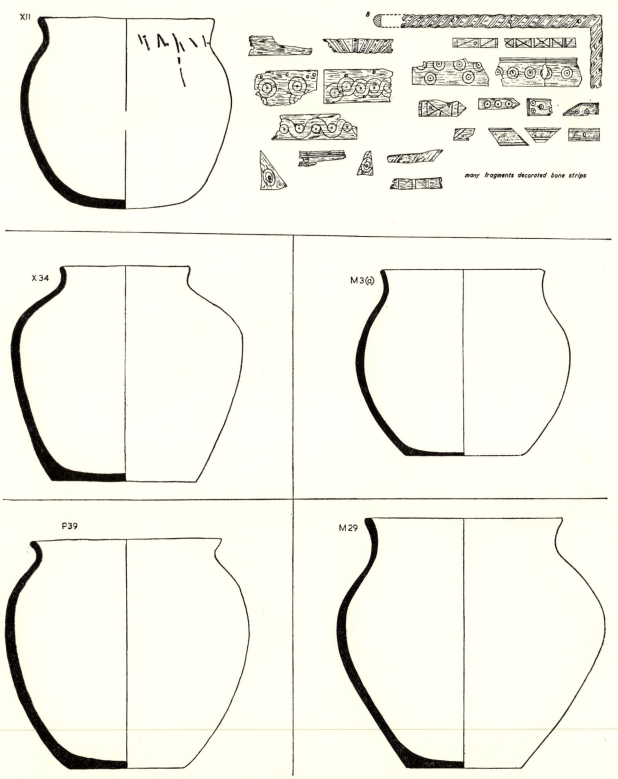

For M 3(a) read M 3(b). FIG. 27. Urns from Caistor-by-Norwich (scales: urns ¼, grave goods ½).

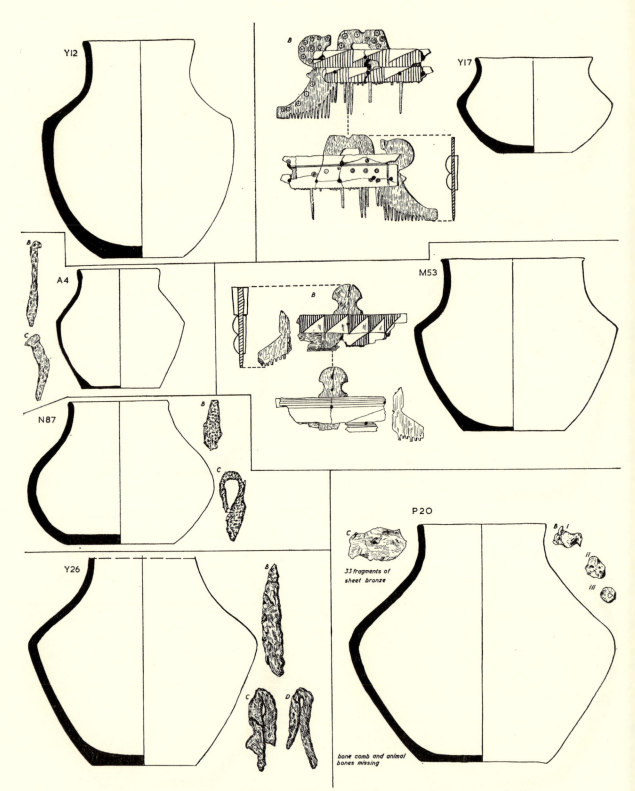

FIG. 28. Urns from Caistor-by-Norwich (scales: urns ¼, grave goods ½).

The following labels appear within the figure:

Y12
B
Y17
A4
B
C
M53
B
N87
B
C
Y26
B
C
D
P20
C
33 fragments of sheet bronze
bone comb and animal bones missing
B i
ii
iii

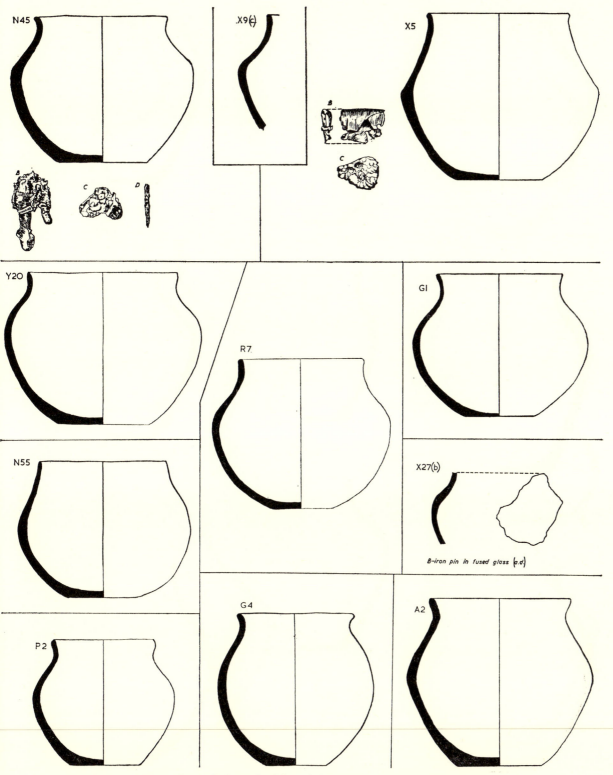

FIG. 29. Urns from Caistor-by-Norwich (scales: urns ¼, grave goods ½).

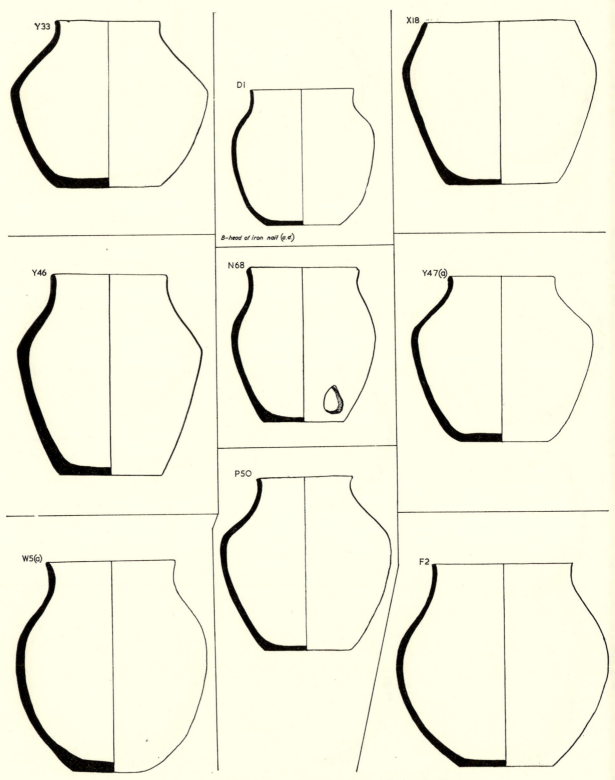

Y33   XI8

DI

B–head of iron nail (a.d.)

Y46   N68   Y47(a)

P5O

W5(a)   F2

FIG. 30. Urns from Caistor-by-Norwich (scale $\frac{1}{4}$).

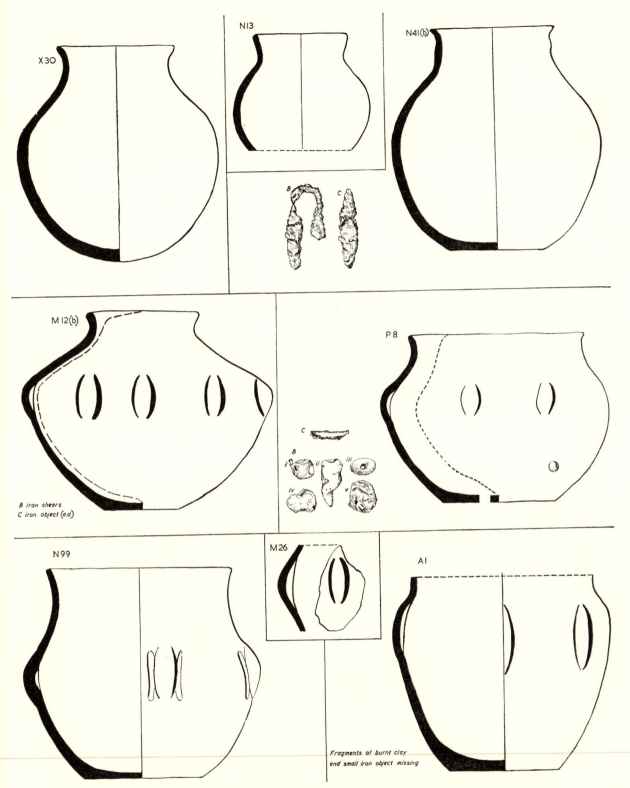

FIG. 31. Urns from Caistor-by-Norwich (scales: urns ¼, grave goods ½).

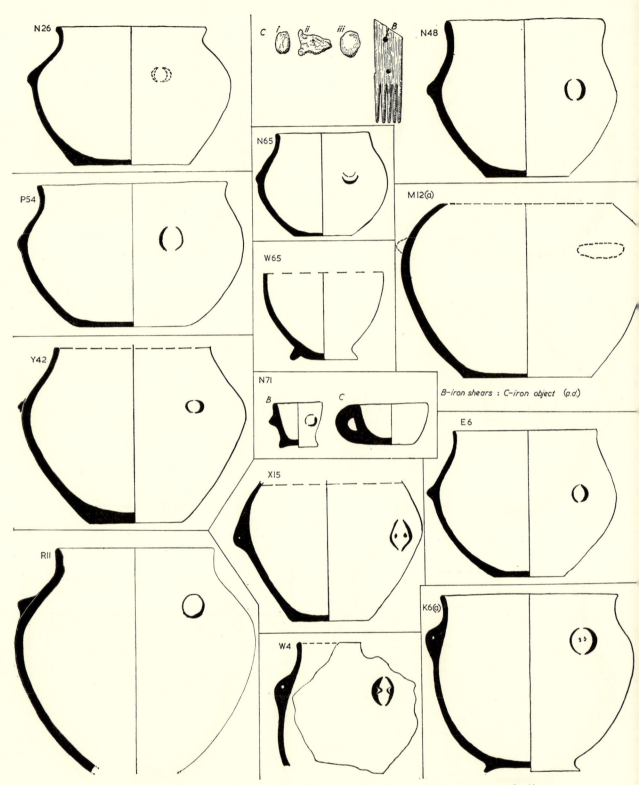

FIG. 32. Urns from Caistor-by-Norwich (scales: urns ¼, grave goods ½).

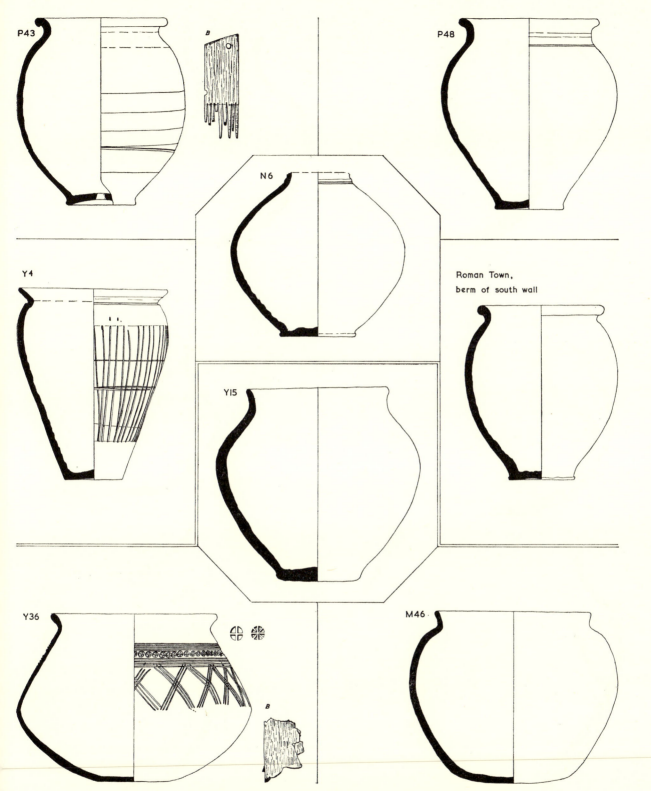

FIG. 33. Urns, including Roman pots, from Caistor-by-Norwich
(scales: urns ¼, grave goods ½).

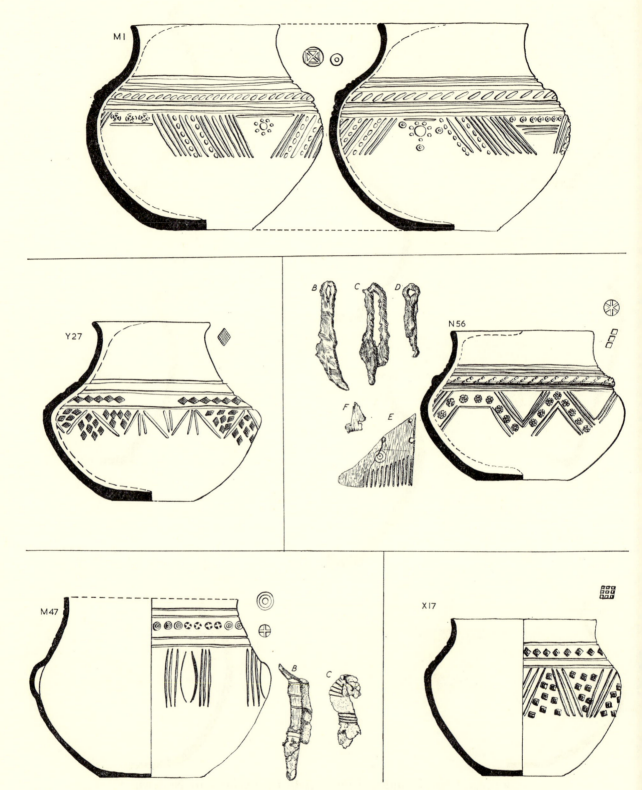

Fig. 34. Urns from Caistor-by-Norwich (scales: urns ¼, stamps and grave goods ½).

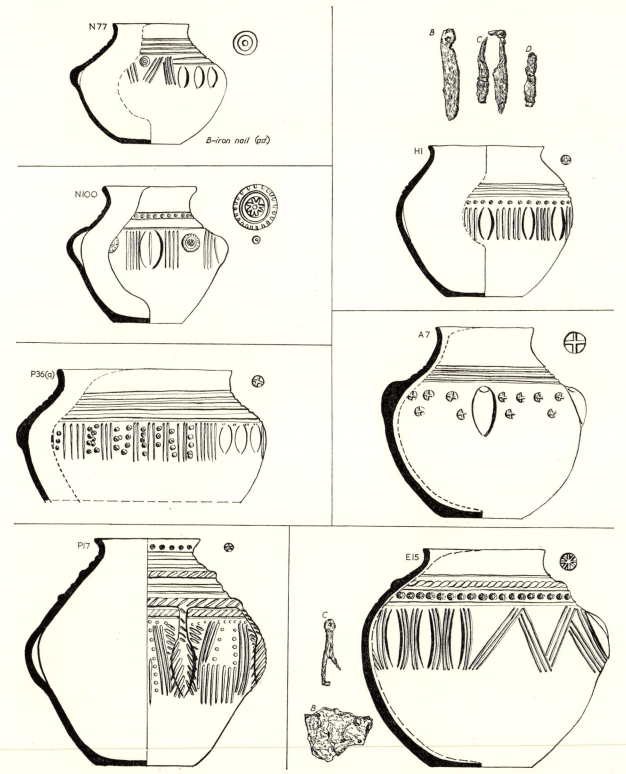

FIG. 35. Urns from Caistor-by-Norwich (scales: urns ¼, stamps and grave goods ½).

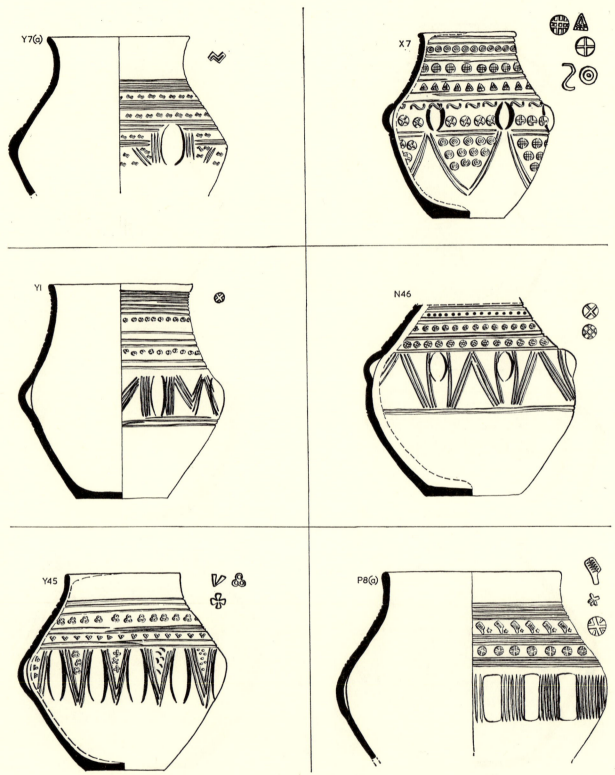

FIG. 36. Urns from Caistor-by-Norwich (scales: urns ⅟₄, stamps ½).

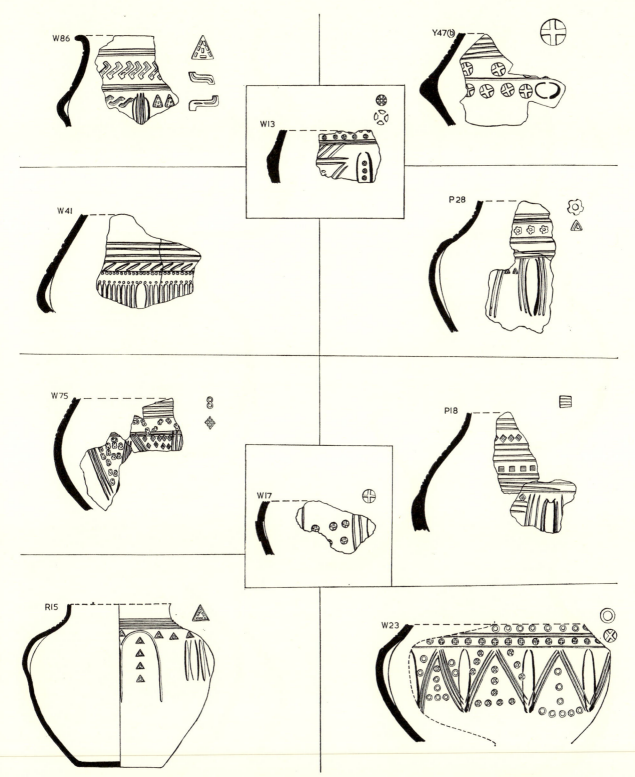

FIG. 37. Urns from Caistor-by-Norwich (scales: urns ¼, stamps ½).
A lead mend from P 28 is on fig. 60 (no. 15). For Y 47(b) read Y 47(c).

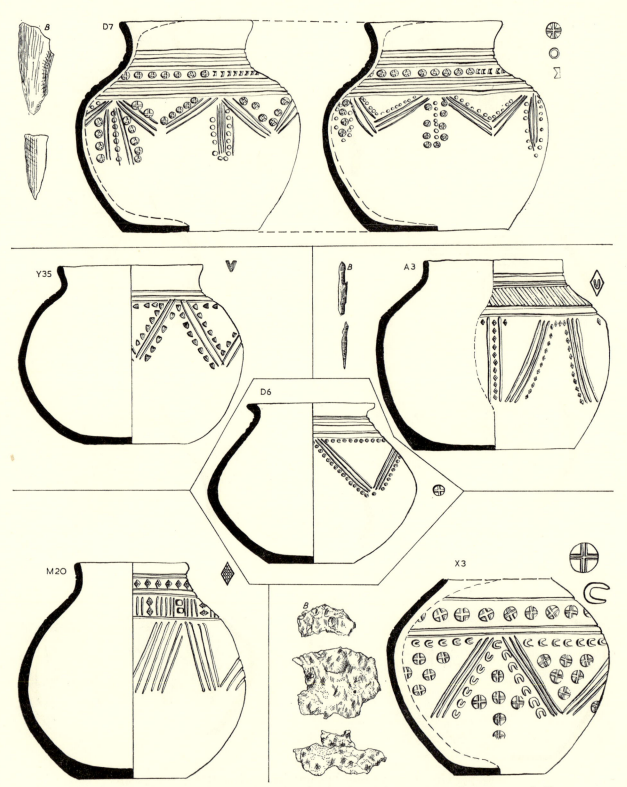

FIG. 38. Urns from Caistor-by-Norwich (scales: urns ¼, stamps and grave goods ½).

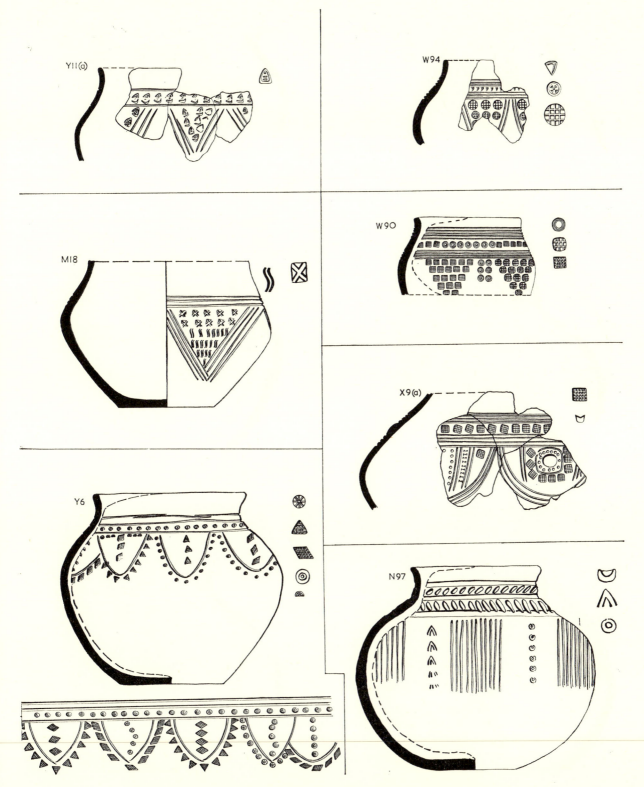

FIG. 39. Urns from Caistor-by-Norwich (scales: urns $\frac{1}{4}$, stamps $\frac{1}{2}$).
X 9(a) is part of W 92 (fig. 46).

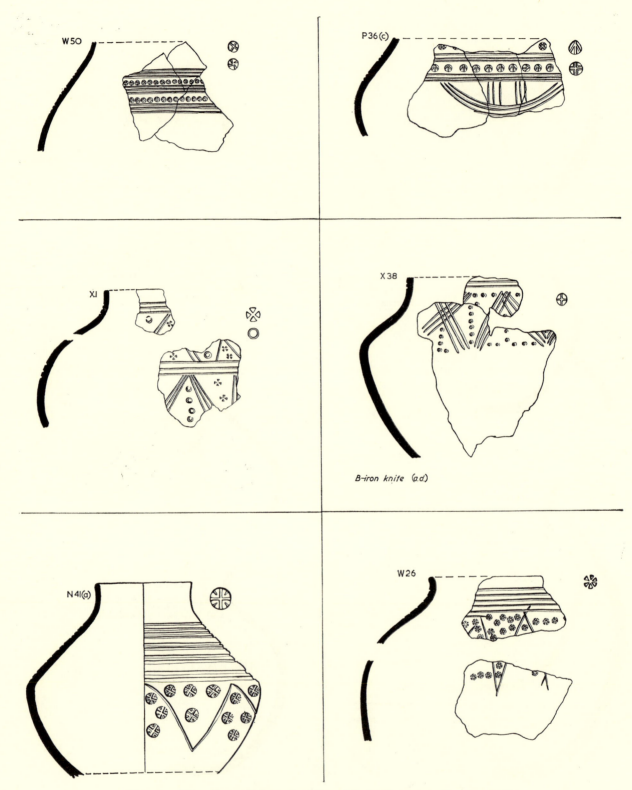

W 50

P 36(c)

X J

X 38

B–iron knife (a.d.)

N 41(a)

W 26

FIG. 40. Urns from Caistor-by-Norwich (scales: urns $\frac{1}{4}$, stamps $\frac{1}{2}$).

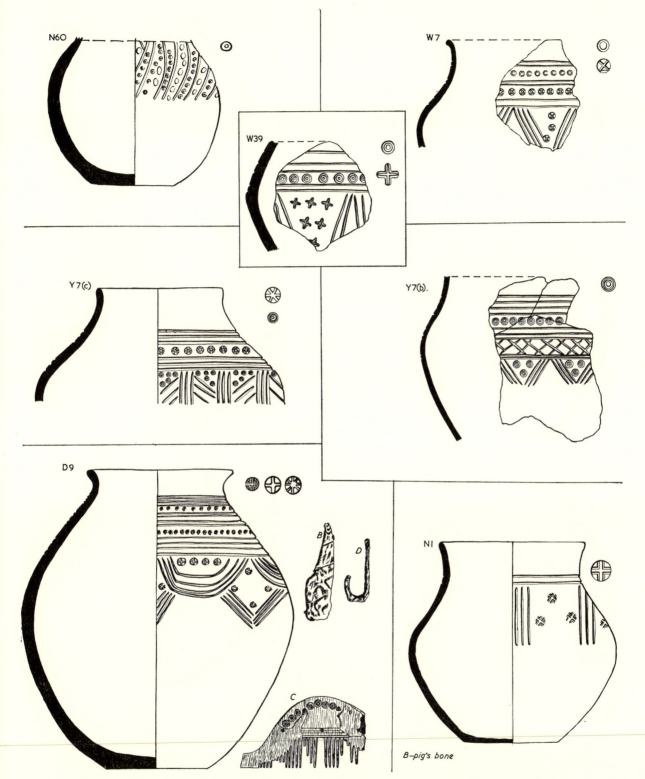

FIG. 41. Urns from Caistor-by-Norwich (scales: urns ¼, stamps and grave goods ½).

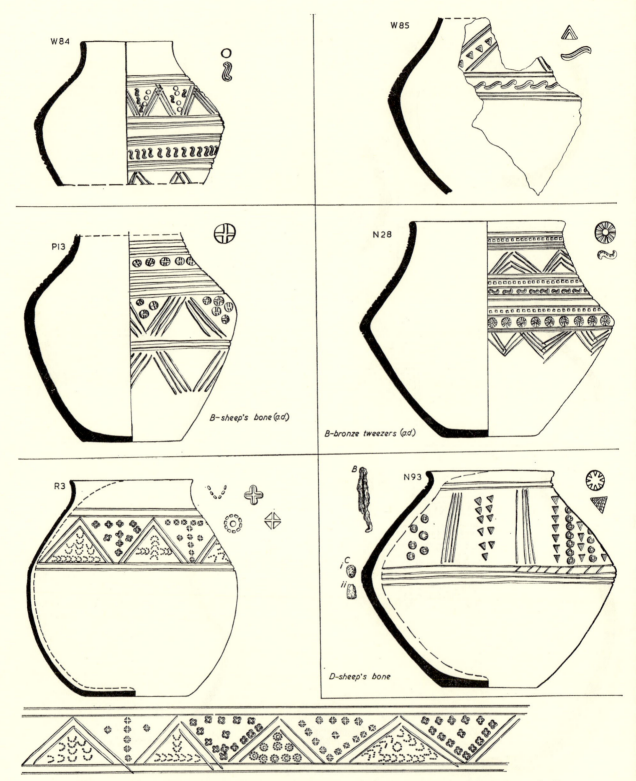

FIG. 42. Urns from Caistor-by-Norwich (scales: urns ¼, stamps and grave goods ½).

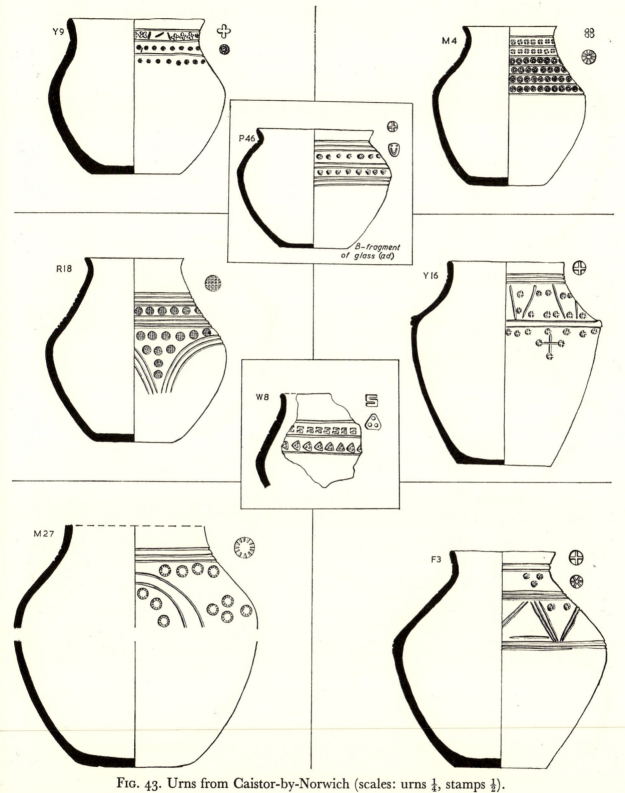

FIG. 43. Urns from Caistor-by-Norwich (scales: urns ¼, stamps ½).

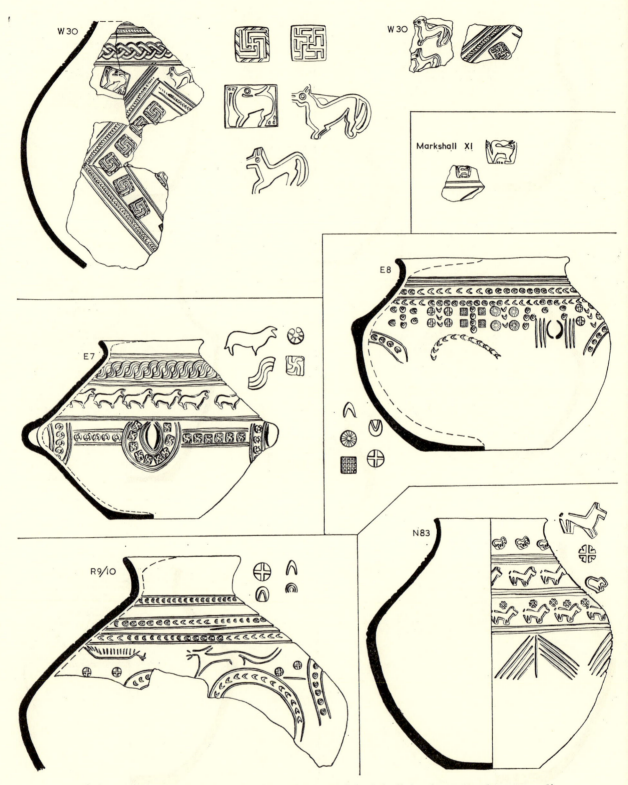

FIG. 44. Urns from Caistor-by-Norwich and Markshall (scales: urns ¼, stamps ½).

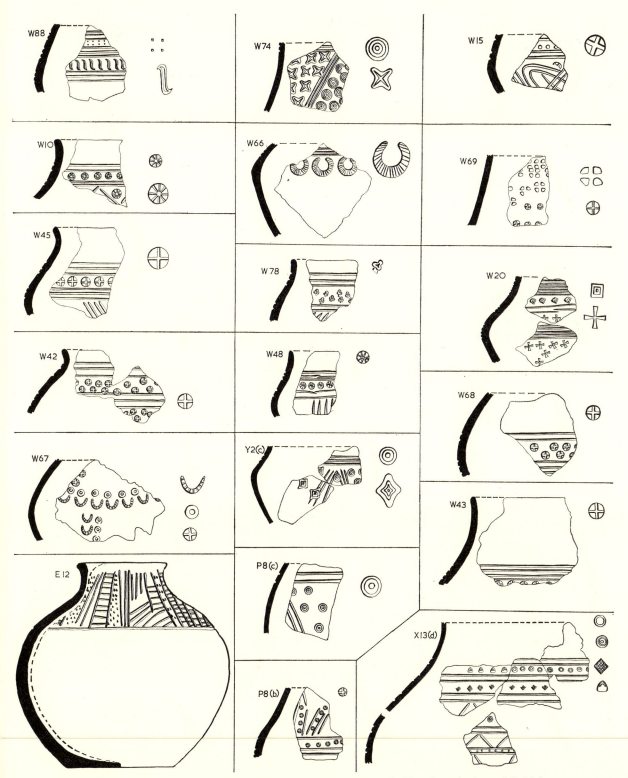

FIG. 45. Urns from Caistor-by-Norwich (scales: urns ¼, stamps ½). For description of P 8(c) see p. 170.

FIG. 46. Urns from Caistor-by-Norwich (scales: urns ¼, stamps ½).
W 92 is part of X 9(a) (fig. 39)

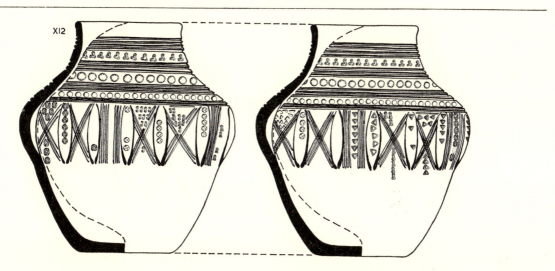

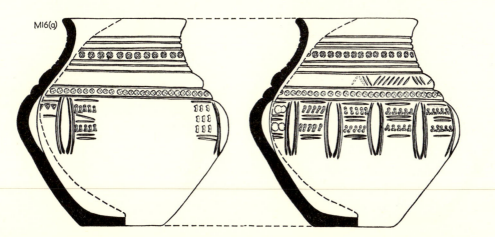

FIG. 47. Urns from Caistor-by-Norwich by Potter I (scales: urns ¼, stamps ½).

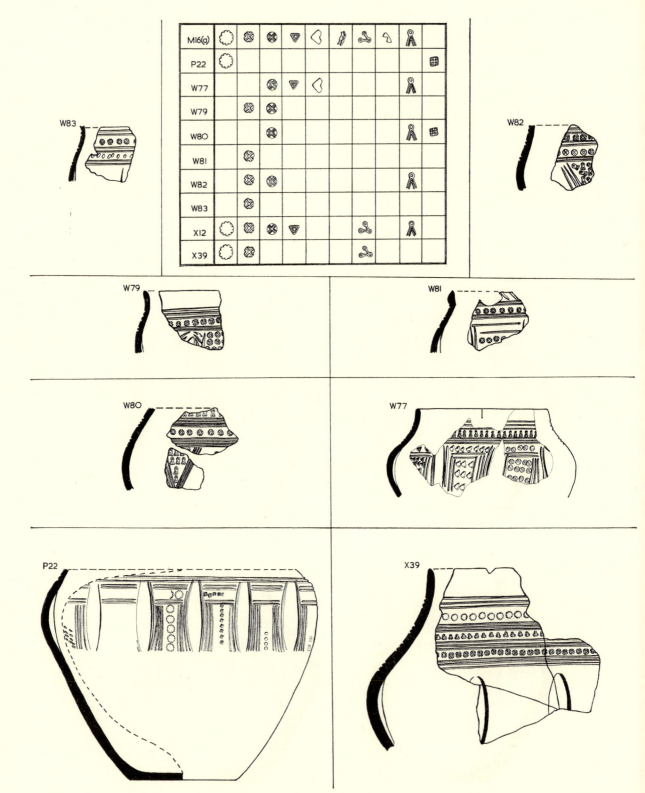

MI6(q)	⚬	✳	✳	▽	◁	𝄞	⚛	⚲	𝓐	
P22	⚬									⊞
W77			✳	▽	◁				𝓐	
W79		✳	✳							
W80			✳						𝓐	⊞
W81		✳								
W82		✳	✳						𝓐	
W83		✳								
XI2	⚬	✳	✳	▽			⚛		𝓐	
X39	⚬	✳					⚛			

FIG. 48. Urns from Caistor-by-Norwich by Potter I (scales: urns ¼, stamps ½).

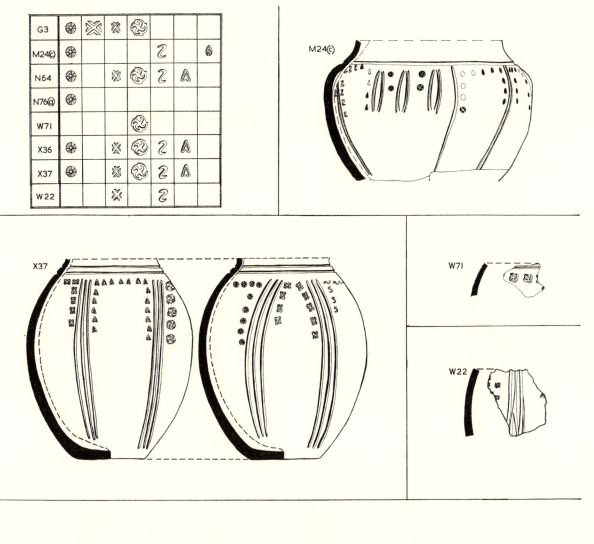

G3	⊕	⊠	⊞	⊚			
M24(c)	⊕				ζ		◮
N64	⊕		⊞	⊚	ζ	◭	
N76(c)	⊕						
W71				⊚			
X36	⊕		⊞	⊚	ζ	◭	
X37	⊕		⊞	⊚	ζ	◭	
W22			⊞		ζ		

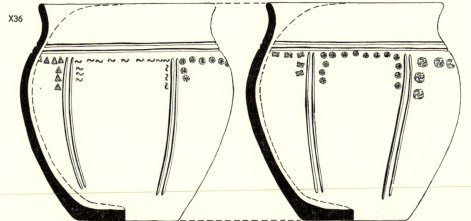

Fig. 49. Urns from Caistor-by-Norwich by Potter II (scales: urns ¼, stamps ½).

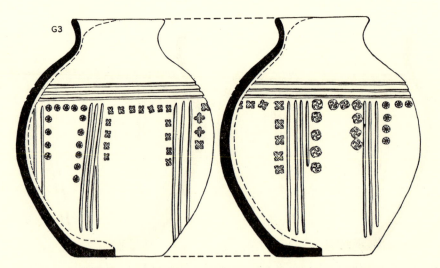

FIG. 50. Urns from Caistor-by-Norwich by Potter II (scales: urns ¼, stamps ½).

Chart (stamp types by urn):

Urn						
G3						
M24(c)						
N64						
N76(i)						
W71						
X36						
X37						
W22						

N76(i)

N64

G3

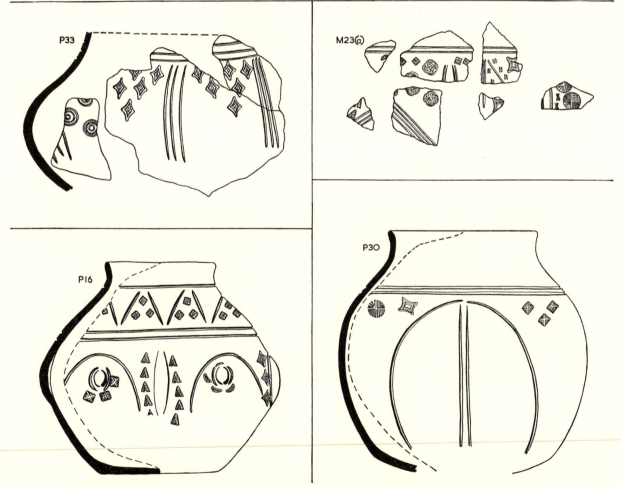

M23(a)	✦	◈	◻	◹	⌒	▦	⌗			
M31			◻					◎		
M32								◎		
M57			◻					◎		◉
P16		◈	◻	◹	⌒				✕	
P30			◻			▦			✕	
P33			◻					◎		

Fig. 51. Urns from Caistor-by-Norwich by Potter III (scales: urns ¼, stamps ½).

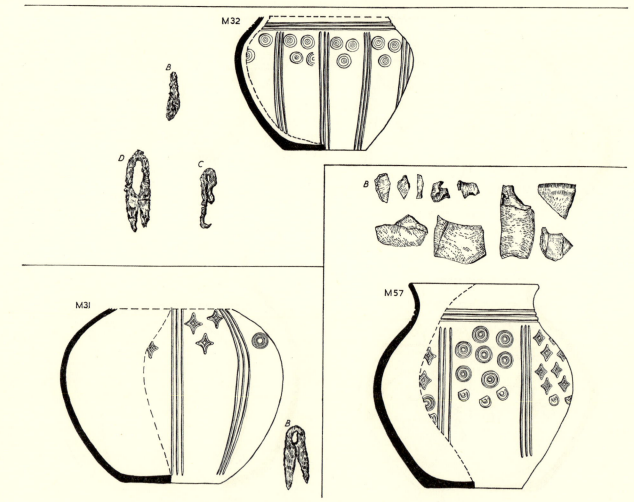

FIG. 52. Urns from Caistor-by-Norwich by Potter III (scales: urns ¼, stamps and grave goods ½)

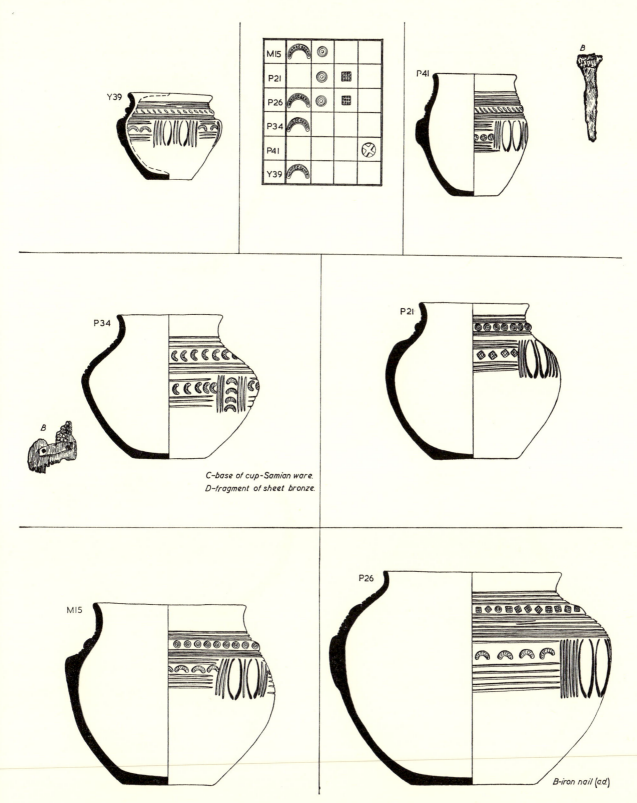

M15	⌒	◎	
P21		◎	▦
P26	⌒	◎	▦
P34	⌒		
P41			⊗
Y39	⌒		

C–base of cup–Samian ware.
D–fragment of sheet bronze.

B–iron nail (ad)

FIG. 53. Urns from Caistor-by-Norwich by Potter IV (scales: urns $\frac{1}{4}$, stamps and grave goods $\frac{1}{2}$).

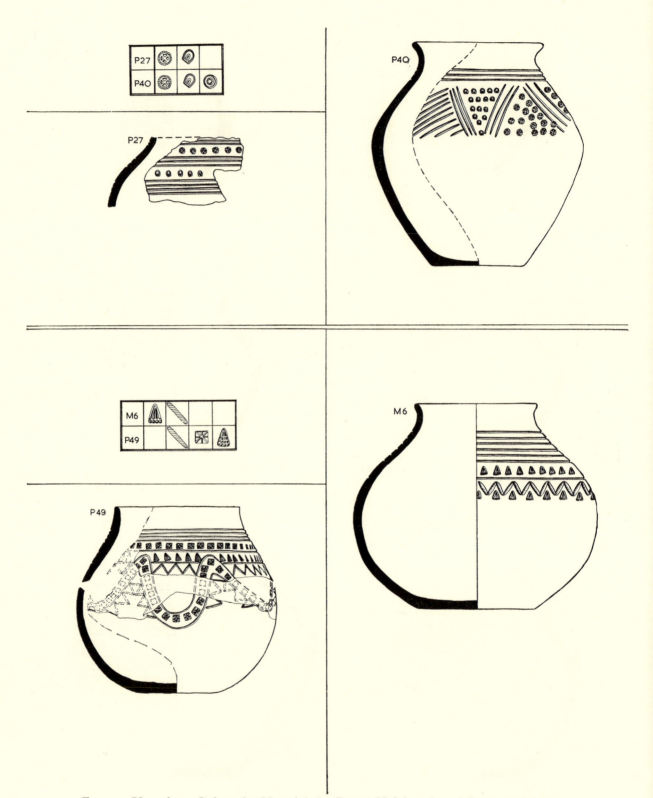

FIG. 54. Urns from Caistor-by-Norwich by Potter V (above) and Potter VI (below) (scales: urns ¼, stamps ½).

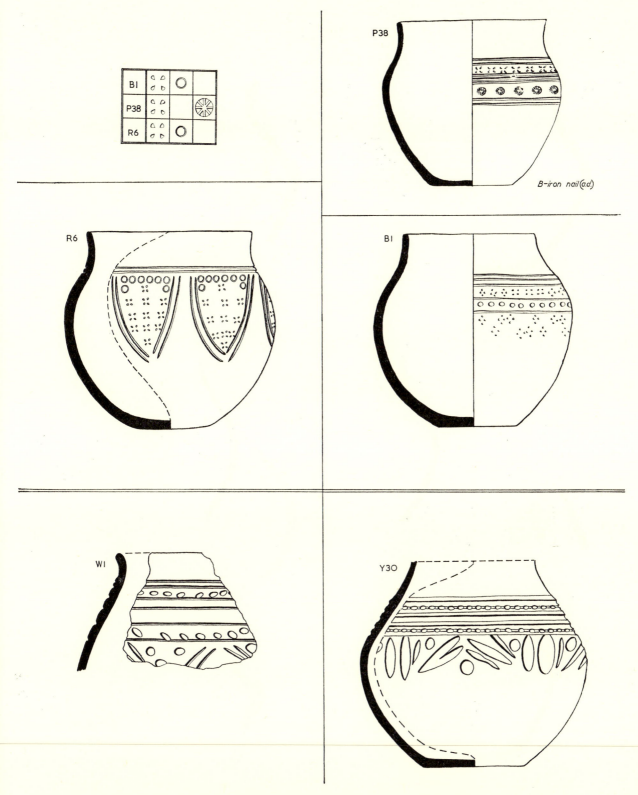

FIG. 55. Urns from Caistor-by-Norwich by Potter X (above) and Potter VII (below) (scale: urns ¼, stamps ½).

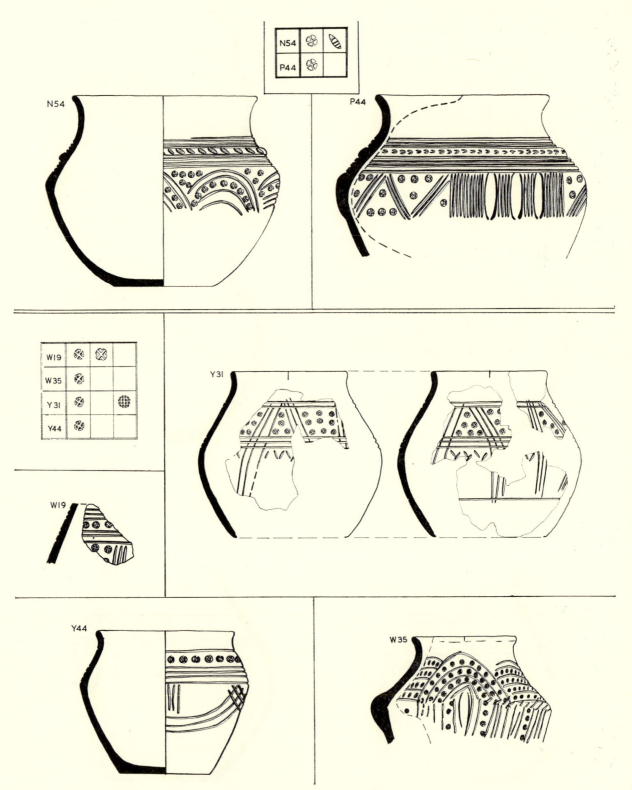

FIG. 56. Urns from Caistor-by-Norwich by Potter VIII (above) and Potter IX (below) (scales: urns ¼, stamps ½).

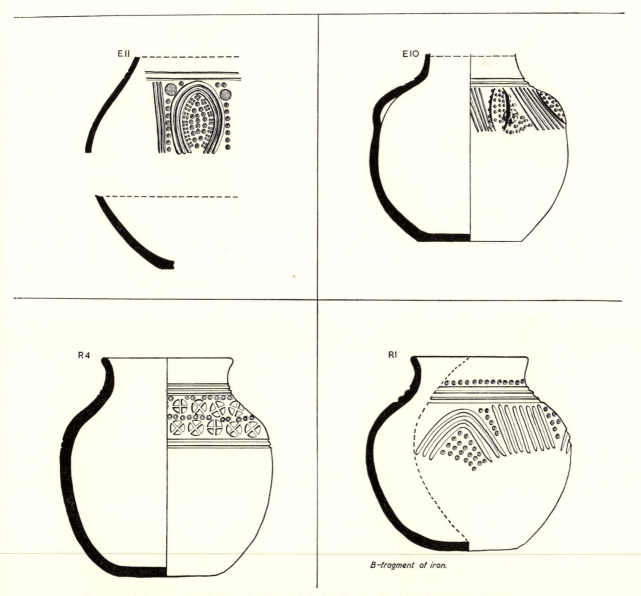

E10	◎	⊕		
E11	◎		⊟	●
R1	◎			
R4	◎	⊕		

B-fragment of iron.

Fig. 57. Urns from Caistor-by-Norwich by Potter XI (scales: urns ¼, stamps ½).

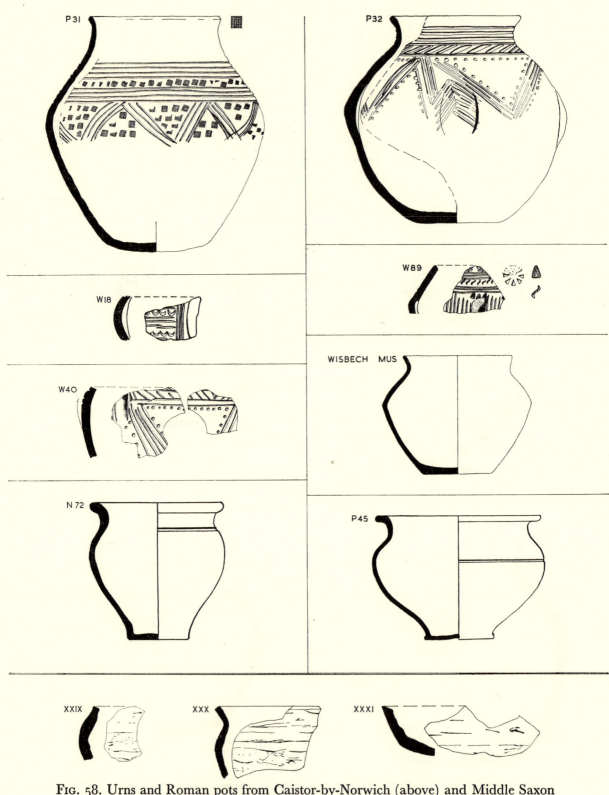

FIG. 58. Urns and Roman pots from Caistor-by-Norwich (above) and Middle Saxon pottery from Markshall (below) (scales: pottery $\frac{1}{4}$, stamps $\frac{1}{2}$).

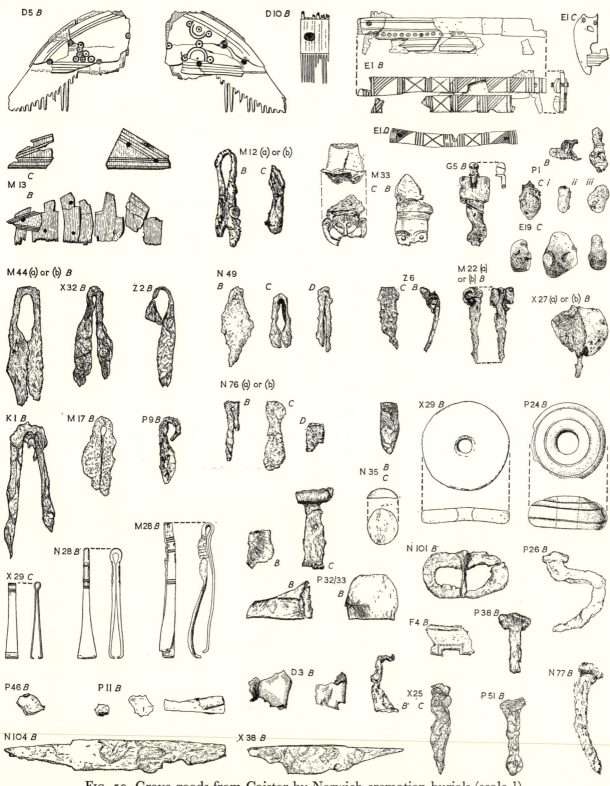

FIG. 59. Grave goods from Caistor-by-Norwich cremation burials (scale ½).
Two views of D5 B are shown.

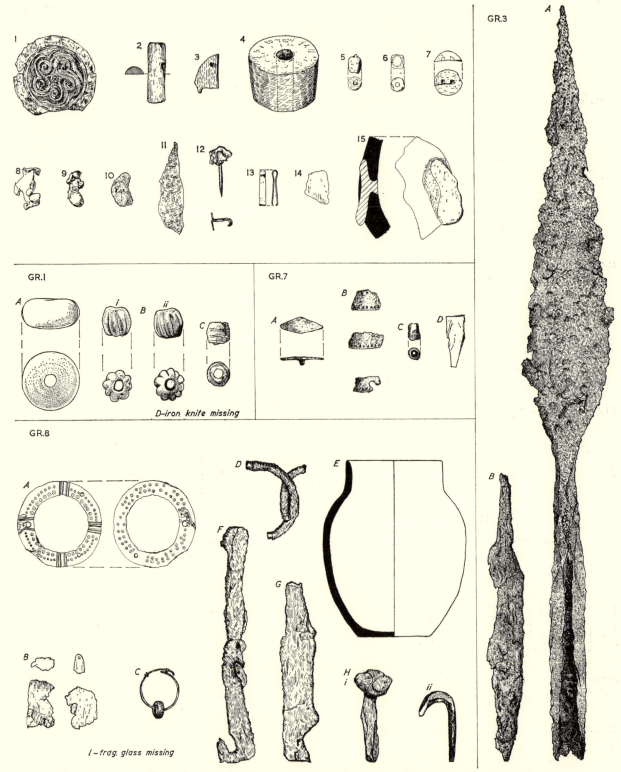

FIG. 60. 1–14: Stray finds from Caistor-by-Norwich, probably from cremation burials;
15: lead mend from urn P 28 (see fig. 37). Grave goods from inhumation burials at
Caistor-by-Norwich. (Scales: $\frac{1}{2}$, except pot, Grave 8 E, $\frac{1}{4}$).

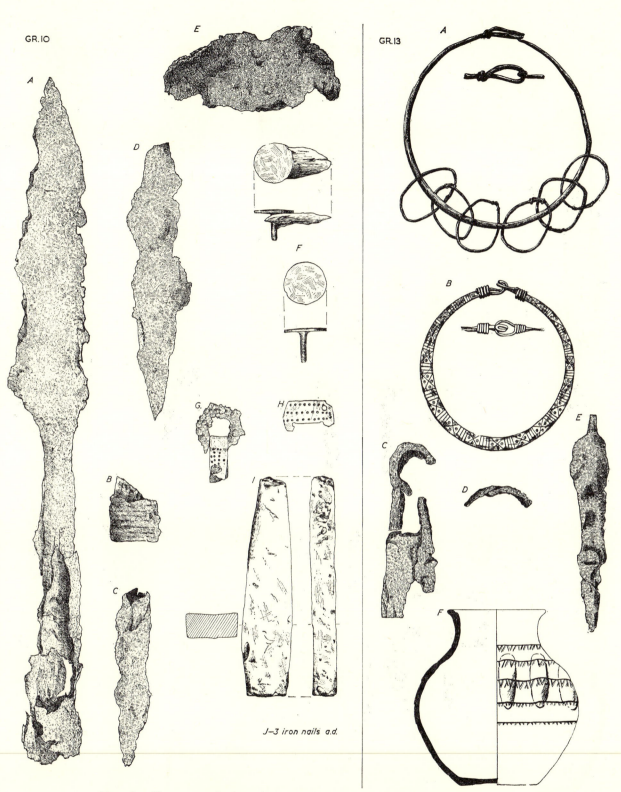

GR.10

E

GR.13

A

D

F

G.

H

B

C

I

E

C

D

B

A

F

J–3 iron nails a.d.

FIG. 61. Grave goods from inhumation burials at Caistor-by-Norwich
(scales: $\frac{1}{2}$, except pot, Grave 13 F, $\frac{1}{4}$).

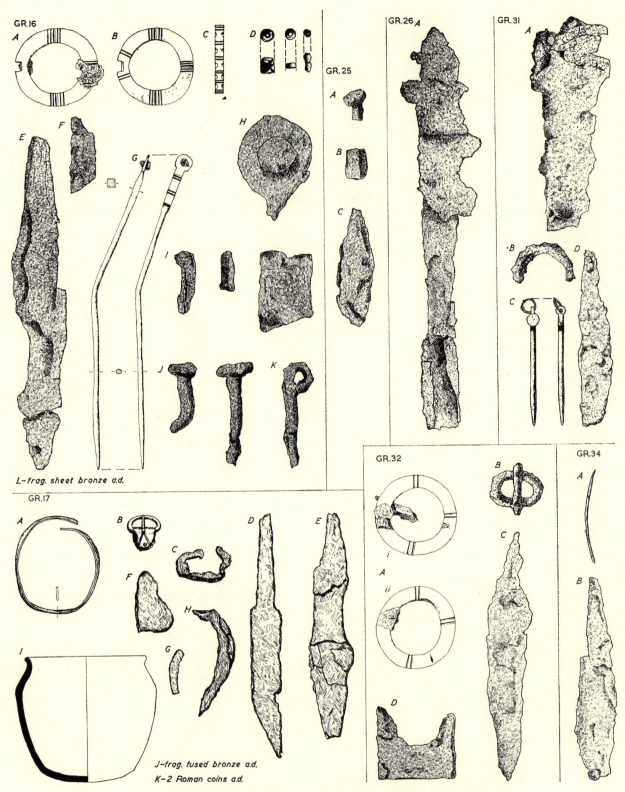

FIG. 62. Grave goods from inhumation burials at Caistor-by-Norwich (scales: $\frac{1}{2}$, except pot, Grave 17 I, $\frac{1}{4}$).

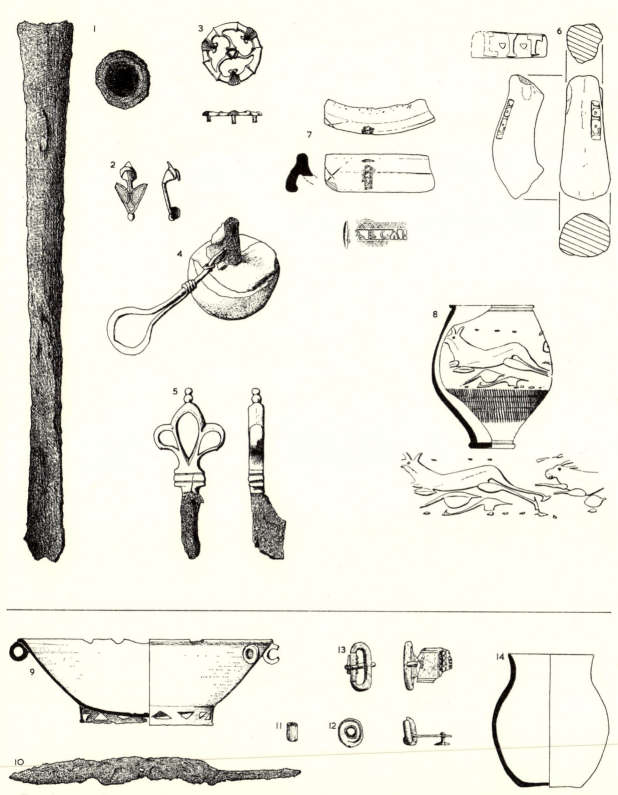

FIG. 63. 1–8: Roman objects from the Caistor-by-Norwich cemetery site; 9: bronze Coptic bowl; 10–14: stray finds from Caistor-by-Norwich, probably from inhumation burials (scales: 6–9 and 14, $\frac{1}{4}$; stamps and other objects, $\frac{1}{2}$).

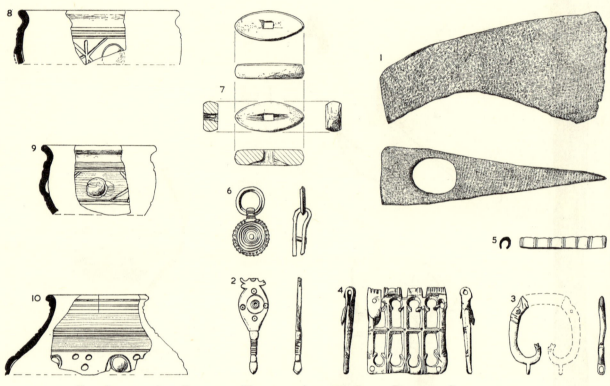

FIG. 64. 1–7: late Roman military equipment; 8–10: Romano-Saxon pottery;
all from *Venta Icenorum* (scales: ½, except pottery, ¼).

FIG. 65. Urns from Markshall (scales: urns ¼, stamps ½).

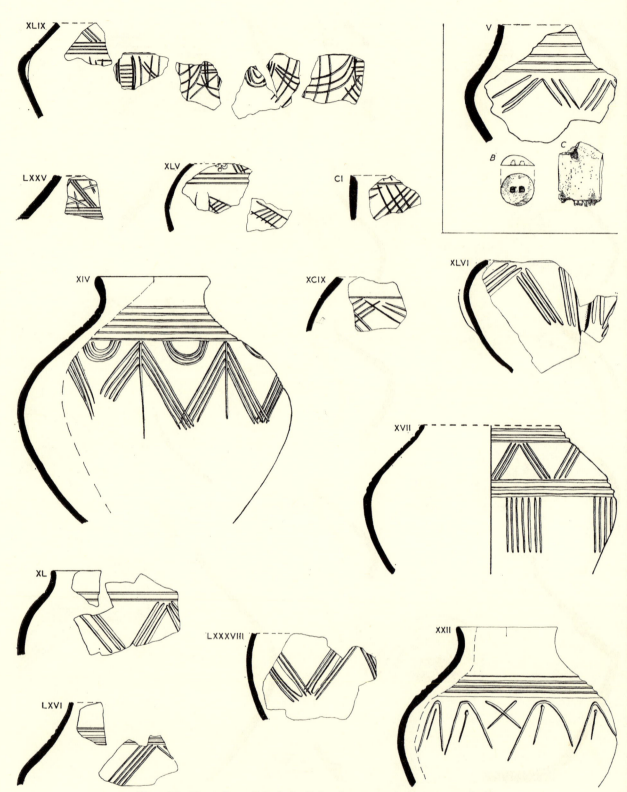

FIG. 66. Urns from Markshall (scales: urns ¼, grave goods ½).

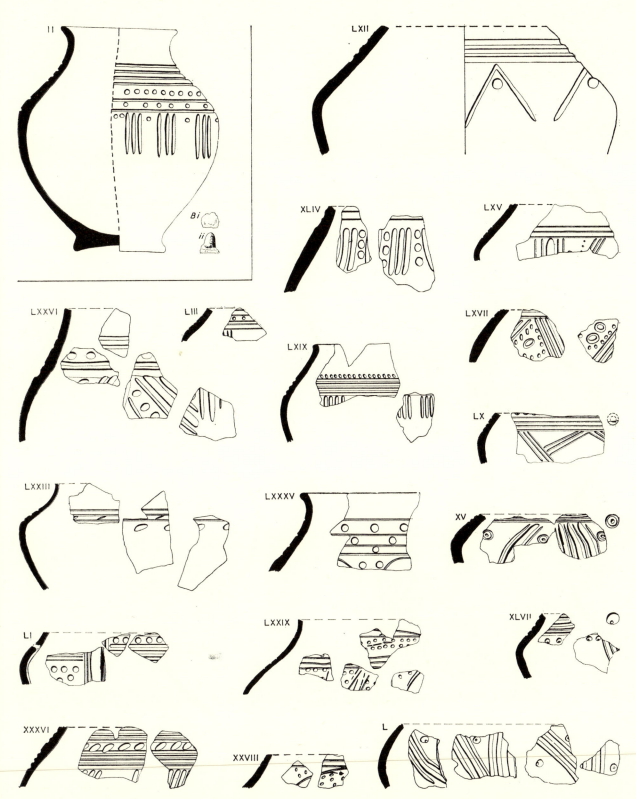

FIG. 67. Urns from Markshall (scales: urns ¼, stamps and grave goods ½).

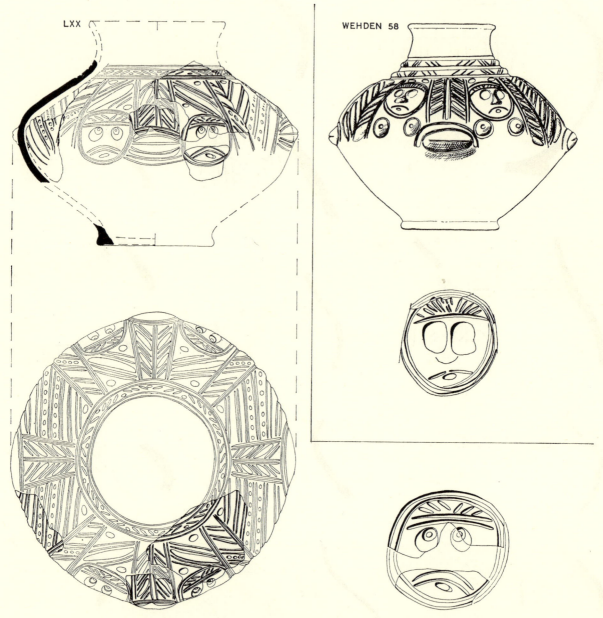

FIG. 68. Urn LXX from Markshall and urn 58 from Wehden (scales: urns ¼, faces ½).

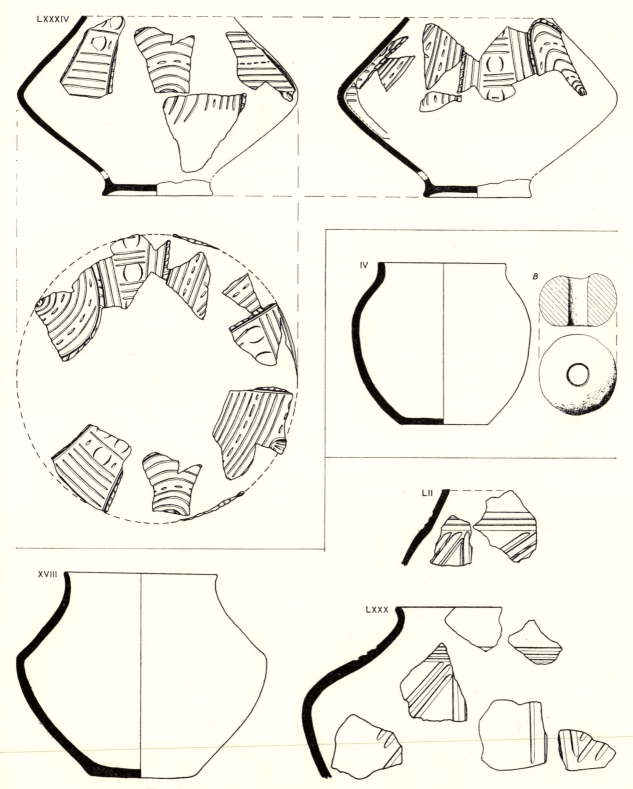

FIG. 69. Urns from Markshall (scales: ¼, grave goods ½).

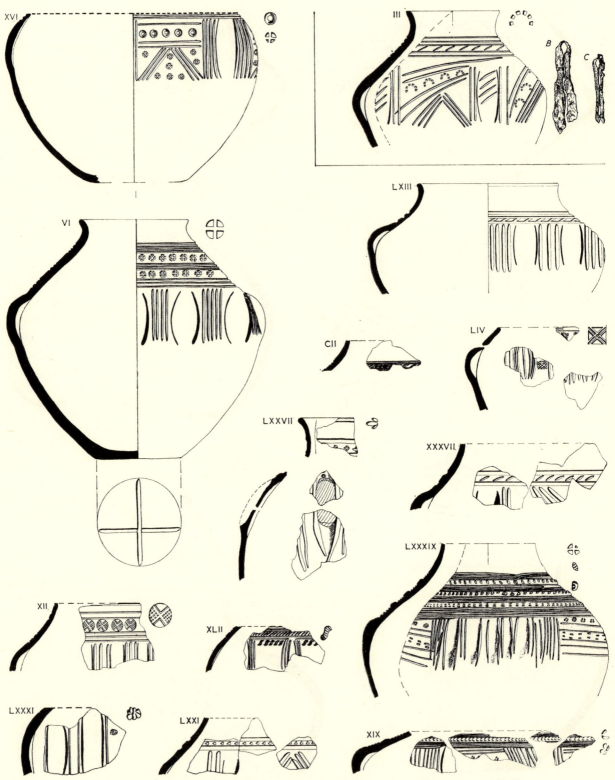

FIG. 70. Urns from Markshall (scales: urns ¼, stamps and grave goods ½).

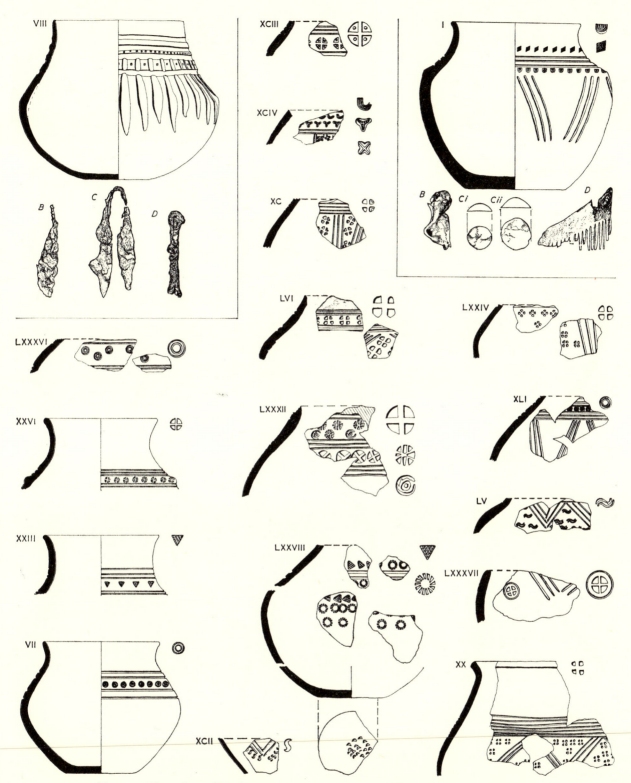

Fig. 71. Urns from Markshall (scales: urns ¼, stamps and grave goods ½).

INDEX

PLATES

PLATE I

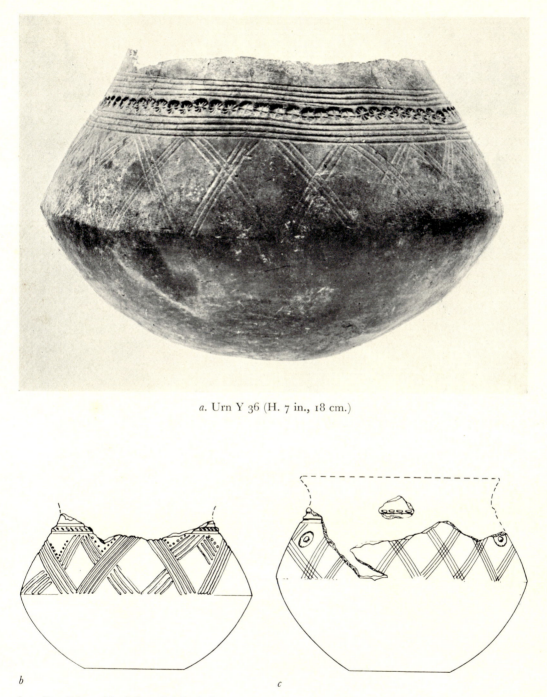

a. Urn Y 36 (H. 7 in., 18 cm.)

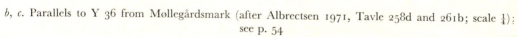

b   *c*

b, c. Parallels to Y 36 from Møllegårdsmark (after Albrectsen 1971, Tavle 258d and 261b; scale $\frac{1}{4}$): see p. 54

PLATE II

a. Urn P 15 (H. 6·75 in., 17 cm.); see pp. 43–4

b. Urn N 54 (H. 8 in., 20·3 cm.); see p. 55

PLATE III

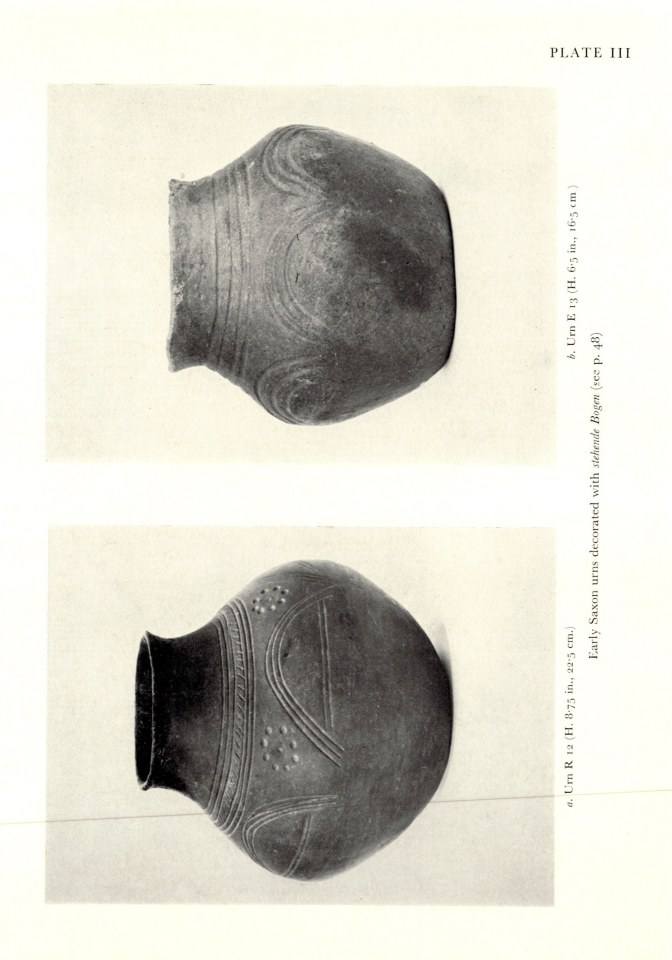

a. Urn R 12 (H. 8·75 in., 22·5 cm.)

b. Urn E 13 (H. 6·5 in., 16·5 cm)

Early Saxon urns decorated with *stehende Bogen* (see p. 48)

PLATE IV

a. Urn M 54 (H. 5·5 in., 14 cm.)

b. Urn N 14 (H. 6·25 in., 16 cm.)

Corrugated Anglian urns (see pp. 45–7)

PLATE V

a. Urn N 51 (H. 6·5 in., 16·5 cm.)

b. Urn R 8 (size unknown as now missing)

Anglian urns (see pp. 45–7)

PLATE VI

a. Urn R 9/10 (H. 10 in., 25·5 cm.); see pp. 61–2, 118

b. Urn E 7 (H. 7 in., 18 cm.); see p. 60

Urns with animal decoration

PLATE VII

a. Urn W 30 (scale about ½)

b. Urn N 83 (H. 10·5 in., 26·5 cm.)

Urns with animal stamp decoration (see pp. 59–61)

PLATE VIII

a. Urn B 2 (size unknown); see p. 47

b. Sörup, Kr. Flensburg

Anglian bossed and corrugated urns

PLATE IX

a. Hammoor, Holstein (KS 12084)

b. Süderbrarup, Kr. Schleswig

Continental Anglian bossed and corrugated urns (parallels to urn B 2); see p. 47

PLATE X

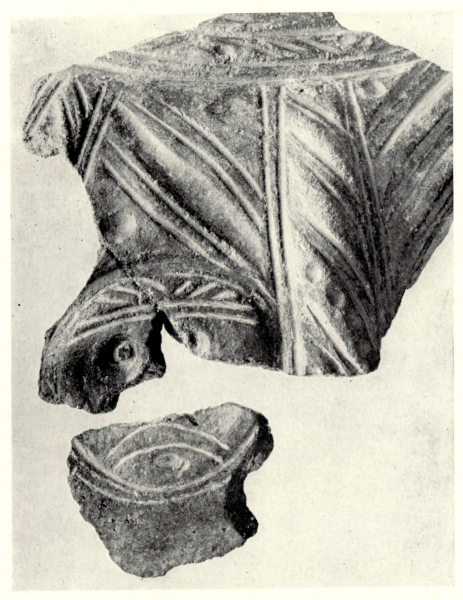

Markshall LXX (scale ⅓); see p 237

PLATE XI

a

b

a. Urn 58 from Wehden, N. Germany (H. 8·5 in., 21·5 cm.) as restored and *b*, the surviving sherd with face decoration (scale ¼)

(*Photographs: Niedersächsisches Landesmuseum, Hanover*)

PLATE XII

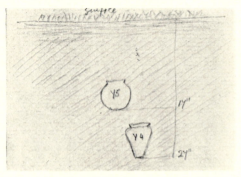

a. Relation of Y4 to Y5 (see pp. 74–6)

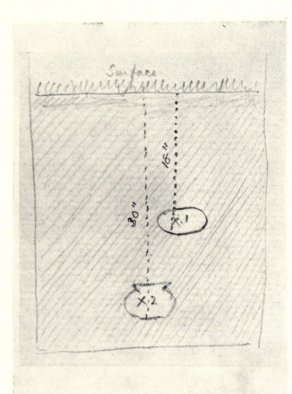

b. N10 as found (see p. 150)

c. The X1/2 group (see p. 56)

d. A7 and detached boss (see p. 123)

Sketches from F. R. Mann's notebooks

PLATE XIII

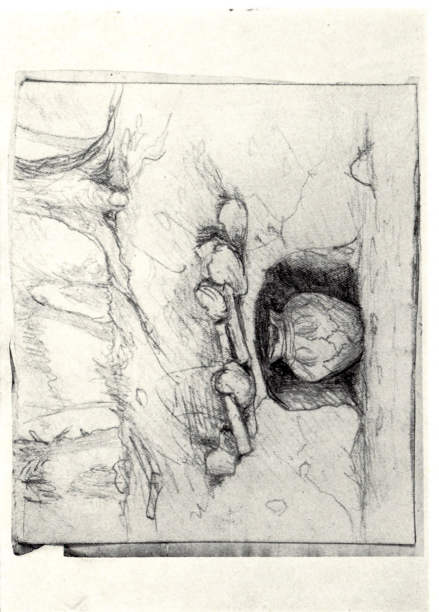

Urn A 8 *in situ*—sketch from F. R. Mann's notebooks (see p. 123)

PLATE XIV

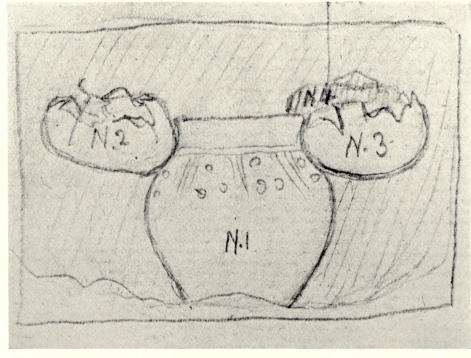

a. The N1–4 group (see p. 50, n. 6)

b. N16/17 group (see p. 52)

Sketches from F. R. Mann's notebooks

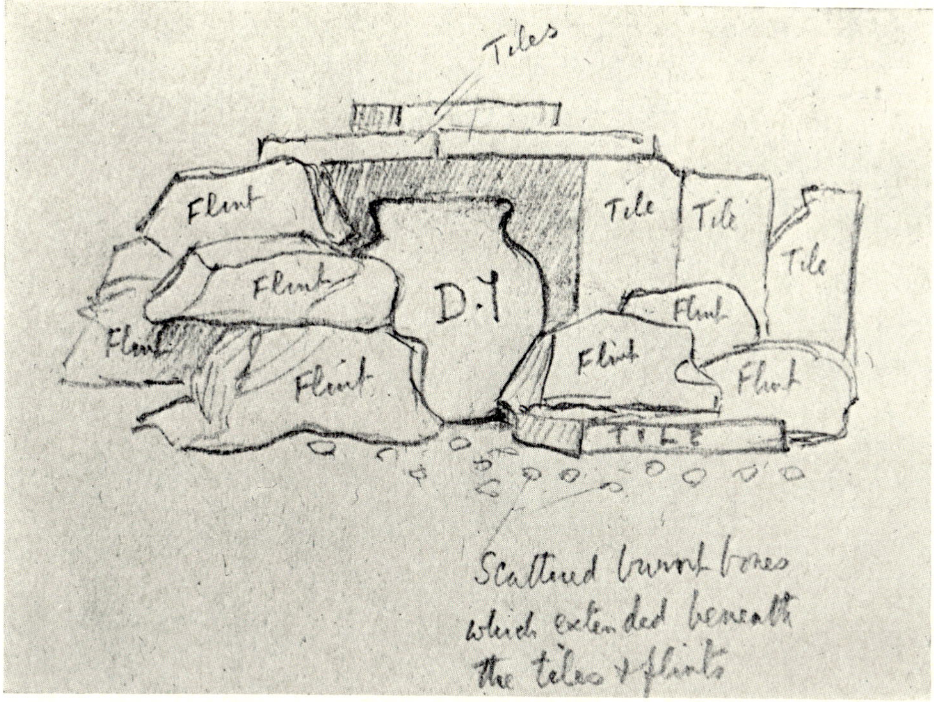

PLATE XV

a. D7 in cist as found

b. The Y9 group (see pp. 56–7)

Sketches from F. R. Mann's notebooks

PLATE XVI

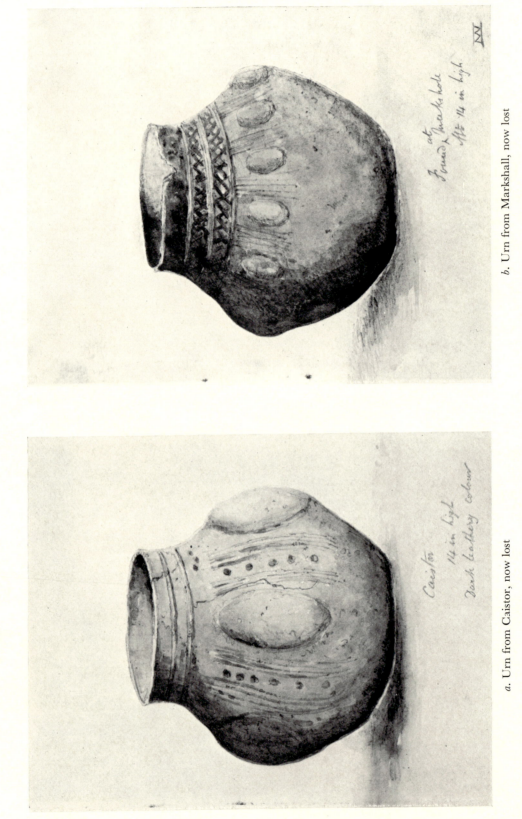

PLATE XVII

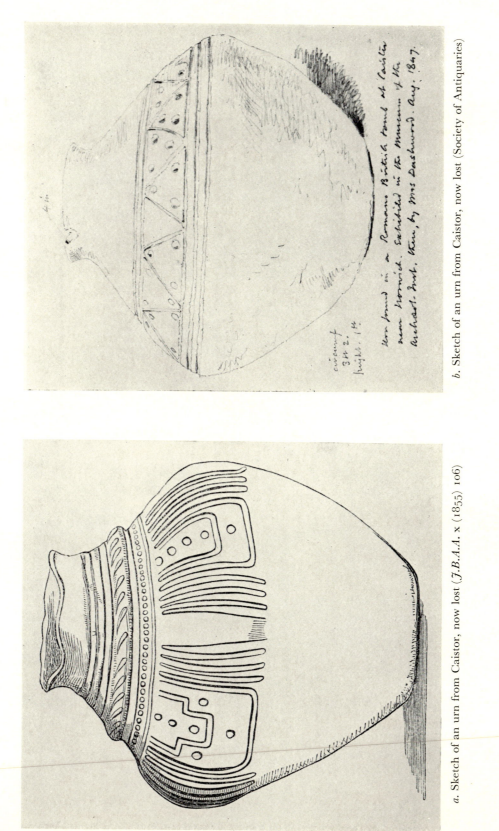

b. Sketch of an urn from Caistor, now lost (Society of Antiquaries)

a. Sketch of an urn from Caistor, now lost (*J.B.A.A.* x (1855) 106)

PLATE XVIII

Sketch of an urn from Caistor, now lost (Dawson Turner Collection, B.M. Add. MSS. 23,027 f. 92)

(Photograph: British Museum)

PLATE XIX

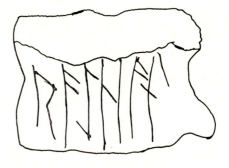

a. Glass cone-beaker from urn E 19 (H. 5·9 in., 15 cm.); see p. 132

b. Roe-deer astragalus from urn N 59 (L. 1·1 in., 2·85 cm.) with detail of runic inscription (see pp. 114–17)

c. Bronze saucer-brooch (diam. 1·8 in., 4·6 cm.); see p. 207, No. 1

d. Openwork bronze mount from Roman Pit 10 (diameter 1·25 in., 3·1 cm.); see p. 27

Small finds from Caister

PLATE XX

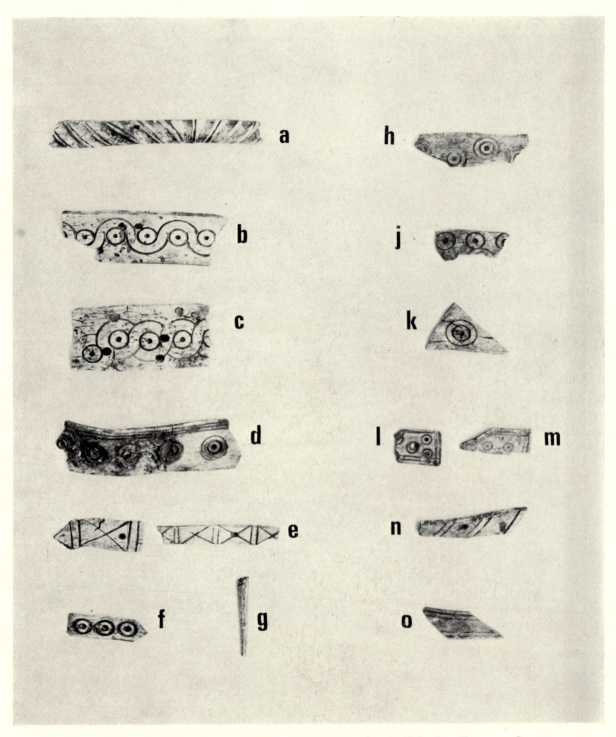

Bone mounts from urn X 11, illustrating the range of decorative motifs (scale *c.* 3/4); see pp. 85, 191–2

PLATE XXI

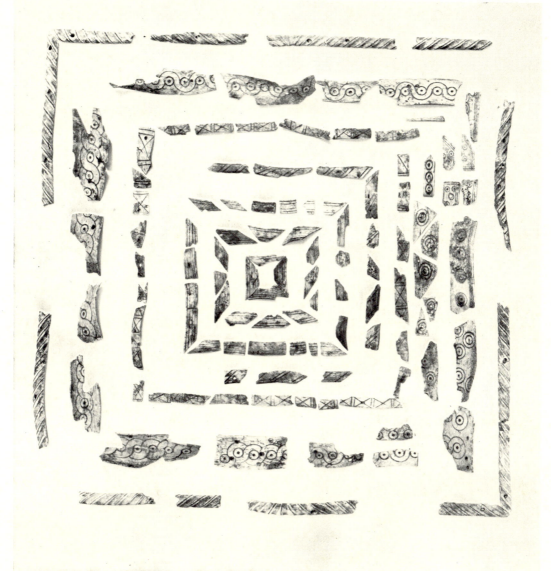

A possible arrangement of the bone mounts from urn X 11 as decoration for a casket (details and dimensions uncertain)

PLATE XXII

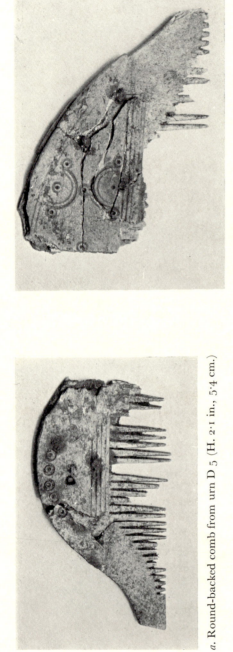

a. Round-backed comb from urn D 5 (H. 2·1 in., 5·4 cm.)

b. Round-backed comb from urn D 9 (H. 1·5 in., 3·8 cm.)

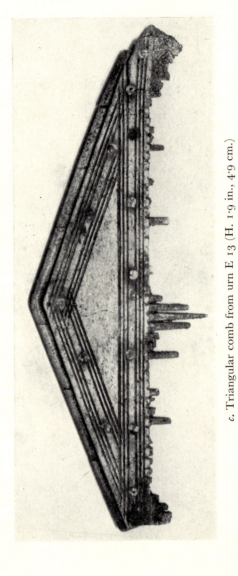

c. Triangular comb from urn E 13 (H. 1·9 in., 4·9 cm.)

Bone combs from Caistor

PLATE XXIII

f. Part of the centre-plate of a triangular comb from urn Y 23 (H. 1·3 in., 3·4 cm.)

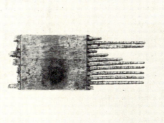

e. Miniature comb from urn R 12 (H. 1·43 in., 3·7 cm.)

b. Frisian barred comb from Hoogebeintum

(Photograph: Prof. A. Vollgraf)

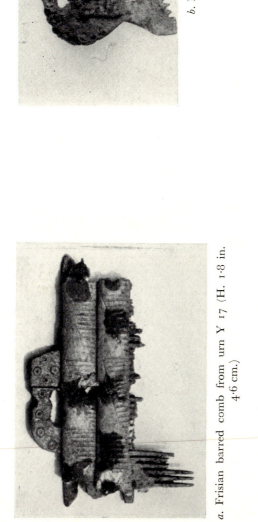

a. Frisian barred comb from urn Y 17 (H. 1·8 in. 4·6 cm.)

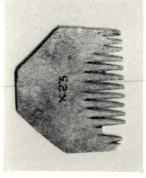

d. Part of a double-sided comb from urn D 10 (H. 1·5 in., 3·8 cm.)

c. Miniature comb from urn X 23 (H. 1·2 in., 3·1 cm.)

Bone combs

PLATE XXIV

a. Pot from inhumation grave 13 (H. 7·4 in., 18·8 cm.); see p. 215

b. Bronze Coptic bowl (H. 3·5 in., 8·3 cm.); see p. 230